D1330567

# BUSINESS AND THE
# SUSTAINABILITY CHALLENGE

In today's green-minded environment, it is vitally important for businesses to have a holistic understanding of the many issues surrounding and shaping sustainability, from competitors to government and political factors, to economics and ecological science. This integrated textbook for MBA and senior-level undergraduates offers a comprehensive overview of the issues of sustainability as they relate to business and influence corporate strategy. It also features a wide range of cases and an extensive discussion of tools to incorporate sustainability issues into strategic decision making, helping instructors and students to build and then apply a solid understanding of sustainability in business.

**Peter N. Nemetz** is a Professor of Strategy and Business Economics in the Sauder School of Business at The University of British Columbia, Canada.

# Other Books by the Author

Editor, *Energy Policy: The Global Challenge*, Butterworth & Co. (Canada) Ltd., for the Institute for Research on Public Policy, Montreal, 1979.

Editor, *Resource Policy: International Perspectives*, Institute for Research on Public Policy, Montreal, 1980.

Editor, *Energy Crisis—Policy Response*, Institute for Research on Public Policy, Montreal, 1981.

*Economic Incentives for Energy Conservation*, Wiley-Interscience, New York, 1984 (with Marilyn Hankey).

Editor, *The Pacific Rim: Investment, Development and Trade*, U.B.C. Press, 1987.

Editor, *The Pacific Rim: Investment, Development and Trade*, U.B.C. Press, 2nd revised edition, 1990.

Editor, *Emerging Issues in Forest Policy*, U.B.C. Press, 1992.

Editor, *The Vancouver Institute: An Experiment in Public Education*, JBA Press, 1998.

Editor, *Bringing Business On Board: Sustainable Development and the B-School Curriculum*, JBA Press, 2002, co-sponsored by the National Round Table for the Environment and the Economy. [Distributed by UBC Press]

Editor, *Sustainable Resource Management: Reality or Illusion?* Edward Elgar, 2007.

## FRONT COVER PICTURE ACKNOWLEDGMENT

Floor mosaic, Piazza Armerina, Sicily. Photograph courtesy of Professor Roger Wilson, Department of Classical, Near Eastern and Religious Studies, University of British Columbia.

# BUSINESS AND THE SUSTAINABILITY CHALLENGE

An Integrated Perspective

**Peter N. Nemetz**

**LIS LIBRARY**

| Date | Fund |
|------|------|
| 4-7-14 | bS_WAR |

Order No

2528575

University of Chester

Routledge
Taylor & Francis Group

NEW YORK AND LONDON

First published 2013
by Routledge
711 Third Avenue, New York, NY 10017

Simultaneously published in the UK
by Routledge
2 Park Square, Milton Park, Abingdon, Oxon OX14 4RN

*Routledge is an imprint of the Taylor & Francis Group, an Informa business*

© 2013 Taylor & Francis

The right of Peter Nemetz to be identified as author of this work has been asserted by him/her in accordance with sections 77 and 78 of the Copyright, Designs and Patents Act 1988.

All rights reserved. No part of this book may be reprinted or reproduced or utilized in any form or by any electronic, mechanical, or other means, now known or hereafter invented, including photocopying and recording, or in any information storage or retrieval system, without permission in writing from the publishers.

**Trademark Notice:** Product or corporate names may be trademarks or registered trademarks, and are used only for identification and explanation without intent to infringe.

*Library of Congress Cataloging-in-Publication Data*

Nemetz, Peter N., 1944–
Business and the sustainability challenge : an integrated perspective / Peter Nemetz.
    p. cm.
  Includes bibliographical references and index.
    ISBN 978-0-415-88240-8 (hardback : alk. paper) —
ISBN 978-0-415-88241-5 (pbk. : alk. paper) —
ISBN 978-0-203-10747-8 (ebook : alk. paper)    1. Business enterprises—Environmental aspects.    2. Sustainable development.    3. Sustainability.
4. Economic development—Environmental aspects.    I. Title.
HD30.255.N46    2013
338.9'27—dc23          2012032154

ISBN: 978-0-415-88240-8
ISBN: 978-0-415-88241-5
ISBN: 978-0-203-10747-8

Typeset in Stone Serif
by Apex CoVantage, LLC

*To my dearest wife, Roma, and daughter, Fiona, whose love and support have made my work possible, and to the thousands of students I have taught during my academic career, who have reciprocated in kind with their knowledge and experience in an intellectual collaboration that has spanned over four decades.*

# Contents

# Tables

# *Figures*

# *Preface*

The rationale for undertaking the daunting task of producing this textbook arose after many years of teaching courses in environmental policy; energy economics; and, more recently, sustainability and business. The subject matter of sustainable development is, by definition, multidisciplinary, and this presents numerous challenges to the amassing of its diverse subject matter within the covers of one book. It is a tribute to the power of the modern concept of sustainability that so many books are now available on this subject. However, instructors tasked with distilling this material within a classroom setting whether for junior- and senior-level undergraduates or masters students in business schools, economics departments, and schools of public policy and government, must grapple with the lack of any relatively comprehensive treatment of the subject. The large array of books on the subject tend to fall into one of two general categories: (a) highly specialized, unidisciplinary studies in such areas as marketing and accounting; or (b) broad and generally exhortatory works on sustainability and corporate strategy.

I suspect that most instructors in the area of sustainability and business, like me, have been forced to cobble together a broad range of snippets from articles and books rather than being able to rely to some degree on a single work as a core source of material. This textbook is an attempt to fill this gap. In fact, the material presented here represents little more than half of the original proposed content. The publisher, in his wisdom, suggested that the large residual devoted to specific areas of study such as fisheries, energy, global warming, forestry, agriculture, etc., be reserved for a second textbook at some date in the future. As such, the work included here has, out of necessity, omitted not only the above mentioned resource-based areas of study, but also certain business subdisciplines such as sustainable marketing, which are addressed in much greater detail in textbooks devoted solely to their analysis. As explained in the introduction, this textbook focuses primarily on the interrelated areas of science, policy, economics, and corporate strategy.

Despite these disclaimers, the production of this work has been a labor of love, driven by hundreds of hours of lively classroom interaction with students with inquiring and open minds from the United States, Canada, and a broad range of countries in Latin America, Europe, and Asia. It is because of them that I undertook this task that, in retrospect, was much more work than I ever realized. In addition to the many students who have inspired me to continue teaching in this field for almost four decades, I owe a deep debt of gratitude to numerous individuals who have contributed in one way or another to this book. To name but a few: the late Ray Anderson, Ken Baker, David Brand, Bill Cafferata, Duncan Dow, Ian Gill, Bettina von Hagen, John Lampman, Cassie Phillips, Rob Prins, Andrew Simms, Michael Vitt, and Donovan Woolard. I also owe thanks to my academic colleagues, Werner Antweiler, Linda Coady, John Grace, Charlie Krebs, David Shindler, and Peter Timmer. Finally, I wish to single out several former students in particular who have been of immense help in this undertaking: Jana Hanova, Simon Bager, Patrick Dore, Cristina Infante, Jane Lister, Miles Panz, Judy Feng, and Rebecca Gu. It goes without saying that all of these individuals must be absolved of any responsibility for any oversights or errors that I may have committed. I also am very grateful to five anonymous reviewers whose detailed comments have significantly improved this work.

Finally, I owe my deepest gratitude to the two most important people in my life: my daughter, Dr. Fiona Danks, who brought her scientific expertise to the task of proofreading chapters for errors in both science and grammar; and especially to my wife, Roma, who provided both intellectual and moral support during the production of innumerable manuscript drafts.

Peter N. Nemetz
*Vancouver, B.C.*
*January 2013*

# Book Outline and Rationale

WHY STUDY SUSTAINABILITY IN A BUSINESS SCHOOL? This is a legitimate question for an undergraduate or master's-level student who has chosen his/her specific discipline within business and is finishing all course requirements in anticipation of graduation and impending employment. The principal answer to this question and the message of this book is fourfold: (1) there is a significant probability that within the next decade or two at most, the national and international business environment will be radically different from today; (2) this may be, in no small part, because of the enormous ecological challenges facing the globe and the feedback effects they have on our economic systems; (3) by necessity, issues of sustainability will be central to the *strategic* decision making of mid-sized and major corporations; and (4) any middle-level or senior manager unfamiliar with the issues, both theoretical and empirical, will be placing themselves and their firms at a serious competitive disadvantage.

It can be argued that the goal of achieving sustainable development is probably the greatest challenge that humankind has ever faced. It will require a concerted and coordinated effort among consumers, business, and government. If sustainable development is indeed to be achieved, it can also be argued that the sine qua non is the education of the emerging business elite in the fundamental principles of sustainability, for only with the active engagement of the business community is there any realistic hope that our economic, social, and ecological systems can achieve sustainability.

This presents a major challenge within the confines of a business school as traditional business education has adopted the reductionist approach pioneered by the sciences. This model has withstood the test of time, producing highly educated young graduates who are focused on the theory and empirical data of their chosen discipline. The study of sustainability, within business as in other subject areas, represents a fundamental divergence from this traditional model. This new educational model requires multidisciplinary integration across a wide range of disciplines in the areas of business, economics, social issues, and ecology. Aside from the occasional *capstone* course at the end of a business degree, there are few, if any, precedents for this holistic approach.

The mission of business schools is to lead in the area of business education, developing new theory, and exploring the significance of a vast array of empirical data. It is also their mission, however, to identify and respond to emerging trends in their environment. One need only read the national press, business magazines, and corporate reports themselves to see the emergence of a dramatic change in the environment of business. Issues of sustainability have been the focus of recent

| RANK | COMPANY | CSR REPORT | SUSTAINABILITY REPORT | IN DOW JONES SUSTAINABLITY INDEX |
|------|---------|------------|------------------------|-----------------------------------|

**TABLE 1.1**

*Top 50 Fortune 500 companies in 2011*

| RANK | COMPANY | CSR REPORT | SUSTAINABILITY REPORT | IN DOW JONES SUSTAINABLITY INDEX |
|------|---------|------------|------------------------|-----------------------------------|
| 17 | American International Group | | | |
| 27 | Amerisource Bergen | | | |
| 35 | Apple | YES | | |
| 39 | Archer Daniels Midland | YES | YES | |
| 12 | AT & T | YES* | YES* | |
| 9 | Bank of America Corp | YES* | YES* | YES |
| 7 | Berkshire Hathaway | | | |
| 47 | Best Buy | YES | YES | |
| 36 | Boeing | YES | YES | |
| 19 | Cardinal Health | YES | | |
| 3 | Chevron | YES* | YES* | YES |
| 14 | Citigroup | YES | YES | YES |
| 4 | ConocoPhilips | YES | YES | |
| 28 | Costco Wholesale | YES* | YES* | |
| 21 | CVS Caremark | YES | YES | |
| 41 | Dell | YES* | YES* | YES |
| 45 | Dow Chemical | YES | YES | |
| 2 | Exxon Mobil | YES* | YES* | |
| 5 | Fannie Mae | | | |
| 1- | Ford Motors | YES | YES | YES |
| 20 | Freddie Mac | YES | YES | |
| 6 | General Electric | YES | YES | YES |
| 8 | General Motors | YES | YES | |
| 11 | Hewlett Packard | YES | YES | |
| 30 | Home Depot | YES | YES | |
| 18 | International Business Machines | YES | YES | YES |
| 40 | Johnson & Johnson | YES | YES | YES |
| 13 | JP Morgan Chase and Co | YES | YES | |
| 15 | KcKesson | YES* | YES* | |
| 49 | Kraft Foods | YES | YES | YES |
| 25 | Kroger | YES | YES | |
| 50 | Lowe's | YES* | YES* | |
| 29 | Marathon Oil | YES* | YES* | |

| RANK | COMPANY | CSR REPORT | SUSTAINABILITY REPORT | IN DOW JONES SUSTAINABLITY INDEX | |
|---|---|---|---|---|---|
| 34 | Medco Health Solutions | | | | **TABLE 1.1**<br>*continued* |
| 46 | Metlife | | | | |
| 38 | Microsoft | YES | YES | | |
| 43 | Pepsico | YES | YES | YES | |
| 31 | Pfizer | YES | YES | YES | |
| 26 | Procter and Gamble | YES* | YES* | YES | |
| 37 | State Farm Insurance Cos | YES | YES | | |
| 33 | Target | YES | YES | YES | |
| 22 | United Health Group | YES | YES | YES | |
| 48 | United Parcel Service | YES | YES | | |
| 44 | United Technologies | YES | YES | | |
| 24 | Valero Energy | YES | YES | | |
| 16 | Verizon Communications | YES | YES | | |
| 32 | Walgreen | YES | YES | | |
| 1 | Walmart Stores | YES* | YES* | | |
| 42 | Wellpoint | YES* | YES* | | |
| 23 | Wells Fargo | YES | YES | | |

*Company presents both corporate social responsibility and sustainability in the same report
Companies with online material only: ConocoPhilips (4), General Motors (8), Hewlett Packard (YESYES), Freddie Mac (20), Valero Energy (24), Marathon Oil (29), Home Depot (30), Pfizer (3YES), Walgreen (32), Boeing (36), State Farm Insurance Cos (37), Archer Daniels Midland (39), United Technologies (44), Best Buy (47), Kraft Foods (49)
*Source:* corporate websites

cover pages from such high profile journals as *Business Week, The Economist, TIME* magazine, and *Vanity Fair.*

This phenomenon has been mirrored in the proliferation of corporate reports devoted to sustainability and/or corporate social responsibility. Table 1–1, for example, lists the top 50 firms by sales in the Fortune 500. Of these 50, all but 6 have published either stand-alone sustainability or corporate social responsibility (CSR) reports or incorporated significant material on these issues on their websites. Also noteworthy is the fact that 14 of these top 50 appear to be included in the Dow Jones Sustainability Index (DJSI), although this listing may be incomplete since Dow Jones Ltd. stopped publishing the complete list of companies on their DJS indexes recently.

While much of the discussion of sustainability issues within the popular press has focused on negative aspects, it is one of the central arguments of this book that many of these sustainability challenges represent extraordinary opportunities for business. This double-sided interpretation is not new to history. The ancient Chinese phrase for "crisis" is composed of two characters: the first represents "danger," but the second represents "opportunity." The modern reinterpretation of this historical characterization was enunciated by Michael Porter of Harvard University in a *Scientific American* essay of April 1991 where he stated that "the conflict between environmental protection and economic competitiveness is a false dichotomy (p. 168)." This thesis has been further developed by Porter in several seminal articles from the *Harvard Business Review* and the *Journal of Economic Perspectives* (Porter and Kramer 2006, 2011; Porter and van der Linde 1995a and 1995b). The key message of these articles is simple: there has been a false dichotomy between expenditures on pollution control and corporate profitability. The gist of the authors' argument is that corporate strategy—the highest level of decision making within a corporation—which recognizes, addresses, and incorporates issues of sustainability can yield significant and "sustainable" competitive advantage.

Several major corporations have already adopted the language of sustainability, if not recognized and internalized this transformative principle. For example, Shell Canada's stated corporate goals are threefold: (1) growth, (2) profitability, and (3) sustainable development. To quote: "over the past decade, issues of sustainability have moved from the periphery of corporate decision making to the centre of corporate strategy" (Symonds 2006). Few industries have been more affected by issues of sustainability than the forest sector. One corporate giant in this sector, Catalyst Paper, lists four reasons why they have moved aggressively to implement sustainability: (1) profit—Catalyst has reduced greenhouse gases by 71% since 1990, saving $16 million per year in fossil fuels; (2) branding—Catalyst has seen the impact of negative press coverage on corporate sales and profitability, which has affected such high-profile companies as Nike and Victoria's Secret [see, for example, Figure 1–1 and Berman 2011]; (3) market share—a differentiation strategy based on sustainability performance has the proven capacity to attract not only retail consumers, but can also influence B-to-B sales; and (4) stability—there are few things that the corporate sector values more than stability and predictability (Kissack 2007). Leading customers', competitors', and government regulatory agencies' proactivity in the area of sustainability holds the promise of long-term gains.

The holistic approach to sustainability advanced by this textbook is based on three interrelated components. First and foremost is corporate strategy. But the formation and execution of such strategy cannot be understood without knowledge and appreciation of the economic and political environment in which this strategy must be crafted. Hence, the second major component is government policy—incorporated in legislation and regulations, as well as economic and political theory that help to shape much of this immediate corporate environment. Finally is the scientific framework, largely in the form of ecological theory, which at least in principle provides the intellectual rationale for a significant portion of government policy relating to sustainability issues.

The structure of this textbook is designed to facilitate the understanding of these three principal interlocking components. Several major case studies—one drawn from the manufacturing sector (Interface), one for the renewable resource sector (Ooteel Forest Products), and one from the non-renewable resource sector

**FIGURE 1.1**

*Sample attack ad*

© ForestEthics, reproduced with permission.

(Suncor)—are used to introduce many of the relevant concepts. Numerous other shorter cases are used to illustrate other important principles. Appendix 1 provides a short note for instructors and students on possible ways to approach the analysis of the cases presented in this textbook.

## WHAT IS SUSTAINABLE DEVELOPMENT?

It is useful to begin a discussion of sustainable development with a *thought experiment* from a seminal work by William McDonough and Michael Braungart in the *Atlantic Monthly* of October 1998 entitled "The Next Industrial Revolution."

If someone were to present the Industrial Revolution as a retroactive design assignment, it might sound like this:
Design a system of production that

- puts billions of pounds of toxic material into the air, water, and soil every year
- measures prosperity by activity, not legacy
- requires thousands of complex regulations to keep people and natural systems from being poisoned too quickly
- produces materials so dangerous that they will require constant vigilance from future generations
- results in gigantic amounts of waste
- puts valuable materials in holes all over the planet, where they can never be retrieved, and
- erodes the diversity of biological species and cultural practices.

Eco-efficiency instead:

- releases *fewer* pounds of toxic material into the air, water, and soil every year
- measures prosperity by *less* activity
- *meets* or *exceeds* the stipulations of thousands of complex regulations that aim to keep people and natural systems from being poisoned too quickly
- produces *fewer* dangerous materials that will require constant vigilance from future generations
- results in *smaller* amounts of waste
- puts *fewer* valuable materials in holes all over the planet, where they can never be retrieved
- standardizes and homogenizes biological species and cultural practices

This quotation cogently describes the path that the Western industrialized world has followed for the last two centuries. It has clearly yielded enormous economic benefits for many nations and, yet, it is clearly the authors' intent to argue that such a path is unsustainable. This view is reflected in the challenging piece by the well-known Harvard biologist E.O. Wilson entitled "Is Humanity Suicidal?" (*New York Times Magazine*, June 20, 1993).

The challenge of sustainability is to find another path for business and government that will continue to generate wealth but with considerably less environmental impact. Two other brief quotations help set the stage for the definition of sustainable development.

1. "Only 7% of physical U.S. throughput winds up as product, and only 1.4% is still product after six months" (Friend 1996).
2. "Business has ignored its major product lines: pollution and waste. Why would anyone set out to produce something which it cannot sell, for which it has no conceivable use, and for which it might be potentially liable?" (Smith 2007, p. 306).

The phrase "sustainable development" emerged from the report of the World Commission on Environment and Development (also known as the Brundtland Report after its chairperson, Prime Minister Gro Harlem Brundtland of Norway). The report was published as *"Our Common Future"* in 1987 by Oxford University Press. The definition is beguilingly simple: "development that meets the need of the present without compromising the ability of future generations to meet their own needs." As originally conceived, sustainable development has three components: (1) the economy, (2) society, and (3) the environment. All must achieve sustainability for the general goal to be realized.

The Brundtland Commission took a fairly optimistic view of the possibilities for *decoupling* economic activity and environmental impact, thereby permitting increased economic development in the Third World. To some, this is overly optimistic, and the concept "sustainable development" is an oxymoron. One of the major conceptual problems raised by the theory of sustainable development is how to define it in a manner that can be operationalized. There are numerous studies of sustainable development, many with their own more precise definition than the Brundtland Commission. Several common conceptual threads run throughout these studies:

(1) a direct or indirect articulation of the concept of *natural capital*—where maintenance of a constant natural capital stock (including the renewable resource base and the environment) yields an indefinite stream of output or "income"; (2) a focus on social stability, empowerment, and equity with particular emphasis on reducing poverty and maintaining an adequate quality of life for all global inhabitants alive and to be born (i.e., both intra and intergenerational equity); (3) a critical distinction between qualitative and quantitative changes in the utilization of our technology and natural resource base (i.e., development versus growth); for example, technological advances which may permit us to raise our standard of living without increasing the throughput of material and energy resources—sometimes defined as *dematerialization*; and (4) the *precautionary principle*—which states that society cannot wait for definitive scientific proof of a potential threat to the global ecosystem before acting if that threat is both large and credible. The underlying theory is based on scientific principles, largely associated with the pioneering work of ecologists such as C.S. Holling (Allen and Holling 2008; Gunderson and Holling 2001; Holling 2005), that suggest that by the time one recognizes or begins to feel the tangible effects of certain types of ecological threats, it may be too late to act to prevent or reverse serious negative effects.

One central concept of sustainability is the proposition that our generation must leave the next generation a stock of capital no less than this generation has now. Implicit in this proposition is that we must, to the best of our ability, live off the "interest" on this capital stock and not draw it down. If part of this capital is drawn down, it must be replaced by substitute capital. The ability to achieve this goal hinges on which of two major definitions of sustainable development is adopted: *weak* sustainability or *strong* sustainability. Under the *Weak Sustainability Constant Capital Rule*, our society may pass on less environment to future generations so long as this loss is offset by increasing the stock of roads and machinery, or other man-made (physical) capital. In contrast, under the *Strong Sustainability Constant Capital Rule*, perfect substitution among different forms of capital is not a valid assumption. Some elements of the natural capital stock cannot be substituted for (except on a very limited basis) by man-made capital. Many of the functions and services of ecosystems are essential to human survival; they are life support services (such as biogeochemical cycling) and cannot be replaced. To implement a policy of sustainable development, it is necessary to have more accurate measures of the various types of capital (natural, human, and physical). Without these measures, society cannot make the right decisions. One of the key challenges addressed in this textbook is applying the definition of sustainability to the corporate sector. What is a sustainable corporation? How might we create it? And how can we use this new paradigm to generate wealth?

## A MENU OF SUSTAINABILITY ISSUES AND NON-ISSUES

While much of public attention has been focused on global warming, the broad challenge of sustainable development includes other major ecological threats to the continued viability of global economic systems. Significant local, regional, and global pressures on the earth's renewable resource base are occurring in fisheries, forestry, biodiversity, agriculture, and water supply as well as human health.

When a topic such as sustainability achieves a prominent place in public discourse, it inevitably falls prey to distortions, misunderstandings, and modern myths. Some of these have achieved wide public currency. Where possible, this textbook will identify and attempt to correct some of the more glaring of these misconceptions. Consider a sampling of these such as the following:

MYTH #1—Countries can grow their way out of pollution. [See chapter 3.]

MYTH #2—A significant number of people and politicians feel that investing in major greenhouse gas reduction is too expensive, now and probably in the future. This book will offer and defend the counterintuitive proposition that even if you do not believe that global warming is likely, it is still worthwhile investing in GHG reduction. [See chapter 9.]

MYTH #3—It is conventional wisdom among some environmental groups that all companies large and small can move immediately to a more sustainable business model and profit therefrom. [See chapter 15.]

MYTH #4—Technological advances will suffice to achieve sustainability. For example, it is assumed that electric cars are the answer to the energy use and pollution associated with the internal combustion engine in the automotive sector. [See chapter 18.]

MYTH #5—Individuals and companies can reduce their carbon footprint to zero by buying offsets. [See chapter 24.]

MYTH #6—The adoption of triple bottom line accounting by all companies will make a major contribution toward achieving sustainability. [See chapters 24 and 25.]

## THINKING ABOUT SUSTAINABILITY AND SYSTEMS ANALYSIS

As stated, the principal goal of this textbook is to introduce students to the broad range of sustainability issues they will encounter in their business careers. The concepts and examples presented in this volume are intimately linked under the general rubric of *integration*—a key characteristic of sustainability. In approaching the broad range of material covered in this volume, students are encouraged to adopt a *systems-theory* approach to their analysis. This approach can be applied within or among the disparate disciplines of business, economics, policy analysis, strategic management, and ecology. The critical question to address in any analysis of a policy, strategy, or event is "what are its effects on other system components and how has it, in turn been affected by other policies, strategies or events?" Many of the tools and theories described in this volume specifically address these questions, including among others, life cycle analysis (LCA), revenge theory (or the law of unintended consequences), input-output, the ecological footprint, net energy analysis, trophic cascades, nonlinear dynamics and feedback, tipping points, industrial ecology, and a range of economic, ecological, and cross-disciplinary modeling techniques. Even the basic economic concept of externalities represents a manifestation of systems thinking as it embodies the potentially system-wide effects of an economic transaction between two parties where these effects are invisible to the market. The adoption of a systems-theory perspective frequently highlights and clarifies the complex interrelationships among disparate disciplinary spheres such as ecology and economics. Appendix 2 to this chapter provides a simple example of this concept, and Appendix 3 discusses the similarities of economic and ecological systems.

After reading this textbook, students should, at a minimum, be comfortable in addressing the following set of fundamental issues in sustainable development.

1. Be able to define sustainable development as originally enunciated and be familiar with key components such as natural capital, intergenerational equity, development versus growth and dematerialization, the precautionary principle, weak vs. strong sustainability.

2. Be familiar with the debate over the meaning of standard economic measures of well-being (such as GDP/capita) and some of the proposed alternatives.

3. Be familiar with the basics of environmental economics (esp. the principles of public goods and externalities, and common property resources vs. open-access resources) as well as some of the basic methods of measuring environmental benefits and the debate over appropriate social discount rates.

4. Be familiar with some of the basic principles of ecological economics (especially how ecological principles are integrated into this new discipline, and the measurement problems associated with ecological services).

5. Have a working knowledge of some fundamental ecological issues such nonlinear dynamics, positive feedback loops, thresholds, and tipping points.

6. Be conversant with major policy tools such as pollution taxes, marketable permits, and offsets.

7. Be familiar with some of the new metrics and data sources associated with sustainable development such as ecological and carbon footprints, the U.S. Toxic Release Inventory (TRI), Canada's National Pollutant Release Inventory (NPRI), and greenhouse gas databases.

8. Have a basic knowledge of some of the metrics and analytical methodologies used in the corporate sphere (eco-efficiency, cradle-to-grave vs. cradle-to-cradle, life-cycle analysis, environmental management systems, product certification, chain of custody, triple bottom line accounting, sustainability reporting, risk assessment matrices).

9. Have a basic knowledge of some major market responses to climate change (European Trading System, Green portfolios, Dow Jones Sustainability Indices, and others).

10. Have a working knowledge of the basic concepts and issues around social enterprise.

## STRUCTURE OF THE TEXTBOOK

The textbook is divided into two major sections. Part I (Foundations—chapters 2 to 10) provides an overview of key economic and ecological principles essential to understanding sustainable development and its relationship to government policy and corporate strategy. Part II (chapters 11 to 28) focuses on the private sector, specifically the tools for assessing, implementing, and communicating corporate sustainability, with an additional discussion of social enterprise and the challenge of determining its rate of return.

## CITED REFERENCES AND RECOMMENDED READINGS

Allen, Craig R. and C.S. Holling (2008) *Discontinuities in Ecosystems and Other Complex Systems*. New York: Columbia University Press.

Berman, Tzeporah (2011) *This Crazy Time: Living Our Environmental Challenge*. Toronto: Knopf.

Brundtland Report (1987) *Our Common Future*. New York: Oxford University Press.

Edwards, Steven F. et al. (2004) "Portfolio Management of Wild Fish Stocks." *Ecological Economics*, 49, pp. 317–329.

Ehrenfeld, John (2003) "Putting a Spotlight on Metaphors and Analogies in Industrial Ecology." *Journal of Industrial Ecology*, 7(1), pp. 1–4.

*Fortune Magazine* (2011) "Fortune 500" (www.fortune.com).

Friend, Gil (1996) "A Cyclical Materials Economy: What goes around comes around . . . or does it?" *New Bottom Line*, 5(6), March 12.

Gunderson, Lance H. and C.S. Holling (2001) *Panarchy: Understanding Transformations in Hunan and Natural Systems*. Washington, DC: Island Press.

Hamel, Gary and Liisa Valikagnas (2003) "The Quest for Resilience," Harvard Business Review, September, pp. 52–63.

Hoffman, Andrew J. (2005) "Business Decisions and the Environment: Significance, Challenges, and Momentum of an Emerging Research Field," in G. Brewer and P. Stern (eds.) *Decision Making for the Environment: Social and Behavioral Science Research Priorities*. Washington, DC: National Research Council, National Academies Press, pp. 200–229.

Holling, C.S. (2005) *Adaptive Environmental Assessment and Management*. Caldwell, NJ: Blackburn Press.

Holling, C.S. and Lance H. Gunderson (2002) "Resilience and Adaptive Cycles," in Lance H. Gunderson and C.S. Holling (eds.) *Panarchy. Understanding Transformations in Human and Natural Systems*. Island Press: Washington, pp. 25–62.

Kambhu, John et al. (2007) *New Directions for Understanding Systemic Risk*. National Research Council, Washington, D.C.

Kissack, Graham (2007) "How to Monetize Sustainability Performance in Business," presentation to Commerce 495 class in the Sauder School of Business, September 26.

Levin, Simon A. (1998) "Ecosystems and the Biosphere as Complex Adaptive Systems." *Ecosystems*, 1, pp. 431–436.

May, Robert M. et al. (2008) "Ecology for Bankers." *Nature*, 451 (Feb. 21), pp. 893–895.

McDonough, William and Michael Braungart (1998) "The Next Industrial Revolution." *The Atlantic Monthly*, October, pp. 82–92.

Porter, Michael E. (1991) "America's Green Strategy." *Scientific American*, April, p. 168.

Porter, Michael E. and Claas van der Linde (1995a) "Green and Competitive: Ending the Stalemate." *Harvard Business Review*, September/October, pp. 120–134.

Porter, Michael E. and Claas van der Linde (1995b) "Toward a New Conception of the Environment-Competitiveness Relationship." *Journal of Economic Perspectives*, 9(4), pp. 97–118.

Porter, Michael E. and Mark R. Kramer (2006) "Strategy & Society: The Link between Competitive Advantage and Corporate Social Responsibility." *Harvard Business Review*, December, pp. 78–92.

Porter, Michael E. and Mark R. Kramer (2011) "Creating Shared Value." *Harvard Business Review*, January/February, pp. 62–77.

Sanchirico, James N. et al. (2006) "An Approach to Ecosystem-Based Fishery Management." Discussion Paper 06–40, September, Resources For the Future, Washington, D.C.

Schumpeter, Joseph (1950) *Capitalism, Socialism and Democracy*. Harper & Row: New York.

Soramaki, Kimmo et al. (2006) "The Typology of Interbank Payment Flows." Federal Reserve Bank of New York Staff Report 243, March.

Smith, William G.B. (2007) "Accounting for the Environment: Can Industrial Ecology Pay Double Dividends for Business?," in Peter N. Nemetz (ed.) *Sustainable Resource Management: Reality or Illusion*? Cheltenham: Edward Elgar, pp. 304–341.

Symonds, Rob (VP Foothills, Shell Canada Ltd.) (2006) Personal communication, November 1.

Walker, Brian and David Salt (2006) *Resilience Thinking*. Island Press: Washington.

Wilson, E.O. (1993) "Is Humanity Suicidal?" *New York Times Magazine*, June 20.

Zolli, Andrew and Ann Marie Healy (2012) *Resilience. Why Things Bounce Back*. Free Press: New York.

## APPENDIX ONE

# A Brief Note on Case Analysis

This book presents several major cases that are used to introduce key concepts and tools of sustainability within the corporate sector. These cases should be approached critically with an eye to what lessons may be drawn from them. Each of the major case chapters begins with a list of concepts and relevant analytical tools, and proceeds to describe the basic characteristics of the firm and the challenges it faces. This is followed by several chapters that elaborate on the concepts and methodologies relevant to the case analysis. As an aid to analysis and in-class discussion, there are at least two distinct ways to approach these cases: (1) through the use of structured questions provided at the end of each case, or (2) a combination of role playing and analysis. In this latter approach, it is suggested that students assume the role of stock analysts who are making recommendations to a group of potential investors. The analysts are to make a case for BUY or SELL with the following considerations: if BUY, is this a short-term, medium-term, or long-term recommendation? If the companies in question are not public, then the analysts will be advising venture capitalists on the value of the potential investment. Comments should be addressed to several potential classes of investors: (1) traditional investors interested in maximizing financial returns; (2) triple bottom line (TBL) investors interested in funding those activities that achieve financial objectives while advancing social and environmental goals; and (3) social enterprise investors interested in social and environmental returns subject to a minimum financial return constraint.

The earliest description of what has more recently been called a *triple bottom line* investor is to be found in Porter and van der Linde's seminal 1995 article in the *Harvard Business Review* entitled "Green and Competitive: Ending the Stalemate." The authors argue that firms can gain sustainable competitive advantage by incorporating social and environmental goals into their strategic planning. In other words, being sustainable can yield the highest long-term profitability. It is important to distinguish between companies that are truly triple bottom line and those who merely report social and environmental indicators along with their financial results.

One way to characterize this tripartite typology is represented in Table 1–2. As stated above, it is ultimately necessary to "bring business on board," for only with the support of the corporate sector is there any chance of achieving sustainability. In this respect the upper left hand cell in Table 1–2 is the most important. There is ample evidence that sustainable investors and sustainably oriented corporations are

| | TRADITIONAL INVESTOR | |
|---|---|---|
| | YES | NO |
| Sustainable Investor  YES | Triple Bottom line: Michael Porter's model (see: Michael E. Porter and Claas van der Linde, "Green and Competitive: Ending the Stalemate" in *Bringing Business on Board*) | Social entreprise: focus on social and environmental aspects with minimum economic return constraint |
| NO | focus solely on economic returns | |

**TABLE 1.2**

*Typology of Investment Strategies with Respect to Sustainability*

ANTICIPATING STRATEGIC DECAY (REF. HAMEL AND VALIKANGAS, HBR SEP. 2003)

| REPLICATION | SUPPLANTATION | EXHAUSTION | EVISCERATION |
|---|---|---|---|
| Is our strategy losing its distinctiveness? | Is our strategy in danger of being superceded? | Is our strategy reaching the point of exhaustion? | Is increasing customer power eviscerating our margins? |
| Does our strategy defy industry norms in an important way? | Are there discontinuities (social, technical or political) that could significantly reduce the economic power of our current business model? | Is the pace of improvement in key performance metrics (cost per unit or marketing expense per new customer, for example) slowing down? | To what extent do our margins depend on customer ignorance or inertia? |
| Do we possess any competitive advantages that are truly unique? | Are there nascent business models that might render ours irrelevant? | Are our markets getting saturated; are our customers becoming more fickle? | How quickly, and in what ways, are customers gaining additional bargaining power? |
| Is our financial performance becoming less exceptional and more average? | Do we have strategies in place to co-opt or neutralize these forces of change? | Is our company's growth rate decelerating, or about to start doing so? | Do our productivity improvements fall to the bottom line, or are forced to give them back to customers in the form of lower prices or better products and services at the same price? |

**TABLE 1.3**

*Concept of Strategic Decay*

*Source:* Hamel and Valikangas 2003, p. 59

*Status*: Reproduced by permission of *Harvard Business Review*. Copyright 2003 by the President and Fellows of Harvard College, all rights reserved.

increasing in numbers, but this is not sufficient to achieve the massive transformation required. Only if traditional investors see sustainability as the avenue to profitability, will the principal impediments be overcome.

From a strategic perspective, it is also useful to adopt Hamel and Valikangas's (2003) concept of strategic decay as illustrated in Table 1–3. Their typology of analytical questions falls into four main categories: *replication, supplantation, exhaustion*, and *evisceration*. The analyst should examine the corporation in light of each of these critical issues.

Finally, it is worthwhile to consider whether the corporation should be included in a green or social portfolio to reflect its environmental and social record.

## APPENDIX TWO

# A Simple Example of Systems Theory

The forest sector has made, and continues to make, a significant contribution to economic activity in the U.S. Pacific Northwest, Southeast, Northeast, and several

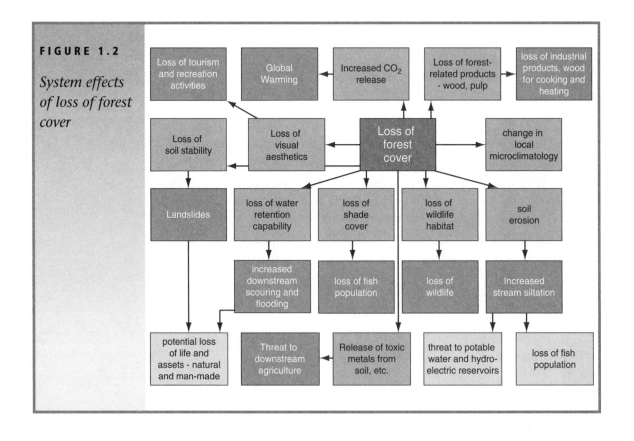

**FIGURE 1.2**

*System effects of loss of forest cover*

provinces of Canada. The traditional view of this sector focused on the economic value from the exploitation of dimensional timber and fiber for pulp and paper. The resulting economic decision-making framework focused on the rate of harvest, subject to a constraint based on maintaining a sustainable yield of forest products for the indefinite future. This historical view has been supplanted by a more extensive and nuanced view of the broad contributions from forests including not only marketable non-timber values, but also the complex interlinkages with both ecological systems and other disparate economic and social activities. Figure 1–2 illustrates some of the more important of these linkages and focuses specifically on the effects of loss of forest cover. Such loss can be due to excessive harvesting with inadequate replacement, or natural or anthropogenic phenomena such as forest fires, disease, and insect predation. What is apparent from this systems graphic is that the effects of the loss of forest cover are multifaceted and have an ultimately significant negative impact across a broad spectrum of economic values and business activity. The nature of these complex linkages are, in many cases, just now being thoroughly researched. What is missing in this diagram—and a subject discussed in chapter 10—are the multiple feedback loops and irreversibilities in this system, which can make system restoration and recovery exceedingly difficult.

## APPENDIX THREE

# Business and Ecosystems as Complex Adaptive Systems

One of the fundamental contributions of the discipline of environmental economics (see chapter 5) was the realization that economic systems, and business in particular, have profound, measurable, and monetizable impacts on the environment. With the emergence of ecological economics (see chapter 6) as a companion discipline, the circle of influence was completed with the identification of ecological systems as providing the underpinnings of economic activity. In fact, both economic and ecological systems have profound similarities and much to learn from each other. Both are manifestations of what have been described as *complex adaptive systems*. Levin (1998, p. 432) defines such systems by three essential components: "sustained diversity and individuality of components; localized interactions among those components; and an autonomous process that selects from among those components, based on the results of local interactions, a subset for replication or enhancement." Walker and Salt (2006, pp. 34–35) focus on a critical characteristic of such systems, namely their *emergent behaviour* (i.e., a characteristic that forecloses the opportunity to predict system behaviour solely from the observation of the "individual mechanics of its component parts or any pair of interactions. . . . Changes in one component can sometimes result in complete

| TABLE 1.4 | PHASE | CHARACTERIZATION | ECOLOGICAL MODEL | BUSINESS MODEL |
|---|---|---|---|---|
| *Business and Ecosystems as Complex Adaptive Systems* | r phase — Exploitation or rapid growth | System components weakly interconnected and the internal state is weakly regulated | Weeds, alder, dock and pigweed on newly exposed sites or cleared lands | Innovators, entrepreneurs, start-ups |
| | k phase — Conservation | Increasing efficiency and interconnectedness at the cost of resilience. Rigidity increases and redundancy and flexibility decrease | More biomass bound up in unavailable forms stored in tree heartwood and dead organic matter | Greater specialization, greater efficiencies, economies of scale |
| | Omega phase — Release | A sudden regime shift from even a small stimulus if system resilience is low [i.e., a tipping point phenomenon] | Fires, droughts, pests and disease | Emergence of new technology or market shock |
| | Alpha phase — Reorganization | A chaotic state with no stable equilibrium; this state evolves back toward a new r phase | New species, growth from suppressed vegetation, germination of buried seeds | Emergence of new groups in organizations, with new inventions, creative ideas and people |

reconfigurations of the system; the system changes to a different stable state (or regime)."

C.S. Holling, one of the fathers of modern ecological theory, has developed a powerful paradigm for understanding the underlying behaviour of a vast array of disparate systems which are, in essence, all complex and adaptive. Holling and Gunderson (2002, pp. 3–34) identify four critical phases in the evolution of such systems: (1) exploitation or rapid growth (called the r phase), (2) conservation (called the k phase), (3) release (called the omega phase), and (4) reorganization (called the alpha phase). The significance of each phase is best illustrated by reference to Table 1–4 which draws upon the work of Walker and Salt (2006, pp. 75–78) to demonstrate the applicability to both ecological and business models.

It is interesting to note that the underlying theoretical foundation of the omega phase is essentially similar to the *creative destruction* process in economic systems articulated by Joseph Schumpeter in his 1950 work, *Capitalism, Socialism and Democracy*.

In light of such strong similarities between economic and ecological systems, it should come as no surprise that conceptual models used in one area may be transferable in complete or modified form to the other. This two-way exchange has been illustrated in several studies which have attempted to apply financial models to the management of natural resources, such as fisheries. By way of example, Edwards et al. (2004) and Sanchirico et al. (2006) use portfolio theory to recommend a shift from single to multiple species optimization in fisheries management. On the other side of the ledger, Kambhu et al. (2007), Soramaki et al. (2006), and May et al. (2008) illustrate how critical ecological principles can aid the understanding of financial markets, thereby leading to improved methods of controlling large and undesirable effects of systemic risk such as those witnessed in the financial crisis of 2007–2008.

Despite the promising emergence of cross-system learning proffered by the underlying similarity of economic and ecological systems, the analyst and policymaker must also be cognizant of system differences which may attenuate the power of such conceptual transferences. The most obvious difference is that in contrast to ecosystems, economic system are composed of human agents who create as well as respond to system rules (Ehrenfeld, 2003, p. 3; Kambhu et al. 2007, p. 17). Nevertheless, this new avenue of intellectual inquiry has opened up many new possibilities for understanding and influencing the behaviour of superficially distinct, complex adaptive systems.

# PART I

*Foundations*

# A Brief Historical Overview of Economic Development and the Environment—Part I—Pre- and Post-Agricultural Revolution

W E BEGIN WITH AN ALLEGORICAL TALE. [See Figure 2–1.] On Easter Sunday, 1722, Dutch explorers landed on a remote island in the South Pacific Ocean. This land, named appropriately, Easter Island, revealed a remarkable and disconcerting sight to the explorers. Standing astride the shoreline were hundreds of massive stone figurines, as much as 65 feet in height and weighing up to 270 tons (Diamond 2005; Ponting 2007). Clearly the result of a relatively advanced civilization, these statues stood in marked contrast to the decay and desolation that surrounded them. The island's inhabitants were reduced to living in caves or reed huts and verging on the brink of extinction from starvation.

Recent research has been able to reconstruct the rise and fall of Easter Island's civilization. First peopled in the fifth century by Polynesians, the island had witnessed the flowering of a society with elaborate religious rituals. Central to the practice of this religion was the quarrying and carting of massive stones from the center of the island to the coastline where they were erected. Absent wheels and other means of conveyance, it appears that the locals adopted a method of transport used by the ancient Egyptians when building the great pyramids. Logs were used to roll the stones to the coast. The earliest inhabitants also relied on the once flourishing forest cover to provide fuel for cooking, heat for their homes, and canoes for offshore fishing.

The explorers found no such forest—the island had been virtually stripped of all trees, and the inhabitants had lost their capacity to build homes, fish offshore, and provide food from once-fertile soil eroded from loss of forest cover. The inhabitants were trapped on their island, no longer able to reverse the decline of their civilization by escaping back to other distant islands in Polynesia.

While this chronology has become the subject of some debate (Diamond 2007; Hunt and Lipo 2006 and 2011), there is, nevertheless, a profound significance to the apparent plight of the Easter Islanders that resonates to this day. Despite the fact that the islanders could presumably observe the exhaustion of the forest resource that was essential for their survival, they were unable to devise a social-economic-political system that allowed them to find the right balance with their fragile environment.

**FIGURE 2.1**

*Easter Island*

*Photo courtesy of David Wright*

One suggested explanation for this suicidal behavior was the increasingly fierce competition for the remaining dwindling resources among rival groups on the island. This bears a disturbing resemblance to modern day national and international behavior toward dwindling marine resources such as the Atlantic cod and diverse whale species, etc. The dismal history of Easter Island provides a striking example of the dependence of human societies on their ecosystem and the consequences of irreversibly damaging that environment. Like Easter Island, the earth has only limited resources to support human society and all its demands. Like the islanders, the human population of planet earth has no practical means of escape. The economist Kenneth Boulding (1966) coined the phrase "Spaceship Earth" in an attempt to capture the essence of this dilemma faced by mankind.

To place this dilemma in a modern context, consider the challenge facing NASA in their goal to send humans to the planet Mars. For just a one-way trip (Krauss 2009), the space agency would have to provide enough food, water, and oxygen for a small crew of astronauts as well as find a way to dispose of waste from their activities. It is obviously impractical (read impossible) to load this material into one spaceship for the journey. To solve this problem NASA would have to replicate within the spaceship a minor version of the earth, creating the commodities needed for existence and recycling the waste products. To all intents and purposes, this is called an *ecosystem*. Some years ago, NASA conducted a minor experiment as a proof of concept. Illustrated in Figure 2–2 is the result of NASA's first experiment: a small

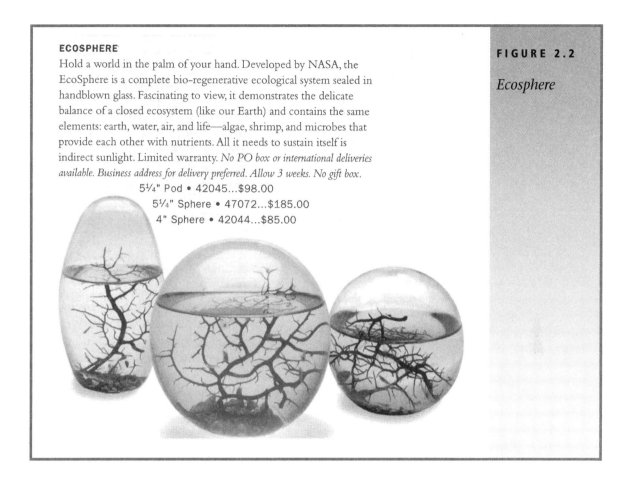

**ECOSPHERE**

Hold a world in the palm of your hand. Developed by NASA, the EcoSphere is a complete bio-regenerative ecological system sealed in handblown glass. Fascinating to view, it demonstrates the delicate balance of a closed ecosystem (like our Earth) and contains the same elements: earth, water, air, and life—algae, shrimp, and microbes that provide each other with nutrients. All it needs to sustain itself is indirect sunlight. Limited warranty. *No PO box or international deliveries available. Business address for delivery preferred. Allow 3 weeks. No gift box.*

5¼" Pod • 42045...$98.00

5¼" Sphere • 47072...$185.00

4" Sphere • 42044...$85.00

**FIGURE 2.2**

*Ecosphere*

glass container or "biosphere" that holds a plant and a small shrimp (www.ecosphere.com). This is basically a closed system like the earth—with the similar exception of the inflow of external energy in the form of sunlight. The process within the container replicates, on a greatly simplified scale, the fundamental principles of a natural ecosystem. The shrimp feeds on the plant, and its detritus acts as a food source for the plant. The system is self-sustaining.

With a proof of concept in hand, the next obvious requirement was to scale up the experiment to reflect more accurately the circumstances and requirements of spaceship travel. In 1991, Biosphere 2 was born in Oracle, Arizona (Schellnhuber 2001; Sherman 1993). Four women, four men, and 3,800 other species of animal and plants were placed within a massive sealed building (see http://www.biospheres.com/images/bio2diagram3.jpg) in an attempt to create a model for space stations on the moon or Mars. Contained within the structure were miniature representations of many of the earth's ecosystems, including a rainforest, coral reef, mangrove wetlands, grasslands and desert (http://www.b2science.org/who/fact). The results of the experiment, if successful, could also meet the requirements of a nine-month space flight. The experiment failed within one year as it was revealed that fresh air was secretly pumped in to compensate for a potentially deadly imbalance that was occurring between oxygen and carbon dioxide, which threatened collapse of all species within Biosphere 2.

The sobering conclusions from this experiment were aptly summarized by Cohen and Tilman (1996, pp. 1150–1151):

> At present there is no demonstrated alternative to maintaining the viability of Earth. No one yet knows how to engineer systems that provide humans with the life-supporting services that natural ecosystems produce for free. Dismembering major biomes into small pieces, a consequence of widespread human activities, must be regarded with caution. Despite its mysteries and hazards, Earth remains the only known home that can sustain life.

At this point, it is legitimate to pose the question: "Why worry?" Modern humankind has achieved the greatest degree of wealth in history; it has proven technical skills that have successfully overcome every serious threat to civilization so far. It is here that one must look outside the fields of technology, politics, and economics and consider the lessons of ecological history. As shall be explored in chapter 6, the global economy is imbedded in a larger system called the earth's ecosystem, which provides the necessary resources for survival. This system is basically "closed" (or finite) and will ultimately constrain the level of human activity. Nature has worked out an elaborate system of checks and balances to maintain some form of equilibrium. A good example of this concept is provided by the relationship between predators and prey, as illustrated in the classic representation of Figure 2–3 (Krebs; see also Forsyth and Caley 2006; Huffaker 1958). Predators (lynx) increase in numbers as their food supply (snowshoe hares) increases, then decrease in number as the prey population is depleted. Prey then increase in the face of the reduced number of predators, and this almost sinusoidal cycle repeats itself indefinitely. When for some reason or another, natural controls are removed on one species, this species may experience exponential growth, until it finally reaches a binding

**FIGURE 2.3**

*Typical predator-prey interaction*

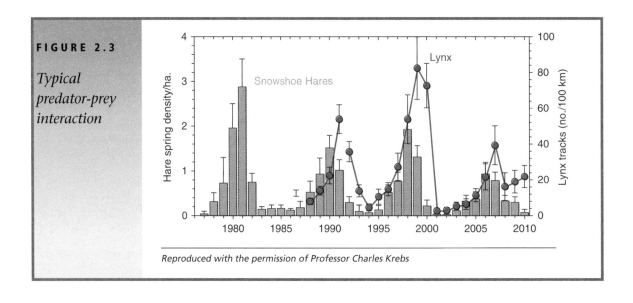

*Reproduced with the permission of Professor Charles Krebs*

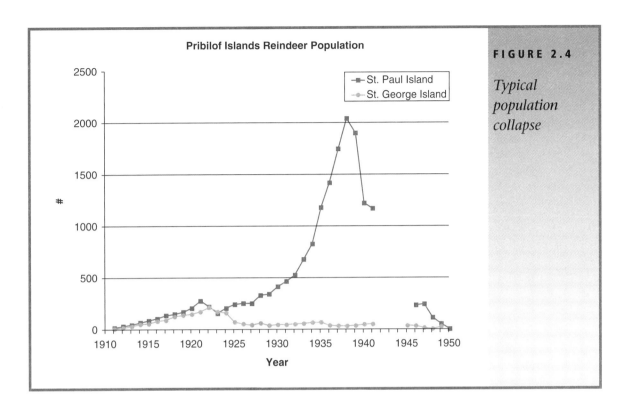

**FIGURE 2.4**

*Typical population collapse*

constraint such as limited food supply. The result is frequently sudden population collapse, as illustrated in Figure 2–4 (derived from Scheffer 1951).

What has this got to do with humanity? Figure 2–5 provides the U.S. Census Bureau's best estimates of global population over the last 500 years. One may posit the rhetorical question: does this look like a state of equilibrium? To understand the significance of this population trend, one must turn to another ecological term known as *carrying capacity*, defined as the number of organisms of a particular species (whether human, animal, or plant) that a geographic area can support without irreversibly reducing its capacity to support them in the future at the desired level of living. Carrying capacity is a function of many interacting factors including food, energy supplies and ecosystem services such as the provision of fresh water and recycling of nutrients. Carrying capacity is ultimately determined by the component that has the lowest capacity. The relevant question is: When will we reach global carrying capacity? The answer to this question is inherently complex (Cohen 1995, Ryerson 2010). But there is some evidence that the Earth may have already passed this point (Brown 2011, Pimental et al. 1999, WWF LPR multiple years). Table 2–1 attempts to determine global carrying capacity in relation to current population (Millman 1991, Uvin 1994). While these numbers are estimates and subject to debate, the general concept holds – capacity is closely related to the standard of living and related levels of energy and material consumption among the human population. Does this mean that the Brundtland Commission's goal of raising the living standard of the vast majority of global inhabitants is unattainable? In Chapter 3 the question is posed whether it is possible to de-link economic growth and environmental despoliation.

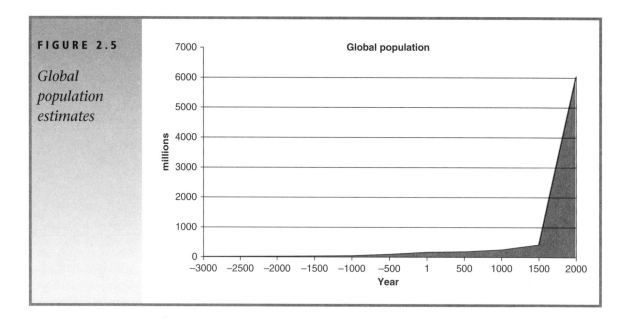

**FIGURE 2.5**

*Global population estimates*

| TABLE 2.1 | CONDITIONS | CARRYING CAPACITY (BILLION PEOPLE) |
|---|---|---|
| *Estimates of Global Carrying Capacity* | If humans gained 25% of their calories from animal protein as is the case with most people in North America | 2.8 |
| | If humans derive 15% of calories from animal products as do many in South America | 3.7 |
| | Using present agro technologies, vegetarian diet only and equal food distribution | 5.5 |
| | CURRENT POPULATION | 7.0 |

The exponential growth of human population in the last 500 years is a central, but not the only, factor that must be considered. Gerard Piel, former publisher of the *Scientific American*, wrote a prescient book entitled *The Acceleration of History*, which discussed the ethical obligations of a citizenry in the face of rapidly advancing science and technology (Piel 1972). A cogent illustration of this modern phenomenon of unprecedented exponential change is provided in historical graphs from Steffen et al. (2005). [See Figure 2–6.] The two most important time series are human population growth [Figure 2–5] and global GDP [Figure 2–7 from De Long 1998]. In contrast to the historical growth of human population represented in Figure 2–5, the scale of the graph of GDP growth is logarithmic, signifying the extraordinary achievement of human ingenuity in creating wealth through the application of technology to the earth's resources.

In 1798, The Reverend Thomas Malthus published the first edition of his *An Essay on the Principle of Population*. This work, more than any other, may have contributed to the characterization of the field of economics as "the dismal science." Malthus hypothesized that humankind would remain in a perpetual state of near starvation as the arithmetic increase in food production would be outpaced by an

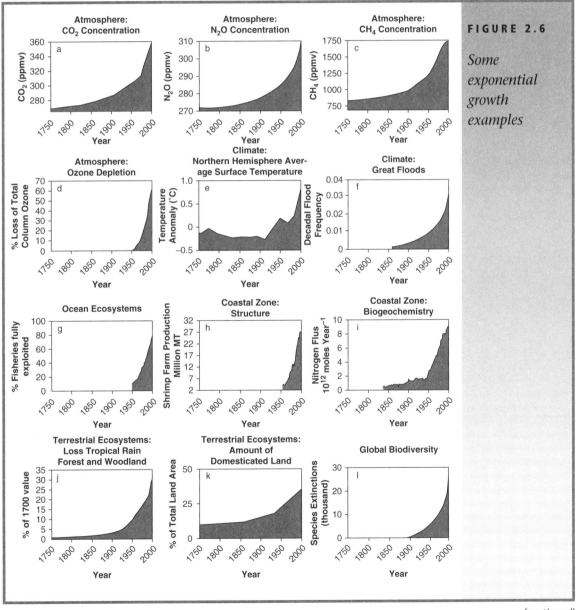

**FIGURE 2.6**

*Some exponential growth examples*

*(continued)*

**FIGURE 2.6**
*continued*

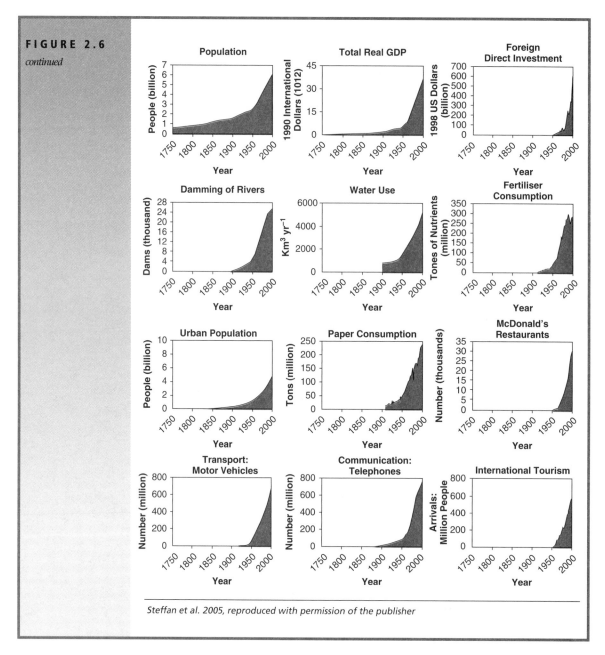

Steffan et al. 2005, reproduced with permission of the publisher

exponential increase in human population. Few works in traditional economics have been so vilified, as generations of economists have declared that Malthus was "wrong," and that increasing production of per capita global food supplies through continued breakthroughs in global food production technology has proved this critique beyond a reasonable doubt.

The United Nations (UN) has projected that global population will continue to increase for the next few decades and eventually stabilize at approximately 9 billion people (UN 2004). If the earth's nations are to feed this growing number of citizens, then major new technological breakthroughs will be required to raise the

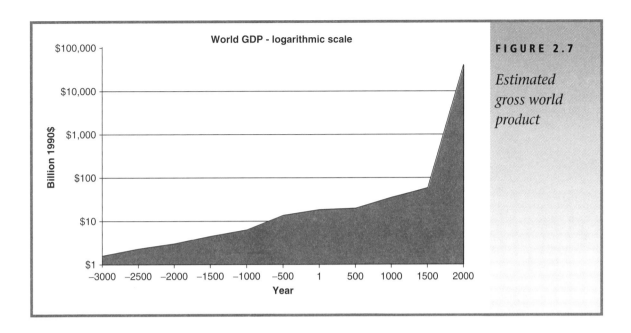

**FIGURE 2.7**

*Estimated gross world product*

yield of current food crops. What are the prospects for these continued advances in technology and its application to food production? One of the great technological advances in agriculture occurred in the period 1950 to 1984 and is referred to as the "Green Revolution." This was a concerted effort on the part of the Western industrialized nations to stimulate staple food production in India and other Third World countries through an agricultural system that relied on five critical factors: hybrid seeds which are high yield, fast growing, and disease resistant; heavy use of fertilizer (e.g., India increased its imports of fertilizer by 600% in 1960–80); increased use of pesticides; mechanization and high energy-intensity agriculture such as tractors, combines, irrigation pumps; and increased reliance on monoculture (UNEP 2011, p. 40).

As with all technological advances, there are both benefits and costs. The benefits were clear: between 1950 and 1984, there was a 2.6-fold increase in world grain output. This represented an average increase of almost 3% per year, and rising per capita production by more than one third. In contrast, world population growth during 1980–85 was only 1.75% per year. The costs, however, have been substantial and include land degradation; ground water contamination; social dislocation due to land aggregation and the displacement of small landowners; and significant costs associated with the production and use of fertilizers, pesticides, and commercial energy products. Initial increases in food production were remarkable, leading to a gradual increase in average grain production per capita at the global level. Since 1985, however, despite the investment of billions of dollars to increase output, supported by the incentive of rising grain prices and the restoration to production of idled U.S. cropland, per capita crop yields have plateaued and appear to be falling, and the declining trend in the proportion of undernourished people in developing countries reversed over the period 2005–2009, although it recovered in 2010

**FIGURE 2.8**

*World per capita grain production*

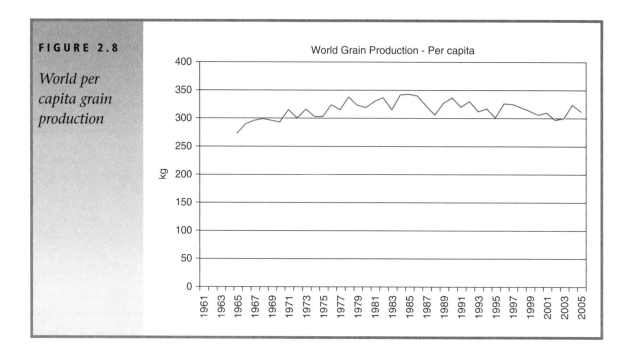

**FIGURE 2.9**

*Percentage of undernourished population in the developing world*

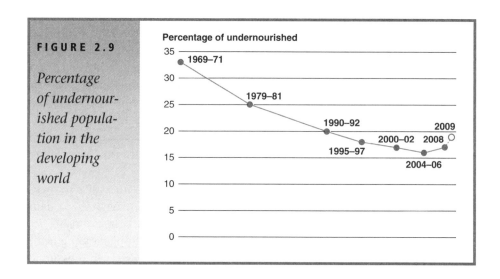

[see Figures 2–8 and 2–9 from FAO 2011]. While other factors aside from inadequate production are at play, such as armed conflict, misdistribution, and spoilage, the trend is not heartening.

## INITIAL CONCLUSION

There are several fundamental forces driving the current pressure on the environment: (1) rising population, (2) increasing industrialization and wealth with its concomitant rise in demand for food and other natural resources, and (3) technological innovations that may have environmentally detrimental effects. The interrelationship among these factors can be captured in the following basic equation:

P × M/P × E/M = total pollution

where P = population, M = material consumption, and E = environmental impact.

The message from this simple relationship is that total pollution can increase from any one of three factors: population growth, increased per capita consumption, and the increased pollution intensity of products. If the goal is to decrease the environmental burden of the planet, it is clearly insufficient to tackle only one or two of these factors; an increase in the residual may offset any positive effects in the others. What does the empirical evidence tell us?

Despite popular opinion to the contrary, it is often the nature of scientific evidence that it is open to divergent interpretations. An optimist would take consolation in the fact that the annual rate of population increase falls as per capita income rises. The underlying dynamic process is referred to as the *demographic transition*, which includes a pattern of changes in birth rates, death rates, and resulting population growth rates that accompany economic development. Net population growth is a function of the phase of economic development. Historically, three such phases have been documented: (1) a pre-industrial phase, characterized by both high birth and death rates, producing low or stable population growth; (2) an industrial phase, marked by high birth rates and major reduction in death rates due to the increased application of public health measures, leading in turn to explosive growth; and (3) a mature or post-industrial phase characterized by both low birth and death rates, producing a return to low or stable population growth rates.

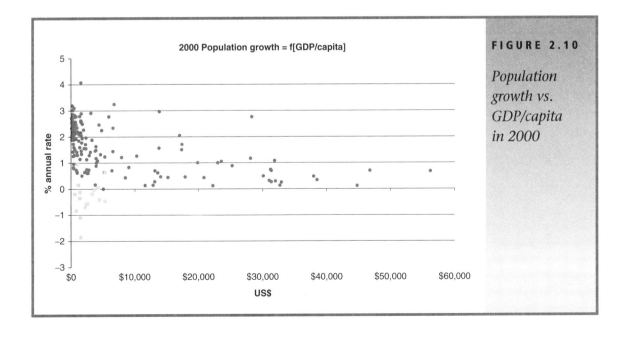

**FIGURE 2.10**

*Population growth vs. GDP/capita in 2000*

**FIGURE 2.11**

*Selected national population pyramids*

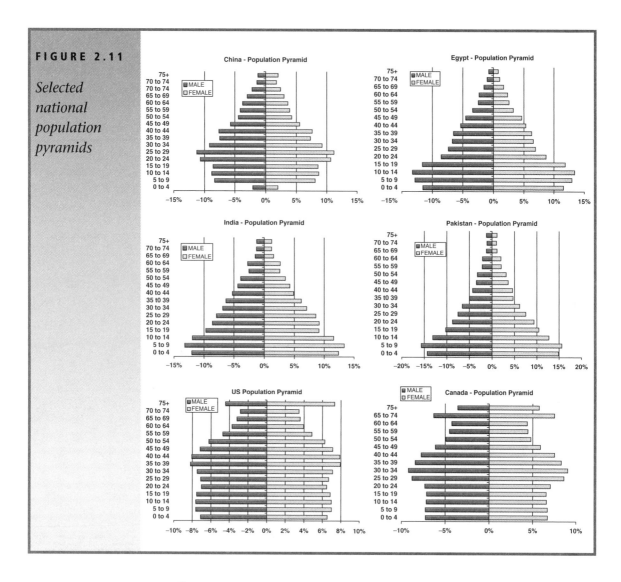

These transitions are based on historical time-series analysis but can also be observed in cross-sectional examination of global nations today that span a broad range of per capita income. The data provided in Figure 2–10 compare the annual growth rates in national population with GDP per capita.[1] It can be hypothesized on the basis of these data that past a certain point in per capita income, population growth rate stabilizes at a low level, in some cases below the level of population replacement. Even more important is the relatively low level of per capita income (at approximately $10,000) at which this stabilization appears to occur. This suggests that it is not necessary to raise the standard of living of the world's poorest countries to the level of the wealthiest in order to solve the problems associated with rapid population increase.

Another way of observing the significantly different national population growth paths is to examine *population pyramids*, which show the percentage of the population, by gender, in each major age category. Figure 2–11 provides sample

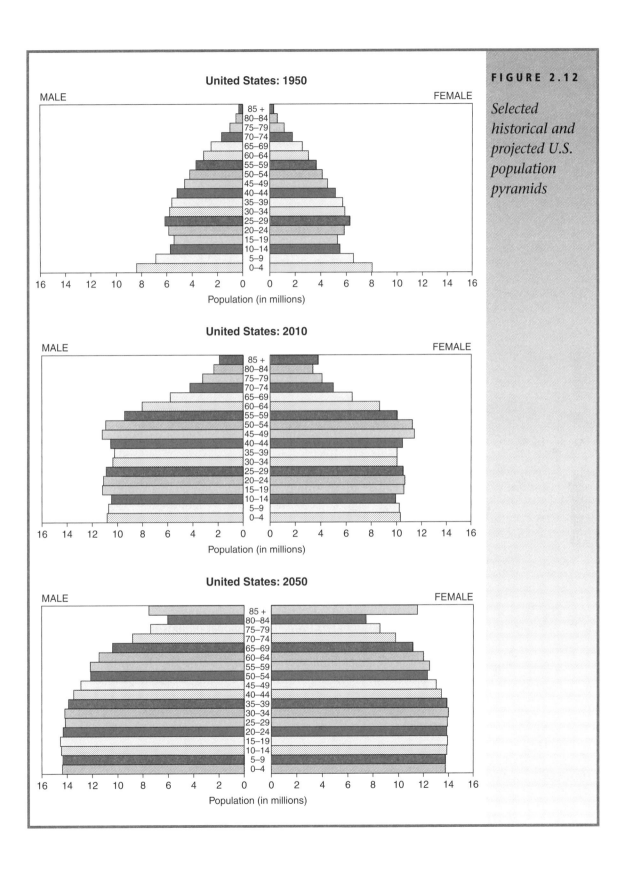

**FIGURE 2.12**

*Selected historical and projected U.S. population pyramids*

international population pyramid data for six countries (U.S. Census Bureau). The two wealthiest countries in this sample, the United States and Canada, have an approximately even age distribution, suggesting a relatively stable population. In contrast, the four developing nations, China, India, Egypt, and Pakistan, have a much greater proportion of their population in their childbearing years, suggesting a potential for a significant continuing increase in population. By raising the standard of living of these countries, it is hoped that they will replicate the historical pattern of the developed world as illustrated in Figure 2–12, which shows how the U.S. population pyramid has shifted over time as national wealth has increased. Nevertheless, the increasing proportion of middle-aged and elderly persons accompanying industrial development tends to generate its own particular challenges, as there is a decrease in the percentage of working people in the total population, putting additional stress on national pension funds.

In sum, the optimist's position is that increased wealth brings reduced population growth and, therefore, by simply raising the standard of living of the rest of the world, the problem of population growth will take care of itself. There are several positive sides to this argument: it seems altruistic and ethical; it may avoid the problem of forced population control, such as China's controversial program to reduce births and the concomitant perverse incentives created by this policy [see chapter 10]; it will avoid the contentious perception that the Industrialized World is forcing population control on the Third World for self-serving reasons; and it may finesse the delicate religious issue of birth control and abortion.

In marked contrast, the pessimist's interpretation of these same data is based on three arguments: first, the process of raising global standards of living will take a long time; second, the drain on essential natural resources (in such areas as fisheries and agriculture) may be enormous and; finally, and perhaps most important, the environment poses a binding constraint in the form of the adequacy of fresh, clean water; the assimilate capacity of air, water, and soil; and the burden on the ecosystem from the increased utilization of energy.

## Summary Overview of Human Historical Impact on the Environment

Throughout the broad sweep of human history, global inhabitants have progressed through four major historical phases: (1) pre-agricultural, (2) agricultural—pre-industrial, (3) industrial, and (4) post-industrial. The last of these phases is restricted to only a subset of modern nations, as the majority of the global population remains in an earlier stage. Figure 2–13 links the exponential increase in population over the least 12,000 years to the major technological transitions. Each of the four principal phases can be associated with specific forms of economic organization, human impacts on the natural environment, and the nature of the risks faced by humankind.

1. **The Pre-Agricultural Period**, characterized by hunting, gathering, and herding, lasted for about 2 million years and was marked by localized ecological disturbance from controlled burning, overhunting, and some resulting extinction of species. The human population remained in relative balance with

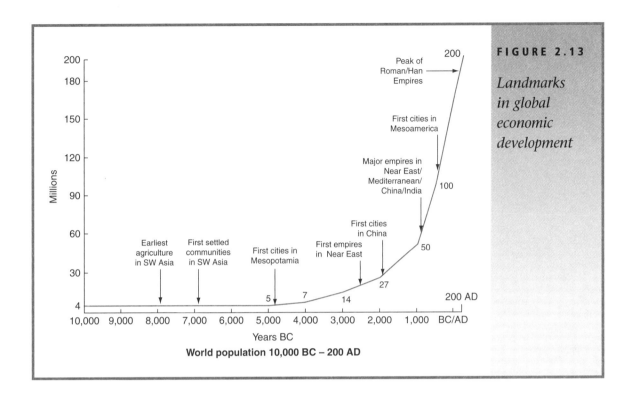

**FIGURE 2.13**

*Landmarks in global economic development*

World population 10,000 BC – 200 AD

resource availability by frequent changes of location, and some measure of population control was achieved through infanticide. A recent study (Doughty et al. 2010) has suggested that even at this early stage of human development, humankind exerted a subtle influence on global climate. It is posited that ancient hunters helped warm the arctic and subarctic regions by intensive hunting of wooly mammoths. By largely eliminating this herbivorous species whose diet consisted largely of leaves, humankind created an ecosystem response that led to the proliferation of dwarf birch trees, changing the reflective surface of the region (i.e., its *albido*) and increasing its heat absorption. This systemic response led to a subtle increase in global warming. This is but one example of the importance of systems analysis not only in the study of ecology, but also in the interrelationship of economic and ecological systems. [See chapter 10 on systems theory.]

2. **The Agricultural Revolution** occurred about 10,000 years ago and represents the most important transition in human history. In the space of a few thousand years, a radically different way of life emerged based on a major alteration to natural ecosystems in order to produce crops and provide pasture for animals. This intensive system of food production was developed separately in three core areas of the world: Mesoamerica, Southwest Asia, and China.

Agriculture allowed the emergence of a large hierarchical social structure supported by, but not engaged directly in, agricultural production, including administration, religion, culture, military forces, and early industrial activity. According to Ponting (1991), the first true cities started to emerge by about 5000 B.C. To quote:

> Human history in the 8000 years or so since the emergence of settled agricultural societies has been about the acquisition and distribution of the surplus food production and the uses to which it has been put. The size of the food surplus available to a particular society has determined the number and extent of other functions . . . the link may have been more obvious in earlier, simpler societies, but it is still present in contemporary societies. (p. 54)

Settled agricultural societies provide the first examples of intensive human alteration of the environment and their major destructive impact. They also provide examples of societies that so damaged the environment as to bring about their own collapse—an event characterized by Jared Diamond (2005) as "Ecocide." At least two major factors associated with agricultural activity had a historically devastating environmental impact: deforestation and irrigation.

**Deforestation**: Forest clearing for agriculture, fuel, and building materials leads to soil erosion, declining crop yields, and eventual the inability to grow enough food. Much of the Mediterranean area, now distinguished by bare rock and deserts, was once covered in forests. In his insightful book on the forest history of the Mediterranean literal, J.V. Thirgood (1981, p.3) observes that

> No other part of the world so strikingly drives home the story of man's failure to maintain his environment. . . . Once the focal point of western civilization, the Balkans, Anatolia, the Levant and North Africa is now economically depressed. Southern Italy, where the Hellenes settled Graecia Magna nearly three thousand years ago (974–443 B.C.) and developed a centre of Grecian culture—where Herodotus, the historian, lived, where Pythagoras advanced the science of Geometry, and where Aeschylus wrote his plays—was a land of forests. It was here in the scorched heart of Sicily at Piazza Armerina, that a mosaic extending over a quarter of an acre was discovered—the floor of a fourth century Roman villa, depicting woodland hunting and wildlife scenes [see the cover of this book]—at a site now surrounded by a landscape of barren grey hills.

Ponting (1991) describes a similar situation in North Africa that "contains a whole series of impressive Roman remains . . . from what were once some of the most flourishing and highly productive provinces of the Roman Empire. But they now lie surrounded by vast deserts, a memorial to widespread environmental degradation brought about by human actions."

One of the most famous and controversial cases of environmental collapse leading to the demise of a society comes from the Maya, who developed in what are now parts of Mexico—Guatemala, Belize, and Honduras—one of the most extraordinary societies of its type found anywhere in the world. The old empire existed during the period 300–900 A.D. Population was estimated to have peaked in 800 A.D. at between 2.7 and 3.4 million. The civilization collapsed within a few decades due to declining food production and to the compound effects of deforestation and drought (Diamond 2005; Fagan 2008; Hodell et al. 1995, 2001; Ponting 2007; Kennett et al., 2012).

***Irrigation***, the process that facilitates the transformation of arid regions to highly productive agricultural areas, is a double-edged sword and has been labeled the second major destructive force of the agricultural era. Its benefits are multifold. In addition to allowing crop production in areas where none could occur before, it permits increased crop yield, allows multiple cropping in a year, and broadens the array of crops that can be cultivated. In contrast, however, its costs are significant, as it can deplete the soil of nutrients and raise the water table, increasing water logging, producing progressive salinization of the soil that can lead to the gradual decline of crop production through lower yields and elimination of salt-intolerant crops such as wheat. The only way this process can be avoided is by very careful use of irrigation, not overwatering, and leaving the ground fallow at periodic intervals. Unfortunately, in many parts of the world, these procedures, especially fallowing, are luxuries as every bit of arable land is required to feed their populations. There are numerous civilizations in human history that are suspected of collapsing due to soil salinization. Among the most prominent of these are the agricultural societies of

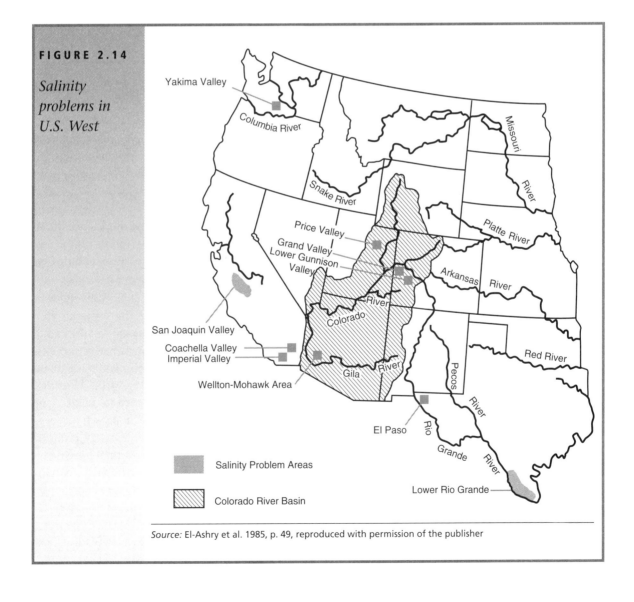

**FIGURE 2.14**

*Salinity problems in U.S. West*

Source: El-Ashry et al. 1985, p. 49, reproduced with permission of the publisher

**FIGURE 2.15**

*Colorado River flows*

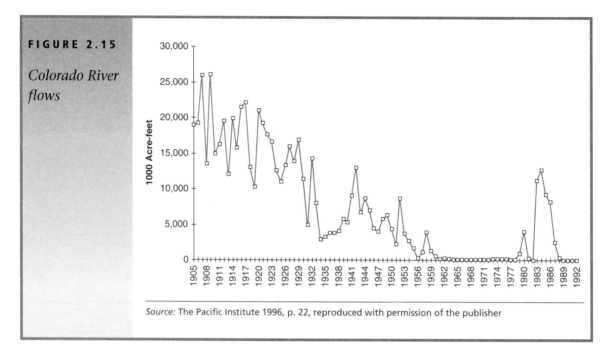

*Source:* The Pacific Institute 1996, p. 22, reproduced with permission of the publisher

ancient Mesopotamia and the Indus valley, now parts of the Middle East and South Asia (Ponting 2007; Turner et al. 1990).

While salinization and other major effects of vast irrigation projects have received relatively little public attention, it is still a critical issue wherever intensive irrigation-based agriculture is practiced in both the Third and Developed Worlds. It is estimated that between 21 and 24% of global arable land is damaged by salt (Lenntech 2011; UNEP 2006). For a cogent example, one need look no further than the United States with the drawdown of the Colorado River and the extensive depletion of the Ogallala aquifer, which have provided vast quantities of water for agriculture and urban development in the Southwest (see Woods et al. 2000; Figure 2–14 from El-Ashry and Gibbons 1986.) Figure 2–15 provides a dramatic example of the effect of excess demand on the Colorado River water over the past century (Morrison et al. 1996). Both of these phenomena represent unsustainable practices that must be resolved if current agriculture and urbanization is to continue in the Western states.

On a positive note, while the San Joaquin Valley in California has lost thousands of acres from cultivation due to irrigation-induced salinization, a recent proposal has offered the promise of using this land in a sustainable manner while contributing to American energy self-sufficiency (*New York Times* Aug. 10, 2010). All critical stakeholders, including farmers and environmentalists, have agreed to use this land for the creation of a 30,000-acre solar energy facility. This novel approach has been termed "the vanguard of a new approach to locating renewable energy projects" overcoming traditional objections to the use of land for nonagricultural purposes.

While both deforestation and irrigation have had devastating impacts on many ancient civilizations, deforestation has been the recent focus of global concern in both tropical and temperate forests—all the way from Brazil, Central America, and Southeast Asia to parts of the Pacific Northwest [see chapter 21]. This is a critical issue today, with immense implications not only directly for global agriculture, but also indirectly for global warming and all its concomitant effects.

# CITED REFERENCES AND RECOMMENDED READINGS

Boulding, Kenneth (1966) "The Economics of the Coming Spaceship Earth" (http://dieoff.org/page160.htm); reprinted as Ch. 5 in Herman E. Daly (ed.) 1973 *Toward a Steady-State Economy*. New York: W.H. Freeman & Co., pp. 121–132.

Brander, James A. and M. Scott Taylor (1998) "The Simple Economics of Easter Island: A Ricardo-Malthus Model of Renewable Resource Use." *American Economic Review*, 88(1), March, pp. 119–138.

Brown, Lester (2011) *World on the Edge:How to Prevent Environmental and Economic Collapse*, Earth Policy Institute, New York: W.W. Norton.

Cohen, Joel E. (1995) *How Many People Can the Earth Support?* New York: W.W. Norton & Co.

Cohen, Joel E. and David Tilman (1996) "Biosphere 2 and Biodiversity: The Lessons So Far." *Science*, 274(15), November, pp. 1150–1151.

De Long, J. Bradford (1998) "Estimates of World GDP, One Million B.C.—Present" (http://econ161.berkeley.edu).

Diamond, Jared (2005) *Collapse. How Societies Chose to Fail or Succeed*. New York: Viking.

Diamond, Jared (2007) "Easter Island Revisited." *Science*, 317, September 21, pp. 1692–1694.

Doughty, Christopher et al. (2010) "Biophysical Feedbacks between the Pleistocene Megafauna Extinction and Climate: The First Human-Induced Global Warming?" *Geophysical Research Letters*, 37, L15703, 5 pages.

El-Ashry, Mohamed et al. (1985) "Salinity Pollution from Irrigated Agriculture." *Journal of Soil and Water Conservation*, 40(1), January–February, pp. 48–52.

Fagan, Brian (2008) *The Great Warming. Climate Change and the Rise and Fall of Civilizations*. New York: Bloomsbury Press.

Food and Agriculture Organization (FAO) (2011) *The State of Food and Agriculture 2010–11*, Rome.

Forsyth, David M. and Peter Caley (2006) "Testing the Irruptive Paradigm of Large-Herbivore Dynamics." *Ecology*, 87(2), pp. 297–303.

Hodell, David A. et al. (1995) "Possible Role of Climate in the Collapse of Classic Maya Civilization." *Nature*, 375, June 1, pp. 391–394.

Hodell, David A. et al. (2001) "Solar Forcing of Drought Frequency in the Maya Lowlands." *Science*, 202, May 18, pp. 1367–1370.

Huffaker, C.B. (1958) "Experimental Studies on Predation: Dispersion Factors and Predator-Prey Oscillations. *Hilgardia*, 27, pp. 343–383.

Hunt, Terry L. and Carl P. Lipo (2006) "Late Colonization of Easter Island." *Science*, 311, March 17, pp. 1603–1606.

Hunt, Terry L. and Carl P. Lipo (2011) *The Statues That Walked. Unraveling the Mystery of Easter Island*. New York: Free Press.

Kennett, Douglas J. et al. (2012) "Development and Disintegration of Maya Political Systems in Response to Climate Change," *Science*, Nov. 9, Vol. 338, pp. 788–791.

Krauss, Lawrence M. (2009) "A One-Way Ticket to Mars." *New York Times*, August 31 Op-Ed.

Krebs, Charles—Personal communication

Lenntech (2011) "Salinity Hazard", Rotterdamseweg, The Netherlands (www.lenntech.com/applications/irrigation/salinity/salanity-hazard-irrigation.htm)

Malthus, Thomas (1798) *An Essay on the Principle of Population*. [Reprinted 2002, Boston: IndyPublish.com.]

Millman, S.R. et al. (1991) The Hunger Report: Update 1991. HR-91–1. Alan Shawn Feinstein World Hunger Program, Brown Univeristy, April.

Morrison, Jason I. et al. (1996) *The Sustainable Use of Water in the Lower Colorado River Basin*. Seattle, WA: Pacific Institute.

*New York Times* (2010) "Recycling Land for Green Energy Ideas," August 10.

Piel, Gerard (1972) *The Acceleration of History*. New York: Alfred A. Knopf.

Pimentel, David et al., (1999) "Will Limits of the Earth's Resources Control Human Numbers?" *Environment, Development and Sustainability* 1, no. 1, March, pp. 19–39.

Ponting, Clive (1991) *A Green History of the World*. Harmondsworth, Middlesex: Penguin Books.

Ponting, Clive (2007) *A New Green History of the World*. London: Vintage Books.

Ryerson, William N. (2010) "Population, The Multiplier of Everything," in Richard Heinberg and Daniel Lerch (eds.) *The Post Carbon Reader: Managing the 21st Century's Sustainability Crises*, Post Carbon Institute, Watershed Media, Healdsburg, CA pp. 153–176.

Scheffer, Victor B. (1951) "The Rise and Fall of a Reindeer Herd." *Science*, 73(6), December, pp. 356–362.

Schellnhuber, H.-J. (2001) "Earth System Analysis and Management," Chapter 2 in Eckart Ehlers and Thomas Krafft (eds.) *Understanding the Earth System. Compartments, Processes and Interactions*. Berlin: Springer, pp. 17–56.

Sherman, Francine Shonfeld (1993) "Biosphere 2: Hard Science of Soft Sell?" in *Encyclopaedia Britannica Yearbook*, p. 166.

Steffen, W. et al. (2005) *Global Change and the Earth System*. Berlin: Springer.

Thirgood, J.V. (1981) *Man and the Mediterranean Forest: A History of Resource Depletion*. London: Academic Press.

Turner, B.L. et al. (1990) *The Earth as Transformed by Human Action: Global and Regional Changes in the Biosphere over the Past 300 Years*. Cambridge: Cambridge University Press.

UN Environment Programme (UNEP) (2006) *Global Environment Outlook 3 (GEO3)*.

UN Environment Programme (UNEP) (2011) *Towards a Green Economy. Pathways to Sustainable Development and Poverty Eradication*.

United Nations (2004) *World Population to 2300*. New York.

U.S. Census Bureau website (http:www.census.gov/)

Uvin, Peter (1994) "The State of World Hunger," *Nutrition Reviews*, Vol. 52, No. 5, pp. 1–17.

Woods J.J. et al. (2000) *Water Level Decline in the Ogallala Aquifer*. Kansas City: United States Geological Service.

World Wildlife Fund (WWF) (multiple years) *Living Planet Report*, Gland, Switzerland. http://www.biospheres.com/images/bio2diagram3.jpg

Wright, David—Photo credit for Easter Island.

www.eco-sphere.com [website of Ecosphere Associates, Inc., Tucson, AZ].

## NOTE

1. Square data points represent former Eastern Bloc countries and republics of the Soviet Union.

# CHAPTER 3

# A Brief Historical Overview of Economic Development and the Environment—Part II—The Industrial Revolution and Sequel

T HE SECOND MOST SIGNIFICANT CHANGE in recent human history was the Industrial Revolution of the late 1700s and early 1800s. This dramatic change in technology, economics, the organization of business and society occurred in England during the period 1760–1840. Termed the "Workshop of the World" (Chambers 1961), the island nation established the framework on which our modern industrial economy rests. This revolution was characterized by a shift from an agrarian to an industrial society where the locus of production shifted from the home and workshop to the factory. The principal features of this radical transformation and its sequelae included over 11 major changes in the technological and nonindustrial spheres:

(1) the use of new basic materials, chiefly iron and steel, (2) the use of new energy sources, including both fuels and motive power, such as coal, the steam engine, electricity, petroleum, and the internal-combustion engine, (3) the invention of new machines, such as the spinning jenny and the power loom that permitted increased production with a smaller expenditure of human energy, (4) a new organization of work known as the factory system, which entailed increased division of labour and specialization of function, (5) important developments in transportation and communication, including the steam locomotive, steamship, automobile, airplane, telegraph, and radio, and (6) the increasing application of science to industry. These technological changes made possible a tremendously increased use of natural resources and the mass production of manufactured goods. (*Encyclopaedia Britannica* 1993, Vol. 6, p. 305)

New developments in nonindustrial spheres included

(1) agricultural improvements that made possible the provision of food for a larger non-agricultural population, (2) economic changes that resulted in a wider distribution of wealth, the decline of land as a source of wealth in

the face of rising industrial production, and increased international trade, (3) political changes reflecting the shift in economic power . . . , (4) sweeping social changes, including the growth of cities, the development of working-class movements . . . , and (5) cultural transformations of a broad order. The worker acquired new and distinctive skills, and his relation to his task shifted; instead of being a craftsman working with hand tools, he became a machine operator, subject to factory discipline. (Ibid.)

From the perspective of environmental sustainability, there were at least four profound and interrelated changes ushered in by the Industrial Revolution: a rapid increase in the flow of materials; a massive increase in the use of energy, particularly fossil fuels; the consequent release of large quantities of anthropogenic greenhouse gases such as carbon dioxide; and the generation and release of a broad range of industrial-based air and water pollutants. Figure 3–1 displays global materials extraction measured from 1900 to 2005 (http://www.ggdc.net/maddison/; Krausmann et al. 2009) Figures 3–2a and 3–2b show the dramatic increase in energy consumption in the United Kingdom (Maddison 2006a and 2006b; Mitchell 2007a; Mitchell and Deane 1962; Warde 2007) and the United States (Maddison 2006; Mitchell 2007; U.S. Dept. of Commerce 1975) over the past several centuries. Both of these figures also display the changing mix of fuel types as fossil fossils established a dominant role in both economies. Figures 3–3 and 3–4 illustrate the inevitable rise

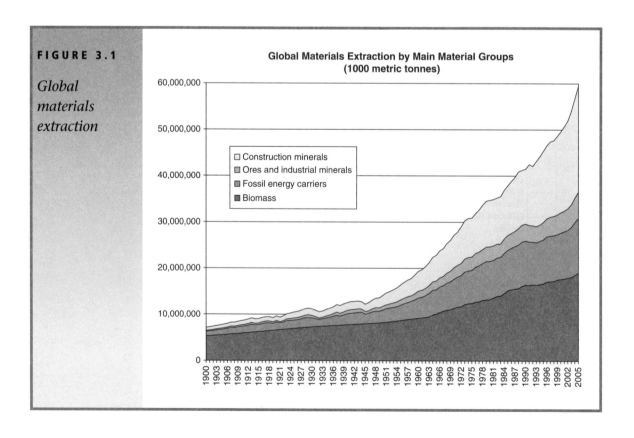

**FIGURE 3.1**

*Global materials extraction*

**Global Materials Extraction by Main Material Groups**
**(1000 metric tonnes)**

Legend:
☐ Construction minerals
▨ Ores and industrial minerals
▨ Fossil energy carriers
■ Biomass

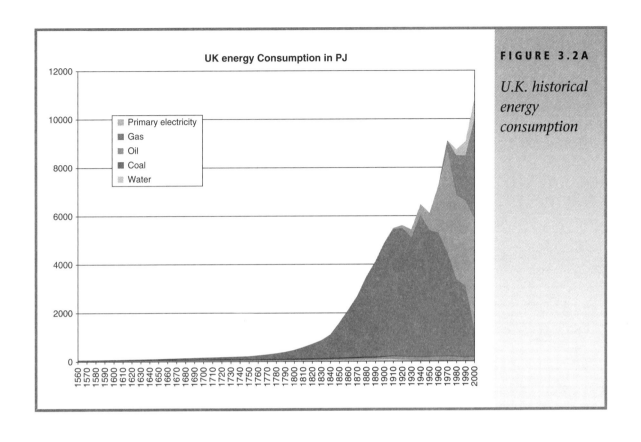

**FIGURE 3.2A**

*U.K. historical energy consumption*

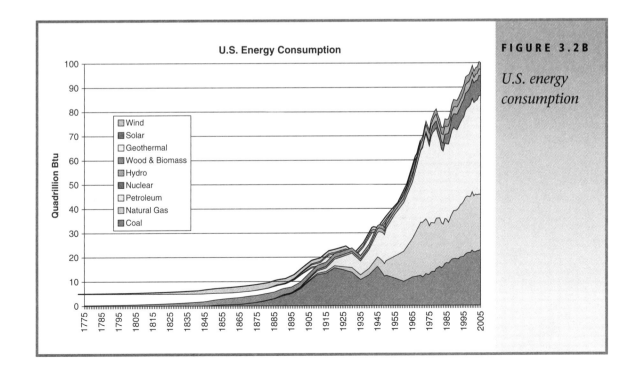

**FIGURE 3.2B**

*U.S. energy consumption*

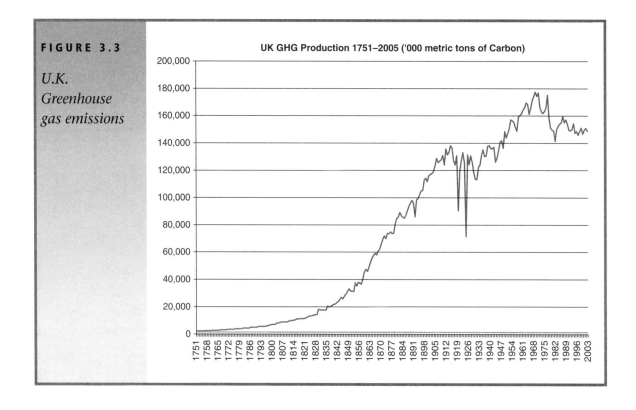

**FIGURE 3.3**

*U.K. Greenhouse gas emissions*

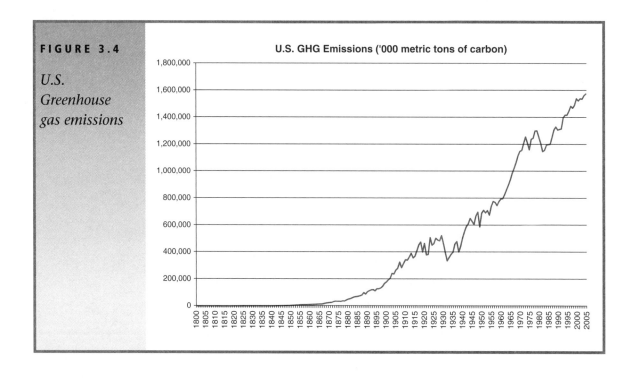

**FIGURE 3.4**

*U.S. Greenhouse gas emissions*

in greenhouse gases, most notably carbon dioxide, as a consequence of this energy consumption (ORNL). The recent apparent decrease in GHG gas emissions in the U.K. is due to two major factors: the backing out of coal by natural gas, and the outsourcing of carbon-intensive manufacturing to overseas producers such as China ) in a process described as "carbon laundering" or "carbon washing" (NEF 2007).

The results of the Industrial Revolution were dramatic, allowing a commensurate increase in wealth and standard of living among the industrializing nations of the world. The fundamental challenge now faced by the global community is how to share this development with the vast majority of world citizens who reside within the Third World without engendering the same deleterious environmental consequences. This challenge can be posited as follows: is it possible to de-link economic growth and environmental despoliation or, more simply, is there more than one path to economic development? It is now generally accepted that raising the standard of living of the Third World to any significant proportion of that experienced by the developed nations would involve massive increases in energy and material flows that would threaten the very foundation of the global ecological system that supports human life and economic activity.

There is a commonly held view that economies can grow their way out of pollution in a manner analogous to the demographic transition. This conventional wisdom is epitomized by the famous *Environmental Kuznets Curve*, named after the late Simon Kuznets of Harvard University's economics department. There are two principal variants of this function. The first class of curves, as illustrated in Figure 3–5a, represents monotonically decreasing environmental problems associated with increasing standards of living, such as the percentage of population without safe water or adequate sanitation. The second class of curves [see Figure 3–5b] are convex functions for such pollutants as airborne particulates and sulfur dioxide. In this case, it is posited that as economies move from primary to secondary and tertiary

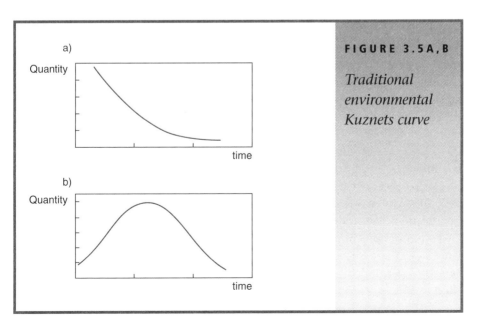

**FIGURE 3.5A,B**

*Traditional environmental Kuznets curve*

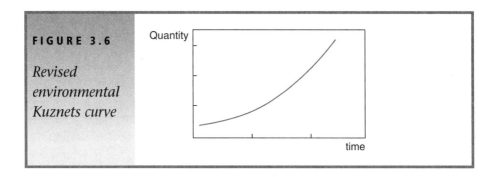

**FIGURE 3.6**

*Revised environmental Kuznets curve*

industry, they can both afford greater pollution control and switch to more environmentally benign production processes.

While these two types of transformations appear to be supported by historical evidence, they portray a seriously incomplete and misleading picture of the environmental consequences of industrialization. Figure 3–6 typifies what is missing. The monotonically increasing functions portrayed in this figure represent the increasing levels of pollutants that rise in tandem with increasing national income: solid waste, radioactive waste, greenhouse gases (GHGs), persistent organic pollutants (POPs), etc. Unlike traditional pollutants associated with the early stages of industrialization, many of these new hazards transcend local or regional effects and pose global-level threats to the environment. While greenhouse gases are the most obvious manifestation of this potential for global impact, another major category includes POPs such as Aldrin, Chlordane, Dieldrin, Dioxins (PCDDs), DDT, Endrin, Furans (PCDFs), Heptachlor, Hexachlorobenzene, Mirex, Polychlorinated biphenyls (PCBs), and Toxaphene. These substances have three critical properties that render them especially problematic: they persist in the environment, they bioaccumulate [see chapter 10] in the food web, and are subject to long-range transport (Breivik et al. 2002, 2007; NRC 2009; UNEP 2007). While many POPs are pesticides, others have been used extensively as solvents and ingredients in both industrial processes and pharmaceutical production.

POPs have multiple diffusion pathways in the environment, and many tend to be transported over long distances and can be deposited far from their point of manufacture or use (EMEP 2005; Ottesen et al. 2010; Wania and Mackay 1993). Several studies of the blood, tissues, and maternal milk of Arctic mammals, including humans, have found pollutant levels many times those of populations in the temperate regions (Indian and Northern Affairs Canada 2003; Schindler November 3, 2007). One research study conducted in the Arctic found a growing gender imbalance among human births, with females far outnumbering males. In one Greenland village, no males were born in the period under study (LOE 2007; Schindler November 3, 2007). In an attempt to understand the potential causal relationships in this phenomenon, one study (UNEP 2004) found a convex relationship between total PCB concentrations in maternal serum and the male/female sex ratio at birth [see Figure 3–7]. There is recent emerging evidence that many of the POPs deposited in the Arctic over the past half century are now being revolatized by climate change (Ma et al. 2011).

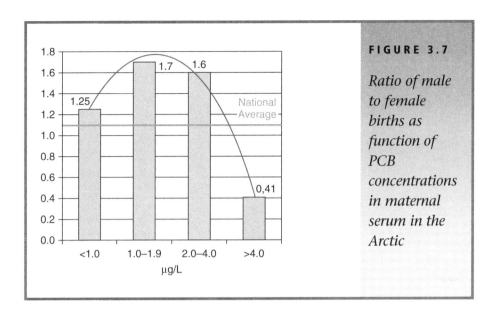

**FIGURE 3.7**

*Ratio of male to female births as function of PCB concentrations in maternal serum in the Arctic*

A recent research paper (Mackenzie 2005) has cited several scientific studies suggesting that changes in human birth sex ratios are not confined to the Arctic regions. One of the principal explanations advanced for this phenomenon is the class of environmental and occupational chemicals called *endocrine disruptors* [EDs], which can interfere with human hormonal systems. [See also James 1996 and Sakamoto et al. 2001.] The most exhaustive study to date on the state of knowledge with respect to ED was published in May 2012 by the European Environment Agency (EEA) (2012). The research suggests that these globally pervasive chemicals can affect multiple human body systems and processes such as reproduction; the thyroid, immune, digestive, cardiovascular, and metabolic systems; as well as neurodevelopmental processes. The report posits a causal relationship between the growth of the global chemical industry and the increasing rates of endocrine diseases and disorders, citing by way of example the decreasing quality of semen quality among many European males where fertility in approximately 40% of males is impaired. A range of similar reproductive-related effects have also been observed in several wildlife species considered to be valuable sentinels of human health. The extent of these "early warning signals" has led the EEA to suggest a precautionary approach [see chapter 9] to the introduction and use of this broad range of chemicals.[1]

Unfortunately the Third World does not escape the impact of chemicals generated in large quantities in the developed nations. Professor Kirk Smith of the University of California at Berkeley has developed the concept of the *environmental risk transition* that describes how Third World countries experience the deleterious impacts of both traditional and modern pollutants. As Figure 3–8 illustrates, many developing nations in the process of industrialization are caught within a zone of risk overlap between traditional and modern risks (Smith 2009; Smith and Ezzati 2005; see also Messerli et al. 2001). A tripartite classification of countries in different stages of development illustrates the major types of morbidity and mortality risks faced by each category.

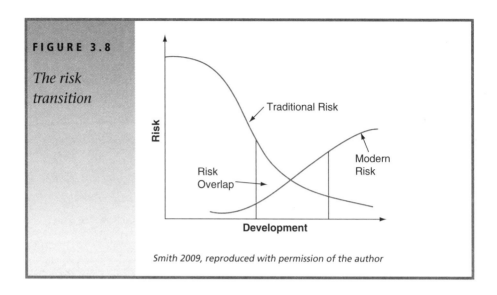

**FIGURE 3.8**

*The risk transition*

*Smith 2009, reproduced with permission of the author*

*Undeveloped Countries*: traditional causes of death are largely from contaminated water, poor sewage disposal, infectious diseases, parasites, and underdeveloped systems of public health.

*Industrializing Countries*: these nations experience a mix of both traditional and modern risk factors with the additional impact of chemical contaminants from uncontrolled industrial processes leading to lung diseases, poisonings, etc.

*Developed Countries*: modern causes of death include heart disease, stroke, and cancer largely associated with longevity, lifestyle (including diet), and exotic contaminants.

The full environmental risk transition (Smith 2009) is presented in Figure 3–9, which shows the shifting environmental burdens from local to global, immediate to delayed, and from risks principally to human health to risks to global life support systems. In sum, the Environmental Kuznets Curve is both oversimplified and misleading. While the original curves purport to show some hypothetical aggregation of pollution, in fact there are a series of curves—each relating to the temporal significance of a particular class of pollutants. If these curves could be aggregated using some common metric, they would portray the overall pollutant level of an economy at any given level of development. The more conceptually correct way of treating these disparate curves would be to include them on one graph in a stacked manner and then take the envelope of these curves to represent the overall burden on the economy and its ecosystem. This final curve would resemble that proposed by Smith in his conceptual model of risk transition where traditional sources of pollution are reduced as new forms of environmental risks emerge, thus leading to a U-shaped function where risk begins to rise again quite rapidly with the nature of the modern industrial system.

Ironically, it is sometimes the case that modern pollutants generated in the developed world that are transported globally by natural processes may have a greater impact on the developing world because of its increased vulnerability due to

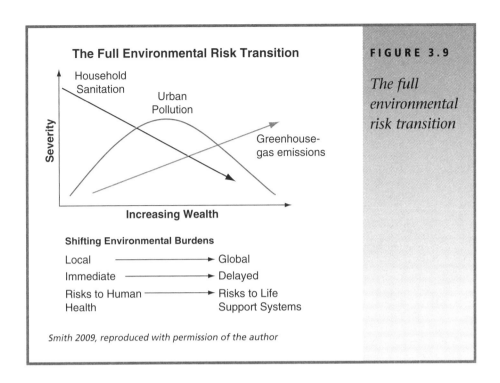

FIGURE 3.9

*The full environmental risk transition*

poverty, malnutrition, and lack of protective institutions and infrastructure (Fussel 2009; IPCC 2001; Yohe et al. 2006; Maplecroft 2011).

## PATHS TO ECONOMIC DEVELOPMENT

The central and critical question emerging from the history of the environmental impact of industrialization is whether it is possible to identify alternative paths of development for the Third World that could successfully raise their standard of living without drastic global ecological consequences. A partial answer to this question requires deconstructing the components of industrialization. There were three essential commodities that launched England on its path to industrialization during the Industrial Revolution: textiles, coal, and iron and steel. There is a distinctive temporal pattern of production and consumption for all of these commodities, as illustrated in Figure 3–10. There is an initial production increase, often accompanied by commensurate exports of related intermediate and finished goods, as the economy first moves through the stages of industrialization, and then a decrease during the post-industrial period that is characterized more by tertiary industry and a service economy. In general, this pattern tends to be repeated for other industrializing economies with some country-specific exceptions. The United States, for example, has seen continued increases in coal and cotton production due to a heavy reliance on coal as a fuel for electricity production and market-distorting subsidies for domestic cotton production. In all cases, however, the continued process

**FIGURE 3.10**

*U.K. historical
data on cotton,
steel and coal*

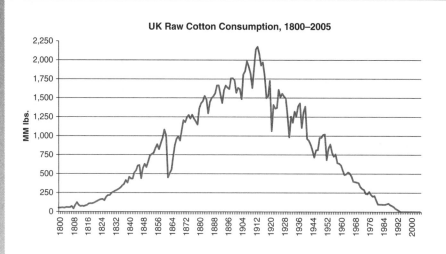

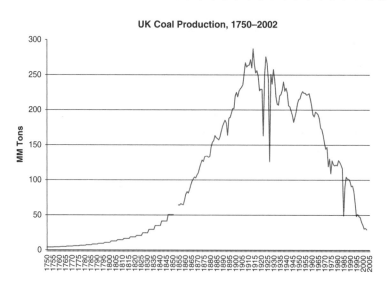

of economic development is marked by steadily increasing releases of greenhouse gases. [See Figures 3–3 and 3–4.]

## CASE STUDY: THE ASIA-PACIFIC

Much of the extraordinary growth in the global economy during the post-World War II era can be attributed to the engine of economic growth in the Asia-Pacific region. What patterns of growth can one observe here, and what implications do these patterns have for the global environment? One model that has been developed to explain the dynamic growth of this region is the *flying geese metaphor* of development. This postwar phenomenon was facilitated by a conscious change in government policy from protectionist import substitution to open market, export promotion. During this transition, the production of labor-intensive and low technology goods is passed from one country to the next as new, more sophisticated technologies/goods are produced in response to changing comparative advantage. This change is based, to a significant degree, on the rising price of labor and availability of other critical inputs such as an educated and trained labor force. Historically, Tier 1 was composed of only one country, Japan, which was the first to engage in massive industrialization in the postwar era. Tier 2 was composed of the *Four Tigers* (Hong Kong, Korea, Taiwan, and Singapore); Tier 3 by four countries in Southeast Asia (Malaysia, the Philippines, Indonesia, and Thailand); and Tier 4 by China, Burma, and Vietnam, but more recently joined by Bangladesh. With sustained double-digit growth, China has moved past most of its Asian neighbors and has recently surpassed Japan as the world's second largest economy after the United States. Illustrative of the flying geese metaphor, rising wage rates in China have forced the movement of certain types of textile production out of China to lower wage countries such as Bangladesh (*Business Week*, March 27, 2006; *New York Times* August 16, 2010, August 14, 2011).

A companion model, entitled the *S Curve*, describes how countries pass through four stages of structural transformation as they travel along an economic growth curve: Stage 1: Primary production; Stage 2a: Labor-intensive manufacturing—typically involving light manufactures like textiles, apparel, and household equipment. In these countries, comparative advantage lies in a large, cheap labor supply; Stage 2b: Heavy Industry; Stage 3: High-tech manufacturing (e.g., electronic chips, consumer electronics, technically sophisticated machinery and equipment); and Stage 4: a post-industrial service economy where comparative advantage is no longer in manufacturing, but rather in domestic and international services, including communication, finance, transportation, and entertainment. This stage usually requires sophisticated technology such as IT, etc.

The result of this dynamic change in comparative advantage is illustrated by the extraordinary rise in Asia-Pacific national GDP in the postwar period. Unfortunately, the environmental impact of this growth is reflected in rapidly rising levels of carbon dioxide. Figure 3–11 plots the ratio of real GDP in 2008 to 1960 values against the ratio of $CO_2$ emissions in 2008 to 1960 values (for Malaysia, the comparative values are 2008:1970). Similar graphs could be generated for other modern industrial-level pollutants. Despite the emergence in the 20th century of what

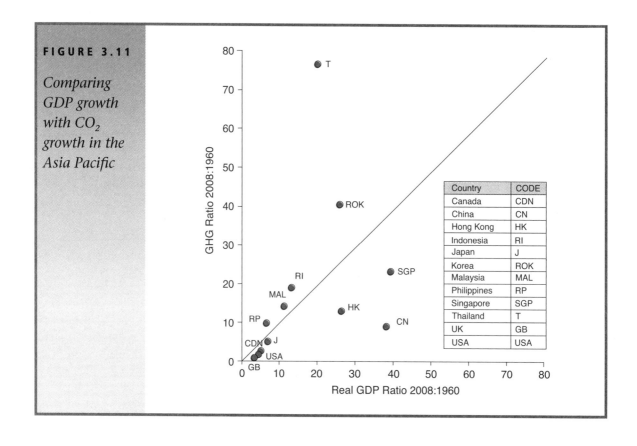

**FIGURE 3.11**

*Comparing GDP growth with CO$_2$ growth in the Asia Pacific*

| Country | CODE |
| --- | --- |
| Canada | CDN |
| China | CN |
| Hong Kong | HK |
| Indonesia | RI |
| Japan | J |
| Korea | ROK |
| Malaysia | MAL |
| Philippines | RP |
| Singapore | SGP |
| Thailand | T |
| UK | GB |
| USA | USA |

has been termed the *Second Industrial Revolution* marked by the production of new natural and synthetic resources such as aluminum, new alloys, and plastics, the environmental pattern associated with continuing production of coal, iron, and steel appears to be repeating. Table 3–1 summarizes the major pollutants from iron, steel, coal, and textile production.

If an alternative path to economic development cannot be found, then raising the living standards of the Third World will have potentially catastrophic impacts on the global ecosystem. Wassily Leontief, the Nobel laureate noted for the invention of Input-Output Analysis [see Appendix to this chapter] conducted an extensive comparison of national economic development and structure in the 1960s (Leontief 1963). He concluded that "The fact is that the choice of alternative technologies hardly exists. The process of development consists essentially in the installation and building of an approximation of the system embodied in advanced economies." Given recent patterns of economic development, there seems to be little reason to believe that this conclusion has changed significantly in the past five decades. This has profound implications for the effect of economic development on the global environment. The challenge of decoupling economic activity and environmental degradation such as climate change remains contentious and has been receiving considerable attention recently (DeCanto and Fremstad 2010; Jackson 2009; Smith et al. 2010; Spence 2011; Victor 2008, UNEP 2011). The next chapter explores the question of what it means to raise gross domestic product—the most common measure of national well-being—and what might be a realistic and desirable target for the Third World.

| | IRON MINING | IRON/STEEL MILLS | COAL MINING | COAL BURNING | TEXTILES |
|---|---|---|---|---|---|
| **AIR POLLUTANTS** | | | | | |
| $CO_2$ | | X | X | X | |
| Fluorides (F) | | X | | | |
| Mercury (Hg) | | | | X | |
| NOx | | X | | X | |
| PM | | X | | | |
| SOx | | X | | X | |
| **WATER POLLUTANTS** | | | | | |
| AOX | | | | | X |
| Arsenic (As) | X | | | | |
| BOD | | | | | X |
| Cadmium (Cd) | X | X | | | |
| Chromium (Cr) | X | X | | | X |
| Cobalt (Co) | | | | | X |
| COD | X | X | | | X |
| Coliform bacteria | | | | | X |
| Copper (Cu) | X | | | | X |
| Cyanide | X | X | | | |
| Iron (Fe) | X | | X | | |
| Lead (Pb) | X | X | | | |
| Mercury (Hg) | X | X | | | |
| Nickel (Ni) | X | | | | X |
| Oil & Grease | X | X | X | | X |
| Pesticides | | | | | X |
| pH | X | X | X | X | X |
| Phenol | | X | | | X |
| Sulphide | | | | | X |
| Temperature | | X | | | X |
| TSS | X | X | X | | X |
| Zinc (Zn) | X | X | | | X |

**TABLE 3.1**

*Major Pollutants from Iron, Steel, Coal and Textile Production*

# CITED REFERENCES AND RECOMMENDED READINGS

Breivik K., Sweetman A., Pacyna J.M., Jones K.C. (2002a) Towards a global historical emission inventory for selected PCB congeners—a mass balance approach 1. Global production and consumption. *The Science of the Total Environment*, 290, pp. 181–98.

Breivik K, Sweetman A, Pacyna JM, Jones KC. (2002b) Towards a global historical emission inventory for selected PCB congeners—a mass balance approach 2. Emissions. *The Science of the Total Environment* 290, pp. 199–224.

Breivik K., A. Sweetman, J.M. Pacyna and K.C. Jones (2007) "Towards a Global Historical Emission Inventory for Selected PCB Congeners—A Mass Balance Approach 3. An Update." *The Science of the Total Environment*, 377, pp. 296–307.

*Business Week* (2006) "How Rising Wages Are Changing the Game in China," March 27.

Chambers, Johnathan D. (1961) *Workshop of the World: British Economic History from 1820 to 1880*. Oxford: Oxford University Press.

Charnes, A. et al. (1972) "Economic Social and Enterprise Accounting and Mathematical Models." *The Accounting Review*, January, pp. 85–108.

*Encyclopaedia Britannica* "Industrial Revolution" (1993), 6, pp. 304–305.

European Environment Agency (EEA) (2012) *The Impacts of Endocrine Disruptors on Wildlife, People and Their Environments*. The Weybridge+15 (1996–2011) report.

European Monitoring and Evaluation Programme (EMEP) (2005) *Regional Multicompartment Model MSCE-POP*, Convention on Long-Range Transboundary Air Pollution, Technical Report 5/2005

Fussel, Hans-Martin (2009) *Development and Climate Change Background Note. Review of Quantitative Analysis of Indices of Climate Change Exposure, Adaptive Capacity, Sensitivity and Impacts*. World Bank.

Global Trade Analysis Project (GTAP), Purdue University website (www.gtap.agecon. purdue.edu).

Hung, Hayley et al. (2010) "Atmospheric Monitoring of Organic Pollutants in the Arctic under the Arctic Monitoring and Assessment Programme (AMAP) 1993–2006." *The Science of the Total Environment*, 408, pp. 2854–2873.

http://www.ggdc.net/maddison/ [website of Groningen Growth and Development Centre, University of Groningen, The Netherlands].

Indian Affairs and Northern Affairs Canada (2003) *Human Health*, Ottawa.

Intergovernmental Panel on Climate Change (IPCC) (2001) *Impacts, Adaptation and Vulnerability—Technical Summary*, Switzerland.

Jackson, Tim (2009) *Prosperity Without Growth. Economics for a Finite Planet*. London: Earthscan.

James, William H. (1995) "Evidence that Mammalian Sex Ratios at Birth Are Partially Controlled by Parental Hormone Levels at the Times of Conception." *Journal of Theoretical Biology*, 180, pp. 271–286.

Krausmann F. et al. (2009) "Growth in Global Materials Use, GDP, and Population during the 20th Century." *Ecological Economics*, 68, pp. 2696–2705.

Lave, Lester B. et al. (1995) "Using Input-Output Analysis to Estimate Economy-wide Discharges." *Environmental Science & Technology* 29(9), pp. 420A–426A.

Leontief, Wassily (1963) "The Structure of Development." *Scientific American*, 20, pp. 148–166.

Leontief, Wassily (1966) *Input-Output Economics*. New York: Oxford University Press.

Living on Earth, podcast September 21, 2007 [www.loe.org].

Ma, Jianmin et al. (2011) "Revolatilization of Persistent Organic Pollutants in the Arctic Induced by Climate Change." *Nature Climate Change*, July 24, pp. 255–260.

Mackenzie, Constanza A. (2005) "Declining Sex Ratio in a First Nation Community." *Environmental Health Perspectives*, 113(1), October, pp. 1295–1298.

Maddison, Angus (2006a) *The World Economy. Volume 1 A Millennial Perspective*. Paris: Development Centre Studies OECD.

Maddison, Angus (2006b) *The World Economy. Volume 2 Historical Statistics*. Paris: Development Centre Studies OECD.

Maplecroft (2011) "World's Fastest Growing Populations Increasingly Vulnerable to the Impacts of Climate Change—4th Global Atlas Reports," (http://mplecroft.com/about/news/ccvi_2012.html).

Messserli, B. et al. (2001) "From Nature-Dominated to Human-Dominated environmental Changes," in Chapter 13 in Eckart Ehlers and Thomas Kraftt (eds.) *Understanding the Earth System*, pp. 195–208.

Mitchell, B.R. (2007a) *International Historical Statistics. The Americas 1750–2005*. Houndmills, Basingstoke, Hampshire: Palgrave Macmillan.

Mitchell, B.R. (2007b) *International Historical Statistics. Europe 1750–2005*, Houndmills, Basingstoke, Hampshire: Palgrave Macmillan.

Mitchell, B.R. and Phyllis Deane (1962) *Abstract of British Historical Statistics*. Cambridge: Cambridge University Press.

Mitchell, B.R. and H.G. Jones (1971) *Second Abstract of British Historical Statistics*. Cambridge: Cambridge University Press.

National Research Council (NRC) (2009) *Global Sources of Local Pollution: An Assessment of Long-Range Transport of Key Air Pollutants to and from the United States*. Washington, DC.

New Economics Foundation and the Open University (2007*) Chinadependence. The Second UK Interdependence Report*, London.

*New York Times* (2010) "China's Labor Tests its Muscle," August 16.

*New York Times* (2011) "Cheap Robots vs. Cheap Labor," August 14.

Oak Ridge National Laboratory (ORNL) Greenhouse Gas website [http://cdiac.ornl.gov/].

Organization for Economic Cooperation and Development (OECD) (n.d.) *The OECD Input-Output Database* [http://www.oecd.org/dataoecd/48/43/2673344.pdf].

Ottesen, Rolf Tore et al. Norges geologiske undersokelse (NGU) (2010) *Geochemical Atlas of Norway Part 2 Geochemical Atlas of Spitsbergen*, Trondheim.

Sakamoto, Mineshi et al. (2001) "Declining Minamata Male Birth Ratio Associated with Increased Male Fetal Death Die to Heavy Methylmercury Pollution." *Environmental Research*, Section A 87, pp. 92–98.

Schindler, David (2007) "A Life with Pesticides," Lecture to The Vancouver Institute, November 3.

*Scientific American* (1981) "Input-Output Chart of the United States Economy in 1980" [poster].

Smith, Kirk (2009) "Combustion, Climate, Health, and the Environmental Risk Transition," September 10–11.

Smith, Kirk and Majid Ezzati (2005) "How Environmental Health Risk Changes with Development: The Epidemiologic and Environmental Risk Transitions Revisited." *Annual Review of Environment and Resources*, pp. 291–333.

Smith, Michael H. et al. (2010) *Cents and Sustainability. Securing Our Common Future by Decoupling Economic Growth from Environmental Pressures*. London: Earthscan.

Spence, Michael (2011) *The Next Convergence. The Future of Economic Growth in a Multi-speed World*. New York: Farrar, Straus and Giroux.

Statistics Canada (2010) *The Input-Output Structure of the Canadian Economy 2006–2007*, Ottawa.

UK Central Statistical Office (various years) *Annual Abstract of Statistics*, London.

U.S. Department of Commerce (1975) *Historical Statistics of the United States*, Washington, DC.

U.S. Department of Commerce, Bureau of Economic Analysis (BEA) (2009) *Concepts and Methods of the U.S. Input-Output Accounts*, Washington, DC.

United Nations Environment Programme (UNEP) (2007) *Global Environment Outlook GEO4*.

United Nations Environment Programme (UNEP) (2011) *Decoupling Natural Resource Use and Environmental Impacts from Economic Growth*.

United Nations Environment Programme (UNEP) Global Environment Facility (GEF) (2004) *Persistent Toxic Substances, Food Security and Indigenous Peoples of the Russian North*.

Victor, Peter A. (2008) *Managing Without Growth. Slower by Design, Not Disaster*. Cheltenham: Edward Elgar.

Wania, Frank and Donald Mackay (1993) "Global Fractionation and Cold Condensation of Low Volatility Organochlorine Compounds in Polar Regions" *Ambio*, 22(1), February, pp. 10–18.

Warde, Paul (2007) *Energy Consumption in England and Wales 1560–2000*. Italy: Cosiglio Nazionale delle Ricerche.

Williams, Florence (2012) *Breasts: A Natural and Unnatural History*, New York: W.W. Norton & Co.

Yohe, Gary et al. (2006) "Global Distributions of Vulnerability to Climate Change." *The Integrated Assessment Journal*, 6(3), pp. 35–44.

## APPENDIX

# A Short Primer on Input-Output Analysis

Developed by Wassily Leontief in the 1930s, Input-Output analysis, sometimes referred to as "inter-industry analysis" is a comprehensive and systematic methodology for representing an economic system, be it local, regional, or national. While the theory has been extant for some time, it was not until the advent of modern computers that the complex computations required to carry out the analysis became possible. Today, these models are used throughout the globe, by both free and centralized planned economies (GTAP, OECD n.d.). Input-output [or I-O] is a model of the flows of goods and services among sectors of the economy. It is represented as a system of simultaneous linear equations that capture the direct and indirect economic interrelationships among all the sectors of the economy, no matter how detailed the degree of disaggregation. A principal use of input-output methodology is to determine the impact on any and all sectors of an economy resulting from an increase or decrease in demand for a final product. For example, what is the economic effect of increasing final (i.e., consumer) demand in the United States for automobiles?

Input-Output can also be used to track the implications of sectoral increases on economy-wide emissions of conventional air, water, and soil pollutants, as well as toxics and greenhouse gases. This requires linkages with environmental databases in the United States such as the Toxic Release Inventory (TRI), U.S. EPA Greenhouse Gas inventory databases, or the U.S. EPA Air Pollution emission inventory. The methodology of measuring system-wide environmental effects involves the use of pollution coefficients in Input-Output tables. This permits the tracking of pollution changes throughout the economy as any one product or sector experiences increased or decreased demand as a result of market forces or government intervention (Lave et al. 1995).

There are three analytical tables associated with traditional Input-Output analysis: the dollar flow table, the coefficient table, and the inverse-coefficient table. Each is briefly described in turn.

The **_dollar flow table_** tracks the sales of goods and services among sectors of an economy. Table 3–2 illustrates a highly simplified representation with an economy divided into three sectors (agriculture and two manufacturing sectors). In the original Leontief square formulation of the input-output table, these sectors are arrayed on both the x-axis and y-axis. Row industries sell to column industries, and column industries buy from row industries. It is important to note that some sectors sell to themselves. This square matrix that forms the core of the I-O analysis is converted into a series of simultaneous linear equations in the next two tables that can be solved algebraically. Note also that there are additional columns and additional rows flanking the square matrix. Their number will depend on the complexity of the model but always include household labor, total inputs, final demand, total output, imports, and exports.

| | AGRICULTURAL SECTOR | MANUFACTURING SECTOR #1 | MANUFACTURING SECTOR #2 | FINAL DEMAND | TOTAL OUTPUTS | |
|---|---|---|---|---|---|---|
| Agricultural sector | $20 | $60 | $40 | $80 | $200 | **TABLE 3.2**  _Sample Input-Output Matrix_ |
| Manufacturing sector #1 | $80 | $60 | $80 | $80 | $300 | |
| Manufacturing sector #2 | $40 | $60 | $120 | $180 | $400 | |
| Household (labour) | $60 | $120 | $160 | $140 | | |
| Total Inputs | $200 | $300 | $400 | | $900 | |

In practice, most extant I-O models, be they regional or national, have subdivided the economy into many more categories. Table 3–3 presents a somewhat great level of disaggregation for the U.S. economy with 81 sectors, although the number may be as large as thousands. The principal challenge in assembling this table is the time and effort required to gather the data for the whole economy. As a consequence, I-O tables frequently incorporate data that may be several years old. There are several limitations to the basic I-O model: first, it represents a snapshot of the economy at one period in time; and, second, the square matrix implies that each category produces one product and that each product is produced by only one industry. This problem has been addressed by the development of rectangular matrices (Statistics Canada 2010).

The **coefficient table** is derived from the dollar flow table and contains the data in a modified form that permits more intensive analysis. Each cell is the ratio of the input from a row industry to the total output of the industry in whose vertical column the cell appears. The algebraic representation is as follows (Charnes et al. 1972):

Each cell in the matrix is derived as follows:

$$X_{ij} = a_{ij} X_j$$

where:

$X_{ij}$ = the amount of goods and services provided by industry in row i to industry in column j

$a_{ij}$ = a constant that relates the activity level of industry j to its requirements from industry i; that is, each unit increase in the total activity of industry j will occasion an input of $a_{ij}$ units from industry i

$X_j$ = total amount of activity of industry j

Each row in the matrix:

$$S\ X_{ij} / y_i = X_i$$

where:

$y_i$ = amount of goods and services flowing from (row) industry i to final demand (rather than to other industries as intermediate inputs)

$X_i$ = total amount of output (or activity) of (row) industry i

Example:

Row #1

$$X_{11} + X_{12} + X_{13} + \ldots + y_1 = X_1$$
or by substitution (Xij = aij Xj) =
$$a_{11} X_1 + a_{12} X_2 + a_{13} X_3 + \ldots + Y_1 = X_1$$

Sample 3—sector table:

$$X_{11} + X_{12} + X_{13} + y_1 = X_1$$
$$X_{21} + X_{22} + X_{23} + y_2 = X_2$$
$$X_{31} + X_{32} + X_{33} + y_3 = X_3$$

**TABLE 3.3**

*Industries in 81-sector U.S. Input-Output Matrix*

81-SECTOR INPUT-OUTPUT MODEL FOR THE USA

**FINAL NON METAL**

1   Footwear and other leather products

2   Misc. furniture and fixtures

3   Household furniture

4   Tobacco manufactures

5   Apparel

6   Misc. fabricated textile products

7   Drugs, cleaning and toilet preparations

8   Food and kindred products

**FINAL METAL**

9   Special industry machinery and equipment

10  Ordnance and accessories

28  Electric lighting and wiring equipment

29  Electric industrial equipment and apparatus

30  Electronic components and accessories

**BASIC METAL**

31  Heating, plumbing and structural metal products

32  Machine shop products

33  Metal containers

34  Stampings, screw machine products and bolts

35  Other fabricated metal products

36  Primary nonferrous metal manufacturing

37  Nonferrous metal ores mining

56  Agricultural, forestry and fishery services

57  Plastics and synthetic materials

58  Chemicals and selected chemical products

59  Chemical and fertilizer, mineral mining

**ENERGY**

60  Petroleum refining and related industries

61  Electricity, gas and water

62  Coal mining

63  Crude petroleum and natural gas

**SERVICES**

64  Federal government enterprises

65  Transportation and warehousing

(Continued)

TABLE 3.3
*continued*

**81-SECTOR INPUT-OUTPUT MODEL FOR THE USA**

| | | | |
|---|---|---|---|
| 11 | aircraft and parts | 38 | Primary iron and steel manufacturing |
| 12 | Misc. transportation equipment | 39 | Iron and ferroalloy ores mining |
| 13 | Radio, television and communication equipment | | **BASIC NONMETAL** |
| 14 | Materials handling machinery and equipment | 40 | Stone and clay products |
| 15 | Misc. manufacturing | 41 | Stone and clay mining and quarrying |
| 16 | Optical, ophthalmic and photographic equipment | 42 | Printing and publishing |
| 17 | Service industry machines | 43 | Glass and glass products |
| 18 | Household appliances | 44 | Paperboard containers and boxes |
| 19 | Scientific and controlling instruments | 45 | Paper and allied products, except containers |
| 20 | Office, computing and accounting machines | 46 | Wooden containers |
| 21 | Farm machinery and equipment | 47 | Lumber and wood products, except containers |
| | | 48 | Forestry and fishery products |

| | |
|---|---|
| 49 | Misc. textile goods and floor coverings |
| 66 | State and local government enterprises |
| 67 | Hotels, personal and repair services, except automobile |
| 68 | Automobile repair and services |
| 69 | Radio and television broadcasting |
| 70 | Amusements |
| 71 | Medical & Educational services, nonprofit organizations |
| 72 | Wholesale and retail trade |
| 73 | Finance and insurance |
| 74 | Communications, except radio and television broadcasting |
| 75 | Business services |
| 76 | Real estate and rental |

**TABLE 3.3**
*continued*

### 81-SECTOR INPUT-OUTPUT MODEL FOR THE USA

| | | | |
|---|---|---|---|
| 22 | Engines and turbines | 50 | Rubber and misc. plastics products |
| 23 | Construction, mining and oil field machinery | 51 | Broad and narrow fabrics, yarn and thread mills |
| 24 | Misc. electrical machinery, equipment and supplies | 52 | Paints and allied products |
| 25 | Metalworking machinery and equipment | 53 | Leather tanning and industrial leather products |
| 26 | Motor vehicles and equipment | 54 | Livestock and livestock products |
| 27 | General industrial machinery and equipment | 55 | Misc. agricultural products |
| | | 77 | Maintenance and repair construction |
| | | | MISC. |
| | | 78 | Research and development |
| | | 79 | Office supplies |
| | | 80 | Business travel, entertainment and gifts |
| | | 81 | Scrap, used and second hand goods |

*Source:* U.S. Department of Commerce, and Scientific American

or

$$a_{11} X_1 + a_{12} X_2 + a_{13} X_3 + y_1 = X_1$$
$$a_{21} X_1 + a_{22} X_2 + a_{23} X_3 + y_2 = X_2$$
$$a_{31} X_1 + a_{32} X_2 + a_{33} X_3 + y_3 = X_3$$

Charnes et al. (1972, p. 89) provide a highly simplified numeric example that divides national output into three commodities: corn, cloth, and shoes.

The third table, the **inverse-coefficient table**, is perhaps the most important, as it allows the tracking of changes in one industry's output throughout the entire economy. In this table, the coefficient in each cell gives, per dollar of delivery to final demand made by the sector listed at the top, the total input *directly and indirectly* required from the industry listed at the left. An illustration follows below.

## BRIEF NUMERICAL EXAMPLE

For convenience of display, the three subtables are sometimes combined in one graph in large Input-Output tables. In Figure 3–12, for example, the sample cell represents the sale of iron ore as an input to the primary iron and steel manufacturing sector in 1980 (*Scientific American* 1981). The dollar flow is $2,775 million; the direct coefficient is 0.0447 (i.e., $2,775 million iron ore input divided by $62,031 million, which is the gross domestic output of primary iron and steel manufacturing); and the inverse coefficient is 0.0579, which is derived by matrix inversion. In contrast to the *direct coefficient*, which represents the increment in iron ore production required as a direct input for one additional unit output of iron and steel, the *inverse coefficient* captures not only the additional direct iron ore input, but also any indirectly induced requirements for iron ore as a consequence of any other sector products required for one additional unit of iron and steel output.

The critical information imparted by the indirect coefficient is illustrated by a second example in Figure 3–13. In this case, the cell captures the relationship between iron ore production and shoe manufacturing. There are no direct sales of iron ore to the shoe manufacturing industry. This does not mean, however, that there are not indirect effects on iron ore demand from the increased production of shoes. For example, the cell representing the dollar sales of iron ore to the shoe manufacturing industry will be zero, as well as the comparable cell in the coefficient table. However, there will be a positive value for the inverse-coefficient since iron ore is used to make steel, and steel is ultimately used in shoe manufacturing (e.g., steel lasts or other shoe components, etc.).

This type of analytical tool can be exceedingly useful. For example, input-output analysis can be used to answer important questions such as (a) how will an industry be affected by increased or reduced demand for any product (e.g.,

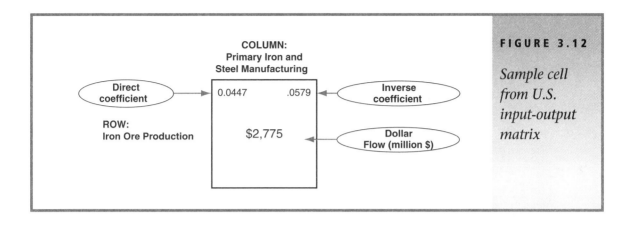

**FIGURE 3.12**

*Sample cell from U.S. input-output matrix*

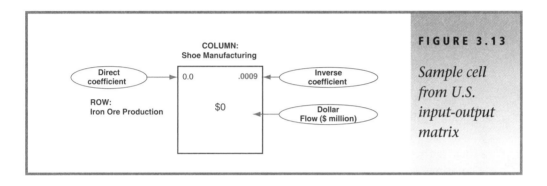

**FIGURE 3.13**

*Sample cell from U.S. input-output matrix*

how will iron ore sales be affected by changes in the demand for shoes)? (b) what is the complete environmental life-cycle impact of selected products? (e.g., what will be the total environmental impact across the economy of an increase in the demand for shoes?); or, at a more conceptual level: (c) are there alternative paths to economic development, or will developing nations have to go through the same pollution-intensive process of development experienced by the developed nations? From a business and sustainability perspective, question (b) is of particular relevance, and the application of I-O analysis to product life-cycle analysis is described in Chapter 20.

## MODERN INPUT-OUTPUT ANALYSIS

While an important breakthrough in the modeling of national economies, the traditional square industry-by-industry matrix invented by Leontief had some significant deficiencies, not the least of which was the handling of secondary products (i.e., products that were produced by an industry in addition to its principal output). A major conceptual advance was achieved in the 1970s in the United States with the adoption of a new System of National Accounts (SNA) developed under the auspices of the United Nations. This led to a major reconceptualization and restructuring of

Input-Output Analysis and the presentation of its component data. As described by the U.S. Bureau of Economic Analysis (2009), the core of the I-O accounts consists of two major tables: a "make" table and a "use" table. To quote (p. 1–2):

> The *make table* shows the production of commodities by industries. The rows present the industries, and the columns display the commodities that the industries produce. Looking across a row, all the commodities produced by that industry are identified, and the sum of the entries is that industry's output. Looking down a column, all the industries producing that commodity are identified, and the sum of the entries is the output of that commodity.
>
> The *use table* shows the uses of commodities by intermediate and final users. In contrast to the make table, the rows in the use table present the commodities or products, and the columns display the industries and final users that utilize them. The sum of the entries in a row is the output of that commodity. The columns show the products consumed by each industry and the three components of "value added"—compensation of employees, taxes on production and imports less subsidies, and gross operating surplus. Value added is the difference between an industry's output and the cost of its intermediate inputs, and total value added is equal to GDP. The sum of the entries in a column is that industry's output.

There are several additional subsidiary tables that are created to assist in studying the ultimate national-level effects of sectoral changes. In fact, variations of these models have been used to study economic activity at a regional level as well.

## Discussion Question

1. Can you think of any country that is not following the Western industrialized model of development? If so, what are the distinguishing characteristics that differentiate this model?

## NOTE

1. The ubiquitous presence of modern chemicals in the environment has been graphically summarized by Williams (2012) in her summary of scientific research on contaminants in human milk: "When we nurse our babies, we feed them not only the fats and sugars that fire their immune systems, cellular metabolisms, and cerebral synapses. We also feed them, in albeit miniscule amounts, paint thinners, dry-cleaning fluids, wood preservatives, toilet deodorizers, cosmetic additives, gasoline by-products, rocket fuel, termite poisons, fungicides, and flame-retardants" (pp. 197–198).

# CHAPTER 4

## *What Are We Trying to Achieve?*
## *Measuring Wealth and Well-Being*

EVER SINCE THE INVENTION OF NATIONAL ACCOUNTS in the 1930s (i.e., methods of measuring the total economic activity of a country), the prevailing worldview has been that the well-being of a society could be measured by looking at the economy and calculating the gross domestic product (or more specifically, the gross domestic product per capita). This fundamental concept has come under increasing scrutiny in the last few decades. Perhaps the most articulate critique was spoken by the late Senator Robert Kennedy who stated in a speech delivered on March 18, 1968, at the University of Kansas:

> Our Gross National Product, now, is over $800 billion dollars a year, but that Gross National Product—if we judge the United States of America by that—that Gross National Product counts air pollution and cigarette advertising, and ambulances to clear our highways of carnage. It counts special locks for our doors and the jails for the people who break them. It counts the destruction of the redwood and the loss of our natural wonder in chaotic sprawl. It counts napalm and counts nuclear warheads and armored cars for the police to fight the riots in our cities. It counts Whitman's rifle and Speck's knife, and the television programs which glorify violence in order to sell toys to our children. Yet the gross national product does not allow for the health of our children, the quality of their education or the joy of their play. It does not include the beauty of our poetry or the strength of our marriages, the intelligence of our public debate or the integrity of our public officials. It measures neither our wit nor our courage, neither our wisdom nor our learning, neither our compassion nor our devotion to our country, it measures everything in short, except that which makes life worthwhile. And it can tell us everything about America except why we are proud that we are Americans. (Kennedy, 1968)

Sustainability requires its simultaneous achievement in all three areas of economy, ecology, and society, yet what we actually measure with national income data is focused solely on the economic. Clearly, there are a significant number of factors that matter to people and are not captured in GDP data. One of these factors surely must be satisfaction or happiness. This has been a difficult variable to measure because of its intangible nature, its cultural characteristics, and its potentially changing components. Fortunately, several outstanding research advances have occurred

*U.S. income and
happiness*

US Happiness Index vs. Median HH Income
(2000$)

$y = -0.0002x + 40.636$

$R^2 = 0.05251$

in the last few years, offering a glimpse of temporal trends in happiness in such countries as the United States as well as permitting cross-national and cross-cultural comparisons (Diener et al. 2010; Graham 2009; Helliwell et al. 2012; Ingelhart 2004). Recent research from the National Opinion Research Center at the University of Chicago (Smith 2011) shows that Americans seem to be no happier than they were 30 years ago despite increased median income (U.S. Census Bureau 2011; see also Helliwell et al. 2012). [See Figures 4–1a and b.] In fact, Figure 4–1c suggests that there may be a modest negative relationship between the two variables in the United States.

A study entitled *The Economics of Happiness* by Mark Anielski (2007) examined several dozen factors that were deemed to be desirable to the average person and then looked at the progress in achieving these goals over the past five decades. As is apparent in Table 4–1, recent quantitative measures of these variables are in most cases worse than they were in 1950. Comparing data from another study (Ingelhart 2004) on happiness in several dozen countries with GNP per capita yields a broad range of values. [See Figure 4–2.] Of particular note is the somewhat counterintuitive nature of the data. While most poor countries have low levels of happiness, several others have unusually high levels—higher than many modern industrialized economies. Many of the countries lying above the trend line are from Latin America, while many below are former members of the communist bloc (Ingelhart 2010). In general, the data suggest that past a certain level of income, there is little improvement in levels of happiness. This is an important finding that we will see elsewhere in our analysis of sustainability since it suggests that one need only raise per capita income levels to between $10,000 and $20,000 per year to achieve a significant degree of happiness—a value considerably lower than the per capita income of much of the industrialized world. A common explanation for the declining marginal increment in happiness is that "more income improves happiness only until basic needs are met. Beyond the point where there is enough income so that people are no longer hungry and absolute poverty has been eliminated, income does not matter for happiness" (Di Tella and MacCulloch 2010).

| WHAT WE WANT MORE OF | PROGRESS INDICATOR | BETTER | WORSE | NO CHANGE |
|---|---|---|---|---|
| Happiness | self-rated happiness | | X | |
| Longer lives | Life expectancy | X | | |
| Overall societal wellbeing | Index for social health | | X | |
| Healthy youth | Youth suicide rate | | X | |
| Prosperous economy | GDP | X | | |
| Healthy markets | Stock market values | X | | |
| More money | Personal income | X | | |
| | Real wages | | X | |
| Genuine Progress | GPI | | X | |
| More material possessions | Consumption expenditures | X | | |
| More leisure time and time with friends & family | Leisure time | | X | |

**TABLE 4.1**

*State of Progress Indicators*

*(Continued)*

**TABLE 4.1**

*continued*

| WHAT WE WANT MORE OF | PROGRESS INDICATOR | BETTER | WORSE | NO CHANGE |
|---|---|---|---|---|
| Strong & healthy relationships | Divorce rate | | X | |
| Healthy farm land | Productive farmland | | X | |
| More time to give to others | Volunteer time | X | | |
| Reduced dependence on fossil fuels | Fossil fuel use vs. Renewables | | X | |
| Debt | US total outstanding debt | | X | |
| Violence | Violent crime rate | | X | |
| Inequality of income & wealth | Gini coefficient | | X | |
| Poverty | Poverty rates | | | X |
| Work | Hours of work | | X | |
| Work-related commuting time | Commuting time | | X | |
| Under-employment | Underemployment rate | | X | |
| Automobile crashes, deaths & injuries | Auto crashes | | X | |
| Long-term environmental damage | Cost of environmental damage | | X | |
| Loss of wetlands | Area of wetlands | | X | |
| Loss of old growth forests | Area of old growth forest | | X | |
| Air pollution | Air quality indices | X | | |
| Reliance on foreign borrowing & debt | Foreign debt outstanding | | X | |

*Source:* Anielski 2007

Richard Layard, in his book *Happiness: Lessons From a New Science* (2006), has identified seven meta-variables that he feels affect happiness: family relationships, financial situation, work, community and friends, health, personal freedom, and personal values. The critical importance of many of these factors has been independently verified in numerous other recent studies.

Once having identified these types of variables and measuring them, the challenge remains as to how such information is to be used. A remarkable effort to use these data to complement GDP figures has been used in the mountain kingdom of Bhutan. In 2008, the country adopted a quantitative *Gross National Happiness Index* (GNH) in order to measure the progress of the government in promoting the emotional well-being of its citizenry. The GNH Index has nine major categories,

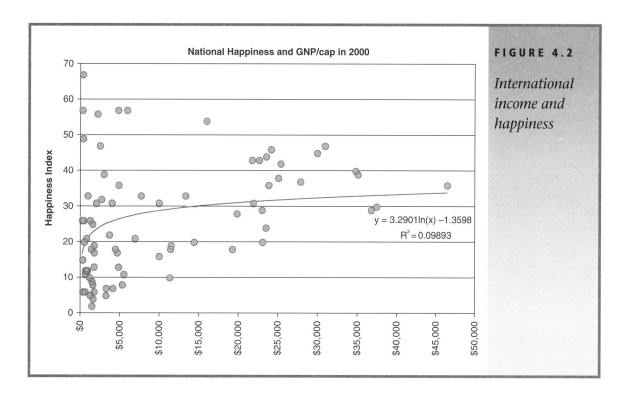

**FIGURE 4.2**

*International income and happiness*

each composed of several subcomponents: psychological well-being, ecology, health, education, culture, living standards, time use, community vitality, and good governance  (www.grossnationalhappiness.com/gnhindex/introductiongnh.aspx). [See Table 4–2.] Table 4–3 displays the subcomponents for the psychological component questions and how they are measured. [See also Ura et al. 2012.]

**GNH INDEX VARIABLES**

| PSYCHOLOGICAL WELLBEING | LIVING STANDARDS |
|---|---|
| 1 General mental health | 1 Household income |
| 2 Frequency of prayer recitation | 2 Income sufficiency to meet everyday needs |
| 3 Frequency of meditation | 3 Food insecurity |
| 4 Taking account of karma in daily life | 4 House ownership |
| 5 Frequency of feeling of selfishness | 5 Room ratio |
| 6 Frequency of feeling of jealousy | 6 Purchase of second hand clothes |
| 7 Frequency of feeling of calmness | 7 Difficulty in Contributing to the Community Festivals |
| 8 Frequency of feeling of compassion | 8 Postponement of urgent repairs and maintainance of house |
| 9 Ferquency of feeling of generosity | |
| 10 Frequency of feeling of frustration | |
| 11 Occurrence of suicidal thought | |

**TABLE 4.2**

*Bhutan's Gross National Happiness Index*

*(Continued)*

**TABLE 4.2**

*continued*

**ECOLOGY COMMUNITY VITALITY**

1 Pollution of rivers
2 Soil erosion
3 Method of waste disposal
4 Names and species of plants and animals
5 Tree plantations around your farm or house

**TIME USE**

1 Total working hours
2 Sleep hours

**HEALTH**

1 Self reported health status
2 Long term disability
3 # of healthy days in the past 30 days
4 Body Mass Index
5 Knowledge of transmission of HIV/AIDS virus
6 Duration for a child to be breast fed only
7 Walking distance to health care centre

**COMMUNITY VITALITY**

1 Sense of trust in neighbours
2 Neighbours helping each other in the community
3 Labour exchange with community members
4 Socialising with friends
5 Members of your family really care about each other
6 You wish you were not part of your family
7 Members of your family argue too much
8 There is a lot of understanding in your family
9 Your family is a real source of comfort to you
10 No. of relatives living in the same community
11 Victim of crime
12 Feelings of safety from human harm
13 Sense of enmity in the community
14 No. of days volunteered
15 Amount of donation in cash value
16 Availability of social support

**ECUCATION**

1 Level of education
2 Literacy rate
3 Ability to understand lozey
4 Historical literacy (Knowledge on local legend and folk stories)

**GOOD GOVERNANCE**

1 Performance of central govt in reducing income gap
2 Performance of central govt in fighting corruption
3 Right to freedom of speech and opinion
4 Freedom from discrimination
5 Trust in central ministries
6 Trust in dzongkhag administration
7 Trust in media

TABLE 4.2

*continued*

GNH INDEX VARIABLES

CULTURE

1 Speaking first language
2 Frequency of playing traditional games
3 Zorig chusum skills
4 Teaching children importance of
   discipline
5 Teaching children importance of
   impartiality
6 Knowledge of mask and other dances
   performed in tshechus
7 Importance of reciprocity as a life
   principle
8 Attitude towards killing
9 Attitude towards stealing

*Source:* www.grossnationalhappiness.com/gnhindex/introductiongnh.aspx

| SL NO | INDICATORS | INDEXES | QUESTION | RANGE | THRESHOLD (DEPRIVED IF VARIABLE IS BELOW THRESHOLD) |
|---|---|---|---|---|---|
| 1 | General mental health | Mental Health Index | General Health Questionnaire | 1(worst) – 37(best) **Categories:** 22–37 Normal mental wellbeing 17–21 Some distress 1–16 Severe distress | 22 (Normal mental wellbeing) |
| 2 | Frequency of prayer recitation | Spirituality Index | Do you say/ recite prayers? | 1(worst) – 3(best) **Categories:** 1 (Never) 2 (Occasionally) 3 (Daily) | 3 (Daily) |
| 3 | Frequency of meditation | Spirituality Index | Do you practise meditation? | 1(worst) – 3(best) **Categories:** 1 (Never) 2 (Occasionally) 3 (Daily) | 2 (Occasionally) |

(Continued)

**TABLE 4.3**

*continued*

| SL NO | INDICATORS | INDEXES | QUESTION | RANGE | THRESHOLD (DEPRIVED IF VARIABLE IS BELOW THRESHOLD) |
|---|---|---|---|---|---|
| 4 | Taking account of karma in daily life | Spirituality Index | Do you consider karma in the course of your daily life? | 1(worst) – 3(best) Categories: 1 (Never) 2 (Occasionally) 3 (Daily) | 3 (Daily) |
| 5 | Frequency of feeling of selfishness | Emotional Balance Index | How often do you experience selfishness? | 1(worst) – 3(best) Categories: 1 (Often) 2 (Sometimes) 3 (Never) | 3 (Never) |
| 6 | Frequency of feeling of jealousy | Emotional Balance Index | How often do you experience jealousy? | 1(worst) – 3(best) Categories: 1 (Often) 2 (Sometimes) 3 (Never) | 3 (Never) |
| 7 | Frequency of feeling of calmness | Emotional Balance Index | How often do you experience calmness? | 1(worst) – 3(best) Categories: 1 (Never) 2 (Sometimes) 3 (Often) | 3 (Often) |
| 8 | Frequency of feeling of compassion | Emotional Balance Index | How often do you experience compassion? | 1(worst) – 3(best) Categories: 1 (Never) 2 (Sometimes) 3 (Often) | 3 (Often) |
| 9 | Frequency of feeling of generosity | Emotional Balance Index | How often do you experience of generosity? | 1(worst) – 3(best) Categories: 1 (Never) 2 (Sometimes) 3 (Often) | 3 (Often) |
| 10 | Frequency of feeling of frustration | Emotional Balance Index | How often do you experience of frustration? | 1(worst) – 3(best) Categories: 1 (Often) 2 (Sometimes) 3 (Never) | 3 (Never) |
| 11 | Occurrence of suicidal thought | Emotional Balance Index | Have you ever seriously thought of committing suicide? | 1(worst) – 2 (best) Categories: 1 (Yes) 2 (No) | 2 (No) |

*Source:* www.grossnationalhappiness.com/gnhindex/introductiongnh.aspx

Several pioneering attempts have been made in the West to create independent measures of national wealth that can be compared to conventional GDP measurements. Figure 4–3 captures the essence of the problem with current economic measures of well-being. Produced by an NGO called Redefining Progress, the figure's accompanying explanatory text reads:

> According to the most popular index of prosperity—the Gross Domestic Product—this family should be celebrating. Their "persona GDP" goes higher every time they have to spend more money, no matter the reason why. Big jump in health insurance premiums? Splendid. Expensive divorce settlements? Even better. Is this any way to measure the real economic progress of a family . . . or a society? We don't think so. That's why we created the Genuine Progress Indicator or GPI. More than 400 leading economists, including several Nobel Prize winners, have called for measures like GPI that offer a more meaningful view of the economic realities most Americans face in their day-to-day lives. Using GDP as a starting point, GPI adds benefits (like the economic value of housework) and deducts costs (like crime and pollution) that GDP ignores. The results are frankly troubling. Both GDP and GPI consistently grew from 1950—the first GPI calculation—until the late 1970s. But for the last 20 years GPI has tumbled, even as total GDP continues to soar. Maybe that's why for too many American families, the "booming" economy doesn't translate into a better quality of life. So the next time politicians and pundits start cheering about the rising GDP, tell them you're still waiting for a measure of genuine progress. (n.d.)

**FIGURE 4.3**

*The downside of GDP growth*

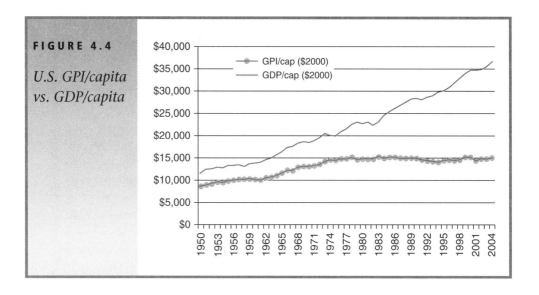

**FIGURE 4.4**

*U.S. GPI/capita vs. GDP/capita*

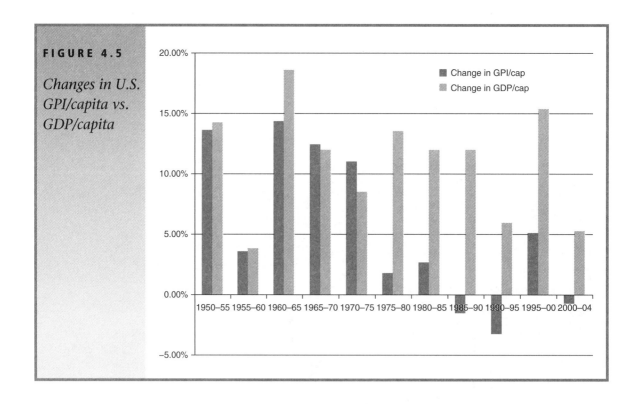

**FIGURE 4.5**

*Changes in U.S. GPI/capita vs. GDP/capita*

A comparison of GDP and GPI per capita for the period following 1950 is presented in Figures 4–4 and 4–5. The calculations behind these figures are reported in Table 4–4 (Talberth et al. 2006). Another, but conceptually similar index has been constructed by a prominent economist Herman Daly, former senior economist

| BILLION $ | 2004 |
|---|---|
| *Personal consumption* | *$7,589* |
| Income distribution | $120 |
| Personal consumption adjusted for income inequality | $6,318 |
| | |
| **ADJUSTMENTS** | |
| Value of housework and parenting | $2,542 |
| Value of higher education | $828 |
| Services of consumer durables | $744 |
| Services of highways and streets | $112 |
| Value of volunteer work | $131 |
| Net capital investment | $389 |
| Cost of household pollution abatement | ($21) |
| Cost of noise pollution | ($18) |
| Cost of crime | ($34) |
| Cost of air pollution | ($40) |
| Cost of water pollution | ($120) |
| Loss of old-growth forests | ($51) |
| Cost of under-employment | ($177) |
| Cost of automobile accidents | ($175) |
| Loss of farmland | ($264) |
| Net foreign borrowing | ($254) |
| Loss of leisure time | ($402) |
| Cost of ozone depletion | ($479) |
| Loss of wetlands | ($53) |
| Cost of commuting | ($523) |
| Cost of consumer durables | ($1,090) |
| $CO_2$ emissions damages | ($1,183) |
| Depletion of nonrenewable resources | ($1,761) |
| *NET GENUINE PROGRESS* | *$4,419* |

*Source:* Talberth et al. 2006

**TABLE 4.4**

*U.S. Genuine Progress Indicator*

for the World Bank; and John B. Cobb, Jr., professor of theology and philosophy at the Claremont Graduate School in California. The results of their measure, called an *Index of Sustainable Economic Welfare*, is compared with per capita GNP in Figure 4–6, and the underlying economic calculations are displayed in Table 4–5 (Daly and Cobb 1994).

FIGURE 4.6

*Index of
sustainable
economic
welfare*

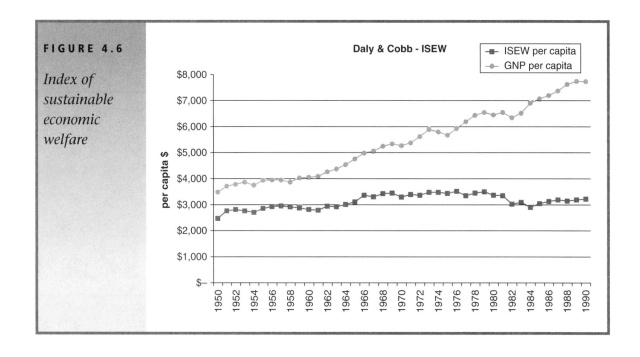

Daly & Cobb - ISEW

TABLE 4.5

*U.S. Index of
Sustainable
Economic
Welfare*

| | BILLION 1992$ |
|---|---|
| Personal consumption | $5,153 |
| Income distribution | $118 |
| Personal consumption adjusted for income inequality | $4,385 |
| | |
| **ADJUSTMENTS** | |
| Value of housework and parenting | $1,911 |
| Services of consumer durables | $592 |
| Services of highways and streets | $95 |
| Value of volunteer work | $88 |
| Net capital investment | $45 |
| Cost of household pollution abatement | −$12 |
| Cost of noise pollution | −$16 |
| Cost of crime | −$28 |
| Cost of air pollution | −$38 |
| Cost of water pollution | −$50 |
| Cost of family breakdown | −$59 |
| Loss of old-growth forests | −$83 |
| Cost of underemployment | −$112 |

| | BILLION 1992$ | TABLE 4.5 |
|---|---|---|
| Cost of automobile accidents | −$126 | *continued* |
| Loss of farmland | −$130 | |
| Net foreign borrowing | −$238 | |
| Loss of leisure time | −$276 | |
| Cost of ozone depletion | −$306 | |
| Loss of wetlands | −$363 | |
| Cost of commuting | −$386 | |
| Cost of consumer durables | −$737 | |
| Cost of long-term environmental damages | −$1,054 | |
| Depletion og nonrenewable resources | −$1,333 | |
| **NET GENUINE PROGRESS** | **$1,770** | |

*Source:* Daly and Cobb 2002

Both of these measures address the social component in sustainable development. Finally, it is necessary to specifically add a focus on natural resource depletion and degradation (i.e., natural capital) to address the ecological component of sustainability. Consider the following quote by Robert Repetto (1989, p. 2), a researcher with the World Resources Institute: "A country could exhaust its mineral resources, cut down its forests, erode its soils, pollute its aquifers, and hunt its wildlife and fisheries to extinction, but measured income would not be affected as these assets disappeared." What are the analytical methodologies that can be used to address this problem?

In his pioneering study conducted for the World Resources Institute in 1989, Repetto used Indonesia, with a major natural resource-based economy, as a case study to demonstrate a new and novel methodology to adjust the country's national accounts to incorporate estimates of the depletion of natural capital. Repetto looked specifically at petroleum, forest, and soil depletion to make adjustments to Indonesia's GDP. The analytical methodology entailed several distinct steps. For petroleum, for example, annual estimates were made of opening and closing physical stocks in barrels of oil considered as economically recoverable reserves. An estimate was then made of economic rent per barrel by subtracting the production costs from the FOB export price. Finally, the physical estimates and rent data were combined in a monetary account to determine the economic value of the opening and closing stocks. The calculation was the following:

Closing stock (m bbl) x rent/bbl = closing stock ($m) + net change in physical stock x rent/bbl = net change in monetary accounts ($m).

Table 4–6 reproduces the results of these calculations for petroleum over the period 1980–1984. As is evident from these data, the value of the physical stock has

**TABLE 4.6**

*Indonesian Petroleum Accounts*

**PHYSICAL ACCOUNTS (MILLION BARRELS)**

|  | 1980 | 1981 | 1982 | 1983 | 1984 |
|---|---|---|---|---|---|
| Opening stock | 11, 742 | 11, 306 | 10,943 | 10,631 | 10,181 |
| Additions | | | | | |
| Discoveries | 141 | 223 | 172 | 71 | 67 |
| Upward revisions | 0 | 0 | 0 | 0 | 0 |
| Depletions | 577 | 586 | 484 | 521 | 517 |
| Net Change | –436 | –363 | –312 | –450 | –450 |
| Closing stock | 11,306 | 10,943 | 10,631 | 10,181 | 9,731 |

**UNIT VALUES (US$/barrel)**

|  | 1980 | 1981 | 1982 | 1983 | 1984 |
|---|---|---|---|---|---|
| FOB Export Price | $28.11 | $35.83 | $35.74 | $34.75 | $31.94 |
| Production costs | $3.80 | $5.50 | $8.59 | $9.15 | $7.64 |
| Rent/barrel | $24.31 | $30.33 | $27.15 | $25.60 | $24.30 |

**MONETARY ACCOUNTS (million US$)**

|  | 1980 | 1981 | 1982 | 1983 | 1984 |
|---|---|---|---|---|---|
| Opening stock | $141,138.80 | $274,848.86 | $331,901.19 | $288,631.65 | $260,633.60 |
| Additions | | | | | |
| Discoveries | $3,427.71 | $6,763.59 | $4,669.80 | $1,817.60 | $1,628.10 |
| Upward revisions | $0.00 | $0.00 | $0.00 | $0.00 | $0.00 |
| Depletions | $14,026.87 | $17,773.38 | $13,140.60 | $13,337.60 | $12,563.10 |
| Net Change | –$10,599.16 | –$11,009.79 | –$8,470.80 | –$11,520.00 | –$10,935.00 |
| Revaluation | $144,309.20 | $68,062.10 | –$34,798.70 | –$16,478.10 | –$13,235.30 |
| Closing stock | $274,848.86 | $331,901.19 | $288,631.65 | $260,633.60 | $236,463.30 |

*Source:* Repetto 1989
REPRODUCED WITH PERMISSION OF THE PUBLISHER

declined over this period in study. A similar methodology is used for the calculation in the changes in the value of forests as a component of Indonesia's natural capital.

Repetto uses a somewhat different methodology for estimating the change in the value of the nation's soils. Again, a multistep calculation is used: first, an annual cost of erosion is based on annual productivity losses from soil erosion; and then these costs are capitalized using a discount rate of 10%. The issue of the appropriate discount rate to use in evaluating natural capital is somewhat contentious, and this issue is discussed further in chapter 7.

Finally, Repetto uses these data to calculate net domestic product (NDP) and net domestic investment (NDI)—representing adjustments to conventional measures of GDP and GDI after adjusting for the value of resource depletion. The results are displayed in Figures 4–7 and 4–8. The conclusions from this landmark study are noteworthy as this methodology can be used to assess the impact of the depletion of natural capital on any nation's real wealth. To quote Repetto: "For resource-based economies, evaluations of economic performance and estimates of macroeconomic relationships are seriously distorted by failure to account for natural resource depreciation. . . . Over the past 20 years [1970–89], Indonesia drew heavily on its considerable natural resource endowment to finance development expenditures (p. 4)."

In fact, the overstatement of Indonesian income and its growth may actually be considerably more than these estimates indicate because only petroleum, timber, and soils on Java are covered. Excluded from this analysis are non-renewables such as natural gas, coal, copper, tin, and nickel, and renewable resources such as non-timber forest products and fisheries. In conclusion: "Should gross investment be less than resource depletion, then, on balance, the country is drawing down, rather than building up, its asset base, and using its natural resource endowment to finance current consumption (p. 5)." If any corporation were to deplete its capital and claim this as income, the management would probably be fired. This is a clear example of how the adoption of certain corporate accounting principles could improve immeasurably the interpretation of government economic data.

This major conceptual advance from a Non-Governmental Organization (NGO) in the private sector was paralleled by work conducted by the World Bank over the

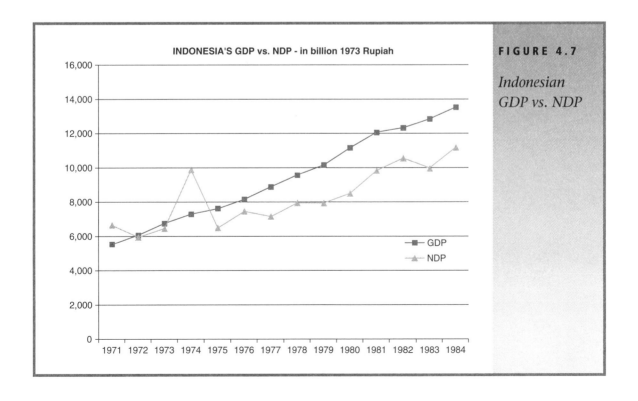

**FIGURE 4.7**

*Indonesian GDP vs. NDP*

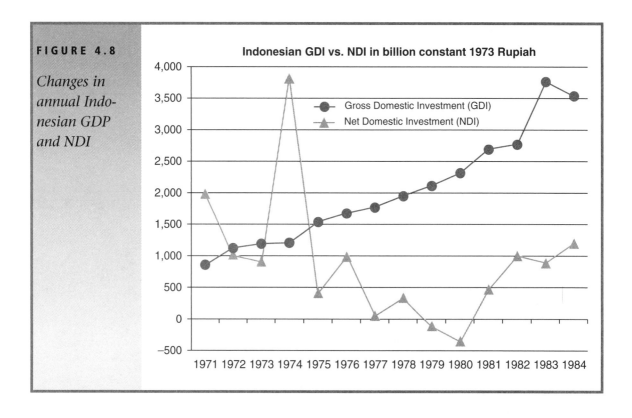

**FIGURE 4.8**

*Changes in annual Indonesian GDP and NDI*

Indonesian GDI vs. NDI in billion constant 1973 Rupiah

- Gross Domestic Investment (GDI)
- Net Domestic Investment (NDI)

past two decades. The bank has produced several methodologies in order to create a more comprehensive measure of the wealth of nations. It began with the recognition that the traditional definition of physical or "produced" capital must be complemented by at least two other types of capital: (1) natural capital, as described above, which includes not only land, fossil-fuel deposits, and other mineral wealth, but also such critical natural resources as clean water and air; and (2) human capital, as embodied in skills, health, and social organization. Table 4–7 presents some example data from the World Bank's original attempt in 1990 to redefine wealth and apply it to a comparison of national economies (Serageldin 1995, Annex 1, pp. 1–4). What are the implications of these revised measures of national wealth? Robert Solow, Nobel Laureate in Economics, has stated that "what we normally measure as capital is a small part of what it takes to sustain human welfare" (*New York Times*, September 19, 1995) Economic development policies have focused on what is easily measured—namely physical capital—to the exclusion of such critical components of national well-being as education, health, social organization, and the environment.

The data in Table 4–7 showed that natural resource-rich countries such as Australia and Canada come out on top on a per capita basis—especially in light of the fact that their resources are shared by a relatively small population base. Such countries as Switzerland and Japan have radically different resource mixes but also ranked near the top because of their investment in human capital. It has been posited that countries that derive most of their wealth from human and social capital are better positioned to create a sustainable economic advantage in the post-industrial era and

| Country | WEALTH per person ($) | COMPOSITION OF WEALTH | | | |
|---|---|---|---|---|---|
| | | NATURAL | | PRODUCED OR MANUFACTURED | HUMAN AND SOCIAL (Education, skills, etc.) |
| | | Land (crops, etc.) | Other (subsoil minerals and water) | | |
| Australia | $835,000 | 64% | 8% | 7% | 21% |
| Canada | $704,000 | 64% | 5% | 9% | 22% |
| Japan | $565,000 | 1% | 0% | 18% | 81% |
| USA | $421,000 | 22% | 3% | 16% | 59% |
| Germany | $399,000 | 3% | 1% | 17% | 79% |
| Singapore | $306,000 | 0% | 0% | 15% | 85% |
| Saudi Arabia | $184,000 | 26% | 28% | 18% | 28% |
| Russia | $98,000 | 34% | 36% | 15% | 15% |
| Mexico | $74,000 | 11% | 5% | 11% | 73% |
| China | $6,600 | 3% | 5% | 15% | 77% |
| India | $4,300 | 2% | 9% | 25% | 64% |
| Vietnam | $2,600 | 2% | 9% | 15% | 74% |
| Ethiopia | $1,400 | 12% | 27% | 21% | 40% |
| **WORLD** | **$86,000** | **15%** | **5%** | **16%** | **64%** |

**TABLE 4.7**

*World Bank's Original Estimates of Total National Wealth 1990*

information age where a high premium is placed on human creativity, education, and technical skills.

The World Bank undertook a major revision and expansion of this analysis first in 2000 and 2006 and then again in 2011. An example of their comparative international data is displayed in Table 4–8. In this case, the categories have been renamed as produced capital, natural capital, and intangible capital. *Produced capital* represents the sum of machinery and structures and development on urban land. *Natural capital* includes energy and mineral resources, timber and non-timber forest resources, crop and pasture land, and protected areas. The category of *intangible capital* is calculated as a residual, representing the difference between total wealth and the sum of produced and natural capital. It includes human capital, institutional infrastructure, and social capital. (Total wealth is defined as the net present value of sustainable consumption. See appendix 1 for the World Bank's calculation of total wealth).

While interesting in and by themselves, these "stock" estimates are considered less important than efforts to estimate national sustainability by incorporating depletion of natural capital. To address this specific issue, the World Bank created a new metric, first called *Genuine Savings* (GSM), more recently labeled *Adjusted Net Savings* (ANS) (World Bank 2011). In conventional national income accounts, the

Source: World Bank 2011

**TABLE 4.8**

*Recent World Bank Estimates of Total National Wealth*

| RANK | COUNTRY | SUBSOIL ASSETS | TIMBER | NONTIMBER FOREST RESOURCES | PROTECTED AREAS | CROP LAND | PASTURE LAND | NATURAL CAPITAL | PRODUCED CAPITAL + URBAN LAND | NET FOREIGN ASSETS | INTANGIBLE CAPITAL | TOTAL WEALTH PER CAPITA |
|---|---|---|---|---|---|---|---|---|---|---|---|---|
| 1 | Luxembourg | $0 | $255 | $85 | $1,413 | $718 | $3,621 | $6,092 | $213,425 | $99,449 | $598,563 | $917,530 |
| 2 | Iceland | $0 | $0 | $103 | $8,382 | $81 | $3,797 | $12,363 | $137,470 | –$45,995 | $799,123 | $902,960 |
| 3 | Norway | $99,706 | $669 | $1,417 | $4,788 | $505 | $3,078 | $110,162 | $183,078 | $36,436 | $532,121 | $861,797 |
| 4 | Denmark | $8,536 | $217 | $587 | $2,463 | $2,808 | $5,005 | $19,616 | $130,827 | $1,288 | $591,224 | $742,954 |
| 5 | Switzerland | $0 | $299 | $155 | $3,521 | $845 | $4,590 | $9,411 | $165,561 | $55,211 | $506,613 | $736,795 |
| 6 | USA | $3,478 | $831 | $462 | $3,625 | $2,598 | $2,827 | $13,822 | $100,075 | –$6,947 | $627,246 | $734,195 |
| 17 | Canada | $12,644 | $3,980 | $4,302 | $11,293 | $2,603 | $2,103 | $36,924 | $89,811 | –$2,977 | $414,938 | $538,697 |
| 44 | Mexico | $3,525 | $1 | $149 | $316 | $1,360 | $1,290 | $6,641 | $21,320 | –$3,085 | $106,508 | $131,385 |
| 101 | China | $804 | $231 | $45 | $107 | $2,501 | $325 | $4,013 | $6,017 | $284 | $8,921 | $19,234 |
| 149 | Ethiopia | $2 | $8 | $48 | $261 | $522 | $281 | $1,123 | $324 | –$97 | $2,089 | $3,439 |
| 150 | Liberia | | $2,012 | $198 | $16 | $955 | $20 | $3,201 | $217 | –$1,709 | $1,659 | $3,368 |
| 151 | Congo Dem. Rep. | $77 | $443 | $546 | $19 | $500 | $14 | $1,599 | $200 | –$183 | $678 | $2,294 |
| 152 | Burundi | $2 | $1,054 | $3 | $13 | $1,541 | $84 | $2,697 | $166 | –$145 | –$527 | $2,191 |

net savings rate is calculated by deducting depreciation of physical capital from gross savings:

$$NS = (GDS—Dp) / GDP$$

where
NS = net savings
GDS = gross domestic savings
Dp = depreciation of physical capital
GDP = gross domestic product
The World Bank's Adjusted Net Savings Rate is calculated as follows:

$$GENSAV = (GDS—Dp + EDU—Rni—CO_2 \text{ Damage}) / GDP$$

where
GENSAV = genuine domestic savings rate
GDS = Gross domestic savings
Dp = depreciation of physical capital
EDU = current expenditure on education
Rni = rent from depletion of i-th natural capital resource (energy, mineral, and forest depletion are included)
$CO_2$ Damage = estimated at US$20 per ton of carbon times number of tons of carbon emitted
GDP = gross domestic product at market prices
Table 4–9 shows the results of these calculations for a selected number of petro states. These countries have widely different genuine savings rates, with many experiencing significant negative values. There is a long-standing debate over the special role of petroleum in economic development and sustainability, frequently referred to as the *Resource Curse* and *Dutch Disease* (see Margonelli 2007 and Maass 2009).

At least one major critique of the original GSM was voiced by Pillarisetti in the journal *Ecological Economics* (2005). According to this author, the metric has both positive and negative features. On the plus side, GSM highlights the need for investment in physical and social capital and subtracts natural resource depletion and environmental damage from conventional measures such as GDP. On the negative side, however, its conceptual problems include the omission of some major pollutants such as sulfur dioxide and nitrogen dioxide, its foundational assumption based on the principle of weak sustainability that the loss of natural capital can be replaced by increased expenditures on other forms of capital [see chapter 1], and because of its components and structure, an apparently misleading impression that many advanced countries are sustainable despite contrary evidence from other major measures such as the *ecological footprint* [see chapter 10]. This critique remains valid for the revised ANS rates.

A special commission was struck in 2009 by the French President Nicholas Sarkozy and co-chaired by two Nobel Laureates, Joseph Stiglitz and Amartya Sen (2009), entitled: "Report by the Commission on the Measurement of Economic Performance and Social Progress." This study is one of the most comprehensive analytical examinations of the issues to date. To quote the authors:

**TABLE 4.9**

*Adjusted Net Savings of Selected Petro States*

| RANK | COUNTRY | ADJUSTED NET SAVINGS |
|---|---|---|
| 12 | Algeria | 21.4 |
| 16 | Iran | 20.0 |
| 30 | Norway | 16.2 |
| 52 | Kuwait | 9.7 |
| 58 | Mexico | 9.0 |
| 68 | Argentina | 7.7 |
| 69 | Canada | 7.6 |
| 79 | Venezuela | 6.5 |
| 82 | Brazil | 5.2 |
| 94 | Kazakhstan | 2.5 |
| 97 | Colombia | 1.5 |
| 98 | Russia | 1.5 |
| 100 | Ecuador | 0.4 |
| 102 | Azerbaijan | −0.1 |
| 110 | Saudi Arabia | −1.8 |
| 111 | Indonesia | −2.4 |
| 127 | Angola | −42.6 |
| 128 | Chad | −49.9 |

*Source:* World Bank 2011

The Commission's aim has been to identify the limits of GDP as an indicator of economic performance and social progress, including the problems with its measurement; to consider what additional information might be required for the production of more relevant indicators of social progress; to assess the feasibility of alternative measurement tools, and to discuss how to present the statistical information in an appropriate way. . . . In effect, statistical indicators are important for designing and assessing policies aiming at advancing the progress of society, as well as for assessing and influencing the functioning of economic markets. . . . Choices between promoting GDP and protecting the environment may be false choices, once environmental degradation is appropriately included in our measurement of economic performance. So too, we often draw inferences about what are good policies by looking at what policies have promoted economic growth; but if our metrics of performance are flawed, so too may be the inferences that we draw. . . . It has long been clear that GDP is an inadequate metric to gauge well-being over time particularly in its economic, environmental, and social dimensions, some aspects of which are often referred to as *sustainability*. . . . The time is ripe for our measurement system to *shift emphasis from measuring economic production to measuring people's well-being. . . . There is a need for a clear indicator of our proximity to dangerous levels of environmental damage (such as associated with climate change or the depletion of fishing stocks).*

The two most recent international efforts to re-cast the debate over the components of well-being have been produced by the United Nations Development Program [UNDP] and the OECD. The first study by UNDP published in 2010 represents the latest version of an attempt by the international body to look beyond the conventional measures of welfare, as typified by GDP/capita, and generate alternative measures of well-being across countries and over time. The first such effort in 1990 was a Human Development Index (HDI) that measured life expectancy at birth, the adult literacy rate, mean years of schooling, and educational attainment. Realizing that the HDI represented only part of the broader picture of well-being, the UNDP

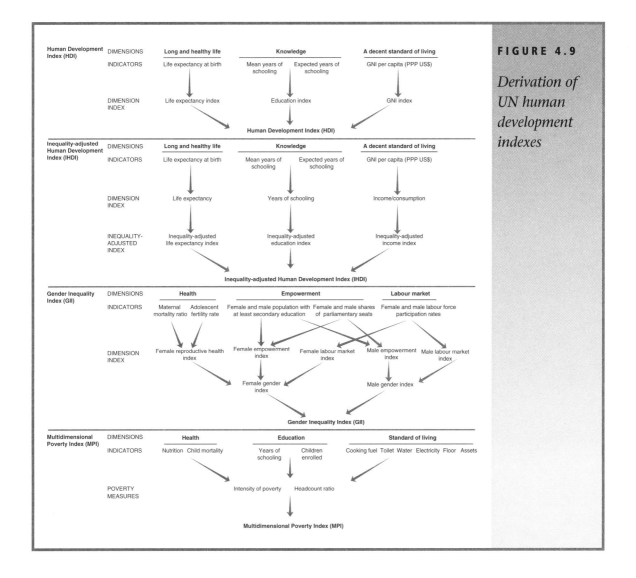

**FIGURE 4.9**

*Derivation of UN human development indexes*

has produced several additional indices: an inequality-adjusted HDI, a Gender In-equality Index (GII), and a Multidimensional Poverty Index (MPI) (UNDP 2010). Figure 4–9 illustrates the components and construction of each of the four indices.

As a parenthetical note, it is important to remember that much of the data re-ported by the UN and relied upon in the construction of these indices is based on surveys conducted by individual countries. As such, the degree of accuracy may be difficult to ascertain. In matters of national pride, such as adult literacy rates, there might be a tendency to err on the upside in the reporting process. Even in most of the developed nations—where literacy rates are considered at 99%, there is a reason to be circumspect. For example, in both the United States and Canada where in-depth analysis has been conducted of disaggregated levels of literacy and numeracy (e.g., proficient, intermediate, basic, and below basic), the results fall far short of 100% [U.S. DoE, NCES, 2005; Statistics Canada 2003]. The UNDP discontinued the use of this variable in its index construction in 2009 and replaced it with mean years of schooling. The underlying lesson from these reports is that the construction of any index—whether it concerns matters social, economic, or ecological—must be based on verifiable data.

The second major study, by the OECD (2011), compared 34 countries across 21 indicators under the general rubrics of "material conditions" and "quality of life" [see appendix 2]. Only six of these variables were conventional measures of economic welfare. The top seven countries (in descending order) were Australia, Canada, Sweden, New Zealand, Norway, Denmark, and the United States.

One additional piece of evidence that suggests that GDP/capita is an inadequate if not misleading indicator of well-being is provided in a controversial new book by Charles Kenny (2011) of the World Bank. In this work, Kenny states that many nations in the Third World are considerably better off than is indicated by their per capita income when one considers the decrease in rates of infant mortality, in-creased school attendance, and general improvement in health including increases in life expectancy. To quote (pp. 10–11): ". . . the biggest success of development has not been making people richer, but, rather, has been making the things that re-ally matter—things like health and education—cheaper and more widely available."

In sum, it is clear that the sustainability challenges we face today—economic, social, and ecological—are the result of the long period of global economic growth, and continuation of this trend poses even greater challenges. As such, it is essential to understand the evolution of modern economic theory designed to address these issues. The next chapter describes the origins and development of the subfield of Environmental Economics, and the following chapter outlines the basic principles of the relatively new discipline of Ecological Economics.

## CITED REFERENCES AND RECOMMENDED READINGS

Anielski, Mark (2007) *The Economics of Happiness: Building Genuine Wealth*. Gabriola Is-land, BC: New Society Publishers.

Canadian Index of Wellbeing (2011) *How Are Canadians Really Doing? Canadian Index of Wellbeing 1.0*. Waterloo, ON: Canadian Index of Wellbeing and University of Waterloo.

Daly, Herman and John Cobb (1994) *For the Common Good*. Boston: Beacon Press.

Daly, Herman and John Cobb (2002) "For the Common Good," in Peter N. Nemetz (ed.) *Bringing Business on Board: Sustainable Development and the B-School Curriculum*. Vancouver: JBA Press, pp. 65–86.

Diener, Ed, John F. Helliwell and Daniel Kahneman (eds.) (2010) *International Differences in Well-Being*. Oxford: Oxford University Press.

Di Tella, Rafael and Robert MacCulloch (2010) "Happiness Adaptation to Income Beyond 'Basic Needs,'" in Ed Diener, John F. Helliwell and Daniel Kahneman (eds.) *International Differences in Well-Being*. Oxford: Oxford University Press, pp. 217–246.

Graham, Carol (2009) *Happiness Around the World: The Paradox of Happy Peasants and Miserable Millionaires*. Oxford: Oxford University Press.

Graham, Carol and Stefano Pettinato (2002) *Happiness & Hardship: Opportunity and Insecurity in New Market Economies*. Washington, DC: Brookings Institute.

Helliwell, John F. and Christopher P. Barrington-Leigh (2010) "Measuring and Understanding Subjective Well-Being." *Canadian Journal of Economics* 43(3), August pp. 729–753.

Helliwell, John F., Richard Layard and Jeffrey Sachs (2102) *World Happiness Report*. The Earth Institute, Columbia University, CIFAR, Centre for Economic Performance, New York.

Ingelhart, Ronald (2004) *Human Beliefs and Values*. Mexico: Siglo Veintiuno editores.

Ingelhart, Ronald F. (2010) "Faith and Freedom: Traditional and Modern Ways to Happiness," in Ed Diener, John F. Helliwell and Daniel Kahneman (eds.) *International Differences in Well-Being*, pp. 351–397. Oxford: Oxford University Press.

Institute of Wellbeing (2009) *How Are Canadians Really Doing? First Report*, University of Waterloo, Ontario.

Kennedy, Robert F. (1968) "Remarks at the University of Kansas," March 18, University of Kansas Library.

Kenny, Charles (2011) *Getting Better: Why Global Development Is Succeeding—and How We Can Improve the World Even More*. New York: Basic Books.

Layard, Richard (2006) *Happiness: Lessons from a New Science*. New York: Penguin.

Maass, Peter (2009) *Crude World: The Violent Twilight of Oil*. New York: Alfred A. Knopf.

Margonelli, Lisa (2007) *Oil on the Brain: Adventures from the Pump to the Pipeline*. New York: Doubleday.

*New York Times* (1995) "The Wealth of Nations: A 'Greener' Approach Turns List Upside Down," September 19.

*New York Times* (2005) "A New Measure of Well-Being from a Happy Little Kingdom," October 4.

Organization for Economic Co-operation and Development (OECD) (2011a) *Compendium of OECD Well-being Indicators*, May, Paris.

Organization for Economic Co-operation and Development (OECD) (2011b) *How's Life? Measuring Well-being*, October, Paris.

Pillarisetti, J. Ram (2005) "The World Bank's 'Genuine Savings' Measure and sustainability." *Ecological Economics*, 55, pp. 599–609.

Redefining Progress (date uncertain) newspaper advertisement, Oakland, CA.

Repetto, Robert (1989) *Wasting Assets: Natural Resources in the National Income Accounts*. Washington, DC: World Resources Institute.

Serageldin, Ismail (1995) *Sustainability and Wealth of Nations: First Steps in an Ongoing Journey*, World Bank, Third Annual World Bank Conference on Environmentally Sustainable Development, September 30.

Smith, Tom W. (2011) "Trends in Well-being, 1972–2010," National Opinion Research Center, University of Chicago, March.

Statistics Canada (2003) *Building on our Competencies: Canadian Results of the International Adult Literacy and Skills Survey*, Ottawa.

Stiglitz, Joseph, Amaryta Sen and Jean-Paul Fitoussi (2009) *Report by the Commission on the Measurement of Economic Performance and Social Progress*. Published as *Mis-Measuring Our Lives.: Why GDP Doesn't Add Up*, 2010. New York: The New Press.

Talberth, John et al. (2006) *The Genuine Progress Indicator 2006: A Tool for Sustainable Development* Oakland: Redefining Progress.

United Nations Development Programme (UNDP) (2010) *Human Development Report 2010.*

Ura, Karma, Sbna Alkire and Tshoki Zangmo (2012) "Case Study" Bhutan. Gross National Happiness and the GNH Index," in John F. Helliwell et al. *World Happiness Report*. The Earth Institute, Columbia University, CIFAR, Centre for Economic Performance.

U.S. Census Bureau (www.census.gov).

U.S. Department of Education (DoE) National Center for Education Statistics (NCES) National Assessment of Adult Literacy (NAAL) (2005) "A First Look at the Literacy of America's Adults in the 21st Century."

World Bank (2006) *Where Is the Wealth of Nations?* Washington, DC.

World Bank (2011) *The Changing Wealth of Nations*. Washington, DC.

www.grossnationalhappiness.com/gnhindex/introductiongnh.aspx [Website of The Centre for Bhutan Studies, Langiophakha, Thimphu, Bhutan].

## APPENDIX ONE

# The World Bank's Calculation of Total Wealth

(World Bank 2011, pp. 142–143, Reproduced with Permission)

## TOTAL WEALTH

Total wealth can be calculated as $W_t = \int_t^\infty C(s) \cdot e^{-r(s-t)} ds$, where $W_t$ is the total value of wealth, or capital, in year $t$; $C(s)$ is consumption in year $s$; and $r$ is the social rate of return to investment. The social rate of return from investment is equal to

$$r = \rho + \eta \, \dot{C}/C$$

where $\rho$ is the pure rate of time preference, $\eta$ is the elasticity of utility with respect to consumption. Under the assumption that $\eta = 1$, and that consumption grows at a constant rate, then total wealth can be expressed as

(A.1) $Wt = \int_t^\infty C(t) \cdot e^{-\rho(s-t)} ds$

The current value of total wealth at time $t$ is a function of the consumption at time $t$ and the pure rate of time preference.

Expression (A.1) implicitly assumes that consumption is on a sustainable path, that is, the level of saving is enough to offset the depletion of natural resources. The calculation of total wealth requires that two issues be considered in computing the initial level of consumption:

- *The volatility of consumption.* To solve this problem we used the five-year centered average of consumption for each of the three years: 1995, 2000, and 2005.

- *Negative rates of adjusted net saving.* When depletion-adjusted saving is negative, countries are consuming natural resources, jeopardizing the prospects for future consumption. A measure of sustainable consumption needs to be derived in this instance.

Hence, the following adjustments were made:

- Wealth calculation for 2005, for example, considered consumption series for 2003–2007.

- For the years in which saving adjusted for depletion of produced and natural capital was negative, this measure of depletion-adjusted saving was subtracted from consumption to obtain *sustainable* consumption, that is, the consumption level that would have left the capital stock intact.

- The corrected consumption series were then expressed in constant 2005 U.S. dollars. Deflators are country specific: they are obtained by dividing gross domestic product (GDP) in current dollars by GDP in constant dollars. This rule was also applied to natural capital and net foreign assets.

- The average of constant-dollars consumption between 2003 and 2007, for example, was used as the initial level of consumption for wealth calculation of 2005.

For computation purposes, we assumed the pure rate of time preference to be 1.5%, and we limited the time horizon to 25 years. This time horizon roughly corresponds to a generation. We adopted the 25-year truncation throughout the calculation of wealth, in particular, of natural capital.

## APPENDIX TWO

# *Well-Being Indicator Variables Used by the OECD (2011)*

A. Material Conditions
   1. Income and Wealth
      a. Household net adjusted disposable income per person
      b. Household financial net wealth per person
   2. Jobs and Earnings
      a. Employment rate
      b. Long-term unemployment rate
   3. Housing
      a. Number of rooms per person
      b. Dwelling with basic facilities
B. Quality of Life
   1. Health Status
      a. Life expectancy at birth
      b. Self-reported health status
   2. Work and Life
      a. Employees working very long hours
      b. Time devoted to leisure and personal care
      c. Employment rate of women with children 6–14 years
   3. Education and Skills
      a. Educational attainment
      b. Students' cognitive skills
   4. Social Connections
      a. Contacts with others
      b. Social network support
   5. Civic Engagement and Governance
      a. Voter turnout
      b. Consultation on rule making
   6. Environmental Quality
      a. Air pollution
   7. Personal Security
      a. Intentional homicides
      b. Self-reported victimization
   8. Subjective Well-Being
      a. Life satisfaction

# CHAPTER 5

# An Overview of Environmental Economics

THE SUBDISCIPLINE OF ENVIRONMENTAL ECONOMICS EMERGED in the 1960s in the wake of the publication of Rachel Carson's *Silent Spring* and the increased awareness of environmental issues among the general public, media, and government. Much of conventional economic thinking concerning environmental degradation focuses on the general concept of "market failure," as expressed in several interrelated issues: externalities, public goods, property rights and issues of common property, and open access resources. Although some of these concepts had been in currency for some time (for example, the English economist Arthur Pigou had discussed the concept of externalities in the 1930s although he did not cast his analysis in terms of environmental degradation), they became central pillars of the new discipline. Despite the new focus on the environment, the subdiscipline was the intellectual child of neoclassical economics and, as such, relied on many of the theoretical constructs of this traditional economic analysis.

*Externalities* are usually defined as unintentional side effects of production and consumption that affect a third party either positively or negatively. The key point is that these effects are not reflected in the price of the good; that is, they do not enter into market transactions. Good examples of positive externalities include clean air and water and beautiful private gardens; and, by contrast, negative externalities include polluted air and water and poorly maintained private residential yards, etc. Because of the existence of externalities, the marginal private cost (MPC) of the activity undertaken does not equal its marginal social cost (MSC). MPC is the cost borne by the producer; MSC is the cost borne by society. When MPC does not equal MSC, goods or activities with negative externalities are underpriced (since the MPC is artificially lower than the MSC) and overproduced, and goods or activities with positive externalities are overpriced and underproduced. The distinction between private and social cost is illustrated in Figure 5–1. Individuals and corporations respond to private costs as they are the direct, visible costs that affect their personal or business decisions. Social cost, in contrast, includes *all costs* associated with the production of a good or service (including externalities) and, as such, are of relevance to government policy that must address the total costs faced by society. In fact, externalities should be of concern to corporations and individual citizens as well since it is their decisions that generate much of the costs. To personalize the concept, one need only ask the question of oneself: "Why should I pay (or incur an additional cost) because someone else has produced or purchased a product or service which may be of little or no interest to me?" The fact that these additional

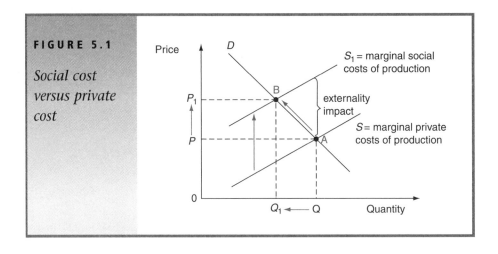

**FIGURE 5.1**

*Social cost versus private cost*

costs often indirectly but ultimately impact such things as personal health, peace of mind, and longevity serves to underscore the importance of externalities.

The majority of environmental goods fall into a category in which market values are not available. These goods, termed *public goods*, generally have two key characteristics: *non-exclusion*—meaning that one person could not prevent (i.e., "exclude") another from consuming the resource, and *joint consumption*—meaning that when a good is consumed by one person, it does not diminish the amount consumed by another person. For example, in theory, one person's consumption of clean air does not diminish any other person's consumption. With non-exclusion and joint consumption, it is never in the interest of a private, profit-maximizing enterprise to produce such a good because the enterprise could not reap the economic rewards of doing so. Consumers would "free ride." Parenthetically, it could be argued that some environmental goods are only quasi-public goods in the sense that consumption by one individual or corporation [of clean river water, for example] may indeed diminish the amount available for others.

Finally, common property resources are those owned by no one and hence over-consumed. The classic elaboration of this theory was provided by Garrett Hardin in a seminal article entitled "The Tragedy of the Commons," which appeared in the December 13, 1968, issue of the prestigious journal *Science*. In this article, Hardin based his assessment on the classic problem faced by English farmers who had un-limited access to the commons to graze their cattle. When farmers took advantage of this opportunity, the inevitable result was overgrazing that impoverished them all. It was Hardin's conclusion that this problem could be solved by the creation of property rights to the commons and the assignment of these rights to a single individual who would have an economic incentive to maintain restricted access, thereby guaranteeing indefinite productivity. This model has been used to explain the continuing overexploitation of global fisheries resources for example. Since the date of its original exposition, however, this theory has been subject to increased scrutiny and criticism.

It is important to note that there are at least two major conceptual problems with Hardin's original formulation. First, Hardin was essentially referring to *open access resources* as opposed to *commons*. The inability to control access to a resource may or may not be characteristic of any one common property resource. In many parts of the Third World, communities have had, or currently have, common property resources that have elaborate institutional mechanisms for preventing excess use and degradation. Examples include former social networks called "water temples" for the coordination of water use on rice fields of Bali, alpine pastures in Switzerland, irrigated rice fields in Northern Philippines ("Zanjera"), historical commons-based irrigation systems in Spain ("Huerta"), some local areas in Africa and Southeast Asia as well as some local fisheries in the South Pacific (Dietz et al. 2003 supplementary material). Unfortunately, many of these functioning commons have been destroyed because of several factors, including increasing population pressure, increasing commercialization of resources resulting from globalization of markets, and the increasing intrusion of remote central government into local forms of government and their traditional means of resource control (even in those circumstances where the intentions are good).

The late Nobel Laureate Elinor Ostrom and colleagues have outlined the criteria for successful management of commons (Dietz et al. 2003; Ostrom et al. 2002): "(i) the resources and use of the resources by humans can be monitored, and the information can be verified and understood at relatively low cost; (ii) rates of change in resources, resource-user populations, technology, and economic and social conditions are moderate; (iii) communities maintain frequent face-to-face communication and dense social networks—sometimes called social capital—that increase the potential for trust, allow people to express and see emotional reactions to distrust, and lower the cost of monitoring behavior and inducing rule compliance; (iv) outsiders can be excluded at relatively low cost from using the resource (new entrants add to the harvesting pressure and typically lack understanding of the rules); and (v) users support effective monitoring and rule enforcement (Dietz et al. 2003, p. 8)." The authors do, however, recognize that there are few locations in the world that meet all of these conditions. Nevertheless, when a constellation of these factors is present, commons management generally can act to control and preserve resources.

The second main critique of Hardin is that single ownership of the resource base is no guarantee that the resources will avoid being degraded or exhausted. For example, if the owner's personal discount rate is higher than the rate of renewal of the resource,[1] it is economically rational (and profit maximizing) for the owner to deplete the resource, take these earnings, and invest them elsewhere (Clark 1973, 1990; Clark and Munro 1978, 1979). Examples abound of entrepreneurs engaging in "high-grading," where they skim off the best of the resource (or deplete most of it) and then abandon the business, taking their profits. This has particularly been the case in the area of forestry. That is the reason why, in North American and most European jurisdictions, there are very strict forestry requirements on how much can be harvested and how much must be replanted each year.

As governments began to respond to perceived environmental threats in the late 1960s, the most common regulatory approach adopted was what has been referred to as "command and control" (CAC). Under this approach, regulatory agencies frequently instruct a company (and specifically a production operation such as a mill, smelter, mine, etc.) to achieve a specific level of pollutant output for each source of air and water pollution, such as a stack or other in-plant source of emissions.

There are several broad sources of economic inefficiency in this approach: first, CAC requires the regulator to spend resources to acquire information about control technology and levels of pollution that corporations already possess; second, industrial operations vary in the ease (i.e., cost) with which they can abate pollution. Therefore, imposing one standard on all is economically inefficient; third, the polluter has no incentive to do better than the standard; and fourth, if the regulations are based on rates of product or effluent output, there is no precise control over total emissions. For example, industrial plants could increase the level of production and concomitant pollution discharges while remaining within the law by meeting standards based on amount of pollutant per unit of output. This is clearly not in keeping with the intent of the original legislation and accompanying regulations that sought to control the environmental impact of an industrial operation.

There is one additional problem associated with command-and-control regulation with its concomitant structure of legal sanctions, most usually fines. In some circumstances, firms may view the regulations as licenses to pollute, with the monetary fine representing the de facto cost of the license. This "cost of doing business" interpretation can be particularly problematic when the amount of the fine is considerably less than the cost of pollutant reduction or avoidance. The problem is compounded by the fact that the probability of being caught is invariably less than 1.0 in any given period, thereby encouraging some firms to adopt a strategy of noncompliance because of the significantly lower expected value of the ultimate financial penalty.

One early solution to the problem of the inefficiency of CAC was the adoption of *performance standards* for some large industrial complexes. Under this approach, often called a bubble regulation, [see Figure 5–2] government may set a limit on the total amount of a particular air pollutant emanating from the complex and let the company achieve that target with the least-cost mix of alternative measures within the complex itself. It is important to note that air emissions can come from point sources (such as stacks), area sources (such as ponds), or fugitive sources (such as pipe leaks and loose fittings). Pollution abatement options may include process changes, changes in the mix of inputs, improvements in "end-of-pipe" control, or any combination thereof.

The bubble approach remains somewhat controversial. For example, the United States Environmental Protection Agency (U.S. EPA) sued the Texas air pollution authority in 2010 to discontinue this practice (*New York Times*, June 11, 2010), however, the concept remains sound. For example, the current use of a cap-and-trade system for the control of sulfur dioxide emissions in the United States [see appendix 1], can be considered a meta-bubble approach with two modifications: (1) the bubble is large enough to encompass a geographic region or the entire country, and (2) the method of achieving the desired performance standard is through the use of marketed permits since *inter-firm* coordination is required as opposed to *intra-firm* optimization in the original one-plant bubble.

One of the first major shifts from command and control toward economic incentives for environmental control was undertaken by the Organisation for Economic Co-operation and Development (OECD) in 1972 under the general rubric of the *Polluter-Pays-Principle* (PPP). The basic tenet of this policy was that the price of the good or service produced should fully reflect its total social cost of production,

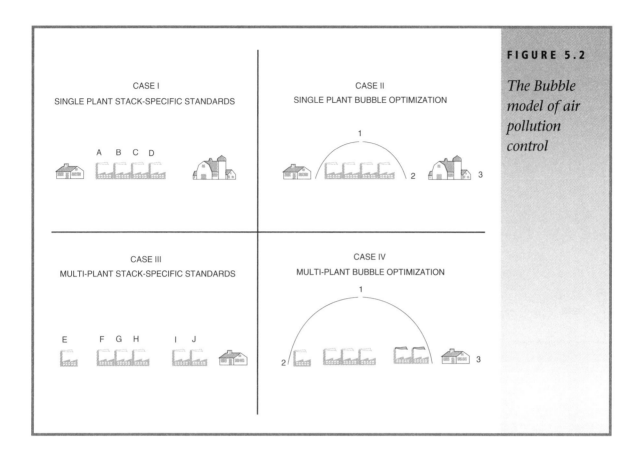

**FIGURE 5.2**

*The Bubble model of air pollution control*

including the cost of all the resources used. In other words, this principle attempts to make polluters "internalize" their externalities so that they and their consumers are ultimately guided by the social cost rather than the private cost of production. There are several critical characteristics of this principle. First, as in all economic decisions, the rational (and efficient) producer is expected to equate marginal costs and marginal revenues (MC = MR), which can also be more generally stated as MC = MB (marginal costs equal marginal benefits). In this case, the scope is widened to consider marginal social costs and benefits rather than marginal private costs and benefits. The rule therefore becomes MSC = MSB. Second, because of the nature of the marginal cost and benefit curves, it will rarely be socially optimal to reduce pollution by 100% [i.e., to have zero levels of pollution]. And, third, the name of the concept is somewhat misleading, as the cost of pollution does not fall exclusively on the producer; instead, the distribution of additional cost will be split between the producer and the consumer depending on the slope of the demand curve faced by the producer. This principle is illustrated in Figure 5–3, which describes the allocation of the tax burden. Two examples illustrate this varying distributional impact. Figure 5–4a represents the case of gasoline, while Figure 5–4b portrays the case for laundry detergent. The underlying variable that determines the ultimate distribution of de facto tax liability is the elasticity of demand for the product itself.[2] Gasoline consumption is considered to be relatively insensitive to price changes

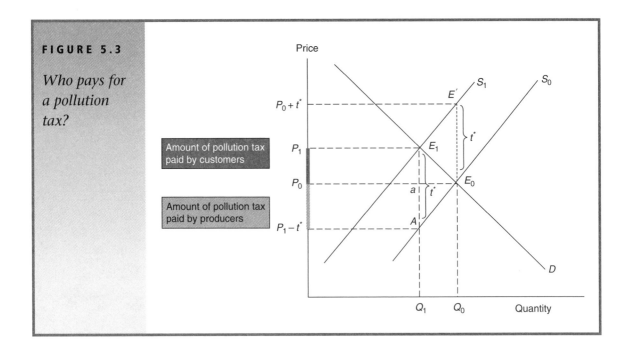

**FIGURE 5.3**

*Who pays for a pollution tax?*

Amount of pollution tax paid by customers

Amount of pollution tax paid by producers

in the short term since most motorists have few options they can pursue short of investing in a new, more fuel-efficient automobile. Interestingly enough, recent experience in the United States with respect to motorists' response to rising gas prices has suggested that there may be more flexibility than previously measured. American motorists have been able to reduce their leisure driving, increase their use of carpooling, and switch where possible to alternative modes of transport, including buses and other forms of mass transit (*New York Times*, May 17, 2011). However, the general principle remains the same: there are some commodities for which there are few substitutes in the short term and, as a consequence, the seller has a better ability to pass along the ultimate incidence of the tax increase. In contrast, in the case of laundry detergent, two factors limit the ability of the manufacturer to pass along the tax: the existence of alternative detergent brands that may vary in their pollution impact, or other non-detergent alternatives such as soap.

There are myriad economic incentives for pollution control already in place in Europe, and a recent United Nations report (2007) has provided a comprehensive summary. Tables 5–1 and 5–2 are drawn from this report and provide a classification of environmental policy instruments as well as examples of those currently in use. [See also OECD 2010b] With so many options available, a critical issue is determining selection criteria for the choice of appropriate policy instruments. When one moves from the world of economic theory to the world of practical use, it is necessary to consider an array of criteria in choosing economic instruments for pollution control. In the "real world," governments consider not only economic efficiency but also important variables such as information requirements, administrative feasibility and costs, distributional equity (such as the effect on different income

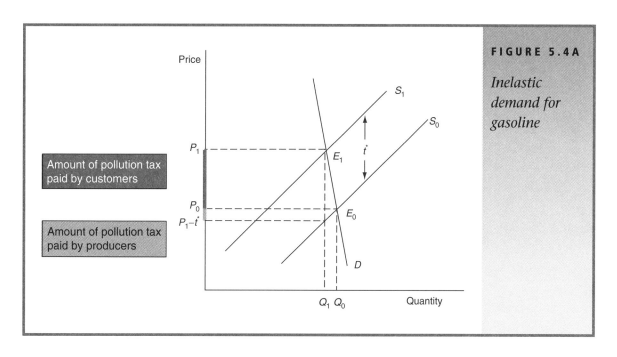

**FIGURE 5.4A**

*Inelastic demand for gasoline*

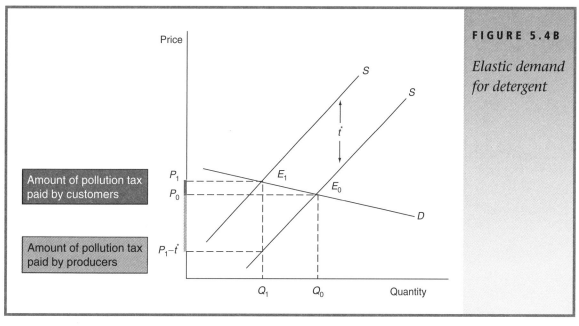

**FIGURE 5.4B**

*Elastic demand for detergent*

groups or regions), dependability, adaptability, dynamic incentives for continuous improvement, political acceptability, and predictability.

Economic incentives in the area of environmental control are generally of four types: effluent charges, marketable permits, miscellaneous charges (such as user charges, product charges, and administrative charges), and subsidies. From an economic perspective, the two most important are emissions fees or taxes (called effluent charges when applied to liquid waste) and marketable emission permits

**TABLE 5.1**

*Classification of Environmental Policy Instruments*

| COMMAND-AND-CONTROL REGULATIONS | DIRECT PROVISION BY GOVERNMENTS | ENGAGING THE PUBLIC AND PRIVATE SECTORS | USING MARKETS | CREATING MARKETS |
|---|---|---|---|---|
| Standards | Environmental infrastructure | Public participation | Remove perverse subsidies | Property rights |
| Bans | Eco-industrial zones or parks | Decentralization | Environmental taxes and charges | Tradeable permits and rights |
| Permits and quotas | National parks, protected areas and recreation facilities | Information disclosure | User charges | Offset programs |
| Zoning | Ecosystem rehabilitation | Eco-labeling | Deposit-refund systems | Green procurement |
| Liability | | Voluntary agreements | Targeted subsidies | Environmental investment funds |
| Legal redress | | Public-private partnerships | Self-monitoring (such as ISO 14000) | Seed funds and incentives |
| Flexible regulations | | | | Payment for ecosystem services |

*Source:* UN GEO4, 2007, p. 468

(generally, but not exclusively, used in the context of air pollution). Jaccard (2005) summarizes some of the trade-offs among the major policy, and Table 5–3 expands upon this analysis by scoring the alternatives by criteria on a three-part scale. Emission fees, marketable permits, and information dissemination with voluntary response are discussed below.

## EMISSION FEES

Derived conceptually from the work of Pigou, such fees or taxes are usually of the form: $x per pound or ton of the target pollutant. At least four principle advantages of this instrument have been expressed in the academic literature:

1. By forcing the polluter to internalize its externalities, this system will drive the level of pollution to its social optimum;
2. Many advocates of this tax instrument claim that since these taxes would be administered via the government's existing tax framework, there is a lower risk

**TABLE 5.2**
*Economic Instruments and Applications*

| | PROPERTY RIGHTS | MARKET CREATION | FISCAL INSTRUMENTS | CHARGE SYSTEMS | FINANCIAL INSTRUMENTS | LIABILITY SYSTEMS | BONDS AND DEPOSITS |
|---|---|---|---|---|---|---|---|
| **Forests** | communal rights | Concession building | Taxes and royalties | | Reforestation incentives | Natural resource liability | Reforestation bonds; forest management bonds |
| **Water Resources** | water rights | water shares | capital gains tax | Water pricing; water protection charge | | | |
| **Oceans and seas** | | Fishing rights; individual quotas; licensing | | | | | Oil spill bonds |
| **Minerals** | mineral rights | | Taxes and royalties | | | | Local reclamation bonds |
| **Wildlife** | | Access fees | | | | Natural resource liability | |
| **Biodiversity** | Patents; Prospecting Rights | Tradeable development rights | | Charges for scientific tourism | | Natural resource liability | |
| **Water pollution** | | Tradeable effluent permits | Effluent charges | Water treatment fees | low-interest loans | | |
| **Land and soils** | Land rights; use rights | | Property taxes; land use taxes | | Soil conservation incentives (such as loans) | | Local reclamation bonds |

(Continued)

TABLE 5.2
*continued*

| | PROPERTY RIGHTS | MARKET CREATION | FISCAL INSTRUMENTS | CHARGE SYSTEMS | FINANCIAL INSTRUMENTS | LIABILITY SYSTEMS | BONDS AND DEPOSITS |
|---|---|---|---|---|---|---|---|
| **Air pollution** | | Tradeable emission permits | Emission charges | Technology subsidies; low-interest loans | | | Deposit refund systems |
| **Hazardous waste** | | | | Collection charges | | | Deposit refund systems |
| **Solid waste** | | | Property taxes | Technology subsidies; low-interest loans | | | |
| **Toxic chemicals** | | | Differential taxation | | | Legal liability; liability insurance | Deposit refund |
| **Climate** | Tradeable emission entitlements; Tradeable forest protection obligations | Tradeable $CO_2$ permits; tradeable CFC quotas; CFC quota auction; carbon offsets | Carbon taxes; BTU tax | | CFC replacement incentives; forest compacts | | |
| **Human settlements** | Land rights | Access fees; tradeable development quotas; tradeable development rights | Property taxes; land use taxes | Betterment charges; development charges; land use charges; road tolls; import fees | | | Development completion bonds |

*Source:* UN GEO4, 2007, p. 31

# TABLE 5.3

*Some Trade-Offs among Policy Instruments for Pollution Control*

| | COMMAND AND CONTROL | EFFLUENT CHARGES OR TAXES | MARKETABLE PERMITS | INFORMATION AND VOLUNTARY RESPONSE | SUBSIDIES |
|---|---|---|---|---|---|
| Effectiveness | Good | Medium | Medium-Good (depending on design) | Poor | Medium |
| Efficiency | Poor | Good | Good | Poor | Poor |
| Administrative feasibility | Good | Good | Medium-Good | Good | Medium |
| Political acceptability | Medium | Poor | Medium | Good | Medium-Good [b] |
| Information requirements | Medium | Medium | Good | Good | Poor |
| Distributional equity (esp. regressivity) | n.a. | Potentially poor [a] | Potentially poor [b] | n.a. | n.a. |
| Dependability | Good | Medium | Medium-Good [b] | Poor | Poor |
| Adaptability | Good - in theory | Good | Good | Good | Poor |
| Predictability (of results) | Good | Medium | Medium-Good [b] | Poor | Poor |
| Dynamic incentives for continuous improvements | Poor | Good | Good | Medium | Poor |

Notes to table:

[a] depending on the nature of the price change in final goods
[b] depending on design

of evasion compared to fixed emissions standards that are policed via irregular on-site inspections;

3. Pollution taxes always provide an incentive for further reductions in emissions, as reducing the amount of emissions means a reduction in the amount of taxes; and

4. Because of #3, firms have an added incentive to devote funds to research and development for new pollution abatement technology.

Despite the potential efficiency gains inherent in this type of regulatory instrument, there are certain problems and complexities in its real-world implementation. First, the assertion that the risk of evasion would be lower (and that monitoring costs would also be lower) with emission fees is false. The government must continue to monitor at the same (or greater) frequency as before in order to determine the quantity of pollutant to be taxed. Second, it is extremely difficult to set the optimal level of tax because of the uncertainty surrounding the actual damage costs associated with any particular pollutant. Therefore, the government requires data on the following: (a) the firm's output of goods, (b) the pollution that this output produces, (c) any long-term accumulation of pollution, (d) human exposure to this pollution, (e) the "damage response function" of this exposure [see chapter 9], and (f) the monetary evaluation of the cost of pollution damage. Third, price changes in the product as a result of pollution charges will probably be regressive; that is, with a bigger relative impact on people with a lower income. Fourth, a pollution tax is less likely to be effective where demand for the final product is inelastic (i.e., unresponsive) to price changes and/or there are few suitable substitutes available. [See Figures 5–4a and b.] And, fifth, countries that unilaterally impose such taxes may face a competitive disadvantage in international trade, losing out to "pollution havens." However, recent evidence suggests that this last point may be less of a problem than first anticipated (Mani and Wheller 1997). Despite these complexities, emission fees or taxes remain a powerful and widely used weapon in the armory of governments seeking to find an efficient method of pollution abatement.

## MARKETABLE PERMITS

The second major economic incentive is marketable pollution permits, of which an important variant is called *cap and trade*. The basic principle is enticingly simple: an acceptable level of pollution is determined for a geographic region, permits are then issued for the level of emissions; that is, up to the allowable level according to some procedure that is deemed equitable, and the holders of such permits (as potential sellers) and other polluters (as potential buyers) are encouraged to form a market and trade these permits.

The emergence of this policy tool can be credited to the theoretical work of Ronald Coase and John Dales. Coase's work (1960) was the first to articulate the critical role that property rights could play in environmental and resource-based issues. Coase's Theorem states that the problem of pollution externalities could be directly addressed through the simple allocation of property rights to *either* the generator or the victim of pollution. Regardless of the allocation of these rights, either one of the parties would have an incentive to seek an agreement between the two that would invariably lead to an efficient economic solution. For example, in the case of a pulp mill upstream of a fishing ground, if the mill had the rights to pollute, a fisherman who suffered the effects of this pollution would have the incentive to pay the polluter to reduce this pollution to the point where the marginal cost to the fisherman equaled his/her marginal benefit from pollution reduction. Conversely, if the fisherman had the right to clean water, the pulp mill would have in the incentive to pay the fisherman to accept the pollution. In practice, however, there would several real-world barriers to the achievement of this result. To quote Coase himself:

> The assumption [is] that there were no costs involved in carrying out market transactions. This is, of course, a very unrealistic assumption. In order to carry out a market transaction it is necessary to discover who it is that one wishes to deal with, to inform people that one wishes to deal and on what terms, to conduct negotiations leading up to a bargain, to draw up the contract, to undertake the inspection needed to make sure that the terms of the contract are being observed, and so on. These operations are often extremely costly, sufficiently costly at any rate to prevent many transactions that would be carried out in a world in which the pricing system worked without cost. (1960, p. 15)

In other words, the achievement of this economically efficient result could be stymied by a range of transaction costs associated with the number of individuals involved, their relative bargaining strength, and asymmetric information, etc. Despite the barriers to the application of this theorem, Coase's seminal contribution relating to property rights and resources, where such resources include clean air and clean water, established a conceptual framework that underpins much of modern environmental economics. It led to the concept of transferable property-like rights that could be extended to the area of environmental control, and Dales (1968) advanced this theory by suggesting it could be operationalized by creating a market for such rights in the form of pollutant permits.

The underlying economic rationale for marketable permits is based on the premise that there is an incentive to SELL permits if a firm's marginal abatement costs are below the ruling price for permits, AND there is an incentive to BUY permits if a firm's marginal abatement costs are above the price of the permits. As a result of this market trading, the control of pollution will tend to be concentrated among those polluters who find it cheapest to control pollution, and permit holding will tend to be concentrated among those who find it expensive to control pollution. Therefore, system-wide, society will have achieved the most efficient, least-cost solution for any desired target level of pollution. Figure 5–5 and 5–6 schematically portray the economic benefits of this type of approach. [Note that the marginal cost curves for pollution removal in this diagram are assumed to be linear for simplicity. In reality, the nature of pollution control technology and economics usually implies non-linearity, with MC rising exponentially as the percentage of pollutant removal approaches 100%.] In this simplified example, the social goal is to remove 100 tons of pollutant from an economy assumed to be composed of three equally sized industrial plants, each with different marginal costs of pollutant removal. These differences may stem from differences in currently installed pollution control capacity, different product mix, or different production technology. The traditional approach of command and control is represented in Figure 5–5 which has a universal standard requiring each firm to remove an equal amount of pollution. The total cost is the summation of the integrals under the three marginal cost curves, here equal to the areas of the triangles AXO + BXO + CXO. Note the radically different marginal pollutant removal costs across the three firms.

In contrast, Figure 5–6 portrays the alternate approach using an economic instrument. All firms face the same effluent price (P) per unit of pollutant. They reduce their pollutant output up to the point where their marginal cost of pollutant

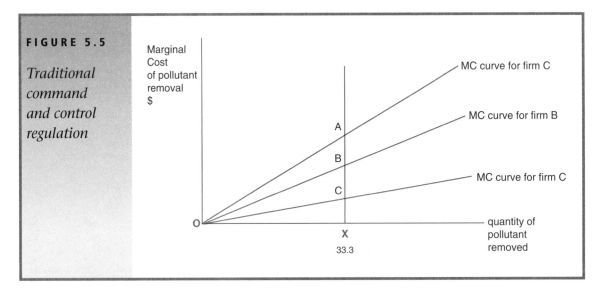

**FIGURE 5.5**

*Traditional command and control regulation*

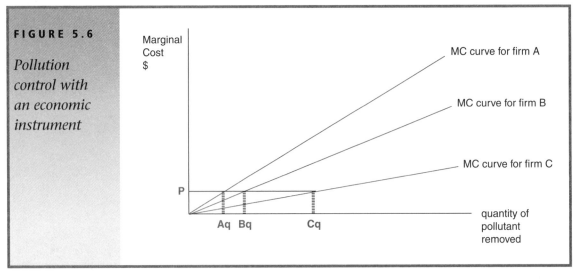

**FIGURE 5.6**

*Pollution control with an economic instrument*

removal equals the market-based effluent price. Why is this so? If their marginal cost were higher than the price, they would rather pay the price at the margin; whereas if the marginal cost were lower than the price, they would sooner reduce the amount of pollutant at the margin. Note that $Aq + Bq + Cq = 100$ tons and that $Aq < Bq < Cq$ (in other words, the firm with the lowest marginal cost of pollutant removal removes the most pollutant, and vice versa). It can be shown by simple geometric or algebraic methods that the economic incentive approach achieves the same total level of reduction at significantly lower total cost simply because the incentive approach encourages economically efficient decisions by each firm and, consequently, across the entire economy. Appendix 1 presents a case study of perhaps the most successful application of marketable permits—the U.S. system of sulfur dioxide trading.

It is important to remember that a marketable pollutant system is not universally applicable and relies on certain characteristics for successful operation. First, there must be a large enough number of industrial plants to act as traders in order to establish a smoothly functioning market for permits. Equally important, however, are certain critical characteristics of the pollutant to be traded that can make or break a market. In his exhaustive study of the theory and practice of emissions trading, Tietenberg (2006) distinguishes among three categories of pollutants: (1) uniformly mixed assimilative pollutants, (2) nonuniformly mixed assimilative pollutants, and (3) uniformly mixed accumulative pollutants.

### 1. *Uniformly mixed assimilative pollutants*

This class of pollutants includes greenhouse and ozone-destroying chemicals. Because they act globally, it does not matter where they are emitted. This spatial equivalence or independence means that the simple conceptual model described above for the efficient allocation of responsibility for abatement is appropriate where the marginal costs of control are equalized across all emitters.

### 2. *Nonuniformly mixed assimilative pollutants*

The simple theoretical model of market-based trading becomes considerably more complex when the environmental impact of pollutant is spatially dependent. Tietenberg identifies common pollutants such total suspended particulates (TSP), sulfur dioxide ($SO_2$), and nitrogen oxides (NOx) as typical of this category. The spatial dependence may derive from two potentially interdependent characteristics: spatial clustering of emitters and spatial "hot spots" where high levels of pollutant may accumulate because of local meteorological or topographical features as well as characteristics of the pollutant that lead to rapid deposition. To quote Tietenberg: "for this class of pollutants, it is not the marginal costs of emissions reduction that are equalized across sources in a cost-effective allocation (as was the case for uniformly mixed assimilative pollutants); it is the marginal costs of concentration reduction at each receptor location that are equalized (2006, p. 34)." This clearly creates a much more complex policy and market challenge, as each receptor represents its own market in which each pollutant emitter must participate.

3. *Uniformly Mixed Accumulative Pollutants*

This classification is typified by pollutants that accumulate in the environment but where the location of discharge is not important. It is unclear how many pollutants in fact satisfy this criterion, as location is critical for many of the chemicals that are accumulative such as lead, cadmium, mercury, and other heavy metals. In these cases, the present value of control costs and benefits must be incorporated into the analysis [see Tietenberg, pp. 38–40 for more details.]

## Real-World Complexities

There are a number of significant empirical complexities that are relevant to the design of marketable pollution permits in the presence of these diverse characteristics of pollutants and the environment into which they are emitted. First, as Tietenberg observes, despite the fact that $SO_2$ clearly falls into category #2, the complexity of the theoretically required policy instrument essentially reduces its applicability. As such, the U.S. EPA has adopted approach #1, which seems to implicitly assume that $SO_2$ is a uniformly mixed assimilative pollutant. The regulatory agency addresses the issue of potential local hot spots through a process called "regulatory tiering" where $SO_2$ emissions must conform to two distinctive regulatory regimes: (a) a national cap and trade, and (b) a set limit on local emissions based on ambient pollutant levels in order to prevent the occurrence of hot spots.

Second, some pollutants have both local and regional or international effects. A large percentage of sulfur dioxide emissions occur in the Ohio River Valley where there are a large number of coal-fired power plants. A significant amount of this pollutant is subject to long-range transport and has been historically responsible for the acidification of soil and water bodies in New England, Upstate New York, and Eastern Canada (*New York Times*, October 22, 1990). Fortunately, the adoption of a cap-and-trade policy across all major emitters of sulfur dioxide in the United States has had a decisive salutary impact on acidified lakes and forests in the Northeast. [See appendix 1] A similar phenomenon of local and long-range transport has been more recently identified with respect to mercury, where significant quantities of this heavy metal found in the high European Arctic have been traced to emissions in North America (Chaulk et al. 2011; Steen et al. 2010).

Third, Tietenberg's categorization misses a fourth class of pollutants that is relevant to the design and application of market-based trading regimes. This category is exemplified by pollutants (such as particulates) that are neither homogeneous nor uniformly mixed. Total suspended particulates can vary in at least two important respects: (a) size—which affects the spatial dimension of deposition and their potential for deep inhalation into the lungs where their effects are much more deleterious, and (b) their toxicity—which varies by their source. For example, the toxicity of particulates will vary markedly if they are produced by road dust, metal smelters, chemical plants, electric power plants, coal-related or petroleum operations, motor vehicles, etc. By way of example, the U.S. EPA lists 40 types of particulate-related health effects from a broad range of sources listed under 9 different rubrics: crustal/soil, salt, secondary sulfate/long-range transport, traffic, oil combustion, coal combustion, other metals, wood smoke/vegetative burning, and miscellaneous unnamed factors (U.S. EPA 2008, pp. 2–21 to 2–23). Under these circumstances, a significant problem may emerge if all of these disparate types of particulates are subject to a cap-and-trade regime that assumes homogeneity in order to facilitate trading. Despite this drawback, several jurisdictions have experimented with a market for particulates expressed as total suspended particulates (TSP) (Atkinson and Lewis, 1974; Montero et al. 2002).

Finally, some innovative hybrid systems have emerged in several areas. One notable example is the Regional Clean Air Incentives Market (RECLAIM) Program in the South Coast Air Quality Management District around Los Angeles, which established a cap-and-trade system for over 300 industrial emitters of $SO_2$ and NOx. One of the principal innovations adopted was the creation of two zones (one coastal and one inland) in order to avoid the creation of hot spots by onshore winds that blow pollution inland from the coast. Within the coastal zone, trades are only permitted internally; by contrast, in the inland zone, trades may occur within and across zones (RECLAIM Annual Report 2007).

Table 5–4 compares these critical attributes for several pollutants: sulfur dioxide; carbon dioxide; particulates; and mercury, the last of which has been recently proposed as a possible candidate for a marketable permits. While the market for sulfur dioxide has worked very well, and so would carbon dioxide, it should be apparent that neither particulates nor mercury satisfy the criteria required for successful operation of a market-based control system. Particulates are a poor candidate because of their heterogeneity. In contrast, while recent research has demonstrated that a significant proportion of mercury can be vaporized and transported as far as the polar regions (Chaulk et al. 2011; Steen et al. 2010), a sizeable remainder of this extremely toxic element may remain near the initial point of emission, creating a local *hot spot*. A situation could develop where an industrial plant with high costs of mercury abatement could chose to purchase permits and continue emitting large quantities of this pollutant, thus exposing the local population to serious health effects.

In addition to emission fees and marketable permits, there is one other related policy instrument that has emerged as a successor to traditional forms of regulation: the mandatory dissemination of pollution emission information to the general

| | $SO_2$ | $CO_2$ | PM | HG | |
|---|---|---|---|---|---|
| Large number of traders | YES | YES | YES | YES | **TABLE 5.4** |
| Homogeneity | YES | YES | NO | YES | *Critical Attributes of Selected Air Pollutants* |
| Non-toxic | Relatively | YES | YES/NO | NO | |
| Favorable meteorological and topographical conditions | Site-dependent | N.A. | Site-dependent | Site-dependent | |
| Capacity to be vaporized and/or dispersed | YES | YES | YES | Partially | |
| Ease of measurement | YES | YES | YES | YES | |

public. While differing from fees and permits by the absence of market prices, this approach has been termed by Konar and Cohen (1997) a system of "market-based incentives." [See appendix 2].

In sum, the development of environmental economics has had a profound impact on government regulation of the environment, as economic instruments have frequently been used to complement or back out traditional regulatory systems of command and control (CAC). This does not mean, however, that CAC has no place in the modern armory of government policy. It still has a valid use in special cases where action is required immediately and/or where the pollutant is exceedingly toxic. In these cases, it is inappropriate to rely on the corporate sector to take time to weigh the relative costs and benefits of voluntarily controlling emissions or releases.

Environmental economics has provided a very important conceptual foundation and policy toolbox for addressing many of the environmental problems faced in recent decades. However, because this area is basically unidisciplinary in nature, it cannot address the broader, multidisciplinary challenges that face us today. To address these issues, a new cross-disciplinary area, known as ecological economics, has emerged in the last two decades and is described in the next chapter.

## CITED REFERENCES AND RECOMMENDED READINGS

Atkinson, Scott E. & Donald H. Lewis (1974) "A Cost-Effectiveness Analysis of Alternative Air Quality Control Strategies." *Journal of Environmental Economics and Management*, 1, pp. 237–250.

Bagley, Constance E. (2006) "Shareholder Primacy Is a Choice, Not a Legal Mandate," in Marc. J. Epstein and Kirk O. Hanson (eds.) *The Accountable Corporation. Volume 1. Corporate Governance*, pp. 85–106.Westport CT: Praeger.

Barde, Jean-Philippe and Nils Axel Braathen (2007) "Green Tax Reforms in OECD Countries: An Overview," Ch. 2 in Peter N. Nemetz (ed.) *Sustainable Resource Management: Reality or Illusion?* pp. 42–87. Cheltenham: Edward Elgar.

Carlos, Ann M. and Stephen Nicholas (1988) "Giants of an Earlier Capitalism," *Business History Review*, 62(3), Autumn, pp. 398–419.

Chaulk, Amanda et al. (2011) "Mercury Distribution and Transport Across the Ocean-Sea-Ice-Atmosphere Interface in the Arctic Ocean." *Environmental Science & Technology*, 45, pp. 1866–1872.

Clark, Colin W. (1973). "The Economics of Overexploitation." *Science*, 181, pp. 630–634.

Clark, Colin W. (1990). *Mathematical Bioeconomics: The Optimal Management of Renewable Resources*. (2nd ed.). New York: Wiley Inter-Interscience, John Wiley and Sons, Inc.

Clark, Colin W., F.H. Clarke and Gordon R. Munro. (1979). "The Optimal Exploitation of Renewable Resource Stocks: Some Problems of Irreversible Investment." *Econometrica*, 47, pp. 25–47.

Clark, Colin W. and Gordon R. Munro. (1978). "Renewable Resource Management and Extinction." *Journal of Environmental Economics and Management*, 5, pp. 198–205.

Coase, Ronald (1960) "The Problem of Social Cost." *Journal of Law and Economics*, 3, October, pp. 1–44.

Conniff, Richard (2009) "The Political History of Cap and Trade." *Smithsonian Magazine*, August.

Cronk, Quentin (2003) "The Thin Green Line: Plants and the Future of Humanity," lecture to The Vancouver Institute, November 22, Vancouver, BC.

Dales, John H. (1968) *Pollution, Property and Prices: An Essay in Policy-Making and Economics*. Toronto: University of Toronto Press.

Davis, G. et al. (1998) UTN: *Chemical Hazard Evaluation for Management Strategies: A Method for Ranking and Scoring Chemicals by Potential Human Health and Environmental Impacts*, University of Tennessee.

Dietz, Thomas et al. (2003) "The Struggle to Govern the Commons." *Science*, 302, December 12, pp. 1907–1912, and supplementary material online at: www.sciencemag.org/cgi/content/full/302/5652/1907/.

duPlessis, Jean Jacques et al. (2011) *Principles of Contemporary Corporate Governance*. Cambridge: Cambridge University Press.

Ellerman, Danny et al. (2000) *Markets for Clean Air: The U.S. Acid rain Program*. Cambridge: Cambridge University Press.

European Environment Agency (EEA) (2008) Application of the Emissions Trading Directive by EU Member States, reporting year 2008, EEA Technical report No. 13.

Europe Environment Agency (2011) *Environmental Tax Reform in Europe: Implications for Income Distribution*, EEA Technical report No. 16.

European Commission (2009) *EU Action against Climate Change. The EU Emissions Trading Scheme*.

Fung, Archon and Dara O'Rourke (2000) "Reinventing Environmental Regulation from the Grassroots Up: Explaining and Expanding the Success of the Toxics Release Inventory." *Environmental Management*, 25(2), pp. 115–127.

Grant, Don Sherman (1997) "Allowing Citizen Participation in Environmental Regulation: An Empirical Analysis of the Effects of Right-to-Sue and Right-to-Know Provisions on Industry's Toxic Emissions." *Social Science Quarterly*, 78(4), December 1997, pp. 859–873.

Hamilton, James T. (1995) "Pollution as News: Media and Stock Market Reactions to the Toxics Release Inventory Data." *Journal of Environmental Economics and Management*, 28, pp. 98–113.

Hamilton, James T. (2005) *Regulation through Revelation: The Origins, Politics and Impacts of the Toxic Release Inventory Program*. Cambridge: Cambridge University of Press.

Hardin, Garret (1968) "The Tragedy of the Commons." *Science*, 162, pp. 1243–1248.

Harrison, Kathryn and Werner Antweiler (2001) "Environmental Regulation vs. Environmental Information: A View From Canada's National Pollutant Release Inventory." University of British Columbia Department of Political Science and Sauder School of Business, Vancouver, BC.

Hertwich, E.G., S.F. Mateles, W.S. Pease and T.E. McKone. (2001) Human Toxicity Potentials for Life Cycle Assessment and Toxics Release Inventory Risk Screening. *Environmental Toxicology & Chemistry*, 20(4), pp. 928–939.

Indiana Clean Manufacturing Technology and Safe Materials Institute, Purdue University. IRCH: Indiana Relative Chemical Hazard Score. (www.ecn.purdue.edu/CMTI/Pollution_Prevention_Progress_Measurement_Method/)

Indiana Relative Chemical Hazard Score—CAS Order (Updated 3/8/04).

Jaccard, Mark (2005) *Sustainable Fossil Fuels. The Unusual Suspect in the Quest for Clean and Enduring Energy*. Cambridge: Cambridge University Press.

Kennedy, Allan A. (2000) *The End of Shareholder Value*. Cambridge MA: Perseus Publishing.

Khanna, Madhu Wilma Rose H. Quimio and Dora Bojilova (1998) "Toxics Release Information: A Policy Tool for Environmental Protection." *Journal of Environmental Economics and Management*, 36, pp. 243–266.

Konar, Shameek and Mark A. Cohen (1997) "Information As Regulation: The Effect of Community Right to Know Laws on Toxic Emissions." *Journal of Environmental Economics and Management*, 32, pp. 109–124.

MacBride, Samantha (2012) *Recycled Reconsidered: The Present Failure and Future Promise of Environmental Action in the United States*, Cambridge, MA: The MIT Press.

Mani, Muthukumra and David Wheeler (1997) "In Search of Pollution Havens? Dirty Industry in the World Economy, 1960–1995." *Workshop 3: Pollution Havens and Pollution Halos*, OECD Conference on FDI and the Environment (The Hague, January 28–29, 1999).

McLean, Brian J. (2007) "Emissions Trading: U.S. Experience Implementing Multi-state Cap and Trade Programs," in Peter N. Nemetz (ed.) *Sustainable Resource Management: Reality or Illusion?* pp. 22–41. Cheltenham: Edward Elgar.

Montero, Juan-Pablo et al. (2007) "A Market-based Environmental Policy Experiment in Chile." *Journal of Law & Economics*, 45(1), April, pp. 267–287.

*New York Times* (1990) "Lawmakers Agree On Rules to Reduce Acid Rain Damage," October 22.

*New York Times* (2010) "Texas and E.P.A. Clash over Air Pollution," June 11.

*New York Times* (2011) "In Consumer Behavior, Signs of Gas Price Pinch," May 17.

Organization for Economic Co-operation and Development (OECD) (2010a) *Principles of Corporate Governance*, Paris.

Organization for Economic Co-operation and Development (OECD) (2010b) *Taxation, Innovation and the Environment*, Paris.

Ostrom, Elinor et al. (2002) *The Drama of the Commons*, National Academy of Sciences, Washington, DC.

Pigou, Arthur (1920) *The Economics of Welfare* [Reprinted 2005, New York: Cosimo].

RECLAIM (REgional CLean Air Incentives Market) (2007) *2005 Annual Audit Report*, March. [see also http://www.epa.gov/airmarkets/resource/docs/reclaimoverview.pdf].

Repetto, Robert (2007) "Better Financial Disclosure Protects Investors and the Environment," Ch. 13 in Peter N. Nemetz (ed.) *Sustainable Resource Management: Reality or Illusion?* pp. 342–375, Cheltenham: Edward Elgar.

Scorecard.org website [http://scorecard.goodguide.com/].

Steen et al. (2010) "Natural and Anthropogenic Atmospheric Mercury in the European Arctic: A Speciation Study." *Atmospheric Chemistry and Physics Discussions*, 10, pp. 27255–27281.

Stephan, Mark Michael E. Kraft and Troy D. Abel (2005) "Information Politics and Environmental Performance: The Impact of the Toxics Release Inventory on Corporate Decision Making," paper prepared for delivery at the 2005 Annual Meeting of the American Political Science Association, Washington, DC, September 1–4.

Thaler, Richard and Cass Sunstein (2009) *Nudge. Improving Decisions about Health, Wealth and Happiness*. London: Penguin.

Tietenberg, T.H. (2006) *Emissions Trading. Principles and Practice* Washington DC: Resources for the Future.

United Nations Millennium Ecosystem Assessment (2005) *Ecosystems and Human Wellbeing: Opportunities and Challenges for Business and Industry*.

United Nations Environment Programme (UNEP) (2001) *Buried Treasure: Uncovering the Business Case for Sustainability*.

United Nations Environment Programme (UNEP) (2007) *Global Environmental Outlook4 (GEO4) Environment for Development. Summary for Decision Makers.*

United Nations Global Compact (2011) Principles for Responsible Investing (PRI) *Report on Progress.*

U.S. Environmental Protection Agency (EPA) (1994) Office of Research and Development, /600/R-94/177 Cincinnati, OH. http://eerc.ra.utk.edu/ccpct/publications.html Values received in Excel file, July.

U.S. Environmental Protection Agency (EPA) (2009a) *Toxics Release Inventory Summary.*

U.S. Environmental Protection Agency (EPA) (2009b) "Toxics Release Inventory—Factors to Consider."

U.S. Environmental Protection Agency (EPA) (2008) *Integrated Science Assessment for Particulate Matter*, First External Review Draft. EPA/600/R-08/139, Research Triangle Park NC.

U.S. Environmental Protection Agency (EPA) Risk-Screening Environmental Indicators (RSEI) website: http://www.epa.gov/opptintr/rsei/pubs/basic_information.html.

U.S. Environmental Protection Agency (EPA) Office of Pollution Prevention and Toxics. (2002) RSEI: *Risk-Screening Environmental Indicators Model: Version 2.1 (1988–2000 TRI reporting data)*. December http://www.epa.gov/opptintr/rsei/index.html) Methodology described in Chapter 1: Introduction to EPAs Risk-Screening Environmental Indicators of the RSEI User's Manual. Values from Technical Appendix A—Available Toxicity Data for TRI Chemicals. (Appendix A last updated December 2002).

U.S. Environmental Protection Agency (EPA) Office of Solid Waste and Office of Pollution Prevention and Toxics. (2000) WMPT: *Waste Minimization Prioritization Tool: Background Document for the Tier III PBT Chemical List. Appendix A: WMPT Summary Spreadsheet*. Washington, DC: EPA, July http://www.epa.gov/epaoswer/hazwaste/minimize/chemlist.htm.

U.S. General Accounting Office (GAO) (1994) *Allowance Trading Offers an Opportunity to Reduce Emissions at Less Cost*. GAO/RCED-95–30.

*Wall Street Journal* (1991) "Right to Know: A U.S Report Spurs Community Action Revealing Polluters," January 2.

World Business Council on Sustainable Development (WBCSD) (2009) *Business and Ecosystems*, Geneva.

World Business Council on Sustainable Development (WBCSD) (2010) *Vision 2050*, Geneva.

World Business Council on Sustainable Development (WBCSD) (2011) *Guide to Corporate Ecosystem Valuation*, Geneva.

# APPENDIX ONE

# Sulfur Dioxide Trading in the United States

With current global concern over greenhouse gas emissions and consequent global warming, significant discussion has been undertaken by policy makers, economists, and market participants with respect to adopting a cap-and-trade system for carbon dioxide emissions in the United States. In fact, such a system already exists in Europe along with a variety of carbon taxes (Barde and Braathen 2007; EEA 2008 and 2011). It is critical to note that American proposals for a $CO_2$ trading system have been inspired by a similar model for sulfur dioxide control that has been operating successfully in the United States for several decades.

Amendments to the U.S. Clean Air Act in 1990, undertaken during the first Bush administration (Conniff 2009) sought to lower levels of acid rain by reducing $SO_2$ emissions by 10 million tons from 1980 levels. The first phase of $SO_2$ emissions reductions was achieved in 1995, with a second phase of reduction accomplished by the year 2000. In Phase I, individual emissions limits were assigned to the 263 most $SO_2$-emission intensive generating units at 110 electric utility plants operated by 61 electric utilities, and located largely at coal-fired power plants east of the Mississippi River. Called cap and trade, the $SO_2$ allowance trading program has achieved an extraordinary degree of success. Full $SO_2$ reductions were expected to be achieved in 2010, entailing a significant benefit to public health because of the reduction in airborne fine particulate matter, much of which is due to sulfates. Monetized benefits from the entire Acid Rain Program (both $SO_2$ and NOx) are estimated at $122 billion annually. In stark contrast to the benefits of the emissions reductions is the much lower cost of compliance. When the Acid Rain Program was being considered by Congress in 1989 and 1990, the estimated cost of the program ranged from $4 billion to over $7 billion per year. But four years after its enactment, an audit of the program by the non-partisan U.S. General Accounting Office concluded that the cost of full implementation was likely to be closer to $2 billion per year. More recent estimates have placed the cost of compliance closer to $1 billion per year. Figure 5–7 shows U.S. experience and projections. There was a major decrease in wet sulfate deposition in large areas of the U.S. Northeast with a concomitant decrease in acidified lakes and rivers (Mclean 2007).

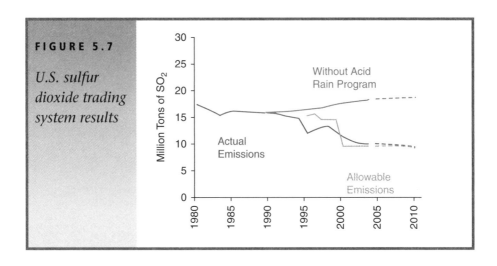

**FIGURE 5.7**

*U.S. sulfur dioxide trading system results*

**APPENDIX TWO**

# The Toxic Release Inventory (TRI) and Its Effects

In 1988 the U.S. government decided to adopt an innovative approach to environmental regulation by instituting a Toxic Release Inventory (TRI) requiring most major industrial plants to reveal the names and quantities of pollutants released to air, water, and soil. The government then made this information freely available to the public in both print and electronic forms. The intent of this novel approach was to mobilize public pressure and "moral suasion" rather than government regulation to help reduce the release of pollution.

Thaler and Sunstein (2009) explicitly cite the TRI in their pathbreaking book *Nudge* that explores the application of behavioral economic principles to many major current policy issues. As defined by the authors, a *nudge* is "any aspect of the choice architecture that alters people's behavior in a predictable way without forbidding any options or significantly changing their economic incentives. To count as a mere nudge, the intervention must be easy and cheap to avoid. Nudges are not mandates." The general phrase used by the authors to describe this innovative approach to policy implementation is *libertarian paternalism*. As Thaler and Sunstein conclude: "the Toxic Release Inventory may be the most unambiguous success story in all of environmental law." Why? Because "without mandating any behavioral change, the law has had massive beneficial effects." [The authors also hypothesize that a similar approach to global warming would work as well through the creation of a Greenhouse Gas Inventory. There are reasons, however, to believe that the success of this approach with the TRI cannot be replicated with greenhouse gases because of the absence of any direct and obvious, localized deleterious effects that would mobilize local community pressure on industrial emitters.]

The positive impact of the TRI on conventional pollutants identified by Thaler and Sunstein has been supported by other authors including Fung and O'Rourke (2000) who state that the "TRI has achieved this regulatory success by creating a mechanism of 'populist maximin regulation'"[3]. Grant (1997) found that "states that have right-to-sue laws or that provide substantial funding for right-to-know programs have significantly lower rates of toxic emissions over time."

Fundamental to the rationale for the establishment of the TRI is the philosophical principle of "license to operate"—a concept which in some respects dates back to the origins of the international trading corporation in the 16th and 17th centuries when European governments granted charters to such companies as the Hudson's Bay Company, the English and Dutch East India companies, the Muscovy Company and the Royal African Company (Carlos and Nicholas 1988). In effect, these companies were granted a license to operate as long as they fulfilled some socially desirable purpose, and their survival was at the discretion of the government. The modern corporation is different in several important respects: it is theoretically immortal and has had many legal benefits conferred upon it that have traditionally been granted to individuals. Nevertheless, a corporation still runs the risk, albeit small, of losing its social license if it alienates a significant number of its key stakeholders, and the range of legally relevant stakeholders has grown in the last few decades (duPlessis 2011; OECD 2010a).

The most dramatic example of this loss of license in recent history is the Union Carbide Corporation, which was eventually swallowed by the Dow Corporation after the world's most devastating nonnuclear industrial accident at Bhopal India on December 2, 1984. As discussed in chapter 11, this marked a sea change in the attitudes and behavior of many corporations toward environmental matters when they suddenly realized that such events could jeopardize not only their profits, but also their continued existence. The increasing pressure on ecosystem services will change the expectations of important constituencies. A broad range of factors can affect a company's, or even an industry's, ability to conduct business in a successful manner. These include failure to meet stakeholder expectations in general but, more specifically, failure to fully disclose the financial implications of a firm's environmental impacts, failure to provide transparency in ecosystem management, and failure to appreciate the risks of regulatory action, investor pressure, and NGO and public boycotts or other media-based campaigns (see, for example, Repetto 2007). Several detailed reports have been published by business and governmental groups detailing the importance of ecosystem management to business (UNEP 2001; WBCSD 2009, 2010, 2011).

## CASE STUDY: SHELDAHL INC. OF NORTHFIELD MINNESOTA

In 1991, the *Wall Street Journal* reported on the case of a small manufacturer of flexible electronic circuits for automobiles and computers. Situated in the college town of Northfield, MN, the company had enjoyed a reputation as a solid corporate citizen. Its manufacturing plant generated no visible signs of pollution. This situation changed radically with the advent of the Toxic Release Inventory. At some point, a local newspaper discovered via the TRI that the apparently innocuous plant was emitting almost 400 tons of methylene chloride (also called dichloromethane), deemed a probable human carcinogen. The ensuing community response convinced the company that its license to operate might be in jeopardy, and it promptly undertook to reduce its emissions of this toxic substance by 90% within two years by changing the mix of chemicals it used in the manufacturing process (*Wall Street Journal*, January 2, 1991). Table 5–5 summarizes the TRI data for the plant for the two years 1987 and 1994, prior to and after the change in technology.

It is obvious from this table that the principal change was a marked decrease in the offending pollutant with an accompanying increase in the output of toluene (another toxic pollutant), albeit at a lower quantity. This raises a paradoxical question: by substituting one toxic compound for another, is it possible to determine whether the company is lowering or raising the total environmental impact of its operations? Answering this question requires a metric that can measure the

| AIR EMISSIONS FROM SHELDAHL PLANT IN NORTHFIELD, MN | | | | | TABLE 5.5 |
|---|---|---|---|---|---|
| CHEMICAL | STACK OR FUGITIVE | 1987 (LBS/YR) | 1994 (LBS/YR) | 1994 AS % OF 1987 | *Sheldahl Ltd. Emissions 1987 and 1994* |
| 1,1,1-Trichloroethane | STK | 48,000 | 0 | 0% | |
| Acetone | STK | 48,000 | 0 | 0% | |
| Ammonia | STK | 29,000 | 7,500 | 26% | |
| **Dichloromethane** | **FUG** | **14,000** | **1,700** | **12%** | |
| **Dichloromethane** | **STK** | **780,000** | **15,300** | **2%** | |
| Freon 113 | FUG | 4,000 | 0 | 0% | |
| Freon 113 | STK | 50,000 | 0 | 0% | |
| Glycol Ethers | FUG | 4,000 | 1,000 | 25% | |
| Glycol Ethers | STK | 54,000 | 8,500 | 16% | |
| Methanol | STK | 44,000 | 5,600 | 13% | |
| Methyl Ethyl Ketone | STK | 84,000 | 20,400 | 24% | |
| Toluene | STK | 9,000 | 24,200 | 269% | |
| **TOTAL** | | **1,168,000** | **84,200** | **7%** | |

*Source:* U.S. TRI

relative toxicity of varying pollutants. Fortunately, there are several risk-based metrics available to make such a comparison. The U.S. EPA, for one, has developed Risk-Screening Environmental Indicators (RSEI) that specifically address this problem (http://www.epa.gov/opptintr/rsei/pubs/basic_information.html). In their description of this tool and accompanying software, the EPA states that

> The Risk-Screening Environmental Indicators (RSEI) model is a computer-based screening tool developed by EPA that analyzes factors that may result in chronic human health risks. These factors include the amount of toxic chemical releases, the degree of toxicity, and the size of the exposed population. RSEI analyzes these factors and calculates a numeric score. To give the score meaning, it must be ranked against other scores also produced by RSEI. The model highlights releases that pose the highest potential risk or potentially pose the highest risk. This way, RSEI helps policy makers and communities quickly identify situations that require further evaluation and set priorities for action. RSEI uses information from the Toxics Release Inventory (TRI), a publicly available database of information on toxic chemical releases and other waste management activities from industrial and federal facilities arrayed by facility, zip code, county, industry, and many other variables. RSEI combines TRI information on the amount of releases with the other risk factors: estimates of toxicity and exposed populations. In addition to ranking numerous

release situations, RSEI can quickly sort results in a number of ways and provide trends by chemical, industry, location, etc. RSEI considers the following information: Amount of chemical released, Location of that release, Toxicity of the chemical, Fate and transport through the environment, Route and extent of human exposure, Number of people affected. This information is used to create numerical values (RSEI scores), which can be added and compared in limitless ways to other RSEI scores to assess the relative hazard and risk of chemicals, facilities, regions, industries, or many other factors. The scores are for comparative purposes and are only meaningful when compared to other scores produced by RSEI. Again, the result does not provide a detailed or quantitative risk assessment, but offers a screening-level perspective for relative comparisons of chemical releases.

In addition to the U.S. EPA RSEI database, there are several other evaluative data sets, including

1. Environmental Defense Fund (EDF) Scorecard Risk Scoring System (Hertwich et al. 2001);
2. Indiana Relative Chemical Hazard Score (IRCH), Indiana Clean Manufacturing Technology and Safe Materials Institute (http://www.ecn.purdue.edu/CMTI/Pollution_progress_measurement_method/values);
3. University of Tennessee (UTN) Chemical Hazard Evaluation for Management Strategies (Davis et al. 1994); and
4. U.S. EPA—Waste Minimization Prioritization Tool (WMPT) (U.S. EPA Office of Solid Waste, 2000).

The Environmental Defense Fund's scorecard.org website has created an integrated evaluation tool that combines the results of these different risk measures to produce rankings for human health and ecological health effects. Table 5–6 summarizes the scorecard.org scores for the two key TRI-reported emissions from Sheldahl: toluene and dichloromethane. It does appear that Sheldahl responded to community sentiment by reducing many of its emissions of toxic compounds. However, while the release of the most contentious pollutant, dichloromethane, decreased by 98% from stack-specific sources and 88% for fugitive sources, the use of toluene increased by over 250%, and its integrated environmental ranking on the IRCH and UTN total hazard value scores is similar to that of dichloromethane. In sum, it is clear that these types of toxicity databases are indispensable in determining not only the direction and magnitude of toxic compound releases from changes in industrial processes, but also in determining the change in the total environmental burden of any specific industrial operation.

This issue of relative pollutant toxicity has been a challenge to the interpretation of the TRI list of major pollutant discharges. [See, for example, MacBride 2012] For example, Table 5–7 lists the top 10 pollutants by total discharge for the first TRI reporting year, 1987; and the most recent year reported, 2009. In 1987, over half of the total output of pollutants was accounted for by one compound, sodium sulfate. 118 firms in the Paper & Allied Products sector accounted for 29% of this output, and 340 firms in the Chemical & Allied Products sector accounted for 61%.

| | DICHLOROMETHANE | TOLUENE | |
|---|:---:|:---:|---|
| **Human Health Rankings** | | | **TABLE 5.6** |
| Toxicity only - Ingestion Toxicity weight (RSEI) | 15 | 3 | *Toxicity* |
| Toxicity only - Inhalation toxicity weight (RSEI) | 3 | 5 | *Scores for* |
| Human Health effects Score (UTN) | **5** | **2** | *Dichloro-* |
| Toxicity and persistence human health risk screening score (WMPT) | **6** | n.a. | *methane* |
| *Toxicity and exposure potential* | | | *and Toluene* |
| Cancer risk score - air releases (EDF) | 0 | n.a | |
| Cancer risk score - water releases (EDF) | 0 | n.a | |
| NonCancer risk score - air releases (EDF) | 7 | 1 | |
| NonCancer risk score - water releases (EDF) | **4** | **1** | |
| Worker Exposure Hazard Score (IRCH) | **24** | **18** | |
| **Ecological Health Rankings** | | | |
| Toxicity only Ecological effects score (UTN) | 2 | 5 | |
| *Toxicity and persistence* | | | |
| Environmental Hazard Value Score (IRCH) | 110 | **130** | |
| ecological risk screening score (WMPT) | **6** | n.a. | |
| **Integrated Environmental Rankings** | | | |
| *Combined human and ecological scores* | | | |
| Total Hazard Value Score (IRCH) | **30** | **29** | |
| Total Hazard Value Score (UTN) | 36 | 36 | |

RSEI = US EPA Risk screening environmental indicators model

UTN = U of Tennessee Center for Clean Products and Clean Technologies Hazard Evaluation System

EDF = Environmental Defence Fund Risk Scoring System

IRCH = Indiana Pollution Prevention and Safe Materials Institute Pollution Prevention Progress Measurement System

WMPT = US EPA Office of Solid Waste - Waste Minimization Prioritization Tool

*Source:* Scorecard.org

It is noteworthy that one plant, owned by IMC Chemicals Inc., was responsible for 40 percent of all releases of sodium sulfate. The company discharged almost 1.85 million tons of this compound into a tailings pond on their property near Trona, in San Bernardino County, California. The magnitude of the discharges of sodium sulfate and their presence on the TRI list was ultimately deemed to be misleading,

## TABLE 5.7

*TRI—Top 10 Releases 1987 and 2009*

TOTAL RELEASES –TRI – 1987

| CHEMICAL | WITH Na$_2$SO$_4$ | | WITHOUT Na$_2$SO$_4$ | |
| --- | --- | --- | --- | --- |
| | TOTAL RELEASES (LBS.) | % OF TOTAL | TOTAL RELEASES (LBS.) | % OF TOTAL |
| Sodium Sulfate (Na$_2$SO$_4$) | 9,038,489,991 | 56.3% | n.a. | n.a. |
| Ammonium sulfate (solution) | 819,811,808 | 5.1% | 819,811,808 | 11.7% |
| Hydrochloric acid | 629,430,160 | 3.9% | 629,430,160 | 9.0% |
| Methanol | 475,580,381 | 3.0% | 475,580,381 | 6.8% |
| Sulfuric acid | 461,180,636 | 2.9% | 461,180,636 | 6.6% |
| Ammonia | 407,877,084 | 2.5% | 407,877,084 | 5.8% |
| Toluene | 374,224,061 | 2.3% | 374,224,061 | 5.3% |
| Phosphoric acid | 349,150,324 | 2.2% | 349,150,324 | 5.0% |
| Acetone | 257,737,211 | 1.6% | 257,737,211 | 3.7% |
| Xylene (mixed isomers) | 212,014,063 | 1.3% | 212,014,063 | 3.0% |
| Methyl ethyl ketone | 200,222,071 | 1.2% | 200,222,071 | 2.9% |
| Other | 2,824,016,241 | 17.6% | 2,824,016,241 | 40.3% |
| TOTAL | 16,049,734,031 | 100.0% | 7,011,244,040 | 100.0% |

Quantities of TRI Chemicals in Waste (in pounds), for facilities in All Industries, for All Chemicals, U.S., 2009

| CHEMICAL | TOTAL PRODUCTION-RELATED WASTE MANAGED | PERCENTAGE OF TOTAL |
| --- | --- | --- |
| METHANOL | 1,957,462,442 | 9.75% |
| HYDROCHLORIC ACID | 1,453,597,049 | 7.24% |
| TOLUENE | 1,228,455,136 | 6.12% |
| ZINC COMPOUNDS | 1,182,354,843 | 5.89% |
| AMMONIA | 1,042,978,876 | 5.19% |
| ETHYLENE | 1,017,455,962 | 5.07% |
| LEAD COMPOUNDS | 866,934,014 | 4.32% |
| N-HEXANE | 827,208,108 | 4.12% |
| SULFURIC ACID | 712,429,616 | 3.55% |
| NITRATE COMPOUNDS | 634,853,233 | 3.16% |
| OTHER | 9,160,975,829 | 45.61% |
| Total | 20,084,705,106 | 100.00% |

*Source:* U.S. EPA - TRI

and the U.S. EPA removed this chemical from the list in the following year as it was considered largely inert and harmless. When making comparisons between the total pollutant load on both lists it is important to note that they are not strictly comparable since, over time, the TRI has expanded its list to include more pollutants, a larger number of industrial operations, and lower emission cutoffs for inclusion.

As stated, the U.S. EPA now recognizes that the interpretation of these data cannot be undertaken without consideration of relative toxicity. As such, the agency has developed a toxicity weighting metric that combines a toxicity rating with the total quantity of pollutant release. There are two scales: one for cancer, the other for non-cancer-related health effects. In 2009, the EPA determined that two chemicals accounted for 925 of the total toxicity-weighted pounds of cancer effects: asbestos (78%) and arsenic and its compounds (14%). For non-cancer health effects, three chemicals accounted for 80 percent of the weighted total releases: manganese and its compounds (39%), arsenic and its compounds (21%), and lead and its compounds (20%). Arsenic appears on both lists because of its unusually toxic chemical properties (U.S. EPA 2009a).

In sum, the interpretation of the TRI data is complicated by at least seven factors: the aforementioned issue of relative toxicity; the persistence of the chemical in the environment; the form in which the chemical is released, which impacts the routes of exposure such as inhalation, ingestion, and absorption; the potential for bioconcentration in the food chain [see chapter 10]; the type of disposal or release (whether to air, water soil, or underground injection); the type of off-site facility receiving the chemical; the efficiency of waste management practices; and the on-site waste management of the toxic chemical (U.S. EPA 2009b).

## Final Observations Concerning the TRI

The TRI not only influences decisions relating to the risk to license to operate, it can also have a bearing on more short-term financial issues facing a corporation. It has been observed that banks and insurance companies are much less willing to insure or lend to companies who may be facing environmental risks associated with the releases of environmental contaminants. In a book entitled *Regulation through Revelation*, James T. Hamilton (2005) used regression analysis to explore the effect on stock prices of the public release of TRI emission data. His results, based on event analysis, were quite dramatic. To quote:

> For companies that reported TRI data to the EPA, the average abnormal returns on the day this information was made public was negative and statistically significant. In terms of the dollar values of the abnormal returns, firms reporting TRI information lost on average $4.1 million in stock value on the first day the data were released. . . . The release of the TRI clearly provided new information to two communities: print journalists writing about pollution and investors concerned about the impact of pollution on financial performance. It remained to be seen how the information might be used by others, including the communities that contained facilities that generated TRI reports.

The findings reported in this book confirm the results of earlier research conducted by several other authors including Khanna et al. (1998) and Konar and Cohen (1997). Despite the apparently beneficial impact of information disclosure through the TRI, it is useful to look for any empirical evidence to support its relative effectiveness in reducing national pollutant releases. Few studies have directly addressed this question. A paper by Stephan, Kraft, and Abel (2005) employed a survey instrument of 1,000 national manufacturing facilities to elicit their views on the role of the TRI in motivating pollutant reduction. Their findings were rather surprising, as they concluded that "the role of the TRI as a motivator for community-level direct action seems to be fairly low. . . . [U]ltimately, the bottom line may come back to the anchor points for U.S. environmental policy: regulation and the threat of liability."

Only one other study was found in the literature that attempts to address this same question with a rigorous analytical methodology. Although based on a similar instrument to the TRI in Canada (called the National Pollution Release Inventory), there is reason to believe that the findings of this study might apply to the United States as well. In this study, Harrison and Antweiler (2001) found that "the vast majority of reductions reported to the inventory to date were found not to be voluntary, as has often been assumed, but are, rather, the result of direct regulation of a relatively small number of polluters." The authors also identified three other unexpected findings: the growth of less visible waste streams through intermedia transfers (e.g., to land disposal and underground injection); the movement of wastes to other communities; and the increasing toxicity of some waste streams despite overall reductions in quantities released.

## CITED REFERENCE AND RECOMMENDED READING

www.epa.gov/oppt/rsei/pubs/rsei_methodology_v2.3.1.pdf [website for US EPA: Risk-Screening Environmental Indicators].

## NOTES

1. See chapter 7 for further discussion of personal discount rates.
2. The price elasticity of demand measures the response in quantity of a product demanded to changes in the price of the product. It is formally defined as

   $\%\Delta Q$ / $\%\Delta P$, where $\Delta$ = change, Q = quantity of product demanded, P = product price.

3. "Maximin" is defined by the *Oxford English Dictionary* as "the largest of a set of minima," or "in Game Theory designating a strategy that maximizes the smallest gain that can be relied on by a participant in a game or other situation of conflict."

# CHAPTER 6

# A Brief Outline of Ecological Economics

ONE OF THE GREAT STRENGTHS *and* weaknesses of environmental economics is its emergence from neoclassical economics—a discipline that grew and thrived in an era largely unaware of and unconcerned about environmental issues. Figure 6–1, familiar to all first-year economics students, captures the essence of the neoclassical economic model of the economy. It is basically a closed system with mutual exchanges between firms and households. Consumers provide their labor to producers, and they, in turn, sell the resulting goods back to consumers. As illustrated in Figure 6–2, environmental economics made a major addition to this model by adding another entity to this simple flowchart: the environment, which sits principally beside the producer's side and represents the repository for the waste generated by the industrial system of production. Table 6–1 lists the principal types of pollutants that have been the common focus of environmental economics. The goal is to internalize externalities in order to reduce economic inefficiency from a social perspective. The overall goal of maximizing economic growth to increase human welfare remains the central thrust. This is fundamentally neoclassical economics with minor modifications.

In contrast, Figure 6–3 captures the essence of the *ecological economics* model that makes three major modifications to the environmental economics model: (1) waste products generated by both consumers and producers have a feedback loop, which means that such products have the capacity to negatively impact the production system from which they are generated; (2) there is a specific inclusion of certain natural resources as inputs such as clean air, clean water, and assimilative capacity; and (3) most important, there is an ecological system that includes at least 17 *ecological services*. The fundamental premise of this major conceptual revision is that the economic system is embedded in the ecological system, cannot function without it, and is ultimately subject to the same laws and constraints that apply to natural systems.

The import of this schematic is captured in the words of Herman Daly, a former chief economist of the World Bank and one of the founders of the new disciple of ecological economics. Daly states:

> It is interesting that so much should be at stake in a simple picture. Once you draw the boundary of the environment around the economy, you have implicitly admitted that the economy cannot expand forever. . . . The notion of an

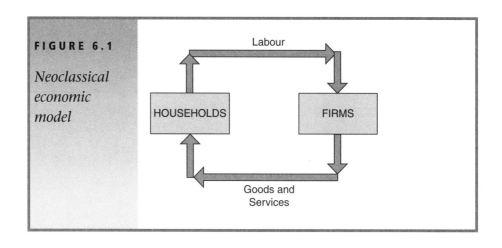

**FIGURE 6.1**

*Neoclassical economic model*

Labour

HOUSEHOLDS

FIRMS

Goods and Services

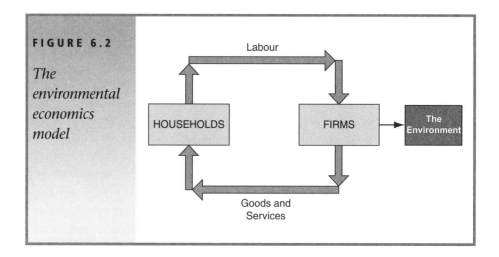

**FIGURE 6.2**

*The environmental economics model*

Labour

HOUSEHOLDS

FIRMS

The Environment

Goods and Services

**TABLE 6.1**

*Some Typical Pollutants Considered in Environmental Economics*

|  | LOCAL | REGIONAL | GLOBAL |
|---|---|---|---|
| AIR | smoke/particulates | photochemical smog | greenhouse gases (recently) |
|  | noxious odours | acid rain | ozone depletion (recently) |
|  |  | pesticide deposition | pesticide deposition |
|  |  | heavy metal deposition | heavy metal deposition |
| WATER | oil spills | airborne deposition of pesticides & heavy metals | oil contamination |
|  | sewage discharge | petroleum pollution |  |

|  | LOCAL | REGIONAL | GLOBAL |
|---|---|---|---|
|  | pesticide runoff | forest runoff |  |
|  | fertilizer runoff | urban runoff |  |
|  | heavy metal discharges | agricultural runoff |  |
|  | suspended solids |  |  |
|  | BOD |  |  |
| SOIL | toxic contamination | erosion | loss of fertility from erosion & overuse of fertilizer |
|  | municipal solid waste | salinization |  |
| RADIATION | localized waste storage contamination from nuclear accidents | contamination from nuclear accidents | contamination from nuclear accidents |

**TABLE 6.1**
*continued*

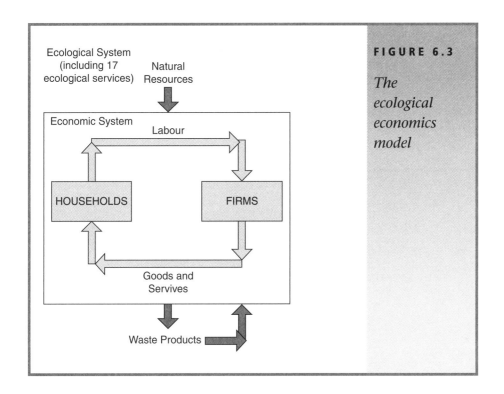

**FIGURE 6.3**

*The ecological economics model*

optimal scale for an activity is the very heart of microeconomics. Yet for the macro level, the aggregate of all microeconomic activities, there is no concept of an optimal scale. The notion that the macroeconomy could become too large relative to the ecosystem is simply absent from macroeconomic theory. The macroeconomy is supposed to grow forever. Since GNP adds costs and benefits together instead of comparing them at the margin, we have no macro-level accounting by which an optimal scale could be identified. Beyond a certain scale, growth begins to destroy more values than it creates—economic growth gives way to an era of anti-economic growth. But GNP keeps rising, giving us no clue as to whether we have passed that critical point! (Daly 1999)

Figure 6–4, based on Daly's work, represents the transfer of the concept of optimal scale from micro to macroeconomics (Daly 2005). Past the point of optimal production and consumption, we enter an area of what Daly terms *uneconomic growth*, where disutility exceeds utility and where humankind may face a potential ecological and economic catastrophe. This critical problem is confounded by the fact that it is not clear at which point this transfer will occur. One of the most persuasive articulations of the dilemma we face was voiced by Ronald Colman (2007) who stated that

Scientists recognize that the only biological organism that has unlimited growth as its dogma is the cancer cell, the apparent model for our conventional economic theory. By contrast, the natural world thrives on balance and equilibrium, and recognizes inherent limits to growth. The cancer analogy is apt, because the path of limitless growth is profoundly self-destructive. No matter how many cars we have in the driveway or how many possessions we accumulate, the environment will not tolerate the growth illusion even if we fail to see through it.

One of the principal challenges posed by ecological economics is that it forces us to examine the specific interlinkages and interdependencies of our economic and ecological systems. What does the ecological system provide that we need? There are at least four components: (1) a natural resource base, including both

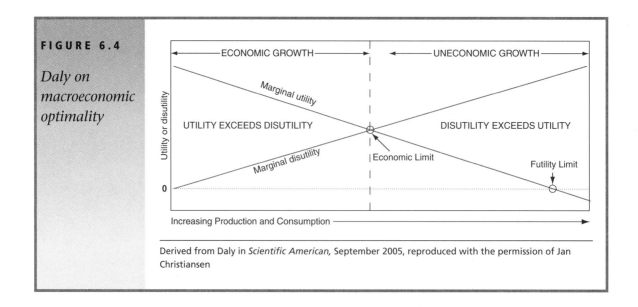

**FIGURE 6.4**

*Daly on macroeconomic optimality*

Derived from Daly in *Scientific American,* September 2005, reproduced with the permission of Jan Christiansen

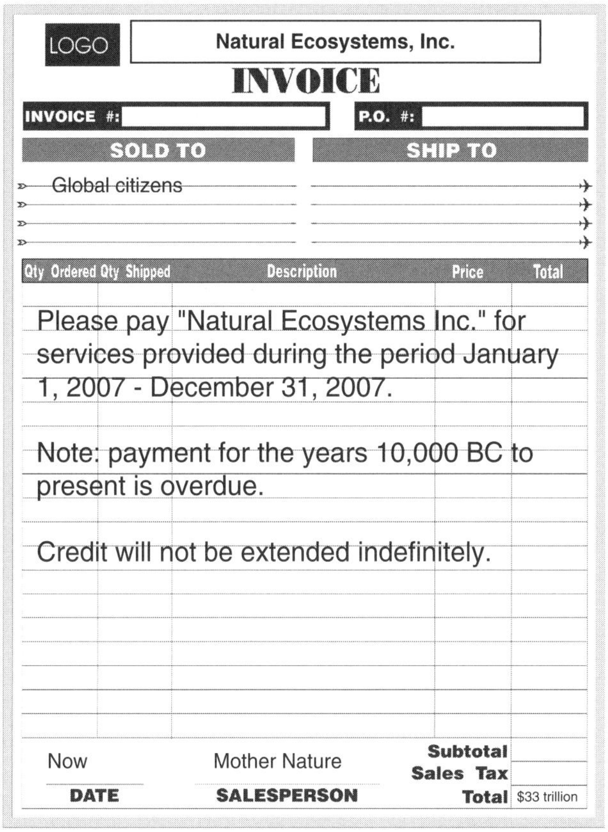

LOGO

Natural Ecosystems, Inc.

**INVOICE**

INVOICE #:

P.O. #:

SOLD TO

Global citizens

SHIP TO

| Qty Ordered | Qty Shipped | Description | Price | Total |
|---|---|---|---|---|

Please pay "Natural Ecosystems Inc." for services provided during the period January 1, 2007 - December 31, 2007.

Note: payment for the years 10,000 BC to present is overdue.

Credit will not be extended indefinitely.

Now

DATE

Mother Nature

SALESPERSON

Subtotal

Sales Tax

Total $33 trillion

**FIGURE 6.5**

*Nature's bill for ecosystem services*

renewable and non-renewable resources. Note that "renewable" may be a misnomer as it is just as easy, if not easier, to deplete a renewable as a non-renewable resource base; (2) a set of natural goods, such as landscape and amenity resources; (3) a waste assimilation capacity that is finite in extent; and, most important, (4) a life support system. Quintin Cronk, formerly of London's world-renowned Kew Gardens, has provided a tongue-in-cheek version of this issue, which is reproduced in Figure 6–5. The total bill amounts to the staggering average figure of $33 trillion, with a range of between $16 and 54 trillion. Where does this figure come from?

In 1997, a multidisciplinary research team composed of scientists and social scientists under the leadership of Robert Costanza published a landmark article in the leading English scientific journal, *Nature*. The article, entitled "The value of the world's ecosystem services and natural capital," was the first major and comprehensive effort to attach a dollar figure to the ecological services that sustain the planet. To place this total estimated value of $33 trillion in context, the global gross

| TABLE 6.2 | ECOSYSTEM SERVICES | BIOMES |
|---|---|---|
| *Ecosystem Services and Biomes* | Nutrient cycling | **MARINE** |
| | Cultural | Open Ocean |
| | Waste treatment | Coastal |
| | Disturbance regulation | Estuaries |
| | | Seagrass / algae beds |
| | Water supply | Coral reefs |
| | Food production | Shelf |
| | | |
| | Gas regulation | **TERRESTRIAL** |
| | Water regulation | Forest |
| | Recreation | Tropical |
| | Raw materials | Temperate / boreal |
| | Climate regulation | Grass / rangelands |
| | | Wetlands |
| | Erosion control | Tidal marsh mangroves |
| | Biological control | Swamps / floodplains |
| | Habitat/refugia | Lakes and Rivers |
| | Pollination | Desert |
| | Genetic resources | Tundra |
| | Soil formation | Ice / rock |
| | | Cropland |
| | | Urban |

*Source:* Costanza et al., 1997, p. 256

| TABLE 6.3 | ECOSYSTEM SERVICE | ESTIMATED VALUE |
|---|---|---|
| *Estimated Value of Ecosystem Services (1997)* | | (billion $) |
| | Nutrient cycling | $17,075 |
| | Cultural | $3,015 |
| | Waste treatment | $2,277 |
| | Disturbance regulation | $1,779 |
| | Water supply | $1,692 |
| | Food production | $1,386 |
| | Gas regulation | $1,341 |

| ECOSYSTEM SERVICE | ESTIMATED VALUE | TABLE 6.3 |
|---|---|---|
| Water regulation | $1,115 | *continued* |
| Recreation | $815 | |
| Raw materials | $721 | |
| Climate regulation | $684 | |
| Erosion control | $576 | |
| Biological control | $417 | |
| Habitat/refugia | $124 | |
| Pollination | $117 | |
| Genetic resources | $79 | |
| Soil formation | $53 | |
| **TOTAL** | **$33,266** | |

*Source:* Costanza et al., 1997 supplementary material

national product in that year was estimated at $18 trillion. The calculation was accomplished by aggregating estimates across 17 ecosystem services for 16 *biomes* [see Table 6–2], and the breakdown of values by ecosystem service is provided in Table 6–3.

The study by Costanza et al. was a meta-type analysis that relied largely on extracting economic estimates from dozens of studies using a broad range of analytical methodologies. A short list of the estimation methods used is provided in Table 6–4, with some of the most commonly used methodologies highlighted in boldface type. Chapter 7 describes in more detail how some of these methodologies are used in practice. The authors recognized that the value of some ecosystem services will be infinite (i.e., no life would be possible on earth without them). As a consequence, Costanza et al. focused on changes in incremental value from the goods and services provided by existing natural capital resources. Figure 6–6, drawn from the U.N.'s Millennium Ecosystems Report (www.maweb.org) provides a graphical summary of the earth's ecosystems and some of the major services they provide. [See appendix 1 for a study on the value of North America's boreal forests, and appendix 2 for the application of this theory to Third World shrimp cultivation.]

As an addendum to this estimate of the value of global ecological services, UNEP commissioned a report published in October 2010 that attempted to estimate the annual environmental *costs* from global human activity. The report arrived at an estimate of $6.6 trillion (www.teebweb.org).

**TABLE 6.4**

*Analytical Methodologies for Estimating Ecosystem Values*

| | |
|---|---|
| donations | price of alternatives |
| energy analysis | productivity effects |
| expenditures | property value |
| external costs | real estate value |
| gross revenues | regional income |
| **hedonic demand** | **replacement cost** |
| marginal cost of reduction | revenues |
| marginal value | shadow price |
| market value | substitution cost |
| net income | surrogate market price |
| net rent | **TCM - travel cost methodology** |
| net revenue | TEV - total enterprice value |
| NPV current expenditures | treatment costs |
| opportunity cost | TVM - time value of money |
| option value | **WTP - Willingness to Pay** |
| preservation payments | **[contingent valuation]** |

*Source:* Derived from Costanza et al., Nature 1997

---

**FIGURE 6.6**

*Ecosystem services*

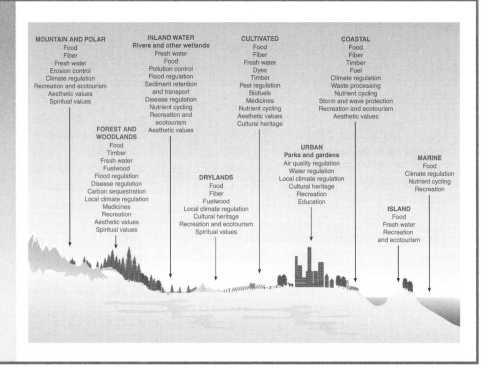

# COMPARING ENVIRONMENTAL AND ECOLOGICAL ECONOMICS

Table 6–5 summarizes the critical differences between environmental and ecological economics. It has been commonly assumed that while the theoretical interpretations of distribution and scale differ markedly between the two fields, the basic neoclassical concept of allocative efficiency[1] remains the same in both areas. In fact, it can be argued that this accepted theory is incorrect and that ecological economics brings a critically important modification (called *resilience*) borrowed from the field of ecology to the concept of allocative efficiency. Resilience refers to the ability of natural systems to rebound from shocks. As illustrated in Figure 6–7, the problem posed by focusing solely on the traditional definition of allocative efficiency is that it may be achieved by decreasing system resilience. There is a trade-off between efficiency and resilience, and ecological economics specifically recognizes this distinction. [See, for example, Goerner et al. 2009.] Consider two simple examples drawn

|  | ENVIRONMENTAL ECONOMICS | ECOLOGICAL ECONOMICS |
| --- | --- | --- |
| **Allocative Efficiency** | principal focus | accepted theory |
| **Distribution** | secondary focus (essentially left to the political process) | prominent focus (both intra- and inter-generational) |
| **Scale (macro level)** | the more, the better | central - i.e. the physical volume of throughput - concept of optimality |

**TABLE 6.5**

*Comparing Environmental and Ecological Economics*

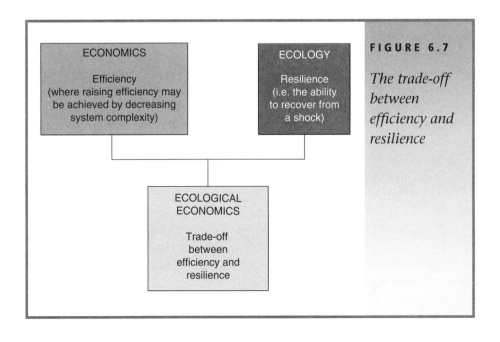

**FIGURE 6.7**

*The trade-off between efficiency and resilience*

from the fields of ecology and economics: advanced agricultural production, and the global trading and financial system.

As will be discussed in greater detail in chapter 10, the modern agricultural system typical of American farming, and often referred to as *industrial agriculture*, has achieved extraordinary levels of productivity, creating vast surpluses of food available for both domestic and international consumption. One of the principal characteristics of industrial agriculture, which contributes to its productivity, is a reliance on monoculture. This highly efficient system of agricultural production relies on a cropping protocol which has little, if any, resilience. It is highly vulnerable to insect attacks and plant diseases. As such, economic efficiency—narrowly defined to exclude systemic considerations—is achieved at the expense of resilience.

One can argue that a similar sacrifice of resilience for the sake of efficiency has been achieved through the use of just-in-time inventory control where such systems are extremely vulnerable to breakdowns at any point in the supply chain. But, perhaps, the most important example of the critical trade-off is the inherent characteristics of the vast and complex international systems of trading and finance, often referred to as globalization. These highly efficient institutions and processes for the movement of large amounts of goods and services as well the concomitant vast daily financial flows that make this possible are also extremely vulnerable to system shocks. Examples in the last two decades (including inter alia the Mexican peso crisis of 1994–95, the 1997 Asian financial flu, and the subprime market meltdown of 2008 and its sequelae) demonstrate how the consequences of events that in previous times could be geographically isolated to the locus of their generation now have the capacity to threaten the functioning of the entire global financial system.

## SUMMARY

The field of ecological economics is still in its infancy, and major conceptual advances are being made annually. There are, however, at least four basic points of consensus in ecological economics. As summarized by Costanza et al. (1997), they are (1) the earth is a thermodynamically closed and nonmaterially growing system. This implies that there are limits to biophysical throughput of resources; (2) the future goal is a sustainable planet with a high quality of life for all its inhabitants (humans and other species). This includes both the present and future generations; (3) a complex system, such as the earth, where fundamental uncertainty is large and irreducible and certain process are irreversible, requires a fundamentally *precautionary* stance [see chapter 9]; and (4) institutions and management should be proactive rather than reactive and should result in simple, adaptive, and implementable policies based on a sophisticated understanding of the underlying systems that fully acknowledges their inherent uncertainties. In light of this new focus on ecosystem services, the central question that arises concerns their significance for business. This fundamental issue is addressed in part 2 of this volume.

The next chapter describes some of the most important analytical tools used in environmental and ecological economics for the measurement of environmental and ecological benefits.

# CITED REFERENCES AND RECOMMENDED READINGS

Aburto-Oropeza, Octavio et al. (2008) "Mangroves in the Gulf of California Increase Fishery Yields." *Proceedings of the National Academy of Sciences*, 105(30), July 29, pp. 10456–10459.

Anielski, Mark and Sara Wilson (2005) *Counting Canada's Natural Capital: Assessing the Real Value of Canada's Boreal Ecosystems*. Calgary AB: Pembina Institute.

Brander, James A. (2006) *Government Policy toward Business*, Fourth Edition Mississauga, ON: John Wiley & Sons.

Colman, Ronald (2007) "Measuring Genuine Progress," in Peter N. Nemetz (ed.) *Sustainable Resource Management: Reality or Illusion*? Cheltenham: Edward Elgar.

Common, Michael and Sigrid Stagl (2005) *Ecological Economics: An Introduction*. Cambridge: Cambridge University Press.

Costanza, Robert et al. (1997) "The Value of the World's Ecosystem Services and Natural Capital." *Nature*, 387, May 15, pp. 253–260, and supplementary material.

Costanza, Robert et al. (1997) *An Introduction to Ecological Economics*. Boca Raton, FL: St. Lucie Press.

Cronk, Quintin (2003) "The Thin Green Line: Plants and the Future of Humanity," Address to The Vancouver Institute, University of British Columbia, Vancouver, BC, November 22.

Daly, Herman (1999) *Ecological Economics and the Ecology of Economics: Essays in Criticism*. Cheltenham: Edward Elgar.

Daly, Herman (2005) "Economics in a Full World." *Scientific American*, September, pp. 100–107.

Daly, Herman and Joshua Farley (2011) *Ecological Economics: Principles of Application*. Second edition. Washington, DC: Island Press.

Eriksson, Ralf and Jan Otto Andersson, (2010) *Elements of Ecological Economics*. London: Routledge.

Goerner, Sally J. et al. (2009) "Quantifying Economics Sustainability: Implications for Free-Enterprise Theory, Policy and Practice." *Ecological Economics*, 69, pp. 76–81.

National Academies of Science (2012) *Ecosystem Service: Charting a Path to Sustainability*, Interdisciplinary Research Team Summaries: conference, Arnold and Mabel Beckman Center. Irvine, California, November 10–11, 2011; The National Academies Keck Futures Initiative.

Sathirathai, Suthawan and Edward B. Barbier (2004) "Comparative Returns of Mangroves for Shrimp Farming and Local Direct and Indirect Uses in Surat Thani Province," in *Shrimp Farming and Mangrove Loss in Thailand*, edited by Edward B. Barbier and Suthawan Sathirathai. [See also Sathirathai, Suthawan and Edward B. Barbier (2001) "Valuing Mangrove Conservation in Southern Thailand." *Contemporary Economic Policy*, 19(2), April, pp. 109–122.]

Thornton, Coralie et al. (2003) "From Wetlands to Wastelands: Impact of Shrimp Farming," Environmental Justice Foundation, London (www.ejfoundation.org).

UK (2011) *National Ecosystem Assessment 2011*.

UN Comtrade database [http://comtrade.un.org/db/].

UN Millennium Ecosystem Assessment (2005) *Ecosystems and Human Well-Being. Opportunities and Challenges for Business and Industry*.

UN Environment Programme (UNEP) et al. (2006) *In the Front Line. Shoreline Protection and Other Ecosystem Services from Mangroves and Coral Reefs.*
www.maweb.org [Millennium Ecosystem Assessment website].
www.teebweb.org [website for The Economics of Ecosystems and Biodiversity].

## APPENDIX ONE

# *Valuing Ecosystem Services of North America's Boreal Forest*

Figure 6–8 illustrates the extent of the disappearance of global boreal forests over the past 8,000 years. Stretching from Alaska eastward through Northern Europe and

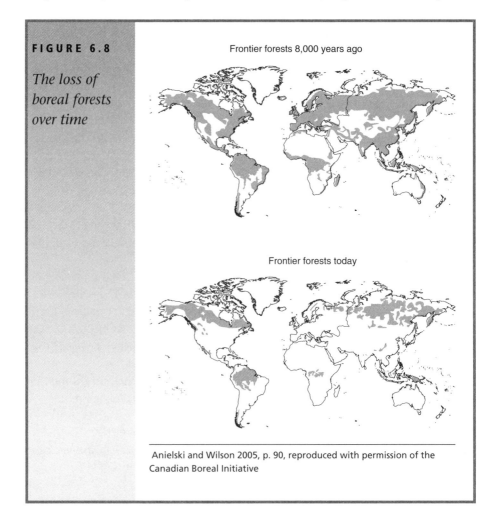

**FIGURE 6.8**

*The loss of boreal forests over time*

Frontier forests 8,000 years ago

Frontier forests today

Anielski and Wilson 2005, p. 90, reproduced with permission of the Canadian Boreal Initiative

| BOREAL ECOSYSTEM WEALTH NATURAL CAPITAL ACCOUNTS | VALUES AND COSTS* |
|---|---|
| **Forests** | |
| *Market Values:* | |
| estimated market value of forestry-related GDP in the boreal region (est. 2002) | $14.9 billion |
| Costs: | |
| estimated cost of carbon emissions from forest industry activity in the boreal | $150 million |
| region (deduction against forestry-related GDP) | |
| *Non-market values:* | |
| value of pest control services by birds | $5.4 billion |
| nature-related activities | $4.5 billion |
| annual net carbon sequestration (excludes peatlands) | 1.85 billion |
| subsistence value for Aboriginal peoples | $575 million |
| non-timber forest products | $79 million |
| watershed service (i.e. municipal water use) | $18 million |
| passive conservation value | $12 million |
| **Wetlands and peatlands** | |
| *Non-market values:* | |
| flood control and water filtering by peatlands only | $77.0 billion |
| flood control, water filtering, and biodiversity value by non-peatland wetlands | $3.4 billion |
| estimated annual replacement cost value of peatlands sequestering carbon | $383 million |
| **Minerals and subsoil assets** | |
| *Market values:* | |
| GDP from mining, and oil and gas industrial activities in the boreal region (est. 2002) | $14.5 billion |
| Costs: | |
| federal government expenditures as estimated subsidies to oil and gas sector in the boreal region | $541 million |
| government expenditures as estimated subsidies to mining sector in the boreal region | $474 million |
| **Water resources** | |
| *Market values:* | |
| GDP for hydroelectric generation from dams and reservoirs in the Boreal Shield ecozone (est. 2002) | $19.5 billion |
| **Waste production (emissions to air, land, and water)** | |
| *Costs:* | |

**TABLE 6.6**

*Summary of Natural Capital Economic Values for Canada's Boreal Region*

(Continued)

**TABLE 6.6**
*continued*

| BOREAL ECOSYSTEM WEALTH NATURAL CAPITAL ACCOUNTS | VALUES AND COSTS* |
|---|---|
| estimated air pollution costs human health | $9.9 billion |
| **TOTAL market values (forestry, mining, oil and gas activity, and hydroelectric generation)** | $48.9 billion |
| **Less cost of pollution and subsidies:** | |
| Air pollution costs | –$9.9 billion |
| Government subsidies to mining sector | –$474 million |
| Federal government subsidies to oil and gas sector | –$541 million |
| Forest sector carbon emission costs | –$150 million |
| **NET market value of boreal natural capital extraction** | $37.8 billion |
| **TOTAL market value of boreal ecosystem services** | $93.2 billion |
| **RATIO of non-market to market values** | 2.5 |

\* Monetary Economic Values and Regrettable Costs (@2002$ per annum)
i.e. These are either environmental or societal costs associated with market-based activities; e.g., forest industry operations.
*Source:* www.grossnationalhappiness.com/gnhindex/introductiongnh.aspx

all the way to Siberia, these forests are considered among the most productive and important on the earth's surface and, yet, the absence of any explicit valuation of their ecosystem services precludes any rational cost-benefit analysis of the degree to which this vast resource base should be transformed for human development. A recent study by the Pembina Institute of Alberta (Anielski and Wilson 2005) entailed the creation of a Boreal Ecosystem Wealth Accounting System (BEWAS) in an attempt to identify, inventory, and measure the full economic value of the ecological goods and services provided just by Canada's portion of this forest. Table 6–6 presents a summary of the findings. One important and innovative technique was to compare the net market value of boreal natural capital extraction (at $37.8 billion) with the total nonmarket value of boreal ecosystem services (at $93.2 billion). The ratio of non-market to market values is approximately 2.5:1, reinforcing the critical conclusion that the omission of these more comprehensive economic estimates from development plans would lead to seriously distorted and economically inefficient decisions.

## APPENDIX TWO

# Case Study of Thai Shrimp Farming

The importance of valuing ecosystem services is graphically illustrated by research on the global loss of mangrove forests and their associated ecosystem services in both hemispheres (Aburto-Oropeza et al. 2008). Thailand's exports of crustaceans have been increasing exponentially since the mid-1970s (UN Comtrade database) to meet market demand in the industrialized countries, particularly the United States. This new and profitable application of aquaculture comes at the expense of vast areas of mangrove swamps that have been cut down to make way for shrimp ponds. The amount of mangrove globally lost to aquaculture, logging, use of wood for fuel and charcoal production, diseases and storms varies from 35–80% by country

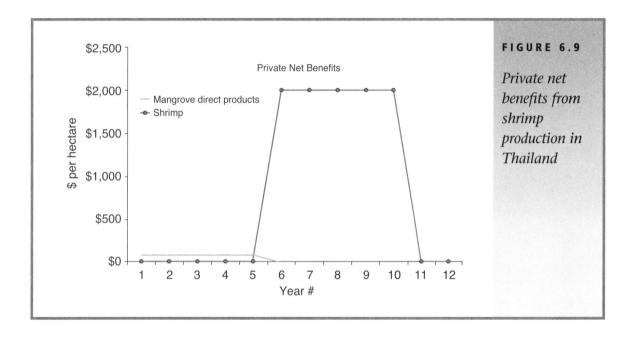

**FIGURE 6.9**

*Private net benefits from shrimp production in Thailand*

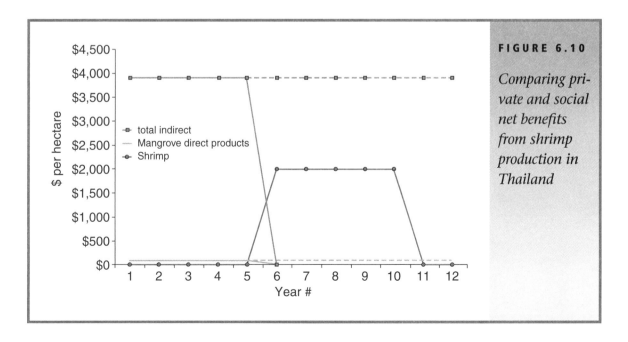

**FIGURE 6.10**

*Comparing private and social net benefits from shrimp production in Thailand*

(UNEP et al. 2006) and, in Thailand alone, the loss has ranged from 50–65% due to shrimp aquaculture (Thornton et al. 2003). There are several major consequences of the replacement of mangroves with fish ponds: One is the exposure of coastal areas to erosion, flooding, increased storm damage, altered natural drainage patterns, increased salt intrusion, and removal of critical habitats for aquatic and terrestrial species. The impacts of mangrove forest loss were clearly illustrated during the devastating 2004 tsunami that completely eradicated countless coastal villages and killed up to 250,000 people in South East Asia.

The business model for shrimp farming makes good economic sense to a private entrepreneur. While the yield from the ponds may last for only 5–10 years, generally followed by abandonment of the land, there is a positive net present value to this investment. Once one area has been ecologically devastated, the business can move to a new unspoiled area and repeat the process. Sathirathai and Barbier (2004) have conducted a detailed analysis of the economics of this type of undertaking and find that private returns are high. Figure 6–9 illustrates the simple economics of the private benefits of this business. In this representation, the net benefits from shrimp production dwarf the value of the direct benefits derived from the mangroves such as a small yield of timber and non-timber products that are terminated once the shrimp fishery begins.

This private sector orientation seriously misrepresents the underlying social costs and benefits of shrimp production as it does not formally account for the value of a standing mangrove forest. Sathirathai and Barbier attempt to value the mangrove ecosystem services including coastline protection and what they term off-shore fishery linkages. This latter term refers to the food and shelter provided to fish as they grow. Also included in their calculation are the external costs of water pollution. Figure 6–10 recasts the economic analysis by comparing the private cost and social cost models. It is clear that once ecosystem services are monetized, what has appeared to be a desirable business venture is not economic, as the indefinite stream of indirect mangrove benefits are lost as well as the much smaller direct benefits. The benefits identified by the authors are lower bound estimates, as they have omitted such important mangrove-related benefits as tourism, carbon fixation, option value, and nonuse values.

## NOTE

1. Allocative efficiency, another term for *Pareto efficiency*, is the cornerstone of neoclassical economic theory. To quote Brander (2006, p. 18), "Pareto efficiency is a broader concept of efficiency than is management efficiency. It requires management efficiency as a necessary condition, but requires additional conditions as well. Ultimately, however, the concept of Pareto efficiency refers fundamentally to the absence of waste. If a situation is Pareto inefficient, it means it is possible to improve the welfare of at least one person without harming anyone else, and it would be wasteful not to do so. Pareto inefficiency means that potential human welfare is being wasted."

# CHAPTER 7

# Cost-Benefit Analysis and Measuring Ecological Benefits

FORESTALLING OR REDUCING THE CONSEQUENCES of pollution is not a cost-free exercise, and, as a result, any proposed policy or regulation should assess the relative benefits as well as costs. Commonly used by governments to choose between competing public projects, cost-benefit analysis (CBA) has been adopted as a useful conceptual framework for assessing policies and projects that have an environmental impact. The mathematical formulation of CBA is straightforward and is represented in equation #1 for any given project:

(1)  $NPV = (B_1 - C_1)/(1+r) + (B_2 - C_2)/(1+r)^2 \dots (B_n - C_n)/(1+r)^n$

    Where:
    $NPV$ = net present value
    $B_i$ = benefits of that project in period i
    $C_i$ = costs of that project in period i
    r = discount rate per period
    n = relevant time horizon

One of the common decision rules of CBA is to choose the project (or projects) with the highest NPV. The central principles of CBA analysis are that (1) all relevant costs and benefits of alternatives must be included and monetized, and (2) all future costs and benefits must be discounted using an appropriate discount rate. There are conceptual challenges to CBA over issues related to intergenerational equity and the choice of an appropriate discount rate. Both of these concerns are addressed later in this chapter.

## QUANTIFYING COSTS AND BENEFITS

While costs of pollution control are relatively easy to estimate as they are usually derived from the market-based prices of inputs such as equipment and labor, the estimation of environmental benefits poses a much more challenging task as the relevant values are rarely, if ever, captured in a market framework; that is, they have no explicit prices since they are not traded. Within a CBA framework, the convention for assessing the economics of pollution control is to define *costs* as those associated

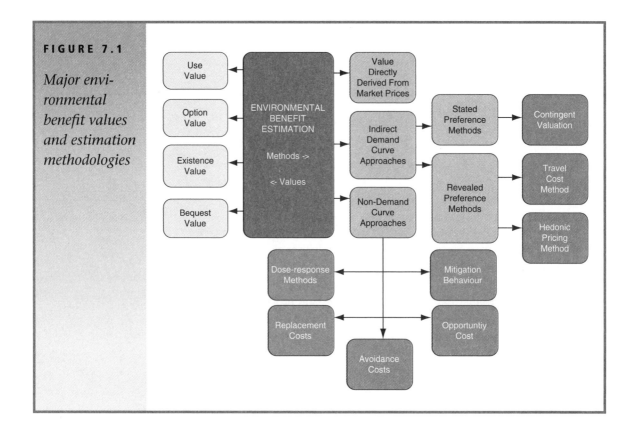

**FIGURE 7.1**

*Major environmental benefit values and estimation methodologies*

with controlling pollution, and *benefits* as the value of the environmental damages avoided through the process of control. The estimation of environmental benefits is one of the most intractable problems in the area of environmental/ecological economics and policy. Figure 7–1 depicts some of the major environmental benefit valuation and estimation methodologies. There are at least four separate types of value: (1) *Use value*—derived from the actual use of the environment; (2) *Option value*—value expressed through the option to use the environment in the future (i.e., the value of not foreclosing future options through development); (3) *Existence value*—value associated with knowing that the environment is being preserved although the person concerned may not actually be using it directly; and a related value: (4) *Bequest value*—a willingness to pay to preserve the environment for the benefit of one's descendants.

There are two general conceptual approaches to estimating benefits: market based and non-market based (also referred to as demand curve and non-demand curve based, respectively). The following is a brief typology of the alternative methodologies [see also Heal 2004; UK NEA 2011]:

**A. Non-Demand Curve-Based Approaches**
1. Dose-response methods; 2. Replacement costs; 3. Mitigation costs; and 4. Opportunity costs

### B. Demand Curve Approach

(1) **Revealed Preference methods**—where demand is revealed by examining individuals' purchases of market-priced goods that are necessary in order to enjoy associated environmental goods. The two most common forms of revealed preference are: (a) **Travel cost method**—for example, using the cost of travel to vacation spots to infer their environmental value; and (b) **Hedonic Pricing method**—for example, using housing prices to determine the value of environmental variables.

(2) **Stated (or Expressed) preference methods**—where demand is measured by examining individuals' stated, or expressed, preferences for environmental goods frequently elicited via surveys and/or questionnaires. The most frequently used stated preference method is: **Contingent valuation**— where the consumer is asked questions that allow the researcher to measure *willingness to pay* (WTP) for the preservation of environmental assets, or *willingness to accept (WTA)* compensation for the loss of these assets.

Each of these techniques is described in turn with accompanying examples.

## NON-DEMAND CURVE APPROACHES

### Dose-Response Methodology

This methodology is frequently used to estimate the extent of damage to human health from exposure to a pollutant. *Dose* refers to the amount of pollutant to which the individual is exposed; *response* measures the extent of consequent human illness (ranging from degrees of morbidity to mortality). This type of analysis frequently requires the complementary use of clinical and epidemiological research and can be complicated by issues of causality and attribution. For example, while it is sometimes—although not always—relatively straightforward to associate workplace exposure to contaminants with subsequent human illness, this process is much more complex within the general public. Several steps are required—each fraught with conceptual difficulties: (1) ambient pollutant levels must be tied to specific emission sources, (2) human illness must be plausibly linked to a specific pollutant, (3) the pathways of exposure must be identified, (4) the pharmacokinetics of the specific interaction of the pollutant and the human body must be elucidated and, finally, (5) the human effects must be monetized. There are standard protocols for assigning dollar values to health effects, and a number of these are reviewed later in this chapter. Some of these protocols, such as those devoted to valuing the loss of life, are somewhat contentious and are discussed in chapter 8.

### Replacement Cost Methodology

This concept is based on the assumption that a damaged environmental good or service can be replaced by some anthropogenic substitute, and that this substitute can be easily valued using current market prices for equipment, land, and labor, etc. While simple in concept, there are certain complications associated with its implementation. Several examples illustrate this point.

| TABLE 7.1 | CROP | TOTAL CROP VALUE (MILLION $) | VALUE OF CROPS DEPENDENT ON HONEY BEE POLLINATION (MILLION $) | % OF TOTAL CROP VALUE |
|---|---|---|---|---|
| *Total Crop Value and Value of Honey Bee Pollinated Crops in the United States* | **DIRECTLY DEPENDENT** | | | |
| | almond | $2,839 | $2,839 | 100% |
| | apple | $2,221 | $1,999 | 90% |
| | soybean | $38,915 | $1,946 | 5% |
| | cherry [sweet] | $721 | $584 | 81% |
| | blueberry [cultivated] | $593 | $534 | 90% |
| | sunflower | $582 | $524 | 90% |
| | orange | $1,935 | $522 | 27% |
| | watermelon | $492 | $310 | 63% |
| | peach | $615 | $295 | 48% |
| | avocado | $322 | $290 | 90% |
| | cranberry | $316 | $285 | 90% |
| | pear | $382 | $240 | 63% |
| | muskmelon [cantaloupe] | $314 | $226 | 72% |
| | canola | $487 | $219 | 45% |
| | grapefruit | $286 | $206 | 72% |
| | cotton [seed] | $1,004 | $161 | 16% |
| | cucumber [fresh] | $194 | $157 | 81% |
| | cucumber [pickled] | $185 | $149 | 81% |
| | raspberry [all (CA)] | $200 | $144 | 72% |
| | tangerine [and mandarins] | $276 | $124 | 45% |
| | prune | $150 | $94 | 63% |
| | nectarine | $129 | $62 | 48% |
| | plum | $78 | $49 | 63% |
| | blueberry [wild] | $51 | $46 | 90% |
| | strawberry | $2,245 | $45 | 2% |
| | raspberry [red] | $56 | $41 | 72% |

**TABLE 7.1**

*continued*

| CROP | TOTAL CROP VALUE (MILLION $) | VALUE OF CROPS DEPENDENT ON HONEY BEE POLLINATION (MILLION $) | % OF TOTAL CROP VALUE |
|---|---|---|---|
| raspberry [red] | $56 | $41 | 72% |
| grape | $3,627 | $36 | 1% |
| muskmelon [honeydew] | $50 | $36 | 72% |
| cherry [tart] | $41 | $33 | 81% |
| apricot | $47 | $27 | 56% |
| Macadamia nuts | $30 | $24 | 81% |
| blackberry | $33 | $24 | 72% |
| kiwifruit | $25 | $20 | 81% |
| squash | $204 | $18 | 9% |
| peanut | $901 | $18 | 2% |
| pumpkin | $117 | $10 | 9% |
| lemon | $381 | $8 | 2% |
| prune and plum | $5 | $3 | 63% |
| tangelo | $7 | $2 | 36% |
| raspberry [black (OR)] | $2 | $2 | 72% |
| boysenberries | $2 | $1 | 72% |
| olive | $113 | $1 | 1% |
| rapeseed | $1 | $1 | 90% |
| **SUB-TOTAL** | **$61,174** | **$12,357** | **20%** |
| **INDIRECTLY DEPENDENT** | | | |
| alfalfa | $7,519 | $2,507 | 33% |
| onion | $1,455 | $1,310 | 90% |
| cotton | $7,318 | $1,171 | 16% |
| broccoli | $649 | $584 | 90% |
| carrot | $597 | $538 | 90% |
| celery | $399 | $319 | 80% |
| cauliflower | $247 | $223 | 90% |
| asparagus | $91 | $82 | 90% |
| sugarbeet | $1,968 | $39 | 2% |
| carrot | $30 | $27 | 90% |
| **SUB-TOTAL** | **$20,274** | **$6,799** | **34%** |
| **GRAND TOTAL** | **$81,448** | **$19,155** | **24%** |

Calderone 2012, reproduced with permission of the author

***The cost of lost pollination***. There have been recent reports of massive die-offs of bee colonies (referred to as *colony collapse disorder*) in the U.S. and elsewhere in the world due to the combined effect of a specific virus and fungus. It now appears that a certain type of pesticide may also be contributing to this serious ecological problem (Henry et al. 2012, Whitehorn et al. 2012). Wood (2012) has argued that the underlying problem is the failure to recognize the nature of systems problems [see Chapter Ten] inherent in modern industrial agriculture. To quote: "Part of what has caused CCD is the immunosuppressive effects of generations of pesticides developed to counter previous threats to bee populations be they microbes or mites. Our chemical intervention in the lifecycle of bees has, in evolutionary terms, 'selected' for a more vulnerable bee. That is, bees' current lack of resilience is a systemic problem in our historical relationship to bees (p. 515)."

The magnitude of the bee colony collapse has forced a re-examination of the critical role that these insects play in crop pollination. The number of crops so pollinated is large and include forage and legume, fruit, vegetables, oilseed crops, and herbs and spices (Klein et al. 2007; Losey and Vaughn 2006; Morse and Calderone 2000; Stipp 2007). The most recent estimate of the value of U.S. crops that rely on honey bee pollination is $19 billion as of 2010 (Calderone 2012, supplementary material, S3, Tables S12–S14). [See Table 7–1.]

In an innovative study in South Africa, Allsopp et al. (2008) attempted to specifically measure the value of pollination of the Western Cape deciduous fruit industry by costing alternative methods to the traditional services provided by insects. These methods include costly equipment- and labor-intensive methods such as aerial spraying or hand pollination. The resulting monetary values represent a significant proportion of the total crop value, reinforcing the conclusion that replacing services provided normally by nature for "free" can be a costly exercise. In contrast, Kasina et al. (2009) have used willingness to pay for pollination services in a study conducted in Western Kenya. They found this analytical methodology preferable to revealed preference in light of the absence of markets for pollination in many developing countries.

In another study considering world agriculture as a whole, Gallai et al. (2009) estimated the total economic value of pollination at 153 billion Euros (approximately $213 billion) and the potential loss of consumer surplus at between 190 and 310 billion Euros (approximately $265–425 billion). The authors add an important qualification, however, that "although our results demonstrate the economic importance of insect pollinators, it cannot be considered a scenario since it does not take into account the strategic response of the market. Producers might have several levels of response strategies in interaction with the intermediate demands of the food supply chain. Moreover, the response of consumers faced to dramatic changes of relative prices would probably be more elaborate than the simple price elasticity can summarize. Short and long term reaction for each crop and in each region would probably be quite different" (p. 820).

***The cost of lost wetlands***. Wetlands are slowly disappearing in the United States as the land is being developed for agricultural purposes, housing, etc. The question is whether it is possible and appropriate to use replacement cost methodology to estimate a value for wetland services. A very important function of wetlands is to filter out excess nutrients and toxics and other biodegradable chemicals from runoff. One possible approach to remedying this problem is to attempt to replace this natural

| SERVICE | COMMENTS AND EXAMPLES | TABLE 7.2 |
|---|---|---|
| **Provisioning** | | *Ecosystem* |
| Food | production of fish, wild game, fruits and grains | *Services* |
| Fresh water | storage and retention of water for domestic, industrial and agricultural use | *Provided by or* *Derived from* |
| Fiber and fuel | production of logs, fuelwood, peat, fodder | *Wetlands* |
| Biochemical | extraction of medicines and materials from biota | |
| Genetic materials | genes for resistance to plant pathogens, ornamental species, and so on | |
| **Regulating** | | |
| Climate regulation | source of and sink for greenhouse gases; influence local and regional temperature, precipitation and other climatic processes | |
| Water regulation (hydrological flows) | groundwater recharge/discharge | |
| Water purification and waste treatment | retention, recovery, and removal of excess nutrients and other pollutants | |
| Erosion regulation | retention of soils and sediments | |
| Natural hazard regulation | flood control, storm protection | |
| Pollination | habitat for pollinators | |
| **Cultural** | | |
| Spiritual and inspirational | source of inspiration; many religions attach spiritual and religious values to aspects of wetland ecosystems | |
| Recreational | opportunities for recreational activities | |
| Aesthetic | many people find beauty or aesthetic value in aspects of wetland ecosystems | |
| Educational | opportunities for formal and informal education and training | |
| **Supporting** | | |
| Soil formation | sediment retention and accumulation of organic matter | |
| Nutrient cycling | storage, recycling, processing, and acquisition of nutrients | |

*Source:* UN 2005, p. 2

ecosystem service with a human-constructed runoff gathering system and filtration plant. In fact, an anthropogenic version of this type of ecosystem is used on a very small scale in some modern green buildings. If a large-scale version of this technological approach were possible, then the replacement cost methodology could be employed to assign a value to lost wetland services. Table 7–2, drawn from a recent report of the UN's Millennium Ecosystem Assessment of 2005 entitled *Ecosystems and Human Well-being: Wetlands and Water* demonstrates that filtering is only one—albeit important—service provided by wetlands. Figure 7–2 (Turner et al. 2000) graphically displays the complex array of interdependent ecosystem services and economic values provided by fully functioning wetlands. The ineluctable conclusion from this table and figure is twofold: (1) the replacement cost methodology outlined above, which focuses solely on filtration benefits, would seriously underestimate the value of the lost wetland; and (2) perhaps, more importantly, replacing all of these vital ecosystem services with anthropogenic counterparts would probably be impossible.

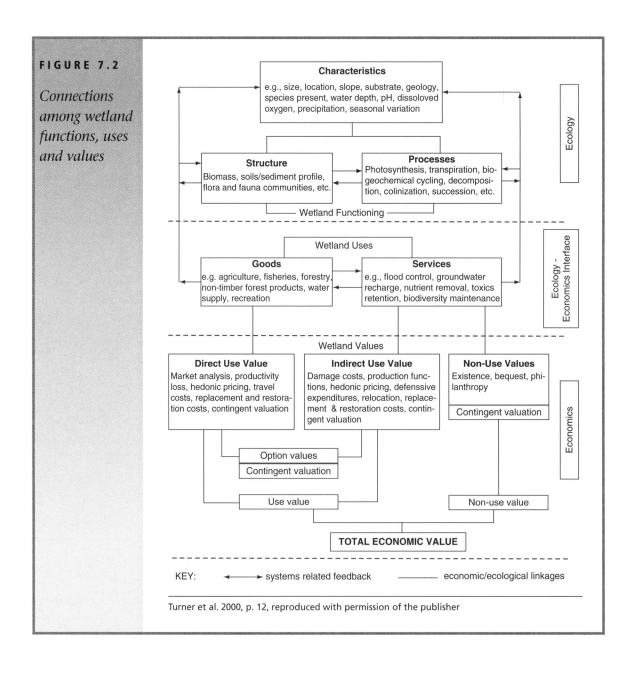

**FIGURE 7.2**

*Connections among wetland functions, uses and values*

Turner et al. 2000, p. 12, reproduced with permission of the publisher

## Mitigation Costing

Similar in concept to replacement cost methods, mitigation costing assigns value to ecosystem services by costing efforts to reduce or offset the negative effects of lost or compromised ecosystem services.

## Opportunity Cost

The opportunity cost methodology focuses on the value of goods and services lost by undertaking a specific course of action. Similar challenges emerge to those identified for replacement costing in measuring the value of all the foregone ecosystem services associated with degrading or destroying a wetlands area.

## DEMAND CURVE-BASED APPROACHES

### The Travel Cost Methodology (TCM)

The travel cost methodology is frequently used to assign a value to ecosystem amenities such as national parks, or changes in recreational quality at these sites. Classified as a revealed preference method, the underlying assumption is relatively simple: the incurred costs of visiting a park (for example, the cost of gasoline used in travel to the site as well as an imputed value to travel time and any other incidental costs such as road tolls) in some way reflect the recreational value of a site. The data on number of visitors and their travel costs can be used with regression analysis to construct a surrogate demand curve for the recreational site from which a measure of total recreational value can be derived. The underlying principle is based on the concept of consumer surplus (CS) illustrated in Figure 7–3, where CS measures the benefit to a consumer, net of the sacrifice he/she has to make, from being able to buy a commodity at a particular price. It is widely used in cost-benefit analysis as an approximate measure of changes in consumer welfare.[1] Graphically, it is the total

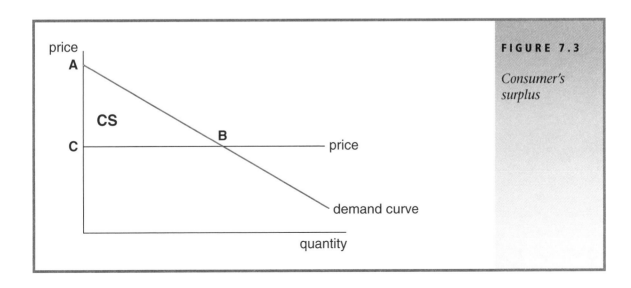

**FIGURE 7.3**

*Consumer's surplus*

(triangular) area ABC between the demand curve and price paid; that is, it is the difference between the total perceived value (i.e., willingness to pay) and the actual price paid.

There are several variants of this methodology. The first, and simplest, called the zonal travel model, estimates the value of the recreational site as a whole derived from average site visit data from predefined geographic zones around the site. The second variant (the individual travel cost approach) uses more disaggregated data based on information gleaned from individual surveys administered at the recreational site itself. The third approach, termed the Random Utility Model (RUM), uses a more detailed and comprehensive statistical approach that permits the valuation of specific characteristics of the recreational site. An excellent example of the RUM model is described in Riera et al. (2011) in a study of Minorca beaches.

There are several conceptual complications associated with the TCM methodology: (a) time costs must be included, as ignoring the implicit cost of time spent traveling to a recreational site may underestimate the value of that site. However, some people enjoy traveling, so for them the journey itself may reflect a benefit rather than a cost; (b) where tourists undertake multiple visit journeys, it is not always simple to apportion travel costs among several recreational sites visited on the same trip. The only methodology that addresses this issue is the RUM model; (c) it can be difficult to differentiate between sites that are visited by people who choose one site in particular and sites that are visited by people who have little choice in sites (and consequently, may value the site less); (d) TCM studies often omit visitors who have not incurred travel costs to reach the site because they live nearby; and (e) a particular challenge is associated with assigning a value when an individual or family values a site so highly that they purchase a home nearby, thereby incurring low travel costs. This last qualification is particularly problematic as it implies an element of endogeneity to the problem of calculating an appropriate value. Bockstael and McConnell (2010), in their extensive theoretical discussion on revealed preference methodologies, identify several other conceptual challenges in applying TCM, especially the definition and construction of a theoretically defensible cost function.

## Hedonic Pricing Methodology

A second major example of a revealed preference analytical technique, hedonic pricing attempts to measure the positive or negative contribution of environmental services to the market price of an asset, usually housing. The methodology is based on the assumption that the environmental effect will be a measurable residual after *all other* factors contributing to housing prices are identified. This analysis is usually conducted in a regression analytic framework, and a typical formulation of the methodology may appear as follows:

> **House price** = f (# bedrooms, # baths, condition of structure, size of structure, zoning, land use, local development policies, type of neighborhood, lot size, access, *environment*), where access is the distance to shops, workplace, etc., and environment is the residual value to be evaluated. A common approach is to look at two neighborhoods that are similar in many respects, allowing the analyst to control for extraneous variables.

## Example #1: Valuing Proximity to a Greenway

Hamilton and Quayle (2002) study how proximity to a greenway affects property values. The regression variables used by the authors are house age (in years), floor area (sq. ft.), prior sale price, lot size (sq. ft.), number of full baths, the total assessed value, and the assessed value of the land only. They also include the variable of particular interest (physical proximity to a greenway) represented as a dichotomous variable (adjacent or near). The authors found a 10–15% increase in economic value for proximity to a greenway after controlling for other factors such as age, location, and other adjacent amenities.

## Example #2: Valuing the Economic Impact of Airport Noise

Helmuth et al. (1997) studied the impact of airport runway noise associated with the SeaTac airport serving the Seattle-Tacoma region of Washington State. Table 7–3 summarizes the results of their analysis. The average drop in house value attributable to local airport noise was in the range of 10%.

Some other useful examples of the application of this technique are provided for evaluating road noise in Norway (Navrud and Strand 2011), and the quality of coral reefs in Hawaii (Brouwer et al. 2007).

## Complexities with the Application of this Methodology

There are several complications with the hedonic pricing model: (a) the statistical challenge is to identify all relevant factors influencing housing and separate the effect of these influences on house prices, and (b) the method assumes that purchasers in the property market have the opportunity to select the combination of house features that they most prefer—an assumption that may be violated by personal income constraints.

| COMMUNITY | ACTUAL AVERAGE ASSESSED VALUE OF HOUSING UNIT | ESTIMATED ASSESSED VALUE WITHOUT AIRPORT | DIFFERENCE ($ LOSS FROM PROXIMITY TO AIRPORT NOISE) | TABLE 7.3 *Hedonic Analysis of Sea-Tac Airport noise* |
|---|---|---|---|---|
| Burien | $129,900 | $143,000 | –$13,100 | |
| Des Moines | $136,100 | $149,800 | –$13,700 | |
| Federal Way | $142,900 | $157,300 | –$14,400 | |
| Normandy Park | $173,600 | $191,100 | –$17,500 | |
| Tukwila | $122,400 | $134,800 | –$12,400 | |

*Source:* Helmuth et al., 1997

## The Contingent Valuation (CV) Methodology

In contrast to the *revealed* preference techniques described above, contingent valuation is a *stated* preference methodology. This method bypasses the need to refer to market prices and is perhaps the most frequently used method for evaluating environmental benefits. It asks individuals explicitly to place values upon environmental assets. The most commonly applied approach is to interview households either at the site of an environmental asset or at their homes and ask them what they are *willing to pay* (WTP) for the preservation of that asset, or what they are *willing to accept* (WTA) in the form of compensation for the loss of the asset. One advantage of this approach is that it can be used to evaluate resources, the continued existence of which people value but never personally visit.

## Example: Measuring the Benefits of Reducing Air Pollution

Air pollution has been identified by numerous research studies conducted by governments and non-governmental organizations (NGOs) over the past few decades as significantly contributing to human illness and death. It is neither feasible nor economically desirable to reduce air pollution to zero levels. As a consequence, it is necessary to utilize a cost-benefit analysis to determine the optimal degree of reduction in ambient levels of air pollutants. This requires an assessment not only of the costs of abatement, but also the monetized benefits associated with reduced damage to human health and other susceptible targets such as plants, animals, water courses, and buildings. In an early landmark study of the California South Coast Air Basin (Hall et al. 1992), the authors assessed a broad range of health effects attributable to ozone and particulate matter among the 12 million residents of the greater Los Angeles area. They found that the residents experienced ozone-related health symptoms on an average of 17 days per year and that particulate exposure led to an increased risk of death of 1/10,000 per year. They concluded that 1,600 lives a year could be saved by additional air pollution control, exclusive of the nonmortal health effects.

The central research question was whether the benefits from increasing air quality levels up to the National Ambient Air Quality Standards (NAAQS) outweighed the costs of pollution control. Negative economic impacts of air pollution were associated with medical costs and work loss, physical discomfort, inconvenience, fear, and impact on others. Three economic measures were used to value pollution-related health effects: the cost of illness (COI), the WTP to avoid the health effects, and the WTA compensation in order to tolerate the continuation of health symptoms. Table 7–4 summarizes their findings for the diverse range of health effects including cough, headache, eye irritation, sore throat, chest congestion, minor restricted activity days (MRAD), multiple minor symptom days (MMSD), and restricted activity days (RAD) including days missed from work, spent in bed, or otherwise measurably constrained.

The total monetary value of the benefits of reducing ozone and particulates was estimated at $10 billion. This figure in and by itself cannot provide a guide to action without a comparison to the costs of achieving this level of control. The authors could find no comparable cost estimate for control but examined several

ADJUSTED DAILY VALUES FOR SYMPTOMS IN 1990 DOLLARS

| EFFECT | VALUE | | |
| --- | --- | --- | --- |
| | LOW | MID | HIGH |
| Cough | $0.50 | $1.50 | $4.50 |
| Headache | $1.00 | $2.75 | $7.25 |
| Eye Irritation | $0.75 | $1.75 | $4.00 |
| Sore Throat | $1.00 | $2.00 | $4.25 |
| Chest Congestion | $1.50 | $3.25 | $6.75 |
| MRAD | $14.50 | $23.00 | $37.25 |
| MMSD | $7.50 | $16.75 | $37.25 |
| RAD | n.a. | $53.00 | n.a. |

MRAD = Minor restricted activity days
MMSD = multiple minor symptom days
RAD = restricted activity days
*Source:* Hall et al. 1992, p. 815, reproduced with permission of Science Magazine, AAAS

**TABLE 7.4**

*Adjusted Daily Values for Air Pollution Symptoms in Los Angeles (1990 dollars)*

related studies that suggested costs up to $13 billion. On the face of it, this would seem to imply that undertaking this level of air pollution reduction would be uneconomic from a social perspective. However, to quote the authors of the original study: "Attainment of the $O_3$ and $PM_{10}$ NAAQS (National Ambient Air Quality Standards) requires control of both NOx and volatile organic compounds (VOCs), but these controls will lead simultaneously to attainment of the $NO_2$ NAAQS, improved visibility, reduced greenhouse gases, and reduced ecosystem effects. Ascribing all control costs to $O_3$ and $PM_{10}$ overstates the costs of meeting these NAAQS standards." In addition, the authors observed that "In this study, no value is ascribed to improvements in visibility, protection of materials or vegetation, or prevention of chronic lung disease. Available information shows that important benefits (including preservation of lung function) are not yet quantifiable in dollars and that current benefit estimates are therefore likely to be underestimates."

Both of these qualifications are illustrative of the fundamental point that cost-benefit analyses—which are critical to the determination of appropriate and economically justifiable public policy—must recognize and incorporate all relevant factors, for failure to do so will lead to socially inefficient policies. The import of this study is that when viewed from a systems perspective, the benefits of air pollution reduction incorporate beneficial outcomes apart from human health. Thus, the benefits clearly outweigh the costs. A series of more recent and inclusive studies have convincingly demonstrated the net benefits of air pollution reduction at the national level. [See Appendix 1 for a summary of the most important of these recent studies produced by the U.S. EPA estimating the net benefits of the Clean Air Act over the period 1990–2020.]

## Complexities Associated with the Contingent Valuation Method (CVM)

As with the other methodologies reviewed above, there are significant conceptual difficulties associated with the use of CVM despite its common usage. These include the following:

(a) *Understating WTP*—the hypothetical nature of CVM scenarios make individuals' responses to them poor approximations of true value. In some cases, people will *free ride*; that is, intentionally understate how much they were willing to pay if they thought they might have to actually pay. Conversely, one could argue that if the individual viewed the question as purely hypothetical, he/she might overstate WTP in order to protect the resource.

(b) *Willingness to pay versus willingness to accept*—researchers have noticed a significant difference in responses when questions are framed in two different ways: "What are you willing to pay (WTP) to receive this environmental asset?" versus "What are you willing to accept (WTA) in compensation for giving up this environmental asset?" WTA has been found to be generally greater than WTP. There has been extensive debate in the economic literature over this discrepancy. Some have argued that this discrepancy is an artifact dependent on experimental design, while others have suggested that there is a legitimate and theoretically defensible explanation for this difference (Georgantzis and Navarro-Martinez 2010; Horowitz and McConnell 2002; Plott and Zeiler 2005; Sayman and Onculer 2005). Several reasons have been advanced for the continued discrepancy between these two measures: (i) there are psychological reasons to indicate that individuals feel the cost of a loss (WTA) more intensely than the benefit of a gain (WTP). This is consistent with the commonly held loss aversion, reference dependence, and the endowment effect associated with Kahneman and Tversky's *Prospect Theory* (Kahneman and Tversky 1979; Kahneman et al. 1990; Rose and Masiero 2010); (ii) because of *moral perceptions* relating to public goods, survey respondents will tend to have a higher WTA/WTP ratio than if the goods are ordinary private goods or money (Biel et al. 2011; Horowitz and McConnell 2002); and, related to the above, (iii) there may be an income (or wealth) constraint that sets an upper bound to how much individuals are willing to pay (Alberini and Kahn 2006; Hanemann 1991). In this vein, the Harvard philosopher Michael Sandel (2012, p. 31) has argued that "willingness to pay for a good does not show who values it most highly. This is because market prices reflect the ability as well as the willingness to pay."

There may be another science-based explanation for the discrepancy between measures of WTA and WTP. Remarkable research results have been generated in recent years from innovative cross-disciplinary studies in the areas of economics, psychology, and neurology under the general rubric of neuroeconomics (Glimcher et al. 2009). Scientists and social scientists have used diagnostic imaging of the brain (e.g., by functional magnetic resonance imaging—fMRI) to observe which portions of the brain are most active during a variety of decisions and emotional states (Fehr et al. 2005; Levine 2011; Singer and Fehr 2005). Using fMRI, for example, De Martino et al. (2009) have found evidence to support Kahneman's theory of reference dependency (i.e., the endowment effect). The scientific support for a legitimate inherent difference between WTA and WTP is further enhanced by neurological imaging studies that suggests that emotional responses to losses occur in a separate part of the brain (such as the amygdala) from reward appreciation (see, for example, Berridge and Kringelbach 2008; De Martino et al. 2010; Lehrer 2010; Shiv et al. 2012). Under these circumstances, there may be no reason to assume that WTA would equal WTP.

Whether WTP or WTA is the appropriate measure depends largely on whether there is an increase or a decrease in an environmental good. The U.S. EPA (2010) has concluded that WTP is the appropriate measure if an individual does not have the good in the baseline case or when an increase in the amount of the good is at issue. In contrast, WTA is the appropriate measure where the individual has the good in the baseline case or when a decrease in the amount of the good is at issue.

(c) *Part-whole bias*: individuals may produce inconsistent answers when asked how much they are willing to pay for either an entire ecosystem or its components. The values may bear no logical relationship to each other, or may even exceed an individual's income or wealth. Consider the example of wildlife in a pond or lagoon in an urban setting as schematically illustrated by the nested Boolean diagram in Figure 7–4. A person answering a CVM survey designed to elicit his or her valuation of bird life may be presented with any of the following survey questions: (1) How much are you willing to pay for one type of duck (e.g., Wood Duck / Mallard / Northern Pintail / Northern Shoveller / American Wigeon / Greater Scaup / Harlequin Duck / Surf Scoter / White-winged Scoter / Common Goldeneye / Barrow's Goldeneye / Bufflehead/Common Merganser)? (2) How much are you willing to pay for one type of bird (e.g., swans / geese / herons / loons / grebes / ducks)? or (3) How much are you willing to pay for all the bird life?, etc. [For other examples, see Bateman et al. 1997; Boyle et al. 1994.]

(d) *Vehicle bias*: respondents may alter their WTP statements according to the specific payment vehicle chosen (e.g., charitable donations versus a tax). While individuals generally dislike paying taxes, many may feel that a tax would be more effective than relying on charitable funds to protect the environment.

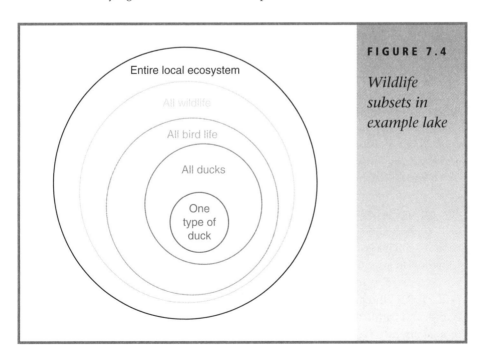

**FIGURE 7.4**

*Wildlife subsets in example lake*

(e) *Starting point bias*: A phenomenon labeled by Kahneman and Tversky as *anchoring* may bias responses. Experiments have demonstrated that a survey's choice of monetary starting point will have a major impact on a respondent's stated willingness to pay for an environmental amenity. For example, there is evidence to suggest that a survey respondent will choose a different value when faced with a range from $10–$100 as opposed to $100–$1,000. Ariely (2008) suggests that the role of anchoring is even more insidious. He has demonstrated that even asking survey participants to think of the last two digits of their social security number before making a choice about a totally unrelated matter will influence their decision.

(f) *Extrinsic vs. Intrinsic motivation*: One of the most interesting studies of the potential theoretical complexities in interpreting the results of CV studies emerges from research by Frey and Oberholzer-Gee (1997) on Swiss residents' response to offers of monetary compensation for accepting the siting of a nuclear waste repository in their community. The authors found that "while 50.8% of the respondents agreed to accept the nuclear waste repository without compensation, *the level of acceptance dropped to 24.6 percent* when compensation was offered [authors' original italics]" (p. 749) The authors conclude that intrinsic motivation is partially destroyed when price incentives [i.e., extrinsic motivation] are introduced. These findings may call into question the relationship between monetary values derived from CV analysis and underlying public evaluation of certain projects where issues of social responsibility are in play.

## Other Methodologies

Several other methodologies have been used to estimate environmental benefits, including conjoint analysis, production functions, and benefits transfer. Brief summaries of these techniques are presented below.

### Conjoint Analysis

A variant of contingent valuation, conjoint analysis (CA) has emerged from the marketing and consumer research literature but is easily transferable to the measurement of environmental benefits (Heal et al. 2004). In contrast to contingent valuation where respondents are asked to assign a monetary value in either a WTP or WTA framework, conjoint analysis infers values by assessing the responses of individuals to a series of detailed choices. CA decomposes the object of choice into a set of attributes, thereby surpassing CVA in the richness of the choice set (Smith 2006). Stewart and Kahn (2006) suggest that CA can avoid some of the inherent bias that may afflict CVA such as part-whole bias [see Figure 7–4] or the hypothetical nature of the questions that can lead to intentional under or overestimation of values. Conjoint analysis has several format variants: ranking, rating, graded-pair comparisons, and dichotomous choices. The most commonly preferred format by economists is the last variant, which asks the respondent to indicate his/her preference among two or more scenarios. In a sense, this approach has some of the attributes of revealed preference.

By way of example, case studies of conjoint analysis are presented by Swallow et al. (1992) who analyze preferences about the location of a landfill site in Rhode Island, and Dohle et al. (2010) who focus on public preferences among attributes of mobile phone base stations in Switzerland.

## Benefits Transfer

Benefits transfer offers an alternative where the application of site-specific revealed or stated preference methodologies cannot be undertaken because of time or resource constraints. The normal procedure involves using monetary estimates from other similar cases and transferring them to the circumstances under study with or without modifications for any site-specific differences between the imported and target cases. Common examples entail the use of recreational values already derived in a different locale. (For other examples, see Morey et al. 2002; Smith et al. 2006). There can be significant problems in guaranteeing the similarity of the source and target circumstances (Barton 2002; Brouwer 2000; Plummer 2009; Spash and Vatn 2006) in which case it may be more appropriate to employ a meta-analysis (e.g., Bergstrom and Taylor 2006; Thomassin and Johnston 2011) that relies on an average of multistudy values or a range bounded by one standard deviation above and below the average value.

## Production Functions

The production function methodology assumes that an environmental good or service serves as a factor input into a good whose market value is measurable (Heal et al. 2004, p. 113). A two-stage approach is required: first, a linkage must be identified and specified between the underlying ecological resource or service and the marketed product or service. Second, by holding other variables constant, the value of the ecological resource or services can be imputed from changes in the price of the marketed good or service and its effect on producer and consumer surplus. Heal et al. use an example of the impact of changes in wetland area on the abundance of crabs. The principal challenge in the application of this methodology is (1) assuring that all the relevant ecological-economic interactions have been identified correctly, (2) taking appropriate notice of the influence of market conditions and regulatory initiatives that will have an influence on the derived values, and (3) determining whether a static or dynamic model is more appropriate for capturing the relationship been the ecological good/services and the marketed product (Heal et al. 2004, p. 114).

## General Conclusions Concerning Economic Valuation Methodologies

There is a broader conceptual challenge with respect to valuation methodologies for environmental resources that rely on either direct or indirect assessment of individual monetary evaluations based on preferences. As Pascual et al. (2010) note, most methodologies in common use are grounded in an anthropocentric view of the world. This has been the subject of some debate, as some authors have suggested a viewpoint referred to as *deep ecology*, which encompasses the inferred values of other living creatures who cohabit the world with the human species (de Steiguer 2006; Devall 1991; *The Ecologist* 1988). Even if one adopts an anthropocentric view, however, the question arises as to what extent the values derived from preference methodologies such as travel costing, hedonic pricing, and contingent valuation can capture the true economic value of the resource. In order to create legitimate estimates of true value, these methodologies must implicitly assume that the human subjects have access to all the relevant information, are science literate, and are rational information processors. Each one of these prerequisites is contentious.

There are at least three types of errors that can arise from the failure to satisfy any one of these prerequisites: (i) incomplete scientific knowledge of system effects, linkages, and *thresholds*; and, specifically, (ii) cumulative effects; and (iii) non-linearities. Brief examples of each type of potential error follow.

**Incomplete scientific knowledge.** In many cases, such information is unavailable to the general public or unknown until after a resource has been damaged or destroyed. Consider the value of *apex or keystone species*. [For more details on this and other scientific concepts and cases mentioned in this section, see chapter 10.] For example, most people have a psychological distaste for sharks and little knowledge about *trophic cascades* associated with the loss of these apex predators. Any economic valuation derived by CV, for example, would grossly underestimate the economic value of this creature, even to humans. Similar cases include such disparate entities as forests [see Figure 1–2], wolves [see Figure 10–6], and salmon. By way example, Cederholm et al. (2000, p. 15) list almost three dozen ocean, estuary and freshwater mammal, fish, insect, bird, and vegetative species who are food web beneficiaries of Pacific Salmon nutrients in the form of juvenile salmon, smolt, fry, eggs, and adult salmon death before and after spawning.

**Cumulative effects.** A good example of potentially misleading economic assessments could stem from valuations placed on the loss of local wetlands. Any one wetland could have a marginal value less than the benefit of development and therefore not worth preserving. Yet, the loss of many such wetlands could have a profound and devastating effect on species such as migratory birdlife, which rely on a network wetlands on their flyways for survival. [See, for example, UNOPS n.d.] Other important examples of cumulative effects include biomagnification and bioaccumulation [see chapter 10].

**Non-linearities.** Not infrequently, land development in wilderness areas impinges on or destroys wildlife habitat. In the absence of detailed ecological information, a survey respondent might assume that reduction in wildlife numbers (such as deer) might be proportional to loss of habitat, and elicited values would reflect this assumption. However, the loss of even a small part of wildlife range can have an effect far out of proportion to its size because of the existence of a threshold effect. This *non-linear effect* can even lead to the total loss of a herd, and a resulting economic effect much greater than the value elicited by contingent valuation (Dykstra 2004; Sinclair 2007).

It should be apparent from the previous discussion that each methodology for evaluating environmental benefits has limitations. A satisfactory resolution to this problem requires a hybrid approach that includes (a) *sensitivity analysis*; and (b) *triangulation*, where several methods are used jointly to arrive at reasonable estimates of benefits.

This chapter concludes with two case studies [see appendices 1 and 2], which demonstrate the value of a comprehensive analysis of environmental costs and benefits. The first is a U.S. EPA assessment of the impact of the *Air Pollution Control Act* over the period 1990–2020; the second is a study conducted for the city of New York that attempted to value the ecosystem services associated with the city's water supply in order to assess the costs of two radically different alternatives.

Finally, it is worth noting that the use of cost-benefit analysis for the assessment of environmental effects is considered most appropriate in circumstances where there are marginal or incremental differences among options and a relatively short time horizon, such as a single generation. The utilization of CBA becomes more problematic when there are potentially major changes from the status quo and when such changes have an impact spanning several generations. This latter issue is particularly germane in the choice of discount rates and discussions of their relevance.

## Discount Rates

The determination of an appropriate discount rate is critical to the choice of an alternative project or course of action in CBA, and this poses some difficult conceptual issues. Figure 7–5 shows just how critical the discount rate can be by comparing the present value (PV) of $1 after $x$ years at various rates. The higher the discount rate, the lower the PV of a dollar received in any future year. With a high enough discount rate (such as 18%), a dollar received after 25 years or more is worth virtually nothing. This has clear implications for decision making among alternative projects that have markedly different temporal profiles of costs and benefits.

There are at least three types of discount rates: personal, corporate, and social. *Personal discount rates* assess individuals' temporal preferences with respect to costs and benefits. Different individuals may have radically divergent discount rates, and many of these may be high for the simple reason that human lives are finite. People generally prefer to realize benefits in the near certain future than in the uncertain

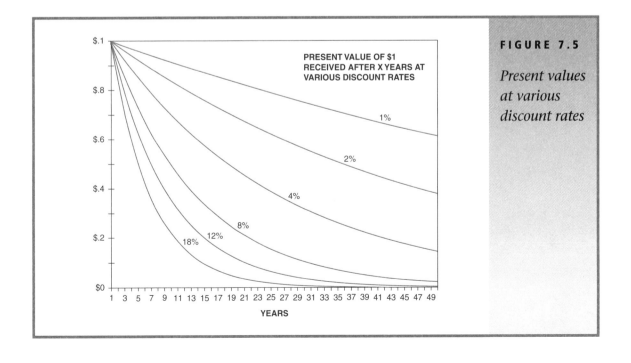

**FIGURE 7.5**

*Present values at various discount rates*

more distant future. Several early studies found individual discount rates as high as 89–300% in the context of consumer purchase decisions for energy efficient appliances (Gately 1980; Hausman 1979).

*Corporate discount rates* are usually calculated as the weighted cost of capital to the firm, as this figure is used to make decisions about the timing and extent of capital investments. As these rates apply solely to private-sector decisions made by companies in the pursuit of profit maximization, this poses a major challenge from a sustainability perspective for there is no reason to believe that corporate time preferences are similar to those held by society in general.

*Social Discount rates.* Since society is assumed to continue in existence indefinitely and that some provision must be made for future generations (i.e., our children, and our children's children, etc.), governments and the society they represent will tend to have a longer view, and this is captured by a lower discount rate.[2] At least two major challenges to sustainability emerge from contrasting corporate and social discount rates. First, since it is perfectly rational for a corporation to adopt a discount rate that is higher than the socially desirable rate, some private-sector projects will be chosen that are either too early or late, too small or large, or not desirable from a social perspective. These projects may include new plant and equipment, new processes, or new products.

Second, given that the social discount rate is the most appropriate to adopt when making important public policy decisions that affect future generations, it is not clear what this rate should actually be. Governmental regulatory agencies in the United States and elsewhere have frequently adopted a social discount rate of 3–4% in contrast to rates within the private sector that may range from 10–15%. A cost-benefit analysis with a sufficiently high discount rate—even 3%—could justify the destruction of a renewable resource that has existed from time immemorial and which could otherwise exist indefinitely into the future. Examples of this can be found in such areas as forestry and fisheries.

In the context of climate change, Brekke and Johansson-Stenman (2008) argue for the use of a risk-free return that they estimate for the United States at 0.4%. In fact, it has been hypothesized that any non-zero discount rate may jeopardize the welfare of future generations and that a zero discount rate must be adopted in some circumstances (Stern 2006). If one assumes that future generations may be worse off than ours—a not totally unreasonable assumption in light of the threats from global warming—then a negative discount rate may be appropriate. Both zero and negative rates pose unusual challenges for project evaluation.

These issues have not been resolved, but extensive research has been conducted on methods to address some of these concerns. Several authors have suggested that the use of a constant discount rate is inappropriate to deal with long-run major threats such as global warming and have proposed the use of *hyperbolic* or *quasi-hyperbolic* discounting (Ainslie 1991; Harvey 1994; Henderson and Bateman 1995; Laibson 1997). This approach is based on empirical evidence that suggests that many individuals in fact use two implicit types of discounting: a high rate for short-term decisions, based on impulsive human instincts; versus a much lower, longer-term or planning rate for decisions in the future. Karp (2005) argues that the application of hyperbolic discounting to long-term issues of major import such as global warming would involve declining social discount rates as the time horizon is extended.

Figure 7–6 presents another alternative to conventional *exponential discounting* from time period zero. The underlying approach of this hybrid (Sumaila 2004; Sumaila and Walters 2005) is that while we make a project decision now, the payoff will look different if such a decision were to be made in any subsequent year. This proposal suggests that such future valuations should be recognized and incorporated more explicitly into decisions today. To quote: "Under the intergenerational discounting approach, the NPV term considers the value of benefits received by the current generation (calculated at a standard discount rate) plus the value of benefits received by an annual influx of new stakeholders. These participants bring with them a renewed perspective on future earnings, partially resetting the discounting clock. The equation requires a standard annual discount factor and a discount factor to evaluate benefits destined for future generations" (Ainsworth and Sumaila 2005, p. 1106). Prager and Shertzer (2006) provide a small clarification to the original formulation emphasizing the distinction between the two types of discount rates: the future-generational discount rate *per generation* and the future-generational discount rate *per year*.

In light of the complex theoretical issues surrounding the choice of an appropriate discount rate or system of rates, Helm (2009) has advanced the argument that the decisions that our society faces today with respect to global climate change must transcend questions of discounting and focus instead on the existence and significance of *fat-tails* (Taleb 2007; Weitzman 2009). This theory posits that the probability distribution of possible future negative outcomes from current GHG emissions contains a long right tail with non-zero probabilities of catastrophic consequences. In essence, the necessity to avoid these possible outcomes at all costs renders debate over the choice of discount rates essentially academic.

**FIGURE 7.6**

*Alternative discounting methodology*

Current Approach

|  | Year 1 | Year 2 | Year 3 | Year 4 | Year 5 | ... | ... | ... | Year n |
|---|---|---|---|---|---|---|---|---|---|
| $NPV0 =$ | $(B_1-C_1)$ / $1+r$ | $(B_2-C_2)$ / $(1+r)^2$ | $(B_3-C_3)$ / $(1+r)^3$ | $(B_4-C_4)$ / $(1+r)^4$ | $(B_5-C_5)$ / $(1+r)^5$ |  |  |  | $(B_n-C_n)$ / $(1+r)^n$ |

The Reality

|  | Year 1 | Year 2 | Year 3 | Year 4 | Year 5 | Year 6 | Year 7 | ... | Year n |
|---|---|---|---|---|---|---|---|---|---|
| $NPV0 =$ | $(B_1-C_1)$ / $1+r$ | $(B_2-C_2)$ / $(1+r)^2$ | $(B_3-C_3)$ / $(1+r)^3$ | $(B_4-C_4)$ / $(1+r)^4$ | $(B_5-C_5)$ / $(1+r)^5$ |  |  |  | $(B_n-C_n)$ / $(1+r)^n$ |
| | $NPV1 =$ | $(B_1-C_1)$ / $1+r$ | $(B_2-C_2)$ / $(1+r)^2$ | $(B_3-C_3)$ / $(1+r)^3$ | $(B_4-C_4)$ / $(1+r)^4$ | $(B_5-C_5)$ / $(1+r)^5$ |  |  | $(B_n-C_n)$ / $(1+r)^n$ |
| | | $NPV2 =$ | $(B_1-C_1)$ / $1+r$ | $(B_2-C_2)$ / $(1+r)^2$ | $(B_3-C_3)$ / $(1+r)^3$ | $(B_4-C_4)$ / $(1+r)^4$ | $(B_5-C_5)$ / $(1+r)^5$ | | $(B_n-C_n)$ / $(1+r)^n$ |
| | | ... | | | | | | | |
| | | | | | | | | | $NPVn$ |

The Proposal

|  | Year 1 | Year 2 | Year 3 | Year 4 | Year 5 | ... | ... | ... | Year n |
|---|---|---|---|---|---|---|---|---|---|
| $NPV0^* =$ | $NPV1$ / $1+r$ | $NPV2$ / $(1+r)^2$ | $NPV3$ / $(1+r)^3$ | $NPV4$ / $(1+r)^4$ | $NPV5$ / $(1+r)^5$ | ... | ... | ... | $NPVn$ / $(1+r)^n$ |

Another study that de-emphasizes the role of the discount rate in decisions concerning the response to possible effects of future climate change has been authored by Sterner and Persson (2008). Drawing upon the work of Weitzman (2007), the authors argue that changing relative prices (specifically the rising relative prices of depleting environmental resources) may outweigh the importance of discount rates in motivating current public policy decisions on greenhouse gas abatement.

In sum, cost-benefit remains an important part of the armory of decision methodologies available to policy makers, but it has been the subject of at least five major critiques. First, CBA was originally intended to compare at the margin public projects with relatively similar effects and timelines; it is inappropriate for making judgments about large-scale issues that affect future generations and the planet as a whole. Second, in parallel with this problem, conventional CBAs focus on efficiency, and its utilitarian roots detracts from its ability to recognize or incorporate matters of distributional equity whether cross-sectional or temporal. Third, CBA will invariably favor projects whose benefits can be more easily monetized despite the fact that some of the most pressing social issues and values are not easily quantified. Under these circumstances, the most appropriate course of action is to supplement this decision methodology with others that have compensatory strengths. One of these is Multi-Attribute Decision Making (MADM), which is briefly described in Appendix 3. Fourth, there are serious concerns about the relevance of conventional cost-benefit analysis in circumstances where ecological systems may face major discontinuities or *tipping points*. The nature of this concern is explored in Chapters 9 and 10, which deal with risk analysis and key ecological concepts. And fifth, while CBA is claimed to be a value-free methodology able to make choices on the basis of objective assessments, several philosophical critiques have challenged the assumption of value neutrality (Ackerman and Heinzerling 2004; Copp and Levi 1982).

## Final Notes on Evaluative Methodologies

The economic evaluation methodologies described above have continued to evolve with increasing recognition of the critical importance of ecosystem services by both corporations and governments. In response to the perceived need for more advanced tools, several recent modeling efforts have been undertaken by universities and nonprofit organizations. These models are specifically designed to permit the rigorous derivation of monetary estimates for ecosystems services at various levels of geographic scale. Foremost among these models are: (a) In-VEST (InVEST website 2011; Kareiva et al. 2011) from Stanford University, the University of Minnesota, and The Nature Conservancy, which utilizes a production function approach to estimation on a geographic information system (GIS) platform; (b) the ARIES Project (Artificial Intelligence for Ecosystem Services) led by the Gund Institute at the University of Vermont, which utilizes the benefit transfer methodology (2011); (c) the European Commission's TEEB (The Economics of Ecosystems and Biodiversity) (TEEB 2010a, 2010b; TEEB website 2011); and (d) MIMES (Multiscale Integrated Models of Ecosystem Services) (see Nelson and Daily 2010).

Much of the previous discussion in this chapter relating to evaluative methodologies has been cast in terms of economic analysis—an approach common to policy makers and businesses in the industrialized world. In the view of Stewart and Kahn (2006, pp. 171–172), however, several of the most commonly used evaluative methodologies are ineffective in a developing world context. For example, the hedonic pricing model assumes the existence of perfect mobility where consumers are free to choose among housing options regardless of location. In addition, the authors doubt the value of information extracted from contingent valuation surveys when respondents have little or no experience of a market economy. Other more situation-appropriate methodologies may be preferable. By way of example, the authors cite a conjoint analysis study conducted in Latin America where respondents are presented with choice sets involving tradeoffs between varying amounts of physical goods (such as diesel fuel and gasoline, and access to health care and education) rather than hypothetical questions of CV analysis designed to elicit estimates of willingness to pay.

Another major issue revolves around the philosophical framework underlying most of the common evaluative methodologies, which is fundamentally anthropocentric, focusing on human preferences and utility, the language of modern economics. There is, however, another major paradigm that focuses on intrinsic ecological values, sometimes termed *biophysical evaluation*. In a comprehensive survey of the economics of valuing ecosystem services and biodiversity, Pascual et al. (2010) elaborate on the critical differences between preference-based and biophysical approaches. Figure 7–7, adapted from their analysis, classifies the principal evaluative methodologies under each of the two rubrics and indicates where each is discussed within this textbook.[3]

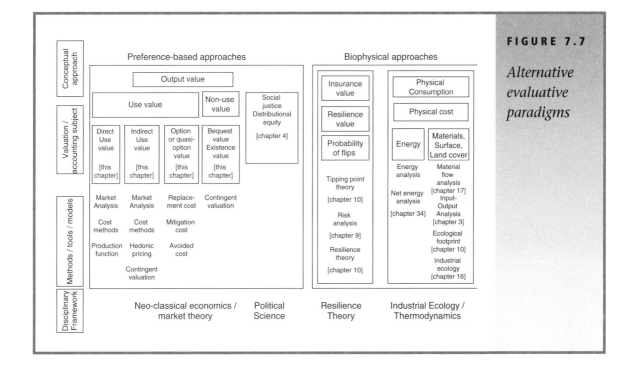

**FIGURE 7.7**

*Alternative evaluative paradigms*

## CITED REFERENCES AND RECOMMENDED READINGS

Ackerman, Frank and Lisa Heinzerling (2004) *Priceless: On Knowing the Price of Everything and the Value of Nothing.* New York: The New Press.

Ainslie, George (1991) "Derivation of 'Rational' Economic Behavior for Hyperbolic Discount Curves." *American Economic Review*, May, pp. 334–340.

Ainsworth, C.H. and U.R. Sumaila (2005) "Intergenerational Valuation of Fisheries Resources Can Justify Long-Term Conservation: A Case Study in Atlantic Cod (*Gadus morhua*)," in *Canadian Journal of Fisheries and Aquatic Sciences*, pp. 1104–1110.

Alberini, Anna and James R. Kahn (eds.) (2006) *Handbook on Contingent Valuation.* Cheltenham: Edward Elgar.

Allsopp, Mike H. et al. (2008) "Valuing Insect Pollination Service with Cost of Replacement." *PlosOne*, September, pp. 1–8.

American Water Works Association (AWWA) (2004) "Conserving Forests to Protect Water." *OpFlow*, 30(5).

Ariely, Dan (2008) *Predictably Irrational: The Hidden Forces That Shape Our Decisions.* New York: Harper-Collins.

Artificial Intelligence for Ecosystem Service (ARIES) website (GUND Institute for Ecological Economics, University of Vermont) (www.uvm.edu/giee/).

Asian Development Bank (ADB) (2002) *Handbook for Integrating Risk Analysis in the Economic Analysis of Projects*, Manila, May.

Barton, David N. (2002) "The Transferability of Benefit Transfer: Contingent Valuation of Water Quality Improvements in Costa Rica." *Ecological Economics*, 42, pp. 147–164.

Bateman, Ian et al. (1997) "Does Part-Whole Bias Exist? An Experimental Investigation." *The Economic Journal*, 107, March, pp. 322–332.

Bennett, Jeff (ed.) (2011) *The International Handbook on Non-Market Environmental Valuation.* Cheltenham: Edward Elgar.

Bergstrom, John C. and Laura O. Taylor (2006) "Using Meta-Analysis for Benefits Transfer; Theory and Practice." *Ecological Economics*, pp. 351–360.

Berridge, Kent C. and Morten L. Kringelbach (2008) "Affective Neuroscience of Pleasure: Reward in Humans and Animals." *Psychopharmacology*, 199, pp. 457–480.

Biel, Anders et al. (2011) "The Willingness to Pay—Willingness to Accept Gap Revisited: The Role of Emotions and Moral Satisfaction," Working Papers in Economics, No. 497, April, University of Gothenburg.

Bockstael, Nancy E. and Kenneth E. McConnell (2010) *Environmental and Resources Valuation with Revealed Preferences.* Dordrecht: Springer.

Boyle, Kevin J. et al. (1994) "In Investigation of Part-Whole Biases in Contingent-Valuation Studies." *Journal of Environmental Economics and Management*, 27, pp. 64–83.

Brekke, Kjell Arne and Olaf Johnsson-Stenman (2008) "The Behavioural Economics of Climate Change." *Oxford Review of Economic Policy*, 24(2), pp. 280–297.

Brouwer, Roy (2000) "Environmental Value Transfer: State of the Art and Future Prospects." *Ecological Economics*, 32, pp. 137–152.

Brouwer, Roy et al. (2011) "A Hedonic Price Model of Coral Reef quality in Hawaii," Ch. 3 in Jeff Bennett (ed.) *The International Handbook on Non-Market Environmental Valuation.* Cheltenham: Edward Elgar, pp. 37–59.

Calderone, Nicholas W. (2012) "Insect Pollinated Crops, Insect Pollinators and US Agriculture: Trend Analysis of Aggregate Data for the Period 1992–2009." *PLoS ONE*, 7(5), May, 27 pages.

Cederholm, C.J. et al. (2000) Pacific Salmon and Wildlife—Ecological Contexts, Relationships, and Implications for Management. Special Edition Technical Report, Washington Department of Fish and Wildlife, Olympia, Washington.

Chestnut, L.G., R.D. Rowe and W.S. Breffle. (2004). *Economic Valuation of Mortality Risk Reduction: Stated Preference Approach in Canada*. Report prepared for Paul De Civita, Health Canada by Stratus Consulting Inc., Boulder, CO, December.

Copp, David and Edwin Levi (1982) "Value Neutrality in the Techniques of Policy Analysis: Risk and Uncertainty." *Journal of Business Administration*, 13(1&2), pp. 161–190.

David Suzuki Foundation (2008) *Ontario's Wealth, Canada's Future: Appreciating the Value of the Greenbelt's Eco-services*, Vancouver BC.

De Martino, Benedetto et al. (2009) "The Neurobiology of Reference-Dependent Value Computation." *The Journal of Neuroscience*, 29(2), March 25, pp. 3833–3842.

De Martino, Benedetto, Colin F Camerer and Ralph Adolphs (2010) "Amygdala Damage Eliminates Monetary Loss Version." *PNAS*, 107(8), Feb. 23, pp. 3788–3792.

De Steiguer, Joseph Edward (2006) *The Origins of Modern Environmental Thought*. Tucson: University of Arizona Press.

Devall, B. (1991) "Deep Ecology and Radical Environmentalism." *Society and Natural Resources*, 4 (3), pp. 247–258.

Dohle, Simone et al. (2010) "Conjoint Measurement of Base Station Siting Preferences." *Human and Ecological Risk Assessment*, 16, pp. 825–836.

Dykstra, P.R. (2004) "Thresholds in Habitat Supply: A Review of the Literature," BC Ministry of Sustainable Resource Management, Victoria, BC.

Fehr, Ernst et al. (2005) "Neuroeconomic Foundations of Trust and Social Preferences" Initial Evidence." *American Economic Review*, 95(2), pp. 346–351.

Frey, Bruno S. and Felix Oberholzer-Gee (1997) "The Cost of Price Incentives: An Empirical Analysis of Motivation Crowding Out." *American Economic Review*, 87(4), September, pp. 746–755.

Gallai, Nicola et al. (2009) "Economic Valuation of the Vulnerability of World Agriculture Confronted with Pollinator Decline." *Ecological Economics*, pp. 810–821.

Gately, Dermot (1980) "Individual Discount Rates and the Purchase and Utilization of Energy-Using Durables: Comment," *The Bell Journal of Economics*, 11(1), Spring, pp. 373–374.

Georgantzis, Nikolaos and Daniel Navarro-Martinez (2010) "Understanding the WTA-WTP Gap through Attitudes, Feelings, Uncertainty and Personality." *Journal of Economic Psychology*, pp. 1–33.

Glimcher, Paul W. et al. (eds.) 2009 *Neuroeconomics:Decision Making and the Brain*. London: Academic Press.

Hall, Jane V. et al. (1992) "Valuing the Health Benefits of Clean Air." *Science*, February 14, pp. 812–817.

Hamilton, Stanley and Moura Quayle (2002) "Corridors of Green: Impact of Riparian Suburban Greenways on Property Values," in Peter N. Nemetz (ed.) *Bringing Business on Board: Sustainable Development and the B-School Curriculum*. Vancouver: JBA Press, pp. 365–390.

Hanemann, W. Michael (1991) "Willingness to Pay and Willingness to Accept: How Much Can They Differ?" *American Economic Review*, June, 81(3), pp. 635–647.

Harvey, Charles M. (1994) "The Reasonableness of Non-Constant Discounting." *Journal of Public Economics*, pp. 31–51.

Hausman, Jerry A. (1979) "Individual Discount Rates and the Purchase and Utilization of Energy-Using Durables." *The Bell Journal of Economics*, 10(1), spring, pp. 33–54.

Heal, Geoffrey M. et al. (2004) *Valuing Ecosystem Services: Toward Better Environmental Decision-Making*. Washington, DC: National Academy of Sciences.

Helm, Dieter (2009) "Climate-change Policy: Why Has So Little Been Achieved?" Ch. 2 in Dieter Helm and Cameron Hepburn (eds.) *The Economics and Politics of Climate Change*. Oxford: Oxford University Press, pp. 9–35.

Helmuth, Obata + Kassabaum, Inc. and Raytheon Infrastructure Services, Inc. (1997) "SEA-TAC International Airport Impact Mitigation Study. Initial Assessment and Recommendations," February.

Henderson, Norman and Ian Bateman (1995) "Empirical and Public Choice Evidence for Hyperbolic Social Discount Rates and the Implications for Intergenerational Discounting." *Environmental and Resource Economics*, 5, pp. 413–423.

Henry, Mickael et al. (2012) "A Common Pesticide Decreases Foraging Success and Survival in Honey Bees." *Science*, 336, April 20, pp. 348–350.

Horowitz, John K. and Kenneth E. McConnell (2002) "A Review of WTA/WTP Studies." *Journal of Environmental Economics and Management*, 44, pp. 426–447.

InVEST website (www.naturalcapitalproject.org) Stanford University.

Kahneman, Daniel (2011) *Thinking, Fast and Slow*. New York: Farrar, Strauss and Giroux.

Kahneman, Daniel and Amos Tversky (1979) "Prospect Theory: An Analysis of Decision Under Risk." *Econometrica* 47(2), March, pp. 263–291.

Kahneman, Daniel et al. (1990) *Journal of Political Economy*, 98(6), pp. 1325–1348.

Kareiva, Peter et al. (2011) *Natural Capital: Theory and Practice of Mapping Ecosystem Services*. Oxford: Oxford University Press.

Karp, Larry (2005) "Global Warming and Hyperbolic Discounting." *Journal of Public Economics*, 89, pp. 261–282.

Kasina, Muo J. et al. (2009) "Measuring Economic Value of Crop Pollination Services. An Empirical Application of Contingent Valuation in Kakamega, Western Kenya," in Pushpam Kumar and Roldan Muradian (eds.) *Payment for Ecosystem Services*, New York: Oxford University Press, pp. 87–109.

Klein, Alexandra-Maria et al. (2007) "Importance of Pollinators in Changing Landscapes for World Crops," *Proceedings of the Royal Society B—Biological Sciences*, 274, pp. 303–313.

Laden, F. et al. (2006) Reduction in Fine Particulate Air Pollution and Mortality: Extended Follow-up of the Harvard Six Cities Study. *American Journal of Respiratory and Critical Care Medicine*, 173, pp. 667–672.

Laibson, David (1997) "Golden Eggs and Hyperbolic Discounting." *Quarterly Journal of Economics*, May, pp. 443–476.

Lehrer, Jonah (2009) *How We Decide*. Boston: Mariner Books.

Levine, David K. (2011) "Neuroeconomics?" March 3, Department of Economics, Washington University, St. Louis.

Losey, John E. and Mace Vaughn (2006) "The Economic Value of Ecological Services Provided by Insects." *BioScience*, 56(4), April, pp. 311–323.

MacCrimmon, Kenneth R. (1968) *Decisionmaking Among Multiple-Attribute Alternatives: A Survey and Consolidated Approach*. Santa Monica, CA: RAND Corporation.

Morey, Edward R. et al. (2002) "Estimating the Benefits and Costs to Mountain Bikers of Changes in Trail Characteristics, Access Fees, and Site Closures: Choice Experiments and Benefits Transfer." *Journal of Environmental Management*, 64, pp. 411–422.

Morse, Roger A. and Nicholas W. Calderone (2000) "The Value of Honey Bees as Pollinators of U.S Crops in 2000." Cornell University, Ithaca, March.

Navrud, Stale and Jon Strand (2011) "Using Hedonic Pricing for Estimating Compensation Payments for Noise and Other Externalities from New Roads," Ch. 2 in Jeff Bennett (ed.) *The International Handbook on Non-Market Environmental Valuation*. Cheltenham: Edward Elgar, pp. 14–36.

Nelson, Erik J. and Gretchen C. Daily (2010) "Modelling Ecosystem Services in Terrestrial Systems." *F1000 Biology Reports*, 2(53), July 22, 6 pages.

Nordhaus, William (2007) "Critical Assumptions in the Stern Review on Climate Change." *Science*, 317, July 13, pp. 201–202.

Nordhaus, William (2007) "The Stern Review on the Economics of Climate Change," May 3 (http://nordhaus.econ.yale.edu/stern_050307.pdf).

Oracle Corporation, Crystalball software (http://www.oracle.com/us/products/applications/crystalball/index.htm).

Palisade Corporation @Risk software (http://www.palisade.com/risk/).

Pascual, Unai et al. (2010) "The Economics of Valuing Ecosystem Services and Biodiversity (TEEB)." *Foundations*, Ch. 5, 133 pages.

Perrot-Maitre, Danielle and Patsy Davis (2001) "Case Studies of Markets and Innovative Financial Mechanisms for Water Services From Forests." *Forest Trends*, May, 48 pages.

Plott, Charles R. and Kathryn Zeiler (2005) "The Willingness to Pay—Willingness to Accept Gap, the "Endowment Effect, Subject Misconceptions, and Experimental Procedures for Eliciting Valuations. *American Economic Review*, 95(3), June, pp. 530–545.

Plummer, Mark L. (2009) "Assessing Benefit Transfer for the Valuation of Ecosystem Services." *Frontiers of Ecology and Economics*, 7(1), pp. 38–45.

Pope, C.A. et al. (2002) "Lung Cancer, Cardiopulmonary Mortality, and Long-Term Exposure to Fine Particulate Air Pollution." *Journal of the American Medical Association*, 287(9), pp. 1132–1141.

Prager, Michael H. and Kyle W. Shertzer (2006) "Remembering the Future: A Commentary on 'Intergenerational discounting: A New Intuitive Approach,'" *Ecological Economics*, 60, pp. 24–26.

Ramsay, F.P. (1928) "A Mathematical Theory of Saving." *Economic Journal*, 38, pp. 543–559.

Richmond, Amy et al. (2007) "Valuing Ecosystem Services: A Shadow Price for Net Primary Production." *Ecological Economics* 2007, 64, pp. 454–462.

Riera, Pere et al. (2011) "Applying the Travel Cost Methodology to Minorca Beaches: Some Policy Results," Ch. 4 in Jeff Bennett (ed.) *The International Handbook on Non-Market Environmental Valuation*. Cheltenham: Edward Elgar, pp. 60–73.

Rose, John M. and Lorenzo Masiero (2010) "A Comparison of the Impacts of Aspects of Prospect Theory on WTP/WTA Estimated in Preference and WTP/WTA Space." *EJTIR*, 10(4), December, pp. 330–346.

Sandel, Michel (2012) *What Money Can't Buy: The Moral Limits of Markets*. London: Allen Lane.

Sayman, Serdar and Ayse Onculer (2005) "Effects of Study Design Characteristics on the WTA-WTP Disparity: A Meta Analytical Framework." *Journal of Economic Psychology*, 26, pp. 289–312.

Shiv, Baba et al. (2012) "Investment Behavior and the Negative side of Emotion." *Psychological Science*, 16(6), pp. 435–439.

Sinclair, Anthony R.E. (2007) "Is Conservation a Lost Cause?" Ch. 8 in Peter N. Nemetz (ed.) *Sustainable Resource Management: Reality or Illusion?* Cheltenham: Edward Elgar, pp. 217–238.

Singer, Tania and Ernst Fehr (2005) "The Neuroeconomics of Mind Reading and Empathy." *American Economic Review*, 95(2), May, pp. 340–345.

Smith, Kirk and Majid Ezzati (2005) "How Environmental Health Risks Change with Development: The Epidemiologic and Environmental Risk Transitions Revisited." *Annual Review of Environment and Resources*, 30, pp. 291–333.

Smith, V. Kerry (2006) "Fifty Years of Contingent Valuation," Ch. 2 in Anna Alberini and James R. Kahn (eds.) *Handbook on Contingent Valuation*, Cheltenham UK: Edward Elgar, pp. 7–65Smith, V. Kerry et al. (2006) "Structural Benefit Transfer: An Example Using VSL Estimates," *Ecological Economics*, 60, pp. 361–371.

Spash, Clive L. and Arild Vatn (2006) "Transferring Environmental Value Estimates: Issues and Alternatives." *Ecological Economics*, 60, pp. 279–388.

Stern, Nicholas (2006) *The Economics of Climate Change*. Cambridge: Cambridge University Press.

Sterner, Thomas and U. Martin Persson (2008) "A Even Sterner Review: Introducing Relative Prices into the Discounting Debate," Review of Environmental Economics and Policy, Vol. 2, issue 1, winter, pp. 61–76.

Stewart, Steven and James R. Kahn (2009) "An Introduction to Choice Modeling for Non-Market Valuation," Ch. 7 in Anna Alberini and James R. Kahn (eds.) *Handbook on Contingent Valuation*. Cheltenham: Edward Elgar, pp. 153–176.

Stipp, D. (2007) Flight of the Honey Bee, *Fortune*, 156(5), pp. 108–116.

Sumaila, Ussif Rashid (2004) "Intergenerational Cost-Benefit Analysis and Marine System Restoration." *Fish and Fisheries*, 5, pp. 329–343.

Sumaila, U.R. and C.J. Walters (2005) "Intergenerational Discounting: A New Intuitive Approach." *Ecological Economics*, 52, pp. 135–142.

Swallow, Stephen K. et al. (1992) "Siting Noxious Facilities: An Approach That Integrates Technical, Economic, and Political Considerations." *Land Economics*, 68(3), pp. 283–301.

Taleb, Nassim Nicholas (2007) *The Black Swan. The Impact of the Highly Improbable*. New York: Random House.

TEEB (2010a) *TEEB—The Economics of Ecosystems and Biodiversity Report for Business—Executive Summary*.

TEEB (2010b) *TEEB—The Economics of Ecosystems and Biodiversity: Mainstreaming the Economics of Nature: A Synthesis of the Approach, Conclusions and Recommendations of TEEB*.

The Economics of Ecosystems and Biodiversity (TEEB) website, UN Environment Programme, Geneva (www.teebweb.org/InformationMaterial/TEEBReports/tabid/1278/Default.aspx).

*The Ecologist* (1988) Vol. 18, No. 4/5 Special Deep Ecology issue.

Thomassin, Paul J. and Robert J. Johnston (2011) "Evaluating Benefit Transfer for Canadian Water Quality Improvements Using U.S./Canada Metadata: An Application of International Meta-Analysis," Ch. 17 in Jeff Bennett (ed.) *The International Handbook on Non-Market Environmental Valuation*. Cheltenham: Edward Elgar, pp. 353–384.

Turner, R. Kerry et al. (2000) "Ecological-Economic Analysis of Wetlands: Scientific Integration for Management and Policy." *Ecological Economics*, 35, pp. 7–23.

United Kingdom (2011) *National Ecosystem Assessment* (NEA).

United Kingdom Treasury (2003) *The Green Book, Appraisal and Evaluation in Central Government*, London.

United Nations (2005) *Millennium Ecosystem Assessment—Ecosystems and Human Well-being: Wetlands and Water*.

United Nations Office for Project Services (UNOPS) (n.d.) "Protecting Migratory Waterbird through Flyway Conservation."

U.S. Environmental Protection Agency (EPA) 2010 *Guidelines for Preparing Economic Analysis*.

U.S. Environmental Protection Agency (EPA) 2011 *The Benefits and Costs of the Clean Air Act from 1990 to 2020*.

Weitzman, Martin L. (2007) "A Review of The Stern Review of the Economics of Climate Change." *Journal of Economic Literature*, 45, September, pp. 703–724.

Weitzman, Martin L. (2009) "On Modeling and Interpreting the Economics of Catastrophic Climate Change." *The Review of Economics and Statistics*, 91(1)1, pp. 1–19.

Whitehorn, Penelope R. et al. (2012) "Neonicotinoid Pesticide Reduces Bumble Bee Colony Growth and Queen Production." *Science*, 336, April 20, pp. 351–352.

Wood, Gillen (2012) "Case Study: Agriculture and the Global Bee Collapse," in Tom Theis and Jonathan Tomkin (eds.) *Sustainability: A Comprehensive Foundation*, Connexions, Rice University, Houston, Texas [http://cnx.org/content/col11325/1.38]

World Wildlife Fund (WWF) (2004) *Running Pure. The Importance of Forest Protected Areas to Drinking Water*.

## APPENDIX ONE

# *Applying Evaluation Methodology— Case Study of the U.S. Clean Air Act*

Table 7–5 presents U.S. EPA estimates of the distribution of a broad range of avoided health effects in 2020 as a result of the implementation of the Clean Air Act (U.S. EPA 2011). Table 7–6 derives mean primary annual benefits for the years 2000, 2010, and 2020. The present value of total monetized benefits of the Clean Air Act as reported in Table 7–7 ranges from $1.4 to $35 trillion. By comparison, the value of direct compliance expenditures (i.e., costs) over the same period equals approximately $0.38 trillion, yielding a central benefit-cost ratio of 32:1.

In its comprehensive study, the EPA makes several important qualifications that strengthen the already persuasive case for the net benefits of the Clean Air Act:

> The most significant known human health effects from exposure to air pollution are associated with exposures to fine particles and ground-level ozone pollution. Many of these effects could be quantified for this study; but other health effects of fine particles and ozone, health effects associated with other air pollutants, and most air pollution-related environmental effects could be quantified only partially, if at all. Future improvements in the scientific and economic information needed to quantify these effects would be expected to further increase the estimated benefits of clean air programs.

**TABLE 7.5**

*Avoided Health Effects from the U.S. Clean Air Act (CAA)*

| ENDPOINT | POLLUTANT | INCIDENCE | | | VALUATION (MILLION 2006$) | | |
|---|---|---|---|---|---|---|---|
| | | 5TH PERCENTILE | MEAN | 95TH PERCENTILE | 5TH PERCENTILE | MEAN | 95TH PERCENTILE |
| MORTALITY | PM, Ozone | 45,000 | 230,000 | 490,000 | $170,000 | $1,800,000 | $5,500,000 |
| MORBIDITY | | | | | | | |
| Chronic Bronchitis | PM | 12,000 | 75,000 | 130,000 | $3,100 | $36,000 | $130,000 |
| Non-fatal Myocardial Infarction | PM | 80,000 | 200,000 | 300,000 | $6,200 | $21,000 | $48,000 |
| Hospital admissions, respiratory | PM, Ozone | 24,000 | 66,000 | 110,000 | $320 | $1,100 | $1,800 |
| Hospital admissions, cardiovascular | PM | 52,000 | 69,000 | 84,000 | $1,400 | $2,000 | $2,600 |
| ER Visits, respiratory | PM, Ozone | 64,000 | 120,000 | 180,000 | $22 | $44 | $69 |
| Acute Bronchitis | PM | –7,000 | 180,000 | 340,000 | –$4 | $94 | $220 |
| Lower Respiratory Symptoms | PM | 1,200,000 | 2,300,000 | 3,300,000 | $18 | $42 | $76 |
| Upper Respiratory Symptoms | PM | 620,000 | 2,000,000 | 3,300,000 | $17 | $60 | $130 |
| Asthma Exacerbation | PM | 270,000 | 2,400,000 | 6,700,000 | $15 | $130 | $390 |
| Minor Restricted Activity Days | PM, Ozone | 91,000,000 | 110,000,000 | 140,000,000 | $3,800 | $6,700 | $10,000 |
| Work Loss Days | PM | 15,000,000 | 17,000,000 | 19,000,000 | $2,300 | $2,700 | $3,000 |
| School Loss Days | Ozone | 2,200,000 | 5,400,000 | 8,600,000 | $190 | $480 | $770 |
| Outdoor Worker Productivity | Ozone | n.a. | n.a. | n.a. | $170 | $170 | $170 |

*Source: US EPA, 2011*

PM = particulates

TABLE 7.6

*Annual Mon-*
*etized Benefits*
*of U.S. CAA*

| BENEFIT CATEGORY | ANNUAL MONETIZED BENEFITS (MILLION 2006$) BY TARGET | | | NOTES |
| --- | --- | --- | --- | --- |
| | 2000 | 2010 | 2020 | |
| **Heath Effects** | | | | |
| PM Mortality | $710,000 | $1,200,000 | $1,700,000 | PM mortality estimates based on Weibull distribution derived from Pope et al. (2002) and Laden et al. (2006). Ozone mortality estimates based on pooled function |
| PM Morbidity | $27,000 | $46,000 | $68,000 | |
| Ozone Mortality | $10,000 | $33,000 | $55,000 | |
| Ozone Morbidity | $420 | $1,300 | $2,100 | |
| Subtotal Health Effects | $750,000 | $1,300,000 | $1,900,000 | |
| **Visibility** | | | | |
| Recreational | $3,300 | $8,600 | $19,000 | Recreational visibility only includes benefits in the regions analyzed in Chestnut and Rowe, 1990 (i.e. California, the Southwest, and the Southeast). |

**TABLE 7.6** *continued*

| BENEFIT CATEGORY | ANNUAL MONETIZED BENEFITS (MILLION 2006$) BY TARGET | | | NOTES |
|---|---|---|---|---|
| | 2000 | 2010 | 2020 | |
| Residential | $1,000 | $25,000 | $48,000 | |
| Subtotal Visibility | $14,000 | $34,000 | $67,000 | |
| **Agricultural and Forest Productivity** | $1,000 | $5,500 | $11,000 | |
| **Material Damage** | $58 | $93 | $110 | |
| **Ecological** | $6.9 | $7.5 | $8.2 | Reduced lake acidification benefits to recreational fishing |
| **Total all categories** | $770,000 | $1,300,000 | $2,000,000 | |

*Source:* US EPA, 2011

| | ANNUAL ESTIMATES | | | PRESENT VALUE ESTIMATE | **TABLE 7.7** |
| --- | --- | --- | --- | --- | --- |
| | 2000 | 2010 | 2020 | 1990–2020 | *Annual Estimates of Benefits and Costs of U.S. CAA* |
| **Monetized Direct Costs (millions 2006$):** | | | | | |
| Low | | | | | |
| Central | $20,000 | $53,000 | $65,000 | $380,000 | |
| High | | | | | |
| **Monetized Direct Benefits (millions 2006$):** | | | | | |
| Low | $90,000 | $160,000 | $250,000 | $1,400,000 | |
| Central | $770,000 | $1,300,000 | $2,000,000 | $12,000,000 | |
| High | $2,300,000 | $3,800,000 | $5,700,000 | $35,000,000 | |
| **Net Benefits (millions 2006$):** | | | | | |
| Low | $70,000 | $110,000 | $190,000 | $1,000,000 | |
| Central | $750,000 | $1,200,000 | $1,900,000 | $12,000,000 | |
| High | $2,300,000 | $3,700,000 | $5,600,000 | $35,000,000 | |
| **Benefit/Cost Ratio:** | | | | | |
| Low | 5 to 1 | 3 to 1 | 4 to1 | 4 to 1 | |
| Central | 39 to 1 | 25 to 1 | 31 to 1 | 32 to 1 | |
| High | 115 to 1 | 72 to 1 | 88 to 1 | 92 to 1 | |
| **Costs per Premature Mortality Avoided (2006$):** | | | | | |
| | $180,000 | $330,000 | $280,000 | not estimated | |

*Source:* US EPA, 2011

Economy-wide modeling was also conducted to estimate the effect of the 1990 Amendments to the Clean Air Act on overall U.S. economic growth and the economic welfare of American households. When some of the beneficial economic effects of clean air programs were incorporated along with the costs of these programs, economy-wide modeling projected net overall improvements in economic growth and welfare. These improvements are projected to occur because cleaner air leads to better health and productivity for American workers, as well as savings on medical expenses for air pollution-related health problems. The beneficial economic effects of these two improvements more than offset the costly effects across the economy of expenditures for pollution control.

## APPENDIX TWO

# Placing a Value on Ecosystem Services—Case Study of New York City's Water Supply

New York City has perennially faced the problem of guaranteeing an ample supply of clean water to its 8 million inhabitants. In the early 1990s, the U.S. EPA introduced new requirements for public water systems that mandated either the construction of filtration systems for unfiltered sources or that the water supplied meet certain criteria in order to avoid filtration. The Catskill/Delaware watershed has provided clean water for New York City since 1915 without the need for filtering and currently meets 90% of the city's demands. In response to the new EPA requirement, city managers had two choices: (1) build a new filtration system; or (2) introduce a comprehensive watershed protection program including land purchase, pollution reduction, and conservation easements that would allow the natural ecosystems to purify the water. It was estimated that the filtration plant would entail a capital expenditure of between $6 and $8 billion with annual operating costs in the range of $300–500 million. In contrast, an innovative program to compensate private landholders in the watershed to reduce their environmental burden would cost only $1–1.5 billion over a 10-year period (AWWA 2004; Heal 2004; Perrot-Maitre and Davis 2001; Richmond et al. 2007; Suzuki Foundation 2008). This was clearly the desirable option, yet there were significant complications to pursuing this second alternative due to the need for an innovative financial model and because of the fragmented nature of land ownership and its diverse use within the watershed. For example, the city owned less than 10%, an additional 25% was devoted to state parks, and the remaining 65% was under private ownership and devoted to small-scale forestry and agriculture. The major environmental concern focused on the potentially negative effects of 400 dairy and livestock farms that could threaten local waterways with runoff containing pathogens, nutrients, and other pollutants. New York City adopted a broad array of instruments to pay for the second option, including the use of taxes, bonds, and trust funds; compensation measures for landowners to adopt best management practices and improved forest management; and property transfer and purchase arrangements that entailed government acquisition and transfer of development rights, conservation easements, and hydrologically sensitive land. Using a discount rate of 7% (the then-current rate on New York City municipal bonds), New York derived a net present value (NPV) for each alternative as presented in Table 7–8. With this discount rate, the NPV of the natural watershed filtration option was less than 8% of the combined capital and operating costs of a new filtration plant. The table also calculates the NPV of both options using an estimated social discount rate of 3%. The decision remains unchanged with this alternative rate.

**TABLE 7.8**

*New York Water Supply Options*

| $ MILLION | | NPV AT 7% | YEAR: 1 | 2 | 3 | 4 | 5 | 6 | 7 | 8 | 9 | 10 | 11 … | 30 |
|---|---|---|---|---|---|---|---|---|---|---|---|---|---|---|
| **30-year time horizon** | | | | | | | | | | | | | | |
| **WATERSHED** | compensation payments | $878 | $125 | $125 | $125 | $125 | $125 | $125 | $125 | $125 | $125 | $125 | $0 | $0 |
| **FILTRATION PLANT** | capital | $7,000 | $7,000 | | | | | | | | | | | |
| | operating | $4,590 | $0 | $400 | $400 | $400 | $400 | $400 | $400 | $400 | $400 | $400 | $400 | $400 |
| | total | $11,590 | | | | | | | | | | | | |
| | Difference at 7% | $10,712 | | | | | | | | | | | | |
| | Difference at 3% | $13,386 | | | | | | | | | | | | |

*Source: Based on data in Perot-Maitre and Davis 2001*

# A Brief Overview of Multi-Attribute Decision Making (MADM)

MADM has been employed to overcome some of the recognized deficiencies of CBA when decisions entail a broad range of social, ecological, and economic issues. There are several variants of this type of decision methodology, but among the most common is the Alternative-Attributes Matrix (AAM). In an AAM, the options or alternatives are arrayed on one axis, and the policy objectives and/or choice criteria are displayed on the other. Each cell of the matrix is filled with a qualitative or quantitative value. The challenge is how to evaluate these data in order to reach a decision, bearing in mind that at first, some criteria may be more important than others; and, second, information may range from a simple "yes" or "no" to a relative value scale from 0–10. A common methodological approach in an AAM is as follows: (1) for each criterion, assign a score (out of 100) for each policy option; (2) assign weights to each criterion; (3) multiply the criteria weights by the policy scores and sum for each policy alternative; and (4) finally choose the policy alternative with the highest score. Table 7–9 illustrates this process. In order to address any concerns among decision makers that the choice of weights may involve uncertainty or a certain degree of arbitrariness, sensitivity analysis may be employed to test for the robustness of the recommended option.

In certain circumstances, it may not be possible to enter a single value in a cell; uncertainty concerning values may necessitate the use of probability distributions. MS Excel add-in software programs such as @RISK [Palisades Corp.] and Crystal Ball [Oracle Corp.] allow the user to enter and evaluate different types of probability distributions in as many alternative-attribute cells as necessary. This involves a four-step process: (1) specifying the type of probability distribution for a cell, (2) entering the parameters of the distributions, (3) running the simulation that processes the model for "n" iterations (this is a type of "Monte Carlo" experiment); and (4) reporting the results of the Monte Carlo simulation as histograms along with the expected value and standard deviation. Cumulative probability distributions may also be generated. (See, for example, ADB 2002).

Under certain circumstances, the decision makers may be unwilling or unable to force each variable to be expressed quantitatively. In its early work for NASA, the RAND Corporation developed a hybrid decision methodology that avoided some of the conceptual problems of reducing all data to a common metric. Table 7–10 reproduces the original problem addressed by this methodology: the choice of an astronaut's pressure suit for the U.S. Apollo space mission. There were five design finalists, and the complexity of the choice process was due to a mix of quantitative and qualitative data as well as attributes with different levels of importance (Mac-Crimmon 1968). The suggested procedure was to sequentially apply three separate decision techniques: (1) satisficing, (2) dominance, and (3) lexicography.

| STEP ONE | ALTERNATIVES - (SCORES OUT OF 100) | | | | | | TABLE 7.9 |
|---|---|---|---|---|---|---|---|
| **ATTRIBUTES OR CRITERIA** | I | II | III | IV | V | VI | *Alternative-Attributes Decision Process* |
| A | 80 | 40 | 50 | 75 | 40 | 10 | |
| B | 25 | 60 | 60 | 35 | 60 | 100 | |
| C | 0 | 40 | 90 | 65 | 30 | 20 | |
| D | 60 | 40 | 15 | 10 | 70 | 70 | |
| E | 40 | 60 | 90 | 25 | 40 | 40 | |
| F | 40 | 10 | 5 | 85 | 90 | 75 | |
| G | 55 | 40 | 20 | 15 | 10 | 100 | |
| H | 50 | 20 | 50 | 75 | 40 | 20 | |
| I | 60 | 40 | 25 | 75 | 60 | 70 | |
| J | 0 | 10 | 30 | 60 | 90 | 5 | |

| STEP TWO | | WEIGHTED ALTERNATIVES | | | | | |
|---|---|---|---|---|---|---|---|
| **ATTRIBUTES OR CRITERIA** | Criteria weights (out of 10) | I | II | III | IV | V | VI |
| A | 1 | 80 | 40 | 50 | 75 | 40 | 10 |
| B | 5 | 125 | 300 | 300 | 175 | 300 | 500 |
| C | 9 | 0 | 360 | 810 | 585 | 270 | 180 |
| D | 2 | 120 | 80 | 30 | 20 | 140 | 140 |
| E | 5 | 200 | 300 | 450 | 125 | 200 | 200 |
| F | 7 | 280 | 70 | 35 | 595 | 630 | 525 |
| G | 7 | 385 | 280 | 140 | 105 | 70 | 700 |
| H | 5 | 250 | 100 | 250 | 375 | 200 | 100 |
| I | 4 | 240 | 160 | 100 | 300 | 240 | 280 |
| J | 8 | 0 | 80 | 240 | 480 | 720 | 40 |
| | TOTAL SCORE | 1680 | 1770 | 2405 | 2835 | 2810 | 2675 |
| | RANK | **6** | **5** | **4** | **1** | **2** | **3** |

Step 1 involved the application of the Satisficing Procedure; that is, comparing the alternatives with the minimal attribute requirements of the decision maker. The purpose of this initial step was to reduce the number of admissible alternatives. For example, it was assumed that the basic requirements were (i) average mobility, (ii) average comfort, (iii) 3-hour life support capacity, (iv) 3.7 psi pressurization,

**TABLE 7.10**

*Choices of Five Pressure Suit Designs for Astronauts*

| ATTRIBUTE | ALTERNATIVE DESIGN | | | | |
|---|---|---|---|---|---|
| | I | II | III | IV | V |
| **Mobility** | average to good | fair to average | poor to fair | fair to good | fair to average |
| Comfort | good, but perhaps minor waste management problems | good, but perhaps some minor hot and cold spots | good, no problems expected | average, minor pressure points expected | average, minor hot and cold spots expected |
| **Life Support (hr)** | 1 to 2 | 3 to 4 | 4 to 5 | 2 to 3 | 2 to 3 |
| Pressurization (psi) | 3.6 – 3.8 | 3.6 – 3.7 | 3.8 – 3.9 | 3.7 – 3.8 | 3.6 – 3.7 |
| Peak Metabolic Tem-perature Load (Btu/ hr) | 1600 – 1900 | 1800 – 2000 | 1900 – 2200 | 2000 – 2200 | 1700 – 2000 |
| Primary flux Meteroid Protection (km/sec) | 25 – 30 | 30 – 35 | 30 – 35 | 27 – 32 | 25 – 32 |
| Maximum Thermal Gain (Btu/hr) | 180 – 240 | 210 – 230 | 150 – 170 | 230 – 270 | 230 – 260 |
| Total ultraviolet radiation (%) | 5 to 6 | 3 to 5 | 1 to 2 | 4 to 7 | 3 to 7 |

*Source:* MacCrimmon 1968

(v) 1900 Btu/hr peak metabolic heat gain, (vi) 30 km/sec primary flux meteoroid protection, (vii) 250 Btu/hr maximum heat gain, and (viii) 5% total ultraviolet radiation. [For "maximum thermal gain" and "total ultraviolet radiation," low values are preferred, while for the other six attributes, high values are preferred.] The result of this first step was that Design I was ruled out because of unsatisfactory life support; and Design III was ruled out because of unsatisfactory mobility.

Step 2 involved the application of a dominance procedure. In this case, the maximum attribute value of II was at least as good as the corresponding minimum attribute value of V and, in some cases, the attribute values of II were better than the corresponding values of V. The result was that Design V was weakly dominated by Design II, therefore Design V was ruled out.

Finally, Step 3 involved the application of the Lexicographic procedure; only then did the decision maker require information about the relative importance of attributes in order to choose among the nondominated, satisfactory alternatives. The result was the final choice of Design II over Design IV since it was assumed, with some justification, that life support was the most important attribute.

## NOTES

1. In economics, total social welfare is composed of both consumer surplus and its mirror concept, producer surplus, measured as the area between the price line and supply curve. Producer surplus is a measure of the excess of what producers receive over the amount of money for which they are willing to sell their product.

2. The social discount rate is composed of two terms: the pure social time preference (or rate) plus the product of the growth rate of consumption and the elasticity of the marginal utility of consumption (Ramsey 1928). The UK Treasury Department (2003, Annex 6, p. 97) explains the rationale for the two components: the first is the rate at which individuals discount future consumption over present consumption on the assumption that no change in per capita consumption is expected; and the second element is included "if per capita consumption is expected to grow over time, reflecting the fact that these circumstances imply future consumption will be plentiful relative to the current position and thus have lower marginal utility. This effect is represented by the product of the annual growth in per capita consumption and the elasticity of marginal utility of consumption with respect to utility." For further discussion of the social rate of discount related to climate change in particular, see Stern (2006, section 2A).

3. In their analysis, Pascual et al. (2010, p. 43) have adopted a specific definition of insurance value. To quote the authors: "Currently, environmental economists interested in valuing resilience of ecosystems regard it not as a property but as natural capital (stock) yielding a 'natural insurance' service (flow) which can be interpreted as a benefit amenable for inclusion in cost benefit analysis."

CHAPTER 8

# Placing a Value on Human Life

A ANY COMPREHENSIVE ASSESSMENT OF THE ECONOMIC EFFECTS of major projects must address the thorny issue of valuing human life. This process raises three central questions: How does one measure the value of life? What are the ethical implications of doing so? And, ethically, should we attempt to attach a dollar value to human life itself? It is argued here that the question of whether we should attach a monetary value to life is basically irrelevant due to the fact that every public project entails some non-zero risk to human life. As a consequence, in making a choice among alternative projects, society is making an implicit judgment about the value of life. Making this value explicit leads to a more efficient, rational, and equitable decision process.

One of the principal objections to this process of monetization is that life is sacrosanct; infinite in value; and, as a consequence, one cannot and must not attach a monetary value to it. If this were the case, then society could not undertake any action at all because of the universality of non-zero risk to human life from all forms of human activity. What are the implications then of refusing to value life and therefore attaching a de facto value of zero to life? Consider the following choice between two alternatives:

**Project A**: net benefits of $10,000,000 with a risk to human life of x

or

**Project B**: net benefits of $11,000,000 with a risk to human life of x + y, where y > 0

If we value human life at zero (by refusing to attach a value to it), then we will always choose Project B, even though it has a higher risk to human life, and *regardless of the size of that risk*. Therefore, to make rational and equitable decisions, we have to be in a position to assess if the extra benefits are worth the extra risk to life. This generally requires valuing life.

Under U.S. Executive Order 12291 issued by President Reagan in February 1981, federal government agencies were required to conduct risk-benefit analyses of proposed regulatory actions. The rationale was that "regulatory action shall not be undertaken unless the potential benefits to society from the regulation outweigh the potential costs to society." Incorporated in these risk-benefit studies are explicit or implicit values for life. In practice, values for human life under the Reagan administration varied markedly by the federal government department. For example, the value for the FAA was $650,083; for the EPA $400,000–$ 7 million; for OSHA $2–$5 million, and for the Office of Management and Budget $22,000. This last figure was both anomalous and contentious as it was intended to estimate the value of life in proposed regulations to increase restrictions on asbestos. This value was based on a figure of $1 million per lost life but discounted over 40 years to represent the average latency period of asbestos-related cancer. It has been suggested that the logic behind this value was a result of political considerations driving science rather than the reverse.

More recent American federal government estimates include the U.S. EPA at $9.1 million, the FDA at $7.9 million, and the Transportation Department at $6 million (*New York Times*, February 16, 2011). In fact, there are a variety of methodologies that have been suggested for the valuation of life. The challenge is to identify a measure that is both economically and ethically acceptable. Table 8–1 lists seven possible measures and the conceptual problems associated with each. Despite the ethical issues associated with the first option, it is commonly used in legal awards and settlements.

| TABLE 8.1 *Alternative Proposals for Valuing Life* | PROPOSALS | PROBLEMS |
|---|---|---|
| | 1. Discounted P.V. of person's expected future earnings | – based on the principle of maximizing GDP as the only criterion<br>– unequal treatment of people by gender, age, occupation, social status, extent of disabilities |
| | 2. Discounted P.V. of losses accruing to others as a result of a particular individual's death | – ignores feelings of potential victims<br>– what about retired people? |
| | 3. Society makes implicit value judgments through the political process in investments | – inconsistent<br>– not determined democratically |
| | 4. The insurance premium that a person is willing to pay | – what if there is no beneficiary? |
| | 5. The chemical value of a body's constituents | – too little ($8.37 — NTY, June 26, 1985)<br>– 5 lbs. calcium, 1.5 lbs. phosphorus, 9 oz. potassium, 6 oz. sulphur, 1 oz. magnesium, > 1 oz. iron, copper and iodine |
| | 6. Infinity | – unworkable because all projects entail some risk to life |
| | 7. The going price for a contract murder | – hardly acceptable on ethical grounds, besides, it varies — $10,000 in NYC or $0 if it is for practice or to establish your credentials |

If each of these seven alternatives is philosophically unacceptable, then one is left with no apparently defensible alternatives. One solution to this dilemma has been provided by the late Ezra Mishan (1971, 1972), an English economist who was a world-recognized expert on cost-benefit analysis. According to Mishan, ethical considerations demand that the value of human life should ultimately be determined by the person whose life is at risk. This value should be based on the minimum sum that a person is "willing to accept" in exchange for giving up his/her life. The question naturally arises as to how this proposal would work in practice. One could certainly not ask each individual how much money he/she is willing to accept to face certain death tomorrow. Mishan proposed a way around this dilemma. If a person is indifferent between (1) not assuming a particular risk, and (2) assuming the risk along with a sum of money "V," then the sum "V" can be used to derive the relevant life value of the person being exposed to that risk. Consider the following example. Assume that a worker is in a high-risk industry where the risk of death is 1/10,000 per year. Assume also that the worker was offered another job where the risk is marginally higher (say, 2/10,000 per year) and is willing to do so for another $300 per year in pay. Then the implicit value that worker is putting on his/her life is: $300/.0001 = $3,000,000. The problem that this approach raises is that it is impractical for the government to ask everyone affected by a particular policy decision to go through a similar exercise as this process would be extremely time consuming and expensive.

One possible solution to this problem is to approach it statistically by looking at the job choices made by large groups of people where one knows both the wages/salaries and risks associated with the jobs. Professor Kip Viscusi, an economist at Duke University, has attempted this large-group, statistical approach to valuing human life (Viscusi 1983, 2002). For example, if a certain job carries a fatality risk of 1 in every 10,000 workers in a year, and if workers are willing to face that risk for $300 in additional pay, then that group of workers values one of its members' lives at $3 million ($300 x 10,000 workers). Viscusi's empirical results have ranged from a low of $600,000 per statistical life for workers in high-risk industries such as mining and oil rigging where the death rate is 1/1000/year to a high of $7–$10 million for white collar workers.

There are at least four conceptual challenges to the application of Viscusi's theoretical approach: (1) society must be able to determine the relevant level of risk with some precision; (2) this information must be available to the worker; (3) society must be convinced that the worker understands the significance of the risk data; and (4) workers must have the freedom to choose, free of any external constraints, such as job availability. In sum, in order to operationalize this theory, one must assume (a) a highly accurate method of determining risks; (b) a perfect market in information; (c) rational information processing by individuals; and (d) a perfect, smoothly functioning labor market. None of these conditions is usually satisfied in practice.

In 2010 the U.S. EPA published a report that included a survey of over six dozen American and international studies that valued mortality risk reductions. This survey included both stated preference data and hedonic wage data. The values ranged from $0.04–$76 million per statistical life with an average of $9.24 million.

In an attempt to skirt the thorny issue of placing a value on life for use in a cost-benefit or risk-benefit analysis, an alternative approach has evolved known as the

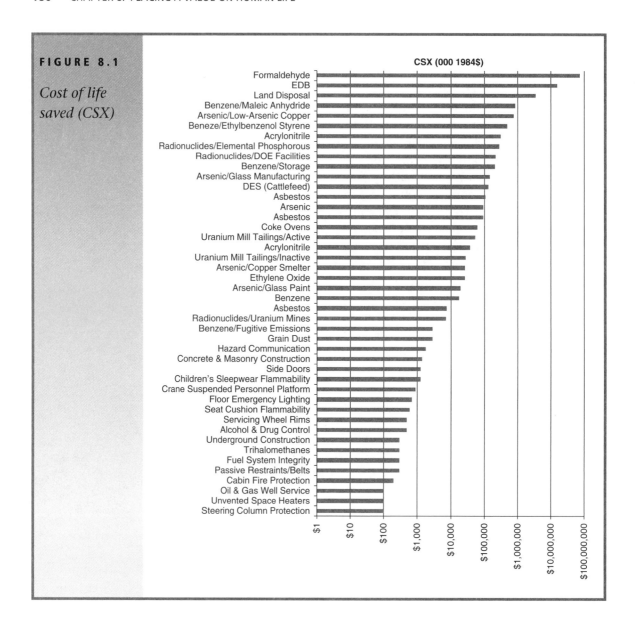

**FIGURE 8.1**

*Cost of life saved (CSX)*

*cost of life saved* (CSX). This methodology is supposedly a type of cost-effectiveness analysis that examines the different values placed by society on life in different contexts and attempts to suggest an efficient reallocation of scare societal resources in order to save the most lives (Morrall 2003; Tengs et al. 1995). When one examines these implicit values, one sees vast differences. [See Figure 8–1.] There is one deficiency with this CSX graph, as lives are never "saved" per se, merely prolonged. So instead of net additional cost (in $) per life saved, we should consider the net additional cost (in $) per life-year saved. This dollar amount is calculated as the quotient of the cost per life saved and the average life expectancy gained by individuals whose lives are saved/prolonged. This type of revised calculation preserves the rank ordering of alternative regulations, but the risk values are significantly lower.

There are at least three conceptual problems with the CSX methodology. First, this methodology ignores risks other than human life and death (e.g., nonfatal health problems); second, counting life-years lost instead of lives lost discriminates against older people (i.e., a measure that saves the lives of the elderly/middle aged is not as good as one that saves the lives of the middle aged/young); and, third, CSX is basically cost-benefit analysis masquerading as cost effectiveness. The critical assumption in CSX is that the benefits (i.e., the value of a life) are held constant, and only the costs of saving or prolonging that life vary. That is, the critical assumption is that each and every human life is equivalent in value under all circumstances—society views the loss of one life in all circumstances in an equivalent manner (i.e., a risk is a risk).

However, we know this to be invalid. Individuals and society implicitly and explicitly place a value on human life that varies by time, place and type of risk. By way of example, in 2008, there were 37,261 vehicle accident deaths in the United States (Ward's Automotive Group 2010). Imagine an equivalent number of deaths from a series of medium-range commercial jets crashes *every day of the year* with an average loss of life of 102 people per crash (i.e., 365 x 102 = 37,230). Society is clearly not indifferent between these two scenarios. Figure 8–2 addresses this apparent anomaly by outlining the numerous characteristics of risks that cause them to be perceived or valued differently.

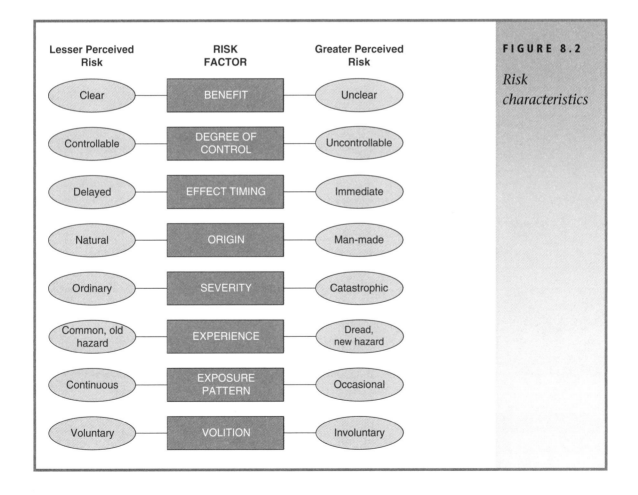

| Lesser Perceived Risk | RISK FACTOR | Greater Perceived Risk |
|---|---|---|
| Clear | BENEFIT | Unclear |
| Controllable | DEGREE OF CONTROL | Uncontrollable |
| Delayed | EFFECT TIMING | Immediate |
| Natural | ORIGIN | Man-made |
| Ordinary | SEVERITY | Catastrophic |
| Common, old hazard | EXPERIENCE | Dread, new hazard |
| Continuous | EXPOSURE PATTERN | Occasional |
| Voluntary | VOLITION | Involuntary |

**FIGURE 8.2**

*Risk characteristics*

In conclusion, the practice of placing an economic value on human life seems like an inescapable necessity, yet most methods of so doing present either conceptual or empirical problems of implementation. The remedy is to choose one or more methods carefully, fully explain the assumptions therein, and attempt to arrive at a reasonably robust estimate that is ethically defensible. Some progress in this direction has already been achieved by government agencies that assign values to life independent of gender, age, or physical condition.

The most important distinction is between two radically different uses of this methodology: (a) government-based cost-benefit analyses that incorporate estimates of the value of human life with the express purpose of reducing the number of lives at risk, and (b) those analyses that incorporate such estimates in order to justify policies that may endanger lives. Several well-known examples of the latter include corporate calculations concerning gas tanks placement in the Ford Pinto, GM trucks, and Boeing jetliners (Birsch and Fielder 1994; Negroni 2000; *New York Times*, July 10, 1999). Perhaps the most notorious example of the dubious ethical application of this methodology is associated with a report prepared for the government of Czechoslovakia in 1999 by Philip Morris (Little 2000) and used to justify the sale and use of tobacco in that country. A brief summary of this report is provided in the appendix to this chapter.

## CITED REFERENCES AND RECOMMENDED READINGS

Birsch, Douglas and John Fielder (1994) *The Ford Pinto Case*, New York: State University of New York Press.

Hahn, Robert W. and Paul C. Tetlock (2008) "Has Economic Analysis Improved Regulatory Decisions," *Journal of Economic Perspectives* Vol. 22, No. 1, Winter, pp. 67–84.

Little, Arthur D. (2000) "Public Finance Balance of Smoking in the Czech Republic," report commissioned by Philip Morris CR.

Mishan, Ezra (1971) *Cost-benefit Analysis: An Introduction*, New York: Praeger Publishers.

Mishan, Ezra (1972) *Elements of Cost-benefit analysis*, London: George Allen & Unwin.

Morrall, John F. (2003) "Saving Lives: A Review of the Record," *Journal of Risk and Uncertainty* 27(3), pp. 221–237.

Negroni, Christine (2000) *Deadly Departure: Why the Experts Failed to Prevent the TWA Flight 800 Disaster and How It Could Happen Again*, New York: Cliff Street Books.

*New York Times* (1999) "Jury awards family $4.9B Against GM," July 10.

*New York Times* (2011) "As U.S. Agencies Put More Value on a Life, Businesses Fret" February 16.

Tengs, Tammy O. et al. (1995) "Five-Hundred Life-Saving Interventions and their Cost-effectiveness," *Risk Analysis* 15(3), pp. 369–390.

U.S. Environmental Protection Agency (EPA) (2010) *Regulatory Impact Analysis (RIA) for Existing Stationary Compression Ignition Engines NESHAP*.

Viscusi, W. Kip and Joseph E. Aldy (2002) "The Value of a Statistical Life: A Critical Review of Market Estimates throughout the World," Harvard Law School [see also same title NBER 2003 WP 9487].

Ward's Automotive Group (2010) *Motor Vehicle Facts & Figures*, Southfield MI.

## APPENDIX

# Philip Morris's Report to the Government of Czechoslovakia

In 1999, Philip Morris Ltd. commissioned a study to measure the budgetary implications of smoking in the Czech Republic (Little 2000). The specific aim of this report was to "determine whether costs imposed on public finance by smokers are offset by tobacco-related tax contributions and *external positive effects of smoking*" [italics added]. The last phrase was curious since, outside the confines of the tobacco industry, it is probably fair to say that there are few, if any, perceived positive effects of smoking. Table 8–2 summarizes Philip Morris's categories of both negative and positive results of smoking with their estimated monetary values. It is apparent that this report considers the shorter life expectancy of smokers as a benefit to the public treasury due to a reduction in health-care costs and pensions. Needless to say, Philip Morris attempted to remove this report from public circulation after the negative response to the macabre conclusions became apparent.

| INCOME AND POSITIVE EXTERNAL EFFECTS | 21,463 MIL CZK | | |
|---|---|---|---|
| Savings on housing for elderly | 28 mil CZK | | **TABLE 8.2** |
| Pension and social expenses due to early mortality | 196 mil CZK | | |
| Health care costs savings due to early mortality | 968 mil CZK | | *Philip Morris'* |
| Customs duty | 354 mil CZK | | *Estimates of* |
| Corporate income tax | 747 mil CZK | | *the Monetary* |
| Value-added tax | 3,521 mil CZK | | *Effects in* |
| Excise tax | 15,648 mil CZK | | *Smoking in the Czech Republic* |
| | | | |
| **SMOKING RELATED PUBLIC FINANCE COSTS** | **15,647 mil CZK** | | |
| Fire induced costs | 49 mil CZK | | |
| Lost income tax due to higher mortality | 1,367 mil CZK | | |
| Days out of work related public finance costs | 1,667 mil CZK | | |
| ETS related health care cots | 1,142 mil CZK | | |
| Smoking (first hand) related health care costs | 11,422 mil CZK | | |
| **NET BALANCE** | **5,815 mil CZK** | | |

*Source:* Arthur D. Little 2000, p.2

# CHAPTER 9

# Risk Analysis and the Precautionary Principle

Because risks are ubiquitous, risk analysis is a common tool used by government, business, and individuals, whether consciously or not. Risk (R) is defined as the product of accident consequences (C) and accident probability (P); that is, R = C x P. For example, if the probability of an accident is $10^{-1}$/year, and the average number of deaths per accident is 100, then the risk is 1/10 x 100 = 10 deaths/year. The discussion in this chapter focuses on technological risk and the threat to human health and life, rather than financial risk.

One of the most notorious public pronouncements on the subject of risk was enunciated by the former Secretary of Defense under the Bush administration, Donald Rumsfeld (2002), when he stated in the context of dangers in Iraq: "Reports that say that something hasn't happened are always interesting to me, because as we know, there are known knowns; there are things we know we know. We also know there are known unknowns; that is to say we know there are some things we do not know. But there are also unknown unknowns—the ones we don't know we don't know." While the public and press were perplexed by this apparently bizarre statement, in fact, Rumsfeld had enunciated a fundamental principle of risk analysis.

Table 9–1 presents some crucial concepts and terminology in the field of risk analysis. Note their correspondence to the speech given by Rumsfeld. This table builds upon the work of Frank Knight (1921) by dividing the nature of risks into four categories: (1) Certainty—which is not technically risk per se—where we are aware of the consequences of an event or decision and know that consequence is certain to occur; that is, its probability is 1.0. (2) Risk—where the consequences of an event or decision are known but not with precision. In this case, a probability distribution is used to define the outcomes. (3) Uncertainty—a situation where the consequences are known but the probability of occurrence is unknown. (4) "Wicked Problems"—a series of outcomes that society does not even know the existence of, let alone their probability. Table 9–2, drawn from a recent study commissioned by the European Environment Agency (Harremoes 2001) provides an example of each category.

The concept of risk can be used effectively in informing both governmental and corporate decision making. The World Economic Forum (2011) has produced a report that focuses on the broad range of global risks facing both public and private sector decision makers. Figure 9–1 places these multifaceted risks, many of which are environmentally related, in an impact-likelihood framework. Of particular usefulness to corporate decision making is a risk matrix that subdivides, or decomposes,

**TABLE 9.1**

*Some Risk Analysis Terminology*

| | CONSEQUENCES (SINGLE OR MULTIPLE) | PROBABILITY OF OCCURRENCE |
|---|---|---|
| **CERTAINTY** | known | 1 |
| **RISK** | known | probability distribution |
| **UNCERTAINTY** | known | unknown |
| **"WICKED" PROBLEMS** | unknown | unknown |

**TABLE 9.2**

*Examples of Categories in Risk Analysis*

| | CASE STUDY EXAMPLES |
|---|---|
| **RISK** | *Known impacts and known probabilities:*<br>e.g., **asbestos** causing respiratory disease, lung and mesotheliomat |
| **UNCERTAINTY** | *Known impacts and unknown probabilities:*<br>e.g., **antibiotics in animal feed** and development of bacterial resistance |
| **IGNORANCE or "WICKED" PROBLEMS** | *Unknown impacts and therefore unknown probabilities:*<br>e.g., surprises of **CFCs** and their destruction of the ozone layer |

*Source:* Harremoes 2001, p. 192

the consequences and frequency of outcomes, as illustrated in Figure 9–2. Each cell in the matrix is given a color to signify its importance or potential threat to corporate operations and profitability. Figure 9–3 applies example numerical data to demonstrate how this matrix could be operationalized. The critical nature of the results progresses from the lower left of the matrix—where results are considered unambiguously acceptable—to the upper right, where results are progressively the following: acceptable with controls, undesirable, highly undesirable, and totally unacceptable. While it may seem intuitively obvious that a firm would wish to minimize its risks, there is frequently a linkage between opportunities and risks, inducing firms to balance potential gains and losses in light of their degree of risk tolerance or aversion.

## PROBABILISTIC RISK ASSESSMENT

A central methodology in risk analysis is probabilistic risk assessment (PRA), which measures the probability and severity of major threats to human life, safety, and the environment. PRA is of particular usefulness today because of complex modern technologies and their capabilities to cause a large degree of damage—either by

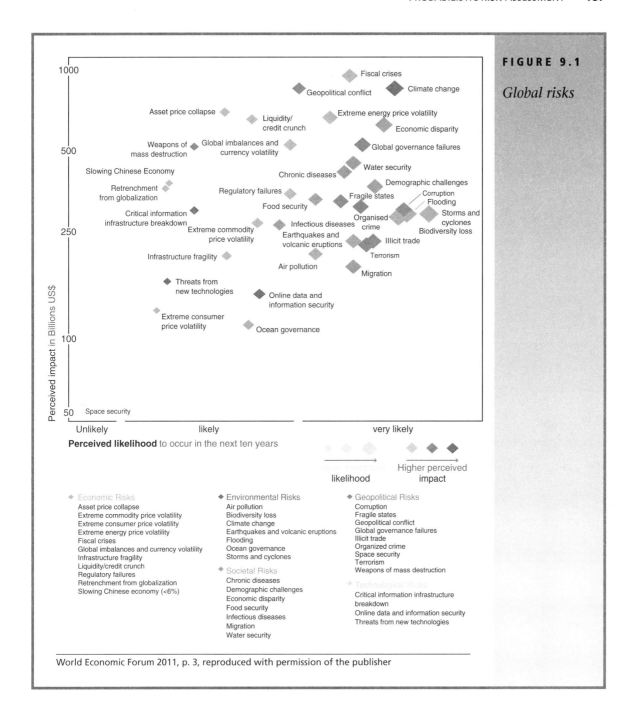

World Economic Forum 2011, p. 3, reproduced with permission of the publisher

accident or intentionally. Examples of PRA include studies of hydrodams, nuclear power plants, chemical factories, etc. There are a number of ways to derive probability estimates used in this type of analysis:

(a) *The Actuarial Method* is used in cases where there is substantial recorded experience, and the accident probability can be determined directly from these data.

(b) *Fault trees* start with the definition of the undesired event whose probability is to be determined, then the analysis works backward to examine all possible

**FIGURE 9.2**

*Risk matrix*

|  | Negligible | Marginal | Serious | Very Serious |
|---|---|---|---|---|
| Frequent | IV | II | I | I |
| Probable | IV | III | II | I |
| Occcasional | V | IV | III | II |
| Remote | V | V | IV | III |

**FIGURE 9.3**

*Risk matrix with possible values*

|  | Injury or illness $2K-$10K OR damage $0.1-$1M | Injury or illness $10K-$200K OR damage $1-$10M | Permanent disability or illness $200K-$1M OR damage $10-$100M | Death or total disability >$1M OR damage >$100M |
|---|---|---|---|---|
| $> 10^{-1}$ | Acceptable as is | Highly Undesirable | Unacceptable | Unacceptable |
| $10^{-1}-10^{-2}$ | Acceptable as is | Undesirable | Highly Undesirable | Unacceptable |
| $10^{-2}-10^{-3}$ | Acceptable as is | Acceptable with controls | Undesirable | Highly Undesirable |
| $10^{-3}-10^{-4}$ | Acceptable as is | Acceptable as is | Acceptable with controls | Undesirable |

contributory causes (U.S. NRC 1981). Figure 9–4 illustrates a highly simplified fault tree that depicts the possible precursors to the release of radioactive wastes to the biosphere (McGrath 1974). The final probability can be computed from the probabilities assigned to each of the preceding risk factors. The U.S. Nuclear Regulatory has produced numerous studies utilizing fault tree analysis to estimate the probability of both minor and major accident sequences at American reactors. One of the first and most detailed of these was the *Reactor Safety Study. An Assessment of Accident Risk in U.S. Commercial Nuclear Power Plants* (WASH-1400), which established baselines for subsequent analyses (U.S. NRC 1975). While this was a generic study, some more recent reports have attempted to generate risk estimates on a plant-specific basis (U.S. NRC 1991). The findings of these reports indicated a marked disparity in potential system risk depending upon, inter alia, susceptibility to flooding, proximity to geological faults, and high population density. Because much of the data used to construct fault trees is the result of expert opinion that is subjective in nature, and because such uncertainties can be compounded by the serial multiplication of probabilities throughout the fault tree, the results can have a significant degree of imprecision. This issue has been particularly contentious with respect to the U.S. NRC's estimates of serious reactor accidents such as core melts (Cochrane 2011; Lochbaum 2011; U.S. NRC 1978). This type of problem was graphically illustrated by the 2011 Fukishima reactor accident in Japan where the sequence of events that led to the catastrophic meltdowns in four nuclear reactors had been totally unanticipated.

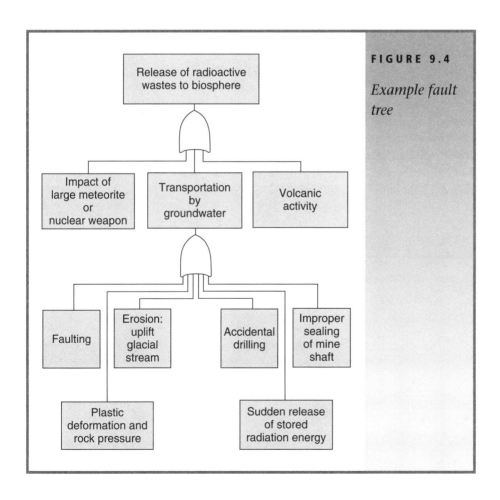

**FIGURE 9.4**

*Example fault tree*

(c) *Event trees* are similar to fault trees, but the logic is used in reverse; that is, the event tree starts with an initiating event and asks to what states of the system it might lead.

Figure 9–5 is a highly simplified version of the most probable sequence for a catastrophic failure in a Nuclear Pressurized Water Reactor (PWR) (Crouch and Wilson 1980; Wilson and Crouch 1982). The overall probability of the accident is the product of all probabilities along the branches of the tree. In this example, probabilities are derived from a number of sources, including actuarial data on pipe breaks and unfavorable weather from past experience, and expert opinion where a sufficiently accurate actuarial database cannot be constructed. There are two basic assumptions in event tree analysis: (i) the analysis is assumed to be complete; that is, the event trees calculated include all possible accident paths; or at least all those with a major contribution to risk; and (ii) the probabilities are assumed unrelated to one another (e.g., that $p_1$, $p_2$, $p_3$, and $p_4$ are in fact independent). If interdependencies are known, then these can be formally incorporated into the analysis. The validity of PRA can be compromised by the existence of unknown correlation between paths, commonly referred to as *common mode failures*. Two archetypal examples of this type of failure are the 1975 accident at the Tennessee Valley Authority's Brown's Ferry nuclear reactor accident in Alabama (U.S. NRC 1975), and the March 2011 Fukushima reactor accident in Japan. In the first case, when a worker used a candle to check for air leaks in the basement of the reactor building, the flame ignited a tray of plastic covered cables, burning through all of them. It turned out that multiple system power cables had been routed through this one tray leading to the simultaneous disabling of supposedly independent safety systems.

In the second case, Japan's Fukishima reactors had been designed to sustain the shock from an earthquake event and had an independent diesel back-up power system outside the reactor building to provide emergency power in the case that power was lost. The unanticipated common mode failure on March 11, 2011, was the combined effect of (i) the direct earthquake shock to the reactor, which disabled the primary power source; and (ii) the indirect effect of the earthquake, which induced a tsunami. The resulting massive ocean wave breeched protective seawalls,

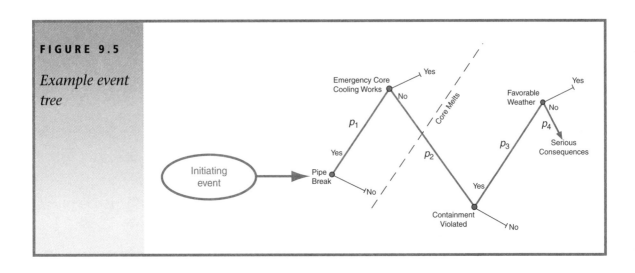

**FIGURE 9.5**

*Example event tree*

inundating and disabling the diesel power units located close to the shore at too low of an elevation.

## RISK-BENEFIT ANALYSIS (RBA)

RBA combines PRA and Cost-Benefit Analysis (CBA) in social decision making. This methodology received a major impetus in February 1981 when President Reagan issued Executive Order 12291 (subsequently modified by President Clinton), which required federal government agencies to conduct risk-benefit analyses of proposed regulatory actions. The stated rationale was that "regulatory action shall not be undertaken unless the potential benefits to society from the regulation outweigh the potential costs to society" (U.S. Archives 1981). Figure 9–6 presents an idealized model of RBA, which a government agency would be expected to employ in determining whether a given project or undertaking was worth pursuing. RBA is principally a modification of CBA to explicitly account for risk. CBA entails the discounting of a stream of anticipated costs and benefits that can be subject to some uncertainty. In those cases, expected values (EV) of outcomes are generally used, where EV is the summation of the products of probability and consequences across all outcomes. In RBA, there are at least two major differences: (1) the "costs" may entail risks to health and life of plants, animals or ecosystems; and (2) the outcomes and their probabilities are much less certain (e.g., uncertainty and "wickedness"). In such circumstances, it is common practice to use wide uncertainty bands or safety factors. There are at least two major generic uses of RBA in the public sector: (i) before introducing a new product (such as a pesticide) with *known benefits but uncertain costs*; or (ii) before introducing a new regulation (such as tightening a pollution standard inside or outside a factory), with *known costs but uncertain benefits*.

Aside from the problems associated with measuring and predicting risk, there are several other major complexities once questions of risk enter the arena of public decision making: (a) the perception of risk, (b) the valuation of risk, and (c) the manner in which the risk is calculated or framed.

The objective measurable risk of an accident (if such an objective measurement is possible) is not necessarily equivalent to perceived risk by the public. Consider the empirical data in Figure 9–7 comparing the perceptions of experts and the general public (Lichtenstein et al. 1978). There is a clear bias in the discrepancy between the perception of the public and that of experts who frequently base their assessments on empirical data. The general pattern is one of public overestimation of high visibility, high dread but rare events; and underestimation of conventional, more frequent events. There are several explanations for this deviation. For example, the media tend to focus on rare events that elicit a high emotional response from the public (Lichtenstein et al. 1978).

The underlying question is whether differences in public attitudes toward the severity of risk are due to ignorance—which can be corrected with education—or a legitimate aspect of public values to be considered in social decision making (Schrader-Frechette 1991). There are numerous characteristics of risks that cause them to be perceived and/or valued differently, as illustrated in Figure 8.2. The timing and magnitude of risk appear to play an important role in their assessment

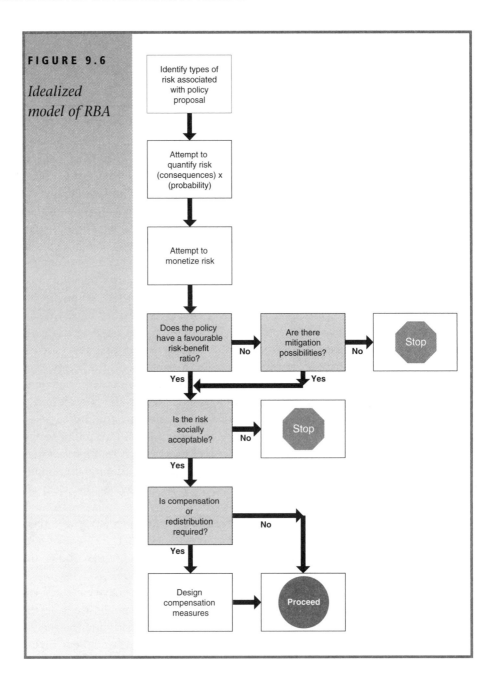

**FIGURE 9.6**

*Idealized model of RBA*

by the general public. Consider how the public might perceive two radically different accident scenarios: *Scenario #1*: 39,800 traffic deaths per year—the actual number of such occurrences in the United States in 2008 (Wards 2010); or *Scenario #2*:
one fatal crash per day of a midsized jet, each carrying an average of 109 passen-
gers. From a simple risk perspective, these are equivalent. In each of the scenarios,
the same number of people die per year, yet it is clear that the public would react
quite differently in each case. In fact, the chances are that public travel by airplane
would fall significantly after as few as 3 or 4 crashes in succession. Why should this
be so? The answer is based on the aforementioned characteristics of risk, which

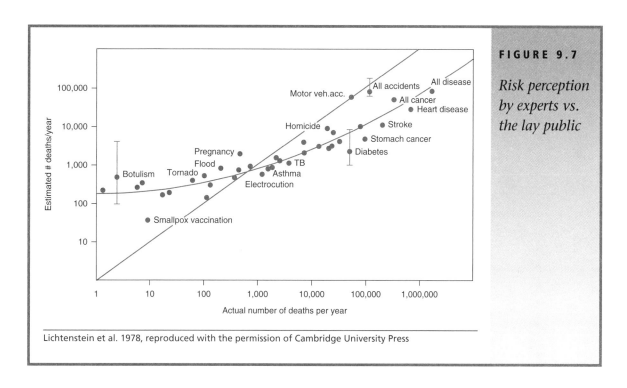

Lichtenstein et al. 1978, reproduced with the permission of Cambridge University Press

**FIGURE 9.7**

*Risk perception by experts vs. the lay public*

elicit different public reactions. In this case, they include: (a) a dread factor; (b) a control factor—people tend to assign a greater risk to flying because of a lack of control, as opposed to a common, and erroneous, sense that they can control the risk of accidents in an automobile because they are driving; and (c) a frequency factor—automobile accidents are common and taken for granted; airplane accidents are not.

Regardless of whether these perceptions are considered rational, there is one additional factor that appears to have unambiguous legitimacy. Rare accidents with large numbers of injuries or fatalities pose a greater risk to the fabric of a society—whether it be a local community or the nation as a whole. This is one manifestation of the *zero-infinity dilemma* where the expected value of an accident may be low, but the consequence predominates. A cogent example is the rare occurrence of nuclear reactor accidents. At least one public agency (the U.S. Nuclear Regulatory Commission) has incorporated this nonlinear public perception of risks into its decision making. Called the *Alpha Model*, the methodology constructs what is termed the *Equivalent Social Cost*, defined as (Frequency) x (Consequences)$^a$, where the exponent on the consequences term a > 1. One of the examples used by the NRC to illustrate the application of this methodology recognizes the important perceptual difference between early deaths after a nuclear accident compared to deaths from the delayed onset of radiation-induced cancer. In the NRC model, the social costs for delayed cancer deaths have a value of 1.0, but the social costs for early deaths have a value of 1.2. Even such an apparently low exponent as 1.2 can have a major impact on the value of the equivalent social cost if the consequences (in this case, deaths) are large in number (Griesmeyer and Okrent 1981; Okrent et al. 1981).

The alpha model presaged the emergence of radically new thinking in the area of public sector decision making in the face of low probability-high consequence events. The traditional rational choice model assumes that governments will calculate the expected values of possible events (i.e., probability x consequence) and choose the option with the highest net benefits. The underlying assumption is that because of their size and long-term view, governments can be risk neutral in decisions that affect society as a whole. With the emergence of ecological scenarios that include rare, but possibly catastrophic consequences, the calculus of decision making has evolved. In probabilistic terms, the terminology for such events is called *fat tails*, referring to the extreme right tail of the probability distribution of outcomes. Such phenomena are not uncommon and are found in such diverse areas as flood insurance claims, crop loss, natural disasters, hospital discharge bills, finance, and nuclear power (Cooke and Nieboer 2011, Mandelbrot and Hudson 2004). In the context of climate change, Kousky et al. (2009) observe that "Catastrophes are of particular concern because, while an exact quantification is not possible, the most extreme adverse impacts from climate change (e.g., the worst 1% of scenarios) may account for a large portion of expected losses. Consequently, focusing primarily on more likely or anticipated (albeit serious) outcomes may miss much of the problem in terms of risks from climate change."

The framing of risk calculations also entails significant complexities. The critical importance of the issue of *framing* was first recognized by Kahneman and Tversky in their seminal work on the rationality of (or lack thereof) the human mind in perceptions and decision making (Tversky and Kahneman 1974, 1981; Kahneman et al. 1982). Consider the simple question of which mode of travel is riskier: cars or airplanes? Many people have a pathological fear of flying and are convinced that aircraft travel is inherently much riskier than travel by automobile. Table 9–3 presents comparative data for both travel modes for two years: 2001 and 2007. On a simple calculation of number of *deaths per billion passenger miles* in both years, the risk of death from driving far outweighs the risk of flying in commercial aircraft. In contrast, if one calculates the number of *deaths per billion hours of travel*, the same marked disparity in risk appears in 2007—a very safe year for flying—but, surprisingly for 2001, when 531 people were killed in commercial airplane crashes, the ratios are quite similar. These calculations are sensitive to the assumed average speed of both modes of transport; nevertheless, the framing chosen to portray the relative risks is clearly an important consideration. These comparisons might be quite different if the much less safe accident record of all air flights, including general aviation, were to be included.

In another example of the importance of framing, Slovic and Weber (2002) describe nine ways that fatality risks associated with chemical manufacturing can be measured: (1) deaths per million people in the population, (2) deaths per million people within x miles of the source of exposure, (3) deaths per unit of concentration, (4) deaths per facility, (5) deaths per ton of air toxin released, (6) deaths per ton of air toxin absorbed by people, (7) deaths per ton of chemical produced, (8) deaths per million dollars of product produced, and (9) reduction in life expectancy associated with exposure to the hazard. The authors cite a major report by the National Research Council (Stern and Fineberg 1996) when they observe that

|  | CARS | | PLANES | | **TABLE 9.3** |
| --- | --- | --- | --- | --- | --- |
| **2007** | | | | | *Comparative* |
| # DEATHS | 43,100 | 43,100 | 1 | 1 | *Risk Data for* |
| BILLION PASSENGER-MILES | 2,640.60 | 2,640.60 | 607.50 | 607.50 | *Automotive* |
| # DEATHS PER BILLION PASSENGER MILES | 16.32 | 16.32 | 0.002 | 0.002 | *and Airplane* |
|  | | | | | *Travel 2001* |
| *ASSUMED AVERAGE SPEED* | 27.60 | 35.00 | 350.00 | 300.00 | *vs. 2007 in the* |
| THEREFORE # BILLION HOURS OF TRAVEL | 95.67 | 75.45 | 1.74 | 2.03 | *USA* |
| # DEATHS PER BILLION HOURS OF TRAVEL | 450.49 | 571.27 | 0.58 | 0.49 | |
|  | | | | | |
| **2001** | | | | | |
| # DEATHS | 42,196 | 42,196 | 531 | 531 | |
| BILLION PASSENGER-MILES | 2,556.00 | 2,556.00 | 486.50 | 486.50 | |
| # DEATHS PER BILLION PASSENGER MILES | 16.51 | 16.51 | 1.09 | 1.09 | |
|  | | | | | |
| *ASSUMED AVERAGE SPEED* | 27.60 | 35.00 | 350.00 | 300.00 | |
| THEREFORE # BILLION HOURS OF TRAVEL | 92.61 | 73.03 | 1.39 | 1.62 | |
| # DEATHS PER BILLION HOURS OF TRAVEL | 455.64 | 577.80 | 382.01 | 327.44 | |

*Sources:* Wards 2010 and US Bureau of Transportation Statistics website

Each way of summarizing deaths embodies its own set of values. For example, "reduction in life expectancy" treats deaths of young people as more important than deaths of older people, who have less life expectancy to lose. Simply counting fatalities treats deaths of the old and young as equivalent; it also treats as equivalent deaths that come immediately after mishaps and deaths that follow painful and debilitating disease or long periods during which many who will not suffer disease live in daily fear of that outcome. Using "number of deaths" as the summary indicator of risk makes no distinction between deaths of people who engage in an activity by choice and have been benefiting from that activity and deaths of people who are exposed to a hazard involuntarily and get no benefit from it. One can easily imagine a range of arguments to justify different kinds of unequal weightings for different kinds of deaths, but to arrive at any selection requires a value judgment concerning which deaths one considers most undesirable. To treat the deaths as equal also involves a value judgment.

Appendix 1 presents two classic examples of how framing can have a transformative influence on risk perception and response thereto.

## PATHOLOGIES OF PRA AND RBA

Despite the powerful tools that both PRA and RBA bring to decision making, there are numerous conceptual difficulties, or pathologies, with both of these methodologies that, on balance, suggest a more modest and supplementary role for these tools in public decision making rather than one of preeminence. Figure 9–8 has recast Figure 9–6 to portray the presence and potential role of each of these issues. There are several types of pathologies that can afflict PRA and RBA (Fairley 1977): (1) not assigning probabilities to credible threats that are difficult to quantify, (2) inadequate treatment of multiple risks and possible synergistic effects, (3) not choosing the most appropriate measure of risk, (4) common mode failures, (5) past analytical errors or oversights in the data, (6) not determining the correct dose-response relationships, (7) inability to anticipate all accident scenarios, and (8) inaccurate estimation of probabilities of anticipated accident scenarios (especially underestimates). Each of these is reviewed briefly below.

 *PRA Pathology #1: Not assigning probabilities to credible but difficult-to-quantify risks.* Estimates of the "probability" of an accident must include, explicitly or implicitly,

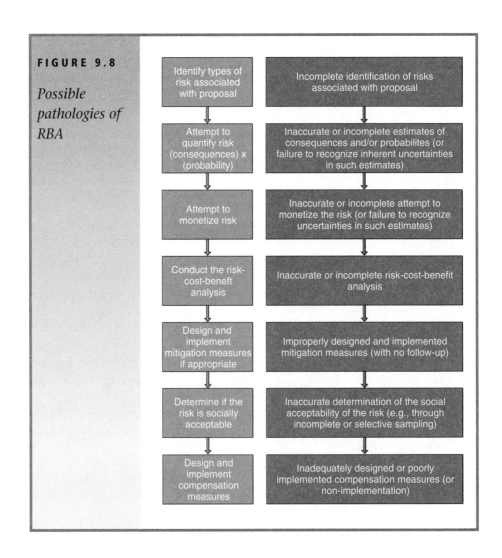

**FIGURE 9.8**

*Possible pathologies of RBA*

contributions from all possible accident sources. Consider a simple game of stud poker, and ask what is the probability of seeing at least one royal flush in a single round of play (Fairley 1977). Assume specifically that one hand is dealt, and there are four players each of whom receives five cards. Using simple combinatorial arithmetic, the probability is 1 in 162,338. Now consider recasting this problem as occurring in an environment where you do not know the other players. The probability of seeing at least one royal flush in the poker hand depends on two probabilities: the probability of the royal flush appearing naturally plus the probability of the royal flush appearing dishonestly. The probability of the royal flush appearing naturally is known: (1/162,338), but the probability of it appearing dishonestly is unknown. However, the chance of it appearing dishonestly is much greater than it appearing naturally. Therefore, a subjectively assessed probability of it appearing dishonestly, roughly set at 1/10,000 for example, swamps the natural probability: p = 1/162,338 + 1/10,000 = approximately 1/10,000.

The message from this simple exercise is that not assigning probabilities to credible but difficult-to-quantify risks is a potentially significant pathology of PRA. Estimates of the "probability" of an accident must include, explicitly or implicitly, contributions from all possible sources of an accident. Real-world examples of this type of potential error are associated with terrorism and threats to public facilities such as nuclear power reactors. The U.S. Nuclear Regulatory Commission's first comprehensive assessment of risks to nuclear power plants called WASH-1400 (U.S. NRC 1974) did not include flooding and sabotage, yet (i) flooding appears to be a potentially significant contributor to risk at some sites since nuclear plants must be located near ample supplies of water for cooling; and (ii) there seems to be little basis for justifying the probability of sabotage by terrorists as being small compared to the estimated frequency of a core melt accident (i.e., WASH-1400's estimate of 1 in 20,000 per reactor year).

Another cogent example is proved by the infamous terrorist attack on the World Trade Center on September 11, 2001. Table 9–4 speculates how an insurer might assess potential risks in the period prior to the attack. This is an archetypical

| EVENT | PROBABILITY | CONSEQUENCES FOR WTC | |
|---|---|---|---|
| Hurricane | low | none | **TABLE 9.4** |
| Earthquake | very low | very low | *Assumed* |
| Conventional explosives | low | low | *Insurer Assess-* |
| Aircraft impact - Empire State Building experience, July 28, 1945, B-25 bomber, $1 million damage, 14 dead | low | low | *ment ex ante 9–11* |
| suitcase atomic bomb | very low | very high | |
| Large jet aircraft - like Sept. 11, 2001 | unanticipated | very high | |
| other? | | | |

example of a *wicked problem* where the event was totally unanticipated yet the consequences were enormous.

*PRA Pathology #2: Multiple risk exposure.* Almost all risk analyses focus on the probability and consequences of single threats such as chemicals with potential mutagenic, teratogenic, and carcinogenic properties. However, the population is rarely exposed to single risk sources. The general pattern is exposure to a multitude of chemical agents that may act additively, synergistically, or antagonistically. Consider the example in Table 9–5 of the super-additive risk of esophageal cancer from the combined exposure of tobacco and alcohol, a not infrequent pattern of behavior (Olsen 1983, p. 223). The importance of this synergistic reaction (where

**TABLE 9.5**

*Super-Additive Risk of Tobacco and Alcohol Consumption*

| | | TOBACCO (G/DAY) | | | | ADJUSTED FOR TOBACCO |
|---|---|---|---|---|---|---|
| | | 0 TO 9 | 10 TO 19 | 20 TO 29 | 30 + | |
| Alcohol (g/day) | **0 to 39** | 1.0 | 3.0 | 4.2 | 12.0 | 1.0 |
| | **40 to 79** | 8.2 | 5.9 | 11.3 | 46.1 | 3.9 |
| | **80 to 119** | 11.9 | 22.7 | 18.0 | 159.3 | 8.0 |
| | **120 +** | 37.4 | 53.0 | 77.8 | 240.7 | 17.6 |
| | **Adjusted for alcohol** | 1.0 | 1.2 | 1.5 | 7.9 | |

*Source:* Olsen 1983

**FIGURE 9.9**

*Synergistic effects of alcohol and tobacco use on risk of esophageal cancer*

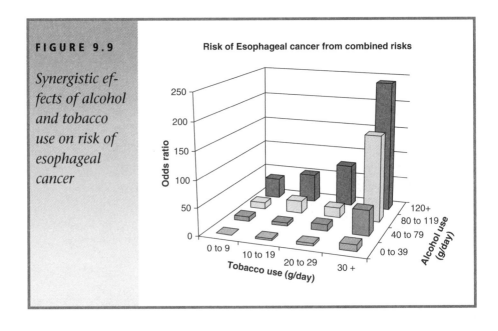

Risk of Esophageal cancer from combined risks

the combined risk is greater than the sum of the individual risks) is graphically portrayed in Figure 9–9.

*PRA Pathology #3: Choosing the right measure of risk.* See the example cited above that compares the risk of driving and flying using two different measures: deaths per billion passenger miles versus deaths per billion hours of travel.

*PRA Pathology #4: Common mode failures.* As described above, event/fault tree analysis is built on the assumption of the independence of branches. Where interdependence can be identified, it is included. Some general types of examples of events that can trigger common mode failure are flooding and earthquakes. Two of the best examples of common mode failures resulting from errors in engineering design were the aforementioned 1975 accident at Brown's Ferry nuclear reactor in the United States and the Fukushima nuclear disaster in 2011.

*PRA Pathology #5: Choosing the correct dose-response function.* This function measures damage to human health in response to a given dose of pollutant. There are several major uncertainties associated with the construction of meaningful dose-response functions. For example, the effects of short-term acute doses of pollutants can be measured reasonably well; however, it is much more difficult to measure the effects of long-term, chronic pollution exposure. Most observational data sets are based on high dosage levels within an occupational setting, and it is therefore necessary to extrapolate back to infer the shape of the dose-response function at low levels of exposure. Figure 9–10 depicts some alternative functions. There are at least two major characteristics of these functions (convexity–concavity; threshold–no threshold), which can have a profound impact on the choice of the appropriate response to a particular pollutant. Figure 9–11 provides an example of the regulatory confusion surrounding the status of saccharin as a possible carcinogen prior to the conclusion that this compound did not, in fact, pose a risk of cancer (U.S. HHS

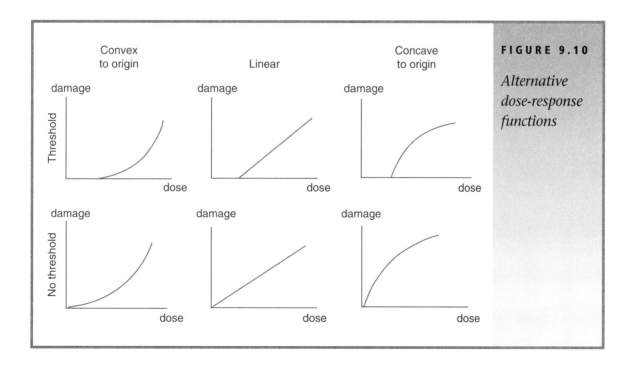

**FIGURE 9.10**

*Alternative dose-response functions*

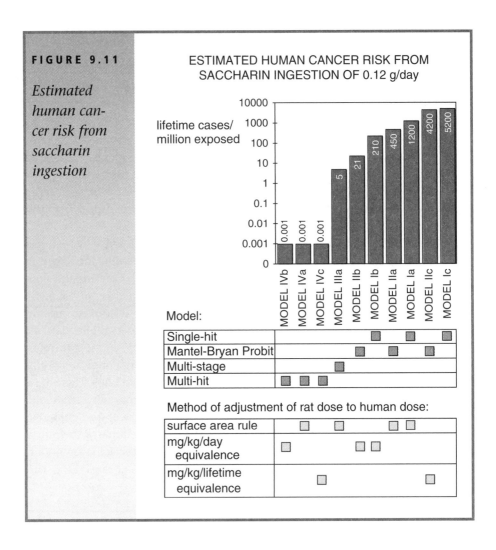

**FIGURE 9.11**

*Estimated human cancer risk from saccharin ingestion*

2011). Two conceptual issues bedeviled this analysis: first, the choice of an appropriate biological model of carcinogenesis; and, second, the method of extrapolating the dose-response of test rats to humans. When these two factors were taken into consideration, the estimated risk of cancer from a given dose of saccharin varied by almost seven orders of magnitude—obviously rendering impossible a scientifically defensible regulation.

*PRA Pathology #6: Past analytical errors or oversights in the data.* Post-WWII radiation standards were initially based on epidemiological data drawn from cancer victims who initially survived the atomic bombs dropped on Hiroshima and Nagasaki. Subsequent discovery of major errors in the calculation of gamma ray and neutron radiation forced a major reexamination of these standards. In deriving the dose-response functions that measure the level of cancer risk associated with a given level of radiation exposure, it was assumed that a large group of workers in a Mitsubishi steel factory in Nagasaki had been standing outside the factory. The Mitsubishi building was made of steel and concrete and contained heavy machinery. However,

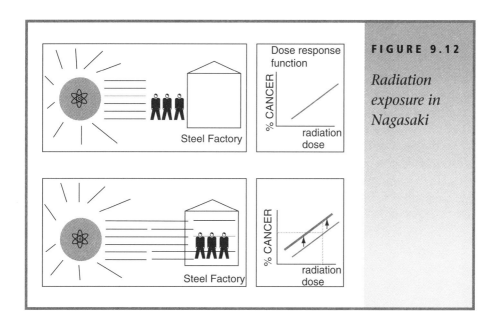

**FIGURE 9.12**

*Radiation exposure in Nagasaki*

Dose response function

% CANCER

radiation dose

Steel Factory

% CANCER

radiation dose

Steel Factory

many of the workers were actually inside the factory and shielded from much of the radiation (*Science* 1981). Figure 9–12 is a schematic representation of the error and its consequences for the standard-setting process. The recalibration of the estimated dose received by the workers shifted the dose-response function to the left, thereby necessitating a revision of standards.

*PRA Pathology #7: The inability to anticipate all accident scenarios.* Two relatively recent examples illustrate this pathology. The first was the existence of operator error in the near meltdown of the Three Mile Island nuclear reactor in Pennsylvania in 1979 (Stephens 1980, Report of the President's Commission 1979). This case was particularly instructive in the reexamination of assumptions considering the normal operation of modern technology. It highlighted the critical problem of understanding the nature of the human-machine interface and human behavior in conditions of boredom, disease, fatigue, stress, deviation from standard operating procedures, etc. The second example was the catastrophic failure of cargo doors on DC-10 jet airlines in the 1970s. Unlike other aircraft, the cargo door of the DC-10 was designed to open out rather than in. The first problem was revealed in 1972, when American Airlines Flight 96 lost its aft cargo door after takeoff from Detroit. On Flight 96, airport employees had forced the door shut, weakening the locking pin and causing the door to blow out as it reached altitude. In 1974 another DC-10, owned by Turkish Airlines, crashed into a forest shortly after leaving Paris's Orly Airport and killed 346 people. A modified seating configuration on the Turkish aircraft caused its control cables to be severed when the cargo door was lost, rendering the aircraft uncontrollable (Fielder and Birsch 1992). The design team that built the DC-10 had been unable to identify these scenarios as possible risks despite conducting an a priori risk analysis.

*PRA Pathology #8: Inaccurate estimation of probabilities of anticipated accident scenarios (especially underestimates).* There is a fundamental problem in assigning probabilities to accidents that might be anticipated but have not yet occurred. A number of examples of this pathology have emerged from the nuclear power industry. For example, a small-break loss of coolant accident (LOCA) occurred at the Ginna nuclear plant near Rochester, New York, on January 25, 1982. Based on data in WASH-1400, the NRC's comprehensive risk analysis, this type of accident should happen about once every 40 years in the U.S. with 75 operating reactors. (i.e., once per every 3,000 reactor-years). In the 5-year period 1975–1982, there were 4 accidents of this type. In another case, the NRC had calculated that the simultaneous failure of 2 independent systems to prevent a core meltdown would occur with a probability of 1/17,000 per year, yet it happened twice in 4 days at 2 reactors in New Jersey in 1991 (*New York Times*, March 29, 2011). Although the events in both of these cases were not technically inconsistent with the original probabilistic estimates, it is much more likely that there were errors in the original risk analysis.

This discussion concludes with a brief description of two monumental failures of risk analysis to predict the nature and extent of the risks involved: the Chernobyl nuclear catastrophe of 1986, and the Challenger space shuttle disaster of the same year.

*The Chernobyl Nuclear Disaster.* On April 29, 1986, the *New York Times* headlined the Soviet announcement of a major accident at one of its nuclear power plants in the Ukraine. The subsequent massive release of radioactive material spread throughout Western Europe prompting major restrictions on the consumption of certain food products. It is unclear if a formal PRA had ever been conducted prior to the accident but, if it had, it would have provided no indication of the probability or consequences of the accident. Figure 9–13 illustrates what a risk analysis might have looked at and what it would have missed given the state of the science at the time. None of the seven major events or consequences was, or could have been, anticipated in a formal risk analysis. Despite the uniqueness of the Soviet reactor design, this is a sobering message for risk assessments of other currently operating reactors worldwide. (See also Medvedev 1989.)

*The Challenger Space Shuttle Disaster.* An equally problematic risk analysis was revealed by the United States' most devastating space accident, the loss of the Challenger spacecraft on January 28 1986. In this case, NASA had carried out an extensive risk analysis prior to the accident and calculated the risk of disaster at 1 in 10,000. This implied that NASA could launch a space shuttle every day for 25 years and not expect any equipment-based disaster. The renowned Caltech physicist, Richard Feynman, was appointed by the U.S. government to lead the investigation of the disaster (Feynman 1986; Feynman and Leighton 2001). He examined the historical data and found that of 2,900 solid rocket boosters launched, the number that failed was 121, yielding a failure ratio of 1 in 24. It is ironic but statistically meaningless that the shuttle exploded on its 25th flight. As brilliantly described in his postmortem of the accident, Edward Tufte (1997) of Yale University graphically demonstrated how NASA had completely misinterpreted its own data by graphing the historical record in a manner that was totally misleading. When Tufte reconceptualized and replotted the graphical information, the risk of the misguided launch became painfully obvious. Tufte's work is a brilliant example of the critical role that good or bad graphical information can play in decision making.

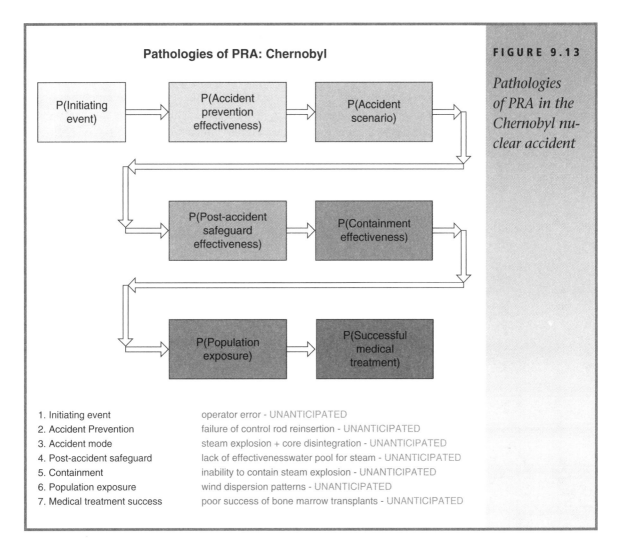

FIGURE 9.13

*Pathologies of PRA in the Chernobyl nuclear accident*

In sum, while PRA and RBA are powerful tools for the interpretation of risk, their use must be tempered by a realization of their inherent conceptual flaws. In a manner similar to CBA, these methodologies can and should be used to inform the decision-making process but not act as a sole guide to the choice of alternatives, especially those with major potential impacts on human health and the global ecosystem.

## THE PRECAUTIONARY PRINCIPLE

In light of the complexities associated with risk analysis and the diverse range of threats faced by modern society, especially catastrophic outcomes in *fat tails*, the challenge is to find a decision rule that can help protect the ecosystem and current and future generations of humanity. The *precautionary principle* is one such rule. Simply stated, it is based on the premise that we live in an uncertain world and that society cannot wait for definitive scientific proof of a potential threat before acting if that threat is both large and credible. The underlying theory is based on scientific principles largely associated with the work of ecologists such as C.S. Holling. [See further discussion in chapter 10.] Holling has demonstrated that ecosystems are nonlinear and when under stress do not necessarily adjust slowly and steadily, but may jump suddenly between alternative equilibrium states, some much less hospitable for human activity than others. The import of this theory is that by the time one recognizes or begins to feel the tangible effects of certain types of ecological threats, it may be too late to forestall or reverse the negative effects.

Variations of the precautionary principle have already been incorporated into legislation and regulation in several countries within the OECD—mostly in Europe but also in the United States. Table 9–6 lists some major examples of this principle in some international treaties and agreements. Harremoes et al. (2001) and Tickner et al. (n.d.) list 12 other such international agreements. Table 9–7 cites 4 examples of its application in the United States (Harremoes et al. 2001; UNESCO 2005).

Perhaps the most important distinction with respect to the application of the precautionary principle rests with the divergent approach to the introduction of new chemical compounds in Europe and the United States. The U.S. Toxic Substances Chemical Act (TSCA) "does not require companies to test chemicals before they notify EPA of their intent to manufacture the chemicals" (U.S. GAO 2007). To

---

**TABLE 9.6**

*Some Examples of the Precautionary Principle in International Treaties and Agreements*

| YEAR | TREATY | KEY WORDING |
|------|--------|-------------|
| 1987 | Montreal Protocol on Substances that Deplete the Ozone Layer | Parties to this protocol . . . determined to protect the ozone layer by taking **precautionary measures** to control equitably total global emissions of substances that deplete it . . . |
| 1990 | Third North Sea Conference | The participants . . . will continue to apply the **precautionary principle,** that is to take action to avoid potentially damaging impacts of substances that are persistent, toxic, and liable to bioaccumulate even where there is no scientific evidence to prove a causal link between emissions and effects |
| 1987 | London Declaration (Protection of the North Sea | Accepting that, in order to protect the North Sea from possibly damaging effects of the most dangerous substances, a precautionary approach is necessary which may require action to control inputs of such substances even before a causal link has been established by absolutely clear scientific evidence |
| 1992 | The Rio Declaration on Environment and Development | In order to protect the environment, the **Precautionary Approach** shall be widely applied by states according to their capabilities. Where there are threats of serious or irreversible damage, lack of full scientific certainty shall not be used as a reason for postponing cost-effective measures to prevent environmental degradation. |

| YEAR | TREATY | KEY WORDING |
|------|--------|-------------|
| 1992 | Framework Convention on Climate Change | The parties should take **precautionary measures** to anticipate, prevent or minimise the causes of climate change and mitigate its adverse effects. Where there are threats of serious or irreversible damage, lack of full scientific certainty should not be used as a reason for postponing such measures, taking into account that policies and measures to deal with climate change should be cost-effective so as to ensure global benefits at the lowest possible cost. |
| 1992 | Treaty on European Union (Maastricht Treaty) | Community policy on the environment . . . shall be based on the **precautionary principle** and on the principles that preventive actions should be taken, that the environmental damage should as a priority be rectified at source and that the polluter shall pay. |
| 2000 | Cartagena Protocol on Biosafety | In accordance with the **precautionary approach** the objective of this Protocol is to contribute to ensuring an adequate level of protection in the field of the safe transfer, handling and use of living modified organisms resulting from modern biotechnology that may have adverse effects on the conservation and sustainable use of biological diversity, taking also into account risks to human health, and specifically focussing on transboundary movements. |
| 2000 | EU communication on the Precautionary Principle | The precautionary principle applies where scientific evidence is insufficient, inconclusive or uncertain and preliminary scientific evaluation indicates that there are reasonable grounds for concern that the potentially dangerous effects on the environment, human, animal or plant health may be inconsistent with the high level of protection chosen by the EU. |
| 2001 | Stockholm Convention on Persistent Organic Pollutants (POPs) | Precaution, including transparency and public participation, is operationalised throughout the treaty, with explicit reference in the preamble, objective, provisions for adding POPs and determination of best available technologies. The objective states: Mindful of the **Precautionary Approach** as set forth in Principle 15 of the Rio Declaration on Environment and Development, the objective of this Convention is to protect human health and the environment from persistent organic pollutants. |

*Source:* Harremoes et al. 2001, p. 14

**TABLE 9.6**
*continued*

the General Accounting Office—an independent branch of the U.S. Congress—this provides "only limited assurance that health and environmental risks are identified." In contrast, a European Union program entitled REACH (Registration, Evaluation and Authorization of Chemicals) reverses the onus of proof (http://ec.europa.

| TABLE 9.7 | ISSUE | PRECAUTIONARY PREVENTION |
|---|---|---|
| *Some U.S. Examples of the Precautionary Principle* | **Food safety (carcinogenic additives)** | The **Delaney Clause** in the Food, Drug and Cosmetics Act, 1957-96, which banned animal carcinogens from the human food chain |
| | **Food safety (BSE)** | A ban on the use of scrapie-infected sheep and goat meat in the animal and human food chain in the early 1970s which may have helped the Untied States to avoid **BSE ("mad cow disease)** |
| | **Environmental safety (CFCs)** | A ban on the use of chlorofluorocarbons (**CFCs**) in aerosols in 1977, several years before similar action in most of Europe |
| | **Public health (DES)** | A ban on the use of **DES** as a growth promoter in beef, 1972–79, nearly 10 years before the EU ban in 1987 |

*Sources:* Unesco 2005, Harremoes et al. 2001, p. 12

eu/environment/chemicals/reach/reach_intro.htm). In contrasting the two disparate approaches to chemical regulation, the U.S. GAO concludes: "TSCA places the burden of proof on EPA to demonstrate that a chemical poses a risk to human health or the environment before EPA can regulate its production or use, while REACH generally places a burden on chemical companies to ensure that chemicals do not pose such risks or that measures are identified for handling chemicals safely." Despite this apparent contrast between the United States and European regulatory approaches toward the introduction of new chemicals, Wiener and Rogers (2002) have argued that the use of the precautionary principle is less an issue of geography than one of circumstance. They identify cases in which either Europe or the United States has taken a more proactive role. To quote: "sometimes the EU is more precautionary than the US (such as regarding hormones in beef), while sometimes the US is more precautionary than the EU (such as regarding mad cow disease in blood). Thus, neither the EU nor the US can claim to be categorically 'more precautionary' than the other. The real pattern is complex and risk-specific" (p. 317).

The issue of potential risks related to industrial chemicals is particularly important as there are in excess of 100,000 such chemicals currently in use in the world today, and their production had increased from 1 million tonnes in 1930 to over 400 million tonnes by 2001 (CEC 2001). A U.S. EPA report (1998) on the availability of data concerning potential chemical hazards reported that 2,863 organic chemicals (i.e., excluding polymers or inorganic chemicals) were either produced or imported at or above 1 million pounds per year in the United States. The report observed that: "EPA's analysis found that no basic toxicity information, i.e., neither human health nor environmental toxicity, is publicly available for 43% of the high volume chemicals manufactured in the US and that a full set of basic toxicity information is available for only 7% of these chemicals. The lack of availability of basic toxicity information on most high volume chemicals is a serious issue" (p. 2).

A recent report on the class of pervasive chemicals known as endocrine disruptors [see chapter 3] has prompted the European Environment Agency (2012) to strongly recommend the adoption of a precautionary principle with respect to their introduction and use in light of their potentially devastating impact on hormonal systems within humans and other animal species.

Another major technological development that has prompted calls for the application of the precautionary principle is in the emerging area of nanotechnology and nanomaterials (NAS 2012) where insufficient data are available on risks associated with materials that may play an increasing important role in a broad range of human activities such as energy, medicine, electronics, and clean technologies. As of 2009, the nanotechnology sector had already achieved approximately $25 billion in product sales (NAS 2012, p. 3).

The application of the precautionary principle is not an arbitrary exercise, but one that must follow strict rules of logic and proof. Table 9–8 provides a quick summary of varying levels of proof required by several national and international bodies with respect to the precautionary principle (Harremoes et al. 2001). To demonstrate the usefulness of the principle, in 2001, the European Environmental Agency published a landmark study that reexamined the history of 14 controversial cases—many involving the introduction of new chemicals—from the late 1800s to this century ((Harremoes et al. 2001). Included among these case studies were major public policy and regulatory decisions concerning fisheries, radiation, benzene, asbestos, Polychlorinated byphenols (PCBs), Halocarbons, the drug Diethylstilbestrol (DES), antimicrobials such as antibiotics added to animal feed as growth promoters, sulfur dioxide, the gasoline additive Methyl tert-butyl ether (MTBE), Great Lakes contamination, Tributyltin (TBT) antifoulants, estrogen mimickers, and Mad cow disease. It was concluded that in many of the cases (1) "early warnings" and even "loud and late" warnings were clearly ignored; (2) the scope of hazard appraisal was too narrow; and (3) regulatory actions were taken without sufficient consideration

| VERBAL DESCRIPTION | EXAMPLES | |
|---|---|---|
| "Beyond all reasonable doubt" | Criminal law; Swedish chemical law, 1973 (*for evidence of safety from manufacturers*) | **TABLE 9.8** *Various Examples of Evidentiary Proof* |
| "Balance of evidence" | Intergovernmental Panel on Climate Change (IPCC), 1995 and 2001 | |
| "Reasonable grounds for concern" | European Commission communication on the precautionary principle | |
| "Scientific suspicion of risk" | Swedish chemical law, 1973, for evidence required for regulators to take precautionary action on potential harm from substances | |

*Source:* Harremoes et al. 2001, p. 184

| | | | |
|---|---|---|---|
| **TABLE 9.9**<br><br>*Timeline of Regulatory Actions Relating to Growth Promoters* | 1970s | Concerns about growth promoters' safety, as DES confirmed a human carcinogen | CAUTION |
| | 1972 | Peakal publishes that DES likely to affect a wide range of species in the environment (wildlife) but this was ignored until the late 1980s | CAUTION |
| | 1972 | DES banned as a hormone growth promoter in the United States | STOP |
| | 1974 | Use of DES reinstated in the United States | GO |
| | 1976 | US Food and Drug Administration (FDA) sets the minimum detectable level of DES | STOP |
| | 1979 | DES banned again on the grounds of the impossibility of identifying levels below which it would not be carcinogenic | STOP |
| | 1982 | EU expert working group (Lamming Committee) concludes that some growth promoters are safe | GO |
| | 1985 | First EU ban is adopted, ignoring results from the Lamming Committee because the scope of their assessments had not been broad enough | STOP |
| | 1987 | Lamming Committee disbanded by EU and their results were not published | |
| | 1988 | Ban of several growth promoters throughout the EU based on uncertainty of their effects on humans | STOP |
| | 1988 | WHO/FAO Joint Expert Committee on Food, using standard risk assessment, reaches same conclusions as Lamming Committee | GO |
| | 1989 | EU ban extended to other growth promoters and to imports from third world countries | STOP |
| | 1989 | Pimenta Report finds illegal use of growth promoters in some Member States | GO |
| | 1989-96 | USA takes unilateral retaliatory measures on EC exports | STOP |
| | 1995 | European Commission organises an international conference on growth promoters and meat production where uncertainties remain regarding effects on the immune system, endocrine system and cancer | GO |
| | 1999 | The EU Scientific Committee on Veterinary Measures Relating to Public Health publishes a report concluding that no threshold can be defined for six growth promoters | CAUTION |
| | 2000 | International workshop on hormones and endocrine disrupters in food and water confirms impacts on the environment (wildlife) of veterinary drugs | CAUTION |
| | 2001 | EU still suffers from sanction to its exports of around EUR 160 million per year | GO |

*Source:* Derived from Harremoes et al. 2001

of alternatives, or of the conditions necessary for their successful implementation in the real world. By way of example, Table 9–9 provides a timeline of the history of regulatory actions around hormones as growth promoters in the last several decades (Harremoes et al. 2001). The stop-go nature of the regulatory response represents the type of failure that the precautionary principle is designed to address.

The EEA report concluded with 12 major recommendations:

1. Acknowledge uncertainty and risk in technology appraisal and public policy making.
2. Provide adequate long-term environmental and health monitoring and research into early warnings.
3. Identify and work to reduce "blind spots" and gaps in scientific knowledge.
4. Identify and reduce interdisciplinary obstacles to learning.
5. Account for real-world conditions in regulatory appraisal.
6. Scrutinize the claimed justifications and benefits alongside the potential risks.
7. Evaluate a range of alternative options for meeting needs alongside the option under appraisal, and promote more robust, diverse, and adaptable technologies so as to minimize the costs of surprises and maximize the benefits of innovation.
8. Use "lay" and local knowledge as well as relevant specialist expertise in the appraisal.
9. Account for assumptions and values of different social groups.
10. Maintain regulatory independence from interested parties while retaining an inclusive approach to information and opinion gathering.
11. Identify and reduce institutional obstacles to learning and action.
12. Avoid "paralysis by analysis" by acting to reduce potential harm when there are reasonable grounds for concern.[1]

Table 9–10, based on the EEA report (Harremoes et al. 2001), illustrates how the precautionary principle could be applied to the three major categories and examples of risk identified in Table 9–2. Two additional studies by Raffensperger and Tickner (1999) and Tickner (2002) provide numerous examples where the principle has been applied in a diverse range of industries and countries. Perhaps the most persuasive use of the precautionary principle is in the area of global warming. [See appendix 2.]

Despite these diverse applications of the precautionary principle, some decision makers, policy analysts, and business persons have expressed concern that the general principle is too imprecise to permit an economically efficient determination of the appropriate timing and magnitude of anticipatory action (Marchant and Mossman 2005). In contrast to these concerns, Pittinger and Bishop (1999, p. 960) from Procter & Gamble state that "neither the practice of risk assessment nor the elements of the precautionary principle are 'new' or 'revolutionary.' For decades, they have been important elements in the design, manufacture and marketing of new consumer products. They also have long been embodied in the frameworks used to regulate the introduction of new products, globally. Due precaution is entirely consistent with sound, cost-effective management of the risks and uncertainties inherent in new technologies."

In response to the concern over issues of operationalizing what appears to be a vague principle, numerous researchers have proposed several methodologies that can bring analytical rigor to the study and application of the precautionary

| | EXAMPLES | POSSIBLE ACTIONS |
|---|---|---|
| **TABLE 9.10**<br><br>*Examples of the Application of the Precautionary Principle to Major Risk Categories* | | |
| **RISK** | Known impacts and known probabilities; e.g., **asbestos** causing respiratory disease, lung and mesothelioma | **Prevention:** reduce known risks, such as asbestos dust |
| **UNCERTAINTY** | Known impacts and unknown probabilities; e.g., **antibiotics in animal feed** and development of bacterial resistance | **Precautionary prevention:** reduce potential hazards by reducing or eliminating human exposure of antibiotic residues in foods |
| **IGNORANCE or "WICKED" PROBLEMS** | Unknown impacts and therefore unknown probabilities; e.g., surprises of **CFCs** and their destruction of the ozone layer | **Precaution:** action taken to anticipate, identify and reduce the impact of surprises.<br><br>For example, use properties of chemicals such as persistence or bioaccumulation as predictors of possible harm; use of robust, diverse and adaptable technologies |

*Source:* Harremoes et al. 2001, p. 192

principle (see, for example, Sandin 1999; Sandin and Hansson 2002; Vardas and Xepapadeas 2010). The continuing debate over the principle sometimes loses sight of the fact that it is not a "one size fits all" approach that can hamper the development of potentially useful new technologies and products but is instead a more nuanced concept with several dimensions. Cameron (2006) and others (Cooney 2005; Peterson 2006; Wiener and Rogers 2002) have identified three distinct versions (weak, moderate, and strong) of the precautionary principle, each tied closely to different evidentiary standards. To quote Cameron (2006, pp. 12–13):

**Weak Version**

The weak version is the least restrictive and allows preventive measures to be taken in the face of uncertainty, but does not require them. To satisfy the threshold of harm, there must be some evidence relating to both the likelihood of occurrence and the severity of consequences. Some, but not all, require consideration of the costs of precautionary measures. Weak formulations do not preclude weighing benefits against the costs. Factors other than scientific uncertainty, including economic considerations, may provide legitimate grounds for postponing action. Under weak formulations, the requirement to justify the need for action (the burden of proof) generally falls on those advocating precautionary action. No mention is made of assignment of liability for environmental harm.

## Moderate Version

In moderate versions of the principle, the presence of an uncertain threat is a positive basis for action, once it has been established that a sufficiently serious threat exists. Usually, there is no requirement for proposed precautionary measures to be assessed against other factors such as economic or social costs. The trigger for action may be less rigorously defined, for example, as "potential damage," rather than as "serious or irreversible" damage as in the weak version. Liability is not mentioned, and the burden of proof generally remains with those advocating precautionary action.

## Strong Version

Strong versions of the principle differ from the weak and moderate versions in reversing the burden of proof. Strong versions justify or require precautionary measures, and some also establish liability for environmental harm, which is effectively a strong form of "polluter pays." Reversal of proof requires those proposing an activity to prove that the product, processs, or technology is sufficiently "safe" before approval is granted. Requiring proof of "no environmental harm" before any action proceeds implies the public is not prepared to accept any environmental risk, no matter what economic or social benefits may arise. At the extreme, such a requirement could involve bans and prohibitions on entire classes of potentially threatening activities or substances.

There is clearly a continuum, from weak to strong, along which the various forms of the precautionary principle may apply. Shamir et al. (2007) have linked two locations on this continuum in particular to accepted rules of evidence: the midpoint is equivalent to "the balance of probabilities" concept typical of civil litigation, while the strong point is equivalent to the criminal law's use of "beyond a reasonable doubt." The fundamental challenge is determining which point on the continuum (i.e., which degree of precaution) is appropriate for any given problem. The incorrect placement of any particular problem on this continuum, can lead *in extremis* to one of two pathologies: suppression of a course of action that has net benefits to society, or accession to a course of action that poses a serious threat. There is a clear need for a rigorous analytical methodology that can address and resolve this ambiguity. *Fuzzy logic* may offer such a solution.

Originally conceived by Professor Lofti Zadeh (1965 and 1973), formerly of the University of California, Berkeley, fuzzy logic is a system for "describing the vagueness of the real world" (Kosko and Isaka 1993). In contrast to conventional Boolean sets where an object is either in a set or not, "a fuzzy set is a class of objects with a continuum of grades of membership. Such a set is characterized by a membership (characteristics) function which assigns to each object a grade of membership ranging from zero and one" (Zadeh 1965). Fuzzy logic is a system that uses such sets to arrive at analytically rigorous solutions to apparently imprecise problems by "1) use of so-called 'linguistic' variables in place of or in addition to numerical variables; 2) characterization of simple relations between variables by fuzzy conditional statements; and 3) characterization of complex relationships by fuzzy algorithms (Zadeh 1973, p. 28).

Numerous studies have already been published on how the concept of fuzzy logic can be applied to the precautionary principle (see, for example, Cameron and Peloso 2001 and 2005; Jablonowski 2006; Marusich 2009; Shamir et al. 2007; Takacs 2010). Perhaps the clearest explanation and application of fuzzy logic to the precautionary principle is the work by Shamir et al (2007).

In conclusion, the essence and importance of the comments of the former U.S. Secretary of Defense Donald Rumsfeld about "unknown unknowns" has been echoed in recent books by prominent scientists and economists, including Benoit Mandelbrot's *The (Mis)behavior of Markets: A Fractal View of Financial Turmoil* (2004), Nassim Taleb's *The Black Swan: The Impact of the Highly Improbable* (2007), and John Quiggin's *Zombie Economics: How Dead Ideas Still Walk Among Us* (2010). To quote Quiggin (p. 70), "The implications [of these types of events] are profound. One is that in environments where surprises are likely to be unfavorable, it makes sense to apply a precautionary principle to decision-making. In such environments, we should prefer simple and easily understood choices to those that are complex and poorly understood, even when the complex option appears to offer greater net benefits."

## A BRIEF NOTE ON RISK-RISK TRADE-OFFS AND THE PRECAUTIONARY PRINCIPLE

One of the principal challenges to the use the precautionary principle has been the emergence of the concept of *risk-risk trade-offs*. Simply stated, this theory states that any action or policy to curtail or prevent the use of a product or technology motivated by the desire to reduce potential risks by invoking the precautionary principle must be tempered by the consideration of the risks associated with abandoning or not adopting such technology. Clearly enunciated in a book by Graham et al. (1997) entitled *Risk vs. Risk: Tradeoffs in Protecting Health and the Environment*, the theory has been applied to several case studies by other authors. Marchant and Mossman (2004) examine the use of the precautionary principle in the European Union Courts, focusing, by way of example, on the use of antibiotics in animal feed. This is a controversial subject that has received a large degree of scientific scrutiny. Antimicrobials are used to promote rapid animal growth and counteract natural forces that increase the likelihood of bacterial infection in animals due to artificially high stocking density in a feedlot environment. Mathematical epidemiological models of disease spread (Anderson and May 1979; May and Anderson 1979) identify density as one of the critical determining factors in the development of epidemics, their spread, and endurance. There is strong evidence that one of the major causes of emerging bacterial resistance to antibiotics is overuse of these pharmaceuticals in both livestock and aquaculture (AAM 2002; FAO 2006; FAO-WHO-OIE 2007; Hawkey and Jones 2009; Mellon et al. 2001; Pew 2008; U.S. HHS 2010). The position advanced by Marchant and Mossman is that discontinuance of the use of these drugs in current modes of livestock production poses a greater threat than their continued use because of the increased chances that human consumers will be exposed to a greater level of bacteria from the food production system. This risk trade-off is part of a generic argument that presumably could apply in other cases where the precautionary principle is being considered.

However, there is a logical fallacy with the argument advanced in this particular case study because of an incorrect definition of system boundaries. In essence, the argument is that the current system of livestock production achieves significant economic efficiencies but has some inherent risks that require offsetting actions such as the use of antibiotics. Cessation of this preventative measure will expose consumers to the inherent system risk. The implicit assumption—and logical pitfall—is that the current system of meat production is a given, and that no other alternatives are possible or economically desirable. If one expands the range of alternatives to include range-fed rather than feedlot-based production systems, then a comprehensive life-cycle systems analysis that recognizes and incorporates all externalities might suggest that the feedlot system is less economically efficient from a societal perspective than the alternative. This issue is part of the larger debate over the costs and benefits of what has been termed *industrial agriculture* (Kimbrell 2002). [See also chapter 10.]

The logical conclusion is that any situation with a potential risk-risk trade-off should be considered on a case-by-case basis with a clear delineation of the appropriate system boundaries to avoid the logical inconsistencies inherent in too narrow an analysis of alternatives.

## CITED REFERENCES AND RECOMMENDED READINGS

American Academy of Microbiology (AAM) (2002) *The Role of Antibiotics in Agriculture*, Washington, DC.

Bowen, Mark (2008) *Censoring Science. Inside the Political Attack on Dr. James Hansen and the Truth of Global Warming.* New York: Dutton.

Cameron, Enrico and Gain Francesco Peloso (2001) "An Application of Fuzzy Logic to the Assessment of Aquifer's Pollution Potential." *Environmental Geology*, 40, pp. 1305–1315.

Cameron, Enrico and Gain Francesco Peloso (2005) "Risk Management and the Precautionary Principle: A Fuzzy Logic Model." *Risk Analysis*, 25(4), pp. 901–911.

Cameron, Linda (2006) *Environmental Risk Management in New Zealand—Is There Scope to Apply a More Generic Framework?* New Zealand Treasury Policy Perspectives Paper 06/06, July.

China.org.cn (2012) "Economic Losses from Pollution Account for 10% of GDP," accessed May 1.

Cochran, Thomas B. (2011) "Statement of Thomas B. Cochran, Ph.D. on the Fukushima Nuclear Disaster and Its implications for U.S. Nuclear Power Reactors," Joint Hearings of the Subcommittee on Clean Air and Nuclear Safety and the Committee on Environment and Public Works, United States Senate, April 12, Natural Resources Defense Council (NRDC).

Commission of the European Communities (CEC) (2001) "Strategy for a Future Chemicals Policy," white paper, Brussels, February 27, COM(2001) 88 final.

Cooke, Roger M. and Daan Nieboer (2011) "Heavy-Tailed Distributions: Data, Diagnostics, and New Developments," Resources for the Future. Washington DC, DP 11–19, March.

Cooney, Rosie (2005) "From Promise to Practicalities: The Precautionary Principle on Biodiversity Conservation and Sustainable Use," in Rosie Cooney and Barney Dickson (eds.) *Biodiversity and the Precautionary Principle: Risk and Uncertainty in Conservation and Sustainable Use*. London: Earthscan, pp. 3–17.

Cooney, Rosie and Barney Dickson (eds.) (2005) *Biodiversity & The Precautionary Principle: Risk and Uncertainty in Conservation and Sustainable Use*. London: Earthscan.

Crouch, Edmund and Richard Wilson (1980) "Estimates of Risks," in Peter N. Nemetz (ed.) *Resource Policy: International Perspectives*, pp. 299–318, Montreal: Institute for Research on Public Policy.

Dyer, Gwynne (2009) *Climate Wars*. Toronto: Vintage.

European Environment Agency (2012) *The Impacts of Endocrine Disruptors on Wildlife, People and Their Environments. The Weybridge+15 (1996–2011) report*.

Environment Agency (EEA) (2013) *Late lessons from early warnings: science, precaution, innovation,* Copenhagen.

Fairley, William B. (1977) "Evaluating the 'Small' Probability of a Catastrophic Accident from the Marine Transportation Liquefied Natural Gas," in William B. Fairley and Frederick Mosteller, *Statistics and Public Policy*. Reading, MA: Addison-Wesley, pp. 331–354.

FAO-WHO-OIE (2007) *Joint FAO/WHO/OIE Expert Meeting on Critically Important Antimicrobials*, November 26–30, Rome.

Food and Agriculture Organization (FAO) (2006) *Livestock's Long Shadow. Environmental Issues and Options*, Rome.

Feynman, Richard (1986) Appendix F to *Report of the Presidential Commission on the Space Shuttle Challenger Disaster*.

Feynman, Richard and Ralph Leighton (2001) *What Do You Care What Other People Think? Further Adventures of a Curious Character*. New York: W. W. Norton & Co.

Fielder, John H. and Douglas Birsch (eds.) (1992) *The DC-10 Case. A Study in Applied Ethics, Technology and Society*. New York: State University of New York Press.

Graham, John D. et al. (1997) *Risk vs. Risk: Tradeoffs in Protecting Health and the Environment*. Cambridge, MA: Harvard University Press.

Greene, Joshua D. et al. (2001) "An fMRI Investigation of Emotional Engagement in Moral Judgment." *Science*, 293, September 14, pp. 2105–2108.

Griesmeyer, J. Michael and David Okrent (1981) "Risk Management and Decision Rules for Light Water Reactors." *Risk Analysis*, 1(2), pp. 121–136.

Harremoes, Poul et al. (2001) *Late Lesson from Early Warnings: The Precautionary Principle 1896–2000*, European Environment Agency.

Hawkey, Peter M. and Annie M Jones (2009) "The Changing Epidemiology of Resistance." *Journal of Antimicrobial Chemotherapy*, 64. Suppl. I, pp. i3–i10.

Hoggan, James (2009) *Climate Cover-Up. The Crusade to Deny Global Warming*. Vancouver: Greystone.

Jablonowski, Mark (2006) *Precautionary Risk Management*. New York: Palgrave Macmillan.

Kahneman, Daniel and Amos Tversky (1981) "The Framing of Decisions and the Psychology of Choice." *Science*, 211, January 30, pp. 453–458.

Kahneman, Daniel and Amos Tversky (1982) "The Psychology of Preferences." *Scientific American*, January 30, pp. 160–173.

Kahneman, D., P. Slovic and A. Tversky (1982) *Judgment Under Uncertainty: Heuristics and Biases*. New York: Cambridge University Press.

Kimbrell, Andrew (ed.) (2002) *Fatal Harvest:The Tragedy of Industrial Agriculture*. Washington, DC: Island Press.

Knight, Frank (1921) *Risk, Uncertainty and Profit*, [reprinted in 2010, Kissimee, FL: Signalman Publishing].

Kosko, Bart and Satoru Isaka (1993) "Fuzzy Logic." *Scientific American*, July, pp. 76–81.

Kousky, Carolyn et al. (2009) "Responding to Threats of Climate Change Mega-Catastrophes," Kennedy School, Harvard University, October 19.

Lichtenstein S., P. Slovic, B. Fischhoff, M. Layman and B. Combs (1978) Judged Frequency of Lethal Events. *Journal of Experimental Psychology: Human Learning and Memory*, 4, pp. 551–578.

Lochbaum, David (2011) *The NRC and Nuclear Plant Safety in 2010: A Brighter Spotlight Needed*. Cambridge, MA: Union of Concerned Scientists.

Mandelbrot, Benoit and Richard L. Hudson (2004) *The (Mis)Behavior of Markets*. New York: Basic Books.

Marchant, G. and K. Mosman (2005) *Arbitrary and Capricious, The Precautionary principle in the European Union Courts*. Washington, DC: AEI Press.

Marusich, Lourdes Juarez (2004) *The Application of Fuzzy Logic Analysis to Assessing the Significance of Environmental Impacts: Case Studies from Mexico and Canada*, Canadian Environmental Assessment Agency.

McGinn, Anne Platt (2000) *Why Poison Ourselves? A Precautionary Approach to Synthetic Chemicals*. Worldwatch Working Paper 153. November.

McGrath, P.E. (1974) "Radioactive Waste Management: Potentials and Hazards from a Risk Point of View." Report EURFNR-1204 (KFK 1992). US-EURATOM Fast Reactor Exchange Program, Karlsruhe, Germany.

Medvedev, Grigori (1989) *The Truth About Chernobyl*. New York: Basic Books.

Mellon, Margaret et al. (2001) *Hogging It:Estimates of Antimicrobial Abuse in Livestock*. Cambridge, MA: Union of Concerned Scientists, January.

Michaels, David (2008) *Doubt Is Their Product: How Industry's Assault on Science Threatens Your Health*. Oxford: Oxford University Press.

National Academy of Sciences (NAS) (1978) *Saccharin: Technical Assessment of Risks and Benefits*, Washington, DC.

National Academy of Sciences (NAS) (1989) *Improving Risk Communication*, Washington, DC.

National Academy of Sciences (NAS) (2012) *A Research Strategy for Environmental, Health, and Safety Aspects of Engineered Nanomaterials*, Washington, DC.

*New York Times* (2011) "When All Isn't Enough to Stop a Catastrophe," March 29.

Olsen, J. (1983) "Epidemiological Approach to Assessment of Combined Effects: Theoretical Background," in World Health Organization (WHO) *Health Aspects of Chemical Safety. Combined Exposures to Chemicals*. Interim Document 11, pp. 211–225.

Okrent, D. et al. (1981) "Industrial Risks," *Proceedings of the Royal Society of London A*, 376, pp. 133–149.

Oreskes, Naomi and Erik M. Conway (2010) *Merchants of Doubt: How a Handful of Scientists Obscured the Truth on Issues from Tobacco Smoke to Global Warming*. New York: Bloomsbury Press.

Organization for Economic Co-operation and Development (OECD) (2008) *Costs of Inaction on Key Environmental Challenges*. Paris: OECD.

Peterson, Deborah C. (2006) "Precaution: Principles and Practice in Australian Environments and Natural Resource Management," Presidential address, 50th Annual Australian Agricultural and Resource Economics Society Conference, Manly, New South Wales, February 8–10.

Pew Commission on Industrial Food Animal Production (2008) *Putting Meat on the Table: Industrial Farm Animal Production in America*, Washington, DC.

Pittinger, Charles A. and William E. Bishop (1999) "Unraveling the Chimera: A Corporate View of the Precautionary Principle." *Human and Ecological Risk Assessment*, 5(5), pp. 951–962.

Pooley, Eric (2010) *The Climate War: True Believers, Power Brokers, and the Fight to Save the Earth*. New York: Hyperion.

Quiggin, John (2010) *Zombie Economics: How Dead Ideas Still Walk Among Us*. Princeton, NJ: Princeton University Press.

Raffensperger, Carolyn and Joel Tickner (1999) *Protecting Public Health and the Environment. Implementing the Precautionary Principle*. Washington, DC: Island Press.

Registration, Evaluation, Authorisation and Restriction of Chemicals (REACH) website: http://ec.europa.eu/environment/chemicals/reach/reach_intro.htm.

*Report of the President's Commission on the Accident at Three Mile Island* (1979).

Rumsfeld, Donald (2002) news conference transcript, February 12: http://www.defense.gov/Transcripts/Transcript.aspx?TranscriptID = 2636.

Sandin, Per (1999) "Dimensions of the Precautionary Principle." *Human and Ecological Risk Assessment*, 5(5), pp. 889–907.

Sandin, Per and Sven Ove Hansson (2002) "The Default Value Approach to the Precautionary Principle." *Human and Ecological Risk Assessment*, 8(3), pp. 463–471.

*Science* (1981) "Japanese A-Bomb Data Will be Revised" October 2, pp. 31–32.

Shamir, Mirit et al. (2007) "The Application of Fuzzy Logic to the Precautionary Principle." *Artificial Intelligence and Law*, 15, pp. 411–427.

Shrader-Frechette, K.S. (1991) *Risk and Rationality: Philosophical Foundations for Populist Reforms*. Berkeley: University of California Press.

Slovic, Paul and Elke U. Weber (2002) "Perceptions of Risk Posed by Extreme Events," conference paper for "Risk Management Strategies in an Uncertain World." Palisades, New York, April 12–13.

Stephens, Mark (1980) *Three Mile Island*. New York: Random House.

Stern, Nicholas (2006) *The Economics of Climate Change*. Cabinet Office—HM Treasury, London.

Stern, Paul C. and Harvey V. Fineberg (eds.) (1996) *Understanding Risk: Informing Decisions in a Democratic Society*, U.S. NRC Committee on Risk Characterization, Washington, DC.

Sterner, Thomas and U. Martin Persson (2008) "An Even Sterner Review: Introducing Relative Prices into the Discounting Debate." *Review of Environmental Economics and Policy*, 2(1), Winter, pp. 61–76.

Takacs, Marta (2010) "Multilevel Fuzzy Approach to the Risk of Disaster Management." *Acta Polytechnica Hungerica*, 7(4), pp. 91–102.

Taleb, Nassim Nicholas (2007) *The Black Swan. The Impact of the Highly Improbable*. New York: Random House.

Tickner, Joel A. (ed.) (2003) *Precaution. Environmental Science and Preventive Public Policy, Washington: Island Press*.

Tickner, Joel, Carolyn Raffensperger and Nancy Myers (n.d.) "The Precautionary Principle in Action. A Handbook." Written for the Science and Environmental Health Network.

Tufte, Edward (1997) *Visual Explanations*. Cheshire, CT: Graphics Press.

Tversky, A.; Kahneman, D. (1974) "Judgment under Uncertainty: Heuristics and Biases." *Science* 185(4157), pp. 1124–1131.

Tversky, Amos and Daniel Kahneman (1981) "The Framing of Decisions and the Psychology of Choice." *Science* 211(4481), pp. 453–458.

UNESCO (2005) *The Precautionary Principle*.

U.S. Archives (1981) Text of Executive Order 12291.

U.S. Bureau of Transportation Statistics website [http://www.bts.gov/].

U.S. Department of Health and Human Services (U.S. HHS), Food and Drug Administration, Center for Veterinary Medicine (2010) *The Judicious Use of Medically Important Antimicrobial Drugs in Food-Producing Animals*, June 28.

U.S. Department of Health and Human Services (U.S. HHS), Public Health Services, National Toxicology Program (2011) "Report on Carcinogens Review Group Actions on the Nomination of Saccharin for Delisting from the Report on Carcinogens," in *Report on Carcinogens, 12th edition*, pp. 467–469.

U.S. Environmental Protection Agency (EPA) (1998) *Chemical Hazard Data Availability Study*, Office of Pollution Prevention and Toxics, April.

U.S. Nuclear Regulatory Commission (NRC) (1974) *Reactor Safety Study. An Assessment of Accident Risks in U.S. Commercial Nuclear Power Plants—WASH 1400*.

U.S. Nuclear Regulatory Commission (NRC) (1978) *Risk Assessment Review Group Report to the U.S. Nuclear Regulatory Commission*, H.W. Lewis et al.

U.S. Nuclear Regulatory Commission (NRC) (1981) *Fault Tree Handbook*.

U.S. Nuclear Regulatory Commission (NRC) (1991) *Severe Accident Risks: An Assessment for Five U.S. Nuclear Power Plants*.

Varas, Giannis and Anastasios Xepapadeas (2010) "Model Uncertainty, Ambiguity and the Precautionary Principle: Implications for Biodiversity Management." *Environmental and Resource Economics*, 45, pp. 379–404.

Von Neumann, John and Oskar Morgenstern (1953) *Theory of Games and Economic Behavior*. Princeton, NJ: Princeton University Press.

Ward's Automotive Group (2010) *Motor Vehicle Facts & Figures 2010*, Southfield, MI.

Weitzman, Martin L. (2007) "A Review of the Stern Review on the Economics of Climate Change." *Journal of Economic Literature*, XLV, September, pp. 703–724.

Wiener, Jonathan B. and Michael D. Rogers (2002) "Comparing Precaution in the United States and Europe." *Journal of Risk Research* 5(4), pp. 317–349.

Wilson, Richard and Edmund Crouch (1982) *Risk/Benefit Analysis*. Cambridge, MA: Ballinger Publishing.

World Bank (2007) *Cost of Pollution in China. Economic Estimates of Physical Damages*.

World Economic Forum (WEF) (2011) *Global Risks 2011* Sixth Edition. An Initiative of the Risk Response Network, Geneva.

Zadeh, Lofti (1965) "Fuzzy Sets." *Information and Control*, 8, pp. 338–353.

Zadeh, Lofti (1973) "Outline of a New Approach to the Analysis of Complex Systems and Decision Processes." *IEEE Trans. Systems, Man and Cybernetics*, 2, pp. 28–44.

---

1. In 2013, the EEA issued a second volume to their original study of 2001 entitled: "Late Lessons from Early Warnings: Science, Precaution, Innovation." The report included twenty new case studies as well as addressing criticism that the original report had omitted studying "false positives." Of eighty identified cases of false alarms, the report found only four clear cut cases [U.S. swine flu, saccharin, food irradiation and southern leaf corn blight] and these turned out to be real risks, cases where the "jury is still out," unregulated alarms, or risk-risk tradeoffs rather than false positives. On balance, the 20 major case studies in this report reinforce earlier conclusions of the necessity of adopting the precautionary principle, especially in light of the fact that the more rapid take-up of new technology today entails risks which spread more quickly and are more widely disseminated than before.

**APPENDIX ONE**

# Two Classic Examples of Risk Framing

In the first example, Daniel Kahneman and Amos Tversky (1981, 1982) ask two separate groups of respondents how they would respond to one of the following two scenarios.

> Imagine that the U.S. is preparing for the outbreak of an unusual Asian disease, which is expected to kill 600 people. Two alternative programs to combat the disease have been proposed. Assume that the exact scientific estimate of the consequences of the programs is as follows:
>
> QUESTION 1: If Program A is adopted, 200 people will be saved. If Program B is adopted, there is a 1/3 probability that 600 people will be saved, and 2/3 probability that no people will be saved. Which of the two programs would you favour?
>
> QUESTION 2: If Program C is adopted, 400 people will die. If Program D is adopted, there is a 1/3 probability that nobody will die, and 2/3 probability that 600 people will die. Which of the two programs would you favour?

In test after test of these scenarios, the authors found a consistent pattern. Program A is overwhelmingly preferred to B. "The majority choice in this problem is risk averse: the prospect of certainly saving 200 lives is more attractive than a risky prospect of equal expected value; that is, a one-in-three chance of saving 600 lives." However, Program D is overwhelmingly preferred to C. "The majority choice in [this formulation of the decision] . . . is risk taking: the certain death of 400 people is less acceptable than the two-in-three chance that 600 will die." The authors conclude that "the preferences in [these two problem choices] . . . illustrate a common pattern: choices involving gains are often risk averse and choices involving losses are often risk taking. However, it is easy to see that the two problems are effectively identical. The only difference between them is that the outcomes are described in [the first choice] . . . by the number of lives saved, and in [the second choice] . . . by the number of lives lost. Inconsistent responses . . . arise from the conjunction of a *framing effect* with contradictory attitudes toward risks involving gains and losses" (1981, p. 453). Kahneman and Tversky conclude that "We have considered a variety of examples in which a decision, a preference or an emotional reaction was controlled by factors that may appear irrelevant or inconsequential. The difficulty people have in maintaining a comprehensive view of consequences and their susceptibility to the vagaries of framing are examples of such impediments. The descriptive study of preferences also presents challenges to the theory of rational choice because it is often far from clear whether the effects of decision weights, reference points, framing and regret should be treated as errors or biases or whether they should be accepted as valid elements of human experience" (1982, p. 173).

The second example is equally macabre and addresses the issue of how individuals might respond when they have the opportunity to influence some else's impending death (Greene et al. 2001). Again two slightly different questions are asked of two randomly selected groups: QUESTION A: A runaway trolley is hurtling toward five people. They will all be killed—unless you throw a switch that will steer the trolley onto a spur, where it will kill just one other person instead of five. Should you throw the switch? QUESTION B: A runaway trolley is hurtling toward five people. You are standing next to a large stranger on a footbridge that arches over the tracks. The only way to save the five is to push the stranger off the bridge onto the tracks below; it is certain that he will die, but his heavy body will stop the trolley, saving the five others. Should you push the stranger to his death?

A vast majority of people say yes to Question A, according to moral philosophers and psychologists who have posed the question over many years. It is morally acceptable to throw the switch to save five innocent lives at the expense of one. But most people say no to Question B; in this case it is morally wrong to kill one person to save five.

After many years of debate, moral philosophers have been unable to arrive at a set of principles to explain why people treat the two situations differently. There appears to be no rational explanation for the difference.

The study by Greene et al. (2001) relies on magnetic imaging of the brain while subjects are making their choice of action. The runaway trolley study finds that the two-trolley car problem formulations engage different parts of the brain. In Choice A, the idea of throwing a switch is impersonal; it is processed by a location in the neocortex that deals mainly with memory, part of the cognitive processing part of the brain. In Choice B, by contrast, the notion of personally pushing a stranger to his death activates the limbic region of the brain that deals with emotions, temporarily suppressing the memory areas. The conclusion is that issues of moral judgment contain both rational and emotional components. The degree to which either emotion or rationality will be dominant depends in part on the nature of the moral dilemma; especially the difference between what has been called "moral-personal" (i.e., "up close and personal") situations and "moral impersonal" situations.

## APPENDIX TWO

# The Precautionary Principle and Global Warming

While a solid consensus has emerged among members of the scientific community that global warming is occurring and that it is anthropogenic, there are a few doubters left in the general public, and this theme has been adopted by certain special interest groups who face the loss of business revenue from any measures undertaken to reverse the emission of carbon dioxide and other greenhouse gases (Bowen 2008;

Dyer 2009; Hoggan 2009; Michaels 2008; Oreskes and Conway 2010; Pooley 2010). It can be demonstrated, however, that it is ultimately in the interest of even non-believers to recognize and act against the threat of global warming. Consider Table 9–11, which analyzes the global warming problem using Von Neumann-Morgenstern game theory (1953). In this representation of the standard two-person game theoretic, Player #1 is society in general, and Player #2 represents nature.

The figure presents a simple 2 x 2 decision matrix that represents two states of nature (global warming is/is not occurring) and two possible courses of action (act/not act). Each of the four matrix cells entails markedly different "payoffs." Given the enormous costs of nonresponse to global warming, a "maximin" strategy is warranted, where society (here denoted as Player #1) chooses a course of action that minimizes potential losses. Acting on the assumption that global warming is occurring may entail significant opportunity costs if global warming is not occurring, but avoids the potentially catastrophic consequences of not acting if, in fact, global warming is occurring.

Up until recently, there were no reasonable estimates of the benefits or costs available to attach to this matrix. In October 2006, a pathbreaking study commissioned by the prime minister and chancellor of the exchequer in the United Kingdom was published. It was—and remains—the most exhaustive and comprehensive analysis of the economics of global climate change. Organized by Sir Nicholas Stern, head of the Government Economic Service and former chief economist of the World Bank, the report was portentous, yet essentially optimistic. To quote: "There is still time to avoid the worst impacts of climate change, if we take strong action now" (Stern, p. vi). One of the most important outcomes of the Stern Report (2006) was the ability to, for the first time, assign credible numbers to both benefits and costs of attempts to control the process of global warming. Table 9–12 recasts the decision matrix in terms of actual economic projections. To place these data in context, global GDP at the time of the Stern Report's publication in 2006 was estimated at $48 trillion. It is clear from this analysis that even if the probability of global warming is deemed to be unlikely (i.e., with a low probability of occurrence), it is still

| **TABLE 9.11**<br><br>*Von Neumann and Morgenstern Game Theoretic Approach to Global Warming* | | | **PLAYER #2 (IN THIS CASE, UNKNOWN STATES OF NATURE)** | |
| --- | --- | --- | --- | --- |
| | | | **GLOBAL WARMING IS NOT OCCURRING** | **GLOBAL WARMING IS OCCURRING** |
| | Player #1 (in this case, society) Possible actions | We assume global warming is occurring and act on it | Generally unproductive investment COSTS: significant BENEFITS: marginal | COSTS: significant BENEFITS: We can slow or possibly reverse the damage |
| | | We assume global warming is NOT occurring and do nothing | COSTS: none BENEFITS: none | **COSTS: enormous BENEFITS: none** |

| | | PLAYER #2 (IN THIS CASE, UNKNOWN STATES OF NATURE | | **TABLE 9.12** |
| | | GLOBAL WARMING IS NOT OCCURRING | GLOBAL WARMING IS OCCURRING | *Table 9–11 with Stern's Estimates* |
| **Player #1 (in this case, society) Possible actions** | **We assume global warming is occurring and act on it** | Generally unproductive investment **COSTS:** 1% of global GDP / year. **BENEFITS:** marginal | **COSTS: 1% of global GDP/year. BENEFITS: between $6 trillion/ year and 20% of global GDP** | |
| | **We assume global warming is NOT occurring and do nothing** | **COSTS:** none **BENEFITS:** none | **COSTS: between $6 trillion and 20% of Global GDP BENEFITS: none** | |

rational behavior to engage in avoidance behavior because of the extraordinary costs of not acting should global warming actually occur. Parenthetically, it should be noted that Stern's maximum estimated GDP loss of 20% (Stern 2007, p. 162) associated with massive climate change may be overly sanguine, in light of the fact that China has recently admitted that environmental despoliation is already costing it as much as 10% of its GDP (China.org.cn; see also World Bank 2007).

Some researchers have even considered Stern's estimates of GDP loss as overly optimistic. Sterner and Persson (2008) observe that Stern's calculations are based on an assumed deviation from a continuing economic growth path that remains positive despite the potential negative effects of increasing greenhouse gas emissions. Citing the work of Weitzman (2007) and the non-zero probability of catastrophic climate change, Sterner and Persson suggest the possibility of global climate change making us "significantly worse off" (p. 63) than we are today. This possibility suggests an even more rigorous application of the precautionary principle with respect to this global threat.

# CHAPTER 10

## Some Relevant Ecological Principles

### STABILITY AND RESILIENCE, NONLINEARITIES, THRESHOLDS, AND TIPPING POINTS

One of the founders of ecological theory, C.S. Holling, was instrumental in elucidating concepts that have played a pivotal role in our modern understanding of the functioning of ecological systems and how they are influenced by anthropogenic behavior. Among the concepts developed by Holling are principles of stability and resilience, nonlinearities, thresholds, and tipping points.

*Stable systems* are systems that are not easily disturbed by shocks from their current state or path. In contrast, *resilient systems* are those that, if disturbed by shocks, tend to return to their previous state or path. Figure 10–1 presents one of Holling's classic representations of types of ecological systems (Holling 1973). In this model, there is a central *domain of attraction* (demarcated by the shaded area within the dashed line) where disturbances of sufficiently small magnitude move the system only temporarily away from the point of equilibrium. The system has a certain amount of resilience. However, with a sufficiently large shock, the system passes a *threshold* and jumps from one equilibrium state to another (i.e., there is a *nonlinear response*). The crucial point is that this second state may be less desirable from a human perspective than the first.

In a major report on Valuing Ecosystem Services (2004), the National Academy of Sciences highlighted the challenges facing conventional economic analysis in assessing thresholds. To quote:

> Severe disturbance of an aquatic ecosystem may lead to an abrupt, and possibly very substantial disruption in the supply of one or more ecological services. This "break" in supply is often referred to as a *threshold effect*. The problem for economic valuation is that before the threshold is reached, the marginal benefits associated with a particular ecological service may either be fairly constant or change in a fairly predictable manner with the provision of that service. However, once the threshold is reached, not only may there be a large "jump" in the value of an ecological service, but how the supply of the service changes may be less predictable. Such ecosystem threshold effects pose a considerable challenge, especially for ex ante economic valuation using revealed-preference methods—that is, when one wants to estimate the value of an ecological service that takes into account any potential threshold effects. Since such severe and abrupt changes have not been experienced, peoples' choices in response to them have not been observed.

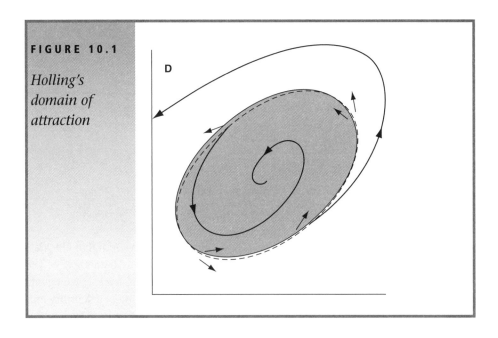

**FIGURE 10.1**

*Holling's domain of attraction*

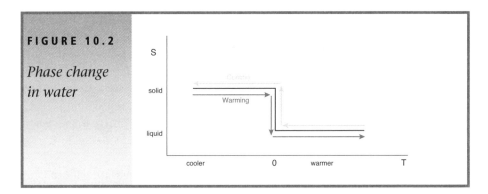

**FIGURE 10.2**

*Phase change in water*

In its simplest form, a nonlinear response may appear as in Figure 10–2, which portrays the phase changes in water as it freezes or thaws. In this figure, S is a state variable (which may take at least two values: solid or liquid), and F is a forcing variable (e.g., T = water temperature in degrees Celsius.) This figure addresses the critical question of whether such a sudden change at the threshold is reversible over some time period of interest. In this case, the answer is clearly "yes." Water and ice change back and forth very quickly with modest changes in temperature.

What happens when one considers transformations of potential greater ecological consequence, such as possible changes in sea level driven by global warming? Figure 10–3 portrays the effect of two possible drivers of sea level rise: (1) a steady expansion in volume due to warming, and (2) a possible sudden increment in sea level driven by catastrophic loss of land-based Antarctic or Greenland ice sheets. In this figure, L = sea level, and T = global temperature. The critical question is again one of reversibility and, in this case, the answer is different. The figure contrasts the

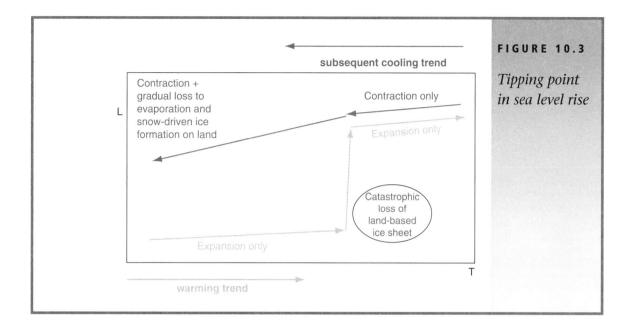

**FIGURE 10.3**

*Tipping point in sea level rise*

potentially rapid sea level rise accompanying global warming with the slow reversal of this trend should there be a subsequent cooling trend. The point of inflection is often referred to as a *tipping point*, which, in layperson's terms, represents a sudden, nonlinear, and usually unfavorable change that is not reversible in the short to medium term.

A critical contributor to nonlinear system dynamics are *feedback loops*, which can be either negative or positive—or what Meadows (2008) has called *balancing* versus *accelerating* feedback. An archetypal example of a *negative feedback* system is the homeostatic system that regulates body temperature. There is a natural tendency to return to the equilibrium temperature of 98.6 Fahrenheit (or 37 degrees Celsius) after any deviation—*as long as* this deviation is not too large (i.e., the temperature does not fall outside the domain of attraction that brings it back to normality).

In contrast, a *positive feedback* system can occur when a shock sets up a process where the system continues to move further away from the point of equilibrium, frequently at an increasing velocity (i.e., the response is nonlinear). Recent greenhouse gas-related examples include melting Arctic ice and Siberian permafrost. In the former case, increasing global temperature reduces ice cover on the Arctic Ocean, thereby reducing its albedo (i.e., the capacity to reflect sunlight). As a consequence, the ocean absorbs more heat, and the melting of sea ice is accelerated. This process is self-reinforcing and nonlinear.

A similar mechanism is posited to exist in Siberia and other Arctic regions that have large areas of permafrost overlaying peat bogs (*The Guardian*, August 11, 2005; Ise et al. 2008). The concern is that global warming will melt the permafrost, releasing large quantities of entrained methane that is 20 times more powerful than carbon dioxide as a greenhouse gas. Recent research has suggested the existence of potentially massive methane reservoirs beneath Antarctica which, if released by global warming, could also lead to a strong positive feedback loop on climate change (Wadham et al. 2012). While still the subject of ongoing scientific debate, these scenarios are non-zero probability, potentially catastrophic events that could lead to a rapid and uncontrolled rise in global temperature, threatening many vulnerable parts of the world.

Recent studies of possible ecological tipping points include a broad range of examples across the globe, including the Amazon rainforest, the North Atlantic "conveyor" current, the Greenland ice sheet, the ozone hole, the Antarctic circumpolar current, the Sahara desert, the Tibetan plateau, the Asian monsoon, methane clathrates, ocean acidity levels, El Niño, the West Antarctic ice sheet, and salinity valves (Broecker and Kunzig 2008; WWF and Allianz 2009). While many of these scenarios remain the subject of speculation with an indeterminate time frame, several local or regional ecological tipping phenomena have already been identified. Some of these examples concern sudden loss of forests in Alaska, the Southwest United States, and British Columbia (Kurz et al. 2008) due to predation by massive insect outbreaks attributed to the effects of global warming, and the loss of fish species and their impact on ecosystems through *trophic cascades* (Eisenberg 2010; Estes et al. 2011; Terborgh and Estes 2010). An illustration of this phenomenon is presented later in this chapter. A well-documented case of a significant phase shift associated with a tipping point concerns coral reefs in the Caribbean. Hughes (1994) documents how overfishing, inter alia, led to a virtually total collapse of reefs near Jamaica and the emergence of an altered ecosystem dominated by fleshy macroalgae. This dramatic change has major impacts on ecotourism and other revenue streams associated with healthy coral reef-based ecosystems [see also Pandolfi et al. 2011].

A major study undertaken in 2009 (Rockstrom et al. 2009a, b) identified and attempted to quantify nine planetary boundaries that, if crossed, could lead to unacceptable environmental damage. The authors admitted the existence of a large degree of uncertainty in this initial research effort but were, nevertheless, able to draw a number of important conclusions. First, they estimated that three planetary boundaries had already been crossed: (i) climate change measured as atmospheric $CO_2$ concentrations; (ii) the rate of biodiversity loss measured as the extinction rate per year; and (iii) the nitrogen cycle measured as the amount of $N_2$ removed from the atmosphere for human use). In addition, it is estimated that our planet may be approaching boundaries for four other categories: global freshwater use, change in land use, ocean acidification, and interference with the global phosphorous cycle.

From a business perspective, a critical question revolves around the economic effects of crossing a "tipping point." The ecological, economic, and social effects of losing a *keystone species* or central system component such as a forest can be momentous. [See, for example, Figure 1–2.]

## SYSTEM BOUNDARIES AND INTERDEPENDENCIES

Central to the study of systems—be they in ecology, economics, business, or society—is the correct definition of system boundaries. A detailed example of the importance of boundaries with respect to the life-cycle analysis of commercial products is presented later in this book. The illustrations in this section are confined to examples derived from ecology and some of the economic consequences thereof.

## The Case of American Agriculture

U.S. agriculture is considered one of the most economically efficient and productive agricultural systems in the world. But just how "efficient" is it? It all depends on where one draws the system boundary—both spatially and temporally. Figure 10–4 presents a schematic representation of the American agricultural system. If the analysis is confined solely to the direct costs of U.S. farm output and its high productivity, the system can be considered to be highly efficient in a traditional sense. There are, however, three other system components that must be considered when calculating the total true (i.e., social) costs: (a) government subsidies; (b) indirect, long-term costs, ultimately borne by the agricultural sector but generally ignored or invisible in the short term; and (c) externalities, principally environmental, which are borne by other sectors. Figure 10–5 summarizes the major groups of uninternalized, agricultural externalities. Once this broader definition of system boundaries is adopted, the "efficiency" and indeed sustainability of U.S. agriculture becomes debatable. The U.S. farming system has been labeled "industrial agriculture" (Altieri 2007; Kimbrell 2002), which relies on massive inputs of energy both directly and indirectly for mechanization, irrigation, and the production of herbicides, pesticides, and fertilizer. Several studies have characterized the American diet as "eating oil" because of this massive reliance on the products of fossil energy (Green 1978; Pfeiffer 2006).

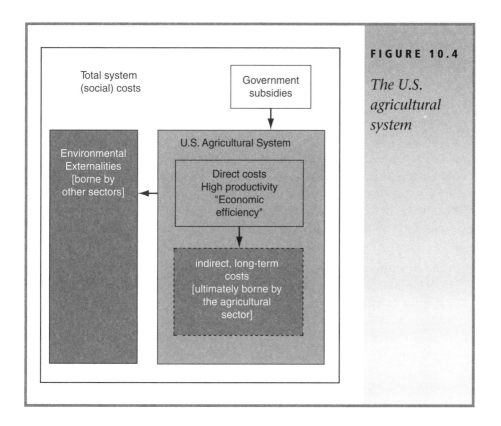

**FIGURE 10.4**

*The U.S. agricultural system*

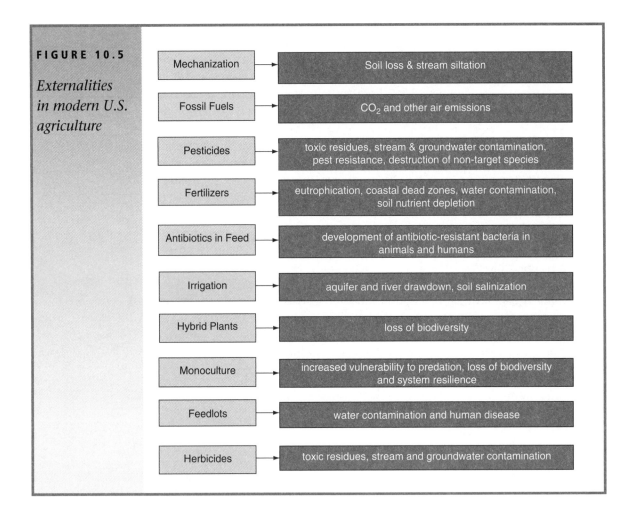

**FIGURE 10.5**

*Externalities in modern U.S. agriculture*

| | |
|---|---|
| Mechanization | Soil loss & stream siltation |
| Fossil Fuels | $CO_2$ and other air emissions |
| Pesticides | toxic residues, stream & groundwater contamination, pest resistance, destruction of non-target species |
| Fertilizers | eutrophication, coastal dead zones, water contamination, soil nutrient depletion |
| Antibiotics in Feed | development of antibiotic-resistant bacteria in animals and humans |
| Irrigation | aquifer and river drawdown, soil salinization |
| Hybrid Plants | loss of biodiversity |
| Monoculture | increased vulnerability to predation, loss of biodiversity and system resilience |
| Feedlots | water contamination and human disease |
| Herbicides | toxic residues, stream and groundwater contamination |

### Other Case Studies

Systems are characterized by interdependencies, both obvious and counterintuitive. *Trophic levels* refer to the position in a food chain inhabited by an organism. *Trophic cascades* are the effects of additions or deletions of an apex predator (i.e., a predator at the top of a food chain), which ripple through and alter an ecosystem. Estes and colleagues (2011) summarize the critical importance of this concept as follows:

> Until recently, large apex consumers were ubiquitous across the globe and had been for millions of years. The loss of these animals may be humankind's most pervasive influence on nature. Although such losses are widely viewed as an ethical and aesthetic problem, recent research reveals extensive cascading effects of their disappearance in marine, terrestrial, and freshwater ecosystems worldwide. This empirical work supports long-standing theory about the role of top-down forcing in ecosystems but also highlights the unanticipated impacts of trophic cascades on processes as diverse as the dynamics of disease, wildfire, carbon sequestration, invasive species, and biogeochemical cycles.

These findings emphasize the urgent need for interdisciplinary research to forecast the effects of trophic downgrading on process, function, and resilience in global ecosystems.

In a typical food chain, each trophic level feeds on the level below and is fed upon by the level above. To understand the complexity of trophic cascades and system interdependencies, consider several recent examples drawn from the American Midwest, East Coast, and Pacific regions. The underlying similarity in all of these cases is the unexpected linkages that ultimately derive from our limited understanding of the complexity of ecosystems and our interactions with them.

The first example illustrates the unanticipated system effects of the controversial reintroduction of wolves into Yellowstone National Park. While the impact on domestic and farm animals was partially anticipated, little was known about the possible effect on fish and birdlife, if any. Figure 10–6 diagrams the rather complex chain of events that led to an increase in trout, Yellow Warbler, and Lincoln Sparrow populations as an indirect result of the reintroduction of wolves.

The second example, with unpredicted but tangible economic impacts on commercial fisheries, focuses on the loss of sharks off the East Coast of the United States. Sharks have largely been considered undesirable because of their tendency to predate on more valuable species and the occasional human. Myers et al. (2007) traced the trophic cascade associated with loss of the shark as an apex predator. The intentional and unintentional killing of 11 species of large sharks that typically feed on rays, skates, and smaller sharks led to an explosion in the population of their prey that was no longer under predator pressure. This, in turn, led to a massive predation of bay scallops, the next lower trophic level. The result was the total physical and economic collapse of the scallop fishery that had existed for over a century. To place this in context, the value of total scallop landings in the United States over the period 2003–2007 was approximately $350 million (Stokesbury 2009).

In addition to the critical role of sharks as an apex species maintaining ecological balance within the complex food chain that they dominate, recent research has suggested that they have an economic value in and by themselves in the important growth area of ecotourism. A Pew-funded study conducted in the Pacific island state of Palau contrasted the value of a single shark sold on the market for food at $108 with its lifetime value as a reef-based tourist attraction that equaled $179,000 in a single year or $1.9 million over its lifetime (Vianna et al. 2010).

The third example is also related to a commercial fishery with significant economic benefits: the Pacific Salmon whose range extends from California in the South to Alaska in the North. Considered a keystone species, the salmon play an essential role in the maintenance of a thriving ecosystem. Salmon of the Pacific Northwest and Alaska are under increased stress from global warming as these fish require relatively cool water temperatures in which to reproduce and thrive. The loss of this apex species would have a cascading and detrimental effect on a large array of mammals, insects, and plants that rely on its central ecological role (Cederholm et al. 2000). Included among these are many creatures with tangible economic benefits from hunting or tourism, including the grizzly and black bear, bald eagle, Caspian tern, coon merganser, harlequin duck, killer whale, and osprey, as well as 129 other mammals, birds, reptiles, and amphibians.

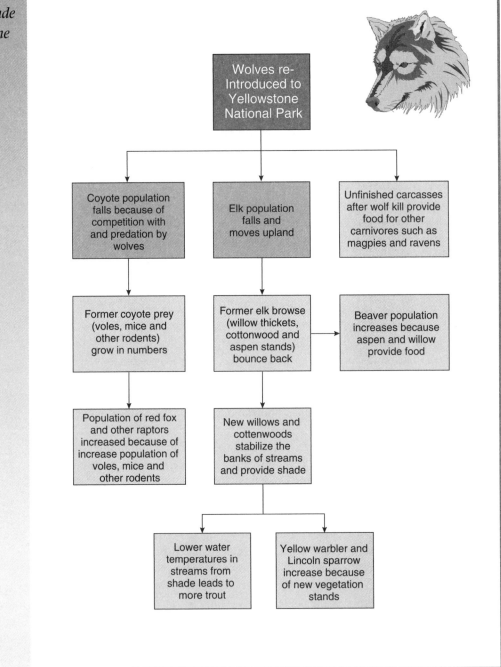

**FIGURE 10.6**

*Trophic cascade in Yellowstone Park*

Wolves re-Introduced to Yellowstone National Park

Coyote population falls because of competition with and predation by wolves

Elk population falls and moves upland

Unfinished carcasses after wolf kill provide food for other carnivores such as magpies and ravens

Former coyote prey (voles, mice and other rodents) grow in numbers

Former elk browse (willow thickets, cottonwood and aspen stands) bounce back

Beaver population increases because aspen and willow provide food

Population of red fox and other raptors increased because of increase population of voles, mice and other rodents

New willows and cottenwoods stabilize the banks of streams and provide shade

Lower water temperatures in streams from shade leads to more trout

Yellow warbler and Lincoln sparrow increase because of new vegetation stands

The fourth and fifth examples are drawn from the Hawaiian Islands. In the early 1980s, the islands had to import milk powder from the U.S. mainland because of unacceptably high levels of the pesticide Heptachlor in the milk from local dairy herds. The question arose as to how milk became contaminated since there were strict rules in place to prevent the exposure of dairy cattle to toxic pesticides. The answer was that Heptachlor was used on pineapple plants. The tops (or crowns) of these plants were cut off before processing and, following the dictum that "waste is lost profits," were fed to dairy cattle, generating additional revenue for pineapple growers. It was not immediately obvious that residual levels of Heptachlor would be found in the pineapple crowns and that this pesticide would find its way into the milk supply because of the circuitous path of contamination.

The second example from the Hawaiian Islands is drawn from the late 1980s and 1990s. Biologists found strange tumors (nonmalignant but life threatening nevertheless) on green sea turtles off the island of Maui [see Figure 10–7]. These tumors, which grow in soft tissue, can block the mouth, eyes, and other vital areas, leading to death from starvation and related causes. Historically, turtles (up to four or five feet in length) have been revered as gods by the Hawaiians and made the subject of art and mythology. In 2003, a book, entitled *Fire in the Turtle House* (Davidson 2003) was published outlining the nature of the problem and possible causes. The tumors are the result of infection by papilloma viruses, but three hypotheses emerged, all anthropogenic in origin: (1) immunosuppression from

**FIGURE 10.7**

*Stricken sea turtle, Maui*

agricultural chemical run-off, (2) forced change in diet of the turtles as a result of agricultural run-off of nutrients and sediment that destroy traditional food sources such as sea grasses and favor the growth of potentially toxic algae, and (3) global warming with increased nutrient and sediment loading, also shifting the diet of the turtles to more toxic food. The crucial scientific question was how to choose among these three possible explanations. In discriminating among hypotheses, it is important to remember that correlation is a necessary but not sufficient condition for causality. Table 10–1 summarizes the three hypotheses and the observed recent trends in the prevalence of tumors. Each hypothesis has a driver that must be analyzed for consistency with the empirical evidence. In this case, global warming has been ruled out in favor of the decrease in agricultural activity. Only by conducting this type of analysis can plausible, but incorrect, hypotheses be eliminated. [See Van Houtan et al. 2010 for a more detailed description of the epidemiological underpinnings of this analysis.]

Systems theory can also inform the discussion of the perceived benefits of eating locally, an idea that has received wide currency after the publication of the national bestseller *The 100-Mile Diet* (Smith and MacKinnon 2007). A key concept in this public debate is the concept of *food miles*; that is, the distance food has to travel from point of production to point of consumption. Central to this calculation is the amount of energy expended (and associated greenhouse gases produced) in the transportation of this food. In general, the conclusion is that "local is better" since less energy is consumed—and fewer greenhouse gases are produced—in the transportation of the food.

A recent study from New Zealand critically reexamines this theory by analyzing the total system effects of transporting lamb from that country to the United Kingdom (Saunders et al. 2006). If one relies solely on food miles as the desideratum,

| TABLE 10.1 *Alternative Hypotheses for Sea Turtle Pathogenesis* | HYPOTHESIS | RECENT TRENDS IN TURTLE TUMOURS | RECENT TRENDS IN HYPOTHESIZED DRIVERS | CONSISTENCY OF HYPOTHESES WITH RECENT TRENDS IN TUMOURS |
|---|---|---|---|---|
| | **Immunosuppression from agricultural run-off** | the incidence of this condition appears to have decreased in recent years (from personal observation) from about 25-40% to about 10% now. | Agricultural land is being increasingly displaced by residential vacation housing | **CONSISTENT** |
| | **Forced change of diet from loss of traditional foods due to agricultural sediment run-off** | | | |
| | **Global warming causing increased nutrient and sediment loading** | | Global warming is continuing | **INCONSISTENT** |

*Source:* derived from Davidson 2003

then clearly it makes more sense to consume domestically produced lamb in the UK. The gist of the New Zealand study is that food miles are an incomplete measure of environmental impact. It includes only the distance food travels and is misleading because it doesn't consider total energy use throughout the production process. In contrast, the New Zealand study takes a much broader view of the environmental impact of lamb and some other major food exports. The environmental impact calculations are based upon a *life-cycle assessment* (LCA) [see chapter 18] and include the energy use and $CO_2$ emissions associated with production and transport to the UK. This is a much more valid comparison than just distance traveled as it reflects differences in the two countries' production systems. Table 10–2 (Saunders et al. 2006) summarizes this system-wide reanalysis that reveals the counterintuitive result that New Zealand lamb has a lower total energy and $CO_2$ profile than UK lamb even after transportation of imported lamb to the UK is factored into the analysis. A similar conclusion concerning the deficiencies of food miles is reached by two other studies by Smith et al. (2005) and Chi et al. (2009).

Clearly, in order to assess the true overall effect and sustainability of a product, it is necessary to develop a methodology that looks at the problem from a systems perspective. Two major types of this approach are life-cycle analysis [which will be discussed in great detail in chapter 18, and see Garnett 2008 for its application to food] and the *Ecological Footprint* discussed later in this chapter.

## REVENGE THEORY

In 1996, Edward Tenner of Harvard University published a book entitled *Why Things Bite Back. Technology and the Revenge of Unintended Consequences*. The central hypothesis advanced by Tenner was that we know very little about the complexity of systems (natural and even some man-made). As a consequence, any attempt to intervene in one location to fix a problem can lead to another totally unanticipated problem somewhere else. Through casual observation it is possible to see a plethora of supporting examples of this persuasive theory.

One of the most famous of these is the story of malaria control in Borneo. While several variants of this tale have been related in the literature, the message is the same: unintended consequences—sometimes very serious—can emerge from what are considered benign interventions designed to cure major problems; in this case, a global disease that affects over one quarter of a billion people and kills almost one million annually (WHO 2011). In the immediate postwar period, the World Health Organization encouraged the widespread use of DDT—considered a benign pesticide—for the control of malaria. Vast swaths of the Third World, including Borneo, were sprayed with this chemical—with little understanding of its ultimate ecological effects. Figure 10–8 illustrates one of the cascades of totally unexpected consequences of this spraying (See, for example, Conway 1972). The initial effect was a marked reduction in the number of mosquitoes and consequent incidence of malaria. However, the spraying of DDT, especially in residence huts, led to the mortality of both cats and small lizards, which controlled rats and caterpillars respectively. This led, in turn, to a marked increase in the numbers of both these pests, the former carrying such diseases as plague and typhus; the latter

**TABLE 10.2**

*Systems Analysis of UK and New Zealand Lamb*

| ITEM | QUANTITY (HECTARES) | | ENERGY (MJ / TONNE CARCASS) | | CO$_2$ EMISSIONS (KG CO$_2$ / TONNE CARCASS) | |
|---|---|---|---|---|---|---|
| | NZ | UK | NZ | UK | NZ | UK |
| **Direct** | | | | | | |
| Fuel, electricity and oil (l of diesel equiv) | | 128 | | 17,156 | | 1,116.9 |
| Fuel use (l of diesel) (including contracting) | 15.5 | | 3,565 | | 244.9 | |
| Electricity use (kWh) | 13.8 | | 594 | | 11.4 | |
| **Direct sub total** | | | **4,159** | **17,156** | **256.3** | **1116.9** |
| | | | | | | |
| **Indirect** | | | | | | |
| Nitrogen (kg) | 5.7 | 76 | 1,953 | 16,147 | 90.1 | 807.4 |
| Phosphorus (kg) | 12.5 | 7 | 985 | 336 | 59.1 | 20.2 |
| Potassium (kg) | 0.5 | 15 | 29 | 498 | 1.7 | 29.9 |
| Sulfur (kg) | 12.3 | | 323 | | 19.4 | |
| Lime (kg) | 22.3 | 87 | 71 | 170 | 50.6 | 122.7 |
| Agri-chemicals (l ai) | 0.6 | 1.5 | 338 | 1,549 | 20.3 | 92.9 |
| Concentrate (kg of dry matter) | | 681 | | 7,432 | | 457.5 |
| Forage, fodder and bedding (kg grass silage) | | 271 | | 1,319 | | 76.5 |
| **Indirect sub total** | | | **3,699** | **27,451** | **241.2** | **1,607.1** |
| | | | | | | |
| **Capital** | | | | | | |
| Vehicles and machinery kg) | 0.8 | | 273 | | 25.4 | |
| Farm buildings (sq m) | 0.1 | 13.1 | 198 | 1,251 | 19.8 | 125.1 |
| Fences (m) | 1.9 | | 194 | | 17.5 | |
| Stock water supply | | | 66 | | 3 | |
| **Capital sub total** | | | **731** | **1,251** | **65.7** | **125.1** |
| | | | | | | |
| **Total Production** | | | **8,589** | **45,858** | **563.2** | **2,849.1** |
| | | | | | | |
| **Yield (kg lamb carcass)** | **190** | **308** | | | | |
| | | | | | | |
| **Post Production** | | | | | | |
| Shipping NZ to UK (17,840 km) | | | 2,030 | | 124.9 | |
| | | | | | | |
| **Total production energy input / emissions** | | | **10,619** | **45,858** | **688.1** | **2,849.1** |

*Source:* Saunders et al. 2006, p. 61

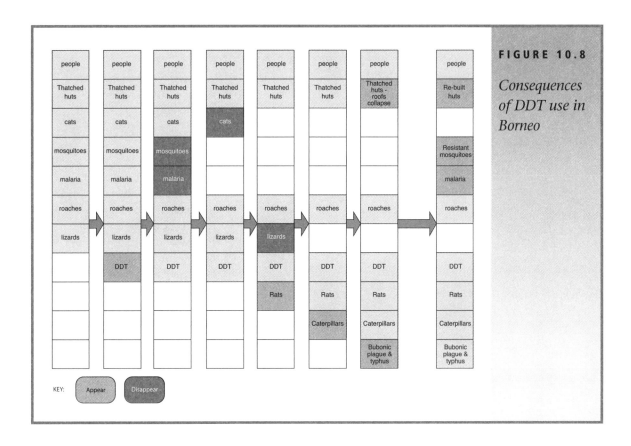

FIGURE 10.8

*Consequences of DDT use in Borneo*

feeding on thatched roofs, leading to roof collapse. Finally, through the process of Darwinian natural selection, the most resistant mosquitoes were able to reproduce. On balance, this initial attempt to eliminate malaria was totally counterproductive, leading ultimately to the return of the disease accompanied by several other pests and diseases.

There are numerous, more recent examples of revenge theory—all the consequences of well-intentioned but ill-informed interventions as matters of public policy. They are summarized in Table 10–3. One of the best known examples is China's one-child policy devised in an attempt to control the multifaceted negative consequences—political, economic, social, and ecological—of uncontrolled population growth in a country whose population already exceeds 1.25 billion (Hudson and Den Boer; 2004 World Bank 2011). Another example is the attempt to encourage people to purchase more energy-efficient commodities, such as cars and white goods. The method adopted to encourage this switch in consumption patterns is absolutely critical. If attempted with a sole reliance on increased efficiency standards without concomitant price increases for energy, the increased energy efficiency will ultimately save consumers money that can, in turn, be used to purchase other energy-using equipment. This novel phenomenon—now labeled the *rebound effect*—was first anticipated in 1865 by the English economist William Jevons who argued that increases in fuel efficiency could ultimately lead to an increase rather than a decrease in fuel use. This phenomenon has been subsequently referred to as

| TABLE 10.3 | REVENGE THEORY EXAMPLE | ORIGINAL GOAL | POLICY/ACTION | UNINTENDED CONSEQUENCE |
|---|---|---|---|---|
| *Examples of Revenge Theory* | Bangladesh drinking water | to find alternative sources to surface water contaminated with fecal coliform and other pollutants | deep well drilling | deep well water in Bangladesh contains arsenic, a known carcinogen |
| | Mississippi River Levees | to reduce the incidence of flooding | installing and raising the levees | levees trap sediment which would normally flow over the banks during flooding and restock local soils; to counter the rise of river levels from the build-up of silt, constant dredging is required along with levee raising. As levees become higher, there is a great risk of breeching and undermining |
| | Lyme disease | to eliminate wolves | wolf kills | reduction in wolves less to explosion in deer population which hosts Lyme vectors |
| | China's population control policy | to control population growth | one-child policy | Rural populations, in particular, require male children for labor. Female children are aborted or abandoned; leading to 30 million excess males known as "Bare Branches" with potentially disruptive influence on social stability |
| | Mad cow disease | to find cheaper food and faster ways to fatten cattle | adding animal byproducts (including spinal and neurological tissue) to the diet of cattle | turning herbivores into carnivores has unintended effects; one of which is the inadvertent contamination of cattle feed with scrapie virus, leading to BSE and possible transmission to humans in the form of Creutzfeldt-Jakob disease |
| | Forest fire prevention | desire to reduce forest fires, especially in national parks | intensive effort to extinguish fires, even those from natural sources such as lightning | the interruption of the natural cycle of forest fires which can play a critical role in forest and ecosystem regeneration leads to the build up of old trees and inflammable waste on the forest floor. When a spark starts a fire, there is a resulting conflagration because of the unnatural accumulation of flammable material |

the *Jevon's Paradox*. Although originally concerned with coal, it remains critically relevant today for all fossil fuels (Alcott 2005; Herring and Sorrell 2009; Sauders 2000; Sorrell 2010; UKERC 2007).

One of the most graphic examples of revenge effects is associated with hydroelectricity—long considered one of the most benign of all energy supply alternatives. As with all energy sources, benefits come with associated costs, and large hydroelectric dams are no exception (Ackermann et al. 1973; Goldsmith and Hildyard 1984; Scudde 2006). The archetypal illustration of the law of unintended consequences is the high Aswan Dam completed in Egypt in 1965. The benefits to this large but economically undeveloped country were substantial—in excess of 10,000 MW electricity capacity and conversion of over 700,000 acres from flood to canal irrigation, permitting double and triple cropping. The construction costs exceeded $1 billion but were expected to yield benefits many times that in magnitude. It soon became apparent, however, that there were numerous unanticipated externalities from the dramatic change in water flows and drastically reduced sediment transport in the Nile River: (1) the loss of natural river water flushing of salts from the soils of the fertile Nile Delta, requiring the construction of an extensive network of drainage tile systems costing $1 billion; (2) loss of soil building and natural fertilizing in the Delta requiring chemical fertilization costing over $100 million per year; (3) increased salinity and seawater intrusion in the Delta; (4) increased coastal erosion; (5) increased river bank and bottom scouring that threatened the integrity of over 500 bridges built over the previous decade, requiring $250 million in mitigation measures; (6) reduction in plankton and organic carbon levels in the Eastern Mediterranean that had traditionally sustained a large and productive sardine fishery; (7) less water downstream because of evaporation and seepage; and (8) loss of dry periods between floods that normally controlled the prevalence of water snails. These snails carry schistosomiasis (or bilharziasis), a debilitating disease that affected a significant proportion of the rural Egyptian population (Stanley and Warne 1993; Sterling 1973, Vorosmarty and Sahagian 2000).

In a related manifestation of the revenge effect, a cascade of consequences affected fisheries productivity off the mouth of the Nile Delta in the decades following the construction of the High Aswan Dam. First, the initial collapse in the fishery was reversed in the late 1980s as the dual impact of fertilizer and sewage run-off produced a surge in nutrient levels and fish populations. But the fishery has declined once again from increased levels of eutrophication (low oxygen) due to the accumulated impacts of the aforementioned fertilizer and sewage discharges (Oczkowski and Nixon 2008; Oczkowski et al. 2009).

The most recent example of electricity-related revenge issues is associated with the world's largest hydroelectric installation on China's Yangtze River. The Three Gorges Dam, built at a cost of over $24 billion to provide 20,000 MW of electricity and prevent the reoccurrence of historically devastating floods has been deemed an environmental catastrophe not only requiring the displacement of 1.2 million people, but also creating landslides, induced seismicity, water pollution, reduced biodiversity, altered weather patterns, drops in downstream water tables with saltwater intrusions, jellyfish blooms, and a rise in the number of cases of schistosomiasis (Hvistendahl 2008, *New York Times*, May 19, 2011).

In a controversial new book entitled *Techno-Fix: Why Technology Won't Save Us or the Environment*, Huesemann and Huesemann (2011) detail the unintended consequences of technological advances in a broad range of areas including industrial agriculture, genetic engineering, automobiles, high-technology warfare, and high-tech medicine.

## SOME OTHER IMPORTANT ECOSYSTEM CHARACTERISTICS

As already noted, ecosystems are characterized by nonlinear dynamics and tipping points. One related characteristic is the presence of lags. Figure 10–9 illustrates this phenomenon with the percolation of a soil disinfectant, 1,2-DCP, into groundwater long after spraying (Meadows et al. 1992, 2004). This phenomenon is of concern for the simple reason that the deleterious effects may be neither anticipated nor immediately obvious. By the time these effects are manifested, reactive policies are too late to stop the medium-term accumulation of physical—and ultimately—economic losses.

Two other concepts are of particular relevance to global fauna—including humans; namely, *bioaccumulation* and *biomagnification* in food chains. Figure 10–10

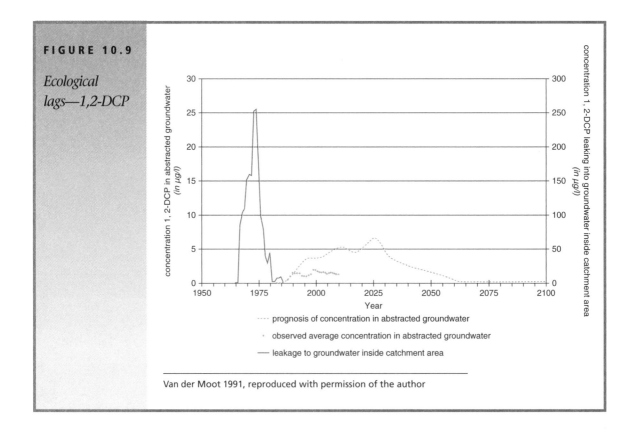

**FIGURE 10.9**

*Ecological lags—1,2-DCP*

········ prognosis of concentration in abstracted groundwater

·   observed average concentration in abstracted groundwater

——— leakage to groundwater inside catchment area

Van der Moot 1991, reproduced with permission of the author

demonstrates the different processes inherent in each of these concepts. Bioaccumulation represents the gradual accumulation of toxic chemicals in fish or animals as they age, whereas biomagnification represents the increasing concentration of toxics as they rise through the food chain. Figure 10–11 illustrates how this process works by showing the dramatic increases in concentrations of organochlorines such as DDT and PCB in a North Pacific food chain, ranging from seven to eight orders of magnitude (based on data in Noble and Elliott 1986; Tanabe et al. 1984). What may appear to be a harmless concentration in seawater becomes potentially toxic at upper levels of the food chain—frequently, animals consumed as food by humans. By way of example, the U.S. EPA issued fish eating guidelines in 2005 recommending that people not consume shark, swordfish, King Mackerel, or Tilefish because of bioaccumulated levels of mercury—a known neurotoxin.

There are, in fact, many pathways of human exposure to toxic chemicals aside from consumption of food products. Figure 10–12 is an EPA-generated flow diagram of the multiple routes of lead exposure from three major sources through air, soil, as well as surface and groundwater (U.S. EPA 2006).

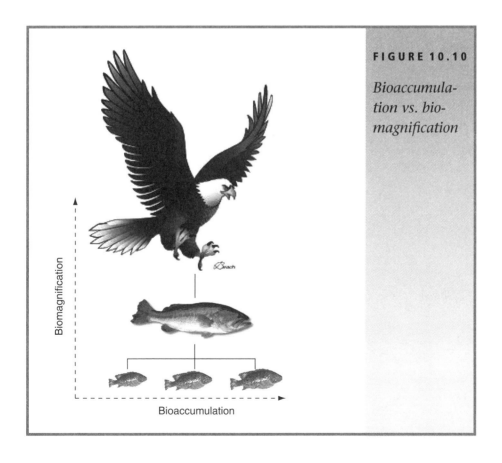

**FIGURE 10.10**

*Bioaccumulation vs. biomagnification*

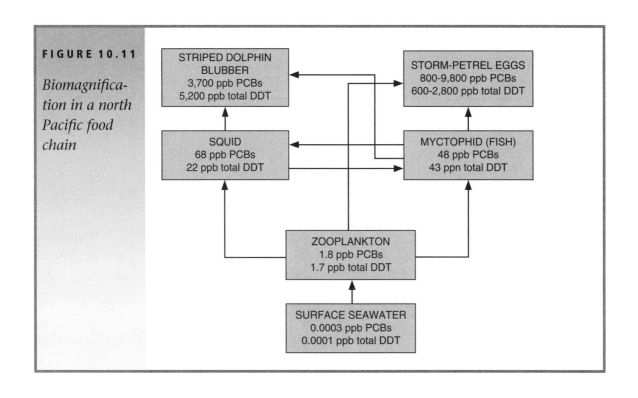

**FIGURE 10.11**

*Biomagnification in a north Pacific food chain*

STRIPED DOLPHIN BLUBBER
3,700 ppb PCBs
5,200 ppb total DDT

STORM-PETREL EGGS
800-9,800 ppb PCBs
600-2,800 ppb total DDT

SQUID
68 ppb PCBs
22 ppb total DDT

MYCTOPHID (FISH)
48 ppb PCBs
43 ppn total DDT

ZOOPLANKTON
1.8 ppb PCBs
1.7 ppb total DDT

SURFACE SEAWATER
0.0003 ppb PCBs
0.0001 ppb total DDT

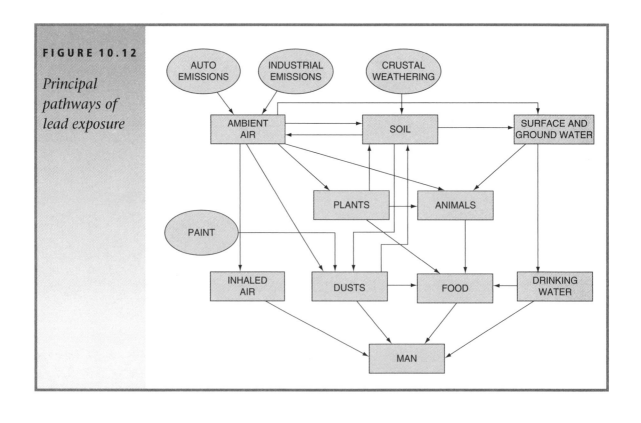

**FIGURE 10.12**

*Principal pathways of lead exposure*

AUTO EMISSIONS

INDUSTRIAL EMISSIONS

CRUSTAL WEATHERING

AMBIENT AIR

SOIL

SURFACE AND GROUND WATER

PLANTS

ANIMALS

PAINT

INHALED AIR

DUSTS

FOOD

DRINKING WATER

MAN

## THE ECOLOGICAL FOOTPRINT

While many of the theories discussed above remain largely in the realm of scientific discourse, one concept that has gained wide currency among public agencies, NGOs, and even the general public is that of *the ecological footprint*, which is an attempt to create a summary, system-level measure of the impact of human activity on the ecosystem. (See www.footprintnetwork.org.) The ecological footprint is a measure of the actual physical stocks of natural capital necessary to sustain a given human population within a given geographic region such as a city. It is sometimes expressed as a ratio; for example, if the ecological footprint of an urban area is 10.0, this implies that the land "consumed" by the urban region is 10 times greater than contained within its political boundaries. A full definition of the ecological footprint for a region—its EF (Ecological Footprint) or ACC (appropriated carrying capacity)—is the land (and water) area in various categories required exclusively by the people in this region: (a) to continuously provide all the *resources* they currently consume, and (b) to continuously absorb all the *wastes* they currently discharge. This land is either borrowed from the *past* (e.g., through the use of fossil fuels), or appropriated from the *future* (e.g., as contamination, plant growth reduction through reduced UV radiation, soil degradation, etc.) (see Rees 2007).

While the EF is frequently used to measure the impact of urbanization, it is also applicable to larger geographic areas such as regions or nations. Consider the ecological footprint of a larger geographic area such as the Netherlands. This country now consumes six times its domestically available biocapacity, up from two times in 1961 (www.footprintnetwork.org).

Perhaps the most important level of EF analysis is at the global level which measures the total impact of all human activity on our earthly environment. As the authors of the EF observe, the total land area of Earth is just over 13 billion hectares (ha), of which only 8.8 billion ha is productive cropland, pasture, or forest. The most important observations flowing from this global-level EF analysis are that the industrialized world appropriates far more than its fair share of global carrying capacity, and if the Third World were to achieve living standards comparable to those experienced in the First World, we would require two additional planet Earths (World Wildlife Fund 2010).

The World Wildlife Fund (WWF) has formally incorporated EF analysis into its *Living Planet Reports*. Figures 10–13 to 10–15 are derived from WWF reports and present the contrasting EFs of some of the wealthiest and poorest nations. Figure 10–16 indicates that as of 1987, the footprint of Earth's population for the first time exceeded global carrying capacity (WWF 2010) and will continue to rise under a business-as-usual scenario.

Finally, EF analysis can be used to assess the ecological impact (or sustainability) of commercial products. In a study conducted in the 1990s, Wada (1993) used footprinting to compare the relative merits of hothouse and field-grown tomatoes. The rationale of the study was to critically examine the view of "technological optimists" that there are no practical constraints to food production and that "industrialized hydroponic greenhouse farming can increase agricultural output per hectare

**FIGURE 10.13**

*National
ecological
footprints*

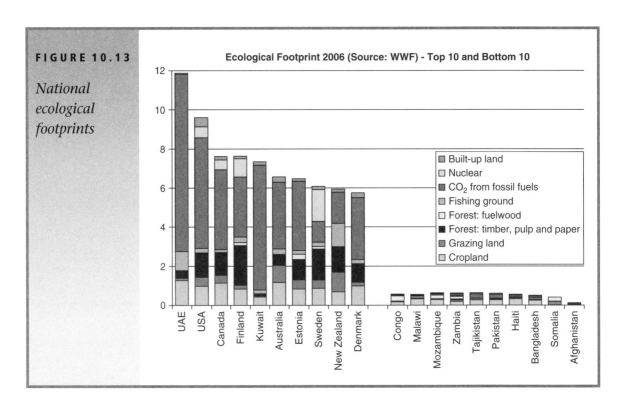

**FIGURE 10.14**

*National
ecological
footprints—
components
percentages*

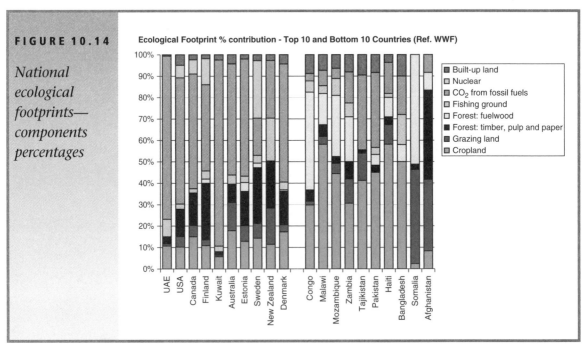

of land far beyond that of conventional field agriculture." The methodology used EF to convert energy inputs and embodied energy into their land equivalents in order to compare their ACC. Table10–4 contrasts the conventional economic analysis of the two alternative growing processes with the EF results. While greenhouse

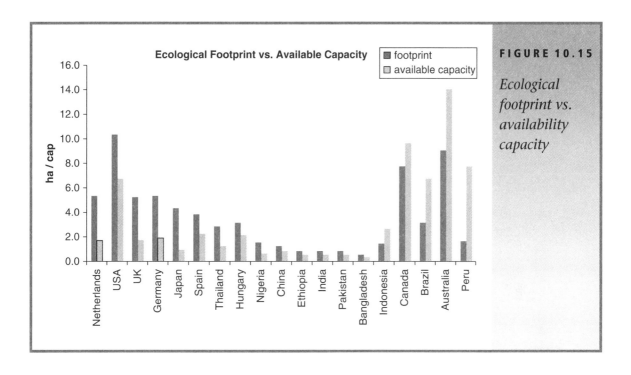

**FIGURE 10.15**

*Ecological footprint vs. availability capacity*

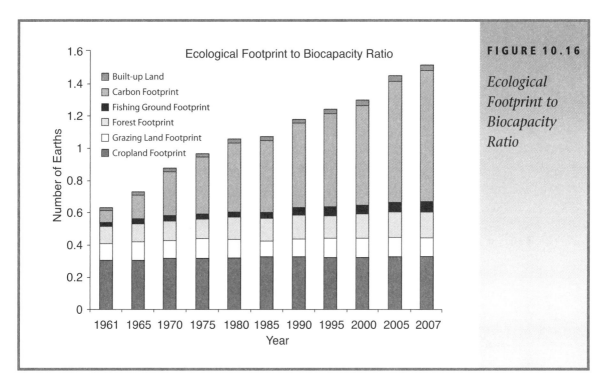

**FIGURE 10.16**

*Ecological Footprint to Biocapacity Ratio*

cultivation produced much better economic results, the hydroponic greenhouse had an ecological footprint 14–21 times greater than a comparable field operation.

The conclusion of this study is particularly germane to the theoretical underpinnings of this textbook, which stress the need for a transeconomic systems perspective that incorporates elements of ecology and social values. To quote:

| TABLE 10.4 | ECOLOGICAL FOOTPRINT OF B.C. TOMATO PRODUCTION | | | | | |
|---|---|---|---|---|---|---|
| | VARIABLE | UNITS | GREENHOUSE A | GREENHOUSE B | FARM A | FARM B |
| *Ecological Footprint of BC Tomato Production* | **Conventional Economic Measures:** | | | | | |
| | Revenue | $1000/ha/yr | 680 | 601 | 53 | 72 |
| | Profit | $1000/ha/yr | 206 | 123 | 23 | 54 |
| | Growing area needed | ha/1000 tonne/yr | 2.02 | 2.29 | 17.84 | 12.14 |
| | Productivity of growing area | tonne/ha/yr | 494 | 437 | 56 | 82 |
| | **Ecological Footprint results:** | | | | | |
| | EF/ACC | ha/1000 tonne/yr | 919 | 765 | 56 | 43 |
| | Productivity of total EF land area | tonne/ha/yr | 1.09 | 1.31 | 17.86 | 23.26 |

*Source:* derived from Wada 1993

This research reveals a conflict that is invisible to conventional economic analysis. Greenhouse farmers make a higher monetary profit per hectare of growing area than field farmers (from 2 to 9 times more). However, using the EF/ACC approach it becomes clear that greenhouse operations are not ecologically sound or sustainable. This study shows that typical economic analysis does not necessarily lead to ecologically satisfactory conclusions. The underpricing of depletable energy, fertilizer, and other inputs to hydroponic production enables operators to profit while unconsciously appropriating the productive capacity of a landscape vastly larger than their own physical plant. (Wada 1993)

The EF plays an important role in a relatively new international indicator of sustainability known as the *Happy Plant Index* (HPI) (happyplanetindex.org). Developed in 2008 as another radical departure from conventional GDP accounting [see chapter 4], this index is composed of three principal measures: life expectancy, a life satisfaction index, and a national ecological footprint. The results of this analysis parallel those reported in chapter 4 from the *Genuine Progress Indicator* and the *Index of Sustainable Economic Welfare*. In essence, national GDP accounts provide an incorrect and misleading signal with respect to sustainability, as many nations with increasing GDP have witnessed significant losses on their HPI. To quote: "the countries that are meant to represent successful development are some of the worst-performing in terms of sustainable well-being" (NEF 2009, p.4). Included among these are China, India, the United States, and many of the OECD countries.

A hopeful message from this analysis is that many middle-income countries, such as Costa Rica (with the highest national HPI index of 76.1 out of a possible 100), have higher HPI scores than their richer counterparts, suggesting that

| RANK | COUNTRY | LIFE EXP (YRS) | LIFE SAT (/10) | FOOTPRINT (GHA) | HPI | |
|------|---------|----------------|----------------|-----------------|------|---|
| 1 | Costa Rica | 78.5 | 8.5 | 2.3 | 76.1 | **TABLE 10.5** |
| 2 | Dominican Republic | 71.5 | 7.6 | 1.5 | 71.8 | |
| 3 | Jamaica | 72.2 | 6.7 | 1.1 | 70.1 | *Happy* |
| 4 | Guatemala | 69.7 | 7.4 | 1.5 | 68.4 | *Planet Index* |
| 5 | Vietnam | 73.7 | 6.5 | 1.3 | 66.5 | |
| 13 | Saudi Arabia | 72.2 | 7.7 | 2.6 | 59.7 | |
| 20 | China | 72.5 | 6.7 | 2.1 | 57.1 | |
| 23 | Mexico | 75.6 | 7.7 | 3.4 | 55.6 | |
| 35 | India | 63.7 | 5.5 | 0.9 | 53.0 | |
| 37 | Nepal | 62.6 | 5.3 | 0.8 | 51.9 | |
| 43 | Netherlands | 79.2 | 7.7 | 4.4 | 50.6 | |
| 49 | Singapore | 79.4 | 7.1 | 4.2 | 48.2 | |
| 51 | Germany | 79.1 | 7.2 | 4.2 | 48.1 | |
| 52 | Switzerland | 81.3 | 7.7 | 5.0 | 48.1 | |
| 53 | Sweden | 80.5 | 7.9 | 5.1 | 48.0 | |
| 69 | Italy | 80.3 | 6.9 | 4.8 | 44.0 | |
| 71 | France | 80.2 | 7.1 | 4.9 | 43.9 | |
| 74 | UK | 79.0 | 7.4 | 5.3 | 43.3 | |
| 75 | Japan | 82.3 | 6.8 | 4.9 | 43.3 | |
| 76 | Spain | 80.5 | 7.6 | 5.7 | 43.2 | |
| 88 | Norway | 79.8 | 8.1 | 6.9 | 40.4 | |
| 89 | Canada | 80.3 | 8.0 | 7.1 | 39.4 | |
| 102 | Australia | 80.9 | 7.9 | 7.8 | 36.6 | |
| 103 | New Zealand | 79.8 | 7.8 | 7.7 | 36.2 | |
| 105 | Denmark | 77.9 | 8.1 | 8.0 | 35.5 | |
| 108 | Russia | 65.0 | 5.9 | 3.7 | 34.5 | |
| 114 | USA | 77.9 | 7.9 | 9.4 | 30.7 | |
| 139 | Burundi | 48.5 | 2.9 | 0.8 | 21.8 | |
| 140 | Namibia | 51.6 | 4.5 | 3.7 | 21.1 | |
| 141 | Botswana | 48.1 | 4.7 | 3.6 | 20.9 | |
| 142 | Tanzania | 51.0 | 2.4 | 1.1 | 17.8 | |
| 143 | Zimbabwe | 40.9 | 2.8 | 1.1 | 16.6 | |

*Source:* NEF 2009

high GDP per capita and economic growth are not prerequisites to sustainability. Table 10–5 presents a selection of countries with component and total scores for HPI (NEF 2009). The HPI value is derived from the formula $(LE*LS/10*6.42) / (FP + 3.35)$, where LE = life expectancy; LS = life satisfaction; and FP = ecological footprint.

The development of ecological footprinting has led to the emergence of similar and equally useful concepts in related types of analyses. Foremost among these is carbon footprinting, a concept explored in great detail in chapter 19.

## CITED REFERENCES AND RECOMMENDED READINGS

Ackermann, William C. et al. (1973) *Man-Made Lakes: Their Problems and Environmental Effects*, Washington, DC: American Geophysical Union.

Alcott, Blake (2005) "Jevons' Paradox," *Ecological Economics* 54, pp. 9–21.

Altieri, Miguel A. (2007) "Fatal Harvest: Old and New Dimensions of the Ecological Tragedy of Modern Agriculture," in Peter N. Nemetz (ed.) *Sustainable Resource Management: Reality or Illusion?* Cheltenham: Edward Elgar, pp. 189–213.

Beyer, Hawthorne L. et al. (2007) "Willow on Yellowstone's Northern Range: Evidence of a Trophic Cascade, *Ecological Applications*, 17(6), pp. 1563–1571.

Broecker, Wallace S. and Robert Kunzig (2008) *Fixing Climate. What Past Climate Changes Reveal About The Current Threat—And How to Counter It*, New York: Hill & Wang.

Cederholm, C. Jeff et al. (2000) *Pacific Salmon and Wildlife. Ecological Contexts, Relationships, and Implications for Management*, Washington State Department of Fish and Wildlife.

Chi, Kelly Rae et al. (2009) *Fair Miles. Recharting the food miles map*. International Institute for Environment and Development (IIED) and Oxfam, Cowley, Oxford.

Conway, Gordon R. (1972) "Ecological Aspects of Pest Control in Malaysia," in M. Taghi Farvar and John P. Milton, *The Careless Technology. Ecology and International Development*, Garden City, NY: Natural History Press, pp. 467–488.

Davidson, Osha Gray (2003) *Fire in the Turtle House. The Green Sea Turtle and the Fate of the Ocean*, New York: Public Affairs.

Eisenberg, Cristina (2010) *The Wolf's Tooth. Keystone Predators, Trophic Cascades, and Biodiversity*, Washington, DC: Island Press.

Elkington, John (1998) *Cannibals With Forks. The Triple Bottom Line of 21st Century Business*, Gabriola Island, BC: New Society Publishers.

Estes, James A. et al. (2011) "Trophic Downgrading of Planet Earth," *Science*, July 15, pp. 301–306.

Garnett, Tara (2008) *Cooking up a storm: Food, greenhouse gas emissions and our changing climate*. Food Climate Research Network, Centre for Environmental Strategy, University of Surrey, September.

Goldsmith, Edward and Nicholas Hildyard (1984) *The Social & Environmental Effects of Large Dams*, San Francisco, CA: Sierra Club Books.

Green, Maurice B. (1978) *Eating Oil. Energy Use in Food Production*, Boulder, CO: Westview Press.

*The Guardian* (2005) "Warming hits 'Tipping Point,'" August 11.

Happy Planet Index website (www.happyplanetindex.org) [website based at The New Economics Foundation, London].

Herring, H. and S. Sorrell (2009) *Energy Efficiency and Sustainable Consumption. The Rebound Effect*, Houndmills, Basingstoke, Hampshire: Palgrave Macmillan.

Holling, C.S. (1973) "Resilience and Stability of Ecological Systems," *Annual Review of Ecology and Systematics*, pp. 1–23.

Holling, C.S. (1979) "Myths of Ecological Stability: Resilience and the Problem of Failure," in C.F. Smart and W.T. Stanbury, *Studies in Crisis Management*, Montreal: Instiwtute for Research on Public Policy, pp. 97–109.

Hudson, Valerie and Andrea M. Den Boer (2004) *Bare Branches: The Security Implications of Asia's Surplus Male Population*, Cambridge, MA: MIT Press.

Huesemann, Michael and Joyce Huesemann (2011) Techno-Fix. Why Technology Won't Save Us or the Environment, New Society Publishers, Gabriola Island, B.C.

Hughes, Terence P. (1994) "Catastrophes, Phase Shifts, and Large-Scale Degradation of a Caribbean Coral Reef," *Science*, 26, September 9, pp. 1547–1551.

Hvistendahl (2008) "China's Three Gorges Dam: An environmental Catastrophe?" *Scientific American*, March 25 online at scientificamerican.com.

Ise, Takeshi et al. (2008) "High Sensitivity of Peat Decomposition to Climate Change through Water-Table Feedback," *Nature Geoscience*, published online 12 October.

Jevons, Stanley (1865) *The Coal Question* [reprinted 2012, Charleston, SC: Nabu Press].

Kimbrell, Andrew (ed.) (2002) *Fatal Harvest. The Tragedy of Industrial Agriculture*, Washington, DC: Island Press.

Krebs, Charles (2008) *The Ecological World View*, Berkeley, CA: University of California Press.

Kurz, W.A. et al. (2008) "Mountain Pine Beetle and Forest Carbon Feedback to Climate Change," *Nature* Vol. 452, April 24, pp. 987–990.

Meadows, Donella (2008) *Thinking in Systems*, White River Junction, VT: Chelsea Green Publishing.

Meadows, Donella and Jorgen Randers (2001) "Adding the Time Dimension to Environmental Policy," *International Organization*, pp. 213–233.

Meadows, Donella et al. (1972) *The Limits to Growth*, New York: Universe Books.

Meadows, Donella et al. (1992) *Beyond the Limits*, Post Mills, VT: Chelsea Green Publishing.

Meadows, Donella et al. (2004) *Limits to Growth: The 30-Year Update*, White River Junction, VT: Chelsea Green Publishing.

Myers, Ransom A. et al. (2007) "Cascading Effects of the Loss of Apex Predatory Sharks from a Coastal Ocean," *Science* 31, pp. 1846–1850.

National Academy of Sciences (2004) *Valuing Ecosystem Services—Toward Better Environmental Decision-Making*, Washington, DC.

*Nature* (2007) "Is the Global Carbon Market Working?" Vol. 445, February 8, pp. 595–596.

The New Economics Foundation (NEF) (2009) *Happy Planet Index 2.0*, London, p. 4.

*New York Times* (2011) "China Admits Problems with Three Gorges Dam," May 19.

*New York Times* (2012) "Carbon Credits Gone Awry Raise Output of Harmful Gas," August 8.

Noble, D.G. and J.E. Elliott (1986) "Environmental Contaminants in Canadian Seabirds, 1968–1985: Trends and Effects," *Canadian Wildlife Service Technical Report Series*, No. 13, Ottawa.

Oczkowski, Autumn and Scott Nixon (2008) "Increasing Nutrient Concentrations and the Rise and Fall of a Coastal Fishery: A Review of Data from the Nile Delta, Egypt," in *Estuarine, Coastal and Shelf Science* 77, pp. 309–319.

Oczkowski et al. (2009) "Anthropogenic enhancement of Egypt's Mediterranean Fishery," in *Proceedings of the National Academy of Sciences* February 3, 106(5), pp. 1364–1367.

Pandolfi, John M. et al. (2011) "Projecting Coral Reef futures Under Global Warming and Ocean Acidification," *Science*, 333, July 22, pp. 418–422.

Pfeiffer, Dale Allen (2006) *Eating Fossil Fuels: Oil, Food and the Coming Crisis in Agriculture*, Gabriola Island, BC: New Society Publishers.

Rees, William (2007) "Is Humanity Fatally Successful? in Peter N. Nemetz (ed.) *Sustainable Resource Management: Reality or Illusion*? Cheltenham: Edward Elgar, pp. 392–419.

Ripple, William J. and Robert L. Beschta (2004) "Wolves, Elk, Willows, and Trophic Cascades in the Upper Gallatin Range of Southwestern Montana, USA, *Forest Ecology and Management*, 200, pp. 161–181.

Ripple, William J. and Robert L. Beschta (2007) "Restoring Yellowstone's Aspen with Wolves," *Biological Conservation*, 138, pp. 514–519.

Rockstrom, Johan et al. (2009a) "A Safe Operating Space for Humanity," *Nature*, 461, September 24, pp. 472–475.

Rockstrom, Johan et al. (2009b) "Planetary Boundaries: Exploring the Safe Operating Space for Humanity," *Ecology and Science*, 14(2) 32 [online], URL: http:www.ecolog yandociety.org/vol14/iss2/art32/.

Saunders, Harry D. (2000) "A View from the Macro Side: Rebound, Backfire and Khazoom-Brookes," *Energy Policy* 28, pp. 439–449.

Saunders, Carolie et al. (2006) *Food Miles—Comparative Energy/Emissions Performance of New Zealand's Agricultural Industry*. AERU. Lincoln University Research Report No. 285, July.

Scudder, Thayer (2006) *The Future of Large Dams*, London: Earthscan.

Smith, Alisa and J.B. (2007) MacKinnon *The 100-Mile Diet*, Random House Canada.

Smith, Alison et al. (2005) *The Validity of Food Miles as an Indicator of Sustainable Development*. Final Report produced for DEFRA (the U.K. Department for Environment, Food and Rural Affairs), July.

Sorrell, Steven (2010) "Energy, Economic Growth and Environmental Sustainability: Five Propositions," *Sustainability2010*, 2, pp. 1784–1809.

Stanley, Danile Jean and Andrew G. Warne (1993) "Nile Delta: Recent Geological Evolution and Human Impact," *Science*, 260(5108), April 30, pp. 628–634.

Sterling, Claire (1973) "The Trouble with Superdams," in *Britannica Yearbook of Science and the Future, 1974*, pp. 112–127.

Stokesbury, Kevin D.E. (2009) "SMAST Cooperative Scallop Video Survey and Fisheries Management," Department of Fisheries Oceanography, School for Marine Science and Technology, University of Massachusetts, February 2—PowerPoint presentation.

Tanabe, Shinsuke et al. (1984) "Polychlorobiphenyls, SDDT, and Hexachlorocyclohexane Isomers in the Western North Pacific Ecosystem," *Archives of Environmental Contamination and Toxicology*, 13, pp. 731–738.

Tenner, Edward (1996) *Why Things Bite Back. Technology and the Revenge of Unintended Consequences*, New York: Alfred A. Knopf.

Terborgh, John and James A. Estes (2010) *Trophic Cascades. Predators, Prey and the Changing Dynamics of Nature*, Washington, DC: Island Press.

UK Energy Research Centre (ERC) (2007) *The Rebound Effect: An Assessment of the Evidence for Economy-Wide Energy Savings from Improved Energy Efficiency*.

US Environmental Protection Agency (EPA) (2006) *Air Quality Criteria for Lead*, October.

van der Moot, N.L. WMD (2011) updated from "Geo-hydrologisch modelonderzoek en 1,2-dcp-voorspelling pompstation Noordbargeres"; WMD/Kiwa; Assen/Nieuwegein December 1991.

Van Houtan, Kyle S., Stacy H. Hargrove and George H. Balazs (2010) "Land Use, Macroalgae, and a Tumor-Forming Disease in Marine Turtles," *PLoS ONE*, September, 5(9), e1 2900, pp. 1–9.

Vianna, G.M.S. et al. (2010) *Wanted Dead or Alive? The relative value of reef sharks as a fishery and an ecotourism asset in Palau.* University of Western Australia, Australian Government and Australian Institute for Marine Science.

Vorosmarty, Charles J. and Dork Sahagian (2000) "Anthropogenic Disturbance of the Terrestrial Water Cycle," *BioScience* 50(9), pp. 753–765.

Wada, Y. (1993) "The Appropriated Carrying Capacity of Tomato Production: Comparing the Ecological Footprints of Hydroponic Greenhouse and Mechanized Field Operations," M.A. Thesis. University of British Columbia, School of Community and Regional Planning.

Wadham, J.L. et al. (2012) "Potential Methane Reservoirs beneath Antarctica," *Nature*, 488, August 30, pp. 633–637.

World Bank (2011) *World Development Report 2012*, Washington, DC.

World Health Organization (WHO) (2011) *World Health Statistics*, Geneva.

World Wildlife Fund (WWF) (2010) *Living Planet Report*, Gland, Switzerland.

World Wildlife Fund and Allianz (2009)—Tyndall Centre. *Major Tipping Points in the Earth's Climate System and Consequences for the Insurance Sector*, Berlin, Germany. www.footprintnetwork.org [website of Global Footprint Network, Oakland, CA].

www.footprintnetwork.org/en/index.php/GFN [website for Global Footprint Network].

# PART II

## The Private Sector

# CHAPTER 11

# A Brief History of Corporate Response to Sustainability Issues

I N MANY RESPECTS, THE BEGINNING OF THE MODERN environmental move-ment began with the publication of Rachel Carson's *Silent Spring* in 1962. The following decade was characterized not only by increased public awareness of the issues, but also by extensive and bipartisan governmental legislative initiatives. Environmental legislation passed under U.S. President Lyndon Johnson included Clear Air, Water Quality and Clean Water Restoration Acts and Amendments, Wilderness Act of 1964, Endangered Species Preservation Act of 1966, National Trails System Act of 1968, Wild and Scenic Rivers Act of 1968, Land and Water Conservation Act of 1965, Solid Waste Disposal Act of 1965, Motor Vehicle Air Pollution Control Act of 1965, National Historic Preservation Act of 1966, Aircraft Noise Abatement Act of 1968, and the National Environmental Policy Act of 1969. Johnson's successor, President Richard Nixon, implemented more wide-ranging legislation such as the Clean Air Act of 1970, amendments to the Federal Water Pollution Control act in 1972, as well as establishing the Environmental Protec-tion Agency, the Occupational Safety and Health Administration, the Council on Environmental Quality, and the Consumer Product Safety Commission.

The decades following Rachel Carson's monumental work were also marked by numerous landmark events in the postwar environmental context of business: a major industrial accident in Seveso, Italy, in 1976 marked by the extensive release of dioxin, a recognized carcinogen; the shipwreck of the tanker Amoco Cadiz off the shores of Brittany in 1978, spilling 1.6 million barrels of oil, the largest marine di-saster of its kind; a serious civilian nuclear plant accident with the partial meltdown of the Three Mile Island nuclear reactor in Pennsylvania on March 28, 1979; the re-lease of the toxic chemical methyl isocyanate at Union Carbide's chemical plant in Bhopal, India, on December 2, 1984, leading to the death of thousands of residents in the immediate area as well as serious injury to tens of thousands of others; the world's worst nuclear power accident at Chernobyl on April 26, 1986; the loss of 250,000 barrels of crude oil in the pristine waters of Prince William Sound, Alaska, when the Exxon Valdez was grounded; the loss of approximately one half million barrels of crude from the sinking of the tanker, Prestige, off the coast of Spain on November 13, 2002; and, more recently, the massive oil spill in the Gulf of Mexico from a drilling platform owned by British Petroleum and the nuclear reactor melt-down in Fukushima, Japan.

Many of the physical effects of the early accidents remain to this day, and the psychological impact on the conduct of business has been unprecedented. In a landmark study entitled "Corporate Strategy: The Avalanche of Change since Bhopal," Bruce Piasecki (1995) argues that the toxic release of gas from the Union Carbide mill was a watershed in corporate attitudes toward environmental risk and the need to create new strategic initiatives for addressing such risks. In this case, the risks were substantial—not only the immense human tragedy, but also the threat to corporate license to operate, as Union Carbide, the owner of the plant no longer exists as a corporate entity. There is still an extant arrest warrant in India for the company's CEO, and in 2010, India renewed its request for the extradition of the chief executive (*New York Times* 2011). The U.S. government also felt the necessity to react. In 1986, the U.S. Congress enacted EPCRA (the Emergency Planning and Community Right to Know Act), which required most major industrial facilities to gather and publicize their emissions to land, air, and water. The Toxic Release Inventory [see chapter 5] created a major impetus to the reduction in industrial pollution in the United States.

Clearly, much has changed from the halcyon days of the immediate postwar years. The business environment in which firms operate has been transformed significantly in the last few decades. The factors that have contributed most strongly to this new context are globalization; several economic crises; the continuing geopolitical problem of global poverty; increased global environmental degradation; and, accompanying this, the emergence of environmental awareness among the general public and, as a consequence, government at all levels from municipal to federal.

Fischer and Schot (1993) have broken down the history of corporate response to environmental pressures into two periods: 1970–1985, and post 1985. According to the authors, the first period was characterized largely by corporations resisting or reluctantly adapting to external pressure for environmental control. Three different substrategies were evinced: (1) crisis-oriented environmental management that was ad hoc and reactive in nature, (2) cost-orientated management characterized by the common view that environmental control was a cost to be minimized and a drag on corporate profitability, and (3) early environmental enlightenment where a small number of corporations were beginning to perceive that environmental issues might be successfully and profitably addressed in new corporate strategic initiatives. In general, however, this era was characterized by a lack of willingness to internalize environmental problems and a reliance on cost-centered, end-of-pipe pollution control rather than fundamental changes in process and products that could potentially enhance profitability.

The second era identified by Fischer and Schot following 1985 represents the first glimmerings of strategic adjustments most notably by a handful of large corporations and multinationals. Willams et al. (1993) identified the following drivers of this corporate response: (1) increasingly stringent environmental legislation and enforcement; (2) increasing costs associated with pollution control, solid waste, and effluent disposal; (3) increasing commercial pressure from the supply, consumption, and disposal of both intermediate and final products; (4) increasing awareness on the part of investors of companies' environmental performance in view of the cost implications associated with liability, and the *polluter pays principle* [see chapter 5]; (5) increasing training, personnel and information requirements; and (6) increasing expectations on the part of the local community and workforce of the environmental performance of firms and their impact on the local environment. Each of these factors set the stage for Porter's conceptual leap, which promised to transform these potential costs into sustainable competitive advantage. [See chapter 1.]

A similar, but somewhat more disaggregated, analysis of the transformation in corporate attitudes relating to the environment is presented in Hoffman's work entitled *From Heresy to Dogma, An Institutional History of Corporate Environmentalism* (2001). To Hoffman, the transformation occurred over four periods: (1) 1960–1970—a period of "industrial environmentalism" where industry considered these issues largely peripheral to its business and had the latitude to handle pollution problems itself largely without government interference; (2) 1970–1982—a period of "regulatory environmentalism," marked by the establishment of the U.S. EPA and new federal environmental regulation and technical compliance by industry; (3) 1982–1988—a period of "environmentalism as social responsibility" where industry became more proactively involved in the public debate and rule-setting processes addressing environmental degradation. Hoffman describes a change from technical compliance to managerial compliance where more corporate institutional processes and structures were established to deal with environmental matters; and (4) 1988–1993, a period "strategic environmentalism," which elevated environmental issues to the level of corporate strategy and the recognition of the explicit role major stakeholders such as investors, insurers, and competitors in environmental issues.

This last period represented the birth of a major change that has radically altered the strategic calculus of corporate decision making—namely, the emergence of *stakeholders* as key players in the corporate environment, replacing the sole reliance on *shareholders* as the ultimate focus of corporate decision making. The OECD *Principles of Corporate Governance* endorsed by OECD Ministers in 1999 states that "In all

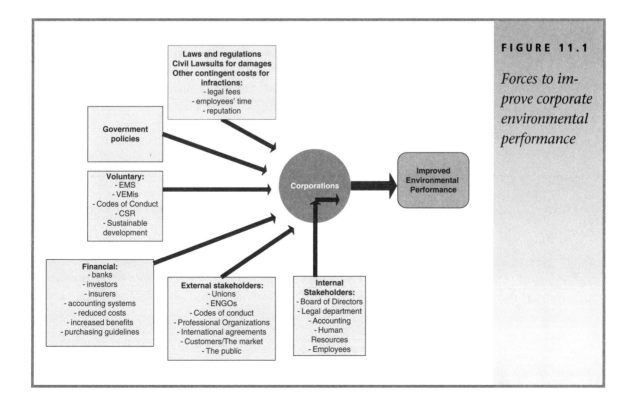

**FIGURE 11.1**

*Forces to improve corporate environmental performance*

OECD countries, the rights of stakeholders are established by law (e.g., labour, business, commercial and insolvency laws) or by contractual relations" (OECD 2010, see also du Plessis et al. 2011). This diverse range of additional players who both constrain and empower corporate action include bondholders, debtors, creditors, insurers, employees, suppliers, customers, regulators, and the general public. All combine to make both enrich and increase the complexity of the corporate environment in which both short-term and long-term decisions must be made. Figure 11–1 summarizes the driving forces acting on corporations to improve environmental performance [derived from Thompson 2002].

The critical question is how this process of transformation in corporate strategy impacted corporate value. This issue is specifically addressed by Dunphy (2007) who identifies six specific evolutionary phases in strategy and links them directly to a value continuum that ranges all the way from value destruction to value creation and sustainability [see Table 11–1]. It is important to bear in mind that none of the rubrics of corporate environmental strategy suggest a mechanical progression of each and every firm through stages of increased engagement with sustainability issues. Rather, they are intended to reflect differing corporate attitudes that may characterize some, but certainly not all, firms in several distinctive periods in the last half century. Clearly, much remains to be accomplished. In one of the modern classics of environmentalism and business entitled *Cannibals With Forks*, John Elkington (1998) identified 7 revolutions that are transforming corporate attitudes and behavior in the realm of sustainable business: (1) increased domestic and international competition, (2) a global shift in human and societal values to include concern for social and ecological issues in addition to economic matters, (3) growing pressures for transparency, (4) the increasing adoption of life-cycle technology and measurement, (5) the emergence of new forms of partnerships especially among NGOS and corporations, (6) the increasing need to take a longer view with respect to the impact of business decisions, and (7) dramatic changes in the philosophy of corporate governance. Elkington concludes his book with an extensive list of 39 steps required to shift business toward sustainability based on the 7 revolutions he has identified. [See Table 11–2]

| **TABLE 11.1** *Six Evolutionary Phases in Strategy and Sustainability* | WAVE | PHASE | CHARACTERIZATION | EFFECT ON CORPORATE VALUE |
|---|---|---|---|---|
| | 1st | Opposition | Rejection | value destroyers |
| | | Ignorance | Non-responsiveness | Value limiter |
| | 2nd | Risk | Compliance | value conservers |
| | | Cost | Efficiency | value creators |
| | | Competitive Advantage | Strategic Proactivity | |
| | 3rd | Transformation | The sustaining corporation | sustainable business |

*Source:* Derived from Dunphy et al. 2007, p. 17

| # | RUBRIC | OLD PARADIGM | NEW PARADIGM |
|---|--------|--------------|--------------|
| 1 | Governance | financial bottom line | triple bottom line |
| 2 | | physical and financial capital | economic, human, social, natural |
| 3 | | tangible, owned assets | intangible, borrowed assets |
| 4 | | downsizing | innovation |
| 5 | | exclusive governance | inclusive governance |
| 6 | | shareholders | stakeholders |
| 7 | Time | wider | longer |
| 8 | | extraction | restoration |
| 9 | | tactics | strategy |
| 10 | | plans | scenarios |
| 11 | | time bandits | time guardians |
| 12 | Partners | deregulation | reregulation |
| 13 | | enemies | complementors |
| 14 | | subversion | symbiosis |
| 15 | | unconditional loyalty | conditional loyalty |
| 16 | | rights | responsibilities |
| 17 | | green business networks | sustainability keiretsu |
| 18 | Life-cycle technology | responsibility to factory gate | stewardship throughout life cycle |
| 19 | | sales | lifetime customer value |
| 20 | | product and waste | co-products |
| 21 | | environmental LCAs | triple bottom line LCAs |
| 22 | | product | function |
| 23 | | trial and error | biometrics |
| 24 | Transparency | closed, except financial reports | open, triple bottom line reports |
| 25 | | need to know | right to know |
| 26 | | facts and science | emotions and perceptions |
| 27 | | one-way, passive communication | multi-way, active dialogue |
| 28 | | promises | targets |
| 29 | Values | careless, uncaring | careful, caring |
| 30 | | control | stewardship |
| 31 | | me | we |
| 32 | | monocultures | diversity |

**TABLE 11.2**

*Elkington's Prerequisites for Sustainability*

(Continued)

| TABLE 11.2 | # | RUBRIC | OLD PARADIGM | NEW PARADIGM |
|---|---|---|---|---|
| *continued* | 33 | | growth | sustainability |
| | 34 | Markets | externalization of costs | internalization of costs |
| | 35 | | compliance | competitive advantage |
| | 36 | | country-by-country standards | global consistency |
| | 37 | | adding volume | adding value |
| | 38 | | production growth | sustainable consumption |
| | 39 | | disruptive NGO campaigns | disruption as commercial strategy |

*Source:* Derived from Elkington 1998, Chapter 12

## CITED REFERENCES AND RECOMMENDED READINGS

Carson, Rachel (1962) *Silent Spring*, Boston: Houghton Mifflin.

Du Plessis, Jean Jacques, Anil Hargovan and Mirko Bagaric (2011) *Principles of Contemporary Corporate Governance*, Cambridge: Cambridge University Press.

Dunphy, Dexter (2007) *Organizational Change for Corporate Sustainability*, London: Routledge.

Fisher, Kurt and Johan Schot (1993) *Environmental Strategies for Industry: International Perspectives on Research Needs and Policy Implications*, Washington, DC: Island Press.

Hoffman, Andre J. (2001) *From Heresy to Dogma, an Institutional History of Corporate Environmentalism*, Stanford, CA: Stanford Business Books.

*New York Times* (2011) "Bhopal (Chemical leak)" updated January 13 at http://topics. nytimes.com/top/news/international/countriesandterritories/india/Bhopal/index. html?8qa.

Organization for Economic Co-operation and Development (OECD) (2010) *Principles of Corporate Governance*, Paris.

Piasecki, Bruce (1995) *Corporate Environmental Strategy: An Avalanche of Corporate Change since Bhopal*, New York: John Wiley & Sons.

Thomson, Dixon (2002) *Tools for Environmental Management*, Gabriola Island, BC: New Society Publishers.

Williams, Hugh E., James Medhurst and Kirstine Drew (1993) "Corporate Strategies for a Sustainable Future," Ch. 4 in Kurt Fisher and Johan Schot (eds.), Environmental Strategies for Industry: International Perspectives on Research Needs and Policy Implications, Washington, DC: Island Press, pp. 117–146.

# CHAPTER 12

# Waste to Profits: The Case of Consolidated Mining and Smelting Ltd.

M ICHAEL PORTER AND CLAAS VAN DER LINDE'S SEMINAL *Harvard Business Review* article of 1995 made a powerful argument about the false dichotomy between environmental control and profitability. As evidenced by recent corporate annual reports, numerous large corporations are beginning to appreciate this argument and are starting to make significant modifications to their corporate strategies to simultaneously advance the cause of corporate profitability and sustainability. It is interesting to note, however, that there is at least one example of a major international company that arrived at this conclusion over half a century ago and adjusted its strategy accordingly, driven by a powerful force of circumstance that threatened its very existence.

The Consolidated Mining and Smelting Company (renamed Cominco in 1966) was formed in 1906 and four years later bought the Sullivan Mine, the world's largest silver-lead-zinc ore body, located at Kimberley in the southeast corner of the Canadian province of British Columbia, which borders on the American states of Washington, Idaho, and Montana. The complex sulfite ore was shipped to the company's newly acquired and redesigned smelter in Trail, B.C., some 160 km to the southwest in the Columbia River valley. As the lead and zinc concentrates contained from 17–33% sulfur, their smelting produced significant quantities of sulfur dioxide as a waste product that was off-gassed from a 409-foot tall stack. By 1930, these releases had reached a high of 651 tons per day of $SO_2$ (or 325.5 tons as sulfur).

The topography of the Trail region presented some unusual challenges and problems, as "the Trail Smelter lies in a deep gorge cut out by the Columbia River. The region is decidedly rugged and the Columbia is flanked on either side by mountains sufficiently high to preclude a diffusion of smoke fumes to east or west" (Howes and Miller 1929, p. 6). The net result of this topographical configuration was a funneling of $SO_2$ waste gases 11 miles down the Columbia River valley into Northeast Washington State (Trail Smelter Arbitration Tribunal 1941, p. 8). In 1926, citizens of the town of Northport in Stevens County, Washington, complained that the toxic fumes were destroying crops, killing their cattle, corroding their barbed wire fences and galvanized roofs, and peeling building paint. The U.S. government complained to Canada, and both countries agreed to take the case to arbitration under the International Joint Commission [IJC], marking the first time that an issue of air pollution came before an international tribunal.

The IJC found against the smelter in 1931, recommending that financial compensation of $350,000 be paid and that the company be required to reduce the massive amounts of $SO_2$ released into the atmosphere. The U.S. government rejected the commission's recommendations as inadequate, and the issue was not finally settled until March 1941 when a special panel (the Trail Smelter Arbitration Tribunal), established in 1936, issued its "Final Decision." Well before the date of settlement, the Consolidated Mining and Smelting Company had hit upon an answer to the problem and had installed several new industrial processes at their site in Trail. The solution was to extract sulfur from the gaseous emissions and produce sulfuric acid ($H_2SO_4$), which could then be used to manufacture fertilizer.

On the face of it, being forced to expend large sums of money on the control of waste products, estimated in excess of $20 million, posed a significant financial challenge to the smelting company. Fortuitously, the system designed to use sulfur dioxide to produce fertilizer addressed a number of critical issues facing the company at the time: (1) most importantly, the new control procedures essentially removed a threat to the continued operation of the smelter; (2) it provided a more diversified product base that allowed the company to weather falling metal prices in the Great Depression; and (3) it allowed the company to capitalize on an emerging market for synthetic fertilizers, both nationally and internationally.

The production of fertilizer was largely based on the conversion of $SO_2$ to $H_2SO_4$, which was used, in turn, to produce fertilizers such as ammonium sulfate, ammonium phosphate, and superphosphate. Figure 12–1 presents a simplified schematic representation of part of the company's extensive industrial complex in the immediate post-WW II period. Not shown here are separate components devoted to the production of nitric acid (and subsequently, ammonium nitrate), a chlor-alkali plant, and facilities for iron and steel production.

On a volume basis, Cominco's historical metal production has been largely dominated by lead and zinc [Figure 12–2], and this has also been reflected in corporate metal-based revenues [Figure 12–3]. Metal prices are notoriously erratic, and the effects of price declines in the Depression [Figure 12–4] are evidenced in Cominco's revenues.

The unusual set of circumstances that forced the smelter to undertake extensive and costly pollution control led to a transformation in the strategic direction of the company. Once fertilizer production was underway in 1930, it continued an almost steady increase until the mid-1960s [see Figure 12–5]. Figure 12–6 details the extraordinary changes in sulfur emissions and feed that occurred at the Trail smelter over the period from 1900 to 1999. Figure 12–7 summarizes the contribution of fertilizer production to company finances. These contributions peaked in 1944 with fertilizer revenue as a percentage of total revenue at 31.7% and the comparable percentage for profit at 42.7 percent.

As Figure 12–6 illustrated, the release of sulfur dioxide from Cominco's operations at Trial has declined steadily since the company instituted waste gas recovery in the late 1920s. Despite the enormous reductions in $SO_2$ emissions, the nature of the ore and smelting technology precluded the total elimination of this pollutant.

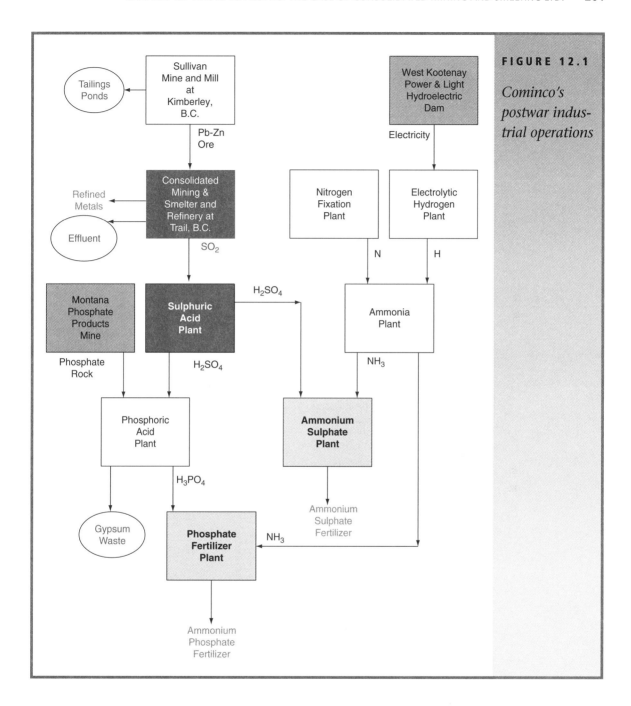

**FIGURE 12.1**

*Cominco's postwar industrial operations*

As a result, Cominco instituted a unique system of air pollutant monitors located downwind of the smelter to provide telemetric feedback on ambient $SO_2$ levels, which vary by season and time of day, depending on temperature, winds, and other atmospheric conditions. Any levels of $SO_2$ deemed excessive led to a temporary curtailment of smelting operations.

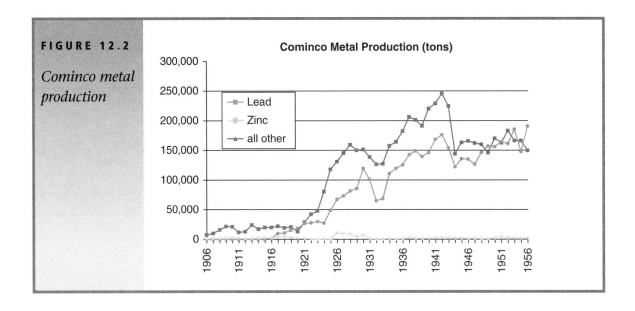

**FIGURE 12.2**

*Cominco metal production*

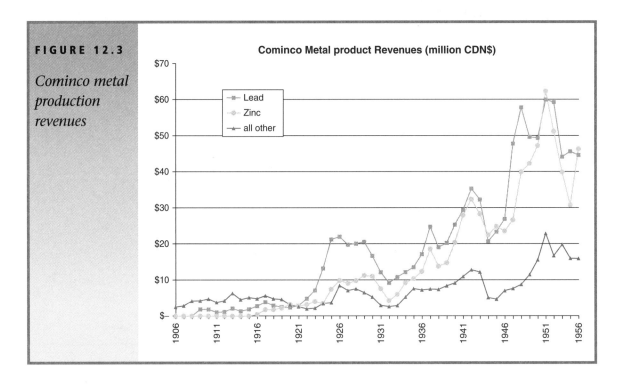

**FIGURE 12.3**

*Cominco metal production revenues*

While numerous examples have been produced of recent efforts by companies in a broad range of industrial activities to convert waste to profits, less attention has been paid to Cominco's pioneering experience from many decades ago. This unusual historical example provides a cogent argument for reconceptualizing the opportunities that may lie hidden in ostensible threats to corporate profitability and survival. It seems clear that even if waste product recovery had not made a contribution to

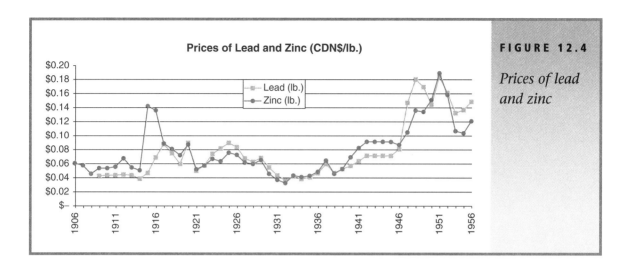

**FIGURE 12.4**

*Prices of lead and zinc*

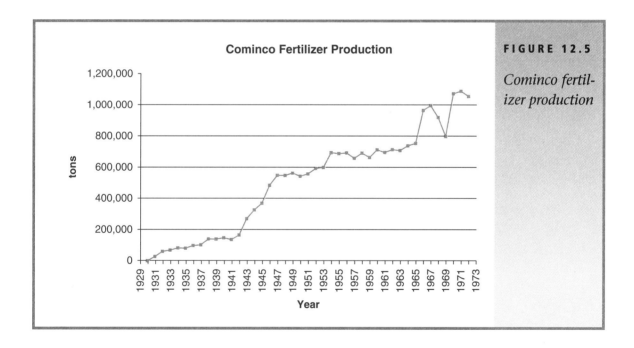

**FIGURE 12.5**

*Cominco fertilizer production*

profit at the company, pollution control would still have be justified—as it essentially eliminated the threat of plant closure and permitted the continued operation of all other corporate activities.

The recognition that waste is lost profit is a concept that is slowly being manifested in corporate strategy among several sectors of the economy. Of particular note in this regard is the petrochemical industry. The conversion of waste to usable intermediate or final product can be conducted at the plant level but is sometimes facilitated by what are called *industrial parks*, where manufacturing plants either

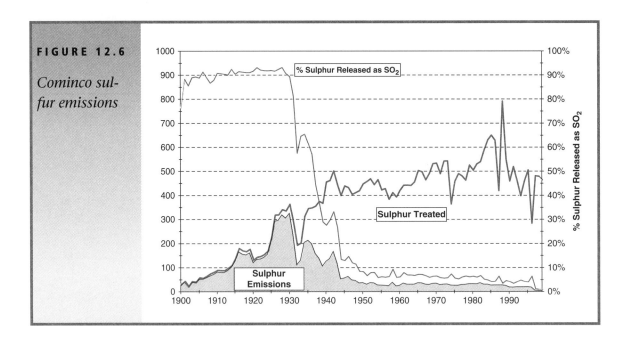

**FIGURE 12.6**

*Cominco sulfur emissions*

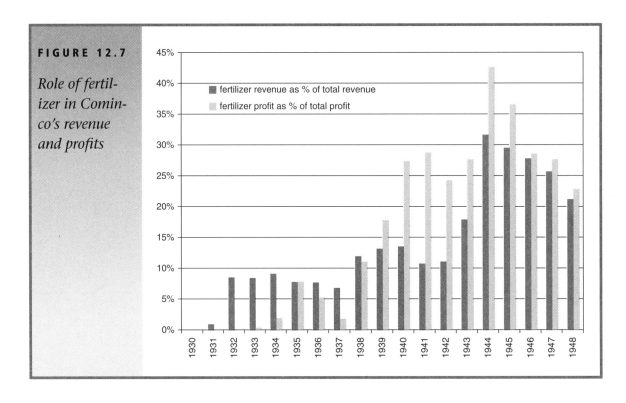

**FIGURE 12.7**

*Role of fertilizer in Cominco's revenue and profits*

within one industry or across industries situate in close proximity to each other. Under these circumstances, waste streams previously considered cost centers can be sold to each other as essential inputs, thereby yielding a source of revenue as well as reducing environmental discharges. This concept is described in greater detail in chapter 16 under the rubric of *industrial ecology*.

While Cominco and numerous petrochemical companies have been able to convert major waste streams to profit, it is not realistic to expect that all companies will have such extraordinary opportunities. Key ingredients include, inter alia, technological complementarities and a favorable market environment. Chapter 15 describes the circumstances under which a radical transformation in the market environment can open up a range of opportunities to adopt sustainable business practices among large numbers of small- to medium-sized businesses.

## CITED REFERENCES AND RECOMMENDED READINGS

Agent for the Government of Canada (1936) "Statement of Facts Submitted by the Agent for the Government of Canada, May 3, 1936," in *Trail Smelter Question*, Government of Canada, King's Printer, Ottawa.

Anon (1938) "RWD Memorandum to Mr. S.G. Blaylock, Vice-President & General Manager," Consolidated Mining and Smelting Company, March 14, V.F. No. 661.12, Trail, BC.

Anon (c.1948) "Producing of Chemical Fertilizers by The Consolidated Mining and Smelting Company of Canada Limited," Trail, BC.

BC Ministry of Environment, Lands and Parks and Environment Canada (1993) *State of the Environment Report for British Columbia*, Victoria, BC and Ottawa, ON.

Howes, Dean E.A. and Dean F.G. Miller (1929) "Trail Smelter Question, Appendix A1, The Deans' Report. Final Report to the International Joint Commission," King's Printer, Ottawa.

International Joint Commission (IJC) (1931) "Report of the International Joint Commission, Signed at Toronto, February 28, 1931,"Appendix A3, *Trail Smelter Question*, Government of Canada, King's Printer, Ottawa, 1936.

Murray, Keith A. (1972) "The Trail Smelter Case: International Air Pollution in the Columbia Valley," *BC Studies*, 15, Autumn, pp, 68–85.

Porter, Michael and Claas van der Linde (1995) "Green and Competitive: Ending the Stalemate," *Harvard Business Review*, 73(5), Sept./Oct., pp. 120–134.

Read, John E. (1963) "The Trail Smelter Dispute," in Charles B. Bourne (ed.) *The Canadian Yearbook of International Law*, 1, pp. 213–229, Vancouver, BC: UBC Press.

Trail Smelter Arbitration Tribunal (1941) "Decision reported on March 11, 1941, to the Government of the United States of America and to the Government of the Dominion of Canada by the Trail Smelter Arbitration Tribunal, under the convention signed April 15, 1935."

CHAPTER 13

# Designing the Corporation of the 21st Century—Case Study of Interface Inc.

## INTERFACE LTD.

Interface is the world's largest producer of carpets for the commercial sector. Tables 13–1 to 13–3 present recent financial data: profit and loss, balance sheet, and cash flow statements, while Figures 13–1 to 13–2 present key historical data: stock price, sales, and net income. The critical individual in Interface was the late Ray Anderson who founded the company in 1973. Anderson has written several books and articles (Anderson, 1999, 2007; Anderson and White 2009) explaining his radical conversion to the cause of sustainability when he realized that he and his company were a "plunderer of the earth." They "were part of the endemic process that is going on at a frightening, accelerating rate worldwide to rob our children and all their descendents of their futures." Anderson described this revelation as tantamount to a "spear through the heart," and he undertook to convert his company into the world's most sustainable enterprise. Figure 13–3 depicts Anderson's view of the typical company of the 20th century. Figure 13–4 shows his view of how modern corporations must be redesigned to achieve sustainability, and Figure 13–5 is the final idealized output of this radical redesign. Anderson has identified seven fronts on which serious change must be achieved for sustainability: Link #1—zero waste; Link #2—benign emissions; Link #3—renewable energy; Link #4—closed loop recycling; Link #5—resource efficient transportation; Link #6—a "sensitivity hookup," which includes service to the community and closer relations with employees, suppliers, and customers; and Link #7—a redesign of commerce itself that entails "the acceptance of entirely new notions of economics, especially prices that reflect full costs. To us, it means shifting emphasis from simply selling products to providing services; thus, our commitment to downstream distribution, installation, maintenance and recycling. These are all aimed at forming cradle-to-cradle relationships with customers and suppliers, relationships based on delivering, via the Evergreen Service Agreement™, the services our products provide, in lieu of the products themselves" (2007, pp. 104–105). In sum, Anderson's conceptualization of the prototypical company of the 21st century is one that is "strongly service-oriented, resource-efficient, wasting nothing, solar-driven, cyclical (no longer take–make–waste linear), and strongly connected to our

| | | | | | |
|---|---|---|---|---|---|
| **TABLE 13.1** | CONSOLIDATED STATEMENTS OF OPERATIONS AND COMPREHENSIVE INCOME (LOSS) | | | | |
| *Interface P&L* | INTERFACE, INC. AND SUBSIDIARIES | | | | |
| | CONSOLIDATED STATEMENTS OF OPERATIONS | | | | |

| | **Fiscal Year** | | |
|---|---|---|---|
| | **2010** | **2009** | **2008** |
| | (In thousands, except per share data) | | |
| Net sales | $ 961,827 | $ 859,888 | $ 10,82,344 |
| Cost of sales | 625,066 | 576,871 | 710,299 |
| Gross profit on sales | 336,761 | 283,017 | 372,045 |
| Selling, general and administrative expenses | 240,901 | 218,322 | 258,198 |
| Impairment of goodwill | — | — | 61,213 |
| Restructuring charges | 3,131 | 7,627 | 10,975 |
| Income from litigation settlements | — | (5,926) | — |
| Operating income | 92,729 | 62,994 | 41,659 |
| Interest expense | 33,129 | 34,297 | 31,480 |
| Bond retirement expenses | 44,379 | 6,096 | — |
| Other expense | 657 | 576 | 1,652 |
| Income from continuing operations before tax expense | 14,564 | 22,025 | 8,527 |
| Income tax expense | 4,494 | 9,352 | 43,040 |
| Income (loss) from continuing operations | 10,070 | 12,673 | (34,513) |
| Loss from discontinued operations, net of tax | (736) | (909) | (5,154) |
| Net income (loss) | 9,334 | 11,764 | (39,667) |
| Net income attributable to noncontrolling interest in subsidiary | (1,051) | (846) | (1,206) |
| Net income (loss) attributable to Interface, Inc. | $ 8,283 | $ 10,918 | $ (40,873) |
| Income (loss) per share attributable to Interface, Inc. common shareholders — basic | | | |
| Continuing operations | $ 0.14 | $ 0.19 | $ (0.58) |
| Discontinued operations | (0.01) | (0.01) | (0.08) |
| Net income (loss) per share attributable to Interface, Inc. common shareholders — basic | $ 0.13 | $ 0.17 | $ (0.67) |
| Income (loss) per share attributable to Interface, Inc. common shareholders — diluted | | | |
| Continuing operations | $ 0.14 | $ 0.19 | $ (0.58) |
| Discontinued operations | (0.01) | (0.01) | (0.08) |

TABLE 13.1

*continued*

CONSOLIDATED STATEMENTS OF OPERATIONS AND COMPREHENSIVE INCOME (LOSS)

INTERFACE, INC. AND SUBSIDIARIES

CONSOLIDATED STATEMENTS OF OPERATIONS

| | | | |
|---|---|---|---|
| Net income (loss) per share attributable to Interface, Inc. common shareholders — diluted | $ 0.13 | $ 0.17 | $ (0.67) |
| Basic weighted average shares outstanding | 63,794 | 63,213 | 61,439 |
| Diluted weighted average shares outstanding | 64,262 | 63,308 | 61,439 |

*Source:* U.S. Securities and Exchange Commission, submission by Interface of form 10-K for the period ending December 31, 2010, pp. 41–44

---

TABLE 13.2

*Interface Balance Sheet*

INTERFACE, INC. AND SUBSIDIARIES

CONSOLIDATED BALANCE SHEETS

| | 2010 | 2009 |
|---|---|---|
| | (In thousands) | |
| **ASSETS** | | |
| Current | | |
| Cash and cash equivalents | $69,236 | $115,363 |
| Accounts receivable, net | 151,463 | 129,833 |
| Inventories | 136,766 | 112,249 |
| Prepaid expenses and other current assets | 24,362 | 19,649 |
| Deferred income taxes | 10,062 | 9,379 |
| Assets of businesses held for sale | 1,200 | 1,500 |
| Total current assets | 393,089 | 387,973 |
| Property and equipment, net | 177,792 | 162,269 |
| Deferred tax asset | 53,022 | 44,210 |
| Goodwill | 75,239 | 80,519 |
| Other assets | 56,291 | 52,268 |
| | $755,4333 | $727,239 |

(Continued)

| **TABLE 13.2** *continued* | INTERFACE, INC. AND SUBSIDIARIES CONSOLIDATED BALANCE SHEETS | | |
|---|---|---:|---:|
| | **LIABILITIES AND SHAREHOLDERS' EQUITY** | | |
| | Current liabilities | | |
| | Accounts payable | $ 55,859 | $ 35,614 |
| | Accrued expenses | 112,657 | 101,143 |
| | Current portion of long-term debt | — | 14,586 |
| | Total current liabilities | 168,516 | 151,343 |
| | Senior notes | 282,951 | 145,184 |
| | Senior subordinated notes | 11,477 | 135,000 |
| | Deferred income taxes | 7,563 | 7,029 |
| | Other | 36,054 | 42,502 |
| | Total liabilities | 506,561 | 481,058 |
| | Commitments and contingencies | | |
| | Shareholders' equity | | |
| | Preferred stock | — | — |
| | Common stock | 6,445 | 6,328 |
| | Additional paid-in capital | 349,662 | 343,348 |
| | Retained deficit | (49,770) | (55,332) |
| | Accumulated other comprehensive loss — foreign currency translation | (26,269) | (24,057) |
| | Accumulated other comprehensive loss — pension liability | (31,196) | (33,186) |
| | Total shareholders' equity — Interface, Inc | 248,872 | 237,101 |
| | Noncontrolling interest in subsidiary | — | 9,080 |
| | Total shareholders' equity | 248,872 | 246,181 |
| | | $ 755,4333 | $ 727,239 |

*Source:* U.S. Securities and Exchange Commission, submission by Interface of form 10-K for the period ending December 31, 2010, pp. 41-44

constituencies—our communities (building social equity), our customers, and our suppliers—and to one other (p. 105)."

Two central parts to operationalizing Interface's sustainability strategy are first the adoption of a leasing system (called an *Evergreen Lease*) where the carpet is not owned by the customer but by Interface instead; and, second, the use of carpet

TABLE 13.3

*Interface Cash Flows*

INTERFACE, INC. AND SUBSIDIARIES

CONSOLIDATED STATEMENTS OF CASH FLOWS

| | Fiscal Year | | |
| --- | --- | --- | --- |
| | 2010 | 2009 | 2008 |
| | (In thousands) | | |
| OPERATING ACTIVITIES: | | | |
| Net income (loss) | $ 9,334 | $ 11,764 | $ (39,667) |
| Loss on discontinued operations | 736 | 909 | 5,154 |
| Income (loss) from continuing operations | 10,070 | 12,673 | (34,513) |
| Adjustments to reconcile income (loss) to cash provided by operating | | | |
| activities | | | |
| Impairment of goodwill | — | — | 61,213 |
| Depreciation and amortization | 27,927 | 25,189 | 23,664 |
| Premium paid to repurchase senior and senior subordinated notes . . . . | 36,374 | 5,264 | — |
| Bad debt expense | 2,031 | 2,214 | 4,180 |
| Deferred income taxes and other | (6,772) | (5,634) | 13,480 |
| Working capital changes: | | | |
| Accounts receivable | (21,418) | 20,978 | 11,891 |
| Inventories | (23,103) | 20,831 | (11,351) |
| Prepaid expenses and other current assets | (5,970) | 78 | 5,072 |
| Accounts payable and accrued expenses | 28,241 | (27,143) | (18,540) |
| Cash provided by operating activities | 47,380 | 54,450 | 55,096 |
| INVESTING ACTIVITIES: | | | |
| Capital expenditures | (31,715) | (8,753) | (29,300) |
| Other | (5,328) | 1,399 | (4,158) |
| Cash used in investing activities | (37,043) | (7,354) | (33,458) |
| FINANCING ACTIVITIES: | | | |
| Borrowing of long-term debt | 275,000 | 144,452 | — |
| Dividends paid | (2,721) | (634) | (7,562) |
| Debt issuance costs | (5,930) | (6,301) | — |
| Repurchase of senior and senior subordinated notes | (279,966) | (138,002) | (22,412) |
| Premium paid to repurchase senior and senior subordinated notes | (36,374) | (5,264) | — |
| Purchase of noncontrolling interest | (11,488) | — | — |
| Proceeds from issuance of common stock | 3,103 | 499 | 1,479 |
| Cash used in financing activities | (58,376) | (5,250) | (28,495) |

*(Continued)*

**TABLE 13.3**

*continued*

### INTERFACE, INC. AND SUBSIDIARIES
### CONSOLIDATED STATEMENTS OF CASH FLOWS

| | | | |
|---|---:|---:|---:|
| Net cash provided by (used in) operating, investing and financing activities | (48,039) | 41,846 | (6,857) |
| Effect of exchange rate changes on cash | 1,912 | 1,760 | (3,761) |
| CASH AND CASH EQUIVALENTS: | | | |
| Net increase (decrease) | (46,127) | 43,606 | (10,618) |
| Balance, beginning of year | 115,363 | 71,757 | 82,375 |
| Balance, end of year | $   69,236 | $   115,363 | $   71,757 |

*Source:* U.S. Securities and Exchange Commission, submission by Interface of form 10-K for the period ending December 31, 2010, pp. 41–44

**FIGURE 13.1**

*Interface stock price history*

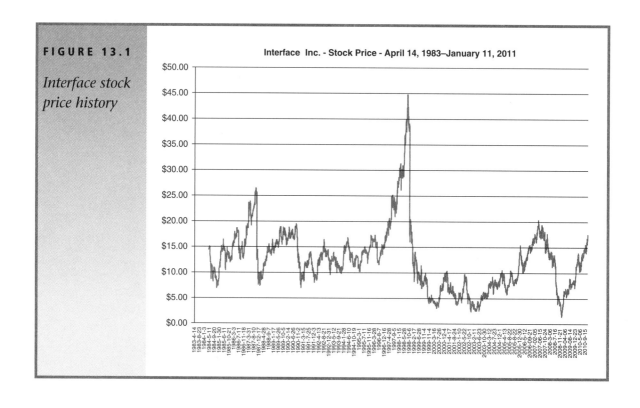

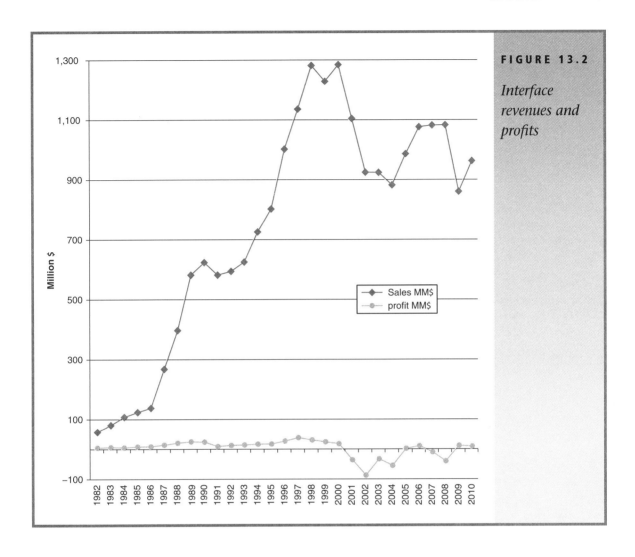

**FIGURE 13.2**

*Interface revenues and profits*

tiles. When a carpet starts to show signs of fading, wear or damage, individual tiles are removed—rather than the entire carpet—and returned to Interface for recycling into new carpet. This is a type of *reverse logistics*, as defined by Sarkis (2010) as a system "for the recovery of products or packaging from the consumer, or supply chain member." This process is formalized in Interface's Clause 6 of its Evergreen Lease that reads: "During the lease term [7 years], nothing contained herein shall give to Customer any right, title or interest in or to the Carpet except as a lessee. At all times, legal title to the Carpet shall remain with Interface, and the Carpet shall not be considered a fixture for any purpose regardless of the degree of its installation in or affixation to real property" (Anderson and White 2009, p.288).

**FIGURE 13.3**

*Anderson's view of the typical company of the 20th century*

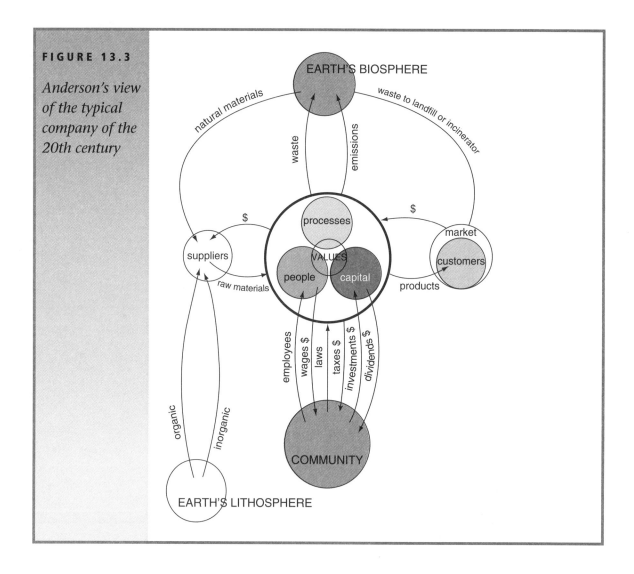

## INTERFACE'S ACHIEVEMENTS

On their corporate website, Interface presents a number of graphics that show how they have progressed in their attempts to reduce their ecological impact. These fall into several categories and are reproduced in Figures 13–6 to 13–14 under the headings of waste elimination, use of renewable energy, greenhouse gas emissions, energy consumption by type, recycled and bio-based materials, water intake, and waste elimination.

## RISK FACTORS

In making a sustainability assessment, it is useful not only to examine closely the financial statements of the company but also to consult filings by the corporation

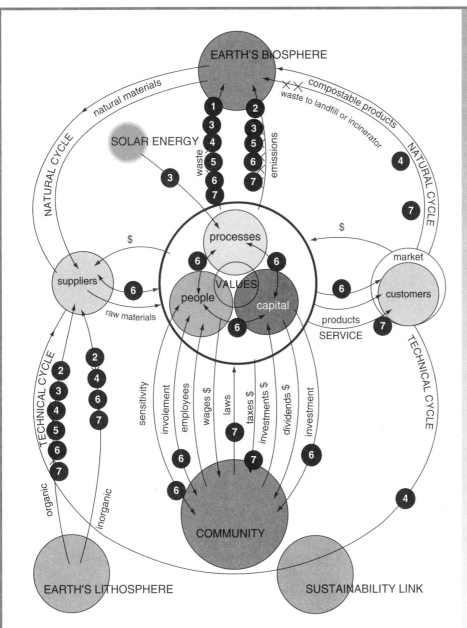

FIGURE 13.4

*Anderson's view of how modern corporations should be redesigned for sustainability*

EARTH'S BIOSPHERE

natural materials

compostable products

waste to landfill or incinerator

NATURAL CYCLE

NATURAL CYCLE

SOLAR ENERGY

waste

emissions

processes

VALUES

$

$

suppliers

market

people

capital

customers

raw materials

products

SERVICE

TECHNICAL CYCLE

TECHNICAL CYCLE

sensitivity

involement

employees

wages $

laws

taxes $

investments $

dividends $

investment

organic

inorganic

COMMUNITY

EARTH'S LITHOSPHERE

SUSTAINABILITY LINK

| LINK # | DESCRIPTION |
|--------|-------------|
| 1 | Zero waste |
| 2 | Benign Emissions |
| 3 | Renewable energy |
| 4 | Closing the loop |
| 5 | Resource-efficient transportation |
| 6 | Sensitivity hookup - service to community, closer relations among stakeholders |
| 7 | Redesign of commerce itself |

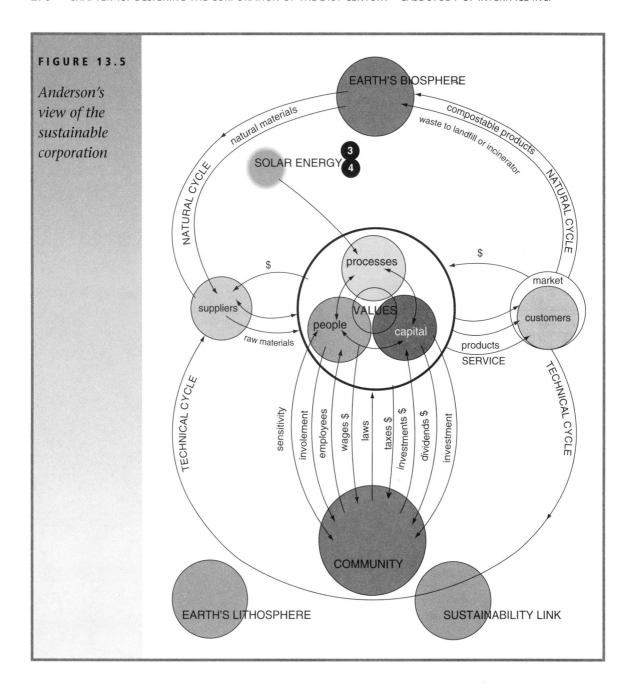

**FIGURE 13.5**

*Anderson's view of the sustainable corporation*

required by the U.S. Securities and Exchange Commission (SEC). Of these filing requirements, the 10-K form is frequently the most informative as it requires the corporation to disclose, among other things, all major current and anticipated risks. It is important to bear in mind, however, that a corporation may be inclined to include or overstate risks solely for the purpose of avoiding any future legal challenges that they have not disclosed all material facts. In spite of this caveat, however, the

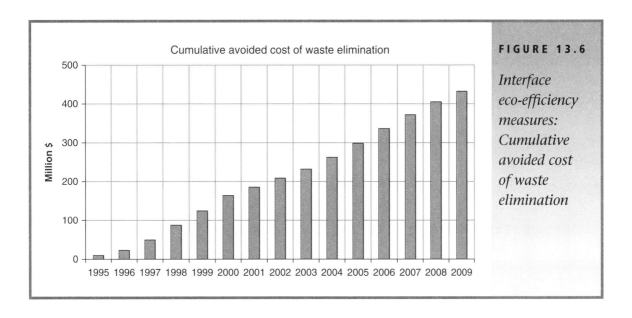

**FIGURE 13.6**

*Interface eco-efficiency measures: Cumulative avoided cost of waste elimination*

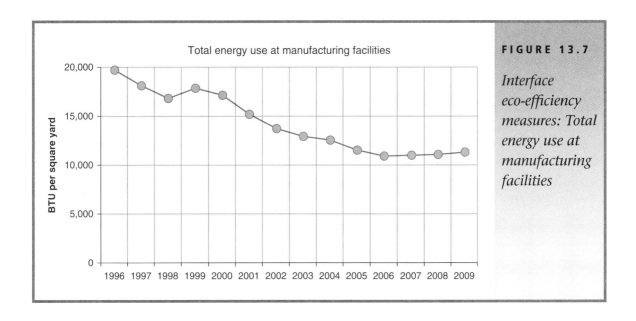

**FIGURE 13.7**

*Interface eco-efficiency measures: Total energy use at manufacturing facilities*

10-K provides critical information on the state of the corporation. The most recent 10-K section on risk for Interface (US SEC 2010) states:

ITEM 1A. RISK FACTORS

*You should carefully consider the following factors, in addition to the other informa-*
*tion included in this Annual Report on Form 10-K and the documents incorporated*

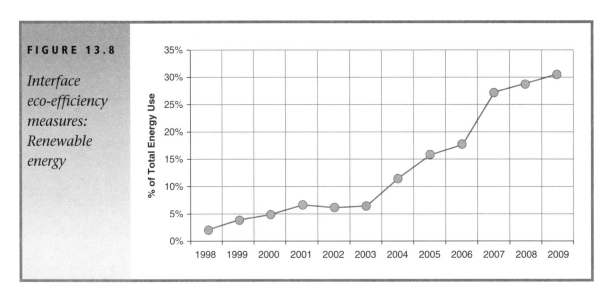

**FIGURE 13.8**

*Interface eco-efficiency measures: Renewable energy*

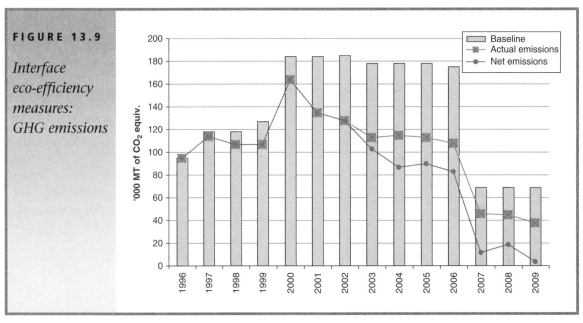

**FIGURE 13.9**

*Interface eco-efficiency measures: GHG emissions*

herein by reference, before deciding whether to purchase our common stock. Any or all of the following risk factors could have a material adverse effect on our business, financial condition, results of operations and prospects.

- Sales of our principal products have been and may continue to be affected by adverse economic cycles in the renovation and construction of commercial and institutional buildings.

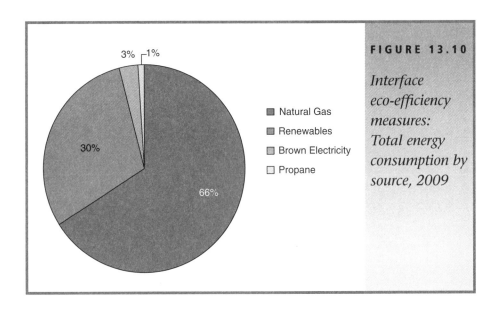

**FIGURE 13.10**

*Interface eco-efficiency measures: Total energy consumption by source, 2009*

- Natural Gas
- Renewables
- Brown Electricity
- Propane

3%   1%
30%
66%

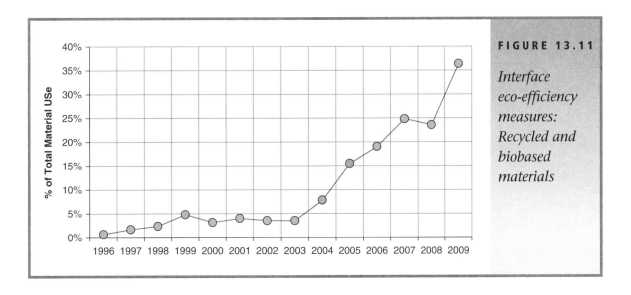

**FIGURE 13.11**

*Interface eco-efficiency measures: Recycled and biobased materials*

- The recent worldwide financial and credit crisis could have a material adverse effect on our business, financial condition, and results of operations.

- We compete with a large number of manufacturers in the highly competitive commercial floor covering products market, and some of these competitors have greater financial resources than we do.

- Our success depends significantly upon the efforts, abilities and continued service of our senior management executives and our principal design consultant, and our loss of any of them could affect us adversely.

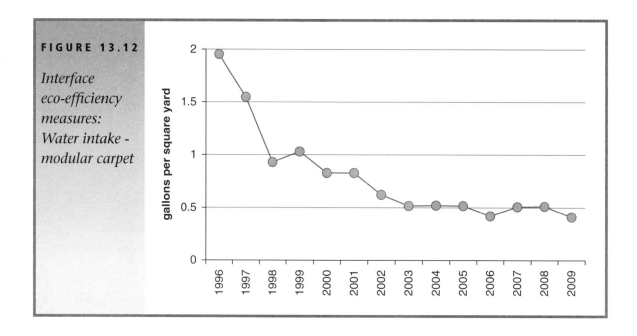

**FIGURE 13.12**

*Interface eco-efficiency measures: Water intake - modular carpet*

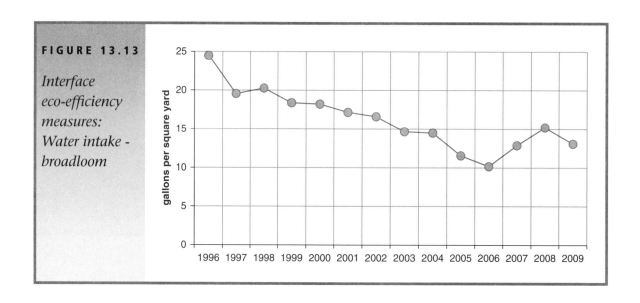

**FIGURE 13.13**

*Interface eco-efficiency measures: Water intake - broadloom*

- Our substantial international operations are subject to various political, economic, and other uncertainties that could adversely affect our business results, including by restrictive taxation or other government regulation and by foreign currency fluctuations.

- We have a significant amount of indebtedness, which could have important negative consequences to us.

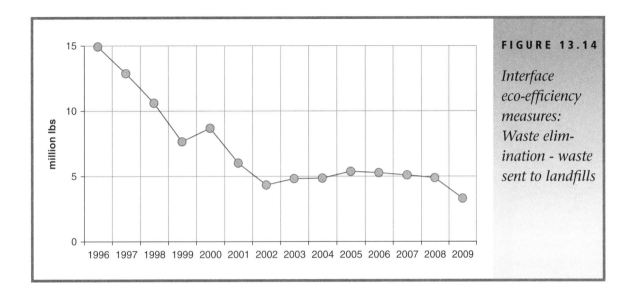

**FIGURE 13.14**

*Interface eco-efficiency measures: Waste elimination - waste sent to landfills*

- The market price of our common stock has been volatile, and the value of your investment may decline.

- Our earnings in a future period could be adversely affected by noncash adjustments to goodwill, if a future test of goodwill assets indicates a material impairment of those assets.

- Our chairman currently has sufficient voting power to elect a majority of our board of directors.

- Our rights agreement could discourage tender offers or other transactions for our stock that could result in shareholders receiving a premium over the market price for our stock.

- Large increases in the cost of petroleum-based raw materials could adversely affect us if we are unable to pass these cost increases through to our customers. Petroleum-based products comprise the predominant portion of the cost of raw materials that we use in manufacturing. While we attempt to match cost increases with corresponding price increases, continued volatility in the cost of petroleum-based raw materials could adversely affect our financial results if we are unable to pass through such price increases to our customers.

- Unanticipated termination or interruption of any of our arrangements with our primary third party suppliers of synthetic fiber could have a material adverse effect on us. The unanticipated termination or interruption of any of our supply arrangements with our current suppliers of synthetic fiber, which typically are not pursuant to long-term agreements, could have a material adverse effect on us because of the cost and delay associated with shifting more business to another supplier. For example, Invista Inc., a

**TABLE 13.4**

*Basic Finan-cial Data for Major Interface Competitors*

| DATA FOR 2012 - U.S. CARPET MILL SEGMENT | INTERFACE | BEAULIEU | MOHAWK | SHAW | CARPET INDUSTRY |
|---|---|---|---|---|---|
| Sales ($mill) | $581.4 | $500 | $2,692 | $3,150 | |
| Net Income ($ mill) | $66.9 | n.a. | $254 | $369 | |
| Net Prrofit on sales | 11.5% | n.a. | 9.4% | 11.7% | 17.6% |
| Market share | 5.8% | 5.0% | 26.7% | 31.1% | |
| GENERAL CORPORATE DATA | | | | | |
| Market Cap ($bill) | $1.05 | n.a. | $6.46 | n.a. | |
| # employees (2011) | 3,702 | n.a. | 26,200 | 30,000 | |

*Sources:* Hoover's corporate reports
IBIS World Corporate reports
MSN Money

subsidiary of Koch Industries, Inc., currently supplies approximately 40% of our requirements for synthetic fiber (nylon) . . . [which] is the principal raw material that we use in our carpet products."

As a final note, it should be recognized that any corporation, short of a monopoly, does not operate in a competitive vacuum. Interface has major competitors in the carpet market, although many have a slightly different market focus. Table 13–4 summarizes some key financial data from 2011 for Interface and its three major competitors: Mohawk Industries, Shaw Industries, and Beaulieu of America.

## Analytical Questions

Some of the key questions facing the analyst are as follows:

(1) Should he/she recommend a BUY or SELL?
(2) Should this stock be promoted for inclusion in a green fund?
(3) What distinguishes Anderson's model of corporate sustainability from normal production models?
(4) How close is Interface to replicating Anderson's model of the prototypical sustainable corporation?
(5) If Interface has not yet achieved the goals set by Anderson, what are the barriers to so doing; can they be overcome; and, if so, how and in what time frame?
(6) Are there discernible trends in the eco-efficiency measures; and, if so, what is their relevance for sustainability?
(7) Is the Strategic Decay Matrix relevant to Interface?

(8) Do any of the risks cited in Interface's 10-K report to the SEC have a bearing on their strategic goal of sustainability?
(9) Can you name any other companies that have successfully dematerialized their product?

## CITED REFERENCES AND RECOMMENDED READINGS

Anderson, Ray (1999) *Mid-Course Correction: Toward a Sustainable Enterprise: The Interface Model*, Atlanta, GA: Peregrinzilla Press.

Anderson, Ray (2007) "Mid-Course Correction: Toward a Sustainable Enterprise," in Peter N. Nemetz (ed.) *Sustainable Resource Management: Reality or Illusion*? Cheltenham: Edward Elgar, pp. 88–114.

Anderson, Ray and Robin White (2009) *Confessions of a Radical Industrialist: Profits, People, Purpose—Doing Business by Respecting the Earth.* (Reissued in 2011 in paperback as *Business Lessons from a Radical Industrialist.*) Toronto: McClelland & Stewart.

Durnil, Gordon K. (1995) *The Making of a Conservative Environmentalist*, Bloomington: Indiana University Press.

Hamel, Gary and Liisa Valikagnas (2003) "The Quest for Resilience," in *Harvard Business Review*, September, pp. 52–63.

Hoover's corporate reports (accessed 2011).

Interface Inc. website and annual reports (www.Interfaceglobal.com).

Porter, Michael and Claas van der Linde (1995) "Green and Competitive: Ending the Stalemate," *Harvard Business Review* Sep/Oct 73(5) pp. 120–134.

Sarkis, Joseph (2010) *Greening the Supply Chain*, London: Springer.

Stahel, Walter (1982) "Product Life Factor" downloadable from http://www.product-life.org/en/major-publications/the-product-life-factor, The Product-Life Institute, Geneva.

U.S. Securities and Exchange Commission (SEC) (2010) Interface Inc. 10-K report, Washington, DC.

# CHAPTER 14

# Assessing Interface Ltd.

## ANDERSON'S RECONCEPTUALIZATION OF THE MODERN CORPORATION

Reengineering a major industrial corporation and reconceptualizing its strategic mission is a daunting undertaking, but Ray Anderson adopted a radical approach to business and economics. The standard economic model subdivides the products of a modern industrial economy into two categories: goods and services. Anderson was among the first to realize that this categorization represents a false dichotomy. With the exception of purchases motivated by concerns over personal prestige, consumers do not buy goods for their physical presence—they buy them for the services they provide. Does one buy a refrigerator, for example, because one likes a large colored metal box in one's kitchen? The answer is no. This good is bought because of the service it provides in the form of refrigeration of food.

By adopting this insightful new and unified view of goods and services, it is possible to focus on the nature of the service provided rather than the physical good itself. Instead of selling carpet per se, Interface made the conceptual jump to selling services. To Interface, the key services that the consumers were buying included color, design, texture, warmth, acoustics, comfort under foot, cleanliness, and improved indoor air quality. The customer benefits in several ways: a smaller amount of carpet is replaced, there is no requirement for waste disposal by the customer, and the carpet can be expensed rather than capitalized. By reclaiming and recycling carpet tiles, Interface is able to lower its material costs, reduce its environmental impact, and lock customers into a longer-term leasing relationship with the vendor rather than a one-off sale.

Figures 14–1, 14–2, and 14–3 represent the transition that Anderson envisages for the emergence of the truly sustainable corporation. Figure 14–1 is the traditional model of industrial production, typically referred to as "once through" or "linear," which relies on virgin raw materials and generates waste in both production and consumption. Figure 14–2 portrays Interface's modular carpet take-back system and its improvements in energy efficiency, material throughout, and waste generation. Figure 14–3 represents the goal that Interface is pursuing: a modern industrial corporation relying exclusively on renewable inputs (both material and energy) and the production of zero waste.

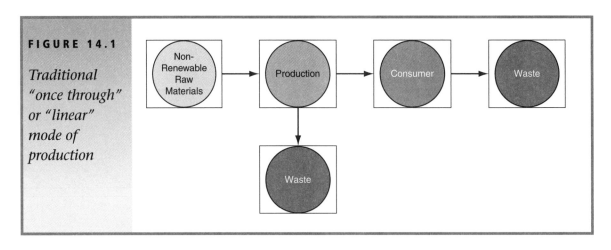

**FIGURE 14.1**

*Traditional "once through" or "linear" mode of production*

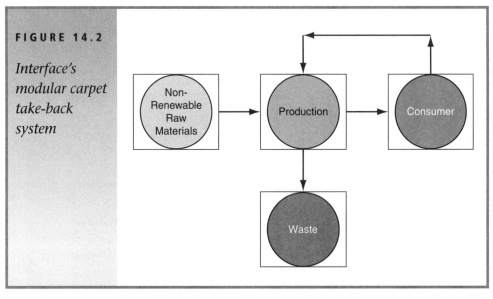

**FIGURE 14.2**

*Interface's modular carpet take-back system*

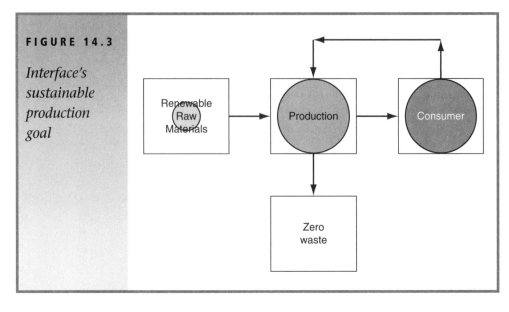

**FIGURE 14.3**

*Interface's sustainable production goal*

## INTERFACE'S RECORD OF PROFITABILITY

While largely profitable in the 1980s and 1990s, Interface has incurred losses during most of the last decade, most recently due to the economic downturn in the United States and global economies. Nevertheless, according to comparative data provided by both Interface and Hoover's (Hoovers.com), the company has appeared to outperform the rest of its industry over much of this period. The problem with this comparative data, however, is that the financial data for two of Interface's largest direct competitors are not available since they are private companies, including Shaw Industries, a wholly owned holding of Warren Buffet's Berkshire Hathaway.

A critical question is to what degree Interface's profitability is influenced—positively or negatively—by its sustainability initiatives. Unfortunately, the publicly available data are not sufficiently disaggregated to answer this question. Some insight into this question can be provided, however, by metrics generated by the company and available on their website [see chapter 13].

## INTERFACE'S SUSTAINABILITY METRICS

Interface's graphed eco-efficiency metrics display somewhat different characteristics. The analyst must determine to what extent these data are relevant or significant for the company's strategic goal of sustainability. The analyst must also determine if there any issues of *strategic decay* (as defined in Table 1–3) relating to the eco-efficiency metrics. Interface has clearly made remarkable strides towards remolding their corporate strategies and technology toward greater sustainability. The issue facing the analyst revolves around the company's future prospects.

## RISKS

In making an assessment of the prospects for Interface's goal of sustainability, it is useful for the analyst to examine Interface's 10-K submission to the SEC on matters of risk and ask whether any of the specifically identified risks appear to be substantive and pose a significant challenge to the reengineering necessary for the company to become truly sustainable. The analyst should bear in mind that not all risks outlined in the 10-K submission are equally significant. There is an incentive for any corporation to err on the side of caution and overreporting of potential risks in order to reduce any possible liability from failure to disclose material facts.

## THE COMPETITIVE ENVIRONMENT

The relevance of the financial assessment of the corporation partly hinges on the state of the competitive environment. If the market is moving toward more sustainable products and Interface has a leadership role in this area, then the assessment of the company's prospects is more positive. This is congruent with Michael Porter's thesis that a sustainability strategy is an important route to building a strong competitive advantage.

As mentioned, the two most significant competitors are Mohawk Industries and Shaw Industries—the former a public company, the latter a private entity. The critical question is whether either of these firms has an equally strong sustainability strategy that can threaten Interface's potential competitive advantage.

## Mohawk Industries

Mohawk Industries has recently produced its first sustainability report (Mohawk-sustainability.com). The report lays out the company's goals in four key areas—reductions in energy use, water use, greenhouse gas emissions, and waste to landfill. The stated intention is to improve upon the performance in each area by 25% by 2020. This is in marked contrast to Interface's "Mission Zero," which aims for a zero environmental impact by 2020. While Interface has provided historical data for several key environmental metrics (see chapter 13), Mohawk presents only its current metrics for the four key areas and the goals for the next decade. This omission of historical data impedes an assessment of the performance of the company in the area of sustainability. This touches on the broader issue of the nature and extent of corporate disclosure of sustainability metrics and the degree of credibility that can be ascribed to the published information. This issue is expanded upon in the appendix to this chapter, which describes a simple methodology for estimating the degree of commitment to sustainability by any one company.

## Shaw Industries

The fact that this company is privately held poses a major challenge to the assessment of corporate sustainability. However, one very important piece of information is available that bears upon the corporation's commitment to, and movement toward, sustainable production. For reasons of cost, many companies in this and numerous other industries rely to a certain degree on recycled rather than virgin material. An excellent example is provided by the pulp and paper industry where recycled paper products are part of a very profitable international market. The principal trade-off is in the nature of the recycling process itself where the fibers tend to degrade with each recycling loop. As such, it is always necessary to make up for this deficiency by supplementing the production process with virgin feedstock. This phenomenon, referred to as *downcycling*, appears superficially to be related to the laws of thermodynamics and has appeared to impose a major constraint on industrial processes.

Recent technological advances have led to the emergence of *upcycling* where waste products are converted into higher value products. Shaw Industries was an early adopter of upcycling, using old carpet fiber to produce new carpet material with no loss of quality (www.iehn.org/publications.case.shaw.php). It is up to the analyst to assess if Shaw Industries has already achieved sustainable competitive advantage with this technological advance. In its recent case study of Shaw Industries, the Investor Environmental Health Network (IEHN) claims that Shaw Industries was prompted to pursue its intensive research into technological innovations to pursue sustainability by the very public commitment to this cause by Interface Inc. and Ray Anderson.

It is instructive to ask if it is possible to conceive of an existing carpet manufacturing process that meets Anderson's criteria for true sustainability. Figure 14–4 suggests one possible answer—a carpet that relies for its raw material on pasture-bred sheep, natural organic dyes, human labor, wooden looms, and produces biodegradable waste. In fact, such carpets have been produced—and continue to be produced—in countries such as Turkey, Iran, Pakistan, and India. On reflection, this model product cannot completely satisfy the criteria of perfect sustainability for at least two reasons: (i) the output is limited; and (ii) the carpets must be shipped from their locus of production to global markets by modern and energy-intensive transport, unless one adopts wind-driven, sea transport, or novel hybrid versions thereof (see, for example, greenUPGRADER.com 2008).

The next two chapters outline additional concepts that bear on this case study. Chapter 15 reviews the principles of eco-efficiency and discusses a more modern carpet production case study that may be the closest to sustainability achieved in the developed world to date. Chapters 16 and following outline other methodologies and metrics for measuring progress toward corporate sustainability, including eco-effectiveness, cradle-to-cradle production systems, life-cycle analysis, industrial ecology, biomimicry, and mass and material balances.

**FIGURE 14.4**

*A sustainable carpet?*

## CITED REFERENCES AND RECOMMENDED READINGS

European Environment Agency (EEA) (2010) *Environmental Disclosures. The Third Major Review of Environmental Reporting in the Annual Report & Accounts of the FTSE All-Share Companies.*

GreenUPGRADER.com (2008) "Tall Ship Belem Delivers Wine by Sail and Saves Carbon," August 17.

Investor Environmental Health Network (IEHN) (2011) (www.iehn.org).

Mohawk Industries website: www.mohawksustainability.com.

Terrachoice (2009) *The Seven Sins of Greenwashing. Environmental Claims in Consumer Markets. Summary Report: North America*, Ottawa, ON, April.

Terrachoice (2010) *The Sins of Greenwashing. Home and Family Edition. A Report on Environmental Claims Made in the North American Consumer Market*, Ottawa, ON.

Valentine, Scott V. (2010) "A Strategic Environmental Management Framework: Evaluating the Profitability of Being Green," in *Sustainability Matters: Environmental Management in Asia*. L.H. Lye, G. Ofori, L.C. Malone-Lee, V.R. Savage and Y.P. Ting. Singapore: World Scientific Publishing, pp. 1–32.

www.iehn.org/publications.case.shaw.php [website of Investor Environmental Health Network].

## APPENDIX

# A Note on Assessing the Credibility of Corporate Sustainability Reporting

With consumers becoming more aware of and sensitive to environmental issues, many businesses are making a concerted effort to make their products "greener." An inevitable consequence of this phenomenon is that some companies will be tempted to exaggerate their claims on behalf of their products. A major new study of 5,296 consumer products in Canada, for example, found that while the news is generally good, there is an active market in *greenwashing*. The report concluded that nearly all "green" consumer products [95.6%] made one false, misleading or unproven environmental claim (Terrachoice 2010; see also Terrachoice 2009). Seven sins of greenwashing have been identified by the report: hidden trade-off, no proof, vagueness, irrelevance, lesser of two evils, fibbing and worshiping false labels. [See Table 14–1.]

Clearly, there is no reason that this pattern would be restricted to advertising. Claims made on behalf of products or production processes by corporations may

| SIN | NATURE | EXAMPLE |
|---|---|---|
| Hidden Trade-off | suggesting a product is green based on an unreasonably narrow set of attributes without attention to other important environmental issues. | Paper, is not necessarily environmentally-preferable just because it comes from a sustainably-harvested forest. Other important environmental issues in the paper-making process, including energy, greenhouse gas emissions, and water and air pollution, may be equally or more significant. |
| No proof | an environmental claim that cannot be substantiated by easily accessible supporting information or by a reliable third-party certification | tissue products that claim various percentages of post-consumer recycled content without providing any evidence |
| Vagueness | claim that is so poorly defined or broad that its real meaning is likely to be misunderstood by the consumer | All-natural products. Arsenic, uranium, mercury, and formaldehyde are all naturally occurring, and poisonous. All natural isn't necessarily green. |
| Irrelevance | an environmental claim that may be truthful but is unimportant or unhelpful for consumers seeking environmentally preferable products | CFC-free is a frequent claim despite the fact that CFCs are banned by law. |
| Lesser of two evils | claims that may be true within the product category, but that risk distracting the consumer from the greater environmental impacts of the category as a whole | Organic cigarettes and fuel-efficient sport-utility vehicles |
| Fibbing | environmental claims that are simply false | products falsely claiming to be Energy Star certified or registered |
| Worshiping False Labels | a product that, through either words or images, gives the impression of third-party endorsement where no such endorsement actually exists; fake labels, in other words | • In the United States, there is a brand of aluminum foil with certification-like images that bear the name of the companys own in-house environmental program without further explanation.<br>• In Canada, one paper towel product uses a certification-like image to make the bold (if vague statement) this product fights global warming.<br>• Several brands of air fresheners give the impression of certification of the claim CFC-free (thereby committing both the Sin of Worshiping False Labels and the Sin of Irrelevance).<br>• A variety of products in both the US and Canada use certification-like images with green jargon including like eco-safe, eco-secure, and eco-preferred. |

**TABLE 14.1**

*Seven Sins of Greenwashing*

*Sources:* derived from Terrachoice 2009 and 2010

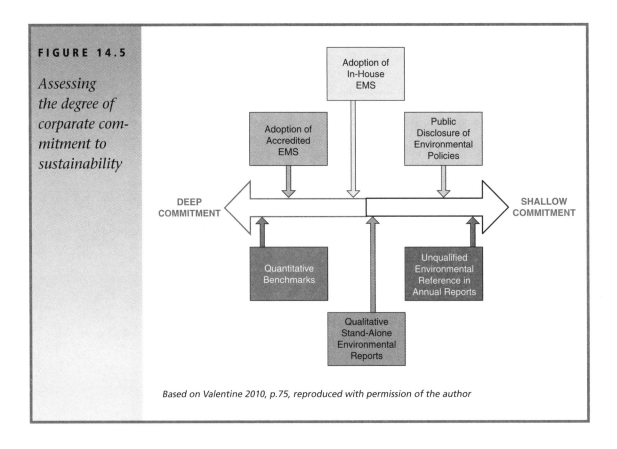

**FIGURE 14.5**

*Assessing the degree of corparate commitment to sustainability*

Based on Valentine 2010, p.75, reproduced with permission of the author

also appear in annual reports and special reports devoted to sustainability. Short of having access to detailed corporate data, there are a limited number of ways that such claims can be verified. One promising new trend is the emergence of third party verification or certification—a topic addressed in chapter 22. Without external verification, analysis of sustainability achievements must rely on a careful reading of a corporation's published information. Valentine (2010) has created a conceptually simple methodology as a first-pass screen for corporate credibility in the area of sustainability. As graphed in Figure 14–5, Valentine arrays the degree of commitment on a horizontal scale from deep commitment at one end to shallow commitment at the other. The contents of the documentation provide by a company in support of its sustainability bona fides can be divided into six categories: (1) unqualified environmental reference in annual reports, (2) public disclosure of environmental policies, (3) qualitative stand-alone environmental reports, (4) adoption of an in-house environmental management system (EMS), (5) adoption of an accredited EMS, and (6) quantitative benchmarks. As Table 14–2 shows, the range of corporate policies can be characterized by five roles: (1) leaders, (2) contenders, (3) trailers, (4) pretenders, and (5) avoiders. While not a definitive determination of the credibility of claims of sustainability [for a counterexample, see chapter 24], this is a useful first-pass screening mechanism.

There are few surveys of corporate reporting that identify how many companies fall into the previous identified categories. However, the European Environment

| LEVEL | ARE DEFINED AS: | WHICH APPEARS IN ENVIRON-MENTAL REPORTS AS: | **TABLE 14.2** |
|---|---|---|---|
| LEVEL 1 - LEADERS | Firms committed to setting quantitative benchmarks in environmental initiatives | Quantitative progress indicators related to environmental issues | *Range of Corporate Policies with Respect to Sustainability* |
| LEVEL 2 - CONTENDERS | Firms which have adopted externally accredited environmental management systems | Specific reference made to ISO14000 or EMAS accreditation | |
| LEVEL 3 - TALKERS | Firms that are currently experimenting with the effectiveness of environmental management initiatives | Qualitative stand-alone environmental reports | |
| LEVEL 4 - PRETENDERS | Firms that understand the threat posed by poor environmental governance. These firms, therefore, endeavor to demonstrate that they meet all binding regulations | Qualitative environmental disclosure over 50 word amidst Annual Reports or on websites | |
| LEVEL 5 - AVOIDERS | Firms that obey environmental regulations because they must. However, they do not see a need to strategically address any environmental issues | Empty space. Firms classified as Avoiders do not disclose any information of environmental issues | |

*Source:* Valentine 2010, p.76, reproduced with permission of the author

Agency (EEA 2010) has conducted periodic reviews of environmental reporting in the annual reports and accounts of FTSE all-share companies. The most recent of these reviews published in 2010 reports the following findings:

- Most companies [99%] are now referring to an environmental topic in their annual reports. However, many of these references are relatively basic, sometimes simply referring to key phrases or topics without any supporting quantitative environmental performance data.

- 67% of FTSE All-Share companies are reporting quantitatively on their environmental impacts. . . . [but] only 28% of companies are providing comparable figures on their environmental impacts.

- Climate change and energy use are the topics with the most quantitative disclosures. Some 62% of companies produced quantitative information on these.

- Companies are increasingly focusing on key environmental issues such as pollution, and 79% of companies referred to this topic in 2009–2010.

- The biggest increase in reporting between 2006 and 2009–2010 was for references and discussion of environmental management systems (EMS), up from 33% to 61%.

- Thirty-three percent of companies referred to environmental procurement. . . . This suggests that companies are growing more aware of both the risks and opportunities of the increasing focus on reducing indirect environmental impacts from supply chains.

- Discussion of biodiversity/land use has increased . . . from 24% in 2004 to 57% in 2009–2010. In contrast, only 45% of companies discussed sustainability or corporate social responsibility, down from 57% in 2006.

# CHAPTER 15

# *Eco-Efficiency and Other Paradigms*

## ECO-EFFICIENCY

ONE OF THE MORE RECENT AND COMMONLY USED SUSTAINABILITY MET-RICS is called *eco-efficiency*. Developed in 1992 by the World Business Council on Sustainable Development (WBCSD) (2005a and 2005b, www.wbcsd.ch), it brings together the essential ingredients necessary for increased economic prosperity—more efficient use of resources and lower emissions. This framework can be used by any business to measure progress toward economic and environmental sustainability.

The methodology provides a common set of definitions, principles, and indicators and is represented by the ratio: (product or service value) / (environmental influence). Commonly used indicators for product/service value are quantity of goods or services produced or provided to customers, and net sales; while those relating to the environmental influence in product/service creation include energy consumption, materials consumption, water consumption, greenhouse gas emissions, and ozone-depleting substance emissions. Figures 15–1 to 15–3 are extracted from a WBCSD report (2005b) demonstrating—for a hypothetical company—how an eco-efficiency ratio is derived. Figure 15–1 presents the numerator data, which focuses on some product or service value; Figure 15–2 represents the denominator, which in this case considers energy consumption and GHG emissions; and, finally, Figure 15–3 calculates the eco-efficiency ratio as net sales per GHG emissions.

These types of eco-efficiency ratios have been used by Interface Inc. in conveying their degree of success in pursuit of sustainability [see chapter 13]. In this respect, it is critical to present a time series in order to create a de facto benchmark. Interface Inc. has been able to do this since they have been tracking these data for over a decade. In contrast, Mohawk Industries has presented only the current estimates and projections with no benchmarking possible at this point.

The principal advantage of this type of metric is threefold: (1) it is relatively easy to compute; (2) it permits not only temporal trend analysis, but also cross-plant and cross-company comparisons; and (3) perhaps, most important, the measure is independent of level of output. For example, a company's total greenhouse gas (GHG) output might decrease solely because the plant has reduced the level of production. The eco-efficiency ratio will signal whether this decrease in product output has been accompanied by relative reductions in GHG, increases, or no change at all.

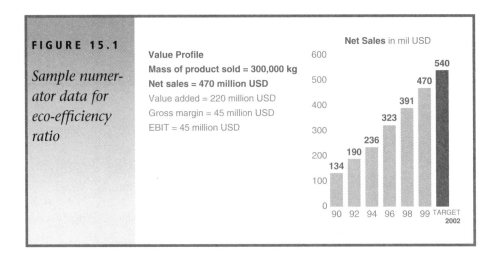

**FIGURE 15.1**

*Sample numerator data for eco-efficiency ratio*

**Value Profile**
**Mass of product sold = 300,000 kg**
**Net sales = 470 million USD**
Value added = 220 million USD
Gross margin = 45 million USD
EBIT = 45 million USD

**Net Sales** in mil USD

**FIGURE 15.2**

*Sample denominator data for eco-efficiency ratio*

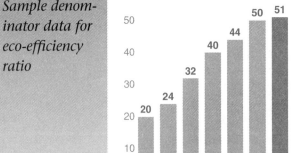

**Energy Consumption** in terajoules

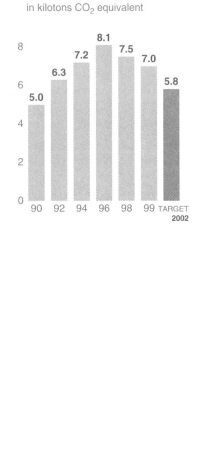

**GHG Emissions**
in kilotons $CO_2$ equivalent

**Environmental Profile**
**Energy consumed = 50,000 gigajoules**
**Material consumed = 4,500 tons**
**Water consumed = 60,000 m$^3$**
**GHG emissions = 7,000 tons $CO_2$ equiv.**
**ODS emissions = 25 tons CFC11 equiv.**
Electricity consumed = 35,300 gigajoules
GHG from upstream
electricity gen. = 4,600 tons $CO_2$ equiv.
Natural gas consumed = 11,500 gigajoules
Acidification emissions = 400 tons $SO_2$ equiv.
VOC emissions = 230 tons
COD effluents = 86 tons
Total waste = 1,450 tons
Waste to landfill = 650 tons

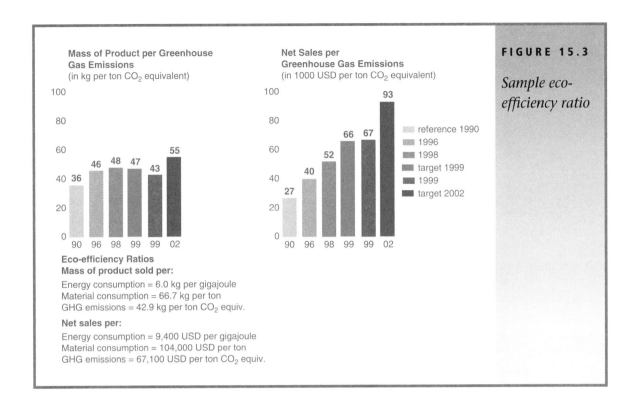

**Mass of Product per Greenhouse Gas Emissions**
(in kg per ton $CO_2$ equivalent)

**Net Sales per Greenhouse Gas Emissions**
(in 1000 USD per ton $CO_2$ equivalent)

reference 1990
1996
1998
target 1999
1999
target 2002

**Eco-efficiency Ratios**
**Mass of product sold per:**

Energy consumption = 6.0 kg per gigajoule
Material consumption = 66.7 kg per ton
GHG emissions = 42.9 kg per ton $CO_2$ equiv.

**Net sales per:**

Energy consumption = 9,400 USD per gigajoule
Material consumption = 104,000 USD per ton
GHG emissions = 67,100 USD per ton $CO_2$ equiv.

**FIGURE 15.3**

*Sample eco-efficiency ratio*

## ALTERNATIVE PARADIGMS

There are two principal criticisms of the eco-efficiency measure. The first is the mirror image of advantage #3 listed above. A firm may be achieving an improved eco-efficiency metric by lowering its GHG per unit of output, but if output is increasing sufficiently, the total level of GHG emissions will rise. Ultimately, from the perspective of society and the ecosystem, it is the total output that matters. This is a nontrivial distinction that lies at the heart of the third major case study on the oil sands in chapter 23. The second critique is even more substantive and lies at the philosophical heart of how we design our modern industrial system. This critique is based on the work of William McDonough and Michael Braungart.

McDonough, an architect and planner; and Braungart, a chemical engineer, first laid out their radical proposals for a total redesign of our modern industrial system of production in an article in the October 1998 edition of *Atlantic Monthly*, entitled "The Next Industrial Revolution." This was followed by an in-depth elaboration of their proposal in a book published in 2002 called *Cradle-to-Cradle: Remaking the Way We Make Things*. They propose a transformation away from our current linear, once-through "cradle-to-grave" production system, which is profoundly inefficient and generates massive amounts of waste. To quote: "Cradle-to-grave designs dominate modern manufacturing. . . . Many products are designed with 'built-in obsolescence,' to last only for a certain period of time. . . . Also, what most people see in their garbage cans is just the tip of the material iceberg; the product itself contains on average only 5 percent of the raw materials involved in the process of making and delivering it" (pp. 27–28).

The fundamental thrust of the innovation proposed by McDonough and Braungart is to redesign our production systems so they mimic nature where there is no waste per se, where virtually all by-products of natural production—with the exception of energy—are recycled into nutrients for the production of other organisms. The industrial challenge is to alter the design process of modern industrial products so that their waste products can be recycled into two streams: what the authors call "biological nutrients" and "technical nutrients" as illustrated in Figure 15–4. There is a key distinction between these two waste streams: the first can reenter the ecosystem without synthetic or toxic components and are thus able to be recycled without altering or contaminating natural cycles; in contrast, the second are recycled in closed loop systems with the production process so that no toxins are released into the environment. This is the essence of the "cradle-to-cradle" system.

The fundamental critique advanced by McDonough and Braungart of current sustainability efforts is that eco-efficiency is focused on reducing the negative environmental impacts of industrial production but does not induce producers to change the basic design of the production process or the products themselves. In the words of the authors, "efficient is not sufficient." Improved technologies that reduce the flow of energy and materials in the cradle-to-grave system do not ultimately eliminate the wastes and toxic products. The approach proposed by McDonough and Braungart is twofold: to replace eco-efficiency with *eco-effectiveness*, and change *downcycling* to *upcycling*—a step that Shaw Industries and some other companies such as Honeywell (McDonough and Braungart 2004) have already undertaken. The authors observe that "in our next Industrial Revolution, regulations can be seen as signals of design failure."

In a reconceptualization similar in spirit to Interface's partial substitution of a service for a good, McDonough and Braungart (1998, p. 90) state: "Imagine what would happen if a chemical company sold intelligence instead of pesticides—that is, if farmers or agro-businesses paid pesticide manufacturers to protect their crops against loss from pests instead of buying dangerous regulated chemicals to use at their own discretion."

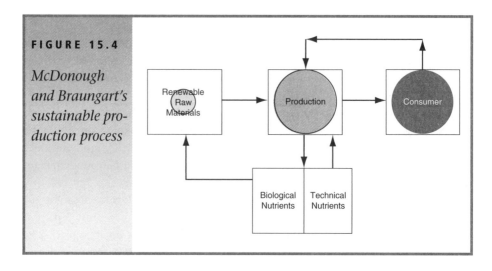

**FIGURE 15.4**

*McDonough and Braungart's sustainable production process*

To advance their agenda of transforming industrial production, McDonough and Braungart formed a consulting company called McDonough Braungart Design Chemistry (MBDC), which offered their services worldwide. While the company has had a number of both successes and failures [F astcompany.com], one of the earliest and most important early success stories was the case of Rohner Textil in Switzerland.

## CASE STUDY: ROHNER TEXTIL AG

A small textile company in Switzerland, Rohner Textil faced many of the similar environmental problems of other companies in the same industry (IEHN 2010). It was under regulatory economic pressure because of the necessity to treat its wastewater and the need to dispose of carpet trimmings deemed toxic by regulatory authorities. The impetus for change came from a textile designer in the United States who requested that the company consider producing a completely biodegradable commercial fabric for office furniture. MBDC was employed as a consultant to the project to transform Rohner's production technology and the nature of the final product. The project was challenging as it involved not only finding new raw material for the textile itself—wool from pasture-bred sheep replaced cotton—but also by the much more imposing task of finding environmentally benign dyes. Only one major chemical company, Ciba-Geigy, was prepared to share its industrial secrets with the company, resulting in the identification of 16 environmentally benign chemicals out of a total of 8,000.

The result of this reengineering process was remarkable, as formerly toxic carpet waste could now be recovered and sold to local farmers as mulch; toxic wastewater was eliminated; and costs were reduced by the elimination of filtering of dyes and chemicals. The new product, called *Climatex Lifecycle*™ became a major contributor to the company's bottom line. This is a classic example of Michael Porter's thesis that sustainability and profitability can be one and the same. Table 15–1 compares Rohner's achievements with the pure model of sustainability posited earlier for handwoven carpets [see Figure 14–4]. In this case, many of the basic ingredients of sustainability have been successfully transferred into a modern, high-volume commercial product capable of meeting the large demands of the international market.

| CHARACTERISTIC | HAND-WOVEN | ROHNER | |
|---|---|---|---|
| fibre | natural (wool) | natural (wool) | **TABLE 15.1** |
| Source of fibre | pasture-bred sheep | pasture-bred sheep | *Characteristics* |
| Type of dyes | natural | Natural | *of Rohner Tex-* |
| Major inputs | labor-intensive | capital and energy-intensive | *til Carpets vs.* |
| Looms | wooden | Metal | *Hand-Woven* |
| Toxic wastes | none | None | *Carpets* |

## THE NATURAL STEP

Formulated by two Europeans, Dr. Karl-Henrik Robert and Dr. John Holmberg, *The Natural Step* principle was introduced into North America by Paul Hawken (Nattrass et al. 1999; Nattrass and Altomore 2002a, 2002b; Robert 2008). It was the goal of Dr. Robert to translate ecological principles into a form that could be implemented throughout a corporation with knowledge and participation at all levels. The Natural Step includes several core processes: (1) perceiving the nature of the unsustainable direction of business and society and the self-interest implicit in shifting to a sustainable direction; (2) strategic visioning through *backcasting*. In contrast to *forecasting*, which starts from the present state and attempts to predict the consequences of current policies, *backcasting* establishes a desirable future goal or state and then attempts to determine the best course of action to achieve that goal; and (3) applying four *System Conditions* for sustainability. These system conditions are focused on preventing the accumulation in the environment of such things as non-renewable materials extracted from the earth; similarly preventing the accumulation of man-made chemicals; preventing the overharvesting of resources and other forms of deleterious intervention in ecosystems; and requiring that resources are used fairly and efficiently in order to meet basic human needs worldwide.

Some major companies or organizations that have adopted the Natural Step include IKEA, Scandic Hotels, Interface Inc., Collins Pine Company, Electrolux, Nike, Starbucks, and CH2M Hill. Figure 15–5 illustrates the implementation of The Natural Step at IKEA, the world's largest retailer of furniture (Nattrass and Altomore 2002b). In some cases, the confluence of sustainability and profit is obvious and simple to achieve. One need only think of the request to guests by major hotel chains to consider using towels more than once or changing bedding every second day. Both the hotel and its guests have made a small contribution to achieving a more sustainable economy while saving the hotel on laundry bills.

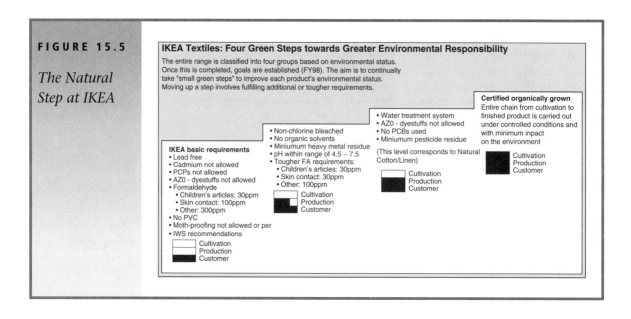

**FIGURE 15.5**

*The Natural Step at IKEA*

## A BRIEF NOTE ON FORCES DRIVING THE DIFFUSION OF SUSTAINABILITY WITHIN THE CORPORATE SECTOR

There is a clear role for government in facilitating the diffusion of sustainable technology, policy, and practices throughout the economy by providing a level playing field that allows these initiatives to compete freely with existing alternative technologies and strategies. Prime examples of this approach can be found in the area of renewable energy sources and demand-side management. However, an equally important phenomenon is the diffusion of sustainability within the corporate sector itself. While much of the popular literature on business and sustainability encourages all companies to incorporate sustainability considerations into their corporate

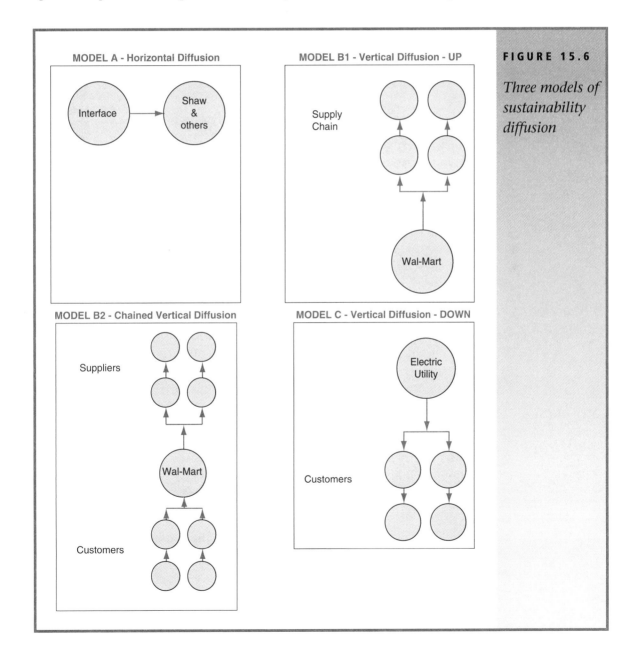

**FIGURE 15.6**

*Three models of sustainability diffusion*

strategy and adopt new and more sustainable production processes and products, this is rarely how new ideas are spread through economies. Figure 15–6 presents three models of diffusion that may be applied to the challenge of moving the industrial system closer to the goal of sustainability. *Model A* represents horizontal diffusion; *Model B* vertical diffusion up the supply chain, and *Model C* vertical diffusion down the supply chain. Each is briefly described in turn below.

## Model A—Horizontal Diffusion

There are several ways in which sustainability innovation and policy can be transferred either directly or indirectly among competitors. The first, illustrated by the case of Interface Inc. and Shaw Industries, is where one company sets the standard and forces other companies to respond. The second case represents the direct transfer of technology either through licensing for a fee or without charge. In the case of Rohner Textil for example, the company offered to share its new nonpolluting technology with other companies in the same industry.

## Model B—Vertical Diffusion Up the Supply Chain

In some respects, this approach potentially represents the most successful model of diffusion for sustainable production technology and strategy. As stated above, it is not realistic to expect all companies to adopt sustainable practices into their business models, especially when they are operating in highly competitive, low-profit margin industries. Suggestions that these firms should adopt new practices that might, on balance, cost many of them lost profits in the short run is not a viable suggestion and is, in fact, counterproductive as it lowers the credibility of sustainability advocate within the business community.

However, this environment can change radically when a major corporation at the bottom of the supply chain mandates that its suppliers must meet sustainability criteria in order to continue to receive orders for their products. Once this *greening of the supply chain* (Sarkis 2010) occurs, the vast array of suppliers who previously might not be able to afford sustainability initiatives can no longer afford *not* to do so. The prime example of this phenomenon is Wal-Mart that has moved aggressively in this area to demand more ecologically friendly products from its approximately 100,000 suppliers. As a consequence, Wal-Mart has been termed a "private regulator," achieving within the business sector what government might be unwilling or unable to attempt. This model represents one of the critical keys to the diffusion of sustainability throughout the economic system as Wal-Mart has come to realize that sustainable business is the key to sustainable profits (Humes, 2011). [See further discussion of the Wal-Mart case in chapter 28.]

## Model C—Vertical Diffusion Down the Supply Chain

In this model, corporations sitting atop or amid a supply chain adopt practices and policies that induce their customers to follow suit. One example of this phenomenon is the adoption by electric power utilities as early as the 1980s of innovative rate structures such as marginal cost pricing (Nemetz and Hankey 1984), which provides a strong incentive to customers within the industrial and commercial sectors to alter their energy use—and perhaps input or product mix—in a more sustainable direction.

## CITED REFERENCES AND RECOMMENDED READINGS

DeSimone, Livio D. and Frank Popoff (1997) *Eco-Efficiency. The Business Link to Sustainable Development*. World Business Council on Sustainable Development, Switzerland.

Hawken, Paul (1993) *The Ecology of Commerce. A Declaration of Sustainability*, New York: Harper Collins.

Humes, Edward (2011) *Force of Nature. The Unlikely Story of Wal-Mart's Green Revolution*, New York: Harper Business.

Investor Environmental Health Network (IEHN) (2010) Case Study. "Rohner Textiles: Cradle-to-Cradle Innovation and Sustainability" (www.iehn.org/publications.case.rohner.php).

McDonough, William and Michael Braungart (1998) "The Next Industrial Revolution," *Atlantic Monthly*, October, pp. 82–92.

McDonough, William and Michael Braungart (2002) *Cradle to Cradle: Remaking the Way We Make Things*, New York: North Point Press.

McDonough, William and Michael Braungart (2004) "The Cradle-to-Cradle Alternative, *State of the World 2004*, Worldwatch Institute, pp.104–105.

Nattrass, Brian and Mary Altomore (2002a) *Dancing with the Tiger: Learning Sustainability Step by Natural Step*, Gabriola Island, BC: New Society Publishers.

Nattrass, Brian and Mary Altomore, (2002b) "IKEA: Nothing is Impossible" in Peter N. Nemetz (ed.) *Bringing Business on Board: Sustainable Development and the B-School Curriculum*, Vancouver, BC: JBA Press, pp.429–458.

Nattrass, Brian and Mary Altomore (1999) *The Natural Step for Business*, Gabriola Island, BC: New Society Publishers.

Nemetz, Peter N. and Marilyn Hankey (1984) *Economic Incentives for Energy Conservation*. New York: John Wiley & Sons.

Robert, Karl-Henrik (2008) *The Natural Step Story. Seeding a Quiet Revolution*, Gabriola Island, BC: New Society Publishers.

Sarkis, Joseph (2010) *Greening the Supply Chain Eco-Efficiency*, London: Springer.

Seiler-Hausmann, Jan-Dirk, Christa Liedtke and Ernst Ulricj von Weizsacker (eds.) (2004) *Eco-Efficiency and Beyond. Towards the Sustainable Enterprise*, Sheffield: Greanleaf.

World Business Council on Sustainable Development (WBCSD) (2005a) *Eco-Efficiency. Creating More Value with Less Impact*, Geneva.

World Business Council on Sustainable Development (WBCSD) (2005b) *Measuring Eco-Efficiency. A Guide to Reporting Company Performance*, Geneva.

World Business Council on Sustainable Development (WBCSD), Geneva [website: www.wbcsd.ch].

# CHAPTER 16

## Closing the Loop—Mimicking Nature

### INDUSTRIAL ECOLOGY (IE)

Smith (2007) summarizes the field of industrial ecology as follows:

> Using nature as a model, industrial ecology views the industrial plant or system as an integrated set of cyclical processes in which the consumption of energy and materials is optimized, waste generation is minimized, and wastes from one process serve as feedstock for other production processes. Industrial ecology views industrial production as a "metabolic" process. It attempts to close the "open materials cycle" characteristic of industrial society, whereby materials and energy are lost to economic use, and harmful toxic substances are released to the environment. Industrial ecology tries to "close the loop" in two ways: (1) by eliminating waste from production processes, and (2) by redesigning wastes as useful by-products that can be used in other processes.

An extensive literature exists on the subject, and there have been numerous applications of its basic principles (Ayres and Ayres 1996, Graedel and Allenby 2010, see also *Journal of Industrial Ecology*). This book reviews some of the key concepts of IE such as eco-efficiency (chapter 15), industrial metabolism (chapter 17) and life-cycle analysis (chapter 18). One of the most advanced applications of the principles of IE, termed *industrial symbiosis*, can be found in *eco-industrial parks*—a grouping of diverse and complementary industrial plants characterized by the mutual exchange of wastes, by-products, and energy. Several examples of operating or proposed parks are drawn from experiences in three countries: Kalundborg, Denmark; Scotsford, Alberta; and Tampico, Mexico. The United States is in the process of developing several parks, but most are still either in the development stage or conceptually simpler than the examples above (http://gei.ucsc.edu/eco-industrial_parks.html).

### KALUNDBORG, DENMARK

The world's first eco-industrial park has been in full operation as a complex interdependent system for over two decades and is located on the coast, 75 miles west of the capital city, Copenhagen. Figure 16–1 presents a schematic of the park that shows the interchange of at least 17 flows among 8 large industrial operations in fields as

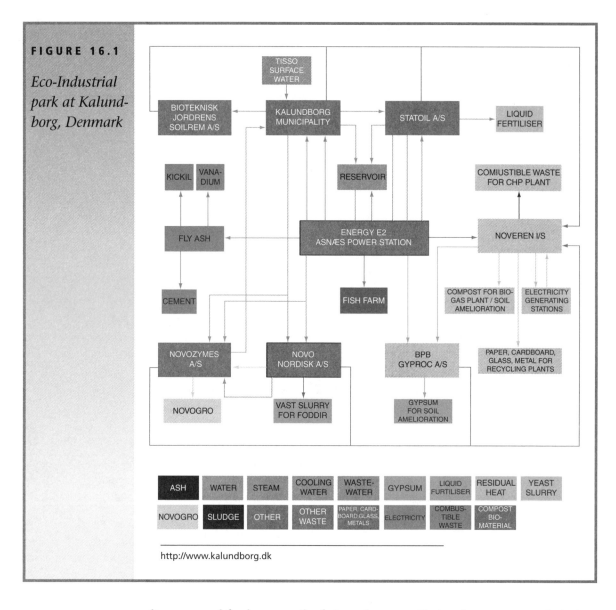

**FIGURE 16.1**

*Eco-Industrial park at Kalundborg, Denmark*

http://www.kalundborg.dk

diverse as coal-fired power, oil refining, pharmaceutical and enzyme manufacturing, and plasterboard. It is noteworthy that it was not the original intention of the participants to create a symbiotic industrial complex. The industrial plants had all been established in relative close proximity but evolved to the current high level of interconnectedness over time as they sought means to reduce waste streams and garner revenue from by-product production (Ehrenfeld and Gertler 1997). The complex has since been expanded to include district heating, conventional agriculture as well as fish farming, and the use of fly ash as a supplement to concrete for roads (Chertow 2007).

## SCOTSFORD, ALBERTA

In some respects, the origins of eco-industrial parks lie in the long-standing practice of petrochemical companies to create conglomerations of industrial operations that interchange feedstocks and utilities. With the principal goal of reducing costs by increasing the utilization of by-products, the fortunate side effect is the reduction of wastes from an otherwise very pollutant-intensive industry. Figure 16–2 illustrates the layout of a major industrial park in Alberta that includes a mixture of oil refineries and chemical plants (McCann 2002). It should be noted, however, that such groupings of petrochemical-related industrial operations pose a disaster risk that would not be present if the plants were not in close proximity. One way that this risk can be reduced is to increase their physical separation and interconnect them with pipelines in those cases where it is possible to use this form of transport without altering the chemical or physical characteristics of the product. This is a viable option and less risky as long as such an undertaking is not so expensive as to offset cost reductions from by-product interchange. Another more likely risk is created by

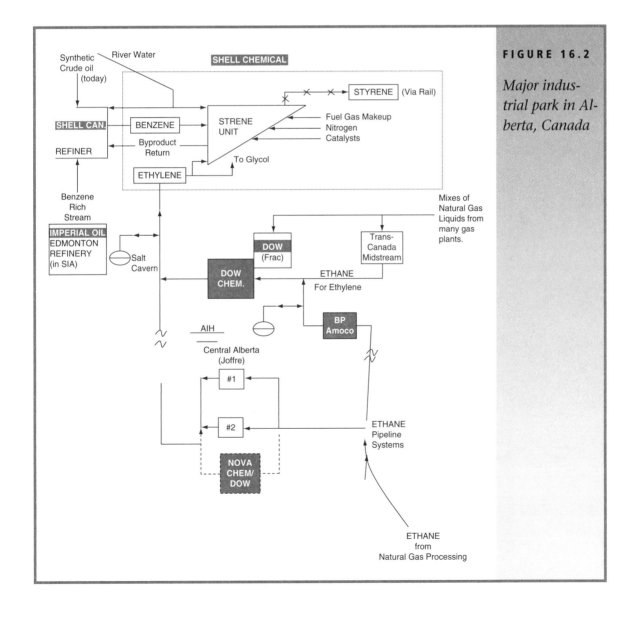

**FIGURE 16.2**

*Major industrial park in Alberta, Canada*

the potential dependence of one plant on the output of another. If one industrial operation were to temporarily cease operation due to accidents or other causes, there is a risk of a cascading impact on all other companies in the park.

## TAMPICO, MEXICO

The first North American effort to create an eco-industrial park based on the concept of by-product synergy was initiated in Mexico with the support of the World

| TABLE 16.1 | COMPANY | PRODUCT |
|---|---|---|
| *Components of Proposed Eco-Industrial Park in Tampico, Mexico* | **Plastics** | |
| | Indelpro S.A. de C.V. | PVC |
| | G.E. Plastics | ABS |
| | Grupo Primex | PVC resin and dust, phtalic anhydride |
| | Policyd | PVC |
| | Polioles | Polystyrene |
| | Pecten Poliesters | Polyethylene |
| | **Industrial Minerals** | |
| | PPG | pure silica |
| | Dupont | $TiO_2$ pigment |
| | **Chemical / Petrochemical** | |
| | Novaquim | chemicals for rubber industry, herbicides |
| | NHUMO | synthetic rubber |
| | INSA-Emulsion | rubber products (tires, hose) |
| | INSA-Solucíon | rubber products (roads, shoes) |
| | Pemex | petroleum refinery products |
| | Petrocel-DMT | dimethyl terephtalate |
| | Petrocel-PTA | phteraphtalic acid |
| | **Metallurgical** | |
| | Sulfamex | manganese sulfate |
| | MineraAutlan | ferromanganese, siliocmanganese |
| | **Miscellaneous** | |
| | Cryoinfra | industrial gases |
| | Grupo Tampico | Coca-cola bottler |
| | Johns Mansville | impermeable membranes |
| | Enertek | electric power |

*Source:* Young et al. 2002, p. 473

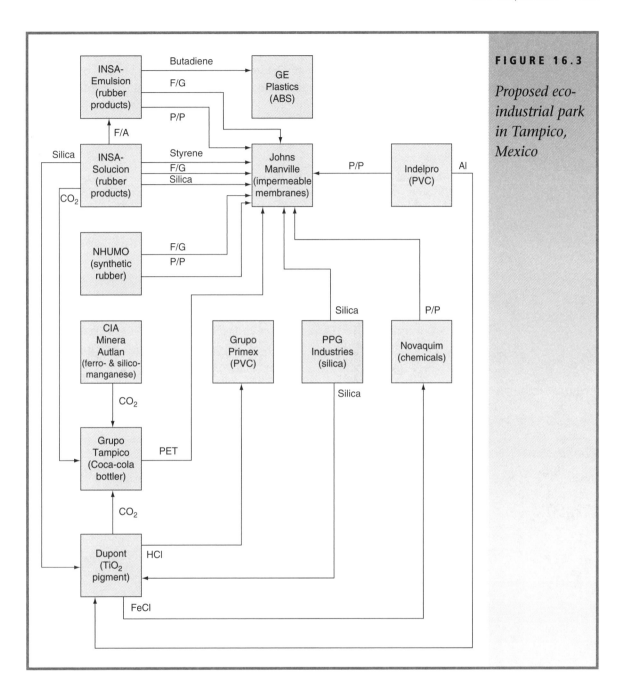

**FIGURE 16.3**

*Proposed eco-industrial park in Tampico, Mexico*

Business Council on Sustainable Development. A diverse range of 21 different companies was encouraged to plan an integrated site, and several small demonstration projects were undertaken. Table 16–1 lists the companies and their products, while Figure 16–3 summarizes the anticipated interplant flows of the critical by-products (Young et al. 2002). A primer on by-product synergy (Mangan 1997) clearly enunciated the challenges facing the establishment of an eco-industrial park, and most of these caveats remain in force today. They include the following. Technical: Is conversion of the by-product technically feasible? Economic: Is it economically feasible? Business: Is it competing against other investment opportunities? Corporate practice: Is the company's decision-making process hindering investment? Regulatory: Are there government-created barriers to synergy? Risk: Could the use of or transportation of what might be considered a waste product lead to increased liability and, if so, who is responsible? Geographic: Can the by-product be economically transported from its generator to its consumer? Trust: Are companies comfortable working together? Time: Is by-product synergy a low or high priority to the company?

In light of this comprehensive list of challenges to the formation of successfully functioning eco-industrial parks (EIPs), it is not surprising that development has been careful and deliberate and that many parks are quite modest, encompassing a relatively small number of plants. Table 16–2 lists some of the most prominent EIPs in the United States at this time. In a study of industrial symbiosis, Chertow (2007) concludes that de novo attempts to create EIPs from scratch have generally been failures; more successful results have evolved from corporations recognizing the potential for synergies with industrial operations already in existence. The author identifies three policies that can facilitate the recognition of these opportunities: "(1) forming reconnaissance teams to identify industrial areas likely to have a baseline of exchanges and mapping their flows accordingly, (2) offering technical

| **TABLE 16.2**<br><br>*Some Major Eco-Industrial Parks in the United States* | 1. Berks Country Eco-Industrial Park in Berks County, PA |
| --- | --- |
| | 2. Brownsville Eco-Industrial Park in Brownsville, Texas |
| | 3. Cabazon Resource Recovery Park in Indio, California |
| | 4. Civano Industrial Eco Park in Tucson, Arizona |
| | 5. Coffee Creek Center in Chesterton, IN |
| | 6. East Shore Eco-Industrial Park in Oakland, California |
| | 7. Fairfield Eco-Industrial Park in Baltimore, Maryland |
| | 8. Franklin County Eco-Industrial Park in Youngsville, North Carolina |
| | 9. The Green Institute in Minneapolis, Minnesota |
| | 10. Plattsburgh Eco-Industrial Park in Plattsburgh, New York |
| | 11. Port of Cape Charles Sustainable Technologies Industrial Park in Eastville, Virginia |
| | 12. Raymond Green Eco-Industrial Park in Raymond, Washington |
| | 13. Riverside Eco-Park in Burlington, Vermont (note: now named Intervale Food Center) |
| | 14. Skagit County Environmental Industrial Park in Skagitt County, Washington |
| | 15. Shady Side Eco-Business Park in Shady Side, Maryland |
| | 16. Trenton Eco-Industrial Complex in Trenton, New Jersey |
| | 17. The Volunteer Site in Chattanooga, Tennessee (note: now named Enterprise South Eco-Industrial Park) |

*Source:* http://gei.ucsc.edu/eco-industrial_parks.html

or financial assistance to increase the number of interactions once some kernels are found to be in place, inspired by managers with a symbiotic mindset, and (3) pursuing locations where common symbiotic precursors already exist, such as cogeneration, landfill gas mining, and waste water reuse, often as one-off activities, to determine whether they may be likely candidates for technical or financial assistance as bridges to more extensive symbiosis" (p. 26).

The most common challenges to the widespread adoption of this type of industrial organization are issues of location, proximity, and complementarity, but a more cogent problem from a sustainability perspective is that EIPs can, by their nature, mimic only part of natural closed cycles. There will still be significant industrial waste associated with these undertakings and, as such, they are vulnerable to the critique of eco-efficiency advanced by McDonough and Braungart. Are there other technologies or technological systems that more closely approximate the sustainable model inherent in natural processes? One approach is *biomimicry*.

## BIOMIMICRY

Derived from the Greek words "bios" (life) and "mimesis (imitation), *biomimicry* is a relatively new set of scientific and engineering principles focused on transferring natural designs and processes into production processes and products (Benyus 1997). One biomimicry website (www.brainz.org/15-coolest-cases-biomimicry/) cites numerous modern inventions based on mimicking nature. These are listed in Table 16–3 (see also www.naturaledgeproject.net).

| AREA OF INNOVATION | INSIRED BY: | PRODUCT NAME | **TABLE 16.3** |
|---|---|---|---|
| Air conditioning | termites | | *Products Inspired by Biomimicry* |
| Economic cluster | rainforest | | |
| Value-added business | nutrient cycling | | |
| Bacterial control | red algae | | |
| Building Material from $CO_2$ | mollusks | | |
| Fog harvesting | a desert beetle | | |
| Economic cluster | the mangrove forest | | |
| Vaccines without refrigeration | resurrection plant | | |
| Fiber manufacture | golden orb weaver spiders | | |
| Water purification | the marsh ecosystem | | |
| $CO_2$ capture | algae | | |
| Pacemaker replacement | humpback whales | | |
| Fire retardant | animal cells | | |
| Plastics from $CO_2$ | plants | | |

*(Continued)*

| TABLE 16.3 *continued* | AREA OF INNOVATION | INSIRED BY: | PRODUCT NAME |
|---|---|---|---|
| | Self-assembling glass | sea sponges | |
| | Wound healing | flies | |
| | Solar cells | leaves | |
| | Friction-free fans | nautilus | |
| | Bacterial control | barberry | |
| | Self-cleaning surfaces | lotus plant | |
| | Optical brighteners | Cyphochilus beetle | |
| | Adhesion without glue | geckos | Gecko Tape ☐ |
| | Adhesive fabrics | cockleburs | Velcor ☐ |
| | Farics with passive humidy control stomata | | Stomatex ☐ |

One of the most prominent emerging applications of biomimicry is architecture in a subfield designated "ecotecture" (*New York Times Magazine*, May 20, 2007; see also *Ecotecture: The Journal of Ecological Design*). Some common examples include rooftop gardens or grass roofs, and vertical gardens or "green walls." Figure 16–4 illustrates the maintenance of a grass roof on a commercial building in Coombs, B.C. One of the most intriguing and visually attractive applications of ecotecture

**FIGURE 16.4**

*Sustainable rooftop maintenance*

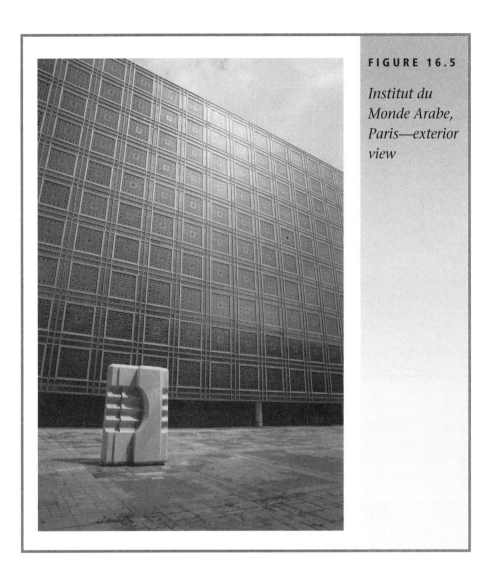

**FIGURE 16.5**

*Institut du Monde Arabe, Paris—exterior view*

is in use of innovative exterior cladding or fabrics on commercial and other buildings. An archetypal example is the outside walls of the Institut du Monde Arabe in Paris. (See Figure 16–5). The exterior wall is composed of 1,600 "irises" designed to replicate the workings of the human eye. More detailed pictures of individual components viewed from both outside and inside the building are reproduced in Figures 16–6 and 16–7. Each mechanical iris opens and shuts depending on the balance of interior and exterior temperatures to let more or less light into the building. In this way, biomimicry can reduce the cost of both heating and cooling.

Biomimicry is not a totally new concept in the area of building design as some ancient buildings incorporated natural processes of cooling by air and water into their architectural design. An archetypal example of this historical phenomenon is provided by the great Alhambra hilltop palace built between 1238 and 1358 by the Moors in Granada, Spain. [See Figure 16–8.] Despite outside temperatures in excess

**FIGURE 16.6**

*Institut du
Monde Arabe,
Paris—exterior
view, close-up*

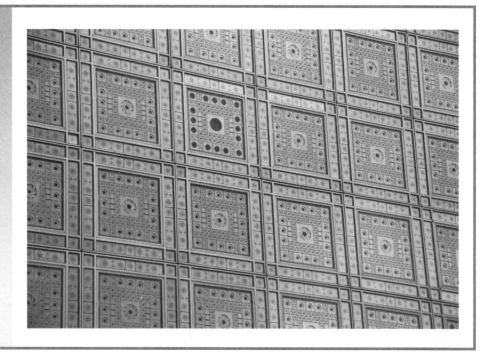

**FIGURE 16.7**

*Institut du
Monde Arabe,
Paris—interior
view, close-up*

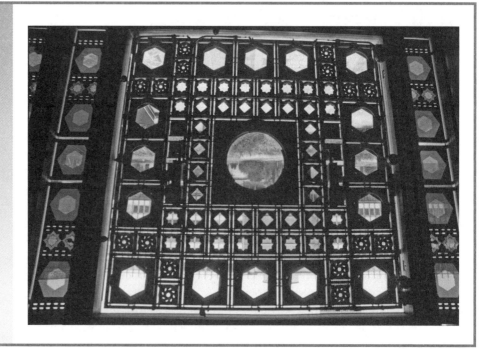

**FIGURE 16.8**

*Alhambra interior, Granada, Spain*

of 100 degrees Fahrenheit, the inside of the palace remains relatively cool because of extensive still and running water and open courtyards and breezeways. This example is suggestive of a broader principle: many ancient civilizations had knowledge that could be of use to us today in the pursuit of sustainability, but many of these historical precedents from such countries as diverse as Ancient Greece, Rome, and China remain ignored or forgotten today (Butti and Perlin 1980; Jordan and Perlin 1979; Needham 1981; Temple 2007).

The following chapters describe in greater detail several other major examples of IE with special application to sustainable industrial production, including mass balances, industrial metabolism, and life-cycle analysis.

## CITED REFERENCES AND RECOMMENDED READINGS

Ayres, Robert U. and Leslie W. Ayres (1996) *Industrial Ecology:Towards Closing the Materials Cycle*, Cheltenham: Edward Elgar.

Benyus, Janine (1997) *Biomimicry: Innovation Inspired by Nature*, New York: Harper Collins.

Butti, Ken and John Perlin (1980) *A Golden Thread. 2500 Years of Solar Architecture and Technology*, Palo Alto, CA: Cheshire Books.

Chertow, Marian R. (2007) "'Uncovering' Industrial Symbiosis." *Journal of Industrial Ecology*, Vol. 11, Number 1, pp. 11–30.

*Ecotecture: The Journal of Ecological Design.* [http://www/ecotecture.com]

Ehrenfeld, John and Nicholas Gertler (1997) "Industrial Ecology in Practice. The Evolution of Interdependence at Kalundborg," *Journal of Industrial Ecology*, 1(1), pp. 67–79.

Graedel, T.E. and B.R. Allenby (2002) *Industrial Ecology, second edition*, Englewood Cliffs, NJ: Prentice Hall.

Graedel, T.E. and B.R. Allenby (2010) *Industrial Ecology and Sustainable Engineering*, Boston: Prentice Hall. http://gei.ucsc.edu/eco-industrial_parks.html. [Green Enterprise Initiative, University of California, Santa Cruz].

Jordan, Borimir and John Perlin (1979) "Solar Energy Use and Litigation in Ancient Times," *Solar Law Reporter*, 1(3), pp. 583–594.

Journal of Industrial Ecology [http://onlinelibrary.wiley.com/journal/10.1111/(ISSN)1530-9290]

Lowe, Ernest A. (2001) *Eco-industrial Park Handbook for Asian Developing Countries*. Report to the Asian Development Bank, Manila.

Lyons, Donald I. (2007) "A Spatial Analysis of Loop Closing Among Recycling, Remanufacturing, and Waste Treatment Firms in Texas," *Journal of Industrial Ecology*, 11(1), pp. 43–54.

Mangan, Andy (1997) *By-product Synergy: A Strategy for Sustainable Development. A Primer*, The Business Council for Sustainable Development, Gulf of Mexico, April.

McCann, T.J. (2002) "Chemical Industry Integration" in Peter N. Nemetz (ed.) *Bringing Business on Board: Sustainable Development and the B-School Curriculum*, Vancouver, BC: JBA Press, pp. 475–492.

Needham, Joseph (1981) *Science in Traditional China*, Cambridge, MA: Harvard University Press.

*New York Times Magazine* (2007) "Eco-tecture," Special Issue, May 20.

Smith, W.G.B. (2007) "Accounting for the Environment: Can Industrial Ecology Pay Double Dividends for Business?" in Peter N. Nemetz (ed.) *Sustainable Resource Management: Reality or Illusion?* Cheltenham: Edward Elgar, pp. 304–341.

Temple, Robert (2007) *The Genius of China*, Rochester, VT: Inner Traditions.

Van Beers, Dick et al. (2007) "Industrial Symbiosis in the Australian Minerals Industry," *Journal of Industrial Ecology*, 11(1), pp. 55–72.

www.community-wealth.org/content/ucsc-university-california-santa-cruz-green-enterprise-initiative [website for UCSC Green Enterprise Initiative, Existing and Developing Eco-Industrial Park Sites in the U.S.].

www.naturaledgeproject.net [website of The Natural Edge Project, Australia].

Young, Rebekah et al. (2002) "Byproduct Synergy: Mexico," in Peter N. Nemetz (ed.) *Bringing Business on Board: Sustainable Development and the B-School Curriculum*, Vancouver, .C: JBA Press, pp. 459–474.

Zhu, Qinghua et al. (2007) "Industrial Symbiosis in China. Case Study of the Guitang Group," *Journal of Industrial Ecology*, 11(1), pp. 31–42.

# CHAPTER 17

# Thinking Systemically (I): Mass Balances and Metabolic Analysis

## MASS BALANCES

The quantification of the total amount of all materials into and out of a process is referred to as a *mass balance*. This type of analysis provides confirmation that all materials have been fully accounted for, and no streams are missing. The fundamental concept is that the total mass flowing into a process should equal total mass flowing out. [See Figure 17–1.] In practice, it is a useful way to identify previously hidden waste streams: if the mass coming out of a process is less than the combined mass of the inputs, then some other stream—most likely waste—must be leaving the process, too. This is a particularly important tool in light of the maxim that "waste is lost profit."

Table 17–1 presents a highly simplified example of mass balance analysis using the drying yield of potatoes (http://www.nzifst.org.nz/unitoperations/matlenerg2.htm). In this case, the 1,000 kg of total input mass in the form of raw potatoes and their constituents is balanced by 1,000 kg of total output mass in the form of dried product and losses. Clearly, a much more complex production process would require an equally complex mass balance analysis.

This type of methodology can be very useful in two specific areas of concern to the corporation: (1) finding a least-cost solution to regulatory requirements for pollution control, and (2) determining if waste streams could be profitably recovered as marketable by-products. Examples of each of these circumstances are presented in case study #1 below. Case study #2 examines a similar problem of total waste cost minimization faced by a local government such as a municipality.

## CASE STUDY #1—MASS BALANCE ANALYSIS TO ASSIST CORPORATE STRATEGY

This case concerns the output of wastes as distinct from the inputs and examines a small rural township with several industrial plants: an abattoir, plywood/sawmill plant, and dairy [Figure 17–2]. The case focuses on the reduction of five-day biochemical oxygen demand ($BOD_5$)—a pollutant whose municipal discharge is dominated by the waste stream from the dairy. Table 17–2 is a simplified and truncated mass balance for the township listing the load into and out of the municipal sewage treatment plant (STP) as well as direct discharges from the three industrial operations.

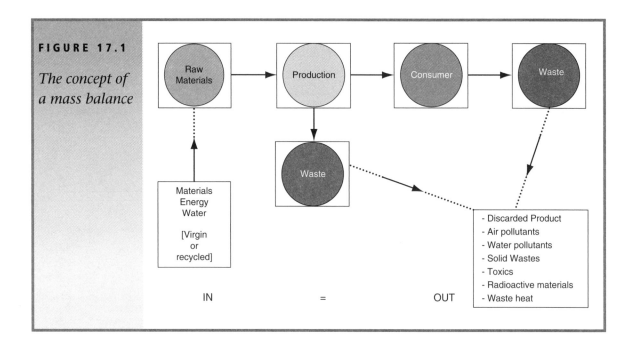

**FIGURE 17.1**

*The concept of a mass balance*

**TABLE 17.1**

*Mass Balance of Potato Drying*

| MASS IN | | MASS OUT | |
|---|---|---|---|
| *Raw Potatoes:* | | *Dried Product:* | |
| Potato solids | 140 kg | Potato solids | 129 kg |
| Water | 860 kg | Associated water | 10 kg |
| | | Total product | 139 kg |
| | | *Losses* | |
| | | Peelings | |
| | | Solids | 11 kg |
| | | Water | 69 kg |
| | | Water evaporated | 781 kg |
| | | Total losses | 861 kg |
| Total | 1000 kg | Total | 1000 kg |

*Source:* www.nzifst.org.nz/unitoperations.matlenerg2.htm

## ABATTOIR

Pollution control in the modeled abattoir presents the richest choice of treatment alternatives among the three major industrial operations and provides a convincing demonstration of the necessity for, and usefulness of, computer programming in arraying and choosing from a multitude of treatment combinations. From the

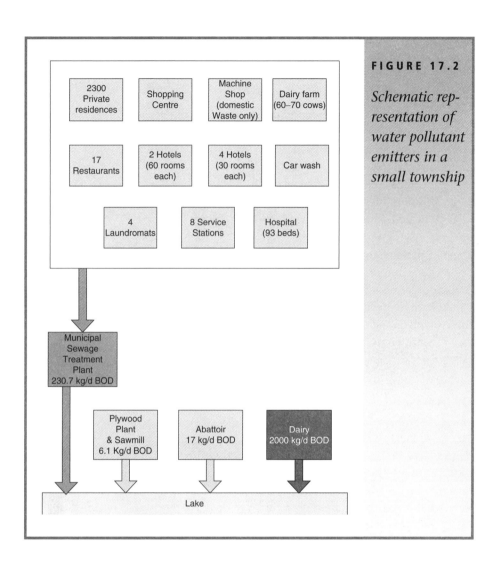

**FIGURE 17.2**

*Schematic representation of water pollutant emitters in a small township*

| | FLOW IN L /d | BOD IN mg /L | TOTAL BOD kg /d |
|---|---|---|---|
| **STP in** | 2,247,392 | 165 | 371 |
| **STP out** | 2,247,392[a] | 22 | 48 |
| **Dairy** | 37,854 | 44,000 | 1,666 |
| **Abattoir** | 11,356 | 1,250 | 14 |
| **Plywood1** | 3,153 | 860 | 3 |
| **Plywood2** | 59,052 | 40 | 2 |
| **Plywood combined** | 62,205 | 82 | 5 |

[a] estimated, exclusive of evaporative losses

**TABLE 17.2**

*Simplified Mass Balance for a Small Township*

literature, three subprocess changes have been identified as well as three add-on alternatives listed as follows (with $BOD_5$ reduction in brackets):

(I) Subprocess changes
    A. Add evaporator to wet rendering system (50% reduction)
    B. Change to dry rendering (60% reduction)
    C. Precede wet clean-up with wet dry clean-up (10% reduction)
(II) Add-on Treatment
    D. Catch basin only (25% reduction)
    E. Trickling filter (65–95% reduction, midpoint 80%)
    F. Activated sludge (85–95% reduction, midpoint 90%)

Some of these alternatives are substitutes, while others are complements. In addition, when computing overall plant $BOD_5$ removal, it is important to recognize the process ordering of specific pollutant reduction technologies. There are, in total, 23 alternative process/treatment combinations that require examination. Eight of these involve total flow reduction as well as $BOD_5$ abatement because of the lower water use inherent in option B.

## DAIRY

The dairy $BOD_5$ waste dominates the system discharge. Traditionally, many small dairies have found it simplest to discharge their high $BOD_5$ organic waste in the form of whey—the portion of the milk remaining after cheese curd is removed—directly to receiving waters. The removal of this option by new regulatory requirements has forced many dairies to consider their waste disposal options. In some cases, the opportunity exists for turning these wastes into profits. Within the last several decades, whey has been transformed from an undesirable waste product into a high-value food additive in baking, candy, sports drinks, animal feed, and calf-milk replacements. Table 17–3 illustrates the type of cost calculation that the dairy farm might conduct in assessing the potential profitability of redirecting its whey from the waste stream to a marketable product. While the incremental value of the recovered whey is not high, this is a relatively small dairy/cheese operation, and the total value of the whey must be combined with the avoided costs of either treating the waste or paying for its discharge to the municipal sewage system. The plywood plant and sawmill have not been included in this analysis as their relatively low-level waste can be accommodated by a simple hookup to the STP with little additional cost.

    The critical importance of corporate-level mass or material balances is demonstrated in chapter 25, which discusses the use of activity-base costing to allocate a corporation's environmentally related costs in a manner that can reduce costs and increase profit potential.

| | | |
|---|---|---|
| # cows | 65 | **TABLE 17.3** |
| lbs of milk per cow | 20,000 | |
| total lbs of milk | 1,300,000 | *Sample Calcu-* |
| percent going to cheese | 50% | *lations of the* |
| milk to cheese | 650,000 | *Economics of* |
| dry whey % | 5.8% | *Whey Recov-* |
| whey butter % | 0.27% | *ery in a Small* |
| total dry whey in lbs | 37,700 | *Dairy Farm* |
| total whey butter in lbs | 1,755 | |
| Price of dry whey / lb Dec 2006 | $0.41 | |
| price of whey butter / lb | $0.60 | |
| (approx 1.5 x dry whey) | | |
| total value of dry whey | $15,457.00 | |
| total value of whey butter | $1053.00 | |
| TOTAL VALUE OF WHEY | $16,510.00 | |

## CASE STUDY #2 — MASS BALANCE ANALYSIS TO ASSIST GOVERNMENT POLICY

Studies of municipal waste treatment cannot be confined to an examination of treatment provided by urban government alone but must address the larger issue of treatment on a system-wide basis that identifies all major waterborne pollutant dischargers within an urban environment and then determines the most efficient combination of treatment installations.

There are basically three steps in the analysis. The first step is to construct a systems materials balance of a few critical parameters such as suspended solids and five-day biochemical oxygen demand ($BOD_5$). The second step involves an assessment of alternative capital and operating costs of treatment at both municipal treatment plants and sites of industrial pollution generation. The third and final step is the identification of the "optimal" treatment solution; that is, the least-cost solution subject to the constraint of maximum permissible effluent discharge to the environment. The list of alternatives should not be restricted to conventional *end-of-pipe* waste treatment processes. Industrial *process changes* or other methods of pollution abatement may be cheaper than conventional end-of-pipe treatment and, consequently, must be included in this analysis. Also, multiple discharge sites, transportation cost savings, and damage changes (increases or decreases) should be considered.

| SOURCE | FLOW (AVG.) IGPD A | BOD[5] (AVG.) LB/DAY | BOD[5] (AVG.) PPM | SUSPENDED SOLIDS (AVG.) LB/DAY | SUSPENDED SOLIDS (AVG.) PPM |
|---|---|---|---|---|---|
| Residential [b,e] | 304,367 | 613.1 | 231 | 719.6 | 271 |
| Commercial and government [c,e] | 46,429 | 202.0 | 498 | 236.0 | 582 |
| Industry | | | | | |
| Brewery [d] | 316,985 | 2,520.0 | 911 | 3,155.0 | 1,140 |
| Sawmill [d] | 35,000 | 105.0 | 344 | 64.5 | 211 |
| Infiltration [e,f] | 658 | 1.0 | 174 | 1.0 | 174 |
| Total estimated sewage treatment plant influent | 703,439 | 3,441.1 | 561 | 4,176.1 | 680 |
| Measured sewage treatment plant influent [d] | 721,520 | 3,138.0 | 498 | 4,289.0 | 681 |
| Percentage error [g] | −2.6% | 8.8% | | −2.7% | |
| Measured sewage treatment plant effluent [d] | − 720,000 | − 75.0 | − 75 | − 950.0 | − 130 |

**TABLE 17.4**

*Materials Balance for an Example Municipal Sewer System*

a Imperial gallons per day
b Represents a population of 3,662
c Includes 115 hotel-motel rooms, 9 restaurants, 3 laundromats, 7 service stations, as well as 20 other small establishments. Also included are a 50-bed hospital and a school population of 1,776.
d Measured
e Estimated
f Infiltration, plus small and unidentified sources and sinks
g An error of this magnitude in the BOD[5] materials balance could be due to an error in estimation of residential, commercial or infiltration BOD[5] loadings, or an unrepresentative sample from the sewage treatment plant. It is assumed that the error is due to the last factor for two reasons: (i) there have been significantly fewer measurements taken by the municipality for influent BOD[5] than flow or suspended solids; and (ii) the adoption of measured BOD[5] at the sewage treatment plant as being representative would imply BOD[5] residential loading coefficients significantly lower than those reported in the literature. Consequently, it is assumed that actual BOD[5] influent to the sewage treatment plant averages 561 parts per million (ppm).

A municipality with a population of approximately 4,000 people has been chosen for this study because of the relative ease of model formulation and solution. Table 17–4 presents a simplified representation of the municipal sewer system with major waste load contributors by type and number.

The least-cost solution on a system-wide basis is found by solving the following two equations:

(1) $dC_R/dQ_R = dC_C/dQ_C = dC_{IA}/dQ_{IA} = dC_{IB}/dQ_{IB} = dC_{STP}/dQ_{STP}$

(2) $Q_R + Q_C + Q_{IA} + Q_{IB} + Q_{STP} = X$

where
    $C$ = cost of pollutant removal,
    $Q$ = quantity of pollutant removed,
    $X$ = total system-wide reduction of pollutant desired.

and subscripts

    R = residential sector,
    C = commercial sector,
    IA = industry A,
    IB = industry B,
    STP = municipal sewage treatment plant.

In other words, the least-cost solution requires that the marginal cost of abatement for all waste treaters be equal, and the summation of all pollutant reductions equals the total desired level of system pollutant removal. There are several problems facing the town chosen as an example, the most important being a planned major increase in brewery production. A revised materials balance reflecting this proposed increase in capacity is presented in Table 17–5.

The economic systems analysis concludes that the least-cost solution to effluent abatement in this municipality entails a division of responsibility for effluent abatement between the town and its principal industrial discharger, the brewery. Clearly, each town or city represents a unique situation with a potentially stronger or weaker argument for industrial pretreatment. What this study demonstrates, however, is that a systems analysis based on mass balances and cost data are critical ingredients in the determination of least-cost solutions to urban wastewater control. Specifically, least-cost solutions cannot be achieved by an examination of alternative

| SOURCE | AVERAGE FLOW | AVERAGE BOD$_5$ | | AVERAGE SUSPENDED SOLIDS | | TABLE 17.5 |
|---|---|---|---|---|---|---|
| | (IGPD) | LB/DAY | PPM | LB/DAY | PPM | *Revised Materials Balance after Proposed Brewery Expansion* |
| Brewery | 1,000,000 | 7,950 | 911 | 9,950 | 11,140 | |
| Other sources | 400,000 | 985 | 282 | 1,107 | 317 | |
| S.T.P. influent | 1,400,000 | 8,935 | 731 | 11,057 | 905 | |

treatment installations by the municipality *alone*, but can be realized only by a broader system perspective that also incorporates treatment alternatives and process changes available to the major dischargers within the urban environment.

An analysis of total system costs is particularly appropriate in light of current water pollution control policies where (i) municipalities are required to charge industrial users of the municipal system for the full costs they impose, and (ii) state agencies pressure many existing sources to connect to existing municipal systems rather than discharge directly to surface waters. The adoption of a comprehensive systems analysis of the urban wastewater treatment problem in North America would be a significant step toward reducing the costs associated with implementation of modern water pollution control policy.

## METABOLIC ANALYSIS

*Metabolic analysis* as used in sustainability studies is the sum of all physical and chemical processes taking place at various levels of geographic scale. One of the most useful applications of this type of mass balances is at the urban, regional, or national levels where flows of energy, materials, and pollutants can be tracked through cites and across national boundaries. Two brief case studies are presented of urban metabolism and the international transport of persistent organic pollutant (POPS).

## CASE STUDY: URBAN METABOLISM

Urban metabolic studies usually focus on several principal flows: water, materials, energy, nutrients, and toxics. The rationale for these studies is to provide a systematic tracking of the total environmental health of a conurbation, as increasing metabolism implies more traffic and pollution as well as a potential displacement or loss of farms, forests, and wildlife. Notable studies have been conducted in such major global cites as Brussels, Tokyo, Hong Kong, Sydney, Toronto, Vienna, London, and Capetown. Figure 17–3 is a particularly data-rich summary of urban metabolism drawn from an early study of Brussels (Kennedy et al. 2007). In 2002, the City of London (www.citylimitslondon.com) commissioned an extensive resource flow and ecological footprint analysis of its urban area with the assistance of five NGOs and professional institutes. [See Figure 17–4.] Without this type of comprehensive systems analysis, it is extremely difficult for a government to identify the major sources of environmental stresses and design appropriate ameliorative measures.

## CASE STUDY: INTERNATIONAL TRANSPORT OF PERSISTENT ORGANIC POLLUTANTS (POPs)

In 2005, the European Community with the assistance of a Russian research center published a complex mass balance report that tracked the transport of selected POPs across Europe (Gusev et al. 2005). The following figures relate to the transport

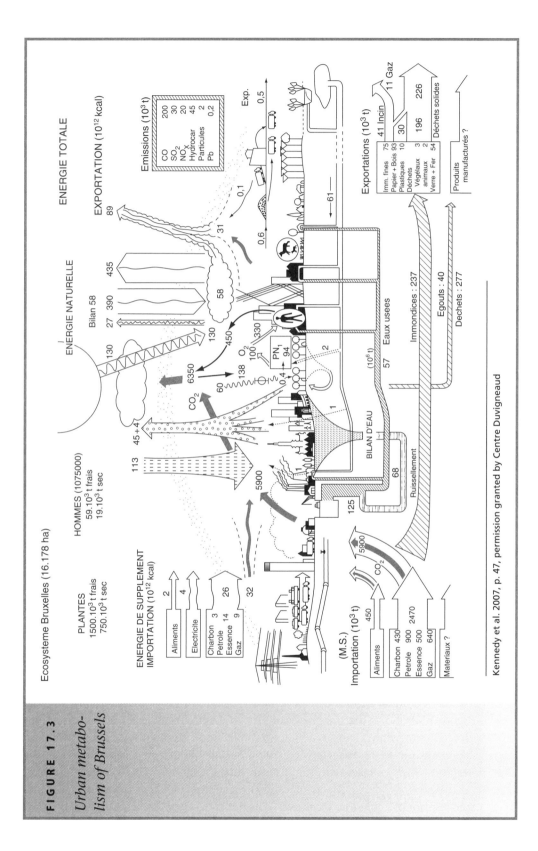

**FIGURE 17.3**

*Urban metabolism of Brussels*

Kennedy et al. 2007, p. 47, permission granted by Centre Duvigneaud

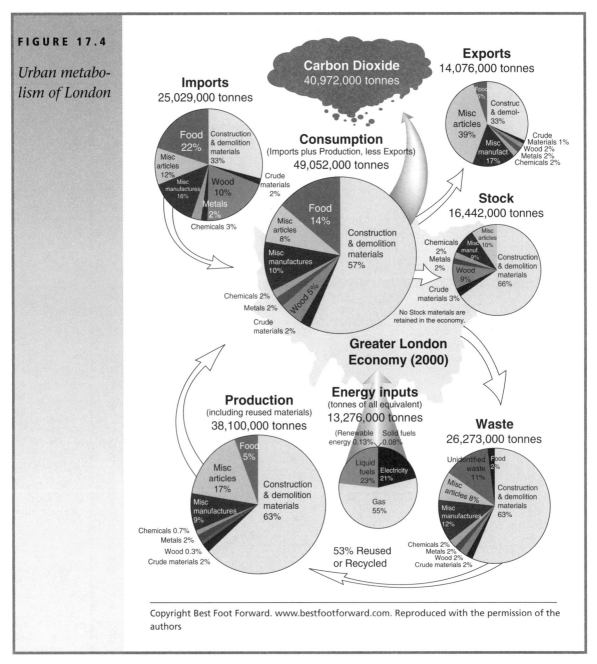

**FIGURE 17.4**

*Urban metabolism of London*

Copyright Best Foot Forward. www.bestfootforward.com. Reproduced with the permission of the authors

of benzo[a]pyrene, a highly carcinogenic product of certain industrial processes; incomplete fossil fuel combustion; and transportation, especially diesel engines. Figure 17–5 shows the origin by country of external sources of B[a]P depositions in Germany, while Figure 17–6 shows the effect of German sources on neighboring countries. More disaggregated data are available that detail the deposition by region within both Germany and its immediate neighbors. These data are essential to the analysis of the effects of various regulatory regimes—whether command-and-control or economic incentives—on the actual level of deposition in any one geographic area. [See also NRC 2009.] This information suggests that any unilateral control measures would probably be ineffective; what is required is a system-wide

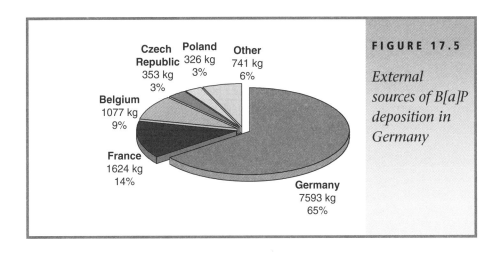

**FIGURE 17.5**

*External sources of B[a]P deposition in Germany*

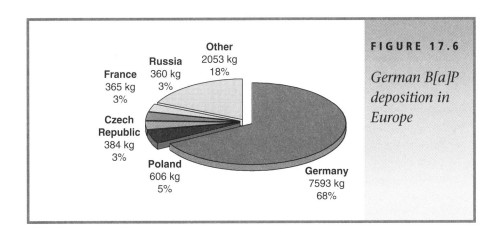

**FIGURE 17.6**

*German B[a]P deposition in Europe*

and integrated multilateral system of controls that lowers deposition levels and eliminates *hot spots* [see chapter 5 for a discussion of these concepts].

The next chapter describes what is probably the most important and useful tool for corporate and government sectors in the assessment of the environmental impact of production processes: life-cycle analysis.

## CITED REFERENCES AND RECOMMENDED REFERENCES

Decker, Ethan H. et al. (2000) "Energy and Material Flow Through the Urban Ecosystem," *Annual Review of Energy and Environment* 2000, pp. 685–740.

Douglas, Ian et al. (2002) "Industry, Environment and Health through 200 Years in Manchester," *Ecological Economics*, 41, pp. 235–255.

European Environment Agency (EEA) (2013) *Environmental pressures from European consumption and production. A study in integrated environmental and economic analysis.* EEA Technical report No 2/2013, Copenhagen.

Gusev, A. et al. (2005) EMEP *Regional Multicompartment Model MSCE-POP*, Meteorological Synthesizing Centre—East, Moscow. Technical Report 5/2005 EMEP/MSC-E.

Hendriks, C. et al. (2000) "Material Flow Analysis: A Tool to Support Environmental Policy Decision Making. Case Studies on the City of Vienna and the Swiss Lowlands." *Local Environment* 5, pp. 311–328.

Huang, S. (1998) Urban Ecosystems, Energetic Hierarchies, and Ecological Economics of Taipei Metropolis. *Journal of Environmental Management* 52, pp. 39–51.

Huppes, Gjalt et al. (2006) "Environmental Impacts of Consumption in the European Union. High-Resolution Input-Output Tables with Detailed Environmental Extensions," *Journal of Industrial Ecology*, 10(3), pp. 129–146.

Kennedy, Christopher et al. (2007) "The Changing Metabolism of Cities," *Journal of Industrial Ecology*, 11(2), pp. 43–59.

Moll, Stephan and Jose Acosta (2006) "Environmental Implications of Resource Use. Environmental Input-Output Analyses for Germany," *Journal of Industrial Ecology*, 10(3), pp. 25–40.

National Research Council (NRC) (2009) Global Sources of Local Pollution. An Assessment of Long-Range Transport of Key Air Pollutants to and from the United States, National Academies Press, Washington, D.C.

Newcombe, Ken et al. (1978) "The Metabolism of a City: The Case of Hong Kong," *Ambio*, 7(1), pp. 3–15.

Newman, Peter W.G. and Jeffrey R. Kenworthy (1989) "Gasoline Consumption and Cities: A Comparison of U.S. Cities with a Global Survey," *Journal of American Planning Association*, 55(1), Winter, pp. 24–37.

Sahely, Halla R. et al. (2003) "Estimating the Urban Metabolism of Canadian Cities: Toronto Area Case Study," *Canadian Journal of Civil Engineering*, April, 30(2), pp. 468–483.

Warren-Rhodes, Kimberley and Albert Koenig (2001) "Escalating Trends in the Urban Metabolism of Hong Kong: 1971–1997," *Ambio*, 30(7), November, pp. 429–438.

www.citylimitslondon.com *City Limits: A Resource Flow and Ecological Footprint Analysis of Greater London* (2002) Commissioned by Chartered Institution of Wastes Management, Environmental Body, Marefair, Northampton.

www.nzifst.org.nz/unitoperations/matlenerg2.htm [website of the New Zealand Institute of Food Science & Technology Inc.]

Zucchetto, James (1975) "Energy-Economic Theory and Mathematical Models for Combining the Systems of Man and Nature, Case Study: The Urban Region of Miami, Florida," *Ecological Modelling*, 1, pp. 241–268.

CHAPTER 18

# *Thinking Systemically (II):*
# *Life-Cycle Analysis*

F IGURE 18–1 IS AN ARCHETYPAL APPLICATION OF Michael Porter's theory of corporate profitability from sustainability [see chapter 1]. Downloaded from Apple's website in 2009, this advertisement embodied a major corporate initiative to seize a competitive advantage on the basis of sustainability. Apple was chafing from ratings (*Newsweek* 2009), which placed its principal rivals Dell and HP as the first and second greenest companies in the United States.

*Business Week*, in an article in its September 24, 2009, edition entitled "Apple Launches Major Green Effort," reported that Apple had launched a major attack on the underpinnings of the green comparative ranking scheme. To quote:

> Apple's real goal is to change the terms of the debate. Company executives say that most existing green rankings are flawed in several respects. They count the promises companies make about green plans rather than actual achievements. And most focus on the environmental impact of a company's operations, but exclude that of its products. HP and Dell put their carbon emissions at 8.4 million tons and 471,000 tons respectively, though both are larger than Apple in terms of revenue. Their numbers exclude product use and at least some manufacturing. The companies have said that including those factors would boost their carbon totals several fold.

The essence of Apple's counterattack was a methodology that has become an essential ingredient in corporate strategy and government policy with respect to sustainability: life-cycle analysis (LCA). Figure 18–1 reports Apple's conclusion that product use accounted for 53% of the total life-cycle emissions of greenhouse gases, a source of emissions ignored by their competitors. The relative significance of product use in total GHG emissions from cradle to grave is often not intuitively obvious. Early research on this subject dates back to pioneering work conducted by R. Stephen Berry and colleagues in the department of chemistry at the University of Chicago. In their exhaustive analysis of life-cycle energy consumption of an automobile, Berry and Fels (1972 and 1973) found that during each year of operation, a typical American car used as much energy as was consumed in its production (i.e. a ratio of 1:1). The largest single contributor to this energy profile (at 38%) was attributable to the cold rolling of steel from iron ore. The GHG profile can be derived directly from the total energy utilization. Since the date of these early studies, there have been significant changes in the fuel economy, size, and distance traveled of

**FIGURE 18.1**

*"Apple and the environment"*

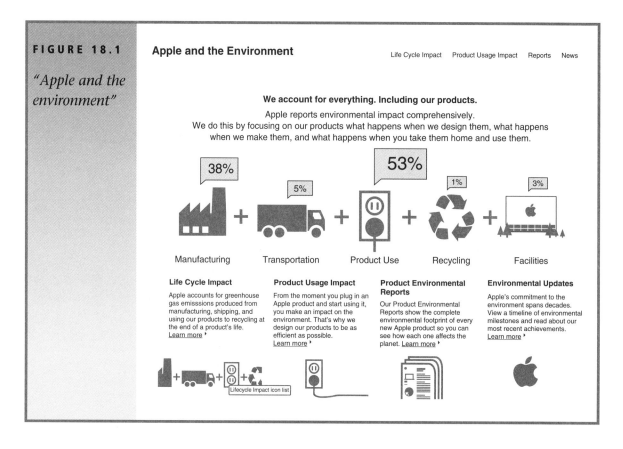

automobiles as well as changes in their production. The modern automobile, for example, uses significantly more aluminum and plastic than its predecessor—both energy-intensive products. [See, for example, Wards, various issues]. More recent research based on information from the United Kingdom has reported the following data (UNESCO 2002):

Average distance travelled each year: 16,000 km
Energy content of fuel: 40 million joules (MJ) per litre
Average fuel consumption: litre per 10 km of travel
Energy required to make and assemble a car: 20,000 million joules (MJ)

A simple arithmetic calculation of energy use based on these data suggests an annual usage/production ratio of 3.2:1, a figure that is significantly different from that of Berry and Fels. A study by Maclean and Lave (1998) from Carnegie Mellon found a ratio of 7.3:1 for lifetime automotive energy use compared to manufacture. The authors also found that the use phase dominates the production process for a wide range of toxic pollutants.

The importance of energy use (and hence GHG production) from the normal operation of modern information and communication technologies (ICT) as well as consumer electronic devices (CE) has only recently become apparent. For example, a major recent study by the International Energy Agency (2009) found that ICT and CE now account for approximately 15% of world residential electricity use, and the

IEA has projected an increase in their energy use by a factor of three within the next two decades. In fact, it is projected that ICT and CE could become the largest energy end-use category in many countries before 2020 (IEA 2009, p. 237).

Figure 18–2 presents a schematic representation of the range of LCA coverage of the production cycle, extending all the way from the production of raw material to a product's final disposal. As displayed here, LCA represents a cradle-to-grave analysis. There is no reason, however, why it could not be enlarged to accommodate the cradle-to-cradle philosophy of McDonough and Braungart [see chapter 15]. According to Graedel and Allenby (1995, 2010), LCA serves three principal purposes: (1) to provide a comprehensive picture of the environmental impact of any product, (2) to assist in identifying reasonable trade-offs in product and process selection, and (3) to help to develop baselines against which future decisions can be made about modifying a product.

In 2009, the *Wall Street Journal* used LCA to measure the total GHG emissions of several well-known consumer products. Four of these are displayed in Figure 18–3: the Toyota Prius, a pair of Timberland boots, Tesco washing liquid, and a Patagonia jacket. One of the most remarkable results of this type of analysis is that both consumers and producers can be surprised by the results, which are often counterintuitive. Consider the *Wall Street Journal*'s report on Timberland's analysis of its shoe line:

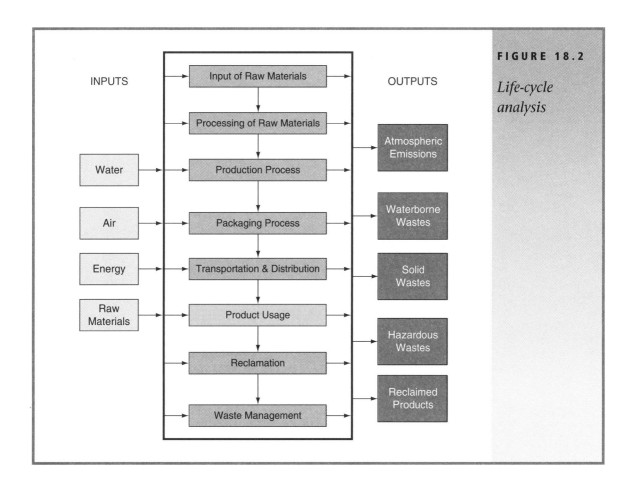

**FIGURE 18.2**

*Life-cycle analysis*

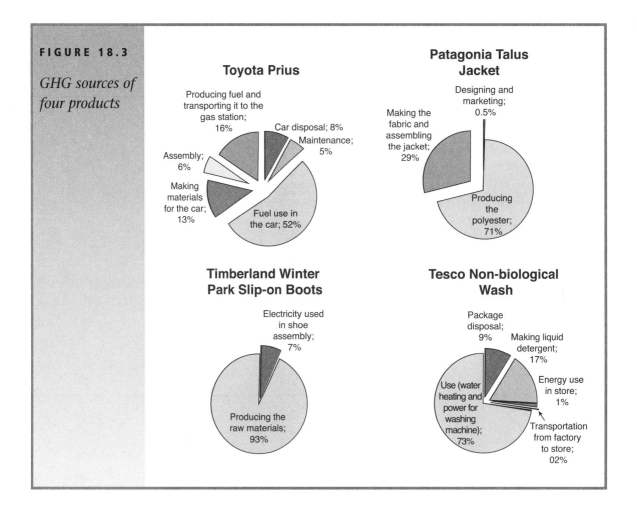

**FIGURE 18.3**

*GHG sources of four products*

By far the biggest contributor [to GHG] is the shoe's raw material. Leather drives the score. The average dairy cow produces, every year, greenhouse gas equivalent to four tons of carbon dioxide. Most of that comes not from carbon dioxide, in fact, but from a more-potent greenhouse gas: methane. Timberland's leather suppliers argue that the carbon hit from a cow should fall not on their ledger, but on the ledger of beef producers. The leather producers reason that cows are grown mainly for meat, with leather as a by-product, so that growing leather doesn't yield any emissions beyond those that would have occurred anyway. But Timberland has determined that 7% of the financial value of a cow lies in its leather. And life-cycle-analysis guidelines used by Timberland say the company should apply that percentage to compute the share of a cow's total emissions attributable to the leather.

This chapter uses a series of case studies to explore the complexities of LCAs and their sometimes counterintuitive results.

## CASE STUDY #1: AN LCA COMPARISON OF AN AMERICAN AND FINNISH OFFICE BUILDING

While LCA can in theory track all major environmental impacts of the production cycle, it is frequently used to measure energy consumption and the associated production of carbon dioxide, sulfur dioxide, nitrogen oxides, and particulates. The U.S. Energy Information Administration (2010) has determined that buildings account for almost 39% of all direct national energy consumption and 38% of $CO_2$ emissions. Such emissions arise principally from the on-site use of fuels for heating and cooking, and from electricity for heating, cooling, and other power needs of buildings. From an LCA perspective, this analysis is incomplete, however, as there are other energy inputs to a building based on indirect and embodied energy. This case study summarizes the results of a more comprehensive, energy-related LCA of two buildings: one in Finland, the other in Minnesota (Junnila et al. 2006). Table 18–1 presents simple comparative data on the two buildings, and Table 18–2 presents the results of the LCA on energy use, $CO_2$, $SO_2$, NOx, and $PM_{10}$.

There are three striking conclusions that can be drawn from this comparison. First, the use phase dominates energy consumption (70%) and all of the pollutant emissions except for $PM_{10}$. Second, overall, the Finnish building performs much better since it uses a third less energy and emits half the $CO_2$, a third of NOx, and a fifth of $PM_{10}$ associated with the U.S. building's life cycle mainly due to the differences in the use phase. And third, the energy used for the operation of the Finnish building is only one-half of the U.S. building, as the emission profiles of energy carriers in Finland are less intensive due to combined heat and power production. Part of the explanation for the variation in pollutant output is due to the different energy source mix in Finland and Minnesota—the former relying on natural gas for 67% and coal for 32% of its supply; the latter relying on a mix of natural gas (22%), coal (21%), and petroleum (40%). From the perspective of GHG and other combustion products, natural gas is considered the best fuel and coal the worst.

| COUNTRY | FINLAND | USA | |
|---|---|---|---|
| # Floors | 4 | 5 | **TABLE 18.1** |
| Floor Area (sq m) | 4,400 | 4,400 | *Data on Two* |
| Volume (Cubic m) | 17,300 | 16,400 | *Buildings—* |
| Structural Frame | steel-reinforced concrete beam and column system | steel-reinforced concrete beam and column system with sheer walls at the core | *Finland and USA* |
| Mass of materials (kg/sq m) | 1,190 | 1,290 | |

*Source:* Junnila et al. 2006

# TABLE 18.2

*Sustainability Data on Two Buildings—Finland and USA*

| PHASE | FINLAND | | | | | MINNESOTA, USA | | | | |
|---|---|---|---|---|---|---|---|---|---|---|
| | Energy GJ | CO₂ Mg | SO₂ kg | NOx kg | PM₁₀ kg | Energy GJ | CO₂ Mg | SO₂ kg | NOx kg | PM₁₀ kg |
| Materials | 15,000 | 1,300 | 2,300 | 4,000 | 2,100 | 31,100 | 2,000 | 9,300 | 8,000 | 2,700 |
| Construction | 4,800 | 200 | 500 | 1,800 | 400 | 5,500 | 400 | 800 | 8,300 | 700 |
| Use | 204,000 | 11,000 | 9,900 | 20,000 | 3,700 | 297,600 | 22,200 | 82,700 | 48,500 | 3,400 |
| Maintenance | 9,500 | 700 | 2,300 | 2,500 | 1,100 | 21,600 | 1,300 | 5,200 | 5,000 | 2,100 |
| End of Life | 800 | 60 | 50 | 700 | 90 | 3,300 | 200 | 400 | 5,800 | 400 |
| TOTAL | 234,100 | 13,260 | 15,050 | 29,000 | 7,390 | 359,100 | 26,100 | 98,400 | 75,600 | 9,300 |
| **PERCENTAGE** | | | | | | | | | | |
| Materials | 6% | 10% | 15% | 14% | 28% | 9% | 8% | 9% | 11% | 29% |
| Construction | 2% | 2% | 3% | 6% | 5% | 2% | 2% | 1% | 11% | 8% |
| Use | 87% | 83% | 66% | 69% | 50% | 83% | 85% | 84% | 64% | 37% |
| Maintenance | 4% | 5% | 15% | 9% | 15% | 6% | 5% | 5% | 7% | 23% |
| End of Life | 0.3% | 0.5% | 0.3% | 2% | 1% | 1% | 1% | 0.4% | 8% | 4% |
| TOTAL | 100% | 100% | 100% | 100% | 100% | 100% | 100% | 100% | 100% | 100% |

*Source:* Derived from Junnila et al. 2006

# CASE STUDY #2: COMPARING ELECTRIC- AND INTERNAL COMBUSTION-POWERED AUTOMOBILES

The principal rationale for the introduction of electric-powered vehicles is to reduce energy use and related GHG emissions. While the market has so far been dominated by electric hybrids, most notably Toyota's Prius, some companies are now moving one step further with the introduction of plug-in hybrids, (the Chevrolet Volt); or pure electric cars (e.g., a modified Prius, Nissan Leaf, and Tesla roadster). An essential ingredient in this new technology is the construction of an integrated electricity supply system that can back out internal combustion engines (ICEs) and support all-electric vehicles. In the pursuit of this strategy, relatively little publicity has been given to a life-cycle analysis of this alternative to conventional powered automobiles. Such a systems-based analysis can cast a crucial light on the choice of alternatives in pursuing a strategy of phasing out ICEs.

Figure 18–4 is a simple schematic of a life cycle of alternative energy sources from origin to final automobile. The critical question in attempting to compare these radically different automotive systems is the choice of performance measure. Three possible categories come immediately to mind: (1) emissions of the U.S. EPA's five criteria air pollutants: CO, NOx, HC, $SO_2$, and PM; (2) total energy use; and (3) greenhouse gas emissions. Table 18–3, drawn from an early study by Graedel and Allenby (1995), compares the two systems on the five criteria air pollutants. The results are mixed, neither propulsion system scoring consistently better than the other. Figures 18–5 to 18–7, drawn from a more recent comparison of plug-in hybrids and internal combustion-powered automobiles (Parks et al. 2007), present results on three pollutants: NOx, $SO_2$, and $CO_2$. In this case, the results appear to unambiguously favor the hybrid electric vehicle.

Systems analysis is critical in arriving at realistic estimates of relative pollutant emissions. First, comparisons will be influenced by the choice of system boundary. If the focus is solely on emissions from the automobile itself, then the electric vehicle is overwhelmingly favored, as it produces no emissions whatsoever. However, a comprehensive LCA adopts a system's perspective by including emissions from power plants that produce the electricity required to power the electric cars. With this inclusion in the analysis, the source of fuel that powers the electric utility's power plant becomes critical as well as the timing of the power draw.

Figure 18–8 depicts the mix of energy sources for the U.S. electric power sector in 2009 (U.S. EIA 2010), indicating that almost 50% of American electricity is produced by the combustion of coal, the least clean of all fossil fuels. The use of an overall average can be misleading, however, when evaluating the environmental impact of electric vehicles at the regional level. The mix of fuel sources varies considerably by geographic region in the United States. For example, the Pacific Northwest derives much of its power from hydroelectric sources, a relatively clean source of energy. A systems analysis of any initiative by Washington or Oregon, for example, to adopt electric vehicles would be misleading, however, if it focused solely on hydropower as a fuel source for electric cars. The relevant source of electricity is neither the dominant regional source nor average mix, but the marginal generating capacity necessary to meet the incremental demand. If the Pacific Northwest

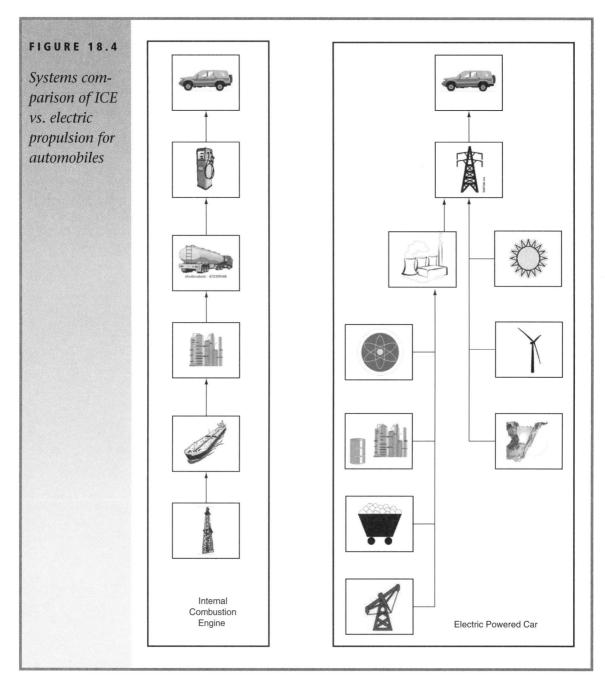

**FIGURE 18.4**

*Systems comparison of ICE vs. electric propulsion for automobiles*

Internal Combustion Engine

Electric Powered Car

sources this incremental power from the interconnected electric grid, then it is necessary to determine what fuel source is providing this additional power. If it were fossil fueled, then the environmental impact would be considerably larger than hydropower.

There are three other factors relating to a LCA that must be considered in comparing ICE vs. electric systems of automobile motive power. First, a comprehensive LCA would also consider the emissions and environmental impacts of the vehicles themselves: their materials, their manufacture, and their eventual recycling. Second,

| POLLUTANT | ELECTRIC | INTERNAL-COMBUSTION | |
|---|---|---|---|
| CO | | **WORSE** | **TABLE 18.3** |
| NOx | | | *Early Comparison of Electric and Internal Combustion Cars* |
| Non-methane HC | | **WORSE** | |
| SOx | **WORSE** | | |
| PM | **WORSE** | | |

*Source:* derived from Graedel and Allenby 1995

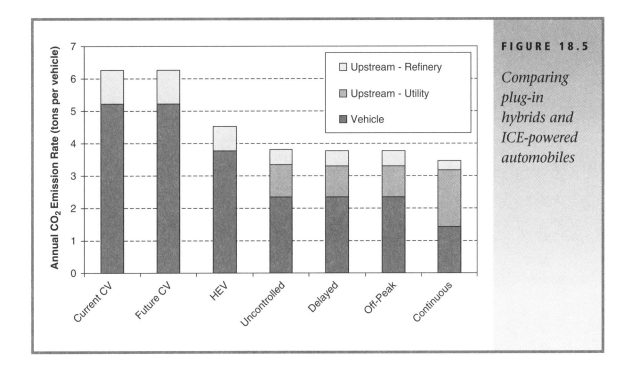

**FIGURE 18.5**

*Comparing plug-in hybrids and ICE-powered automobiles*

the relative environmental impact of the different emissions is not addressed. For example, carbon monoxide emissions are generally considered a problem only in the immediate vicinity of high-volume traffic, while some of the other pollutants such as $SO_2$ and NOx have much more significant effects both locally and regionally. And finally, a comprehensive LCA would have to include the environmental significance of different battery types in electric vehicles, including lead-acid, nickel-cadmium, lithium-ion, etc. Each of these has its own distinctive risks.

The most comprehensive analysis to date of the relative $CO_2$ life cycle of internal combustion and hybrid and all-electric vehicles was published by the Low Carbon Vehicle Partnership in the United Kingdom (Patterson et al. 2011). This report also stressed the critical importance of expanding any comparative analysis

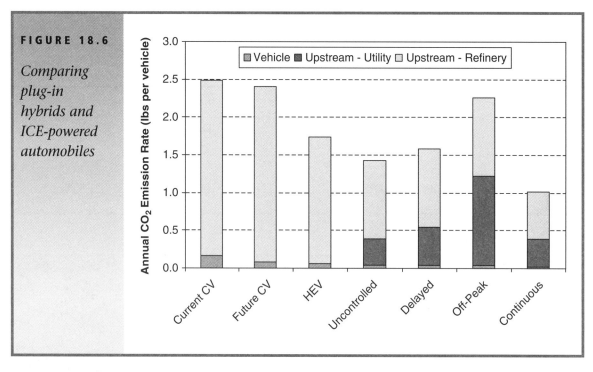

**FIGURE 18.6**

*Comparing plug-in hybrids and ICE-powered automobiles*

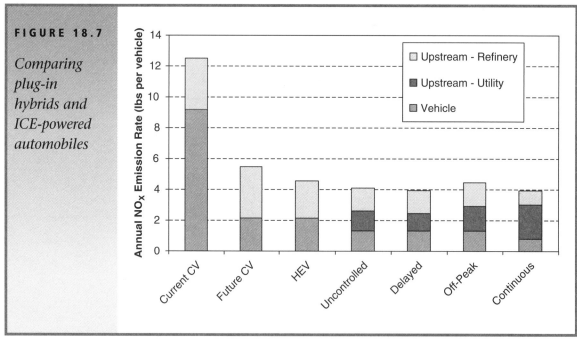

**FIGURE 18.7**

*Comparing plug-in hybrids and ICE-powered automobiles*

beyond a mere focus on tailpipe emissions to include the entire life cycle of alternative vehicular technologies. Electric and hybrid cars have a lower carbon footprint than their fossil-fuel counterparts. Most of the carbon emissions in ICE vehicles are associated with driving, but fully 46% of the carbon footprint of electric vehicles is generated in the production process. This type of analysis clearly identifies areas in all the technical options where the most profitable research can be conducted to reduce system-wide carbon dioxide emissions.

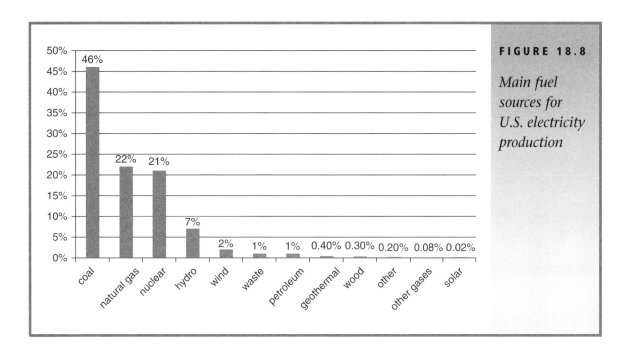

**FIGURE 18.8**

*Main fuel sources for U.S. electricity production*

## CASE STUDY #3: PAPER vs. PLASTIC CUPS

Most major food chains have, in the interest of sustainability, replaced their use of plastic cups with the paper equivalent. Is this really the most sustainable solution? LCA can cast some light on this issue. In an LCA study published in *Science* magazine (1991), Hocking conducted an extensive comparison of the two alternatives on the basis of 25 environmentally related variables. The somewhat surprising results are presented in Table 18–4. On 21 of the 25 variables, the paper product fared less well than the plastic product. On only four variables did plastic come out the loser: the quantity of cooling water, the emissions of metal salts, the release of pentanes, and the extent of biodegradability. Somewhat similar anomalous results emerge from comparisons of paper and plastic shopping bags, despite the frequently successful efforts of some cities and supermarkets to discourage the use of plastic bags. It is estimated that in the United States, more than 380 billion plastic bags are used per year, requiring an estimated 38 million barrels of oil to produce (fooddemocracy.wordpress.com 2008; Royte 2007). Figure 18–9 presents a simple schematic of the life cycle of a shopping bag (Sustainability Victoria 2007). This LCA conducted in Australia found that assumptions about end-of-life treatment (such as recycling) have a major impact on the comparative results. The critical point missed in a simple comparison of paper and plastic bags is that this is an incomplete and misleading dichotomy. It appears that neither product is desirable from a sustainability perspective—hence the increasing use of more environmentally benign reusable fabric and nonwoven polypropylene "green bags" (Sustainability Victoria 2007) commonly used in both the United Kingdom and France, for example.

**TABLE 18.4**

*Paper Cups vs. Plastic Cups*

| | PAPER | PLASTIC |
|---|---|---|
| **RAW MATERIALS USED PER CUP** | | |
| Wood and bark | 3.3 grams | 0 grams |
| Petroleum products | 4.1 grams | 3.2 grams |
| Other chemicals | 1.8 grams | .05 grams |
| Weight per cup | 10.1 grams | 1.5 grams |
| **Per metric ton of material** | | |
| **Utilities** | | |
| Steam (kg) | 9,000 to 12,000 | approx. 5000 |
| Power (kWh) | 980 | 120 to 180 |
| Cooling water (cubic meters) | 50 | 154 |
| **Water effluent** | | |
| Volume (cubic meters) | 50 to 190 | 0.5 to 2 |
| Suspended solids (kg) | 35 to 60 | Trace |
| BOD (kg) | 30 to 50 | 0.07 |
| Organochlorines (kg) | 5 to 7 | 0 |
| Metal salts (kg) | 1 to 20 | 20 |
| **Air emissions** | | |
| Chlorine (kg) | 0.5 | 0 |
| Chlorine dioxide (kg) | 0.2 | 0 |
| Reduced sulfides (kg) | 2 | 0 |
| Particulates (kg) | 5 to 15 | 0.1 |
| Chlorofluorocarbons (CFCs) | 0 | 0 |
| Pentane (kg) | 0 | 35 to 50 |
| Sulfur dioxide (kg) | approx. 10 | approx. 10 |
| **Recycle Potential** | | |
| To primary user | Possible, though washing can destroy | Easy, negligible water uptake |
| After use | Low, hot melt adhesive or coating difficulties | High, resin reuse in other applications |
| **Ultimate disposal** | | |
| Proper incineration | Clean | Clean |
| Heat recovery (MJ/kg) | 20 | 40 |
| Mass to landfill (g) | 10.1 | 1.5 |
| Biodegradable | Yes, BOD to leachate, methane to air | No, essentially inert |

*Source:* Hocking 1991, p. 505 reproduced with permission of Science Magazine, AAAS

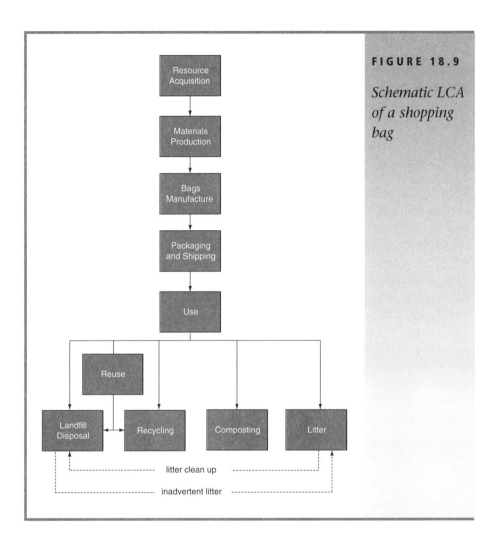

**FIGURE 18.9**

*Schematic LCA of a shopping bag*

A comprehensive LCA can be a time-consuming and resource-intensive exercise. Fortunately, several research groups around the world have already conducted extensive analysis for many products, and their results are available online either for free or a fee. Foremost among these is the *Ecoinvent* database produced by the Swiss Centre for Life Cycle Inventories (Frischknecht et al. 2007, EcoInvent website), which includes approximately 4,000 data sets for products, services, and processes used in many LCA studies.

One of the principal impediments to the use of LCA as a definitive arbiter of total environmental impacts of specific products is the absence of some common metric to compare the relative importance of diverse environmental effects. This challenge is apparent above in the comparison of electric and ICE cars on the basis of the US EPA's five criteria air pollutants, as well as Hocking's comparison of plastic and paper bags. In light of the discussion in chapter 7 on the methodology of monetizing environmental effects, it is tempting to consider converting all the disparate effects into dollar equivalents. Unfortunately, this is a daunting task and open to criticism on the unresolved issues emerging from monetization and discounting. Two analytical techniques currently in use are full-cost accounting (FCA) and life-cycle cost analysis (LCCA). While in theory, these methodologies might be applicable, in practice their use has largely been restricted to easily quantifiable financial costs for non-environmental effects. The next chapter considers another variant on systems analysis, namely, carbon accounting (or carbon footprinting); and the following chapter revisits the controversial question of the system boundaries of the typical LCA.

### A Brief Note on Social Life-Cycle Assessment

All of the discussion above pertains to the environmental effects of products and services and has been labeled E-LCA by the United Nations Environment Programme (UNEP) to differentiate it from a companion measure known as Social Life-Cycle Assessment, S-LCA (UNEP 2009). Developed more recently, the S-LCA tool parallels the framework and analysis of the E-LCA except that its focus is on social and socioeconomic impacts of products and services throughout their entire life cycle from cradle to grave. There are five stakeholder categories (workers, local community, society, consumers, and value chain actors) who are the focus of these studies, and six impact categories (human rights, working conditions, health and safety, cultural heritage, governance, and socioeconomic repercussions). A brief examination of these impact categories suggests why S-LCA is more difficult to perform than a conventional E-LCA where effects may be more obvious and measureable. UNEP lists several limitations that affect S-LCA today but which are the subject of further research (pp. 76–79): novelty of the technique, difficulty in accessing the data, difficulty of quantification and aggregation, ignorance of causal chain relations, skill deficiencies among practitioners, frequent inadequate input from stakeholders, difficult assessment of the product use phase, and inadequate transparency in the communication of results. Despite these limitations, not all of which are specific to S-LCA, the UNEP has emphasized the need for the continued development and refinement of this tool. A prime example cited by UNEP of the potential usefulness of S-LCA would be an assessment of the socioeconomic effects of chemicals in Europe under the terms of the REACH EU directive. [See chapter 9.]

## CITED REFERENCES AND RECOMMENDED READINGS

Berry, R. Stephen and Margaret F. Fels (1972) "The Production and Consumption of Automobiles. An Energy Analysis of the Manufacture, Discard and Reuse of the Automobile and its Component Materials," A Report to the Illinois Institute for Environmental Quality, July.

Berry, R. Stephen and Margaret F. Fels (1973) "The Energy Cost of Automobiles," *Science and Public Affairs*, pp. 11–60.

*Business Week* (2009) "Apple Launches Major Green Effort," September 24.

EcoInvent website (see Swiss Centre for Life Cycle Inventories).

Esty, Daniel and Andrew Winston (2009) *Green to Gold*, Hoboken, NJ: John Wiley & Sons.

Fooddemocracy.wordpress.com [BC Food Systems Network, Powell River, BC].

Frischknecht, Rolf et al. (2007) *Implementation of Life Cycle Impact Assessment Methods*, Swiss Centre for Life Cycle Inventories, St-Gallen, Switzerland.

Graedel, T.E. and B.R. Allenby (1995) *Industrial Ecology*, Englewood Cliffs, NJ: Prentice Hall.

Graedel, T.E. and B.R. Allenby (2010) *Industrial Ecology and Sustainable Engineering*, Boston: Prentice Hall.

Hocking, Martin B. (1991) "Paper versus Polystyrene: A Complex Choice," *Science* Vol. 251, February 1, pp. 504–505.

International Energy Agency (2009) *Gadgets and Gigawatts. Policies for Energy Efficient Electronics*, Paris.

International Organization for Standardization (ISO) (2006a) *ISO 14040 Environmental Management—Life Cycle Assessment—Principles and Framework*, Geneva.

International Organization for Standardization (ISO) (2006b) *ISO 14044 Environmental management—Life Cycle Assessment—Requirements and Guidelines*, Geneva.

Junnila, Seppo et al. (2006) "Life-Cycle Assessment of Office Buildings in Europe and the United States," *Journal of Infrastructure Systems*, March, pp. 10–17.

Maclean, Heather L. and Lester B. Lave (1998) "A Life-Cycle Model of an Automobile," Environmental Science and Technology, July 1, pp. 322–330.

Newsweek.com "Apple and the Environment," accessed September 30 2009.

Parks, K. et al. (2007) *Costs and Emissions Associated with Plug-In Hybrid Electric Vehicle Charging in the Xcel Energy Colorado Service Territory*, National Renewable Energy Laboratory (NREL), Golden, CO.

Patterson, Jane et al. (2011) "Preparing for a Life Cycle $CO_2$ Measure," Low Carbon Vehicle Partnership, London, May 20.

Royte, Elizabeth (2007) "Why the Bag Backlash?" *Huffington Post*, April 8.

Sustainability Victoria (2007) *Comparison of Existing Life Cycle Analysis of Shopping Bag Alternatives*, April 18, report No. 1, Victoria, Australia.

Swiss Centre for Life Cycle Inventories. EcoInvent reports, St-Gallen, Switzerland. (www.ecoinvent.org/documentaiton/reports/).

UK Environment Agency (2005) *Life Cycle Assessment of Disposable and Reusable Nappies in the UK*. May, London.

UN Educational, Scientific and Cultural Organization (UNESCO) (2002) "Module 1: Cars and energy" [http://portal.unesco.org/education/en/file_download.php/a01355752c9e869a63cc5651084cfa30Cars+and+energy.pdf].

United Nations Environment Programme (UNEP) (2009) *Guidelines for Social Life Cycle Assessment of Products*.

U.S. Energy Information Administration (EIA) (2010) *Annual Energy Review*.

*Wall Street Journal* (2009) "Six Products, Six Carbon Footprints," March 1.

Wards Automotive Group, *Motor Vehicle Facts & Figures*. Southfield, MI, Various dates.

# CHAPTER 19

# Thinking Systemically (III): A Brief Note on Carbon Accounting

WITH THE ADVENT OF THE EUROPEAN TRADING SYSTEM (ETS) for greenhouse gases (EC 2008), European corporations have been faced with the necessity of generating accurate estimates of their output of carbon dioxide. A new series of metrics and methodologies have emerged in order to measure the *carbon footprint* of business. Even in the United States, where there is no formal requirement to reduce the emissions of greenhouse gases, the emergence of voluntary exchanges that trade in carbon-based emissions, including the now-defunct Chicago Climate Exchange, has been indicative of the potential importance of this issue to major corporate players in the American economy.

Carbon accounting, or carbon *footprinting*, is a hybrid of life-cycle analysis and the ecological footprint that measures the total quantity of greenhouse gases emitted by an entity—whether it be an individual, plant, firm, or geographic entity. As well as scholarly work on this subject (Pandey et al. 2011), numerous books and articles have been written for the general public, including, inter alia, *How Bad Are Bananas? The Carbon Footprint of Everything* by Mike Berners-Lee (2011) and the "The Cheeseburger Footprint" by Jamais Cascio (http://www.openthefuture.com/cheeseburger_CF.html). This latter study uses detailed data on energy use in the food sector co-developed by Stockholm University and the Swiss Federal Institute of Technology (Carlsson-Kanyama and Faist n.d.) to construct an approximate picture of the magnitude of the greenhouse gases associated with this ubiquitous American product. The results are startling, as the author concludes that "the greenhouse gas emissions arising every year from the production and consumption of cheeseburgers is roughly the amount emitted by 6.5 million to 19.6 million SUVs. There are now approximately 16 million SUV's currently on the road in the U.S."

Carbon accounting is becoming a common metric in the corporate sector for both internal and external use. The giant British food chain, Tesco, has adopted carbon labeling on many of their products (www.tesco.com/climatechange/carbonfootprint.asp). There are at least five reasons why companies would be willing to calculate their carbon footprint in an environment where such an exercise is not legally mandated. According to the Carbon Trust (2008b), measuring the carbon footprint of products across their full life cycle is a powerful way for companies to collect the information they need to reduce GHG emissions; identify cost savings opportunities; incorporate emissions impact into decision making on suppliers, materials, product design, manufacturing processes, etc.; demonstrate environmental/corporate responsibility leadership; meet customer demands for information on product carbon footprints; and differentiate and meet demands from "green" consumers.

Added to this list is a new and powerful incentive in the area of finance. The U.S. Securities and Exchange Commission has recently encouraged corporations to add environmental issues to the list of material risks that they report every year in their reports to the SEC (January 27, 2010). There is a strong possibility that this move is a precursor to making such reporting mandatory. In many respects, the reporting of such risks has already become mandatory in that bank and insurance companies are increasingly loath to fund or insure corporations with unclear potential liabilities emerging from a company's products, processes, and waste management practices. As Repetto states (2007):

> For corporations in environmentally sensitive industries the message is clear. Shareholders are demanding and governments are requiring more transparency regarding the ways in which environmental costs, risks and liabilities are affecting their financial conditions and prospects. There is no reason to believe that these demands will weaken. Well-managed companies will realize that they can benefit from this trend because financial markets clearly reward good corporate governance, and public trust is a valuable business asset.

In a report entitled "Carbon Risks and Opportunities in the S&P 500," Trucost Ltd. has estimated the exposure to carbon costs among large corporations (2009). In their words, "carbon intensity indicates financial risk." This is borne out by the report's calculations by industry sector that indicates that "carbon liabilities could equate to 2% to 17% of EBITDA for Utilities companies in the S&P 500." Because of its reliance on fossil fuels, the utility sector is the most vulnerable sector, while insurance, banks, and other service industries have the least exposure.

Several international standards have been created recently to assist corporations in constructing a carbon footprint. Foremost among these are ISO 14064 and 14065. To quote the International Organization for Standardization (n.d.):

> In March 2006, ISO launched its greenhouse gas (GHG) accounting and verification standards ISO 14064:2006. The complementary new standard, ISO 14065:2007, Greenhouse gases—Requirements for greenhouse gas validation and verification bodies for use in accreditation or other forms of recognition, published on 15 April 2007, details requirements for GHG validation or verification bodies for use in accreditation or other forms of recognition. While ISO 14064 provides requirements for organizations or persons to quantify and verify GHG emissions, ISO 14065 specifies accreditation requirements for organizations that validate or verify resulting GHG emission assertions or claims (www.iso.org/iso/home.html).

Carbon accounting methodology has also been made readily available by such key players as The Carbon Trust, an independent company established in 2001 under the aegis of the government of the United Kingdom (www.carbontrust.co.uk). With the mandate to facilitate the transition to a less carbon intensive economy, the trust has consulted broadly with corporations and NGOs to develop a set of standard protocols. American partners in this process have included Coca-Cola, Coors, Kimberley-Clarke, and Pepsico. The principal product from this work has been the development of PAS 2050 (Carbon Trust 2008c) (where PAS = publicly available specification).

PAS 2050 describes five steps to calculating a carbon footprint: (1) building a process map of a product's life cycle, from raw materials to disposal, including all material, energy, and waste flows; (2) confirming the boundaries of the analysis [i.e., how many suppliers, processes, and inputs to include] and performing a high-level footprint calculation to help prioritize efforts; (3) collecting data on material amounts, activities, and emission factors across all life-cycle stages; (4) calculating the product carbon footprint; and (5) assessing the precision of the footprint analysis. Table 19–1 lists five stages of the cradle-to-grave production process and the data requirements associated with each.

| RAW MATERIALS | MANUFACTURE | DISTRIBUTION/ RETAIL | CONSUMER USE | DISPOSAL/ RECYCLING | TABLE 19.1 |
|---|---|---|---|---|---|
| All inputs used at any stage in the life cycle | All activities from collection of raw material to distribution: all production processes, transport/ storage related to production, packaging, site-related emissions, e.g., lighting, ventilation, temperature | All steps in transport and related storage | Energy required during use phase: storage, preparation, application, maintenance and repair | All steps in disposal: transport, storage, processing | *Data Requirements for Constructing a Carbon Footprint of a Cradle-to-Grave Production Process* |
| Include processes related to raw materials: mining/ extraction of minerals, farming, forestry, pre-processing, packaging, storage, transport | All materials produced: product, waste, co-products (useful byproducts), direct emissions | Retail storage and display | | Energy required in disposal/ recycling process | |
| Account for impact of raw materials: fertilizer production, transport and application, and land use changes | | | | Direct emissions due to disposal/ recycling: carbon decay, methane release, incineration | |

*Source:* Based on Carbon Trust 2008c, p. 14

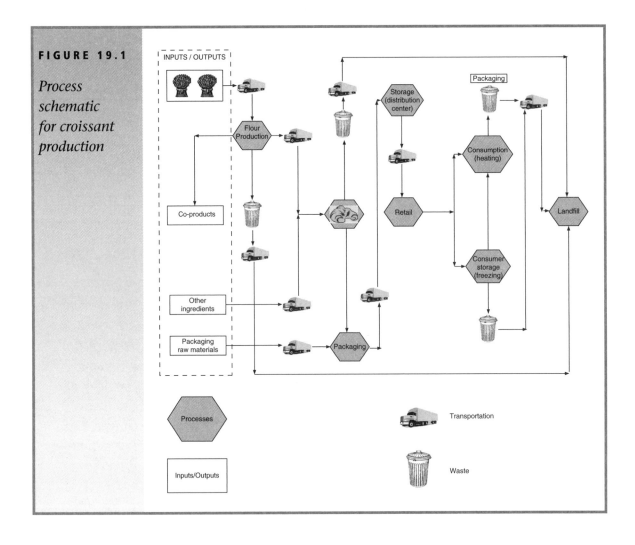

**FIGURE 19.1**

*Process schematic for croissant production*

Figure 19–1 presents a simplified schematic of a PAS 2050 process map for croissant production (Carbon Trust 2008b). Table 19–2 lists the six steps from raw material acquisition to waste disposal, the subcategories of data that are required to compute the overall footprint, and the component results. Figure 19–2 focuses on only one part of the production chain to provide some idea of the nature of the calculations. Commensurate with PWC's focus on the importance of the supply chain, these data reveal that almost half of the carbon footprint of croissant production is due to the nature of raw material production, followed by the manufacturing process itself that accounts for less than one third of the carbon footprint. [Disposal is 14.4%; consumer use 3.6%, and distribution and retail only 0.5%.]

With a clearer understanding of where the challenges lie—and the opportunities for cost reduction and profit increments—a corporation has several generic emission reduction opportunities (Carbon Trust 2008c):

*Energy use.* Change fuels, for example, from electricity to gas; increase the proportion of energy produced by renewables.

| | | | | |
|---|---|---|---|---|
| Raw material cultivation and transport - wheat | 1a | Farming | 450 | **TABLE 19.2** |
| | 1b | Wheat transport | 9 | *Carbon* |
| | | | | *Accounting* |
| Raw material production – wheat | 2a | Flour production - milling | 45 | *for Croissant* |
| | 2b | Flour transport | 7 | *Production* |
| | 2c | Waste transport | 1.4 | |
| | | Waste disposal | 54 | |
| Croissant Production | 3a | Baking | 300 | |
| | 3b | Packaging | 40 | |
| | 3c | Waste transport | 2 | |
| | | Waste disposal | 30 | |
| Distribution and retail | 4a | Transport to distribution centre | 30 | |
| | 4b | Storage | 0.5 | |
| | 4c | Transport to store | 5 | |
| | 4d | Retail | 20 | |
| Consumer Use | 5a | Storage - freezing | 5 | |
| | 5b | Consumption - heating | 36 | |
| Disposal | 6a | Transport to landfill | 0.4 | |
| | 6b | Landfill decomposition | 165 | |
| Total per tonne of croissants (kg $CO_2$ e) | | | 1200 | |
| Total per 12-croissant package | | | 1.2 | |

*Source:* Derived from Carbon Trust 2008b

*Production.* Decrease waste volumes by process changes or by-product recovery for resale; increase the size of manufacturing operations to capitalize on opportunities for economies of scale; decrease the amount of processing; change manufacturing practices and improve efficiency.

*Distribution.* Decrease the degree of energy-intensive heating and/or cooling in storage and transportation; decrease the distances traveled by relocating production and/or distribution facilities.

*General.* Include energy/carbon criteria in purchasing/supplier choices; include energy/carbon criteria in product design, configuration and/or materials; change technology to more energy efficient processes; and improve inventory management.

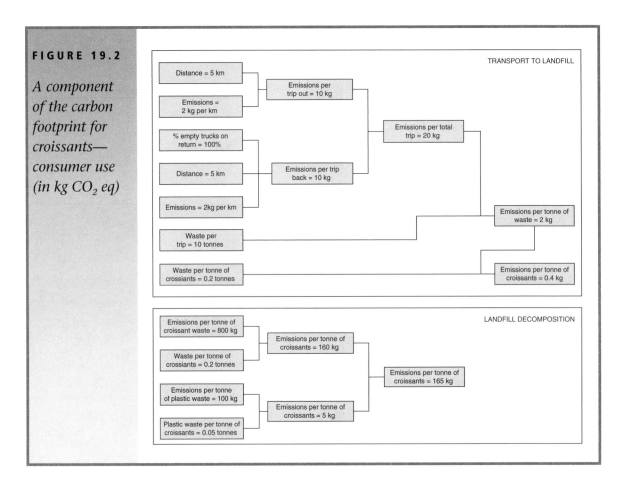

**FIGURE 19.2**

*A component of the carbon footprint for croissants— consumer use (in kg CO$_2$ eq)*

One of the most remarkable findings of this type of analysis is that for some products the greatest reduction in their system-wide carbon footprint lies not within their own operation but among its suppliers—thereby suggesting that a corporation might more profitably direct its attention to reconstructing or modifying its supply chain (Humes 2011; PWC 2009). In addition to providing a metric for calculating carbon footprints, the Carbon Trust also has consulting services available for corporations willing to respond to this initiative. There is a long list of case studies based largely on U.K. companies where significant efficiencies and cost savings have been achieved (Carbon Trust n.d.). For example, at two plants in the U.K., Heinz Ltd. was able to lower their CO$_2$ emissions by 17,600 metric tons over four years with a resulting saving of 13% in their energy budget and a credit of 700,000 UKP on an enhanced capital allowance scheme in one year.

PriceWaterhouseCoopers (Hawksworth 2006) has devoted significant effort to examining the carbon-related issue of supply chain management and has concluded that the benefits are substantial and include short- and long-term cost reductions, improved supplier loyalty, risk management, and maintaining or developing competitive advantage.

The following chapter presents a critique of both LCA and Carbon Footprinting and suggests a hybrid methodology using Input-Output analysis that can overcome some of their deficiencies.

# CITED REFERENCES AND RECOMMENDED READINGS

AXA Investment Managers and Trucost (2010) *Taking Carbon Risk into Account*, London.

Berner-Lee, Mike (2011) *How Bad Are Bananas? The Carbon Footprint of Everything*, Vancouver, B.: Greystone Books.

Carbon Trust (www.carbontrust.co.uk). London.

Carbon Trust (n.d.) London. (http:www.carbontrust.co.uk/abut-carbon-trust/what-we-do/case-studies/Pages/casestudies.aspx).

Carbon Trust (2008a) *Product Carbon footprinting: The New Business Opportunity*, London.

Carbon Trust (2008b) *Guide to PAS 2050*, London.

Carbon Trust (2008c) *PAS 2050:2008 Specification of the Assessment of the Life Cycle Greenhouse Gas Emissions of Goods and Services*, London.

Carbon Trust (2010) *Carbon Footprinting*, London.

Carbon Trust (2011) *Green Your Business for Growth*, London.

Carlsson-Kanyama, Annika and Mireille Faist (n.d.) *Energy Use in the Food Sector: A Data Survey*. Department of Systems Ecology, Stockholm University, Department of Civil and Environmental Engineering, Swiss Federal Institute of Technology (ETH Zurich).

Cascio, Jamais "The Cheeseburger Footprint" (http://www.openthefuture.com/cheeseburger_CF.html).

European Commission (EC) (2008) *EU Action against Climate Change. The EU Emissions Trading Scheme*. 2009 edition.

GreenBiz Group (2011) *State of Green Business 2011*, Oakland, CA.

Hawksworth, John (2006) *The World in 2050. Implications of Global Growth for Carbon Emissions and Climate Change Policy*, PriceWaterhouseCoopers (PWC) London.

Humes, Edward (2011) *Force of Nature: The Unlikely Story of Wal-Mart's Green Revolution*, New York: Harper Business.

International Organization for Standardization ISO (n.d.) www.iso.org/iso/home.html.

Pandey, Divya et al. (2011) "Carbon Footprint: Current Methods of Estimation," *Environmental Monitoring and Assessment*, 178, pp. 135–160.

PriceWaterhouseCoopers (PWC) (2008) *How Your Company Can Prepare to Manage Carbon as an Asset*.

PriceWaterhouseCoopers (PWC) (2009) *Carbon Disclosure Project Supply Chain Report 2009*.

Repetto, Robert (2007) "Better Financial Disclosure Protects Investors and the Environment," in Peter N. Nemetz (ed.) *Sustainable Resource Management: Reality or Illusion?* Cheltenham: Edward Elgar, pp. 342–375.

Trucost (2009) *Carbon Risks and Opportunities in the S&P 500*, Boston, MA.

UK Environment Agency (2011) *Environmental Disclosures. The Third Major Review of Environmental Reporting in the Annual Report & Accounts of the FTSE All-Share Companies*.

U.S. Securities and Exchange Commission (SEC) (2010) "SEC Issues Interpretive Guidance on Disclosure Related to Business or Legal Developments Regarding Climate Change," January 27.

www.tesco.com/climatechange/carbonfootprint.asp. [Tesco, Dundee, UK].

CHAPTER 20

# Thinking Systemically (IV): LCA, Carbon Footprinting and Input-Output Analysis

W HILE LIFE-CYCLE ANALYSIS AND ITS SUBSET, CARBON FOOTPRINTING, are powerful tools for tracking the environmental impact of a product, there are certain inherent theoretical drawbacks to these methodologies (Lave et al. 1995). Perhaps the most important of the limitations to this type of engineering, process-based analysis is the somewhat arbitrary definition of the system boundary. The analysis is usually limited, by necessity, to what are perceived to be the most important negative environmental impacts from the chain of production. This presents a classic systems problem, as it is not always clear how much of the total impact has been captured within the defined boundaries of the analysis. By way of example, Lester Lave of Carnegie Mellon University's Department of Engineering has developed a methodology for expanding the analysis to include, in theory, all the possible impacts of any given pollutant release throughout the entire chain of production. The essence of this analytical approach rests on input-output analysis, which has the capacity to track the multitude of direct and indirect relationships among all sectors of a national economy.

By way of example, Lave has revisited the analysis by Hocking [see Figure 18–7] of the comparative life cycle analyses of paper and polystyrene cups (Lave et al. 1995). The task faced by Hocking—and anyone else attempting a process analysis of this type—is immense because of the vast array of direct and indirect suppliers and inputs associated with every level of the production chain from raw materials to final product. Figure 20–1 is a representation of the narrow boundaries of Hocking's analysis as determined by Lave. This restricted analysis focused on a limited set of direct suppliers. In contrast, once input-output analysis is brought to this problem, the boundary is significantly wider and is represented in Figure 20–2. Lave's conclusions were twofold: (1) while the toxic discharges from all direct suppliers were substantial, indirect suppliers have more than twice the toxic discharges of direct suppliers; and (2) while on a per dollar, or per pound, of output, plastic generates greater toxic discharges than paperboard, on a per cup basis, paperboard generates more toxic waste than plastic. To make this comparison, Lave totaled all toxic releases to air, water, underground, and land in pounds.

While this is an important step in generating a commensurable metric, there is one major problem that is finessed by this analysis—the lack of comparability

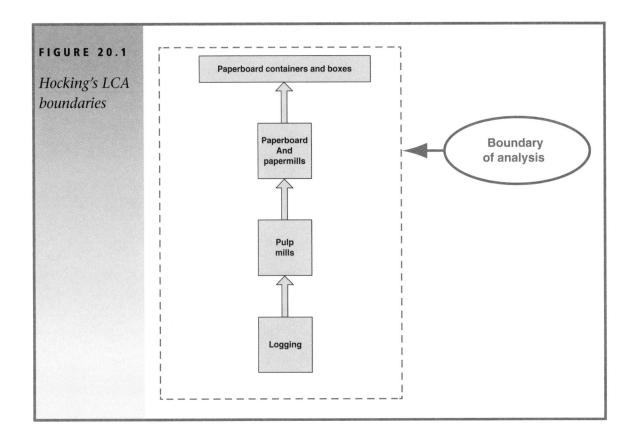

**FIGURE 20.1**

*Hocking's LCA boundaries*

Paperboard containers and boxes

Paperboard And papermills

Boundary of analysis

Pulp mills

Logging

among pollutants. In order to generate a meaningful overall value in pounds of pollutant release, it is necessary to assume that one pound of pollutant *x* has an equivalent health or environmental effect as one pound of pollutant *y*. As discussed in the appendix to chapter 5, this is a tenuous assumption. There are two partial solutions to this problem: first, is to use the U.S. EPA system of toxicity equivalence values, although this pertains principally to human health effects. Second, it is to convert major impacts to monetized value. Although, conceptually, this second approach is much more comprehensive, it is extremely difficult in practice to implement in practice, as outlined in chapter 7.

Carnegie Mellon University has established an extensive, publicly accessible website that facilitates the application of I-O analysis to the study of any major production process (www.eiolca.net). There are six types of industry-specific data available on this EIO-LCA database: (1) economic activity; (2) conventional air pollutants such as $SO_2$, CO, NOx, volatile organic compounds (VOC), lead (Pb), and particulate matter ($PM_{10}$); (3) greenhouse gases such as $CO_2$, $CH_4$, $N_2O$, CFCs, all converted to their global warming potential (GWP);[1] (4) energy by fuel type; (5) toxic releases to air, water, land, underground, both on site and off site; and (6) employment data.

Another comprehensive database is available from the Ecoinvent Centre, the Swiss Centre for Life Cycle Inventories (www.ecoinvent.org). This data set covers

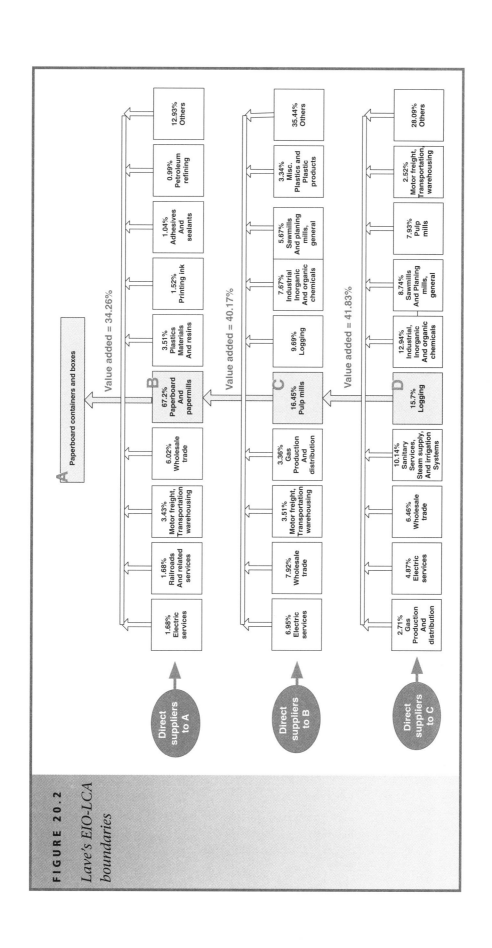

**FIGURE 20.2**

*Lave's EIO-LCA boundaries*

nearly 4,000 industrial processes and, although a charge is levied for use, the website contains several dozen freely downloadable published studies that focus on particular industries and chemicals.

Table 20–1 provides data from the Carnegie Mellon database on the GHG emissions of one example industry, ferrous metal foundries. The key distinction is

| TABLE 20.1 *GHG Emissions from Ferrous Metal Foundries* | | GWP CUMULATIVE MTCO₂E | % |
|---|---|---|---|
| | **TOTAL FOR ALL SECTORS** | **914.17** | **100.0%** |
| | **DIRECT EMISSIONS** | | |
| | 331510     **Ferrous metal foundries** | **81.87** | **9.0%** |
| | **INDIRECT EMISSIONS** | | |
| | 221100     Power generation and supply | 388.08 | 42.5% |
| | 484000     Truck transportation | 66.43 | 7.3% |
| | 562000     Waste management and remediation services | 49.73 | 5.4% |
| | 331111     Iron and steel mills | 43.49 | 4.8% |
| | 331112     Ferroalloy and related product manufacturing | 37.31 | 4.1% |
| | 331419     Primary nonferrous metal, except copper and aluminum | 30.87 | 3.4% |
| | 331312     Primary aluminum production | 21.98 | 2.4% |
| | 212100     Coal mining | 19.97 | 2.2% |
| | S00202     State and local government electric utilities | 17.00 | 1.9% |
| | 211000     Oil and gas extraction | 14.73 | 1.6% |
| | 486000     Pipeline transportation | 11.98 | 1.3% |
| | 327410     Lime manufacturing | 10.66 | 1.2% |
| | 482000     Rail transportation | 8.54 | 0.9% |
| | 481000     Air transportation | 8.51 | 0.9% |
| | 324110     Petroleum refineries | 7.37 | 0.8% |
| | 212230     Copper, nickel, lead, and zinc mining | 6.87 | 0.8% |
| | 221200     Natural gas distribution | 6.19 | 0.7% |
| | 420000     Wholesale trade | 6.13 | 0.7% |
| | 212320     Sand, gravel, clay, and refractory mining | 5.60 | 0.6% |

*Source:* www.eiolca.net

between direct and indirect emissions. In this case, it can be seen that direct emissions account for only 9% of the total of all emissions attributable to this industry. A brief comparison of both process-based LCA and EIO-LCA is provided in Table 20–2 by Hendrickson et al. (2006).

A similar type of in-depth analysis applied to carbon footprinting was reported in a special issue of *Economic Systems Research* in 2009. Six papers addressed the theoretical issues and presented case studies covering land use accounting, corporate footprints, national examples from Australia and Japan, and multiregional analysis.

| | PROCESS-BASED LCA | EIO-LCA | |
|---|---|---|---|
| **Advantages** | results are detailed, process specific | results are economy-wide, comprehensive assessments | **TABLE 20.2** *Comparing EIO-LCA and Process-Based Models* |
| | allows for specific product comparisons | allows for systems-level comparisons | |
| | identifies areas for process improvements, weak point analysis | uses publicly available, reproducible results | |
| | provides for future product development assessments | provides for future product development assessments | |
| | | provides information on every commodity in the economy | |
| **Disadvantages** | setting system boundary is subjective | product assessments contain aggregate data | |
| | end to be time intensive and costly | process assessments difficult | |
| | difficult to apply to new process design | must link monetary values with physical units | |
| | use proprietary data | imports treated as products created within economic boundaries | |
| | cannot be replicated if confidential data are used | availability of data for complete environmental effects | |
| | uncertainty in data | difficult to apply to an open economy (with substantial non-comparable imports) | |
| | | uncertainty in data | |

*Source*: Hendrickson et al. 2006
Copyright 2006 From Environmental Life Cycle Assessment of Goods and Services: An Input-Output Approach by Hendrickson et al. Reproduced by permission of Taylor and Francis Group, LLC, a division of Informa plc.

A paper by Huang et al. (2009) parallels in many respects the analysis of Lave with respect to the potential contributions of I-O analysis to LCA. The authors identify the same problem of arbitrary cutoffs thresholds in LCA that can lead to a serious underestimate of the total environmental impact of a production chain. Huang et al. observe that in an attempt to be as complete as possible, many engineering process LCAs adopt a cutoff of 95–99% percent (i.e. they attempt to include within the boundary of analysis all inputs that have at least a 1% or 5% contribution to the total environmental release of carbon). But, as the authors point out, it is logically impossible to determine if such coverage has been achieved if the total impact is unknown. The true aggregate impact can only be determined by the use of input-output analysis. Huang et al. present several industry-level empirical calculations from Australia and the United States to demonstrate their point, and their results are quite startling. For example, in the U.S. newspaper publishing sector, the top contributor of carbon in the supply chain is electricity used by the publishers themselves with 5% of total contributory emissions. The authors observe that if only items that represented at least 5% or more of total emissions were included, then clearly 95% of total emissions would be missed. The comparable missed total for a 1% cutoff is 72%.

One of the more amusing discoveries yielded by the total systems analysis provided by I-O came from a totally unanticipated source of carbon. To quote:

> In an upstream scope-3 calculation,[2] supply chains start with an emitting upstream sector, and end with the purchasing industry sector under investigation. The meaning of upstream chain is best explained using an example. Consider the supply chain *Beef cattle -> Meat processing -> Restaurant*. The emissions associated with this supply chain are caused, for example, by land clearing or enteric fermentation in animals slaughtered for meat that is supplied to a restaurant's kitchen. Another way of expressing this is to say that emissions from beef-cattle farming become 'embodied' in the restaurant meal. (Huang et al. 2009)

In sum, life-cycle analysis and carbon footprinting both have a serious deficiency—the lack of appropriate system analysis. This obstacle can be largely overcome through the use of input-output analysis that encompasses an entire national economy. There are, however, several drawbacks to a sole reliance on I-O analysis (Huang et al. 2009). These include, first, the degree of sectoral aggregation. Input-output tables can range in size from very small to very large, depending on how finely each sector is defined. For example, the North American Industrial Classification System (NAICS) drills down to the six-digit level of industries, and the greater the disaggregation, the larger the data requirements (www.census.gov/eos/www/naics/). Conversely, the lower the level of disaggregation, the greater the simplifications and possible distortions. Second, these models are generally based on single geographic-political areas and do not account for interregional flows where regions can be subnational or transnational. If, for example, a significant proportion of inputs come from an offshore supplier and no comparable I-O-based pollutant data are available, the final result can be seriously incomplete. Within a national context, however, regional models can be linked more easily. Third, I-O analysis is essentially static and usually relies on data collected several years before the analysis can be completed. Fourth, the lack of price data is problematic since changes in prices clearly influence how an economic system will respond to changes in inputs due to such factors as regulations or economic incentives. Fifth, a simplifying assumption in this type of I-O analysis is one of a fixed, or linear, relationship between physical output and resulting pollution. And, finally, the underlying system of industry classification used in the construction of input-output tables must deal with the sometimes complex problem of primary versus secondary products generated by establishments. While establishments are classified to industries on the basis of their primary products or services, many establishments create other products or services that may be produced or used differently from their primary products. This can produce challenges to the process of classification. In the construction of I-O tables, the U.S. Bureau of Economic Analysis (Horowitz and Planting, 2009, pp. 4–5) addresses this problem through the creation of two sets of "make" and "use" tables called *standard* tables and *supplementary* tables. To quote:

> The *standard tables* closely follow NAICS and are consistent with other economic accounts and industry statistics. The *supplementary tables* are derived from the standard tables by reassigning some secondary products to the industry in which they are the primary products. In most cases, the reassignment decisions are based on comparisons of the production processes for the two industries.

As a result of the limitations of a sole reliance on input-output analysis, it is the measured opinion of Lave, Huang, and others that a hybrid model is appropriate, where both an engineering, process-based LCA and I-O regional model are used to inform the decision-making process. This is a similar conceptual approach to the process of "triangulation" recommended in chapter 7 where no single method of measuring environmental benefits can provide a comprehensive analysis of the issue at hand.

## CITED REFERENCES AND RECOMMENDED READINGS

*Economic Systems Research* (2009) Volume 21, Issue 3 Special issue on Carbon Footprint and Input-Output Analysis, September.

Hendrickson et al. (2006) *Environmental Life Cycle Assessment of Goods and Services: An Input-Output Approach*, Washington, DC: Resources for the Future Press.

http://unfccc.int/ghg_data/items/3825.php [UN Framework Convention on Climate Change].

Horowitz, Karen J. and Mark A. Planting (2009) Concepts and Methods of the U.S. Input-Output Accounts, U.S. Bureau of Economic Analysis, Washington, DC.

Huang, Y. Anny et al. (2009) "The Role of Input-Output Analysis for the Screening of Corporate Carbon Footprints," *Economic Systems Research*, 21(3), September, pp. 217–242.

Lave, Lester et al. (1995) "Using Input-output analysis to estimate economy-wide discharges," *Environmental Science & Technology*, September, 29(9), pp. 420A–426A.

www.census.gov/eos/www.naics/ [U.S. Government Census Bureau website for NAICS].

www.ecoinvent.org [Swiss Centre for Life Cycle Inventories website].

www.eiolca.net [website of Carnegie-Mellon's Green Design Institute].

www.ghgprotocol.org [Greenhouse Gas Protocol website].

## NOTES

1. The global warming potential (GWP) of major greenhouse gases (GHGs) is usually cast in terms of carbon dioxide equivalent ($CO_2$e). The GWPs for the major GHG are defined in Table 20–3 (http://unfccc.int/ghg_data/items/3825.php).
2. *Scope* is a boundary concept associated with the Greenhouse Gas Protocol, a joint initiative of the World Resources Institute and the World Business Council for Sustainable Development. To quote its website (www.ghgprotocol.org):

> The GHG Protocol is the most widely used international accounting tool for government and business leaders to understand, quantify, and manage greenhouse gas emissions. The GHG Protocol is working with businesses, governments, and environmental groups around the world to build a new generation of credible and effective programs for tackling climate change. It provides the accounting

**TABLE 20.3**

*Global Warming Potential of Major GHGs*

| SPECIES | CHEMICAL FORMULA | LIFETIME (YRS) | GLOBAL WARMING POTENTIAL | | |
|---|---|---|---|---|---|
| | | | 20 YEARS | 100 YEARS | 500 YEARS |
| $CO_2$ | $CO_2$ | variable [a] | 1 | 1 | 1 |
| Methane [b] | $CH_4$ | 12+/-3 | 56 | 21 | 6.5 |
| Nitrous oxide | $N_2O$ | 120 | 280 | 310 | 170 |
| HFC-23 | CHF3 | 264 | 9,100 | 11,700 | 9,800 |
| HFC-32 | CH2F2 | 5.6 | 2,100 | 650 | 200 |
| HFC-41 | CH3F | 3.7 | 490 | 150 | 45 |
| HFC-43-10mee | C5H2F10 | 17.1 | 3,000 | 1,300 | 400 |
| HFC-125 | C2F5 | 32.6 | 4,600 | 2,800 | 920 |
| HFC-134 | C2H2F4 | 10.6 | 2,900 | 1,000 | 310 |
| HFC-134a | CH2FCF3 | 14.6 | 3,400 | 1,300 | 420 |
| HFC-152a | C2H4F2 | 1.5 | 460 | 140 | 42 |
| HFC-143 | C2H3F3 | 3.8 | 1,000 | 300 | 94 |
| HFC-143a | C2H3F3 | 48.3 | 5,000 | 3,800 | 1,400 |
| HFC-227ea | C3HF7 | 36.5 | 4,300 | 2,900 | 950 |
| HFC-236fa | C3H2F6 | 209 | 5,100 | 6,300 | 4,700 |
| HFC-245ca | C3H3F5 | 6.6 | 1,800 | 560 | 170 |
| Sulfur hexafluoride | SF6 | 3,200 | 16,300 | 23,900 | 34,900 |
| Perfluoromethane | CF4 | 50,000 | 4,400 | 6,500 | 10,000 |
| Perfluoroethane | C2F6 | 10,000 | 6,200 | 9,200 | 14,000 |
| Perfluoropropane | C3F8 | 2,600 | 4,800 | 7,000 | 10,100 |
| Perfluorobutane | C4F10 | 2,600 | 4,800 | 7,000 | 10,100 |
| Perfluorocyclobutane | c-C4F8 | 3,200 | 6,000 | 8,700 | 12,700 |
| Perfluoropentane | C5F12 | 4,100 | 5,100 | 7,500 | 11,000 |
| Perfluorohexane | C6F14 | 3,200 | 5,000 | 7,400 | 10,700 |

[a] derived from the Bern carbon cycle model Global Warming Potential
[b] The GWP for methane includes indirect effects of tropospheric ozone production and stratospheric water vapor production

*Source:* http://unfccc.int/ghg_data/items/3825.php

framework for nearly every GHG standard and program in the world—from the International Standards Organization to The Climate Registry—as well as hundreds of GHG inventories prepared by individual companies. The GHG Protocol also offers developing countries an internationally accepted management tool to help their businesses to compete in the global marketplace and their governments to make informed decisions about climate change.

With respect to *scope*, the protocol defines direct and indirect emissions as follows:

Direct GHG emissions are emissions from sources that are owned or controlled by the reporting entity. Indirect GHG emissions are emissions that are a consequence of the activities of the reporting entity, but occur at sources owned or controlled by another entity. The GHG Protocol further categorizes these direct and indirect emissions into three broad scopes: Scope 1: All direct GHG emissions. Scope 2: Indirect GHG emissions from consumption of purchased electricity, heat or steam. Scope 3: Other indirect emissions, such as the extraction and production of purchased materials and fuels, transport-related activities in vehicles not owned or controlled by the reporting entity, electricity-related activities (e.g. T&D losses) not covered in Scope 2, outsourced activities, waste disposal, etc.

# CHAPTER 21

# The Search for Innovative Business Models—The Case of Ooteel Forest Products, Ltd.

## CURRENT OPERATIONS AND FUNDAMENTAL CHALLENGES

Ooteel is a forestry company with private land holdings situated on the Pacific Northwest coast of North America. It has been operating a logging operation for several years whose profitability is intimately tied to variations in the market price of its timber. The company is now facing a major challenge. Continuation of its current business model will not guarantee future profitability principally because of the emergence of concerns over environmental sustainability among the general public and its customers in particular. This challenge is manifested in two areas: first, the company's plans to harvest old growth trees has received a major push-back from environmental non-governmental organizations (ENGOs) and the threat of a boycott of its products if this plan proceeds. Second, a lack of forest certification of its current logging operations may threaten access to markets for some of its products. Ooteel has sought the advice of consultants who have generated an innovative, but potentially risky, strategy that may help the company survive. It is now up to Ooteel to assess this new strategic option and determine its economic viability. The new strategic plan is described below with relevant economic data.

## THE PROPOSED STRATEGIC PLAN TO BE EVALUATED

As presented to the management of Ooteel, the new strategic direction has four distinct components: (1) product branding through independent certification of responsible forest practices, (2) the launching of an ecotourism initiative by the company to add an additional source of revenue from the non-harvested forest, (3) marketing of carbon credits from non-harvested timber land that satisfies the "additionality" criterion where the carbon comes from trees in areas that the company is not required by law to set aside, and (4) a companion proposal to market biodiversity credits. The challenge to management is to determine whether these strategic directions alone or in combination are sufficient to guarantee profitability.

## OPERATING DETAILS

Ooteel's land holdings total approximately 150,000 hectares (ha), and the company has been harvesting approximately 300,000 cubic meters of timber annually over the past few years from approximately half this area. This harvest, at a somewhat lower rate (4 cu meters per hectare) than normal because of environmental sensitivities, is composed of approximately 60% high-quality cedar that lends itself to value-added remanufacturing of more expensive appearance grade products; the remaining 40% is a mix of lower-grade wood, principally hemlock with more limited opportunities for high-end manufacturing. When prices for high-grade cedar are up, this proportion of the harvest is guaranteed a market and generates a reasonable profit. The challenge to the company is the uncertain market for its lower-grade products; forest certification holds the promise of guaranteeing that this market will remain open and that Ooteel will have more competitive access to it than companies without an ecolabel. The four strategic initiatives are as follows:

1. *Product branding through certification.* While the company would prefer to receive a price premium for this lumber, premia for certified changes to logging practices vary markedly from 0–10%. What makes certification attractive even without a price premium is more competitive market access for their low-quality product. A consultant has advised the company that without certification, there is a greater than 50–50 chance that this product could not be marketed, putting the corporation into a serious financial crisis. In order to receive certification, Ooteel must change its logging practices and forest management system from clearcutting to variable retention and selective cutting. This will involve a significant increment to its operating costs. One of the principal cost differences is a shift from cable-based logging to a mix of 40% cable and 60% helicopter-based logging. The shift in forest management will also entail a reduction in annual harvest to approximately 100,000 cubic meters. An additional but small cost is required for certification itself, ranging from a median value of $0.27–2.40 per hectare plus $0.12–$0.49 per hectare for annual audits (Cubbage and Moore 2008; Cubbage et al. 2009; Hansen et al 1998; Lister 2011), to 2–3 cents per cubic meter in another (Gullison 2003).
2. *Ecotourism.* Ooteel's coastal forest operations are close to a globally popular existing tourist destination whose activities could be largely viewed as ecological in nature. The consultant's report suggested that Ooteel might be able to generate an ecotourism revenue stream from small-scale, low capital-intensive activities such as boat tours, hiking, camping, nature walks, and wildlife viewing equal to anywhere between 5% and 10% of the gross current regional tourist revenues. This could be undertaken by itself or through strategic partnerships with existing local tourism operators.
3. *Marketing of carbon credits.* There is an emerging market for carbon credits/offsets globally that the company might be able to tap into through the sequestration of carbon in the proportion of their land holdings that will be set aside as non-harvestable. It is estimated that the company could dedicate 50,000–75,000 ha for this purpose. The quantity of standing timber in this area is estimated at 600 cubic meters/ha, and the quantity of carbon sequestered is estimated at approximately 900 tons of carbon per ha.

4. *Marketing of biodiversity credits.* While markets for carbon credits are well along the road to development, comparable institutions for biodiversity are only in their nascent stage. Part of the problem is the difficulty of developing quantifiable indicators for biodiversity. There are a great number of uncertainties at this time, but the consultants suggested that one avenue to pursue would be a per hectare payment by a corporation that is undertaking a development somewhere in North America or the world that may compromise the level of its local biodiversity. The biodiversity credits purchased from Ooteel would act as an offset. The issue is clearly one of determining the appropriate price.

There is obviously a great deal of uncertainty involved with each one of the four components, and the consultants have suggested that the company may wish to hire an analyst to use a Monte Carlo analysis[1] to generate a profile of possible financial outcomes and help the management assess the corporate attitude toward risk. Two common Monte Carlo software packages are @RISK™ and Crystal Ball.™ [See Table 21.3 in Appendix]

## COST PROJECTIONS

The consultants have prepared cost projections based on an annual harvest of 100,000 cu m (cubic meter), and these data are reproduced in Table 21–1.

| **TABLE 21.1** |
|---|

*Ooteel's Cost Structure*

| Logging (Variable) costs | $/cu m |
|---|---|
| Yarding [1] | $49.75 |
| Barge & Tow | $6.00 |
| Other phase [2] | $51.75 |
| Subtotal | $107.50 |
| **Fixed costs** | |
| **Forest Management** | |
| Regulatory compliance & reporting | $154,000 |
| Forestry and engineering [3] | $547,000 |
| Silviculture accrual [4] | $105,000 |
| Subtotal | $806,000 |
| **SG&A [5]** | $307,600 |
| Property taxes per hectare | $7.50 |
| Harvest tax per cubic meter | $6.00 |

These cost categories are composed of the following components.

[1] *Yarding*: The company's former method of logging with clearcutting used cables for the retrieval of downed trees at a cost of $16.25 per cu m. The shift to a more sustainable method of forestry (specifically *ecoforestry*; that is, ultra low-impact forestry) has necessitated a 40% mix of cables and 60% use of helicopters[2], the latter costing $72 per cu m. This averages out at $49.70 per cu m.

[2] *Other phase costs*: include falling, loading, hauling, sorting, booming grounds, roads, and misc. other costs.

## Fixed Costs

[3] Forestry and engineering costs are related to field, professional, and data analysis costs required to plan and execute harvesting, road building, silviculture, and protection activities.

[4] Silvicultural accrual cost is an expected future silviculture cost equal to between $1.75–3.00 /cu m of harvest, at an assumed rate of timber harvest of 50,000–100,000 cu m/yr.

[5] SG&A include personnel, marketing, research, accounting, legal, insurance, training, and misc. other.

In addition, the company faces annual property taxes of $7.50 per hectare as well as a harvest tax of approximately $6 per cu m. Since Ooteel is a private land owner, it pays no stumpage fees.

## REVENUE PROJECTIONS

While there is a fair degree of certainty concerning these cost estimates, the potential revenue side is more uncertain, especially with respect to each of the four proposed components of the new sustainability strategy. The nature and extent of this uncertainty is discussed below.

### Lumber Prices

There are numerous grades of timber, each receiving a different price. Recent average historical prices (in 2009 dollars) for Ooteel's mix of cedar and hemlock logs are presented in Table 21–2. Since there is every reason to assume that this price variability will continue in the future, Ooteel must build this expected variation into its financial projections.

### Ecotourism

The local region currently generates average tourist-related revenues of approximately $40 million, an amount that has been growing at or above the rate of inflation over the last decade. It is assumed that Ooteel could realize a 10–20% contribution to its bottom line from any ecotourism revenues it can capture.

| YEAR | CEDAR | HEMLOCK | TABLE 21.2 |
|------|-------|---------|------------|
| 1999 | $181.62 | $85.57 | *Historical Prices for Cedar and Hemlock (in 2009$ per cu m)* |
| 2000 | $187.86 | $83.95 | |
| 2001 | $172.55 | $74.88 | |
| 2002 | $202.41 | $82.10 | |
| 2003 | $174.58 | $67.85 | |
| 2004 | $148.73 | $68.57 | |
| 2005 | $115.77 | $58.01 | |
| 2006 | $139.09 | $60.04 | |
| 2007 | $179.31 | $66.50 | |
| 2008 | $163.36 | $55.83 | |
| 2009 | $113.40 | $49.98 | |

## Carbon Credits/Offsets

As global markets for carbon credits/offsets are still emerging, the prices are highly variable. Ooteel has been advised by its consultants that current rates run between $6–$8/ton for forest carbon but that these prices are expected to increase annually in light of the rising concern over global climate change and the concomitant increase in carbon markets and trading by corporations, governments, and ENGOs. Recent reports by the U.S. EPA (2009, 2010) have forecasted that the price of these credits will increase at or above the rate of inflation for the next several decades. Forest carbon offsets are measured as any net reduction in forest carbon emissions on an annual basis. While conceptually simple, the calculation of these emission changes is relatively data intensive and subject to a large number of qualifications and exclusions. For simplicity, the consultants have recommended a rather conservative approach to estimation in order to give Ooteel a general idea of the relative magnitude of potential revenues should they be able to capitalize on the market for carbon. In the simplified calculation suggested by the consultants, Ooteel is required to compare the carbon emissions associated with a normal annual harvest (at a conservative 4 cubic meters per hectare per year) with no harvest from the newly dedicated land conservation area. It is important to note that not all carbon is released by harvesting. On average, the consultants have estimated that fully 40% of carbon in the harvested wood remains in the product over a period of 100 years—a time span usually considered relevant for this type of carbon sequestration calculation. Two other adjustments are required in order to estimate the baseline quantity of carbon credits available for offsetting. The first is a risk buffer to account for potential losses from forest fires, insect predation, and land use changes. The second is termed economic leakage (BC 2010) and is described as follows:

Project activities that result in the change in the level of a service (e.g., land use of a given type, amount of wood products produced) provided from within the project boundary may result in changes in the level of those services provided outside the project area . . . due to market forces/activity shifting. Such changes, which are often referred to as "leakage," may result in changes in the amount of carbon stored in forest and/or wood product carbon pools located outside of the project boundary, but that are nonetheless affected by the project activity and that might serve to cancel out to some degree emission reductions or enhanced sequestration achieved by the project within the project boundary.

In light of these three factors, the consultant feels that the company can be credited with only a 50% reduction in carbon emissions by eliminating the harvest.

### Biodiversity Credits/Offsets

A recent report from EcosystemMarketplace (2010) surveys the state of biodiversity markets worldwide by reporting on global offset and compensation programs. There is an extraordinary range of values that can be imputed for biodiversity and related ecological services from the little data that is publicly available. The consultants advising Ooteel have adopted a relatively conservative approach and suggested an annual value of $5–15 per hectare based on the experience of Costa Rica in pricing its environmental services (Castro et al 2000). There is a special opportunity to package and market a customized conservation credit product in a payment for ecoservices (PES) model.

## APPENDIX

**TABLE 21.3**

*Suggested Range of Values for Monte Carlo Simulation*

| VARIABLE | LOWER BOUND | UPPER BOUND |
|---|---|---|
| cedar prices | $113.40 | $202.41 |
| hemlock prices as percentage of cedar prices | 34% | 50% |
| Possible branding premium from certification | 0% | 10% |
| percentage of ecotourism revenue as percentage of gross current regional tourist revenue | 5% | 10% |
| potential profit rate from eco-tourism | 10% | 20% |
| certification costs per hectare | $0.27 | $2.40 |
| auditing costs per hectare | $0.12 | $0.49 |
| current carbon offset prices ($/ton carbon) | $6.00 | $8.00 |
| possible biodiversity offset prices per hectare | $5.00 | $15.00 |

## CITED REFERENCES AND RECOMMENDED READINGS

British Columba (BC) Ministry of Environment (2010) *British Columbia Forest Carbon Offset Protocol, Final Draft for Public Review*, November 22, Victoria, BC.

Castro, Rene et al. (2000) "The Costa Rican Experience with Market Instruments to Mitigate Climate Change and Conserve Biodiversity," *Environmental Monitoring and Assessment*, 61, pp. 75–92.

Cubbage, Fred and Susan Moore (2008) "Impacts and Costs of Forest Certification: A Survey of SFI and FSC in North America," Presentation to 2008 Sustainable Forestry Initiative Meeting, Minneapolis, MN, September 23.

Cubbage, Fred et al. (2009) "Costs and Benefits of Forest Certification in the Americas," in Jeanette B. Paulding (ed.) *Natural Resources: Management, Economic Development and Protection*, pp. 155–183, Hauppauge, NY: Nova Science Publishers, Inc.

EcosystemMarketplace (2010) *Update. State of Biodiversity Markets. Offset and Compensation Programs Worldwide* [www.ecosystemmarketplace.com] Washington, DC.

Gullison, R.E. (2003) "Does Forest Certification Conserve Biodiversity?" *Oryx*, 37(2), pp. 153–165.

Hanson, E. et al. (1998) "Understanding Forest Certification," Oregon State University Extension Service, February. (Available at http://sfp.cas.psu.edu/pdfs/certsht.pdf).

Lister, Jane (2011) *Corporate Social Responsibility and the State. International Approaches to Forest Co-Regulation*, Vancouver, BC: UBC Press.

United Nations Economic Commission for Europe (UNECE) (2011) *Forest Products Annual Market Review 2010–2011*.

U.S. Environmental Protection Agency (EPA) (2009) *EPA Analysis of the American Clean Energy and Security Act of 2009, H.R. 2454 in the 111th Congress*, 6/23/09.

U.S. Environmental Protection Agency (EPA) (2010) *Supplemental EPA Analysis of the American Clean energy and Security Act of 2009, H.R. 2454 in the 111th Congress*, 1/29/2010.

### Analytical Questions

The key questions facing the analyst are as follows:

(1) Should he/she recommend an investment at this time in this private company?

(2) Given that Ooteel's current business model is no longer viable, is it possible to achieve profitability by adopting one or more of the strategic initiatives suggested by the consultant?

(3) Using several of the models of a sustainable corporation described in this text (e.g., Anderson, Natural Step, McDonough-Braungard), assess to what extent the company could be described as sustainable under its new strategic direction.

(4) Will FSC certification provide Ooteel with a sustainable competitive advantage?

## NOTES

1. In Table 21–3 the consultant has listed some of the variables that might enter such an analysis. Since most of the probability distributions are unknown, it is suggested that the analyst adopt either a normal or a continuous uniform distribution. In those cases where sufficient data are available, such as price history, then a probability distribution can be used that approximates the historical data. The price of cedar and hemlock are not independent variables since both are influenced by the state of the economy and world markets and, as such, tend to move in the same direction although hemlock prices have a lower variance than cedar. Under these circumstances, it may be appropriate to use the price of cedar as the principal price variable and determine the corresponding price of hemlock by using a probability distribution on the historical relationship between the two wood prices.
2. While the use of helicopters for logging introduces some technology-specific safety concerns, there are at least four benefits from their use: (1) a reduced need for access roads with their associated environmental disruption, (2) a wider seasonal window for harvesting, (3) elimination of falling damage to the target tree and neighboring trees, and (4) a reduction in occupational hazards associated with felling.

## CHAPTER 22

# Assessing Ooteel's Strategic Options

T HE MAJOR STRATEGIC CHALLENGE FACING OOTEEL LTD. is that continuation of its current business model will not guarantee future profitability because of a radically different business environment with the emergence of concerns
over sustainability among the general public and its customers. A four-pronged innovative strategy has been proposed by consultants that has the potential for both
sustainability and long-term profitability. If successful execution can be realized,
this would represent the operationalization of Michael Porter's seminal hypothesis
[see chapter 1] that sustainability is the key to long-run competitive advantage.
Figure 22–1 displays the goals and inherent challenges facing the company, and
Figure 22–2 presents the detailed business case defined by the strategic initiatives,
tactical targets, and specific constraints, risks and challenges. It is apparent that this
strategy is not without risks, and a fundamental issue is whether the company can
achieve profitability through the success of any one or subset of the four initiatives,

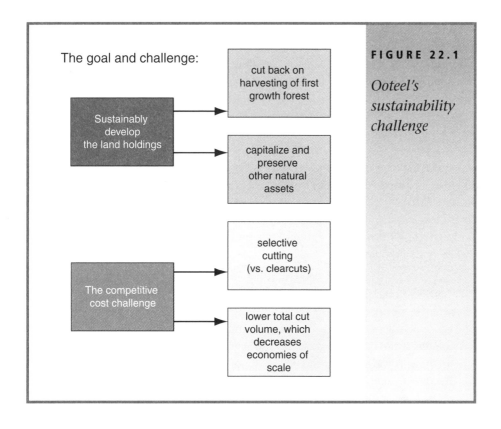

**The goal and challenge:**

Sustainably develop the land holdings → cut back on harvesting of first growth forest

Sustainably develop the land holdings → capitalize and preserve other natural assets

The competitive cost challenge → selective cutting (vs. clearcuts)

The competitive cost challenge → lower total cut volume, which decreases economies of scale

**FIGURE 22.1**

*Ooteel's sustainability challenge*

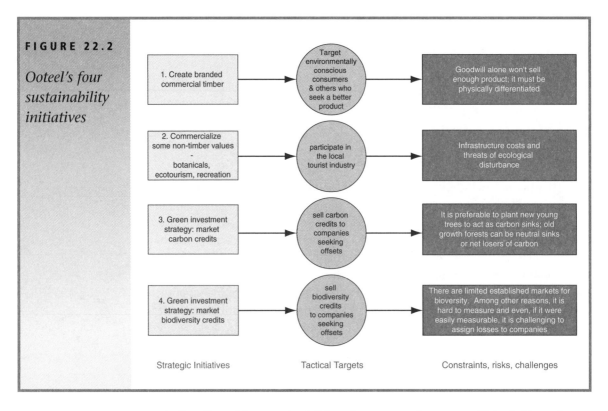

**FIGURE 22.2**

*Ooteel's four sustainability initiatives*

| Strategic Initiatives | Tactical Targets | Constraints, risks, challenges |

or whether the achievement of all four is necessary for success. This challenge is portrayed using a model from electrical engineering in Figures 22–3a and 22–3b. Model A uses an "OR Gate" where satisfying any one of the independent conditions will suffice for success; while Model B uses an 'AND Gate" where all of the independent conditions are necessary for success. The following sections discuss in greater detail the opportunities and risks associated with each of the four strategic thrusts.

## CERTIFICATION

As outlined in the consultant's proposal, the intent of the certification initiative is to create branded commercial timber that could earn a price premium, gain access to new markets, or maintain existing markets that are under emerging scrutiny from customers concerned about sustainability. A recent report on certification has outlined its pioneering role in building a more sustainable economy (SustainAbility 2011a, p. 6). To quote:

> Certification, labeling and the standards-setting organizations . . . have made what was once invisible visible, changed societal and consumer norms, given producers access to new markets, promoted multi-stakeholder collaboration, and driven operational changes among businesses and other large buyers. They are now in widespread use as operational tools for business to make purchasing decisions, manage supply, market and sell to B2B and B2C customers, guide employees, and respond to stakeholders and regulators.

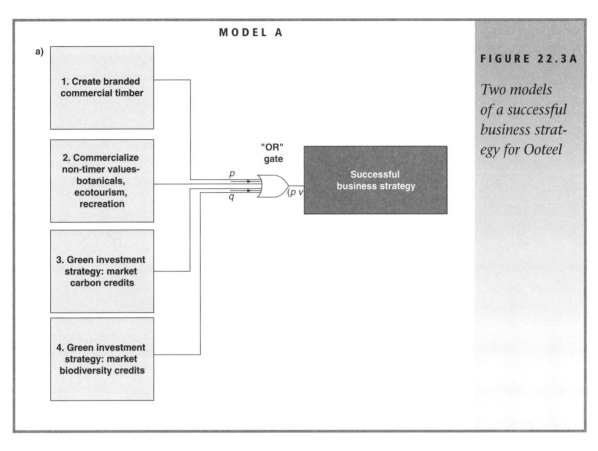

MODEL A

a)

1. Create branded commercial timber

2. Commercialize non-timer values-botanicals, ecotourism, recreation

3. Green investment strategy: market carbon credits

4. Green investment strategy: market biodiversity credits

"OR" gate

$p$

$q$

$(p \lor$

Successful business strategy

FIGURE 22.3A

*Two models of a successful business strategy for Ooteel*

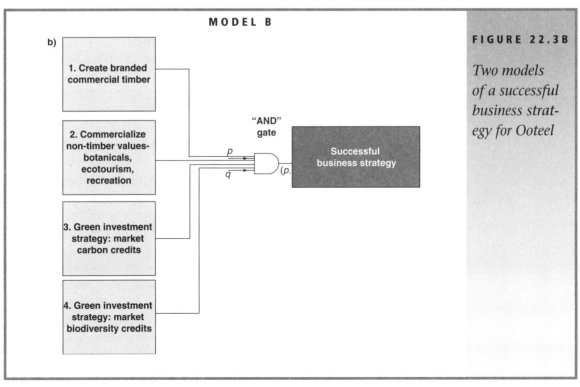

MODEL B

b)

1. Create branded commercial timber

2. Commercialize non-timber values-botanicals, ecotourism, recreation

3. Green investment strategy: market carbon credits

4. Green investment strategy: market biodiversity credits

"AND" gate

$p$

$q$

$(p.$

Successful business strategy

FIGURE 22.3B

*Two models of a successful business strategy for Ooteel*

Certification can take one of three forms: self-certification, industry certification, or third party certification. For obvious reasons, the last of these options is the most likely to be arms length and command the greatest credibility. The essence of certification is verification that the forest company is engaging in responsible forest practices, and this achievement is frequently accompanied by an eco-label attesting to this result. Within the last few decades, several organizations have emerged at the global level to offer forest certification services, foremost among these being the Programme for the Endorsement of Forest Certification (PEFC) and the Forest Stewardship Council (FSC). According to recent data (UNECE 2011) PEFC accounts for over two thirds of global forest certified with 236 million hectares as of May 2011, followed by FSC with 143 million hectares, most of which are in North America and Europe. FSC describes itself as "a non-profit, independent and internationally recognized organization that accredits and monitors independent forest product certifiers. FSC assures consumers that certification labels are consistent and reliable, and that practices adhere to an international set of principles as well as locally developed forest management standards. . . . FSC certification is conducted by independent, credible, nongovernmental organizations. Accreditation ensures that certifiers are independent from the timber trade, that they are qualified to make accurate forest assessments, their standards are consistent with international principles, and their assessments are conducted in a reliable and consistent manner" (http://www.fscoax.org/principal.htm).

If Ooteel proceeds with its reformulated forestry plan, they are virtually guaranteed FSC certification. While the company would be content with the guaranteed market access that this process offers to deliver, the prospect of a price premium enhances the attractiveness of this option. Very little data have been assembled on the extent and magnitude of such premia, but some studies have suggested significant differences among markets. UNECE (2011) and others (e.g., Yuan and Eastin 2007) report premia of 6.3% in Europe, 5.6% in Korea, 5.1% in the United States, and 1.5% in Canada.

FSC certification is based on 10 principles as described in Table 22–1. It is important to note that a significant component of this certification process is performance-based as opposed to process-based. This increases the likelihood that the ultimate sustainability goals will be realized. This is an issue of some importance that is discussed again in chapter 24.

If certification is to succeed, then the ultimate consumers of forest products must be cognizant of the product; be willing to accept it; and, in some cases, be willing to pay the additional price premium. Since forest products are rarely sold directly to final retail consumers, the role of the intermediary is essential to the success of this process. Within the last few years, several home improvement chains, such as Home Depot—the largest in the United States—have chosen to stock and advertise certified timber, thereby significantly increasing the marketing of this product. Their wood purchasing policy is reproduced in Table 22–2. A recent poll by the American Institute of Architects showed that 91% of registered voters would pay a premium for a house if it was deemed to be environmentally beneficial (Germain and Penfield 2010). An additional impetus to this market has been the emergence of *green* architects and builders who are capitalizing on increased public

| # | PRINCIPLE | STRATEGIC ACTIONS REQUIRED BY COMPANY |
|---|-----------|----------------------------------------|
| #1 | Compliance with laws and FSC principles | Forest management shall respect all applicable laws of the country in which they occur, and international treaties and agreements to which the country is a signatory, and comply with all FSC Principles and Criteria. |
| #2 | Tenure and use rights and responsibilities | Long-term tenure and use rights to the land and forest resources shall be clearly defined, documented and legally established. |
| #3 | Aboriginal peoples rights | The legal and customary rights of Aboriginal peoples to own, use and manage their lands, territories, and resources shall be recognized and respected. |
| #4 | Community relations and workers rights | Forest management operations shall maintain or enhance the long-term social and economic well being of forest workers and local communities. |
| #5 | [Multiple] benefits from the forest | Forest management operations shall encourage the efficient use of the forests multiple products and services to ensure economic viability and a wide range of environmental and social benefits. |
| #6 | Environmental impact | Forest management shall conserve biological diversity and its associated values, water resources, soils, and unique and fragile ecosystems and landscapes, and, by so doing, maintain the ecological functions and the integrity of the forest. |
| #7 | Management plan | A management plan – appropriate to the scale and intensity of the operations -shall be written, implemented, and kept up to date. The long-term objectives of management, and the means of achieving them, shall be clearly stated. |
| #8 | Monitoring and assessment | Monitoring shall be conducted – appropriate to the scale and intensity of forest management – to assess the condition of the forest, yields of forest products, chain of custody, management activities and their social and environmental impacts. |
| #9 | Maintenance of high conservation value forests | Management activities in high conservation value forests shall maintain or enhance the attributes which define such forests. Decisions regarding high conservation value forests shall always be considered in the context of a precautionary approach. |
| #10 | Plantations | Plantations shall be planned and managed in accordance with Principles and Criteria 1 - 9, and Principle 10 and its Criteria. While plantations can provide an array of social and economic benefits, and can contribute to satisfying the worlds needs for forest products, they should complement the management of, reduce pressures on, and promote the restoration and conservation of natural forests. |

**TABLE 22.1**

*Ten Principles of FSC Certification*

*Source:* FSC website [http://www.fsc.org/1093.html]

| | |
|---|---|
| **TABLE 22.2**<br><br>*Home Depot's Wood Purchasing Policy* | 1. The Home Depot will give preference to the purchase of wood and wood products originating from certified well managed forests wherever feasible.<br>2. The Home Depot will eliminate the purchase of wood and wood products from endangered regions around the world.<br>3. The Home Depot will practice and promote the efficient and responsible use of wood and wood products.<br>4. The Home Depot will promote and support the development and use of alternative environmental products.<br>5. The Home Depot expects its vendors and their suppliers of wood and wood products to maintain compliance with laws and regulations pertaining to their operations and the products they manufacture.<br><br>*Source:* www.homedepot.com |

concern about the environment and who seek LEED certification that frequently includes certified wood products (CAGBC 2010). The Leadership in Energy and Environmental Design (LEED) program, administered by the U.S. Green Building Council, has established a voluntary certification process for new buildings based on sustainability principles. [See appendix.] The U.S. Green Building Council has estimated that green building products and services in the United States are expected to contribute as much as one-half trillion dollars over the period 2009–2013 (usgbc.org/displaypage.aspx?CMSPageID = 124).

### Assessing the Current and Future Role of Certification

As detailed by Conroy (2007), the modern form of product certification began in the 1980s and 1990s in the forest sector, led by Collins Pine in the United States (Hansen and Punches 1998) and MacMillan Bloedel (since bought by Weyerhaeuser) in British Columbia. This phenomenon has since spread to many other industries such as fisheries, finance and investment, tourism, mining, agriculture, industrial chemicals, clothing, oil and gas, etc. Conroy (p. xiii) divides the recent history of this phenomenon into three distinct phases: "(1) Nonprofit civil organizations create new standards for corporate social and environmental accountability, often in stakeholder negotiations with companies themselves. (2) Companies are moved to adopt these standards, either because of internal corporate culture and the new business opportunities they offer or due to NGO Pressure in the form of tough market campaigns. (3) Newly created, nonprofit, standard-setting organizations implement a credible and efficient method for certifying corporate compliance with the new standards."

As might be expected with the proliferation of third party certifiers, issues will inevitably arise with respect to cross-sectional comparability, quality control, transparency, and changing standards over time (NAS 2010). In some cases, as in fisheries, this can be the source of some controversy (Jacquet et al. 2010). Several studies have already been published in an attempt to assess the current state of certification, and some have identified significant shortcomings (See, for example, Lister 2011; Miljoeko AB and SustainAbility 2001; SustainAbility 2011b; SustainAbilty and Mistra 2004; TerraChoice 2010). In addition to helping consumers choose products, the rating process has been used to link executive compensation to performance and assist asset managers in investment decision making (SustainAbility 2011). An essential component of product certification is *chain-of-custody* (CofC), which allows the final consumer the opportunity to track the product all the way back to the original producer(s), reassuring the consumer that sustainable products and practices have been used at every stage of the supply chain. The more complex the supply chain and the more global components involved, the greater benefit of CofC despite the increased costs associated with possible product segregation and detailed tracking documentation.

As outlined by UNECE (2011), the bulk of forest certification has occurred in Europe and North America, where governments and forestry companies have generally established strong programs of reforestation and forest stewardship. For example, the percentage of European forested area that has received certification is 50.8%, and the comparable number for North America is 32.7%. In stark contrast, however, the certification rates for the rest of the world are considerably lower with Oceania at 6.4%, the former Communist states (CIS) at 5.3%, Latin America at 1.7%, Asia at 1.4%, and Africa at a dismal 1.1% (UNECE 2011, p. 101). This is problematic because of the critical role of tropical forests in the global ecosystem and the large rates of deforestation in the Third World (Dauvergne and Lister 2010; Williams 2006).

## Ecotourism

The essence of this second initiative is shifting from the traditional model of forestry as providing only fiber and timber to capitalizing on non-timber values such as botanicals; recreation; and targeted, low-impact tourism. Each one of these aspects has the capability of generating revenue for landowners and forestry companies. These potential values are independent of the vast array of unpriced ecosystem services that flow from intact forest lands. In evaluating the potential revenue stream from these nontraditional uses of forest lands, Ooteel must assess the market for ecotourism. The International Ecotourism Society (TIES) defines ecotourism as "responsible travel to natural areas that conserves the environment and improves the well-being of local people." This means that those who implement and participate in ecotourism activities should follow the following principles: minimize impact; build environmental and cultural awareness and respect; provide positive experiences for both visitors and hosts; provide direct financial benefits for conservation; provide financial benefits and empowerment for local people; and raise sensitivity to host countries' political, environmental, and social climate (www.ecotoursim.org).

Tourism is the largest sector in the world economy, employing over 230 million people and generating revenues over $6.5 trillion (TIES 2006). As of 2009 there were 880 million international tourist arrivals, down slightly from 919 million in 2008, but these numbers are expected to exceed 1.5 trillion by 2020. The comparable tourist receipts for 2008 and 2009 are $939 billion and $850 billion respectively (UNWTO 2010, p. 12). TIES (2006) has reported an ecotourism annual growth rate of 20–34% over the period 1990–2005, a rate that was three times greater than tourism in general. TIES estimates that sustainable tourism could reach a value of approximately one-half trillion dollars in the near future, representing as much as one quarter of the global travel market. In contrast to regular package tours where 80% of the revenue is returned to international business, as much as 95% of ecotourism revenues end up in the local economy. TIES has estimated the daily expenditure of cultural tourists as over €70/US$90, versus visitors on a touring holiday (€52/US$67), beach holiday (€48/US$62), city break or rural trip (€42/$US$54).

## Marketing Carbon Credits

Various forms of carbon trading have entered the business mainstream. EcosystemMarketplace (2010a and b) has provided an extensive analysis of forest carbon markets. Specific formal mechanisms were established under the Kyoto Protocol with the intent of reducing deforestation in the Third World, leading to the REDD (Reducing Emissions from Deforestation and Degradation) initiative in 2007 at Bali (FAO et al. 2008, 2010). Paralleling this international program has been the emergence of a few regional voluntary carbon exchanges including the now defunct Chicago Climate Exchange, exchanges in Australia and New Zealand, and the recent creation of a global electronic platform for the spot trading of voluntary carbon credits, based in London and Australia (www.carbontrade-exchange.com).

The fundamental principle of all these initiatives is the concept of "offsetting" where a corporation may choose to pay money to an intermediary to invest in a broad range of carbon-reducing activities where such payments are less expensive than carbon emission reduction by the corporation. In the case of forest credits, the payment may be less concerned with reducing current carbon emissions than forestalling any future release from forest harvesting by essentially paying for carbon sequestration and improved forest management. The EcosystemMarketplace report, based on a restricted data set, suggests that the bulk of the estimated $150 million worth of global transactions were conducted in North and Latin America and that this market appears to be expanding. The market for forest-based carbon in North America seems to have escaped many of the major problems surrounding the use of offsets in other industries in the global market.

The determination of carbon credits available for an offset market is a complex process, and some organizations and governments have already produced detailed protocols for their calculation (BC 2011; CAR 2010; IPCC 2006; ISO 14064–2; WBCSD & WRI 2005). For example, the province of British Columbia, which contains some of the largest timber holdings in North America, has produced an extensive and detailed 187-page protocol (BC 2011) which addresses such key issues as offset recognition criteria, appropriate project types, and procedures for microlevel and system-based calculations. The government has identified five key offset recognition criteria: first, the project must be real (i.e., it is an identifiable project, and there are sound methods available to quantify GHG emissions); second, there must be *additionality* (i.e., a reduction of GHG emissions beyond business as usual and regulatory requirements, as well as the ability to overcome economic and technical barriers); third, the undertaking is permanent (i.e., the offset has a lasting impact, measured relative to a 100-year time scale); fourth, the project is verifiable (i.e., it can be quantified, monitored, and audited; and the measurement uncertainty is minimized); and fifth, there is clear ownership (i.e., of the offset attributes by the party claiming them). These are critical criteria, as some of these have been violated in the international offset market for GHG reduction under the Kyoto Protocol.

One of the most useful private sector guides to assessing and estimating forest-based carbon credits has been produced by Climate Action Reserve (CAR 2010). Their extensive guide identifies three categories of eligible offsets: (1) *reforestation*, which "involves restoring tree cover on land that is not at optimal stocking levels and has minimal short-term (30-years) commercial opportunities," (2) *improved forest management*, which "involves management activities that maintain or increase carbon stocks on forested land relative to baseline levels of carbon stocks," and (3) *avoided conversion*, which "involves preventing the conversion of forestland to a non-forest land use by dedicating the land to continuous forest cover through a conservation easement or transfer to public ownership." Each of these three project types has strict eligibility criteria as described in CAR 2010.

In essence, the principal components of a carbon offset assessment involve (a) changes in the carbon sequestration of standing timber—both decreases and accretions, (b) changes in the carbon sequestration of soil and other vegetation, and (c) carbon releases related to the process of forestry itself. Each of these categories may vary in their applicability to each of the three major offset project types as summarized in Tables 22.3a and 3b. As indicated in chapter 21, the degree of carbon sequestered in forest products after harvesting is an important and complex issue. At least one study has attempted to generate these values in an American context (Smith et al. 2005). There are several principal pathways of harvested forest products: to wood products, to paper products, to biofuel, and disposal to landfill. [See Figure 22–4.] The precise estimation of these data is elusive because of the wide range of specific factors that can influence the rate of storage/loss, including type of wood, wood product, end use, location of production and use, and nature of disposal (BC 2011).

Companies contemplating forest-based carbon offsets must also address the "unavoidable risk of reversal," where human- or natural-induced events affect the sequestration of carbon (BC 2011). These risks include wildfire, disease or insect outbreak, wind throw from hurricane or other wind events, illegal harvesting, unplanned harvest, mining activity, or land use change.

**TABLE 22.3A**

*GHG Assessment Boundaries*

| DESCRIPTION | TYPE | GAS | REFORESTATION | IMPROVED FOREST MANAGEMENT | AVOIDED CONVERSION |
|---|---|---|---|---|---|
| *Primary Effect Sources, Sinks and Reservoirs* | | | | | |
| Standing live carbon (carbon in all portions of living trees) | Reservoir / Pool | $CO_2$ | Included | Included | Included |
| Shrubs and herbaceous understory carbon | Reservoir / Pool | $CO_2$ | Included | Optional | Optional |
| Standing dead carbon (carbon in all portions of dead, standing trees) | Reservoir / Pool | $CO_2$ | Included | Included | Included |
| Lying dead wood carbon | Reservoir / Pool | $CO_2$ | Optional | Optional | Optional |
| Litter and duff carbon (carbon in dead plant material) | Reservoir / Pool | $CO_2$ | Optional | Optional | Optional |
| Soil carbon | Reservoir / Pool | $CO_2$ | Optional or included | Optional or included | Optional or included |
| Carbon in in-use forest products | Reservoir / Pool | $CO_2$ | Included | Included | Included |
| Forest product carbon in landfills | Reservoir / Pool | $CO_2$ | Excluded | Excluded when project harvesting exceeds baseline; included when project harvesting is below baseline | Excluded when project harvesting exceeds baseline; included when project harvesting is below baseline |

Source: Derived from CAR 2010, pp. 26-36

**TABLE 22.3B**

## GHG Assessment Boundaries

| DESCRIPTION | TYPE | GAS | REFORESTATION | IMPROVED FOREST MANAGEMENT | AVOIDED CONVERSION |
|---|---|---|---|---|---|
| ***Secondary Effect Sources, Sinks, and Reservoirs*** | | | | | |
| Biological emissions from site preparation activities | Source | $CO_2$ | Included | Included | Included |
| Mobile combustion emissions from site preparation activities | Source | $CO_2$ | Included | Excluded | Excluded |
| | | $CH_4$ | Excluded | Excluded | Excluded |
| | | $N_2O$ | Excluded | Excluded | Excluded |
| Mobile combustion emissions from ongoing project operation & maintenance | Source | $CO_2$ | Excluded | Excluded | Excluded |
| | | $CH_4$ | Excluded | Excluded | Excluded |
| | | $N_2O$ | Excluded | Excluded | Excluded |
| Stationary combustion emissions from ongoing project operation & maintenance | Source | $CO_2$ | Excluded | Excluded | Excluded |
| | | $CH_4$ | Excluded | Excluded | Excluded |
| | | $N_2O$ | Excluded | Excluded | Excluded |
| Biological emissions from clearing of forestland outside the Project area | Source | $CO_2$ | Included | Excluded | Included |
| Biological emissions / removals from changes in harvesting on forestland outside the Project Area | Source / sink | $CO_2$ | Excluded | Included / Excluded | Excluded |
| Combustion emissions from production, transportation, and disposal of forest products | Source | $CO_2$ | Excluded | Excluded | Excluded |
| | | $CH_4$ | Excluded | Excluded | Excluded |
| | | $N_2O$ | Excluded | Excluded | Excluded |
| Combustion emissions from production, transportation, and disposal of alternative materials to forest products | Source | $CO_2$ | Excluded | Excluded | Excluded |
| | | $CH_4$ | Excluded | Excluded | Excluded |
| | | $N_2O$ | Excluded | Excluded | Excluded |
| Biological emissions from decomposition of forest products | Source | $CO_2$ | Included | Included | Included |
| | | $CH_4$ | Excluded | Excluded | Excluded |
| | | $N_2O$ | Excluded | Excluded | Excluded |

*Source:* Derived from CAR 2010, pp. 26-36

**FIGURE 22.4**

*Harvested wood products life cycle*

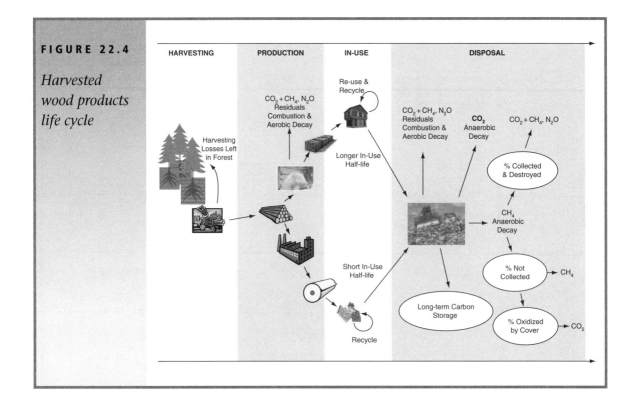

## MARKETING OF BIODIVERSITY CREDITS

This fourth and final initiative proposed to Ooteel by the consultants is the most tentative, yet it holds the promise of future returns as the global markets for biodiversity continue to emerge and mature. Biodiversity is notoriously difficult to quantify, although several outstanding attempts have been made to generate quantitative measures to facilitate the development of monitoring and market making (GRI, 2007; Rio Tinto and Earthwatch 2006). Biodiversity markets have been defined as "any payment for the protection, restoration, or management of biodiversity. Just a small sample includes: biodiversity offsets, conservation easements, certified biodiversity-friendly products and services, bioprospecting, payments for biodiversity management, hunting permits, and eco-tourism" (ecosystemmarketplace 2009, p. 1).

A strong case has already been made that corporate attention to this subject is good for risk reduction and ultimately the bottom line (Bishop et al. 2008; Earthwatch 2000, n.d.; F&C 2004; GRI 2007; IUCN 2004 and n.d.; OECD 2001, 2002, 2003, 2004; Secretariat of the Convention on Biological Diversity 2010). For example, Earthwatch (n.d) lists some of the major components of a business case for a corporate biodiversity-related strategy: managing risks, facilitating legal compliance with new regulations and legislation, improving reputation, attracting and retaining staff, financial benefits from cutting costs, avoiding fines and enhancing sales opportunities from green credentials, gaining and retaining investment, retaining the license to operate, securing sustainable supply chains, and demonstrating a commitment to corporate social responsibility.

Ecosystemmarketplace has produced two recent reports on the state of biodiversity markets (2009, 2010) where they report that the current global market size is at least $2.4–4 billion, with a North American dominance. Only a lower bound estimate of market size is feasible because "80% of existing programs are not transparent enough to estimate their market size" (EcosystemMarketplace 2009, p. iv). The greatest volume of biodiversity-related payments and area in North America relate to U.S. aquatic compensatory mitigation and conservation banking covering 37,700 acres annually.

There have already been a number of major private sector initiatives undertaken to create and maintain a market in biodiversity values. For example, British-based Canopycapital has established a template for investment in ecosystem services including biodiversity (www.canopycapital.co.uk), and a major NGO-corporate collaboration has been established under the rubric of BBOP (Business and Biodiversity Offsets Programme (www.bbop.forest-trends.org, and Forest Trends et al. 2009a). Initiated by Forest Trends, Conservation International, and the Wildlife Conservation Society, this organization has an advisory board from a large group of international agencies, NGOs, and a diverse range of corporate sponsors such as Anglo America, Newmont, Sherritt, Alcoa, Rio Tinto, Shell Oil, etc. The BBOP program provides extensive documentation to assist corporations in participating in this emerging market, including a biodiversity offset cost-benefit handbook (Forest Trends 2009b), biodiversity offset design handbook (Forest Trends 2009c), biodiversity offset implementation handbook (Forest Trends 2009d), and extensive in-depth case studies from the United States (Forest Trends 2009e), Ghana (Forest Trends 2009f), Madagascar (Forest Trends 2009g), etc.

Many of these studies and initiatives appear to be concerned with companies engaging in activities that endanger biodiversity. As a consequence, they fund the creation of biodiversity reserves or activities on- or off-site in order to compensate for this damage. The opportunities that Ooteel might, as a consequence, be able to capitalize on are threefold: (1) offering companies who are reducing biodiversity as a result of their business activities a distant off-site opportunity to offset, (2) offering companies who are engaging in some other form of environmentally detrimental activity the opportunity to "cross offset," or (3) offering companies and other investors an opportunity to invest in biodiversity credits for other reasons—goodwill, desire to protect and preserve the environment, etc.

As mentioned above, the development of quantifiable indicators for biodiversity remains a significant challenge to implementation. To quote the OECD (2002, p. 29):

> The challenge in developing robust quantitative indicators of biodiversity lies in finding those that can be meaningfully applied for policy assessment. Here it is important to note that biodiversity is frequently discussed at different scales. The absence of any discrete cut-off point for determining boundaries between species or ecosystems is still subject to research and discussion. . . . Although there is much interest in the development of indicators or inventories

of ecosystem function, species richness is still the common approach to distilling the available information. . . . Species richness is simply a systematic inventory of the number of species contained within an area. This is the commonest method for rapid impact statements about the change in diversity. In terms of approaches to valuation, species richness is also an easy concept to understand.

The Global Reporting Initiative (GRI 2007) includes five indicators in their list of performance metrics available to participating corporations: EN11—location and size of land owned, leased, managed in, or adjacent to, protected areas and areas of high biodiversity value outside protected areas. EN 12—description of significant impacts of activities, products, and services on biodiversity in protected areas and areas of high biodiversity value outside protected areas. EN13—Habitats protected or restored. EN14—strategies, current action, and future plans for managing impacts on biodiversity. EN15—number of IUCN Red List species and national conservation list species with habitats in areas affected by operations, by level of extinction risk.

A problem sometimes posed by the choice of biodiversity measures is that they are either process variables or do not lend themselves to quantification and monetization for market-based transactions. One of the most exhaustive studies to address the complexities of operationalizing biodiversity-based instruments has been produced by the joint efforts of Rio Tinto and the Earthwatch Institute (2006). Although conceived as an aid to mining operations, this work has implications far beyond this particular sector. The report addresses, in turn, such critical issues as biodiversity values; biodiversity risks; the advantages of going beyond species richness to include abundance, variation and distribution; limitations in the use of nature indicators (including quality of the data, selection and evaluation, optimal conditions and scale); and a list of 40 potential indicators drawn from a range of international sources with critical commentary on each. [See Table 22–4.]

Because of the inherent complexities in arriving at defensible biodiversity indicators, Coady (2002, p. 396) has argued that "to assess the creation of biodiversity values, it makes sense to focus on the elements that sustain biodiversity such as habitat, rather than the biodiversity itself. Because biodiversity is not a thing, but a "cluster of concepts," one cannot purchase an amount of it. Managing for habitat becomes a surrogate for protecting and managing species." Because both the markets for carbon and biodiversity are subsets of the larger concept of paying for ecosystem services (PES), this, in turns, offers the prospect for bundling both of these components in a new, more broadly focused, sustainability instrument focused on habitat management.

The adoption of a PES-based system may be the most productive avenue for Ooteel to pursue in operationalizing this fourth element of its revised corporate strategy. For example, the government of Costa Rica compensates landowners for four environmental services of which biodiversity is one (Castro et al. 2000). [See Table 22–5.] This is just one example of an emerging international market in payments for such services (Jack 2008; Katoomba Group and UNEP 2008; Kumar and Muradian 2009; Wetz-Kanounnikoff 2006; Wunder 2005). Recent studies of this market

| GUIDANCE / INDICATOR | SOURCE | TYPE | COMMENTS |
|---|---|---|---|
| EN6. Location and size of land owned, leased, or managed | GRIc | P | |
| EN28. Number of IUCN Red List species with habitats in areas affected by operations. | GRIa | S | |
| EN7. Description of the major impacts on biodiversity associated with activities and/or products and services in terrestrial, freshwater, and marine environments. | GRIc | PS | *Means of measurement and reporting unclear* |
| EN23. Total amount of land owned, leased, or managed for production activities or extractive use. | GRIa | P | *Low linkage to biodiversity impacts* |
| EN24. Amount of impermeable surface as a percentage of land purchased or leased. | GRIa | P | *Link to biodiversity unclear* |
| EN25. Impacts of activities and operations on protected and sensitive areas. (e.g., IUCN protected area categories 1-4, World Heritage Sites, and Biosphere Reserves). | GRIa | S | *Means of measurement and reporting unclear* |
| EN26. Changes to natural habitats resulting from activities and operations and percentage of habitat protected or restored. Identify type of habitat affected and its status. | GRIa | S | *Means of measurement and reporting unclear. More than one indicator* |
| EN27. Objectives, programmes, and targets for protecting and restoring native ecosystems and species in degraded areas. | GRIa | R | *Means of measurement and reporting unclear* |
| EN28. Number of IUCN Red List species with habitats in areas affected by operations. | GRIa | S | |
| EN29. Business units currently operating or planning operations in or around protected or sensitive areas. | GRIa | P | |
| Native vegetation clearance | ICMM | S | |
| Aquatic habitat destruction | ICMM | S, P | |
| Introduced species (e.g. richness, composition, abundance, distribution) | ICMM | P | |
| Human inhabitancy (e.g. number of employees) | ICMM | P | *Low relevance to biodiversity* |

**TABLE 22.4**

*Typology of Biodiversity Indicators*

(Continued)

**TABLE 22.4**

*continued*

| GUIDANCE / INDICATOR | SOURCE | TYPE | COMMENTS |
|---|---|---|---|
| Fragmentation (e.g. vegetation patch size, area occupied by roads and tracks) | ICMM | P | |
| Extent and condition of native vegetation (e.g. species richness, cover abundance, distribution of species / vegetation, stand-age distribution) | ICMM | S | *Vague and needs to be linked to key features requirements* |
| Extent and condition of terrestrial fauna habitat (e.g. density of logs, tree size density, plant species diversity) | ICMM | S/P | *As above* |
| Extent and condition of aquatic habitats (e.g. water depth, vegetation cover abundance / composition, dissolved oxygen, invertebrate taxa composition / abundance | ICMM | S/P | *As above* |
| Soil condition and nutrient cycling (e.g. nutrient levels, soil infiltration rate, depth of litter layer, ecosystem function analysis) | ICMM | S/P | *Linkage to biodiversity features not very clear* |
| Nutrient conditions of aquatic habitats | ICMM | P | |
| Significant (extinct, endangered, vulnerable, or otherwise threatened) species and communities (flora and fauna) e.g. number of species or area of communities | ICMM | S | *Vague and difficult to measure* |
| Microclimate | ICMM | P | *Linkage to biodiversity features not very clear* |
| Terrestrial, marine, estuarine and wetland protected areas (e.g. hectares or funds committed to management) | GRI, ICMM | Ra | |
| Recovery plans (e.g. ratio of plans for significant species to number of significant species) | ICMM | Ra | *Low value unless actions are reported* |
| Pest plant and animal plans (e.g. implementation of pest management plans, area of weeds controlled) | ICMM | Ra | |
| Rehabilitation plans (e.g. area revegetated, number of new species recorded since implementation) | ICMM | Ra | |
| Extent of area by forest type relative to total forest area | MP | S | |

| GUIDANCE / INDICATOR | SOURCE | TYPE | COMMENTS |
|---|---|---|---|
| Extent of area by forest type and by age class or successional stage | MP | S | |
| Extent of area by forest type in protected area categories as defined by IUCN2 or other classification systems | MP | P | |
| Extent of areas by forest type in protected areas defined by age class or successional stage | MP | P | |
| Fragmentation of forest types | MP | P/S | |
| The number of forest dependent species | MP | S | *Vague and difficult to measure* |
| The status (threatened, rare, vulnerable, endangered, or extinct) of forest dependent species at risk of not maintaining viable breeding populations, as determined by legislation or scientific assessment | MP | S | *As above* |
| Number of forest dependent species that occupy a small portion of their former range | MP | S | *As above* |
| Population levels of representative species from diverse habitats monitored across their range | MP | S | *Need to be linked to objectives* |
| Percent change in number of threatened species in each IUCN Red List category, number of species downlisted, and number | CI | S | *Dependent on many factors and other organizations* |
| Percentage improvement towards achieving downlisting of each threatened species, concentrating on rates of decline, starting with Critically Endangered Species | CI | S | *Difficult to measure, and dependent on many factors and organizations* |
| Percentage and total number of all Key Biodiversity Areas that are protected with (a) legal recognition and (b) biodiversity conservation as an official goal | CI | S | *Dependent on many factors and other organizations* |
| Percentage change in habitat cover at Key Biodiversity Areas | CI | S | *Does not take into account habitat quality* |

**TABLE 22.4**
*continued*

(Continued)

| TABLE 22.4 | GUIDANCE / INDICATOR | SOURCE | TYPE | COMMENTS |
|---|---|---|---|---|
| *continued* | Change in fragmentation statistics | CI | S | |
| | Percentage change in suitable habitat cover for corridor-level species | CI | S | |

TABLE KEY:

GRI 2002 = GRI Sustainability Reporting Indicators; c = core indicator, a = additional
ICMM 2005 = ICMM Good Practice Guidance for Mining and Biodiversity
MP = Montreal Process biological diversity indicators for the conservation and sustainable management of temperate and boreal forests
CI = Conservation International's Outcome Monitoring Indicators
S = State of biodiversity (direct indicator of biodiversity)
P = pressure
R = response Indicator
a = activities
p = processes

*Source:* Rio Tinto and Earthwatch 2006, pp. 31-33

| TABLE 22.5 | ENVIRONMENTAL SERVICE | PRIMARY FOREST | | | SECONDARY FOREST | | |
|---|---|---|---|---|---|---|---|
| *Costa Rican Payment for Ecological Services* | **$/hectare** | **min** | **med** | **max** | **min** | **med** | **max** |
| | Carbon sequestration | 19 | 38 | 57 | 14.63 | 29.26 | 43.89 |
| | Protection of water | 2.5 | 5 | 7.5 | 1.25 | 2.5 | 3.75 |
| | Biodiversity protection | 5 | 10 | 15 | 3.75 | 7.5 | 11.25 |
| | Ecosystem protection | 2.5 | 5 | 7.5 | 1.25 | 2.5 | 3.75 |
| | TOTAL | 29 | 58 | 87 | 20.88 | 41.76 | 62.64 |

*Source:* Castro et al. 2000, p. 82
Reproduced with the permission of Environmental Monitoring & Assessment.

across all sectors (for example, forestry, agriculture, water resources, etc.) have identified over 300 programs worldwide with a value in excess of $6.5 billion (OECD 2010). The UN FAO (2007) and Landell-Mills and Porras (2002) list five principal components of forest sector PES programs (in order of size): carbon sequestration, biodiversity conservation, watershed protection, landscape beauty, and bundled services. The payment for ecosystem services is an archetypal example of the successful application of Coase's Theorem [see chapter 5] where a private exchange between two parties addresses an environmental issue to the satisfaction of both parties (Engel et al. 2008; Farley and Costanza 2010). Wunder et al. (2008) provide one of the most comprehensive analyses of global PES programs: their characteristics, location, design features, payments, factors affecting effectiveness, efficiency, and welfare effects.

## CITED REFERENCES AND RECOMMENDED READINGS

Bishop, Joshua et al. (2008) *Building Biodiversity. Business*. Shell Oil and International Union for Conservation of Nature (IUNC) London and Gland, Switzerland.

Bowyer, Jim L. (2008) "The Green Movement and the Forest Products Industry," *Forest Product Journal*, Vol. 58, No. 7/8, July/August, pp. 7–13.

British Columbia (BC) Ministry of Environment (2011) *Protocol for the Creation of Forest Carbon Offsets in British Columbia*, August 12, Victoria, BC.

Canada Green Building Council (CAGBC) (2010) "Chain of Custody for Certified Wood Products within LEED Canada," Ottawa [http://www.cagbc.org/AM/PDF/FAQ_Certified_Wood_in_LEED_June_2010.pdf].

Castro, Rene et al. (2000) "The Costa Rican Experience with Market Instruments to Mitigate Climate Change and Conserve Biodiversity," *Environmental Monitoring and Assessment*, 61, pp. 75–92.

Climate Action Reserve (CAR) (2010) *Forest Project Protocol for Board Approval*, Version 3.2, Los Angeles, CA, August 20.

Coady, Linda (2002) "Iisaak: A New Economic Model for Conservation-Based Forestry in Coastal Old Growth Forests, B.C.," in Peter N. Nemetz (ed.) *Bringing Business on Board: Sustainable Development and the B-School Curriculum*, Vancouver, BC: JBA Press, pp. 561–576.

Conroy, Michael E. (2007) *Branded! How the Certification Revolution is Transforming Global Corporations*, Gabriola Island, BC: New Society Publishers.

Conservation International (n.d.) *Monitoring Support Program: Monitoring for Conservation Planning and Management*, Arlington, VA.

Dauvergne, Peter and Jane Lister (2010) "The Prospects and Limits of Eco-Consumerism: Shopping Our Way to Less Deforestation?" *Organization & Environment*, 23(2), pp. 132–154.

Earthwatch (2000) *Case Studies in Business & Biodiversity*, Oxford.

Earthwatch (n.d.) *Engaging Businesses with Biodiversity. Guidelines for Local Biodiversity Partnerships*, Oxford.

Earthwatch, International Union for Conservation of Nature (IUCN) and World Business Council for Sustainable Development (2002) *Business & Biodiversity: The Handbook for Corporate Action*, Oxford.

Ecosystemmarktplace (2009) *State of Biodiversity Markets. Offset and Compensation Programs Worldwide*, Washington, DC [www.ecosystemmarketplace.com].

Ecosystemmarktplace (2010a) *Update. State of Biodiversity Markets. Offset and Compensation Programs Worldwide*, Washington, DC [www.ecosystemmarketplace.com].

Ecosystemmarktplace (2010b) *State of the Forest Carbon Markets 2009: Taking Root and Branching Out*, Washington, DC [www.ecosystemmarketplace.com].

Ecosystemmarktplace (2010c) *Building Bridges: State of the Voluntary Carbon Markets 2010*, Washington, DC [www.ecosystemmarketplace.com].

Engel, Stefanie et al. (2008) "Designing Payments for Environmental Services in Theory and Practice: An Overview of the Issues," *Ecological Economics*, 65, pp. 663–674.

European Environment Agency (2012) *Streamlining European biodiversity indicators 2020: Building a future on lessons learnt from the SEBI 2010 process*, EEA Technical report No. 11, Copenhagen.

Food and Agriculture Organization (FAO), UNDP, UNEP (2008) *UN Collaborative Programme on Reducing Emissions from Deforestation and Forest Degradation in Developing Countries (UN-REDD)*. Framework Document, June 20.

Food and Agriculture Organization (FAO), UNDP, UNEP (2010) *The UN-REDD Programme Strategy 2011–2015*.

F&C Management Ltd. (2004) *Is Biodiversity a Material Risk for Companies? An Assessment of the Exposure of FTSE Sectors to Biodiversity Risk*, Edinburgh, UK.

Farley, Joshua and Robert Costanza (2010) "Payments for Ecosystem Service: From Local to Global," *Ecological Economics*, 69, pp. 2060–2068.

Forest Trends, Conservation International and Wildlife Conservation Society (2009a) *Business, Biodiversity Offsets and BBOP: An Overview*, Washington, DC.

Forest Trends, Conservation International and Wildlife Conservation Society (2009b) *Biodiversity Offset Cost-Benefit Handbook*, Washington, DC.

Forest Trends, Conservation International and Wildlife Conservation Society (2009c) *Biodiversity Offset Design Handbook*, Washington, DC.

Forest Trends, Conservation International and Wildlife Conservation Society (2009d) *Biodiversity Offset Implementation Handbook*, Washington, DC.

Forest Trends, Conservation International and Wildlife Conservation Society (2009e) *BBOP Pilot Project Case Study. Bainbridge Island*, Washington, DC.

Forest Trends, Conservation International and Wildlife Conservation Society (2009f) *BBOP Pilot Project Case Study. The Ambatovy Project*, Washington, DC.

Forest Trends, Conservation International and Wildlife Conservation Society (2009g) *BBOP Pilot Project Case Study. Akyem Gold Mining Project, Eastern Region, Ghana*, Washington, DC.

Germain, Rene H. and Patrick C. Penfield (2010) "The Potential Certified Wood Supply Chain Bottleneck and Its Impact on Leadership in Energy and Environmental Design Construction Projects in New York State," *Forest Products Journal*, 80(2), pp. 114–118.

Global Reporting Initiative (GRI) (2002) *Sustainability Reporting Guidelines*, Amsterdam. [https://www.globalreporting.org/resourcelibrary/G3.1-Guidelines-Incl-Technical-Protocol.pdf].

Global Reporting Initiative (GRI) (2007) *Biodiversity. A GRI Reporting Resource*, Amsterdam.

Global Reporting Initiative (GRI) (2006/2007) *Global Reporting Initiative. Sustainability Report*, Amsterdam.

Gullison, R.E. (2003) "Does Forest Certification Conserve Biodiversity?" *Oryx*, 37(2), pp. 153–165.

Hansen, Eric and John Puncher (1998) "Collins Pine: Lessons from a Pioneer. Case study." Oregon State University.

Home Depot website (www.homedepot.com).

International Council on Mining & Metals (ICMM) (2010) *Mining and Biodiversity: A Collection of Case Studies—2010 edition*, London.

International Council on Mining & Metals (ICMM) (n.d.) *Good Practice Guidance for Mining and Biodiversity*, London.

International Ecotourism Society (TIES) (2006) *TIES Global Ecotourism Fact Sheet*, Washington, DC, September.

International Ecotourism Society (2005) *Consumer Demand and Operator Support for Socially and Environmentally Responsible Tourism*, Washington, DC.

International Institute for Environment and Development (IIED) (2001) "Pro-Poor Tourism: Harnessing the World's Largest Industry for the World's Poor," *Opinion*, London, May, pp. 1–8.

International Organization for Standardization (ISO) (2006) *ISO 14064–2 Greenhouse Gases—Part 2: Specification with Guidance at the Project Level for Quantification, Monitoring and Reporting of Greenhouse Gas Emission Reductions or Removal Enhancements*, Geneva.

International Union for Conservation of Nature (IUCN) (2004) *Biodiversity Offsets: Views, Experience, and the Business Case*, Gland, Switzerland.

Intergovernmental Panel on Climate Change (IPCC) (2006) *Guidelines for National Greenhouse Gas Inventories*, Volume 4, Chapter 4, "Forest Land," Geneva.

Jack B. Kelsey et al. (2008) "Designing Payments for Ecosystem Services: Lessons from Previous Experience with Incentive-Based Mechanisms" *PNAS*, 105(28), July 15, pp. 9465–9470.

Jacquet, Jennifer et al. (2010) "Seafood Stewardship in Crisis," *Nature*, 467(2), pp. 28–29.

Katoomba Group, UNEP and Forest Trends (2008) *Payment for Ecosystem Services: Getting Started. A Primer*, Nairobi. [http://www.unep.org/pdf/PaymentsForEcosystemServices_en.pdf]

KPMG LLP, Fauna & Flora International and ACCA (2012) *Is Natural capital a Material Issue? An evaluation of the relevance of biodiversity and ecosystem services to accountancy professionals and the private sector.*

Kumar, Pushpam and Roidan Murdian (2008) *Payment for Ecosystem Services*, Oxford: Oxford University Press.

Landell-Mills, Natasha and Ina. T. Porras (2002) *Silver Bullet or Fools' Gold? A Global Review of Markets for Forest Environmental Services and Their Impact on the Poor*, International Institute for Environment and Development (IIED), London.

Lister, Jane (2011) *Corporate Social Responsibility and the State: International Approaches to Forest Co-Regulation*, Vancouver, BC: UBC Press.

Miljoeko A.B. and SustainAbility (2000) *Screening of Screening Companies*. Socially Responsible Investment, SRI, Report prepared for MISTRA, The Foundation for Strategic Environmental Research, Stockholm.

National Academy of Sciences (2010) *Certifiably Sustainable? The Role of Third-Party Certification Systems*. Report of a workshop, Washington, DC.

National Environmental Research Institute, Denmark (NERI) (1995) *Nature Indicators Survey*.

Organization for Economic Co-operation and Development (OECD) (2001) *Valuation of Biodiversity Benefits. Selected Studies*, Paris.

Organization for Economic Co-operation and Development (OECD) (2002) *Handbook of Biodiversity Valuation. A Guide for Policy Makers*, Paris.

Organization for Economic Co-operation and Development (OECD) (2003) *Harnessing Markets for Biodiversity. Towards Conservation and Sustainable Use*, Paris.

Organization for Economic Co-operation and Development (OECD) (2004) *Handbook of Market Creation for Biodiversity: Issues in Implementation*, Paris.

Organization for Economic Co-operation and Development (OECD) (2010) *Paying for Biodiversity: Enhancing the Cost-Effectiveness of Payments for Ecosystem Services*, Paris.

Rio Tinto and Earthwatch (2006) *A Review of Biodiversity Conservation Performance Measures*, Oxford.

Secretariat of the Convention on Biological Diversity (CBD) (2006) *Global Biodiversity Outlook 2*, Montreal.

Secretariat of the Convention on Biological Diversity (CBD) (2010) *Global Biodiversity Outlook 3*, Montreal.

Smith, James E. et al. (2005) *Methods for Calculating Forest Ecosystem and Harvested Carbon with Standard Estimates for Forest Types of the United States*, USDA, Northeastern Research Station, General Technical Report NE-343.

SustainAbility (2011a) *Signed, Sealed . . . Delivered? Behind Certifications and Beyond Limits*, Washington, DC.

SustainAbility (2011b) *Rate the Raters. Phase Four. The Necessary Future of Ratings*, Washington, DC, July.

SustainAbility and Mistra (2004) Values for Money. *Reviewing the Quality of SRI Research*, London.

TerraChoice (2010) *The Sins of Greenwashing*. Home and Family Edition, Ottawa, ON.

UN Food and Agriculture Organization (FAO) (2007) *The State of Food and Agriculture 2007*, Rome.

UN World Tourism Organization (WTO) (2010) UNWTO *World Tourism Barometer*, 8(3), October.

United Nations Economic Commission for Europe (UNECE) (2011) *Forest Products Annual Market Review 2010–2011*.

Wertz-Kanounnikoff, Sheila (2006) "Payments for Environmental Services—a Solution for Biodiversity Conservation?" *Ressources Naturelles*, 12, pp. 1–16.

Williams, Michael (2006) *Deforesting the Earth. From Prehistory to Global Crisis*, Chicago: University of Chicago Press.

World Business Council for Sustainable Development (WBCSD) and World Resources Institute (WRI) (2005) *The GHG Protocol for Project Accounting*, Geneva.

World Resources Institute (WRI) (2005) *Ecosystems and Human Well-Being: Biodiversity Synthesis*. Millennium Ecosystem Assessment, Washington, DC.

Wunder, Sven (2005) *Payments for Environmental Services: Some Nuts and Bolts*. Centre for International Forestry Research (CIFOR), Jakarta, Occasional paper No. 42.

Wunder, Sven et al. (2008) "Taking Stock: A Comparative Analysis of Payments for Environmental Services Programs in Developed and Developing Countries," *Ecological Economics*, 65, pp. 834–852.

www.Carbontradeexchange.com [website for Carbon Trade Exchange (CTX)].

www.Ecotourism.org [website for International Ecotourism Society].

www.fscoax.org/principal.htm [website for Greenpeace International]

www.usgb.org [website for U.S. Green Building Council].

Yuan, Yuan and Ivan Eastin (2007) "Forest Certification and Its Influence on the Forest Products Industry in China," Center for International Trade in Forest Products (CINTRAFOR), Seattle, WA, Working Paper 110, December.

## APPENDIX

# Leadership in Energy and Environmental Design (LEED)

LEED is a third party certification program and the nationally accepted benchmark for the design, construction and operation of high performance green buildings. Developed by the U.S. Green Building Council in 2000 through a consensus based process, LEED serves as a tool for buildings of all types and sizes. LEED certification offers third party validation of a project's green features and verifies that the building is operating exactly the way it was designed to. LEED certification is available for all building types including new construction and major renovation; existing buildings; commercial interiors; core and shell; schools and homes. LEED systems for neighborhood development, retail and healthcare are currently pilot testing. To date, there is over 4.5 billion square feet of construction space involved with the LEED system. LEED is a point based system where building projects earn LEED points for satisfying specific green building criteria. Within each of the seven LEED credit categories, projects must satisfy particular prerequisites and earn points. The five categories include Sustainable Sites (SS), Water Efficiency (WE), Energy and Atmosphere (EA), Materials and Resources (MR) and Indoor Environmental Quality (IEQ). An additional category, Innovation in Design (ID), addresses sustainable building expertise as well as design measures not covered under the five environmental categories. The number of points the project earns determines the level of LEED certification the project receives. LEED certification is available in four progressive levels according to the following scale: There are 100 base points; 6 possible Innovation in Design and 4 Regional Priority points: Certified 40–49 points, Silver 50–59 points, Gold 60–79 points, Platinum 80 points and above" (http://www.usgbc.org/DisplayPage.aspx?CMSPageID=1991).

# CHAPTER 23

# *Case Study of Suncor, Inc.*

L OCATED IN NORTHERN ALBERTA, Canada, Suncor is a leading producer of synthetic crude oil extracted from large oil sand deposits. This company and other oil sands producers have assumed particular importance because they sit on massive petroleum deposits rivaling those of Saudi Arabia and because they offer an unique opportunity for the United States to access large supplies of oil from a friendly neighbor with minimal risk from disruption due to political, social, or military factors. Tables 23.11 and 23.12 in Appendix 1 contain historical data on Suncor and the other major oil sands producers.

The company originally began exploiting the oil sands in the mid-1960s under the name of Great Canadian Oil Sands Ltd. Corporate profitability is directly related to global petroleum prices, so prospects for the large-scale development of the oil sands had to await the run-up in prices within the last two decades. Figure 23–1 shows the recent history of global oil prices, and Figure 23–2 shows the correlation between Suncor's stock price and oil prices. The raw material, called bitumen, is contained in a sand matrix that has been extracted in a manner similar to conventional strip mining and heated with reactants to create synthetic crude. This process relies on extensive use of natural gas (approximately 750 cu ft per barrel of bitumen) in order to provide the fuel for this energy-intensive technology (Alberta Chamber of Resources 2004). Since most of the deposits of bitumen are inaccessible by conventional mining techniques, the oil sands industry has also invested large sums of capital into developing an alternative method of extraction called *in situ* mining. This alternative recovery process can access deeper deposits by drilling holes into the underground strata and using large quantities of heated water and reagents to force the bitumen to the surface. This process is estimated to require approximately 1,500 cu ft of natural gas per barrel of bitumen (Alberta Chamber of Resources 2004).

The advent of higher priced oil permitted the development of the oil sands that, because of their nature, are considerably more expensive to exploit than conventional crude oil. For traditional investors, Suncor has proven a very productive investment as illustrated by its stock price history reproduced in Figure 23–3. With four stock splits over the period from 1997 to 2008, an initial investment of $22.62 per share in December 1993 would have yielded an equivalent $1,167.20 in May 2008 just prior to the U.S. financial crisis. While the company has a history of extracting other energy resources such as conventional oil and natural gas, it made a strategic decision in late 2009 to shift its principal focus to the continued development and expansion of its oil sands operations. The rationale for this shift is apparent from the five-year financial highlights reproduced in Table 23–1.

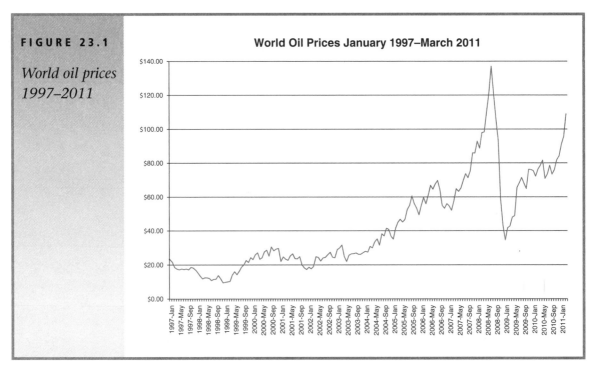

**FIGURE 23.1**

*World oil prices 1997–2011*

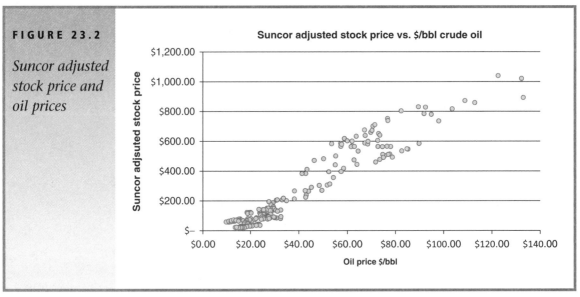

**FIGURE 23.2**

*Suncor adjusted stock price and oil prices*

The corporation has been listed in at least four sustainability indexes: the Dow Jones Sustainability Index for North America, the TD Global Sustainability Fund, the Corporate Knight's 2010 Report on Clean Capitalism, and the *Fortune* list of green giants. The oil sands industry has recently begun a public relations campaign to label its output as "ethical oil" to contrast it with petroleum from other nations with dubious social and political policies that impact human rights (*New York Times* 2011). A major impetus for this campaign is to counter emerging concerns in both Europe and the United States about the environmental impacts of petroleum produced from the oil sands (*New York Times* 2010a; Canada.com 2011).

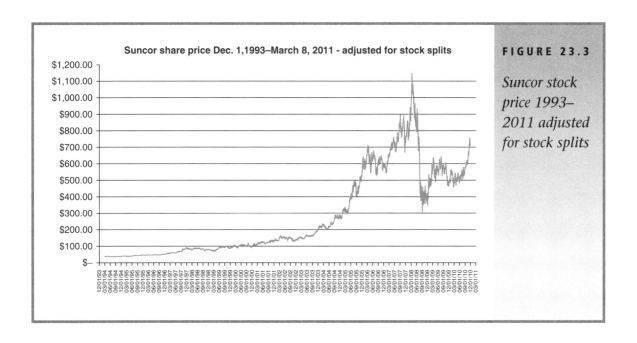

**FIGURE 23.3**

*Suncor stock price 1993–2011 adjusted for stock splits*

| ($ millions) | 2010 | 2009 | 2008 | 2007 | 2006 |
|---|---|---|---|---|---|
| **Revenues from continuing operations** | | | | | |
| Oil Sands | **9 423** | 6 539 | 8 639 | 6 175 | 6 457 |
| Natural Gas | **734** | 423 | 364 | 284 | 313 |
| International and Offshore | **4 323** | 1 217 | — | — | — |
| Refining and Marketing | **21 062** | 11 851 | 9 258 | 8 220 | 7 174 |
| Corporate and eliminations | **(1 192)** | 4818 | 10 185 | 2 492 | 894 |
| | **34 350** | 24 848 | 28 446 | 17 171 | 14 838 |
| **Net earnings (loss) from continuing operations** | | | | | |
| Oil Sands | **1 492** | 557 | 2 875 | 2 474 | 2 775 |
| Natural Gas | **(277)** | (185) | 34 | 7 | 78 |
| International and Offshore | **1 114** | 323 | — | — | — |
| Refining and Marketing | **801** | 407 | (22) | 406 | 227 |
| Corporate and eliminations | **(442)** | 104 | (805) | 78 | (139) |
| | **2 688** | 1 206 | 2 082 | 2 965 | 2 941 |
| **Cash flow from (used in) operations** | | | | | |
| Oil Sands | **2 769** | 1 251 | 3 507 | 3 165 | 3 902 |
| Natural Gas | **445** | 329 | 367 | 251 | 279 |
| International and Offshore | **2 879** | 951 | — | — | — |

**TABLE 23.1**

*Suncor GHG emissions*

| | | | | | |
|---|---|---|---|---|---|
| **TABLE 23.1** *continued* Refining and Marketing | **1 536** | 921 | 220 | 660 | 422 |
| Corporate and eliminations | **(973)** | (653) | (37) | (39) | (57) |
| | **6 656** | 2 799 | 4 057 | 4 037 | 4 546 |
| **Capital and exploration expenditures** | | | | | |
| Oil Sands | **3 709** | 2 831 | 7 413 | 4 566 | 2 463 |
| Natural Gas | **178** | 320 | 342 | 537 | 458 |
| International and Offshore | **1 096** | 666 | — | — | — |
| Refining and Marketing | **667** | 380 | 207 | 351 | 747 |
| Corporate | **360** | 70 | 58 | 175 | 27 |
| | **6 010** | 4 267 | 8 020 | 5 629 | 3 695 |
| **Total assets** | **70 169** | 69 746 | 32 528 | 24 509 | 18 959 |

*Source:* U.S. Securities and Exchange Commission, submission by Suncor of form 40-f, exhibit 99-1 for fiscal year ending December 31, 2010

As indicated in Figures 23–4, the process of upgrading bitumen to synthetic crude oil has numerous environmental impacts in addition to land disturbance from the removal of boreal forest and soil overlaying the deposits. Emissions of $SO_2$ (23,398 tonnes), NOx (12,390 tonnes), and greenhouse gases (GHG) (10,267,989 tonnes) (as well as water use) are greater on a per barrel basis than those associated with conventional petroleum recovery (see Figure 23–5 and NPRI 2012). Table 23–2 shows the predominant role of oil sands production and processing in Suncor's total corporate-level greenhouse gas emissions.

In addition, the oil sands process produces large quantities of wastewater contaminated with toxic pollutants that require storage in large tailings ponds for lengthy periods of time to facilitate settling and evaporation. Canada's National Pollutant Release Inventory (NPRI)—the equivalent of the American Toxic Release inventory—lists several dozen pollutants of concern [see Table 23–3]. There is continuing debate over the existence and severity of leakage from the tailings ponds as well as downwind deposition of pollutants that can influence water quality, aquatic biota, and possibly the health of aboriginals in downstream communities (Kelly et al. 2009 and 2010; Timoney and Lee 2009).

Suncor has major plans to expand its production over the next few years, and this is anticipated to raise levels of pollutant emissions in the future. With respect to GHG, Suncor's emissions ranked third in Canada in 2009 (Environment Canada 2011). The combined GHG emissions of all oil sands producers in this region of Alberta exceed the largest point source of GHG in the United States from Georgia Power's Scherer plant, which emitted 27 million tons in 2007 (EPA 2011) and Europe's largest, PGE Elektrownia Belschatow S.A, in Rogowiec, Poland, at 29.5 million tonnes of $CO_2$. The oil sands emissions are expected to increase by as much as 62 million tons by 2020 as expansion of current operations continues and new oil

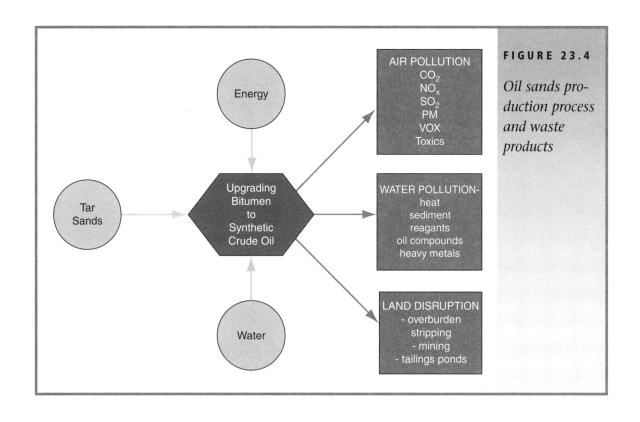

FIGURE 23.4

*Oil sands pro-*
*duction process*
*and waste*
*products*

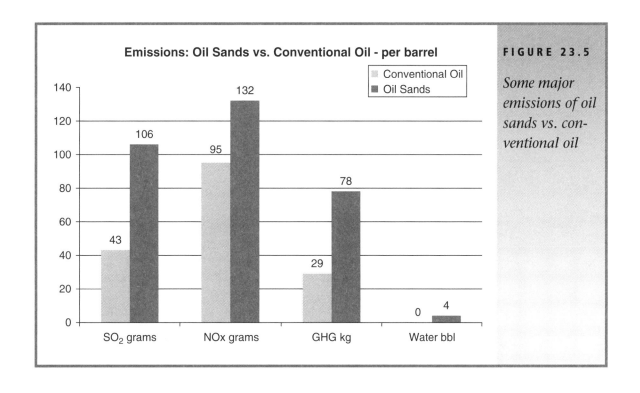

FIGURE 23.5

*Some major*
*emissions of oil*
*sands vs. con-*
*ventional oil*

| TABLE 23.2 | REPORTING COMPANY | FACILITY | CITY | PROVINCE | GHG (TONNES $CO_2E$) |
|---|---|---|---|---|---|
| *Suncor GHG emissions* | Suncor Energy Oil Sands Limited Partnership | Suncor Energy Inc. Oil Sands | Fort McMurray | Alberta | 8,554,881 |
| | Suncor Energy Oil Sands Limited Partnership | Firebag | Ft. McMurray | Alberta | 1,568,206 |
| | Suncor Energy Inc. | Edmonton Refinery | Edmonton | Alberta | 1,322,115 |
| | Suncor Energy Inc. | Raffinerie de Montreal | Montreal | Quebec | 1,228,247 |
| | Suncor Energy Products Inc. | Sarnia Refinery | Sarnia | Ontario | 612,189 |
| | Suncor Energy Inc. | Terra Nova | St. John's | NFLD | 604,227 |
| | Suncor Energy Oil and Gas Partnership | Hanlan Robb Gas Plant | Edson | Alberta | 321,799 |
| | Suncor Energy Oil Sands Limited Partnership | MacKay River, In-Situ Oil Sands Plant | Fort McMurray | Alberta | 144,902 |
| | Suncor Energy Products Inc. | St. Clair Ethanol Plant | Mooretown | Ontario | 82,259 |
| | Suncor Energy Oil and Gas Partnership | Ferrier Gas Plant | Rocky Mountain House | Alberta | 51,974 |
| | | | COMPANY TOTAL | | 14,490,799 |
| | | | OIL SANDS SUBTOTAL | | 10,267,989 |

sands production comes online (Environment Canada 2011; Office of the Auditor General of Canada 2012, chapter 2, p. 45).

Suncor is extremely sensitive to concerns over the environmental impacts of its operations and the public reaction thereto, since these impacts are a potential threat to both current and future markets for Suncor's synthetic crude as well as a possible threat to the company's license to operate. A large degree of negative international publicity resulted from the recent death of several hundred ducks that had landed on the surface of the tailings ponds of another major oil sands producer, Syncrude Ltd. (*New York Times* 2010b). Oil sands tailings ponds, some as high as 300 feet above the adjacent Athabasca River, currently cover over 170 sq km, of which

**TABLE 23.3**

*Major Water Pollutants from Suncor*

| SUBSTANCE | ON-SITE RELEASES | | | | DISPOSAL | UNITS |
|---|---|---|---|---|---|---|
| | AIR | WATER | LAND | TOTAL | ON-SITE | |
| 1,2,4-Trimethylbenzene | 518 | - | - | 518 | - | tonnes |
| 2-Butoxyethanol | - | - | - | - | - | tonnes |
| 7H-Dibenzo(c,g)carbazole - PAH | 823 | - | - | 823 | - | kg |
| Acenaphthene - PAH | 8.8 | - | - | 8.8 | 8,194 | kg |
| Acenaphthylene - PAH | 2.5 | - | - | 2.5 | 0 | kg |
| Aluminum oxide (fibrous forms) | - | - | - | - | - | tonnes |
| Ammonia (total) | 2.6 | 0.322 | - | 2.9 | 1,565 | tonnes |
| Arsenic (and its compounds) | 45 | 18 | - | 63 | 145,538 | kg |
| Benzene | 81 | - | - | 81 | 4.6 | tonnes |
| Benzo(a)anthracene - PAH | - | - | - | - | 3,534 | kg |
| Benzo(a)phenanthrene - PAH | 2.9 | - | - | 2.9 | 29,844 | kg |
| Benzo(a)pyrene - PAH | 0.246 | - | - | 0.246 | 2,257 | kg |
| Benzo(b)fluoranthene - PAH | 0.907 | - | - | 0.907 | 2,998 | kg |
| Benzo(e)pyrene - PAH | 0.556 | - | - | 0.556 | 7,107 | kg |
| Benzo(g,h,i)perylene - PAH | 0.344 | - | - | 0.344 | 2,497 | kg |
| Benzo(j)fluoranthene - PAH | - | - | - | - | 2,998 | kg |

| SUBSTANCE | ON-SITE RELEASES | | | | DISPOSAL OFF-SITE | | UNITS |
|---|---|---|---|---|---|---|---|
| | AIR | WATER | LAND | TOTAL | ON-SITE | RECYCLING | |
| Ethylene | 17 | - | - | 17 | - | - | tonnes |
| Ethylene glycol | - | - | - | - | - | - | tonnes |
| Fluoranthene - PAH | 2 | - | - | 2 | 3,509 | - | kg |
| Fluorene - PAH | 11 | - | - | 11 | 4,182 | - | kg |
| Formaldehyde | 8 | - | - | 8 | - | - | tonnes |
| Hexachlorobenzene | - | - | - | - | - | - | grams |
| Hydrogen sulphide | 727 | - | - | 727 | - | - | tonnes |
| Indeno(1,2,3-c,d)pyrene - PAH | 0.252 | - | - | 0.252 | 1,268 | - | kg |
| Isopropyl alcohol | - | - | - | - | - | - | tonnes |
| Lead (and its compounds) | 495 | 11 | - | 507 | 345,782 | 29,361 | kg |
| Manganese (and its compounds) | 0.297 | 0.705 | - | 1 | 7,803 | 0 | tonnes |
| Mercury (and its compounds) | 45 | - | - | - | - | 1.6 | kg |
| Methanol | - | - | - | - | - | - | tonnes |
| Molybdenum trioxide | - | - | - | - | - | 155 | tonnes |
| n-Hexane | 273 | - | - | 273 | - | - | tonnes |
| Nickel (and its compounds) | 0.6 | 0.768 | - | 1.4 | 831 | 26 | tonnes |

**TABLE 23.3** *continued*

| SUBSTANCE | ON-SITE RELEASES | | | | DISPOSAL | UNITS |
| | AIR | WATER | LAND | TOTAL | ON-SITE | |
|---|---|---|---|---|---|---|
| Benzo(k) fluoranthene - PAH | 0.233 | - | - | 0.233 | 11 | kg |
| Cadmium (and its compounds) | 78 | 5.1 | - | 83 | 1,447 | kg |
| Carbon disulphide | 65 | - | - | 65 | - | tonnes |
| Carbonyl sulphide | 45 | - | - | 45 | - | tonnes |
| Chromium (and its compounds) | 0.381 | 0.027 | - | 0.408 | 716 | tonnes |
| Cobalt (and its compounds) | 0.002 | 0.019 | - | 0.021 | 341 | tonnes |
| Copper (and its compounds) | 0.19 | 0.015 | - | 0.205 | 116 | tonnes |
| Cumene | 50 | - | - | 50 | - | tonnes |
| Cyclohexane | 225 | - | - | 225 | - | tonnes |
| Dibenzo(a,h)anthracene - PAH | 0.037 | - | - | 0.037 | 1,221 | kg |
| Diethanolamine (and its salts) | - | - | - | - | - | tonnes |
| Dioxins and furans - total | - | - | - | - | - | g TEQ |
| Ethylbenzene | 539 | - | - | 539 | 125 | tonnes |

| SUBSTANCE | ON-SITE RELEASES | | | | DISPOSAL OFF-SITE | | UNIT: |
| | AIR | WATER | LAND | TOTAL | ON-S E | RECYCLING | |
|---|---|---|---|---|---|---|---|
| Perylene - PAH | 0.138 | - | - | 0.138 | 8,196 | | kg |
| Phenanthrene - PAH | 26 | - | - | 26 | 28,433 | | kg |
| Phenol (and its salts) | 0.185 | - | - | 0.185 | 283 | | tonnes |
| Phosphorus (total) | - | 0.389 | - | 0.389 | 4,052 | | tonnes |
| Propylene | 75 | - | - | 75 | - | | tonnes |
| Pyrene - PAH | 5.1 | - | - | 5.1 | 15,963 | | kg |
| Sulphuric acid | 258 | - | - | 258 | - | | tonnes |
| Toluene | 1,428 | - | 0 | 1,428 | 174 | | tonnes |
| Total Reduced Sulphur (TRS) *** | 1,144 | - | - | 1,144 | - | | tonnes |
| Vanadium (except when in an alloy) and its compounds | 1.7 | 3.1 | - | 4.8 | 878 | | tonnes |
| Xylene (all isomers) | 2,803 | - | - | 2,803 | 572 | | tonnes |
| Zinc (and its compounds) | 0.743 | 0.058 | - | 0.801 | 434 | 0.148 | tonnes |

*Source:* NPRI

| CODE | METRIC | INCLUDED | NOT INCLUDED |
|------|--------|----------|--------------|
| EC1 | Direct economic value generated and distributed, including revenues, operating costs, employee compensation, donations and other community investments, retained earnings, and payments to capital providers and governments. | X | |
| EC2 | Financial implications and other risks and opportunities for the organization's activities due to climate change. | p | |
| EC4 | Significant financial assistance received from government. | X | |
| EC5 | Range of ratios of standard entry level wage by gender compared to local minimum wage at significant locations of operation. | X | |
| EC6 | Policy, practices, and proportion of spending on locally-based suppliers at significant locations of operation. | X | |
| EC7 | Procedures for local hiring and proportion of senior management hired from the local community at locations of significant operation | p | |
| EC8 | Development and impact of infrastructure investments and services provided primarily for public benefit through commercial, in-kind, or pro bono engagement. | X | |
| EC9 | Understanding and describing significant indirect economic impacts, including the extent of impacts. | | |
| EN1 | Materials used by weight or volume. | X | |
| EN2 | Percentage of materials used that are recycled input materials. | X | |
| EN3 | Direct energy consumption by primary energy source. | X | |
| EN4 | Indirect energy consumption by primary source. | X | |
| EN5 | Energy saved due to conservation and efficiency improvements. | X | |
| EN6 | Initiatives to provide energy-efficient or renewable energy based products and services, and reductions in energy requirements as a result of these initiatives. | X | |
| EN7 | Initiatives to reduce indirect energy consumption and reductions achieved. | | X |
| EN8 | Total water withdrawal by source. | X | |
| EN9 | Water sources significantly affected by withdrawal of water. | X | X |
| EN10 | Percentage and total volume of water recycled and reused. | | X |
| EN11 | Location and size of land owned, leased, managed in, or adjacent to, protected areas and areas of high biodiversity value outside protected areas. | X | |

**TABLE 23.4**

*GRI Indicators Reported by Suncor*

continued

| TABLE 23.4 *continued* | CODE | METRIC | INCLUDED | NOT INCLUDED |
|---|---|---|---|---|
| | EN12 | Description of significant impacts of activities, products, and services on biodiversity in protected areas and areas of high biodiversity value outside protected areas. | X | |
| | EN13 | Habitats protected or restored. | X | |
| | EN14 | Strategies, current actions, and future plans for managing impacts on biodiversity. | X | |
| | EN15 | Number of IUCN Red List species and national conservation list species with habitats in areas affected by operations, by level of extinction risk. | | X |
| | EN16 | Total direct and indirect greenhouse gas emissions by weight. | X | |
| | EN17 | Other relevant indirect greenhouse gas emissions by weight. | X | |
| | EN18 | nitiatives to reduce greenhouse gas emissions and reductions achieved. | X | |
| | EN19 | Emissions of ozone-depleting substances by weight. | X | |
| | EN20 | NO, SO, and other significant air emissions by type and weight. | X | |
| | EN21 | Total water discharge by quality and destination. | X | |
| | EN22 | Total weight of waste by type and disposal method. | X | |
| | EN23 | Total number and volume of significant spills. | | |
| | EN24 | Weight of transported, imported, exported, or treated waste deemed hazardous under the terms of the Basel Convention Annex I, II, III, and VIII, and percentage of transported waste shipped internationally. | | X |
| | EN25 | Identity, size, protected status, and biodiversity value of water bodies and related habitats significantly affected by the reporting organization's discharges of water and runoff. | p | |
| | EN26 | Initiatives to mitigate environmental impacts of products and services, and extent of impact mitigation. | p | |
| | EN27 | Percentage of products sold and their packaging materials that are reclaimed by category. | X | |
| | EN28 | Monetary value of significant fines and total number of non-monetary sanctions for noncompliance with environmental laws and regulations. | X | |
| | EN29 | Significant environmental impacts of transporting products and other goods and materials used for the organization's operations, and transporting members of the workforce. | | X |

*continued*

| CODE | METRIC | INCLUDED | NOT INCLUDED | **TABLE 23.4**<br>*continued* |
|------|--------|----------|--------------|--|
| EN30 | Total environmental protection expenditures and investments by type. | X | | |
| LA1 | Total workforce by employment type, employment contract, and region, broken down by gender. | X | | |
| LA2 | Total number and rate of new employee hires and employee turnover by age group, gender, and region. | X | | |
| LA3 | Benefits provided to full-time employees that are not provided to temporary or part-time employees, by significant locations of operation. | | | |
| LA4 | Percentage of employees covered by collective bargaining agreements. | X | | |
| LA5 | Minimum notice period(s) regarding operational changes, including whether it is specified in collective agreements | X | | |
| LA6 | Percentage of total workforce represented in formal joint management—worker health and safety committees that help monitor and advise on occupational health and safety programs. | X | | |
| LA7 | Rates of injury, occupational diseases, lost days, and absenteeism, and total number of work-related fatalities, by region and by gender. | X | | |
| LA8 | Education, training, counseling, prevention, and risk-control programs in place to assist workforce members, their families, or community members regarding serious diseases. | X | | |
| LA9 | Health and safety topics covered in formal agreements with trade unions | X | | |
| LA10 | Average hours of training per year per employee by gender, and by employee category. | X | | |
| LA12 | Percentage of employees receiving regular performance and career development reviews, by gender. | X | | |
| LA13 | Composition of governance bodies and breakdown of employees per employee category according to gender, age group, minority group membership, and other indicators of diversity | X | | |
| LA14 | Ratio of basic salary and remuneration of women to men by employee category, by significant locations of operation. | X | | |

*Note:* P = Partial

Suncor accounts for approximately 40 sq km (Grant et al. 2010; see also *National Geographic* 2009). It has been estimated that 6 cubic meters of tailings are created for every cubic meter of bitumen recovered (Griffiths 2006).

The company's public image is enhanced by its inclusion in several sustainability indexes cited above, and this inclusion appears to be based on corporate policies in a number of related areas. These include:

1. Use of the Global Reporting Initiative (GRI) G3 guidelines to structure their annual sustainability report. (See Table 23–4 for a list of the GRI performance indicators used by Suncor.)
2. The adoption of a triple bottom line approach to reporting corporate results.
3. The stated intention to restore land cover removed by stripping and mining. This is a complex operation, and the company has initiated a number of test projects in this area that had achieved a 0.2% level of restoration to 2010 (*Journal of Commerce* 2010).
4. An investment in at least two forms of alternative energy: (1) wind power totaling 255 MW (see Table 23–5 for Suncor's wind farm investment data). This investment has cost approximately $500 million; and (2) an ethanol plant in Ontario that was completed in 2006 at a cost of $120 million to produce 200 million liters of ethanol per year. In 2011, Suncor completed a $120 million expansion to increase the output to 400 million liters per year. Revenue from renewable energy was $33 million in 2010.
5. Participation in a number of carbon offsetting programs to compensate for a proportion of the greenhouse gases produced by operations. Wind power offsets currently equal 470,000 tons of $CO_2$eq. Suncor has also participated in the Rio Bravo

| TABLE 23.5 | WIND FARM | | OWNERSHIP INTEREST (%) | SIZE (MW) | TURBINES | COMMISSIONED |
|---|---|---|---|---|---|---|
| *Suncor Wind Farm Data* | Operated by Suncor | | | | | |
| | Wintering Hills | Drumheller, Alberta | 70.0 | 88 | 55 | 2011 |
| | Kent Breeze | Thamesville, Ontario | 100.0 | 20 | 8 | 2011 |
| | Non-operated | Ripley, Ontario | 50.0 | 76 | 38 | 2007 |
| | Ripley | Taber, Alberta | 33.3 | 30 | 20 | 2006 |
| | Chin Chute | Magrath, Alberta | 33.3 | 30 | 20 | 2004 |
| | Magrath | Gull Lake, Saskatchewan | 50.0 | 11 | 17 | 2002 |
| | SunBridge | | | | | |

*Source*: U.S. Securities and Exchange Commission, submission by Suncor of form 40-f, exhibit 99-1 for fiscal year ending December 31, 2010.

| FACTOR | MINING | SAGD |
|---|---|---|
| Overburden depth | < 75 m | > 150 m |
| Reserves (totals 27 million cubic meters; 170 billion bbl) | 20% | 80% |
| Crude bitumen production (total 238,000 cubic meters/ day; 1,500,000 bbl/day in 2009) | 55% | 45% |
| Recovery | > 90% | < 60% |
| Fresh water demand (cubic meters/ cubic meters of | 2 to 3 | ~0.5 |
| Carbon imprint (Kg $CO_2$ equiv/cubic meters SCO) | 820 | 1,100 |
| Direct land disturbance (ha/100,000 cubic meters) | 5.9 | 0.88 |
| Capital cost | high | moderate |

**TABLE 23.6**

*Comparison of Bitumen Production Using Open Pit Mining and In Situ Steam-Assisted Gravity Drainage Method*

*Source:* Gosselin et al. 2010, p. 51

Carbon Sequestration Project in Belize to prevent deforestation and institute sustainable forest management practices. Suncor estimates that its renewable energy initiatives will eventually offset as much as 1 million tons of GHG. Finally, the company is required by the Alberta government under its Specified Gas Emitters Regulation (SGER) to also purchase additional offset credits to comply with provincial requirements pertaining to emission intensity (Alberta Environment 2007). Part of the program sponsored by the government entails the purchase of tillage offsets designed to reduce the emission of carbon dioxide from agricultural practices. A recent report from the Alberta Auditor General (2011) raised concerns, however, about the lack of supporting documentation about the degree to which reduced tillage or no-tillage practices have been adopted. It was also suggested that this program may fail the test of *additionality* [see chapter 5], where eligible offsets must come from programs that are not common practice or required by law.

6. A commitment to hiring some local aboriginal labor as well as funding initiatives in local aboriginal communities in an attempt to increase standards of living and compensate for any loss of livelihood due to reductions in traditional employment associated with trapping, hunting, and fishing. Suncor has stated that in 2009 it spent $273 million on direct purchases from aboriginal businesses, and has bought over $1 billion worth of goods and services from these businesses since 1992, at an average of approximately $60 million per year (Suncor 2011).

7. A commitment to shift toward *in situ* recovery as conventional near-surface deposits are exhausted. The exploitation of these deeper deposits does not require the removal of vegetative cover and stripping of overburden but does entail significant disturbance to the integrity of the local ecosystem due to the large number of bore holes and related infrastructure (Schindler 2009).

8. A commitment to continue investing funds into new technological research to lower the GHG-intensity of synthetic oil. In this regard, a study based on data from the industry has reported a 39% drop in this intensity since 1990 (Gosselin et al. 2010). [See Figure 23–6.]

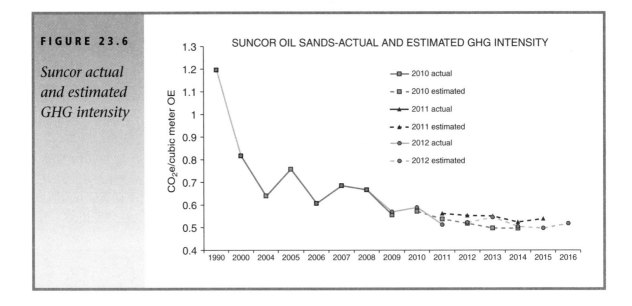

**FIGURE 23.6**

*Suncor actual and estimated GHG intensity*

9. A commitment to reduce water requirements of the production process that currently uses up to 5 barrels of water for every barrel of bitumen extracted (Pembina 2005). As of 2005, all oil sands operators were licensed to divert over 349 million cubic meters of water from the Athabasca River Basin in which the oils sands are located, and fully 90% of water withdrawals are ultimately diverted to tailing impoundments. The total withdrawals represent over 10% of low-flow volumes in the River (Pembina 2006).

10. A commitment by the industry to seek possible alternatives to the large-scale use of high-quality natural gas as an energy source in the production of synthetic crude. One alternative that has been considered is a possible nuclear power plant to provide both electricity and process heat (Dunbar and Sloan 2003; *Globe and Mail* 2005).

11. Plans to utilize currently experimental and largely unproven carbon capture and storage technology in the future in order to reduce its greenhouse gas emissions.

Additional information is provided in the following tables and figures: Table 23–6 lists comparative system-wide greenhouse emission estimates for *in situ* versus conventional surface mining of oil sands; Figure 23–7 is an aerial view of Suncor's oil sands operations compared with a comparable photograph of Manhattan; Figure 23–8 depicts a cross-section profile of one of the company's tailings ponds; Table 23–7 is a copy of the latest consolidated statement of earnings; and Table 23–8 is a copy of a recent risk assessment matrix produced for Suncor (Zhao 2007).

The development of the oil sands is expected to continue into the future for at least two reasons: first, they are a major source of employment and revenue for both the province of Alberta and Canada; and, second, they offer a very attractive investment opportunity not only for traditional oil companies but also for a number of foreign governments who wish to diversify their source of petroleum. Table 23–9 presents a recent forecast of GHG emissions from continued development in the oil and gas sector over the next decade (Environment Canada 2011), and Table 23–10 indicates the potential land area involved in this potential development.

**FIGURE 23.7**

*Google Earth views of Suncor and Manhattan*

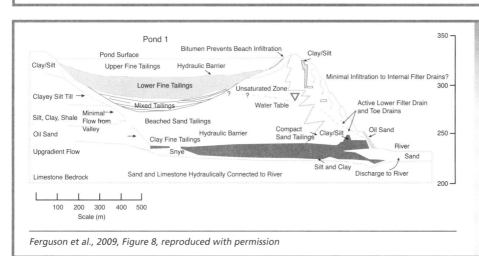

**FIGURE 23.8**

*Vertical cross-section across oil sands tailing pond*

Ferguson et al., 2009, Figure 8, reproduced with permission

**TABLE 23.7**

*Suncor Consolidated Statements of Earnings 2008–2010*

| FOR THE YEARS ENDED DECEMBER 31 ($ MILLIONS) | 2010 | 2009 | 2008 |
|---|---|---|---|
| **Revenues** | | | |
| Operating revenues (note 21) | 33 198 | 17 977 | 17 920 |
| Less: Royalties (note 4) | (1 937) | (1 150) | (822) |
| Operating revenues (net of royalties) | 31 261 | 16 827 | 17 098 |
| Energy supply and trading activities (notes 7 and 21) | 2 700 | 7 577 | 11 320 |
| Interest and other income (notes 3 and 5) | 389 | 444 | 28 |
| | 34 350 | 24 848 | 28 446 |
| **Expenses** | | | |
| Purchases of crude oil and products | 14 911 | 7 388 | 7 606 |
| Operating, selling and general (note 20) | 7 810 | 6 430 | 4 146 |
| Energy supply and trading activities (notes 7 and 21) | 2 598 | 7 381 | 11 323 |
| Transportation | 656 | 396 | 240 |
| Depreciation, depletion and amortization (note 15) | 3 813 | 1 860 | 961 |
| Accretion of asset retirement obligations | 178 | 136 | 60 |
| Exploration | 197 | 209 | 90 |
| Loss (gain) on disposal of assets | (107) | 66 | 13 |
| Project start-up costs | 77 | 51 | 35 |
| Financing expenses (income) (note 8) | (30) | (488) | 917 |
| | 30 103 | 23 429 | 25 391 |
| **Earnings before Income Taxes** | 4 247 | 1 419 | 3 055 |
| **Provisions for (Recovery of) Income Taxes** (note 9) | | | |
| Current | 1 004 | 841 | 514 |
| Future | 555 | (628) | 459 |
| | 1 559 | 213 | 973 |
| **Net Earnings from Continuing Operations** | 2 688 | 1 206 | 2 082 |
| **Net Earnings (Loss) from Discontinued Operations** (note 6) | 883 | (60) | 55 |
| **Net Earnings** | 3 571 | 1 146 | 2 137 |

*Source:* U.S. Securities and Exchange Commission, submission by Suncor of form 40-f, exhibit 99-1 for fiscal year ending December 31, 2010.

## SUNCOR AND LIFE-CYCLE ANALYSIS

The measurement of total greenhouse gas emissions from an oil sands operation is a complex undertaking because of the variety of technologies, emission sources, and choice of appropriate system boundaries (Moorhouse et al. 2011). Two recent issues have arisen with respect to unmeasured GHG emissions: (1) research by Rooney

# TABLE 23.8

## Suncor—Risk Assessment Matrix

**Suncor Energy - Risk Assessment Matrix**

| Likelihood Category | Description | C1 | C2 | C3 | C4 | C5 | C6 |
|---|---|---|---|---|---|---|---|
| Likelihood Category - Frequency Guidelines (Business Unit Basis) | | | | | | | |
| 6 — f >= 1/yr | Occurs once or more per year in BU/facility/project, and is likely to reccur within one year | III | II | I | I | I | I |
| 5 — 0.1 =< f < 1/yr (between 1/yr and 1/10 years) | Expected to occur several times in the BU/facility/project lifetime | III | III | II | I | I | I |
| 4 — 0.01 =< f <0.1/year (between 1/10 and 1/100 years) | Expected to occur in the BU/facility/project lifetime | IV | III | III | II | I | I |
| 3 — 0.001=< f <0.01/year (between 1/100 and 1/1,000 years) | May happen less than once during the BU/facility/project lifetime | IV | IV | III | III | I | I |
| *2 — 0.0001=< f <0.001/year (between 1/1,000 and 1/10,000 years) | *Remote chance of happening | IV | IV | IV | III | III | II |
| *1 — f < 0.0001/year (less than 1/10,000 years) | *Extremely remote chance of happening | IV | IV | IV | IV | III | III |

Likelihood Category — Increasing Likelihood →

Consequence Category — Increasing Consequence →

*Note: Likelihood categories 1 & 2 are typically for facility design purposes

(Continued)

**TABLE 23.8**
*continued*

| | | Incident - no Treatment | First aid/ minor illness | Medical aid, injury or illness/ restricted work/ Nuisance public impact | Temporary disability/ lost time/ | Permanent disability/ fatality/ | Multiple onsite fatalities/ |
|---|---|---|---|---|---|---|---|
| Social | Health & Safety (Public and Employees) | | | | | | |
| Environmental | Environmental | Release to on-site environment, contained immediately | Small uncontained release below legal limit or with minor impacts/ possible cumulative impact on-site | Minor environmental impact, but result in permit violation or administrative penalties | Significant adverse impact, significant long-term liability, enforcement action | Catastrophic impact, material (corporate) longterm liability | |
| Economic | Financial/ Damage (Equipment + Business Interruption) (Business Unit/ Clients) | C < $10k | $10k =< C < $100k | $100k =< C < $1M | $1M =< C < $10M | $10M =< C < $100M | C > $100M |
| Social | Reputation (Political/ Regulatory) | Individual concern/ local media attention/ no impact on Suncor's reputation | Community concern/ regional news/ adverse impact on Suncor's reputation at regional level | Provincial news/ adverse impact on Suncor's reputation at provincial/ state level | National news/ public outrage/ short-term drop in market share and share price | Recurring national attention/ punitive action by government against company/ long-term major impact on market share and share price | |

| TABLE 23.9 | OIL AND GAS SECTOR: EMISSIONS BY PRODUCTION TYPE (MT CO₂E) | | | | | |
|---|---|---|---|---|---|---|
| | | 2005 | 2008 | 2010 | 2020 | ABSOLUTE CHANGE |
| *Projected GHG Emissions from the Oil and Gas Sector in Canada* | Natural Gas | 53 | 53 | 47 | 52 | -1 |
| | Light Oil | 9 | 11 | 10 | 8 | -1 |
| | Heavy Oil | 21 | 17 | 18 | 12 | -9 |
| | Offshore | 1 | 1 | 2 | 2 | 1 |
| | Total Conventional Oil | 31 | 29 | 30 | 22 | -9 |
| | Oil sands — Bitumen In situ | 9 | 16 | 19 | 34 | 25 |
| | Oil sands — Bitumen Mining | 7 | 8 | 9 | 18 | 11 |
| | Oil sands — Bitumen Upgrading | 14 | 16 | 21 | 40 | 26 |
| | Total Oil sands | 30 | 40 | 49 | 92 | 62 |
| | Petroleum Refining | 19 | 19 | 18 | 17 | -2 |
| | Pipelines | 20 | 17 | 15 | 16 | -4 |
| | Total | 153 | 158 | 159 | 199 | 46 |

*Source:* Environment Canada 2011

| TABLE 23.10 | JURISIDICTION | SIZE |
|---|---|---|
| *Relative Size of Projected Area of Oil Sands Operations (in 1000 sq km)* | Alberta | 662 |
| | France | 505 |
| | Sweden | 450 |
| | Norway | 386 |
| | Germany | 357 |
| | UK | 249 |
| | **Oil sands - potential including *in situ*** | **140** |
| | Greece | 131 |

et al. (2012) has provided the first estimates of the impact of open pit mining on carbon storage and sequestration by lost boreal forest and peatlands. The authors conclude that landscape changes due to currently approved surface extraction will release 11.4–47.3 million metric tons of stored carbon (equivalent to 41.8–173.4 tons of $CO_2$); and (2) a report from the Alberta Auditor General (2011) notes that tailings ponds can be a significant source of methane ($CH_4$), a greenhouse gas with a global warming potential (GWP) 23 times that of carbon dioxide. Despite the difficulty of measuring such fugitive emissions, there are some published estimates from Syncrude, another major oil sands producer (Siddique et al. 2008) but none from Suncor. Appendix 2 presents the derivation of total estimates of GHG emissions from the Syncrude tailings pond and its possible application to Suncor.

## CITED REFERENCES AND RECOMMENDED READINGS

Alberta Auditor General of Alberta (2011) *Report of the Auditor General of Alberta*, Edmonton, November.

Alberta Chamber of Resources (2004) *Oil Sands Technology Roadmap: Unlocking the Potential*, Edmonton, January 30.

Alberta Energy Resources Conservation Board (multiple years) ST-39 *Alberta Mineable Oil Sands Plant Statistics Monthly Supplement*, Calgary.

Alberta Energy Resources Conservation Board (multiple years) ST-43 *Alberta Mineable Oil Sands Plant Statistics (Annual)*, Calgary.

Alberta Environment (2007) *Specified Gas Emitters Regulation. Technical Guidance Document for Baseline Emissions Intensity Applications*, Edmonton, July 18.

Canada.com (2011) "Canada Fighting EU Plans to Label Oilsands World's Dirtiest Crude Source," October 19.

Canada Office of the Auditor General (2012) *Report of the Commissioner of the Environment and Sustainable Development to the House of Commons*, Chapter 2. "Meeting Canada's 2020 Climate Change Commitments," Ottawa, Spring.

Corporate Knights (2010) *Report on Clean Capitalism*, Toronto.

Dow Jones Sustainability Index (http://wwwdjindexes.com).

Dunbar, R.B. and T.W. Sloan (2003) "Does Nuclear Energy Have a Role in the Development of Canada's Oil Sands?" Canadian International Petroleum Conference, Calgary, Alberta, June 10–13.

Environment Canada (2011) "Canada's Emission Trends," Ottawa, July.

*Fortune*—list of green giants (www.fortune.com).

Ferguson, G.P. et al., (2009) "Hydrodynamics of a large oil sand tailings impoundment and related environmental implications," *Canadian Geotechnical Journal*, 46, pp. 1446-1460.

*Globe and Mail* (2005) "Oil Sands Players Eye Nuclear Option," September 23.

Gosselin, Pierre et al. (2010) *Environmental and Health Impacts of Canada's Oil Sands Industry*, The Royal Society of Canada, Ottawa.

Grant, Jennifer et al. (2010) *Northern Lifeblood. Empowering Northern Leaders to Protect the Mackenzie River Basin from Oil Sands Risks*. Pembina Institute, Calgary.

Griffiths, Mary (2006) "Water Use in the Oil Patch: The Motivation for Innovation," PTAC Water Innovation in the Oil Patch conference, June 21, Pembina Institute, Calgary.

*Journal of Commerce* (2010) "Suncor Energy's Tailings-Pond Reclamation Claims Questioned," September 29 [www.joconl.com/article/id40807].

Kelly, Erin N. et al. (2009) "Oil Sands Development Contributes Polycyclic Aromatic Compounds to the Athabasca River and Its Tributaries, *PNAS*, December 29, 106(52), pp. 22346–22351.

Kelly, Erin N. et al. (2010) "Oil Sands Development Contributes Elements Toxic at Low Concentrations to the Athabasca River and Its Tributaries," *PNAS*, September 14, 107(37), pp. 16178–16182.

*National Geographic* (2009) "The Canadian Oil Boom," March, [http://ngm.nationalgeographic.com/2009/03/Canadian-oil-sands/kunzig-text].

*New York Times* (2010a) "Backers Rev Up Oil Sands Campaign," December 8.

*New York Times* (2010b) "Alberta's Tar Sands and the Dead Duck Trial," March 10.

*New York Times* (2011) "An Oil Ad Vexes the Saudis," September 25.

NPRI (2011) (www.ec.gc.ca/inrp-npri/) [website of Canada's National Pollutant Release Inventory].

Pembina Institute (2005) *Oil Sands Fever. The Environmental Implications of Canada's Oil Sands Rush*, Calgary.

Pembina Institute (2006) *Troubled Waters, Troubling Trends*, Calgary.

Ramos-Padron, Esther et al. (2011) "Carbon and Sulfur Cycling by Microbial Communities in a Gypsum-Treated Oil sands Tailings Pond." *Environmental Science & Technology*, 45, pp. 439–446.

Rooney, Rebecca C., Suzanne E. Bayley and David W. Schindler (2012) "Oil Sands Mining and Reclamation Cause Massive Loss of Peatland and Stored Carbon," *PNAS*, March 27, 109(13), pp. 4933–4937.

Schindler, David (2009) "The Environmental Impacts of Exploiting the Alberta Tar Sands," Lecture at *The Vancouver Institute*, Vancouver, BC, March 7.

Siddique, Tariq et al. (2008) "A First Approximation Kinetic Model to Predict Methane Generation from an Oil Sands Tailings Settling Basin." *Chemosphere*, 72, pp. 1573–1580.

Suncor (2007) *Report on Sustainability*.

Suncor (2011a) "Climate Change Action Plan."

Suncor (2011b) *Summary Report on Sustainability*.

TD Global Sustainability Fund (www.tdcanadatrust.com/products . . . funds/sustainability-fund.jsp).

Timoney, Kevin P. and Peter Lee (2009) "Does the Alberta Tar Sands Industry Pollute? The Scientific Evidence." *The Open Conservation Biology Journal*, 3, pp. 65–81.

U.S. Environmental Protection Agency (EPA) (2011) (http://www.epa.gov/climatechange/emissions/index.html).

Zhao, John (2007) "Significance of Risk Quantification. The Smart Decision-making Process," Palasade @Risk User Conferences.

## Analytical Questions

(1) Is this company a candidate for investment by a green investor?

(2) Should this company be listed in a sustainability index?

(3) Is it appropriate for the industry to label its output as "ethical oil?"

(4) Can this company be labeled as sustainable relative to other oil companies?

(5) Does this company meet the requirements of sustainability enunciated by Anderson, McDonough-Braungart, or The Natural Step?

(6) What is the significance of Suncor's record of GHG-intensity reduction since 1990?

(7) How significant a role does Suncor's carbon offsets and investments in wind power and ethanol production play in Suncor's sustainability strategy?

**APPENDIX ONE**

# Historical Data on Suncor and Other Major Oil Sands Producers

# TABLE 23.11

## Suncor Historical Data

| YEAR | OIL SANDS MINED (TONNES) | PURCHASED NATURAL GAS (10³M³) | ELECTRICITY PURCHASED (MWH) | ELECTRICITY GENERATED (MWH) | BITUMEN PRODUCTION (M³) | INTERMEDIATE HYDROCARBONS PRODUCTION(M³) | SYNTHETIC CRUDE OIL PRODUCTION (M³) | HEAVY FUEL OIL AND DILUENT NAPHTHA PRODUCTION (M³) | PROCESS GAS PRODUCTION (10³M³) | COKE PRODUCTION (TONNES) | SULPHUR PRODUCTION (TONNES) |
|---|---|---|---|---|---|---|---|---|---|---|---|
| 1967-1995 | 944,039,894 | | | | 101,655,170 | 81,445,311 | 74,055,894 | 1,043,053 | | 22,506,454 | 2,780,317 |
| 1996 | 51,083,345 | 289,396 | 137,295 | 442,709 | 5,646,782 | 4,586,621 | 3,895,213 | 233,937 | | 1,231,613 | 170,648 |
| 1997 | 54,143,321 | 293,459 | 186,351 | 382,690 | 5,729,456 | 4,746,094 | 3,808,828 | 221,842 | | 1,118,487 | 174,978 |
| 1998 | 62,396,984 | 265,458 | 187,022 | 449,464 | 6,559,994 | 5,602,882 | 4,062,511 | 194,159 | | 1,315,952 | 193,298 |
| 1999 | 73,014,843 | 192,239 | 123,164 | 512,758 | 7,576,979 | 6,139,039 | 3,712,106 | 249,898 | | 1,456,361 | 183,948 |
| 2000 | 84,934,388 | 263,929 | 252,583 | 544,608 | 8,289,311 | 6,762,262 | 4,415,597 | 224,606 | | 1,633,204 | 211,566 |
| 2001 | 97,898,571 | 667,115 | 52,217 | 2,371,629 | 8,892,537 | 7,268,553 | 4,536,837 | 287,508 | | 1,739,347 | 221,557 |
| 2002 | 147,255,711 | 805,213 | 743 | 2,596,824 | 15,655,028 | 12,145,549 | 8,049,730 | 308,051 | | 2,896,626 | 402,825 |
| 2003 | 152,469,006 | 720,772 | 0 | 3,183,813 | 15,708,927 | 12,944,156 | 8,181,941 | 288,961 | 1,016,961 | 3,032,932 | 422,641 |
| 2004 | 154,275,510 | 1,572,911 | 6 | 3,027,358 | 15,740,236 | 0 | 12,807,321 | 94,205 | 1,066,569 | 3,098,230 | 439,037 |
| 2005 | 101,636,016 | 1,515,006 | 1,334 | 2,651,881 | 11,358,138 | 0 | 9,370,922 | 45,039 | 717,026 | 2,277,433 | 300,322 |
| 2006 | 149,031,795 | 1,940,651 | 8,623 | 3,002,286 | 17,634,027 | 0 | 14,952,344 | 79,062 | 1,145,206 | 3,736,138 | 462,426 |
| 2007 | 134,389,521 | 2,009,446 | 821 | 2,949,541 | 15,459,686 | 0 | 13,634,111 | 58,239 | 1,058,705 | 3,370,977 | 435,683 |
| 2008 | 124,415,020 | 2,101,049 | 5,124 | 2,808,516 | 14,359,705 | | 13,457,125 | 145,461 | 914,682 | 3,263,210 | 386,102 |
| 2009 | 146,465,679 | 2,224,879 | 352,092 | 2,873,562 | 16,798,837 | | 16,527,376 | 58,338 | 1,242,107 | 4,002,902 | 478,519 |
| 2010 | 143,055,119 | 1,664,265 | 260,100 | 2,856,891 | 15,437,844 | | 14,998,518 | 63,440 | 1,104,032 | 3,598,835 | 0 |

Note: there are a number of accounting changes which make some of the historical data noncomparable

*Source: Alberta government*

**TABLE 23.12**

*Oil Sands Historical Production Data Table*

OIL SANDS MINED (TONNES)

| YEAR(S) | SUNCOR ENERGY INC. | SYNCRUDE CANADA LTD. - MILDRED LAKE | SYNCRUDE CANADA LTD. - AURORA | SHELL - CANADA - ALBIAN SANDS ENERGY INC. | SHELL CANADA ENERGY - JACKPINE MINE | CANADIAN NATURAL RESOURCES LTD. | PETRO-CANADA - FORT HILLS |
|---|---|---|---|---|---|---|---|
| 1967-1995 | 944,039,894 | 1,718,107,078 | 0 | 0 | | | 0 |
| 1996 | 51,083,345 | 149,697,690 | 0 | 0 | | | 0 |
| 1997 | 54,143,321 | 150,981,605 | | 0 | | | 0 |
| 1998 | 62,396,984 | 148,863,142 | 0 | 0 | | | 0 |
| 1999 | 73,014,843 | 162,418,457 | 0 | 0 | | | 0 |
| 2000 | 84,934,388 | 133,203,554 | 13,666,884 | 0 | | | 0 |
| 2001 | 97,898,571 | 131,353,025 | 47,557,881 | 0 | | | 0 |
| 2002 | 147,255,711 | 116,053,778 | 40,560,751 | 2,909,572 | | | 0 |
| 2003 | 152,469,006 | 108,347,364 | 46,748,957 | 45,291,746 | | | 0 |
| 2004 | 154,275,510 | 93,421,458 | 77,664,760 | 79,020,376 | | | 0 |
| 2005 | 101,636,016 | 77,677,758 | 74,226,778 | 93,410,754 | | | 0 |
| 2006 | 149,031,795 | 72,719,400 | 102,317,254 | 79,007,202 | | | 58,465 |
| 2007 | 134,389,521 | 91,893,790 | 103,143,036 | 89,838,790 | | | 0 |
| 2008 | 124,415,020 | 102,031,037 | 90,127,674 | 88,895,212 | | 1,113,978 | 0 |
| 2009 | 146,465,679 | 89,677,030 | 104,192,180 | 85,935,476 | | 41,609,700 | 0 |
| 2010 | 143,055,119 | 94,164,432 | 111,732,646 | 71,010,064 | 12,322,070 | 62,205,945 | 0 |

*Source:* Alberta government

# APPENDIX TWO

# Estimates of GHG Emissions from Oil Sands Tailings Ponds

Siddique et al. (2008) have estimated methane ($CH_4$) emissions from Syncrude's Mildred Lake tailings pond with a surface area of approximately 10 square km and 200 million cubic meters of fluid fine tailings. Estimating fugitive emissions is a difficult task, but it is rendered extremely complex for oil sands tailings ponds because of a high level of uncertainty over the quantity and type of methanogenic bacteria and the presence of low molecular weight hydrocarbons (such as naptha frequently used as a diluent in the processing of the oil sands), which provide carbon and energy for methanogensis (Ramos-Padron et al. 2011). The estimates derived by Siddique et al. for Syncrude range from a low of 6 tons to a high 266 tons of $CH_4$ per day. This is equivalent to a possible range of 50,370–2,233,070 tons per year of $CO_2$eq on a yearly basis in light of the fact that methane has a GWP of 23.

Syncrude has two oil sands operations (Mildred Lake and Aurora) with annual production of 94,164,432 and 111,732,646 tonnes per year respectively. As of 2009, Syncrude's total GHG emissions totaled 9,837,000 tonnes; as such, approximately 4,449,000 of this can be attributed to the Mildred Lake operation. This implies that GHG emissions from Syncrude's Mildred Lake tailings pond represents as little as 1.12% of total Mildred Lake operations or as much as 49.64%. This remarkably large range clearly suggests that much more research is necessary in order to produce a more accurate estimate in line with the requirements of the Alberta Environment ministry. It is unclear to what extent these calculations can be transferred to Suncor, as there are differences in the two oil sands operations' processes and chemicals. Nevertheless, the question remains important as is it ultimately relates to the total GHG footprint of oil sands operation on a system-wide basis.

# CHAPTER 24

## *Assessing Suncor*

## SUSTAINABILITY REPORTING

S UNCOR IS ONE OF MANY CORPORATIONS that have chosen to report not only financial results but also their performance in the two other aspects of sustainability: namely, environment and society. The standard procedure for so doing is to separately list results for a selection of performance indicators in each of these two major areas. In their annual reports on sustainability, Suncor has highlighted their results on such key environmental indicators as air emissions, water consumption and land use, and social variables such as occupational injuries. These types of indicators have been developed by a wide range of organizations— including commercial rating agencies, NGOs, standard-setting bodies, governments, international organizations, and multiple-stakeholder groups—in order to standardize the process of reporting and guaranteeing comparability both temporally and across companies.

One of the largest of these organizations is the Global Reporting Initiative (GRI), which issues sustainability guidelines for reporting on the economic, environmental, and social dimensions of activities, products, and services to a broad array of entities in addition to corporations. The choice of indicators is left to each organization, and it is up to the corporation to seek third party certification of the reported data if so desired.

In addition to the GRI, there are several other prominent agencies with promulgated guidelines or standards, including the United Nations, Organization for Economic Co-operation and Development (OECD), AccountAbility, the International Organization for Standardization (ISO), etc. There are three basic types of standards (Oakley and Buckland 2004, pp. 134–135): (1) *principle-based*, which set out "broad principles of behavior but do not specify how they are to be achieved or how conformity with them can be assessed"; (2) *performance* standards, which measure the actual achievements of the organization on the selected indicator; and (3) *process* standards, which outline processes that an organization should follow in order to achieve sustainability. Table 24–1 summarizes the principal promulgating organizations and how they are categorized. There are clearly trade-offs involved in the choice of standard as outlined by Oakley and Buckland in Table 24–2. The analyst should consider which approach would be more appropriate for Suncor.

| TABLE 24.1 | PRINCIPLES-BASED STANDARDS | PROCESS STANDARDS | PERFORMANCE STANDARDS | HYBRID STANDARDS |
|---|---|---|---|---|
| *Basic Types of Standards* | UN Global Compact | AA1000 | SA8000 | FTSE4Good SIGMA |
| | OECD Guidelines for Multinational Enterprises | ISO14000 ISO9000 | Global Reporting Initiative (GRI and G3) | London Stock Exchange Combined Code |
| | Caux Roundtable Principles for Business | | | Winning with Integrity (Business in the Community) |

*Source:* Oakley and Buckland 2004, p. 135, reproduced with permission

| TABLE 24.2 | TYPES | PROS | CONS |
|---|---|---|---|
| *Trade-Offs in Choice of Standards* | **Principles-based standards** | help to identify the scope of the issues and provide opportunities for external alignment for an organization | often lack details and how they are to be implemented and compliance is often difficult to establish |
| | **Process standards** | they provide practical guidance to organizations and help to establish repeatable processes and behaviours | they do not prescribe performance levels, and may be over-bureaucratic |
| | **Performance standards** | help provide transparency about what is actually being achieved | difficulty of establishing generally applicable targets that are sufficiently sensitive to different operating contexts and of ensuring that like is compared with like. Such standards may have a narrow scope that this may miss the issues that are most important to a given company and its stakeholders. |
| | **Hybrid standards** | combines the best of all approaches: a framework of principles, practical workable guidance on what is to be done, and the ability to assess actual performance. | |

*Source:* Derived from Oakley and Buckland 2004, pp. 134-136, reproduced with permission.

## TRIPLE BOTTOM LINE ACCOUNTING

A corporation or other organizational entity that chooses to report on environmental and social effects of their operations is generally considered to have adopted triple bottom line accounting, but clearly, the choice of standard system, number of indicators, and their level of detail, existence of temporal comparative data, and presence or absence of third party certification all bear upon the question of validity. Perhaps the most critical conceptual difficulty with TBL accounting as currently practiced is that the fact that the three accounts—financial, environmental, and social—are stand-alone lists or statements that lack any form of integration. Under these circumstances, it can be difficult, if not impossible, for shareholders or other stakeholders to obtain any sense of the impact of these variables not only on the financial performance of the company but also on the broader society, economy, and environment in which the corporation operates. This central challenge of sustainability reporting is specifically addressed in chapter 25.

## POLLUTANT INTENSITY VERSUS TOTAL POLLUTANT OUTPUT

The ambiguous impact on the environment of reductions in pollutant intensity has prompted many governmental regulatory agencies to abandon this type of requirement in favor of performance measures that can track total pollutant output. Pollutant-intensity reductions are a necessary but not sufficient criterion for reduced impact on the environment—the ultimate goal of any sustainability policy—because any reduction in pollution intensity can be offset by a compensating increase in product output. The analyst should assess the significance for Suncor's goal of sustainability in light of both its past and anticipated GHG intensity and total GHG pollution.

## SUNCOR AND SUSTAINABILITY INDEXES

As mentioned in chapter 23, Suncor is currently listed on a least four sustainability indexes. In explaining the inclusion of Suncor in its 2010 Clean Capitalism Report Canada, Corporate Knights (2010) describes the company's sustainability priorities as

> *Environment*: It has voluntarily reported GHG emissions since 1995 and has invested in technology, improved energy efficiency and reduced GHG emissions intensity at its oil sands plant by 45% compared to 1990 levels. Suncor has invested in wind power generation in Alberta and Ontario, and water usage has been reduced by 22% over the last six years. *Safety*: Suncor constantly seeks safety improvements with its Journey to Zero safety culture. *Communities*: The

company has an Aboriginal Affairs Policy based on responsibility, recognition and respect; for example, it partners with the Fort McKay First Nation to establish a business incubator to promote economic development and entrepreneurship. It has also donated $24.9 million to hundreds of charitable and non-profit organizations in communities where it operates.

Perhaps the most prominent of the sustainability indexes on which Suncor is listed is the Dow Jones Sustainability Index (DJSI). Table 24–3 lists the criteria and weights adopted by Dow Jones for inclusion in their sustainability index. The criterion of environmental reporting receives a weight of 3%, and environmental performance, as measured by eco-efficiency, receives a weight of 7%. The central question is

**TABLE 24.3**

*DJSI Corporate Sustainability Assessment Criteria*

DOW JONES SUSTAINABILITY INDEXES

| SUSTAINABILITY | ASSESSMENT | INDEXES | DATA | REVIEWS | NEWS | PUBLICATIONS |
|---|---|---|---|---|---|---|

CRITERIA AND WEIGHTINGS

CORPORATE SUSTAINABILITY ASSESSMENT CRITERIA

| DIMENSION | CRITERIA | WEIGHTING (%) |
|---|---|---|
| Economic | Codes of Conduct / Compliance / Corruption&Bribery | 5.5 |
| | Corporate Governance | 5.0 |
| | Risk & Crisis Management | 6.0 |
| | Industry Specific Criteria | Depends on Industry |
| Environment | Environmental Performance (Eco-Efficiency) | 7.0 |
| | Environmental Reporting* | 3.0 |
| | Industry Specific Criteria | Depends on Industry |
| Social | Corporate Citizenship/ Philanthropy | 3.5 |
| | Labor Practice Indicators | 5.0 |
| | Human Capital Development | 5.5 |
| | Social Reporting* | 3.0 |
| | Talent Attraction &Retention | 5.5 |
| | Industry Specific Criteria | Depends on Industry |

*Criteria assessed based on publicly available information only
*Source:* http://www.sustainability-index.cm. Reproduced with permission.

| | | SUNCOR | |
| | | YES? | NO? |
|---|---|---|---|
| Anderson | Strongly service oriented | | |
| | Resource-efficient | | |
| | solar-driven | | |
| | Wasting nothing | | |
| | Cyclical - not linear | | |
| | Strongly connected to constituencies | | |
| | | | |
| Robert | no increase in concentrations of substances extracted from the Earth's crust | | |
| | no systematic increase in concentrations of substances produced as a byproduct | | |
| | no systematic increasing degradation by physical means | | |
| | people not subject to conditions that systematically undermine their capacity to meet their needs | | |
| | | | |
| McDonough and Braungart | Waste equals food | | |
| | Use of current solar income | | |
| | respect for diversity | | |
| | Lack of product and byproduct toxicity, bioaccumulation or persistence | | |

**TABLE 24.4**

*Criteria Defining a Sustainable Corporation*

*Sources:* Anderson 1999, Robert 2008, McDonough and Braungart 2002

whether Suncor should be listed on a sustainability index. The inclusion must rest on either one of two criteria: absolute or relative performance. As detailed in chapters 13 and 14, Ray Anderson (1999), Robert (2008), and McDonough and Braungart (2002) have developed lists of criteria that define a sustainable corporation. These are summarized in Table 24–4.

If Suncor's inclusion is based on its relative performance, then there are five alternative comparisons: all extractive and manufacturing industries, extractive industries only, the energy industry, the oil and gas sector, or the oil sands industry. Table 24–5 lists the range of components of the energy industry. Renewable energy technologies are generally considered to have a lower environmental impact than non-renewable energy sources [see, for example, NAS 2010; OECD 2001; Voss 2009, WEC 2004].

**TABLE 24.5**

*Typology of Energy Technology and Sources*

| | | | |
|---|---|---|---|
| Renewables | solar | conventional thermal | |
| | | thermoelectric | mirror fields |
| | | | central boiler |
| | | photovoltaic | |
| | tidal | barrrier | |
| | | stand-alone units | |
| | wave | | |
| | wind | | |
| | biomass | solid | |
| | | liquid | crop ethanol |
| | | | cellulosic ethanol |
| | | gaseous | |
| | hydro | large scale | |
| | | run-of-river | |
| | | micro | |
| | geothermal | | |
| Non-renewables | Oil | conventional | |
| | | OIL SANDS | |
| | Gas | conventional | |
| | | shale | |
| | Coal | | |
| Nuclear | conventional fission | | |
| | fast breeder | | |
| | fusion | | |
| Energy Efficiency | | | |
| Storage | electric | | |
| | hydrogen | | |
| Secondary methane recovery | coal bed | | |
| | solid waste | | |
| Transmission | conventional AC | | |
| | DC | | |
| | Cryogenic | | |

## CITED REFERENCES AND RECOMMENDED READINGS

AccountAbility, London. (www.accountability.org).

Alberta (2008a) "Alberta to Cut Projected Emissions by 50 Percent Under New Climate Change Plan." Edmonton, News Release, January 24.

Alberta (2008b) *Alberta's 2008 Climate Change Strategy. Responsibility, Leadership, Action*, Edmonton.

Alberta Carbon Capture and Storage Development Council (ACCSDC) (2009) *Accelerating Carbon Capture and Storage implementation in Alberta*. Edmonton, March.

Alberta Environment (2008) "Alberta Air Emissions Trends and Projections." Edmonton, June 18.

Anderson, Ray (1999) *Mid-Course Correction: Toward a Sustainable Enterprise: The Interface Model*. Atlanta: Peregrinzilla Press.

Corporate Knights (2010) *Clean Capitalism Report Canada*, Toronto [www.corporateknights.com].

Dow Jones Sustainability Index (DJSI) (www.sustainability-index.com/).

Environmental Defence (2008) *Canada's Toxic Tar Sands, The Most Destructive Project on Earth*, Toronto, February.

*Globe and Mail* (2012) "Alberta's Carbon Capture Efforts Set Back," April 26.

Global Reporting Initiative (GRI), Amsterdam (www.globalreporting.org).

*The Guardian* (2011) "Longannet Carbon Capture Project Cancelled," October 19.

International Organization for Standardization (ISO) (www.iso.org/iso/iso_catalogue. htm), Geneva.

Kirchsteiger, C. (2008) "Carbon capture and storage – desirability from a risk management point of view," *Safety Science*, 46, pp. 1149–1154.

McDonough, William and Michael Braungart (2002) *Cradle to Cradle: Remaking the Way We Make Things*. New York: North Point Press.

National Academy of Sciences (NAS) (2010) *Hidden Costs of Energy: Unpriced Consequence of Energy Production and Use*. Washington, DC.

*New York Times* (2011a) "Utility Shelves Ambitious Plan to Limit Carbon," July 13.

*New York Times* (2011b) "AEP Move to Stop Carbon Capture and Sequestration Project Shocks Utilities, Miners," July 15.

*New York Times* (2011c) "Obstacles to Capturing Carbon Gas," July 31.

*New York* Times (2012a) "Growing Doubts in Europe on Future of Carbon Storage," January 16.

*New York Times* (2012b) "With Natural Gas Plentiful and Cheap, Carbon Capture Projects Stumble," May 19.

Oakley, Ros and Ian Buckland (2004) "What if Business as Usual Won't Work?" in Adrian Henriques and Julie Richardson (eds.) *The Triple Bottom Line. Does It All Add Up*? London: Earthscan, pp. 131–141.

Organization for Economic Co-operation and Development (OECD) (2001) *Externalities and Energy Policy: The Life Cycle Analysis Approach*, Workshop Proceedings. Paris, November 15–16.

Organization for Economic Co-operation and Development (OECD) (2008) *Guidelines for Multinational Enterprises*. Paris.

Public Broadcasting System (PBS) (2008) "Heat" *Frontline* Transcript, October 21.

Robert, Karl-Henrik (2008) *The Natural Step Story. Seeding a Quiet Revolution*, Gabriola Island, BC: New Society Publishers.

Thomson, Graham (2009) *Burying Carbon Dioxide in Underground Saline Aquifers: Political Folly or Climate Change Fix?* Munk Centre for International Studies, University of Toronto.

UN Global Compact (www.unglobalcompact.org/).

U.S. Environmental Protection Agency (EPA) (2008) *Vulnerability Evaluation Framework for Geologic Sequestration of Carbon Dioxide*, July 10.

Voss, Alfred (2009) "Life Cycle Analysis for Different Energy Sources," Symposium Energy 2050, Stockholm, October 19–20.

Wilday, Jill et al. (2011) "Hazards from carbon dioxide capture, transport and storage," *Process Safety and Environmental Protection*, 89, pp. 482–491.

World Energy Council (2004) *Comparison of Energy Systems Using Life Cycle Assessment*, London, July.

## APPENDIX

# A Brief Note on Carbon Capture and Storage

One potential solution that has been advanced to the increasing problem of carbon emissions is carbon capture and storage (CCS). This technology has received a great deal of international attention, and Suncor is considering it as a partial solution to its long-term carbon dioxide reduction challenges. The Alberta government also considers CCS an integral part of its climate strategy, expecting it to account for as much as 70% of its emission reduction by 2050 (Alberta 2008a; see also Alberta 2008b; Alberta CCSDC 2009; Alberta Environment 2008). In this suggested technological solution, carbon would be captured at the point of emission and then injected into the earth where it would remain indefinitely.

Several critical criteria must be met before this technology can be considered a viable solution. First, the technology would only be useful for large single-point emission sources and inappropriate for distributed or fugitive sources. Second, there must be reasonably proximate favorable geological formations. Third, the costs must be a relatively small proportion of the total cost of energy production. And, finally, there must be some assurance that the geological formations designed to contain the injected $CO_2$ are stable and able to hold the gas indefinitely. The most likely candidates for the application of this technology would be fossil-fueled power plants. One recent in-depth report (Thomson 2009) has concluded that "By one estimate the United States would have to construct 300,000 injection wells at a cost of $3 trillion by 2030 just to keep emissions at 2005 levels."

University of Manitoba energy expert Vaclav Smil has calculated that governments will have to construct $CO_2$ infrastructure about twice the size of the world's crude oil industry just to bury 25% of the world's emissions. For one example, there would be an enormous demand for steel pipe to move the gas, and the production and laying of this pipe is energy and GHG intensive (Smil 2010). These scale-up issues pose among the most imposing challenges to this technology, even if other scientific questions were to be resolved satisfactorily.

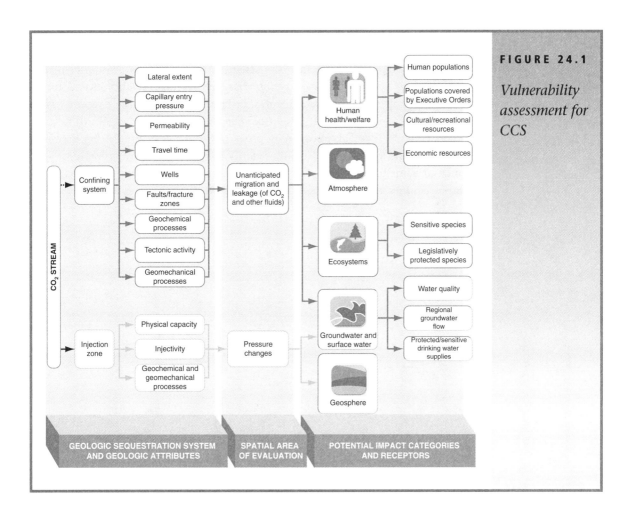

**FIGURE 24.1**

*Vulnerability assessment for CCS*

A fundamental uncertainty remains about the ultimate effectiveness and safety of such a system. It is not known with any certainty how long the $CO_2$ would stay underground, and if it were to escape, the consequences could be potentially very serious. *In extremis*, the sudden release of carbon dioxide from underground storage could lead to an environmental crisis of potentially greater magnitude than the original problem. This type of risk is an excellent example of *revenge theory* [see chapter 10]. Figure 24–1 reproduces a recent U.S. EPA (2008) graphic that illustrates the multitude of scientific uncertainties associated with CCS focusing on the vulnerability of the geological system to unanticipated migration, leakage, undesirable pressure changes, and the possible negative consequences of system failure on human, plant, and animal life. On the basis of cost and risk alone, this option is considered by some experts as not worth pursuing (Thomson 2009).

In an interview granted to PBS (2008), David Ratcliffe, the CEO of Southern Company, one of the nation's largest emitters of GHG from coal, stated that "I think the truth is that we don't know where we have storage capability in this nation at this point in time. We haven't even come close to defining what will be required in storage, what are the legal liabilities and what are the permitting requirements, much less the infrastructure needed to develop that storage and to move the carbon—the $CO_2$ into that storage, whether it's pipelines or trucks or whatever it is. We haven't even scratched the surface yet."

While research continues into the scientific and economic feasibility of this technology, no commercial-scale facility has yet been built, and several recent high-profile projects in the United States, Britain, and Canada have recently been cancelled (*Globe and Mail* 2012; *The Guardian* 2011; *New York Times* 2011a, b, c; 2012a, b). While this technology may prove to be viable in the future, its recent track record and current level of uncertainty suggest that any corporate or governmental plans to rely extensively on this technology for carbon dioxide control entails a significant risk [See also Kirchsteiger 2008, and Wilday et al. 2011].

# CHAPTER 25

# Internalizing Sustainability into Corporate Strategy through Financial Accounts

A FUNDAMENTAL PREREQUISITE TO INTERNALIZING SUSTAINABILITY into corporate strategy is to transform relevant ecological and social data into a form both recognizable to and usable by senior corporate decision makers. As discussed in chapter 24, triple bottom line (TBL) accounting has become the gold standard of sustainability reporting, allowing stakeholders the ability to gauge the degree of corporate success in achieving the elusive goal of sustainability—at least in theory. The challenge is to transform the stand-alone reporting of environmental and social indicators into monetary values that can be unified with a corporation's financial statements. This is a formidable task, as chapter 7 has outlined the conceptual complexities of monetizing just a few key environmental values, excluding a number of critical ecosystem services and social values. This chapter describes some recent advances in this endeavor and promise of future progress.

In a pathbreaking article published in the *American Economic Review*, Muller et al. (2011) have developed a theoretical framework for incorporating air pollution externalities into systems of national accounts. The research develops monetized industry-level estimates of environmental damages based on emissions of the six criteria pollutants ($SO_2$, NOx, VOC, $NH_3$, $PM_{2.5}$, and $PM_{10}$) then compares these results with the corresponding value added of 820 U.S. industries. Not surprisingly, the industries with the largest gross external damages (GED) include coal-fired electric power generation (with a GED of $53.4 billion) followed by crop production; livestock production; and highway, street, and bridge construction. What is surprising, however, is that fact that seven industries have air pollution damages that exceed their value added. These industries are solid waste combustion and incineration (with a GED/VA ratio of 6.72), petroleum-fired electric powered generation (5.13), sewage treatment facilities (4.69), coal-fired electric power generation (2.20), and dimension stone mining and quarrying (1.89). The authors caution the reader about the correct interpretation of these values. First, these damages are confined to air pollution; second, they do not address possible offsetting benefits (such as water pollution control from sewage treatment); and, third and perhaps most important, they do not suggest that the American economy would be better off without these industries. What the data do demonstrate, however, is that the level of pollution control in these industries is far below the social optimum (and, as such, the price of the product does not reflect the marginal cost of pollution, as discussed in chapter 7).

This critique even applies to the pollution reduction already achieved by the cap-and-trade system currently in place to address $SO_2$ and NOx emissions from U.S. power plants.

At least two important conclusions emerge from this analysis. First, it is a confirmation of the central tenet of environmental economics that "getting the price right" is an essential prerequisite to achieve the socially optimal level of pollution control. Second is a realization that some form of environmental accounting is absolutely critical to bringing environmental and ecological values into both public sector and corporate strategic decision making. Without this type of clear economic signal, society runs the very large risk of proceeding down the path of paying lip service to environmental issues but not addressing them in an efficient, effective, and comprehensive manner. This type of challenge applies equally to social values, and that is the subject of chapter 26.

This chapter borrows a fundamental distinction from the accounting literature to frame the discussion: the difference between financial and managerial accounting. The former is designed to signal critical corporate financial information to a company's many external stakeholders such as shareholders, suppliers, purchasers, insurance companies, banks, government regulatory agencies, and the general public. In contrast, the latter is designed to provide senior management with all the information required to make reasoned and efficient decisions concerning products manufactured and marketed, financing, logistics, and resource allocation in general. The next sections discuss these two sustainability-related accounting issues from both an external and internal perspective, bearing in mind that some signals are designed for both types of stakeholders.

## SIGNALING EXTERNAL STAKEHOLDERS

As stated above, the critical challenge to assessing the performance of a firm with respect to sustainability is to balance its conventional measures of economic performance with its positive or negative contributions from a social perspective. This is achieved through a process of monetization, albeit imperfect and incomplete, which takes the three distinct accounts of TBL accounting and achieves some form of synthesis. Only then is it possible to determine whether a company or product is adding to or detracting from total social value. Matthews and Lave (2003) have provided a cogent rationale for this consolidation: "If a company calculated its costs on the basis of social costs, it would see where it was imposing large costs on society and perhaps where it is likely to be regulated in the future. Using social costs would show the firm where corporate citizenship could contribute the most to environmental quality. Having social costs substantially greater than private costs indicates a possible problem."

The first question that comes to mind is why a company would choose to report data relating to sustainability. As Table 1–1 demonstrated, virtually all of the top 50 companies in the U.S. Fortune 500 have chosen to do just that. Figure 25–1, drawn from the work of Schaltegger and Wagner (2006), summarizes the most important factors that drive the decision to report. Figure 25–2 identifies the major external and internal stakeholders and to what purpose the reported sustainability

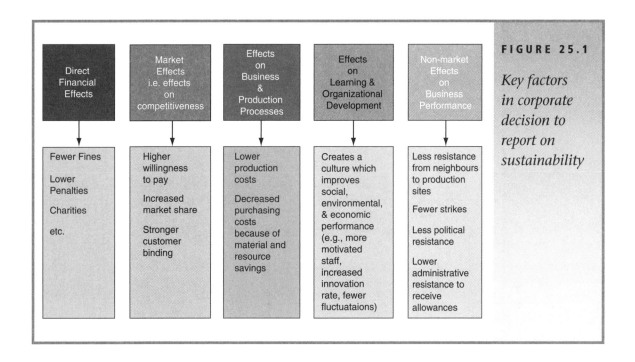

**FIGURE 25.1**

*Key factors in corporate decision to report on sustainability*

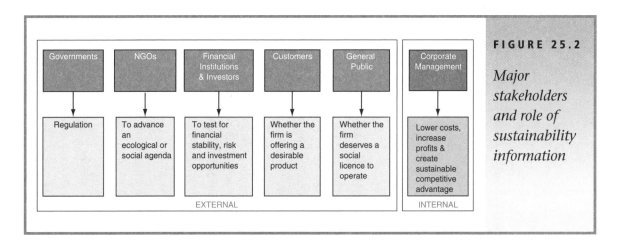

**FIGURE 25.2**

*Major stakeholders and role of sustainability information*

information is ultimately put. Several companies have attempted the consolidation of TBL, although this approach generally focuses on monetizing environmental values to the exclusion of more intractable social values. Table 25–1, drawn from the annual report of Baxter Health, reproduces not only direct environmental costs but also environmental income, savings, and cost avoidance. While not directly incorporated into the corporate profit-and-loss statement, the monetization of these values could easily permit this consolidation.

One of the first companies to attempt a consolidation of environmental costs with corporate financials was Interface Europe. The corporation focused specifically on monetizing the effects of their air emissions and opted to use avoidance and restoration cost methodology in order to simplify their calculations. Table 25–2

**TABLE 25.1**

*Baxter Health—Monetized Environmental Costs and Savings*

ESTIMATED ENVIRONMENTAL COSTS, INCOME, SAVINGS AND COST AVOIDANCE WORLDWIDE[1] (DOLLARS IN MILLIONS)

| ENVIRONMENTAL COSTS | 2007 | 2006 | 2005 | 2004 |
|---|---|---|---|---|
| **Basic Program** | | | | |
| Corporate Environmental - General and Shared Business Unit Costs[2] | $ 1.6 | $ 1.4 | $ 1.5 | $ 1.3 |
| Auditor and Attorney Fees | 0.4 | 0.4 | 0.4 | 0.4 |
| Energy Professionals and Energy Reduction Programs | 1.0 | 1.0 | 1.0 | 1.0 |
| Corporate Environmental - Information Technology | 0.3 | 0.3 | 0.3 | 0.3 |
| Business Unit/Regional/Facility Environmental Professionals and Programs | 7.4 | 7.2 | 6.8 | 6.5 |
| Pollution Controls - Operation and Maintenance | 3.1 | 3.2 | 2.9 | 3.2 |
| Pollution Controls - Depreciation | 0.9 | 0.8 | 0.7 | 0.8 |
| Basic Program Total | 14.7 | 14.3 | 13.6 | 13.5 |
| **Remediation, Waste and Other Response** (proactive environmental action will minimize these costs) | | | | |
| Attorney Fees for Cleanup Claims and Notices of Violation | 0.1 | 0.1 | 0.1 | 0.1 |
| Settlements of Government Claims | 0.0 | 0.0 | 0.0 | 0.0 |
| Waste Disposal | 10.0 | 7.1 | 6.1 | 5.9 |
| Carbon Offsets[3] | 0.1 | 0.0 | 0.0 | 0.0 |
| Environmental Fees for Packaging[4] | 0.9 | 0.9 | 1.1 | 1.0 |
| Environmental Fees for Electronic Goods and Batteries | 0.1 | 0.1 | 0.0 | 0.0 |
| Remediation/Cleanup - On-site | 0.5 | 0.1 | 0.1 | 0.1 |
| Remediation/Cleanup - Off-site | 0.0 | 0.3 | 0.0 | 0.2 |
| Remediation, Waste and Other Response Total | 11.7 | 8.6 | 7.4 | 7.3 |
| **Total Environmental Costs** | $ 26.4 | $ 22.9 | $ 21.0 | $ 20.8 |

**TABLE 25.1**
*continued*

ESTIMATED ENVIRONMENTAL COSTS, INCOME, SAVINGS AND COST AVOIDANCE WORLDWIDE[1] (DOLLARS IN MILLIONS)

| ENVIRONMENTAL COSTS | 2007 | 2006 | 2005 | 2004 |
|---|---|---|---|---|
| Environmental Income, Savings and Cost Avoidance | | | | |
| (see Detail on Income, Savings and Cost Avoidance from 2007 Activities online) | | | | |
| From Initiatives in Stated Year | | | | |
| Regulated Waste Disposal | $ (0.7) | $ 0.3 | $ (0.1) | $ 0.7 |
| Regulated Materials[5] | (2.7) | 0.8 | (0.3) | 2.1 |
| Non-hazardous Waste Disposal | (0.8) | 0.0 | 0.3 | 7.0 |
| Non-hazardous Materials[5] | (0.8) | (2.5) | 5.7 | 4.8 |
| Recycling (income) | 4.8 | 4.7 | 4.3 | 3.0 |
| Energy Conservation | 4.1 | 3.3 | 6.8 | 12.0 |
| Water Conservation | 0.6 | 0.6 | 0.0 | 1.1 |
| From Initiatives in Stated Year Total[6] | 4.4 | 7.2 | 16.7 | 30.7 |
| As a Percentage of Basic Program Costs | 30% | 51% | 123% | 227% |
| Cost Avoidance from Initiatives Started in the Six Years Prior to and Realized in Stated Year[6,7] | 78.2 | 83.8 | 78.7 | 62.2 |
| **Total Environmental Income, Savings and Cost Avoidance in Stated Year** | **$ 82.6** | **$ 91.0** | **$ 95.4** | **$ 92.9** |

*Sources:* Baxter Health 2007, p. 19, reproduced with permission of Baxter Health

**TABLE 25.2**

*Monetized Air Pollution Impacts— Interface Europe*

| TARGET | APPROACH | DETAILS |
|---|---|---|
| **Electricity consumption** | premium of green electricity production over current rates | 1 p per kWh on top of 4 p per kWh current rates |
| **$CO_2$** | sequestering cost in forests - from current market price for warrants | 5.45 UK pounds per tonne |
| **NOX from manufacturing processes** | end-of-pipe treatment costs | 14,000 UK pounds per tonne |
| **VOC from manufacturing processes** | end-of-pipe treatment costs | 7,200 UK Pounds per tonne |
| **NOX and VOC from ground transport** | cost of switching to LPG cars - note that while $CO_2$ is similar for LPG and gasoline-powered cars, NOx is reduced 40% and HC are reduced between 40 and 95% | 1500 UK pounds per vehicle plus total annual fuel savings of 18,000 UK pounds |
| **$SO_2$ from manufacturing processes** | end-of-pipe treatment costs (thermal incineration, scrubbing) | 2,400 UK pounds per tonne |
| **PM (particulates)** | electrostatic precipitators | 2,800 UK pounds per tonne |

*Source:* Derived from Howes 2000

identifies the specific air pollutants and the valuation approach adopted for each, and Table 25–3 displays the consolidated results (Howes 2000). After deducting sustainability costs attributable to corporate air pollution emissions, operating income decreased from 17 million to 15.752 million UK pounds, an adjustment of approximately 7%. This latter figure was deemed a first pass estimate of environmentally sustainable profits. This experimental approach by Interface to reporting the degree of corporate sustainability has since been replaced with an emphasis on eco-efficiency measures, as detailed in chapters 13 and 14, which Interface now feels presents a more accurate and comprehensive picture of their impacts and achievements (personal correspondence, Interface VP sustainability). On their website, Interface has chosen to brand their approach to sustainability as "Mission Zero," which communicates seven areas targeted for sustainability: (1) eliminating all forms of waste in every area of business; (2) eliminating toxic substances from products, vehicles, and facilities; (3) operating facilities with renewable electricity sources—solar, wind, landfill gas, biomass, geothermal, tidal, and low impact/small scale hydroelectric or non-petroleum-based hydrogen; (4) redesigning processes and products to close

| EMISSIONS | TONNES | UNITS | UNIT COST | TOTALS |
|---|---|---|---|---|
| Natural Gas consumption of 26 million kWh equivalent | | | | |
| $CO_2$ | 4,761 | 6 | £28,566 | |
| NOX | 4 | 14,000 | £56,000 | |
| $SO_2$ | 4 | 2,400 | £9,600 | |
| Total | | | | £94,166 |
| | | | | |
| Electricity consumption of 17 million kWh | | | | |
| $CO_2$ | 7,537 | n.a. | | |
| NOX | 20 | n.a. | | |
| $SO_2$ | 43 | n.a. | | |
| Total (avoidance) | | | | £170,000 |
| | | | | |
| Direct Production emissionss | | | | |
| NOX | 3 | n.a. | | |
| $SO_2$ | 0 | n.a. | | |
| VOC | 17 | n.a. | | |
| CO | 4 | n.a. | | |
| Total (avoidance) | | | | £350,000 |
| | | | | |
| Transport distribution of 4.645 million kms | | | | |
| $CO_2$ | 3,079 | 6 | £18,474 | |
| NOX | 34 | 14,000 | £476,000 | |
| VOC | 1 | 7,200 | £7,200 | |
| CO | 9 | 40 | £360 | |
| PM | 2 | 2,800 | £5,600 | |
| Total Haulage/Distribution | | | | £507,634 |
| | | | | |
| Transport (company cars) of 8.875 million kms | | | | |
| $CO_2$ | 2,026 | 6 | £12,156 | |
| NOX (50 percent of 2) | 1 | 14,000 | £14,000 | |
| VOC | low | 7,200 | | |
| PM | low | 2,800 | | |
| LPG Net Conversion costs | | | £265,000 | |
| LPG Annual Fuel Savings | | | -£283,000 | |
| Net | | | -£18,000 | |
| Total Cars | | | | £22,000 |
| | | | | |
| Air travel of 6.397 million kms | | | | |
| $CO_2$ | 1,215 | 6 | £7,290 | |
| NOX | 4 | 14,000 | £56,000 | |
| Total air travel | | | | £63,290 |
| Rounding | | | | £41,000 |

**TABLE 25.3**

*Interface Europe—Calculation of Environmentally Sustainable Profits*

(Continued)

| **TABLE 25.3** *continued* | Total Sustainability Cost | **£1,248,090** |
| --- | --- | --- |
| | Operating Income per the financial Accounts | **£17,000,000** |
| | Environmentally sustainable profits | **£15,751,910** |

*Source:* Howes 2000, p. 234
*Status:* Reproduced with permission of Edward Elgar Ltd.

the technical loop using recovered and bio-based materials; (5) transporting people and products efficiently to reduce waste and emissions; (6) creating a culture that integrates sustainability principles and improves people's lives and livelihoods; and (7) creating a new business model that demonstrates and supports the value of sustainability-based commerce.

Table 25–4 displays the approach to consolidation adopted by Wessex Water Services (2004) in the United Kingdom. The adjustment for environmental costs was approximately 6%, similar in magnitude to the initial estimates by Interface.

A critical question facing a corporation that decides to signal its degree of sustainability to its stakeholders is to what degree this signaling is successful. There is empirical evidence to suggest that signals from third party sources, such as the U.S. Toxic Release Inventory, can have an impact on stock prices [see chapter 5], and that some opinion polls suggest that consumers are more willing to buy products deemed to be green (ecofriendlysites.org, environentalleader.com).

Very little research has been conducted, however, to determine whether consumer perceptions accurately reflect corporate achievements. An initial test of this hypothesis was conducted by a Canadian research organization in 2008 (Change 2008). The stated goal of the experiment was to clarify "how committed Canada's top brands are to the environment. And, how committed consumers think they are. In the world of branding, what is real is only what is perceived to be real. What a brand does, good or bad, only affects its value if those actions change consumer opinion." The results indicate that a sizable number of corporations, many of which are multinationals with high brand recognition, appear to have a negative consumer perception despite their reported high scores on sustainability, and some have a reputation that appears unsupported by a measure of performance.

While a promising attempt to address the question of the effectiveness of corporate communication of sustainability performance, the study raises a number of questions concerning the analytical methodology employed. While consumer attitudes were derived from a consumer attitude survey, the degree of corporate sustainability, against which consumer attitudes were compared, was based on self-reported corporate data rather than third party certification, raising the possibility of bias in the results.

A subsequent report that has narrowed the focus and increased its coverage to specifically address the responses to climate change among 97 American companies in 10 sectors (Change 2010) has overcome the potential problem of

**TABLE 25.4**

*Wessex Water Environmental Accounts*

| ENVIRONMENTAL COST COMPONENT | CONSUMPTION | EMISSIONS (GAS) | EMISSIONS (TONNES) | TARGET LEVEL (TONNES) | DIFFERENCE (TONNES) | COST / TONNE TO AVOID IMPACT (UK POUNDS STERLING) | IMPACT COST 2000/2001 ('000 UK POUNDS STERLING) |
|---|---|---|---|---|---|---|---|
| Fossil fuel grid electricity | 181.2m kWh | $CO_2$ | 77,922 | 36,074 | 41,848 | £5.50 | -£230 |
| | | NOx | 217 | 132 | 85 | £14,000 | -£1,190 |
| | | SOx | 453 | 400 | 53 | £2,400 | -£127 |
| Natural gas | 19m kWh | $CO_2$ | 3,612 | 1,577 | 2,035 | £5.50 | -£11 |
| Diesel oil | 8.9m kWh | $CO_2$ | 2,247 | 616 | 1,631 | £5.50 | -£9 |
| Methane | | $CO_2$ | 63,963 | 28,753 | 35,210 | £5.50 | -£194 |
| Vehicles | | $CO_2$ | 6,999 | 2,176 | 4,823 | £5.50 | -£27 |
| | | Other | 58 | 144 | n.a. | n.a. | |
| Abstraction | Meeting Defra guidance onlow flow rivers at "priority 2" sites | | | | | | -£1,850 |
| Contaminated land | An estimated cost for dealing with land used for sewage disposal. The value is based on the current market cost for remediation | | | | | | -£120 |
| Environmental impact cost | | | | | | | -£3,758 |
| Profit after tax | | | | | | | £63,300 |
| Environmentally sustainable profit | | | | | | | £59,542 |

*Source: Wessex Water Services Limited, 2004, p. 3, reproduced with permission*

**FIGURE 25.3**

*Map of actual and perceived sustainability scores*

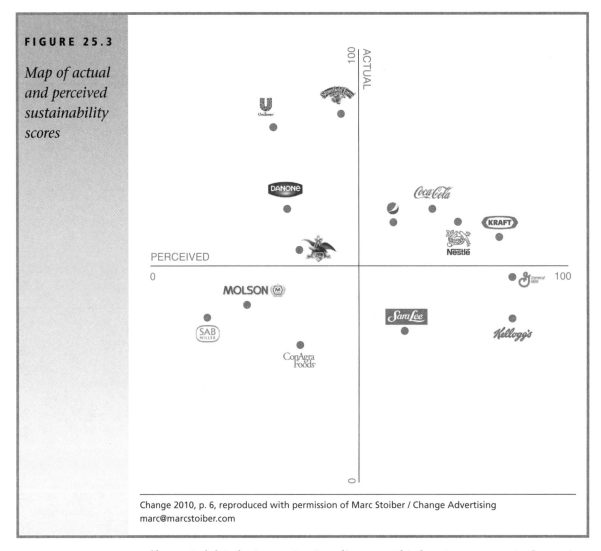

Change 2010, p. 6, reproduced with permission of Marc Stoiber / Change Advertising
marc@marcstoiber.com

self-reported data by increasing its reliance on third party assessments. In particular, the report uses the corporate climate scores of Climate Counts.org (Climate Counts 2011),[1] which, in turn, draws upon the research of the Carbon Disclosure Project (PWC 2011). Figure 25–3 presents the results of the analysis for the Food & Beverage Sector. Clearly, the most desirable quadrant [I] is the upper right hand, where corporations are recognized for their leadership in addressing climate change. The upper left-hand quadrant (II) provides a very useful signal to the corporation that there are unrealized goodwill and related marketing opportunities from doing a better job of communication the success of their climate change policies. The least desirable location from a societal perspective is quadrant IV [the lower right] where firms are trading on a positive reputation they do not deserve.

## SIGNALING MANAGEMENT

In a remarkably insightful study from the World Resources Institute, Ditz et al. (1995) addressed the fundamental challenges that continue to face senior management in internalizing environmental costs into corporate decision making. The basic thesis of their book was that the lack of recognition of the true magnitude and location of all environmental costs can cripple a firm and prevent it from making intelligent resource allocation decisions—either avoiding unnecessary costs or capitalizing on hidden revenue opportunities. The authors identified four major environment-related questions faced by senior corporate management: (1) What are their environmental costs? (2) How large are these costs? (3) Where do these costs arise within the organization? and (4) How can these costs be better managed? Most important, lack of information about these costs can foreclose important strategic opportunities for corporations.

Ditz et al. described how most corporate attention to environmental accounting has been generally concentrated on financial accounting, particularly on the significant liabilities arising from the remediation of contaminated property. However, pollution abatement and control represent only a portion of a firm's environmentally driven costs. Environmental costs associated with other activities can be much greater. For example, a company's choice of raw materials, manufacturing processes, and product design can profoundly affect these costs. There are pathologies of traditional accounting practices in the face of environmental factors. Even to this day, many companies have no conception of the extent and location of environmental costs borne by the firm. Products with *relatively lower environmental costs* will subsidize those with higher environmental costs, and products with *relatively higher environmental costs* may appear profitable but impose significant environmental costs on other parts of the business, and such costs are not attributed to their original source. The result is a major distortion in the process of profit maximization through inefficient resource allocation decisions at the margin. Certain products or processes may be encouraged/discouraged on the basis of such incorrect price signals within the corporation.

To illustrate their hypothesis, Ditz et al. cited the example of a small privately owned company in the Pacific Northwest that has served the global market for stained glass products. As anyone can attest who has visited some of the grand cathedrals in Europe, among the most visually striking components are stained glass windows with orange and red coloring. Artists have long relied on cadmium-based pigments to create these colors, yet cadmium and its compounds are exceedingly toxic, creating significant issues of hazardous solid waste and air emissions. Although ruby-red glass, which relies on cadmium-based pigments, generates more hazardous wastes than other colors, the company had allocated environmental costs equally across all its different glass products, and had not charged a premium for ruby-red glass. The company was paying approximately $3,500 per ton (about $32,500 a year) to dispose of its hazardous waste. The net result of the traditional accounting practice used by the company was that ruby-red glass appeared profitable while, in reality, it was actually making a loss.

The solution to this dilemma is the creation of an Environmental Management Information System (EMIS), which is, in turn, part of a much broader corporate Environmental Management System (EMS) defined as "organizational structure, responsibilities, practices, processes and resources for developing, implementing, achieving, reviewing and maintaining environmental policy" (Sheldon and Yoxon, 2002). To Thompson (2002, p. 20), the central purpose of an EMS is "to improve environmental performance by: setting goals and objectives (policy); identifying, obtaining, and organizing the people, skills, and knowledge, technology, finances, and other resources necessary to achieve the goals and objectives; identifying and assessing options for reaching the goals; assessing risks and priorities; implementing the selected set of options; auditing performance for necessary adjustments by providing feedback to the system; and applying the environmental management tools as required."

| **TABLE 25.5**<br><br>*Basic Components of a Model EFS* | **ENVIRONMENTAL COSTS**<br><br>*Costs of Basic Program*<br>Environmental services (percentage of)<br>Environmental / energy coordinators, etc.<br>Business unit environmental programmes and initiatives (including personnel costs, professional fees, etc.) Waste minimization and pollution prevention - operations and maintenance<br>Waste minimization and pollution prevention - capital costs<br><br>**Total costs of basic program**<br><br>*Remediation, waste and other cots*<br>Fines and prosecutions<br>Waste disposal costs<br>Environmental taxes - e.g., landfill, climate levy<br>Remediation / clean-up costs<br>Other costs, etc.<br>Total remediation, waste and other costs<br><br>**Total environmental Costs**<br><br>**Environmental Savings**<br>*Income, savings and cost avoidance from report year*<br>Reduced insurance from avoidance of hazardous materials<br>Reduced landfill tax and other waste disposal costs<br>Energy conservation savings<br>Water conservation savings<br>Reduced packaging savings<br>Income from sale of recovered and recycled materials<br>Other savings, etc.<br><br>**Total environmental savings**<br>As a percentage of environmental costs<br><br>Summary of savings<br>Savings in report year<br>Savings brought forward from initiatives in prior years<br><br>**Total income, savings and cost avoidance** |
| --- | --- |

*Source:* Derived from Howes 2004, p. 105

EMS procedures have been codified in ISO 14001 (Kuhre 1995) and have been extensively described in numerous works directed at middle and upper management (Hillary 1997; Hunt and Johnson 1995; Sheldon and Yoxon 2002; Starkey 1998). Many of the tools that form an integral part of an EMS are described in detail in this textbook. A critical component of an Environmental Management System is the Environmental Financial Statement (EFS), which allocates costs in a manner that allows a company to identify the location of its costs and opportunities for savings. Howes (2004) lists some of the basic components of a model EFS. [See Table 25–5.] To Matthews and Lave (2003), "a *reasonable* MIS tabulates current environmental costs and likely future liabilities and traces them to the material, product, and process generating them, allowing decision-makers to assess their current status." In contrast, "a *good* MIS would give decision-makers information about how environmental costs and liabilities would change if there were a change in materials, design, or process." It has been estimated that environmental costs can account for as much as 20% of total costs for some companies, depending on their products, production processes, and waste generation (Ditz et al. 1995; Henriques

| ENVIRONMENTAL COSTS | UK POUNDS | |
|---|---|---|
| **Payroll and Labour costs** | | **TABLE 25.6** |
| Apportionment of technical service manager's and others' time | 60,000 | *EMIS from* |
| Other costs? | x | *Dartford and* |
| Costs of basic programme | 60,000 | *Graveshead* |
| **Remediation, waste and other costs** | | *Hospital* |
| Waste disposal costs | 250,000 | |
| Tree protection - metal fencing | 7,500 | |
| Environmental taxes paid - landfill tax, other costs, etc. | x | |
| **Total remediation, waste and other costs** | 257,500 | |
| **Total environmental costs** | **317,500** | |
| **Environmental Savings** | | |
| **Income, savings and cost avoidance** | | |
| Ground stabilization - net savings building materials avoided | 111,500 | |
| Re-use of excavated material on-site - fuel costs avoided | - | |
| Avoided landfill charges / waste disposal costs | 50,000 | |
| Construction of drainage swale - avoided drainage infrastructure costs | 20,000 | |
| Reduced landfill tax and other waste disposal costs | x | |
| Income from sale of recovered and recycled materials | | |
| Other savings, etc. | x | |
| **Total environmental savings** | **181,500** | |
| **Savings as a percentage of environmental costs** | **57%** | |

*Source:* Howes, 2003, p. 12, reproduced with permission of Chartered Institute of Management Accountants

and Richardson 2004). An example of a good EMIS is presented in Table 25–6, which identifies both environmental costs and offsetting environmental savings resulting from the identification and remediation of environmental costs by the Dartford and Gravesham Hospital in Kent, England (Howes 2003, p. 12). This is similar to the experience of Baxter Health [see Table 25–1], which provided critical financial environmental information to both management and external stakeholders.

The critical issue is one of cost allocation, and there are a number of promising methodologies for recognizing and/or incorporating environmental costs into conventional financial analysis. [See, for example, the discussion of full cost accounting in GEMI 1994.] These include, inter alia, activity-based costing; environmental profit and loss accounts; genuine wealth accounting; sustainable balanced scorecard; and ratio-based financial models for sustainability. Each is briefly described below.

## ACTIVITY-BASED COSTING

Table 25–7 summarizes seven reasons provided by the U.S. EPA (1995) why environmental costs and performance are worthy of corporate attention. As indicated earlier, the first challenge is to identify all the types of environmentally related

| **TABLE 25.7**<br><br>*Principal Reasons Why Environmental Costs and Performance Are Worthy of Corporate Attention* | (1) Many environmental costs can be significantly reduced or eliminated as a result of business decisions, ranging from operational and housekeeping changes, to investment in "greener" process technology, to redesign of processes/products. Many environmental costs (e.g., wasted raw materials) may provide no added value to a process, system, or product.<br>(2) Environmental costs (and, thus, potential cost savings) may be obscured in overhead accounts or otherwise overlooked.<br>(3) Many companies have discovered that environmental costs can be offset by generating revenues through sale of waste by-products or transferable pollution allowances, or licensing of clean technologies, for example.<br>(4) Better management of environmental costs can result in improved environmental performance and significant benefits to human health as well as business success.<br>(5) Understanding the environmental costs and performance of processes and products can promote more accurate costing and pricing of products and can aid companies in the design of more environmentally preferable processes, products, and services for the future.<br>(6) Competitive advantage with customers can result from processes, products, and services that can be demonstrated to be environmentally preferable.<br>(7) Accounting for environmental costs and performance can support a company's development and operation of an overall environmental management system. Such a system will soon be a necessity for companies engaged in international trade due to pending international consensus standard ISO 14001, developed by the International Organization for Standardization. |
| --- | --- |

*Source:* US EPA 1995, pp. 1-2

EXAMPLES OF ENVIRONMENTAL COSTS INCURRED BY FIRMS

*POTENTIALLY HIDDEN COSTS*

**TABLE 25.8**

*Examples of Environmental Costs Incurred by Firms*

| Regulatory | Upfront | Voluntary (Beyond Compliance) |
| --- | --- | --- |
| Notification | Site studies Site preparation | Community relations/ |
| Reporting | Permitting | outreach |
| Monitoring/testing | R&D | Monitoring/testing |
| Studies/modeling | Engineering and | Training |
| Remediation | procurement | Audits |
| Recordkeeping | Installation | Qualifying suppliers |
| Plans | | Reports (e.g., annual |
| Training | | environmental reports) |
| Inspections | **Conventional Costs** | Insurance |
| Manifesting | Capital equipment Materials | Planning |
| Labeling | Labor | Feasibility studies |
| Preparedness | Supplies | Remediation |
| Protective equipment | Utilities | Recycling |
| Medical surveillance | Structures | Environmental studies |
| Environmental | Salvage value | R & D |
| insurance | **Back-End** | Habitat and wetland |
| Financial assurance Pollution | Closure/ | protection Landscaping |
| control Spill response | decommissioning Disposal of | Other environmental |
| Stormwater management | inventory Post-closure care | projects |
| Waste management Taxes/ | Site survey | Financial support to |
| fees | | environmental groups |
| | | and/or researchers |

| *Contingent Costs* | | |
| --- | --- | --- |
| Future compliance costs | Remediation Property | Legal expenses Natural |
| Penalties/fines Response to | damage Personal injury | resource damages |
| future releases | damage | Economic loss damages |

| *Image and Relationship Costs* | | |
| --- | --- | --- |
| Corporate image | Relationship with | Relationship with lenders |
| Relationship with customers | professional staff | Relationship with host |
| Relationships with investors | Relationship with workers | communities Relationship |
| Relationship with insurers | Relationship with suppliers | with regulators |

*Source:* US EPA 1995, p. 9

costs associated with corporate operations. Table 25–8 provides a listing of these costs identified by the U.S. EPA under four general rubrics: conventional, potentially hidden, contingent, and image/relationship costs. An emerging methodology to address the complex issue of cost allocation is material-flow-oriented, activity-based costing (ABC). [See chapter 17 for a discussion of mass and material balance

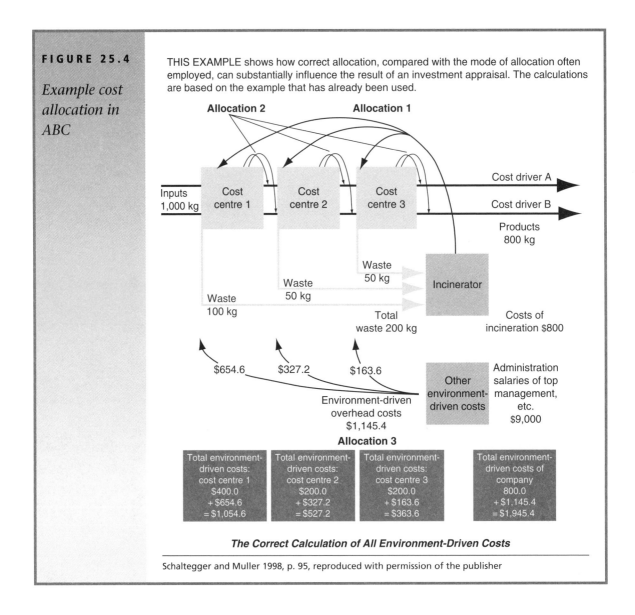

**FIGURE 25.4**

*Example cost allocation in ABC*

THIS EXAMPLE shows how correct allocation, compared with the mode of allocation often employed, can substantially influence the result of an investment appraisal. The calculations are based on the example that has already been used.

*The Correct Calculation of All Environment-Driven Costs*

Schaltegger and Muller 1998, p. 95, reproduced with permission of the publisher

calculations.] Schaltegger and Muller (1998) outline the three-step allocation process in ABC using as an example a production process that relies on an incinerator for waste disposal [See Figure 25–4]: first, allocation from joint environmental cost centers (e.g., an incinerator) to *responsible* cost centers (i.e., production centers); second, from responsible cost centers to final cost objects (i.e., units of final products); and third, the allocation of other environmentally induced (i.e., indirect) costs to both cost centers and cost objects.

While conceptually simple, ABC encounters several practical complexities. The first is the choice of allocation keys that are critical to the analysis. Schaltegger and Muller identify four common keys: the volume of throughput (materials, emissions, and waste treated); the toxicity of emissions and waste treated; the environmental impact added (volume multiplied by the impact per unit of volume of the emissions treated); and the induced costs associated with treating different kinds of throughput (materials and emissions treated). There is no clear best alternative; the choice is situation dependent. Some authors feel, however, that a commonly used metric, namely, direct labor hours, can distort corporate decisions concerning the appropriate mix of factor inputs (Burritt 1998) and should be avoided in instances with environmental impacts.

The second complexity with respect to the implementation of ABC is related to capital expenditures, specifically how to separate out expenditures undertaken to upgrade technology that may also have an improved environmental effect designed to avoid future liabilities or which incorporates new and more efficient and environmentally friendly technology.

Third, cost categories vary in their ease of measurement and ability to be allocated. The U.S. EPA arrays five environmental cost categories from easiest to most difficult to measure: conventional costs, hidden costs, contingent costs, relationship/image costs, and social costs. Figure 25–5 displays the US EPA's four-tier cost and financial protocol recommended for corporations seeking to measure the benefits of pollution prevention (U.S. EPA 1989). It has to be acknowledged that ABC may not always be successful in allocating all relevant costs and that the companion

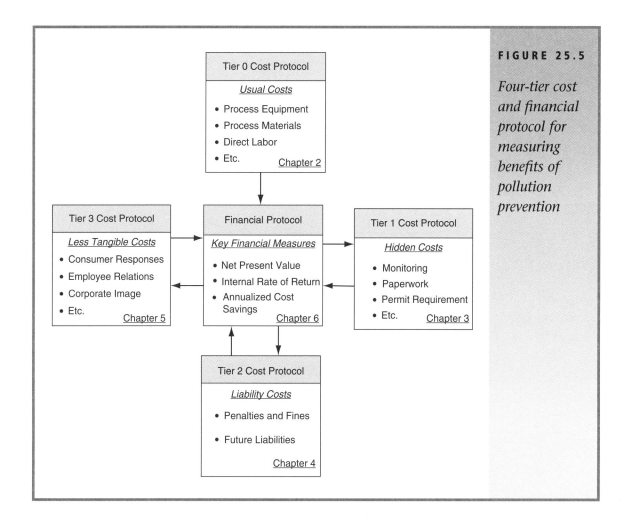

**FIGURE 25.5**

*Four-tier cost and financial protocol for measuring benefits of pollution prevention*

use of eco-efficiency measures is still useful as a signaling device for internal corporate decision making.

Schaltegger and Burritt (2000) conclude with the observation that the implementation of ABC and the realization of the potential costs and profit impacts are contingent on corporations adopting material-flow and energy-flow oriented ecological accounting. The following example drawn from the operations of Interface Inc. addresses both types of practices.

### ABC Case Study: Interface Inc.

Emblemsvag and Bras (2001) have published a comprehensive empirical work on the application of ABC in four major corporate case studies, including Interface Inc. Because of limited time and resources, the authors were only able to perform a preliminary analysis of Interface based on material and energy efficiency, to the exclusion of cost data. However, the case study yields some insightful results that aided the corporation in its own analysis of the sustainability of its operations. The authors were able to track the complex flow of both materials and energy across 6 facilities, 10 product lines, and 49 distinct activities. Table 25–9 presents their summary estimates of resource consumption based on 1997 product and process data. The most remarkable conclusion from this analysis is that over 91% of attributable energy consumption and 97% of attributable waste generation is associated with *material usage in production*; that is, purchased inputs whose environmental impact is outside the boundaries of Interface's production operations. On reflection, however, this is not completely surprising as one important factor is Interface's reliance on synthetic fabrics that are highly energy intensive with respect to production and embodied energy [see chapters 13–14]. It is important to note, however, that the U.S. EPA's Toxic Release Inventory data on environmental releases from Interface's operations show significant plant-level improvements since the TRI commenced data gathering in 1987 (www.epa.gov/tri/).

| **TABLE 25.9**<br><br>*Interface Resource Use Estimates* | RESOURCE CATEGORY | ENERGY CONSUMPTION (MJ/ YEAR) | PERCENTAGE | WASTE GENERATION [PWU/YEAR] | PERCENTAGE |
|---|---|---|---|---|---|
| | Depreciation and Maintenance | 2,567,020 | 0.06% | 1786 | 0.01% |
| | Buildings | 344,008,015 | 8.63% | 700917 | 2.86% |
| | Freight within Troup County | 915,212 | 0.02% | 3837 | 0.02% |
| | Material Usage in Production | 3,637,859,399 | 91.28% | 23827025 | 97.12% |
| | Total | 3,985,349,646 | 100.00% | 24,533,565 | 100.00% |

*Source:* Emblemsvag and Bras 2001, p. 214, reproduced with permission

In light of the important role of Interface's supply chain in the company's overall environmental impact, the challenge is to identify what technology and policy levers are available to the corporation in their goal of moving toward sustainability. Emblemsvag and Bras offer three possible initiatives: first, asking their suppliers to generate information on the embodied energy of their products; second, shifting corporate purchasing decisions toward material with lower embodied energy; and third, increasing the role of recycling in order to reduce reliance on eternal supplies of raw materials. As outlined in chapter 13, Interface has made this a major component of their sustainability strategy as they attempt to close the loop in the manufacturing process. [See also the discussion of Wal-Mart and its supply chain initiatives in Chapter 28].

## ENVIRONMENTAL PROFIT & LOSS [EP&L] ACCOUNTING

The critical importance of the supply chain in the overall environmental impact of corporate operations has been graphically demonstrated by the recent development of a new methodology announced in 2011 by the German sportswear giant, Puma. The company hired PriceWaterhouseCoopers and the environmental research group, Trucost, to collaborate with it in a comprehensive examination of the environmental and social costs and benefits of its business activities. The results demonstrated that

| | WATER USE | GHDs | LAND USE | AIR POLLUTION | WASTE | TOTAL | |
|---|---|---|---|---|---|---|---|
| | € million | € million | € million | € million | € million | € million | % of total |
| | 33% | 32% | 26% | 7% | 2% | 100% | |
| TOTAL | 47 | 47 | 37 | 11 | 3 | **145** | 100% |
| **PUMA** operations | <1 | 7 | <1 | 1 | <1 | **8** | 6% |
| Tier 1 | 1 | 9 | <1 | 1 | 2 | **13** | 9% |
| Tier 2 | 4 | 7 | <1 | 2 | 1 | **14** | 10% |
| Tier 3 | 17 | 7 | <1 | 3 | <1 | **27** | 19% |
| Tier 4 | 25 | 17 | 37 | 4 | <1 | **83** | 57% |
| | | | | | | | |
| **EMEA** | 4 | 8 | 1 | 1 | <1 | **14** | 10% |
| **Americas** | 2 | 10 | 20 | 3 | <1 | **35** | 24% |
| **Asia/Pacific** | 41 | 29 | 16 | 7 | 3 | **96** | 66% |
| | | | | | | | |
| **Footwear** | 25 | 28 | 34 | 7 | 2 | **96** | 66% |
| **Apparel** | 18 | 14 | 3 | 3 | 1 | **39** | 27% |
| **Accessories** | 4 | 5 | <1 | 1 | <1 | **10** | 7% |

**TABLE 25.10**

*Puma— EP&L— Stage 1*

*Source:* Puma.com, reproduced with permission

94% of Puma's environmental costs were attributable to the production of raw materials in its supply chain. The PWC consultant observed that "fundamentally, this analysis is about risk management for the environment, and for business, because you cannot separate the two . . . This is a first for a company to measure and value the impact of its business in this way and gives PUMA a unique and challenging insight into their supply chain. It's a game–changing development for businesses to integrate environmental issues into their current business model like this, because it provides a basis for embedding their reliance on ecosystem services into business strategy" (PUMA and PPR Home joint press release, Munich/London, May 16, 2011).

Table 25–10 summarizes the results of the first phase of the Puma multistage analysis. The total environmental impact measured in this phase is 145 million euros. To place this in the context of total corporate operations, Puma had profits in 2010 of 202.2 million euros on sales of 2,706.4 million euros. The following phase will attempt the more conceptually challenging task of estimating the impact of social factors such as fair wages, safety, and working conditions. Finally, the creation of an integrated profit-and-loss analogue that includes environmental, social, and economic components requires the measurement of any offsetting benefits related to the creation of jobs, tax contributions, philanthropic initiatives, and other value-adding elements.

As indicated in Table 25–10, Puma has focused initially on five environmental impacts: water use, GHGs, land use, air pollution, and waste. Three categorizations have been used: (1) principal product lines, (2) global markets by region, and (3) tiers in the supply chain. Puma core operations include offices, warehouses, stores, and logistics; Tier 1 is the manufacturing of corporate products; Tier 2 represents outsourced processes such as embroiders, printers, and outsole production; Tier 3 is the processing of raw materials, such as leather tanneries, chemical industry and oil refining; and Tier 4 is raw material production such as cotton cultivation and harvesting, natural rubber production, oil drilling, and cattle ranching for leather, which represents the largest contribution to land-use impacts. The company has also reported that the single most important contributor to air pollution is ammonia emissions from animal waste and fertilizers used in agricultural processes. Table 25–11, derived from Puma's online reports, summarizes the major methodologies employed in monetizing the environmental impacts as well as the actual values used.

The development of this innovative methodology has allowed Puma to structure its operations in a more sustainable manner and measure its degree of success on each of the component initiatives. A critical part of this reorientation of its business model and corporate strategy will clearly require extensive collaboration with suppliers. To quote:

> PUMA and PPR Home [its parent company] will look to play a catalytic role in raising awareness that the current business model is outdated and needs decisive reforms, forging partnerships and collaborations to explore new and innovative ways to differentially attribute the responsibilities and equitably share the costs of these, while building capacity at suppliers' factories and developing new materials and products. PUMA and PPR HOME are sharing the results of the EP&L with other industry players and corporations to leverage adopting a new business model that takes the costs of using natural resources within business operations into account. This analysis will also help to better assess

**TABLE 25.11**

*Puma EP&L Components*

| TARGET | VALUATION METHODOLOGY | RANGE OF VALUES | VALUE CHOSEN |
|---|---|---|---|
| **WATER USE** | Focus on scarcity as a result of the indirect use value of water. [Lost value associated with direct consumption not included as it is assumed to be internalized in the price for water extraction and use]. Scarcity is measured by withdrawal from surface and groundwater as a percentage of actual renewable freshwater resources. A sample of 18 studies was used to determine the relationship between scarcity and value. | 0.03 - 18.45 Euros per cubic meter | 0.81 Euros per cubic meter |
| **WASTE** | Values were generated for three different types of disposal: landfill, incineration and recycling. | | |
| **(a) Landfilling** | There are three main externalities: methane emissions, leachate and disamenity costs, including noise, dust, litter, odour, vermin, visual blight and perceived risk. (1) For methane, the social cost of carbon [see "GHG" below] was used to derive a $CO_2$ equivalent value for methane, and a discount rate of 3.4% was used for the stream of future emissions. (2) leachate costs are based on the site-specific cost of clean-up. (3) Disamenty costs were calculated using hedonic pricing methods [see this book Chapter 7]. | 36 - 87 Euros per tone | 73 Euros per tone |
| **(b) Incineration** | There are two principal externalities: air emissions and disamenities. The social cost of carbon was used for GHG emissions; $SO_2$, NOx and PM were valued as outlined below under "Air Pollution", and dioxin and heavy metal emission values were derived from EU 2009. The value of GHG emissions avoided from any energy recovered on site was subtracted. | 35 - 63 Euros per tone | 51 Euros per tone |

*(Continued)*

**TABLE 25.11**

*continued*

| TARGET | VALUATION METHODOLOGY | RANGE OF VALUES | VALUE CHOSEN |
|---|---|---|---|
| **(c) Recycling** | Recycling has environmental benefits as well as negative externalities. Despite the fact that benefits are expected to exceed costs, a conservative approach to valuation was adopted which assumed that the benefits and costs cancelled each other out. | n.a. | 0 Euros per tone |
| **LAND USE** | The analysis focussed on the loss of ecosystem services and biodiversity from land conversion for buildings and agriculture. The values were largely derived from TEEB 2011 and specific to each eco-region (tropical forest, grassland, inland wetland). | 63 - 18,653 Euros per hectare | 347 Euros per hectare |
| **GHG** | The social cost of carbon was used based on estimates from Tol 2009, and a social rate of discount of 3.4 % was used. | n.a. | 66 Euros per ton of $CO_2e$ |
| **AIR POLLUTION** | Six air pollutants are considered: NH3, PM10, $SO_2$, NOx, VOCs and CO. Market values were used where appropriate; otherwise the analysis relied on a literature review of estimates derived from willingness-to-pay studies [see this book chapter 7]. Values were adjusted for site-specific factors. | Euros per tonne. PM10 1,285-191,743; NH3 1,133-5,670; $SO_2$ 7836,422; NOx 664-3,179; VOCs 425-1,998 | Average value per tonne in Euros: PM10 14,983, NH3 1,673, $SO_2$ 2,077, NOx 1,186, VOCs 836 |

*Source: Puma.com, reproduced with permission*

the relative environmental impacts of sourcing from different countries and regions. Down the line it will allow PUMA to improve supply chain management and reduce supply chain risks (PUMA and PPR Home joint press release, Munich/London, May 16, 2011).

## GENUINE WEALTH ACCOUNTING

Once a corporation has adopted a TBL approach to reporting, there are several possible additional steps that may be useful in helping the company realize greater long-term sustainability and profitability. One of these is the adoption of a corporate *Genuine*

**FIGURE 25.6**

*Genuine wealth account attributes for business*

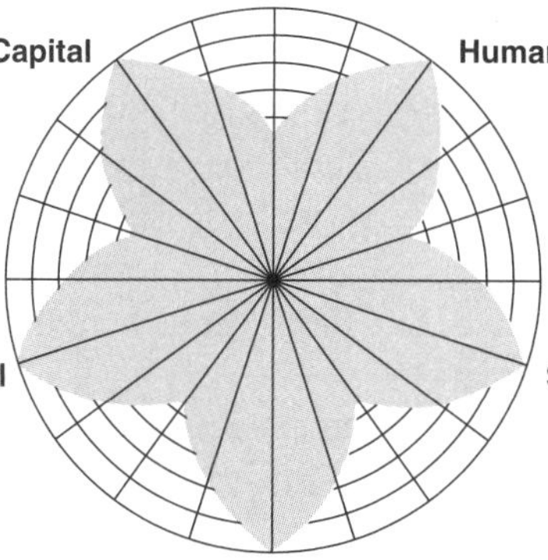

**Financial Assets**
- Current financial assets; cash, accounts receivable, inventories
- Capital assets

**Financial Liabilities**
- Debt (short and long-term borrowings)
- Accounts payable

**Shareholder's Equity**
- Preferred securities
- Share capital
- Retained earnings

**Financial Capital**

- People (employees, contractors, suppliers)
- Intellectual capital: educational attainment, knowledge, skills
- Employment rate
- Labor participation rates
- Full-time, permanaent job rate
- Benefits including work-place interventions
- Creativity and entrepreneurship
- Capabilities
- Motivation

- Productivity
- Happiness (self-rated)
- Time use balance (work, family, leisure, community)
- Health (disease, diet, overall health)
- Physical well-being (fitness)
- Mental well-being
- Spiritual well-being
- Addictions (drugs, alcohol, gambling)
- Workplace safety
- Training and professional development
- Personal self-development

**Human Capital**

**Built Capital**
- Infrastructure; roads, pipelines, transmission lines, other structures
- Buildings
- Machinery and equiment
- Technology
- Patents
- Brands
- Intellectual property (ideas, innovations)
- Management processes
- Production processes
- Databases

**Natural Capital**
- Environmental goods and services
- Natural resources (stocks and flows): land, minerals, oil, gas, coal, forests (trees), fish and wildlife, water, air, carbon sinks
- Ecosystem integrity
- Energy (by type, source, and end-use)

**Social Capital**
- Customer relationships (value, loyalty and commitment by customers)
- Supplier relationships (value and commitment by suppliers)
- Reputation
- Workplace relational capital: employee interrelationships, workplace climate (e.g., stress, excitement, joy), social cohesion (teams and team spirit), workplace climate (happiness with work)
- Equity (incomes, age-sex distribution, women in management)
- Employee family quality of life
- Networks
- Friendships amongst workplace colleagues
- Membership in professional associations, clubs, and other organizations
- Social events with colleagues
- Family outings with workplace colleagues
- Financial investment/giving/donations to the community

Anielski 2007, p. 157, reproduced with permission of the author

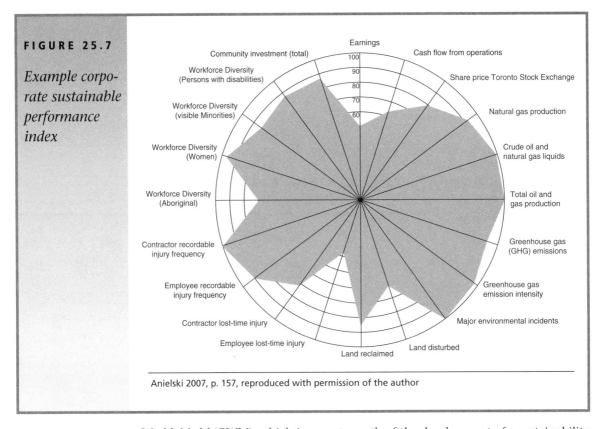

**FIGURE 25.7**

*Example corporate sustainable performance index*

Anielski 2007, p. 157, reproduced with permission of the author

*Wealth Model* (GWM), which is an outgrowth of the development of a sustainability index for public sector entities such as cities (Anielski 2007). The GWM can incorporate physical, qualitative, and monetary conditions of five critical capital assets (i.e., financial, human, social, built, and natural) into the daily operation of an organization. To quote Anielski (2007, p. 155), "such accounts inform directors, shareholders and communities about the effective rate of return to investment in all five capital assets and analyze the efficiency and effectiveness of total capital management. This includes evaluating the integrity or coordination of capital for sustained flows of benefits as well as the annual depreciation or depletion rate of capital." Figure 25–6 presents a conceptual diagram that illustrates the components of each form of capital. Operationalizing this concept requires the companion development of a quantitative sustainable performance index for the firm, as illustrated in Figure 25–7. As the author states, the advantage of this integrated model is that it shows the delicate balance required to achieve genuine sustainability. The challenge in implementation is developing common standards for measurement and reporting to allow both temporal intracorporate tracking, as well as cross-firm and industry comparisons. Despite the fact that the model is a work in progress, there is no reason why an organization could not adopt some variant as a first step to a more comprehensive analysis.

## SUSTAINABLE BALANCED SCORECARD

The concept of the *Balanced Scorecard* was first introduced into the popular business literature by Kaplan and Norton in the *Harvard Business Review* in 1992 and was followed by numerous additional works on the subject by the authors (Kaplan and Norton 1993, 2001, 2004, 2007). Now widely used by corporations, nonprofits, and governments (2GC 2011), this instrument was originally designed to provide managers with a structured series of interlinked indicators that could provide an organization with a comprehensive understanding of its performance. In their original articulation of this concept, Kaplan and Norton developed sets or parameters designed to address four specific questions:

> First, how do customers see your company? Find out by measuring lead times, quality, performance and service, and costs. Second, what must your company excel at? Determine the processes and competencies that are most critical, and specify measures, such as cycle time, quality, employee skills, and productivity, to track them. Third, can your company continue to improve and create value? Monitor your ability to launch new products, create more value for customers, and improve operating efficiencies. Fourth, how has your company done by its shareholders? Measure cash flow, quarterly sales growth, operating income by division, and increased market share by segment and return on equity. The balanced scorecard lets executives see whether they have improved in one area at the expense of another. (Kaplan and Norton 1995, p. 1)

As Figure 25–8 demonstrates (Kaplan and Norton 2007), the questions were presented in four linked tables that enunciated organizational goals and their related performance measures. In Figure 25–9, the authors (Kaplan and Norton 2005) illustrated how the balanced scorecard could be constructed using a hypothetical company (ECI) in the semiconductor industry. This analytical tool has become so popular that it is used globally across a broad spectrum of organizational types. In a recent survey, over 80% of respondents reported use of the balanced scorecard to influence business actions (2GC 2011). The scorecard has been used to aid strategic management, inform decision making and reporting of results, and to drive organizational performance by influencing the actions and behavior of managers and individuals and the way they are appraised (2GC 2011, p. 4).

A balanced scorecard has several critical characteristics (Schaltegger and Burritt 2000): "it measures a set of performance indicators, specifies goals and measures goals in similar terms, removes the focus on a single short-term measure of financial results, and provides physical as well as financial measures of performance. Furthermore, it provides a strategic action process with the following four steps: formulation and implementation of vision and strategy, communicating and linking, business planning, and strategic feedback and learning."

In a subsequent book, Kaplan and Norton (2001) acknowledged that while the original purpose of the scorecard was to solve a measurement problem associated with the inability of traditional financial metrics to measure the value-creating activities from an organization's intangible assets, this was being supplanted by the emerging use of the scorecard to guide the implementation of new corporate strategies. [See also Cobbold and Lawrie 2002.] As is inevitable with an analytical tool with such a large uptake, there is a continual process of evolution. Cobbold and Lawrie describe three distinct generations of balanced scorecards, beginning with the original conceptualization of Kaplan and Norton. The authors describe four key

**FIGURE 25.8**

*Balanced scorecard*

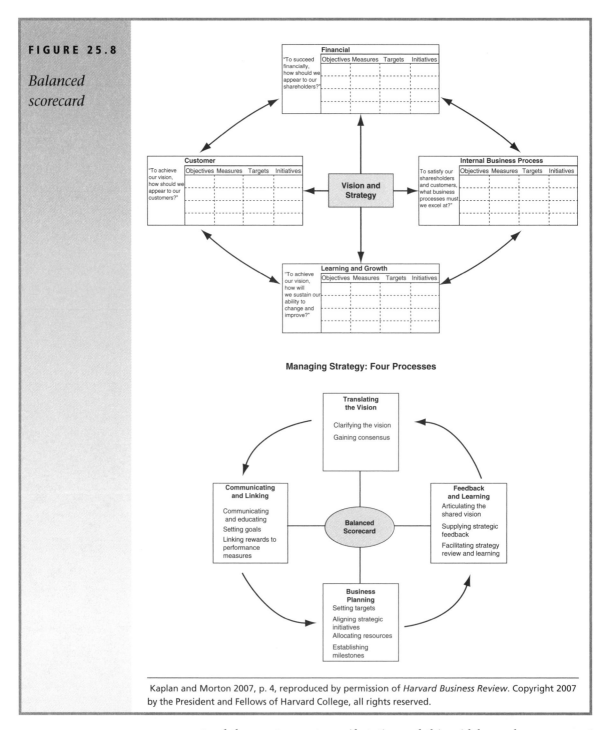

Kaplan and Morton 2007, p. 4, reproduced by permission of *Harvard Business Review*. Copyright 2007 by the President and Fellows of Harvard College, all rights reserved.

components of the most recent manifestations of this widely used management tool: (1) a destination statement that describes what the organization is likely to look like at an agreed future date; (2) an articulation of strategic objectives; (3) a Strategic Linkage Model that incorporates four zones or "perspectives" relating to financial and market characteristics, external relationships, activities and processes, and organization and culture; and, finally, (4) measures and initiatives designed to support management's ability to monitor progress towards goal achievement.

## ECI's Balanced Business Scorecard

**FIGURE 25.9**

*Example balanced scorecard*

### Financial Perspective

| GOALS | MEASURES |
|---|---|
| Survive | Cash flow |
| Succeed | Quarterly sales growth and operating income by division |
| Prosper | Increased market share and ROE |

### Customer Perspective

| GOALS | MEASURES |
|---|---|
| New products | Percentage of sales from new products |
| | Percentage of sales from proprietary products |
| Responsive supply | On-time delivery (defined by customer) |
| Preferred suppliers | Share of key accounts' purchases |
| | Ranking by key accounts |
| Customer partnerships | Number of cooperative engineering efforts |

### Internal Business Perspective

| GOALS | MEASURES |
|---|---|
| Technology capability | Manufacturing geometry versus competition |
| Manufacturing excellence | Cycle time, unit cost, yield |
| Design productivity | Silicon efficiency, engineering efficiency |
| New product introduction | Actual introduction schedule versus plan |

### Innovation and Learning Perspective

| GOALS | MEASURES |
|---|---|
| Technology leadership | Time to develop next generation |
| Manufacturing learning | Process time to maturity |
| Product focus | Percentage of products that equal 80% of sales |
| Time to market | New product introduction versus competition |

Kaplan and Morton 2005, p. 4, reproduced by permission of *Harvard Business Review.* Copyright 2005 by the President and Fellows of Harvard College, all rights reserved.

Clearly, an instrument with this track record offers a potential opportunity in the area of sustainability. Table 25–12 illustrates how Epstein (2008) adapts the balanced scorecard for explicit use by organizations interested in the impact of strategies, policies, products, and procedures on social and environmental responsibilities; competitive advantage; and financial viability. Epstein also states that a corporation may choose to add a fifth dimension to this analysis that includes social and environmental performance indicators linked with the other four components shown in Table 25–8.

Figge et al. (2002) presents a hypothetical case study of a textile company to illustrate how a *Sustainability Balanced Scorecard* can aid in the incorporation of environmental and social factors into high-level corporate strategy. Borrowing

| **TABLE 25.12**<br><br>*Modification of the Balanced Scorecard for Sustainability* | **FINANCIAL DIMENSION** | **STAKEHOLDER DIMENSION** |
|---|---|---|
| | • Percent of sales revenues from "green" products | • Sustainabiliy awards |
| | • Recycling revenues | • Funds donated for community support |
| | • Energy costs | • Number of community complaints |
| | • Fines and penalties for pollution | • Employee satisfaction |
| | **INTERNAL BUSINESS PROCESS DIMENSION** | **LEARNING AND GROWTH DIMENSION** |
| | • Percent of suppliers certified | • Diversity of workforce and management |
| | • Volume of hazardous waste | • Number of volunteer hours |
| | • Packaging volume | • Cost of employee benefits |
| | • Number of community complaints | • Percent of employees trained in sustainability |
| | • Cost of minoritty business purchases | |
| | • Number of product recalls | |

Epstein 2008, p. 138. Reprinted with permission of the publisher. From Making Sustainability Work, copyright© 2008 by Marc J. Epstein, Berrett-Koehler Publishers, Inc., San Francisco, CA. All rights reserved. www.bkconnection.com

from Kaplan and Norton (2001), Figge et al. use the concept of a *Balanced Scorecard Strategy Map* [see also Kaplan and Norton 2004] to create a hierarchical network of cause-and-effect chains for all relevant economic, environmental, and social issues facing their hypothetical firm. [See Figure 25–10.] Once this initial step has been completed, it is possible to proceed to the balanced scorecard process of defining indicator targets and measures. The usefulness of this methodology is illustrated with reference to a hypothetical company producing textiles (p. 26) that wishes to increase its return on capital from 6–8%. To achieve this goal, the company wants to increase its sales margin from 4% to 4.5% and boost its turnover by 20% by increasing its market share from 15% to 20%. The company proposes reaching these goals by adopting several initiatives that will increase customer demand and improve its environmental and social image: (i) a shift to less toxic inputs and more durable products; (ii) ensuring that no child labor is involved in the supplier chain; (iii) increasing efficiency in the use of energy, water, and material; and (iv) adopting measures to increase employee motivation and satisfaction. The strategy map in Figure 25–10 illustrates this integration of environmental and social issues in the Sustainability Balanced Scorecard as "conventional success factors" so that nonmarket issues become part of a mainstream management system.

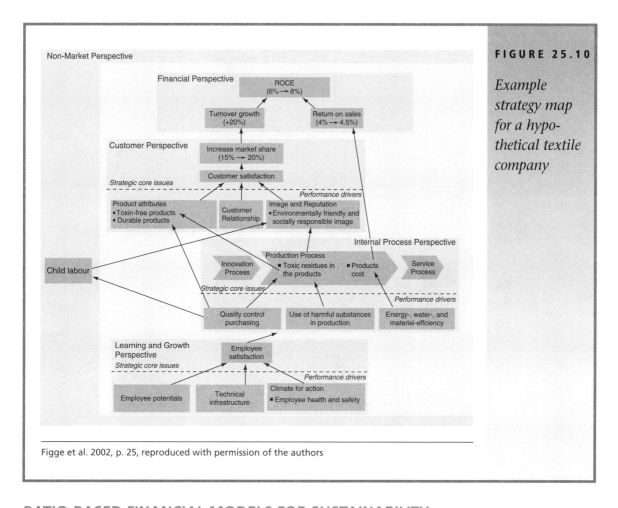

Figge et al. 2002, p. 25, reproduced with permission of the authors

**FIGURE 25.10**

*Example strategy map for a hypothetical textile company*

## RATIO-BASED FINANCIAL MODELS FOR SUSTAINABILITY

Chousa and Castro (2006) have developed *a Model of Financial Analysis of Sustainability* based on the Dupont system of ratio analysis to integrate sustainability considerations into traditional financial models. The distinguishing characteristic of their model is the inclusion of specific ratios that reflect the relationship between physical measures of pollution and more conventional financial values such as sales. Figure 25–11 is used by the authors to demonstrate the value of this hybrid and integrated approach. The authors contrast two alternative approaches: first a focus on the sales/fixed assets ratio and its role in corporate profitability. The relevant path is denoted by the shaded ratios in the area demarcated by the large box with a dashed-line perimeter. To quote (p. 138): "From a traditional perspective, when the value of this ratio is high, it is believed to reflect the efficient use of the capital invested in the company's site and the likely reduction of the financial leverage of the company's capital structure (owing to the improved ROA, which would lead to higher profit that would allow the reduction of total liabilities)."

In contrast, the authors posit that the company may be delaying capital expenditures on necessary pollution control equipment. Conventional financial analysis would not reflect the potentially detrimental impact such a decision might have on

**FIGURE 25.11**

*Expanded financial analysis including environmental factors and influence on profitability*

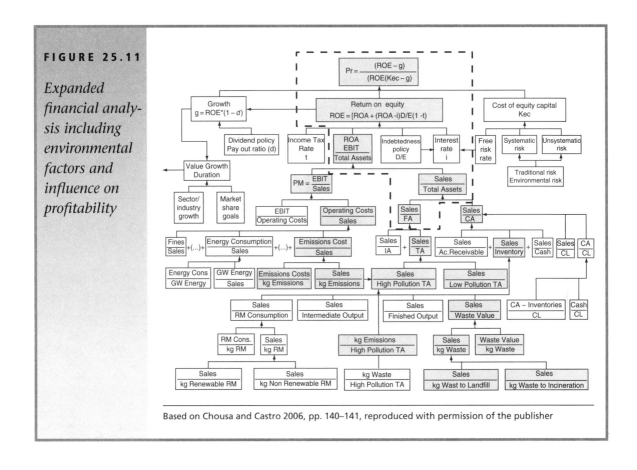

Based on Chousa and Castro 2006, pp. 140–141, reproduced with permission of the publisher

long-run profitability by negatively affecting competiveness or exposing the corporation to environmental liability and governmental regulatory action. The inclusion of all of the shaded ratios outside the dashed-line box allows the analyst to track the cascading effect of the decision to avoid pollution control expenditures all the way through to ROA, ROE, and profitability. To quote:

> The analysis of ratios such as sales/waste value, cost of emissions/sales, environmental fines/sales, etc. can add valuable information to the financial ratio analysis. Although a high sales/fixed assets ratio may be signaling an improved ROA and ROE, other ratios may be signaling the opposite. A high cost of emissions/sales ratio and/or a high environmental fines/sales ratio will limit profit generation and a low sales/waste value ratio will reduce the sales/current assets ratio, this compensating for the high value initially found for the sales/fixed assets ratio. (p. 142)

## TWO OTHER METHODOLOGIES OF NOTE

### Sustainable Value

Figge and Hahn (2005) have developed an interesting valuation methodology to calculate the sustainable value creation of companies and their cost of *sustainability capital.* The essence of the analysis, based on the concept of opportunity cost, measures to what degree any corporation's resources could be used elsewhere in a national economy with a lower environmental impact. The methodology is illustrated by a case study of British Petroleum (BP) laid out in Tables 25–13 and 25–14. In the first step, as illustrated in Table 25–13, relative financial and pollutant emission data are presented for both the UK national economy and BP. BP's *net value added* is defined as "the value created within a company after depreciation. It excluded any value that has been created by suppliers or that will be created by customers." BP's *nonfinancial assets* "were estimated by subtracting all financial assets (e.g., securities) from BP's total assets."

The second step, as illustrated in Table 25–14, involves the creation of two critical ratios: (1) a return on *sustainability capital* for BP calculated by relating BP's estimated value added to all eight forms of *capital* listed in the table. While a pollutant would not normally be considered a form of capital, there is a logic to its use here. For example, a pollutant could be linked to a form of capital in the sense that there is corresponding natural ecosystem capital used to receive, assimilate, disperse, or otherwise respond to the emission of this particular pollutant. (2) A similar ratio for the UK calculates the cost of capital based on the economy as a whole. The difference between the BP and UK ratios is multiplied by BP's performance data to estimate the sustainability value created by BP. The underlying rationale for this analysis is that "BP covers its cost of sustainability capital if and only if it uses its different forms of capital more efficiently than the British economy (p. 53)."

The authors' calculations yield a net sustainability deficit for BP of 72,373 million UK pounds, calculated as the quotient of the total value created (578,984 million UK pounds) divided by 8 (i.e., the number of types of capital under consideration) in order to avoid double counting. This implies that "had the resource been allocated to the British economy on average rather than to BP, an additional 72,373 million UK pounds more value would have been created." Only two of the resources (economic capital and work accidents) make a positive contribution to the company's sustainable value; the other resources create a negative sustainability value. [While this conclusion is readily apparent from the "ratio" column in Table 25–13, the additional analysis conducted by the authors facilitates the allocation of monetary value to the sustainability measures.] In the third and final step, the authors calculate a measure of BP's *sustainability efficiency*. The value is defined as the ratio: (net value added) / (cost of sustainability capital). The resulting value is 0.177 derived from the ratio: (15.563 million UK pounds) / (72,373 + 15.563 million UK pounds). The authors' conclusion is that "BP earns only 17.7 pence per UK pound of opportunity cost of sustainability capital. Consequently its sustainability efficiency is below unity. BP thus falls short of covering its cost of sustainability capital."

This analysis raises at least two interesting issues: first, the choice of the benchmark; and, second, the avenues available for remedying negative sustainable value.

The use of a national economy as a benchmark is potentially problematic as it implies that all those companies with higher efficiency levels than the national economic average are somehow *sustainable*, and that all those companies with lower efficiency levels are *non-sustainable*. This approach does not address the question of whether any country's national average values are necessarily sustainable with respect to any recognizable criteria. The authors recognize this potential dilemma and

**TABLE 25.13**

*BP Sustainable Value—Input Data*

| BP | AMOUNT UNITS | UK | AMOUNT UNITS | RATIOS |
|---|---|---|---|---|
| Net value added | 15,563 UK pounds | Net domestic product | 884,718 million UK pounds | 1.76% |
| nonfinancial assets | 69,885 million UK pounds | total net wealth | 4,375,200 million UK pounds | 1.60% |
| $CO_2$ | 73,420,000 tons | $CO_2$ | 572,500,000 tons | 12.82% |
| $CH_4$ | 367,201 tons | $CH_4$ | 2,195,238 tons | 16.73% |
| $SO_2$ | 224,541 tons | $SO_2$ | 1,125,000 tons | 19.96% |
| NOx | 266,133 tons | NOx | 1,680,000 tons | 15.84% |
| CO | 124,584 tons | CO | 3,966,500 tons | 3.14% |
| Work accidents | 83 number | Work accidents | 132,696 number | 0.06% |
| PM10 | 16,666 tons | PM10 | 178,000 tons | 9.36% |

*Source:* Derived from Figge and Hahn 2005, p. 53, Tables 1 and 2, reproduced with permission of the authors

TABLE 25.14

BP Sustain-
able Value
Calculations

| TYPE OF CAPITAL | BP'S RETURN ON CAPITAL [MIO UK POUNDS /UNIT] | UK RETURN ON CAPITAL [I.E. THE OPPORTUNITY COST] [MIO UK POUNDS / UNIT] | DIFFERENCE IN RETURNS ON CAPITAL [MIO UK POUNDS / UNIT] | BP'S ABSOLUTE AMOUNTS [FROM TABLE 25-12] | VALUE CREATED [MIO UK POUNDS] |
|---|---|---|---|---|---|
| Economic capital | 0.2227 | 0.2022 | 0.0205 | 69,885 | 1,433 |
| $CO_2$ | 0.0002 | 0.0015 | −0.0013 | 73,420,000 | −95,446 |
| $CH_4$ | 0.0424 | 0.4030 | −0.3606 | 367,201 | −132,413 |
| $SO_2$ | 0.0693 | 0.7864 | −0.7171 | 224,541 | −161,018 |
| NOx | 0.0585 | 0.5266 | −0.4681 | 266,133 | −124,577 |
| CO | 0.1249 | 0.2230 | −0.0981 | 124,584 | −12,222 |
| Work accdents | 187.506 | 6.6673 | 180.8387 | 83 | 15,010 |
| PM10 | 0.9338 | 4.9703 | −4.0365 | 16,666 | −67,272 |
| | | | | total | −576,506 |
| | | | | sustainable value | −72,063 |

Source: Figge and Hahn 2005
Status: Reproduced with permission

**FIGURE 25.12A**

*Costing social risks for hypothetical mining company in Third World*

| Schedule A | Cost of social risks |
| --- | --- |

| Risk | Benefit | Cost types | Costs | Like-lihood | Expected value |
| --- | --- | --- | --- | --- | --- |
| Civil unrest surrounding site | $ ......... | • Costs of engaging employers skilled in negotiating with protesters | $ ......... | ......... % | $ ......... |
| | | • Cost of engaging extra security perosnnel | $ ......... | | |
| | | *Reputation-related:* | | | |
| | | • Cost of hiring community relations manager | $ ......... | | |
| | | • Cost of managing activist NGO relations | $ ......... | | |
| Prostituion near site | $ ......... | • Costs of implementing health education for workers to teach about sexually transmitted diseases (to avoid costs related to HIV infection) | $ ......... | ......... % | $ ......... |
| Child labor | $ ......... | *Reputation-related:* | | ......... % | $ ......... |
| | | • Cost of reputaion damage | $ ......... | | |
| | | • Cost of managing boycotts when information reaches activist consumers | $ ......... | | |
| | | • Cost of NGO relations manager | $ ......... | | |
| Infringement of indigenous lands | $ ......... | • Cost litigation in international courts | $ ......... | ......... % | $ ......... |
| | | • Cost of remunerating population | $ ......... | | |
| | | • Cost of work stoppages due to local strike, reputation damage, community protests, work stoppages | $ ......... | | |
| | | *Reputation-related:* | | | |
| | | • Cost of hiring community relations manager | $ ......... | | |
| | | • Cost of managing activist NGO relations | $ ......... | | |
| Reputation costs, including lost sales and profits | | | | | $ ......... |
| NPV | | | | | $ ......... |

Reprinted with permission of AICPA. From Making Sustainability Work, copyright© 2008 by Marc J. Epstein, Berrett-Koehler Publishers, Inc., San Francisco, CA. All rights reserved. www.bkconnection.com

FIGURE 25.12B

*Costing po-*
*litical risks for*
*hypothetical*
*mining com-*
*pany in Third*
*World*

| Schedule B | Cost of political risks |
| --- | --- |

| Risk | Benefit | Cost types | Costs | Like-lihood | Expected value |
| --- | --- | --- | --- | --- | --- |
| Changes in legislation that change the rules of the game | $ .......... | • Lost revenues<br>• Increased taxes and tariffs | $ ..........<br>$ .......... | .............. % | $ .................. |
| Forced contact negotiation with host governement | $ .......... | • Lost profits<br>• Lost investment | $ ..........<br>$ .......... | .............. % | $ .................. |
| Armed insurrection | $ .......... | • Cost of hiring private security<br>• Cost of training local police/military to prevent human rights abuses (if required to use these forces by contract) | $ ..........<br>$ .......... | .............. % | $ .................. |
| Associated reputation risk | $ .......... | • Cost of incentive packages to attract workers to location<br>• Cost of protests, etc. due to potential linkages with human rights abuses | $ ..........<br>$ .......... | .............. % | $ .................. |
| Endemic corruption | $ .......... | • Costs of payoffs and bribes<br>• Costs of potential lawsuits for that activity | $ ..........<br>$ .......... | .............. % | $ .................. |
| Targeted criminal activity | $ .......... | • Costs of protecting personnel, including extra security, reinforcing security at private homes, providing security training to employees and families<br>• Cost of attracting workers, including increased pay, time off, and hardshiop bonuses<br>• Costs of increased security to protest facility<br>• Cost of potential work stoppages | $ ..........<br><br><br><br>$ ..........<br><br>$ ..........<br>$ .......... | .............. % | $ .................. |
| Terrorism | $ .......... | • Cost of reinforcing infrastrucure<br>• Cost of hiring additional security personnel<br>• Cost of rebuilding | $ ..........<br>$ ..........<br>$ .......... | .............. % | $ .................. |
| Reputation costs,including lost sales and profits | | | | | $ .................. |
| NPV | | | | | $ .................. |

Reprinted with permission of AICPA. From Making Sustainability Work, copyright© 2008 by Marc J. Epstein, Berrett-Koehler Publishers, Inc., San Francisco, CA. All rights reserved. www.bkconnection.com

suggest possible alternative benchmarks including the efficiencies of other economic entities "such as national economies, regions, industry sectors, or companies other than the one under examination. On the other hand, one could also use performance targets such as emission reduction targets to form the benchmark efficiencies."

The second, and related, issue is the question of what signals this type of analysis generates for ameliorating poor sustainability performance. In this respect, the analysis of Figge and Hahn is not inconsistent with standard environmental economic theory. A company might be able to improve its efficiency rating by raising the price for its products and thereby lowering their demand. This would move the company closer to the optimal social output for its product. In general, while providing information of this sort for external stakeholders is exceedingly useful, generating signals for management is at least as important—if not more so—for the simple reason that without such internal signals, a company cannot determine the appropriate path to sustainability.

## Social and Political Risk Analysis

The focus of the discussion so far has been on how to incorporate environmental risk into corporate decision making traditionally reliant on convention financial metrics. In many cases, however, corporate risk may extend into both the social and political realms, and it is these additional risks that Epstein (2008) addresses in his book *Making Sustainability Work*. The example he uses is a mining company operating in the Third World, although the general structure of this analysis could easily be expanded to cover corporate operations in the developed world where there are different types

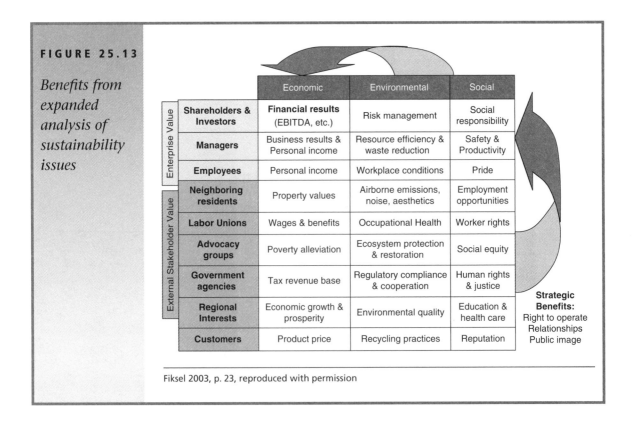

**FIGURE 25.13**

*Benefits from expanded analysis of sustainability issues*

|  |  | Economic | Environmental | Social |
|---|---|---|---|---|
| **Enterprise Value** | **Shareholders & Investors** | Financial results (EBITDA, etc.) | Risk management | Social responsibility |
|  | **Managers** | Business results & Personal income | Resource efficiency & waste reduction | Safety & Productivity |
|  | **Employees** | Personal income | Workplace conditions | Pride |
| **External Stakeholder Value** | **Neighboring residents** | Property values | Airborne emissions, noise, aesthetics | Employment opportunities |
|  | **Labor Unions** | Wages & benefits | Occupational Health | Worker rights |
|  | **Advocacy groups** | Poverty alleviation | Ecosystem protection & restoration | Social equity |
|  | **Government agencies** | Tax revenue base | Regulatory compliance & cooperation | Human rights & justice |
|  | **Regional Interests** | Economic growth & prosperity | Environmental quality | Education & health care |
|  | **Customers** | Product price | Recycling practices | Reputation |

**Strategic Benefits:**
Right to operate
Relationships
Public image

Fiksel 2003, p. 23, reproduced with permission

of social and political risk. Figures 25–12a and b illustrate the calculations that a corporation may employ to generate expected values that could then be incorporated directly into traditional ROI calculations. It should be noted, however, that the use of the simple expected value for each of these risks—which implies risk neutrality—may have to be modified in light of two factors: (1) management's attitude toward risk, especially its degree of risk tolerance or risk aversion [see, for example, Mac-Crimmon and Wehrung 1986]; and (2) the possibility of *fat tail* phenomenon—low probability events that could threaten the survival of the corporation [see chapter 9].

## SUMMARY OBSERVATIONS

The above examples are merely some of numerous efforts to incorporate sustainability considerations into high-level corporate decision making. One organization in particular that has been raising corporate awareness to the long-term benefits of sustainability has been the World Business Council on Sustainable Development (WBCSD)—a collaborative research and information-disseminating association of over 200 major global corporations that is based in Geneva, Switzerland. Much of the published work of the WBCSD is composed of case studies and analytical documents that address key issue in corporate sustainability and help to develop new tools for managerial decision making. Foremost among these tools is the creation of a *Sustainable Business Development Framework* (SBDF), which clearly demonstrates how a focus on sustainability issues can create intangible strategic benefits and improve environmental and social performance, leading to both increased enterprise and external stakeholder value (www.wbcsd.org). Joseph Fiksel (2003; and Fiksel et al. 2002) details the multifaceted benefits in Figure 25–13 from expanding the purview of corporate strategy from the three traditional financially related cells in the top left of the table [i.e., financial results such as EBITDA of interest to shareholders and investors, business results and personal income of concern to managers, and the personal income of employees] to the 24 other cells that address environmental and social issues that benefit not just the enterprise directly, but also all the indirect benefits accruing to the corporation through the broad range of stakeholders.

### A Final Reflection on Triple Bottom Line Reporting and the Integration of Sustainability Accounts

Hahn et al. (2010) have written a provocative article that challenges the emerging view of corporate sustainability. It is their contention that the literature is dominated by what they have termed a "win-win paradigm" where corporate sustainability is achieved through the simultaneous attainment of all three legs of the sustainability "stool": economic, environmental, and social. It is the authors' hypothesis that the complexity of sustainability issues makes this an exceedingly rare accomplishment, and fundamental trade-offs characterize this domain as they do in all other avenues of human endeavor. In many cases, corporate achievement of one aspect of sustainability may come at the expense of another. It is their view that the sole pursuit of all three forms of sustainability, without the realization of the inherent trade-offs, will foreclose many viable and productive options. A central conclusion of their thesis is that corporations can make a significant contribution to sustainability at the societal level by excelling in just one or two forms of sustainability, be they economic, environmental, or social. To quote: "corporate sustainability based on the win–win logic will be restricted to conflict-free solutions with little ambition to fundamentally change core business practices for the sake of sustainable development. . . . By following the win–win paradigm sustainability issues are ultimately judged through the lens of profit maximization rather than being treated as ends in themselves" (p 219). In Figure 25–14, Hahn et al. present a model that lays out the multifaceted nature of trade-offs faced in the pursuit of sustainability. These trade-offs can occur at four levels (individual, organizational, industry, and societal) and in three dimensions (outcome, temporal, and process). Some of these have already been highlighted in this textbook, including the trade-off between efficiency

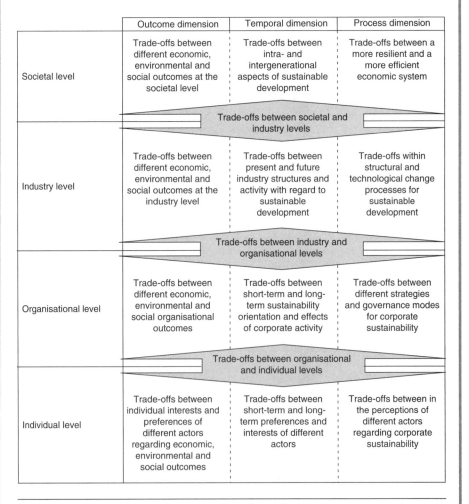

**FIGURE 25.14**

*Analytical framework for trade-offs in corporate sustainability*

| | Outcome dimension | Temporal dimension | Process dimension |
|---|---|---|---|
| Societal level | Trade-offs between different economic, environmental and social outcomes at the societal level | Trade-offs between intra- and intergenerational aspects of sustainable development | Trade-offs between a more resilient and a more efficient economic system |
| | Trade-offs between societal and industry levels | | |
| Industry level | Trade-offs between different economic, environmental and social outcomes at the industry level | Trade-offs between present and future industry structures and activity with regard to sustainable development | Trade-offs within structural and technological change processes for sustainable development |
| | Trade-offs between industry and organisational levels | | |
| Organisational level | Trade-offs between different economic, environmental and social organisational outcomes | Trade-offs between short-term and long-term sustainability orientation and effects of corporate activity | Trade-offs between different strategies and governance modes for corporate sustainability |
| | Trade-offs between organisational and individual levels | | |
| Individual level | Trade-offs between individual interests and preferences of different actors regarding economic, environmental and social outcomes | Trade-offs between short-term and long-term preferences and interests of different actors | Trade-offs between in the perceptions of different actors regarding corporate sustainability |

Hahn et al. 2010, p. 223, reproduced with permission of the authors and resilience (chapter 5); and the trade-off between current and future generations (chapter 7). Hahn et al. are convinced that "truly proactive corporate sustainability strategies are those strategies that do not shy away from taking into account conflicts, but rather accept trade-offs for the sake of substantial sustainability gains at the societal level" (p. 226).

## CITED REFERENCES AND RECOMMENDED READINGS

2GC Active Management (2011) *Balanced Scorecard Usage Survey 2011. Summary of Findings*. Maidenhead, Berkshire.

Anileski, Mark (2007) *The Economics of Happiness: Building Genuine Wealth*. Gabriola Island, BC: New Society Publishers.

Baxter Health (2007) *Sustainability Report*.

Bekefi, Tamara and Marc J. Epstein (2006) *Integrating Social and Political Risk into Management Decision-Making*. Management Accounting Guideline, Certified Management Accountants (CMA) Canada, American Institute of CPAs (AICPA).

Bekefi, Tamara and Marc J. Epstein (2011) "Integrating Social and Political Risk into ROI Calculation." *Environmental Quality Management*, Spring, pp. 11–23.

Burritt, Roger L. (1998) "Cost Allocation," in Martin Bennett and Peter James (eds.) *The Green Bottom Line: Environmental Accounting for Management. Current Practices and Future Trends*. Sheffield: Greenleaf, pp. 152–161.

Change (2008) *MapChange 2008. A Sustainability Brand Map Study*. Vancouver, BC.

Change (2010) *MapChange 2010. A Sustainability Brand Map Study*. Vancouver, BC. [www.maddockdouglas.com.]

Chousa, Juan Pineiro and Noelia Romero Castro (2006) "A Model of Financial Analysis at the Service of Sustainability," in Stefan Schaltegger and Marcus Wagner (eds.) 2006 *Managing the Business Case for Sustainability. The Integration of Social, Environmental and Economic Performance* Sheffield: Greenleaf, pp. 127–145.

Climate Counts (2011) *5th Annual Company Scorecard Report*. Durham, NH, December.

Cobbold, Ian and Gavin Lawrie (2002) "The Development of the Balanced Scorecard as a Strategic Management Tool," 2GC Conference Paper, presented at PMA Conference, Boston, May.

Ditz, Daryl et al. (eds.) (1995) *Green Ledgers: Case Studies in Corporate Environmental Accounting*. Washington, DC: World Resources Institute.

Emblemsvag, Jan and Bert Bras (2001) *Activity-Based Cost and Environmental Management. A Different Approach to the ISO 14000 Compliance*. Boston: Kluwer.

*Environmental Leader. Environmental & Energy Management News* (2010) "U.S. Consumers Still Willing to Pay More for 'Green' Products," March 29. [http://www.environmentalleader.com/2010/03/29/u-s-consumers-still-willing-to-pay-more-for-green-products/]

Epstein, Marc J. (2008) *Making Sustainability Work. Best Practices in Managing and Measuring Corporate Social, Environmental, and Economic Impacts*. Sheffield and San Francisco: Greenleaf Publishing and Berrett-Koehler Publishers.

Figge, Frank and Tobias Hahn (2005) "The Cost of Sustainability Capital and the Creation of Sustainable Value by companies." *Journal of Industrial Ecology*, 9(4), pp. 47–58.

Figge, Frank et al. (2002) "The Sustainability Balanced Scorecard—Theory and Application of a Tool for Value-Based Sustainability Management," Paper presented at the Greening of Industry Network Conference, Gothenburg, on "Corporate Social Responsibility—Governance for Sustainability."

Fiksel, D. et al. (2002) *Toward a Sustainable Cement Industry*, Sub-study 3, Business Case Development, Battelle Report to the World Business Council for Sustainable Development, Geneva.

Fiksel, Joseph (2003) "Revealing the Value of Sustainable Development." *Corporate Strategy Today*, June, pp. 28–36.

Global Environmental Management Initiative (GEMI) (1994) *Finding Cost-effective Pollution Prevention Initiatives: Incorporating Environmental Costs into Business Decision Making A Primer*. Washington, DC.

Hahn, Tobias et al. (2010) "Trade-offs in Corporate Sustainability: You can't have your cake and eat it." Editorial in *Business Strategy and the Environment*, 19, pp. 217–229.

Henriques, Adrian and Julie Richardson (eds.) (2004) *The Triple Bottom line. Does It All Add Up*? London: Earthscan.

Hillary, Ruth (ed.) (1997) *Environmental Management Systems and Cleaner Production*. Chichester: John Wiley & Sons.

Howes, Rupert (2000) "Corporate Environmental Accounting: Accounting for Environmentally Sustainable Profits," in Sandrine Simon and John Proops (eds.) *Greening the Accounts*. Cheltenham: Edward Elgar, pp. 223–245.

Howes, Rupert (2003) *Environmental Cost Accounting: An Introduction and Practical Guide*. London: Chartered Institute of Management Accountants (CIMA Research).

Howes, Rupert (2004) "Environmental Cost Accounting: Coming of Age? Tracking Organizational Performance Towards Environmental Sustainability," in Adrian Henriques and Julie Richardson (eds.) *The Triple Bottom Line. Does It All Add Up*? London: Earthscan, pp. 99–112. http://ecofriendlysites.org/articles/article-18.html.

Hunt, David and Catherine Johnson (1995) *Environmental Management Systems: Principles and Practice*. London: McGraw-Hill.

Kaplan, Robert S. (2002) "The Balanced Scorecard and Nonprofit Organizations," *ON Balance*, Harvard Business School, November–December.

Kaplan, Robert S. and Steven R. Anderson (2007) *Time-Driven Activity-Based Costing: A Simpler and More Powerful Path to Higher Profits*. Boston: Harvard Business School Press.

Kaplan, Robert S. and David P. Norton (1992) "The Balanced Scorecard: Measures that Drive Performance." *Harvard Business Review*, January–February, pp. 71–79.

Kaplan, Robert S. and David P. Norton (1993) "Putting the Balanced Scorecard to Work." *Harvard Business Review*, September–October, pp. 134–147.

Kaplan, Robert S. and David P. Norton (2001) *The Strategy-Focused Organization: How Balanced Scorecard Companies Thrive in the New Business Environment*. Boston: Harvard Business School Press.

Kaplan, Robert S. and David P. Norton (2004) *Strategy Maps: Converting Intangible Assets in Tangible Outcomes*. Boston: Harvard Business School Press.

Kaplan, Robert S. and David P. Norton (2007) "Using the Balanced Scorecard as a Strategic Management System." *Harvard Business Review*, July–August, pp. 150–161.

Kuhre, W. Lee (1995) *ISO 14001 Certification. Environmental Management Systems*. Upper Saddle River, NJ: Prentice Hall.

Lamberton, Geoff (2005) "Sustainability Accounting—A Brief History and Conceptual Framework." *Accounting Forum*, 29, pp. 7–26.

MacCrimmon, Kenneth R. and Donald A. Wehrung (1986) *Taking Risks: The Management of Uncertainty*. New York: Free Press.

Matthews, H. Scott and Lester B. Lave (2003) "Using Input-Output Analysis for Corporate Benchmarking." *Benchmarking: An International Journal*, 10(2), pp. 152–167.

Muller, Nicholas Z., Robert Mendelsohn, and William Nordhaus (2011) "Environmental Accounting for Pollution in the United States Economy." *American Economic Review*, 101(5), pp. 1649–1675.

Niven, Paul R. (2008) *Balanced Scorecard Step-by-Step for Government and Nonprofit Agencies*, Hoboken, NJ: John Wiley & Sons.

PriceWaterhouseCoopers (PWC) (2011) *CDP Global 500 Report 2011. Accelerating Low Carbon Growth*. Report for the Carbon Disclosure Project, London.

Puma.com [website of the Puma corporation].

Schaltegger, Stefan and Roger Burritt (2000) *Contemporary Environmental Accounting. Issues, Concepts and Practice*. Sheffield: Greenleaf.

Schaltegger, Stefan and Kasper Muller (1998) "Calculating the True Profitability of Pollution Prevention," in Martin Bennett and Peter James (eds.) *The Green Bottom Line. Environmental Accounting for Management. Current Practices and Future Trends*. Sheffield: Greenleaf, pp. 86–99.

Schaltlegger, Stefan and Marcus Wagner (eds.) (2006) *Managing the Business Case for Sustainability. The integration of Social, Environmental and Economic Performance*. Sheffield: Greenleaf.

Sheldon, Christopher and Mark Yoxon (2002) *Environmental Management Systems, a Step-by-Step Guide to Implementation & Maintenance*. London: Earthscan. 3rd edition.

Starkey, Richard (ed.) (1995) *Environmental Management Tools for SMEs: A Handbook*. Copenhagen: European Environment Agency, March.

Thompson, Dixon (2002) *Tools for Environmental Management: A Practical Introduction and Guide*. Gabriola Island, BC: New Society Publishers.

U.S. Environment Protection Agency (EPA) (1989) *Pollution Prevention Benefits Manual. Volume I: The Manual. Phase II*, October.

U.S. Environment Protection Agency (EPA) (1995) *An Introduction to Environmental Accounting as a Business Management Tool: Key Concepts and Terms*.

U.S. Environment Protection Agency (EPA) Toxic Release Inventory (TRI) website (www.epa.gov/tri/).

Wessex Water Services Limited (2004) "Wessex Water Environmental Accounts." Bath, UK.

World Business Council for Sustainable Development, Geneva (www.wbcsd.org).

## Analytical Questions

1. Using a public company, apply any one of the metrics outlined in this chapter to reassess the sustainability of the corporate enterprise in question.
2. If possible, apply more than one metric and determine if the results are comparable.

## NOTE

1. Climate Counts (2011, p. 5) uses 22 criteria in 4 general categories: *Review*: whether the company takes inventory of their greenhouse gas (GHG) emissions using an industry accepted accounting protocol; *Reduce*: whether the company has articulated a strategy for reducing GHG emissions and have succeeded in achieving actual reductions; *Policy Stance*: whether the company explicitly supports the need for comprehensive energy and climate policy or there is evidence they oppose such measures; and *Report*: whether the company publicly discloses information about their sustainability efforts and their progress toward carbon neutrality. Of the 136 companies in 16 sectors scored in this report, 79 were deemed to be "striding" toward a low carbon future, 31 were "starting" to address their climate impact, and 26 were "stuck" without a climate strategy.

# CHAPTER 26

# Social Enterprise and the Social Return on Investment

IT HAS BEEN THE PRINCIPAL THRUST OF THIS TEXTBOOK that a truly sustainable economy can be achieved only when both traditional as well as green investors can agree on processes and products that are both profitable and sustainable. [See Figure 26–1.] This does not mean, however, that there is no room for investment opportunities that appeal largely to green investors. In fact, the emergence of the phenomenon of social entrepreneurship signals the viability of this option. The social enterprise is a broad and somewhat amorphous category, as it includes not only traditional nonprofits but also organizations that can be profitable but have as their principal, if not exclusive, focus the advancement of social and environmental objectives. In many cases, any profits that might be generated are reinvested in order to advance the particular social goals of the organization. Another way of viewing the strategic functioning of this type of entity is to see it as maximizing the achievement of social goals with a nonnegative profit constraint. This chapter first provides a brief review of the state of social enterprise in the United States and the United Kingdom, as well as diverse models of social enterprise globally, and then summarizes some of the more common metrics for measuring the success and impact of social enterprise.

One of the principal challenges in studying social enterprise is the varied definitional boundaries (see, for example, Mair et al. 2006). Dacin et al. (2010) have surveyed the literature and concluded that the definitions focus on four key factors: "the characteristics of individual social entrepreneurs, their operating sector, the processes and resources used by social entrepreneurs, and the primary mission and outcomes associated with the social entrepreneur." They believe that "the definition that holds the most potential for building a unique understanding of social entrepreneurship and developing actionable implications is one that focuses on the social value creation mission and outcomes, both positive and negative, of undertakings aimed at creating social value." In Table 26–1, the authors outline the principle distinctions between social and three other forms of entrepreneurship. Young (2001) summarizes the juxtaposition between the organizational identities of social enterprises and the legal forms they may take in Table 26–2.

**FIGURE 26.1**

*The ideal business sustainability investment model*

|  |  | Sustainable Investor | |
|---|---|---|---|
|  |  | **YES** | **NO** |
| **Traditional Investor** | **YES** | **Sustainable Enterprise Economy** | Traditional for-profit enterprise |
|  | **NO** | Social enterprise |  |

**TABLE 26.1**

*Distinction among Types of Entrepreneurs along Mission and Process/Resources Dimensions*

|  | CONVENTIONAL | INSTITUTIONAL | CULTURAL | SOCIAL |
|---|---|---|---|---|
| **Definition** | An agent who enables or enacts a vision based on new ideas in order to create successful innovations | An agent who can mobilize resources to influence or change institutional rules, in order to support or destroy an existing institution, or to establish a new one | An agent who identifies an opportunity and acts upon it in order to create social, cultural, or economic value | An actor who apples business principles to solving social problems |
| **Wealth distribution** | Shareholder | Shareholder and/or stakeholder | Shareholder and/or stakeholder | Shareholder and/or stakeholder |
| **Predominant organizational form** | Profit | Profit | Nonprofit or profit | Nonprofit or profit |
| **Primary goal (or motives)** | Economic | Institutional reform/ development | Cultural diffusion / enlightenment | Social change / well-being |
| **Product** | Create and/or distribute consumer product or service | Establish legitimacy | Establish new norms and values | Promotes ideology / social change |
| **Tensions** | Growth versus survival | Resistance to change (isomorphism versus competitive advantage?) | Commercialization versus culture (authenticity) | Economic sustainability versus social mission |

| | CONVENTIONAL | INSTITUTIONAL | CULTURAL | SOCIAL |
|---|---|---|---|---|
| **Examples** | Business service providers | Edison | Museums | Aravind Eye Clinic |
| | Software developers | Kodak | Folk art festivals | Greyston Bakery |
| | Tourism companies | Apple | Symphony orchestras | Rugmark |

**TABLE 26.1**
*continued*

*Source:* Dacin et al. 2010, p. 44

*Status:* Reproduced with permission of Academy of Management Perspectives

| IDENTITY / LEGAL FORM | NONPROFIT | FOR-PROFIT |
|---|---|---|
| Corporate Philanthropy | major nonprofits competing for market share who find it useful to help other charities as part of corporate strategy | business corporations whose philanthropy is part of a business strategy to enhance profits |
| Social Purpose Organization | nonprofits that undertake commercial activities to generate funds and support social goals | businesses whose owners are focussed on social goals and where the for-profit form is more comfortable or practical |
| Hybrid | nonprofits whose leaders seek both income and social benefits | businesses whose owners sacrifice some profits to achieve social goals |

**TABLE 26.2**

*Organizational Identities of Social Enterprises and Their Legal Forms*

*Source:* Young 2001, p. 7

*Status:* Reproduced with permission

## SOCIAL ENTERPRISE IN THE UNITED STATES

Because of the fuzzy definitional borders of social enterprise, it can be difficult to get a sense of its role in a national economy. The *New York Times* reported in October 12, 2011 on the emergence of hybrid companies, defined as those putting social goals ahead of profit, and the legal challenges these organizations may face at the state level. Corporate law jurisdiction rests at the state rather than the federal level, and most state legislation has enshrined the traditional view that shareholder interests (i.e., profitability) must be paramount. Despite this fact, as many as 14 states such as California have amended their laws to allow 3 variants that facilitate social enterprise (*New York Times* 2011):

*LC3*: a specialized form of limited liability corporation with a primary purpose intended to take investments from foundations.

*Benefit Corporation*: a corporation that emphasizes social impact over profitability. Social and environmental goals must conform to statutory definitions, and directors must consider the impact of corporate decisions on the community and the environment as well as shareholders.

*Flexible purpose corporation*: a corporation with a stated social purpose. Directors are required to keep its social purpose in mind when considering how to maximize shareholder value. Annual reports of social impact and planned future expenditures to achieve that impact are required.

Many of these social enterprises have sought certification, and several nonprofit organizations have emerged in order to facilitate this process. In the United States, a major example is B Lab (or B Corporation) where B stands for benefit as "benefiting workers, the community and the Earth." According to B Lab, there are now in excess of 30,000 social entrepreneurs who generate $40 billion in annual revenue (*Forbes* 2011, B Lab 2011). [See also Young 2001.] Some sense of the size and growth of the social enterprise sector can be gleaned from data published annually by the U.S. Internal Revenue Service (accessed 2012). The IRS produces extensive data under the rubric "SOI Tax Stats—Charities & Other Tax-Exempt Organizations Statistics." Historical data covering the period 1985 to 2006 show total revenue for "Nonprofit charitable Organizations" growing from $268 billion to $1.37 trillion. There is a problem in interpretation of these data, however, as cogently outlined by Kerlin and Pollak (2010) who point out certain critical inclusions and exclusions from this data set. According to the IRS, the data reported above fall under the code 501(c)(3) and include religious, educational, charitable, scientific, or literary organizations, and testing for public safety organizations. Also included are organizations preventing cruelty to children or animals, or fostering national or international amateur sports competition. In their own more selective data set drawn from IRS data, Kerlin and Pollak distinguish between the arts and culture subsector and the human services subsector. Their measure of total revenues for all nonprofits, exclusive of hospitals and institutions of higher learning, over the period 1982 to 2002 range from approximately 45% to 65% of the comparable IRS data. Salamon et al. (2012) have reported that the nonprofit sector as a whole is the third largest sector in the United States, after retail trade and manufacturing, with 10.7 million employees.

## SOCIAL ENTERPRISE IN THE UNITED KINGDOM

Several efforts have been undertaken in the United Kingdom to determine more accurately the number and size of entities with a social entrepreneurial orientation. One of the most comprehensive surveys to date has been produced by IFF Research (2005) for the Small Business Service of the UK Department of Trade and Industry. The survey relied on two principal sources of information but nevertheless was deemed to underestimate the number and size of social enterprises in the United Kingdom. The results found approximately 15,000 social enterprises, representing around 1.2% of all British enterprises with an annual income of 18 billion UK pounds, somewhat less than 1% of all national enterprise income. Employment was nearly one half million people, two-thirds of whom work full time in these endeavors. The principal foci were health and social care (33%), community or social services (21%), real estate/renting (20%), and education (15%). The main groups who are helped by these enterprises are those with disabilities (19%), children or young (17%), the elderly (15%), and those on low incomes (12%). Finally, the main way that people are helped is through training and education at 20% of all social enterprises.

Clearly, the estimated number of such enterprises varies markedly depending on their definition. Lyon et al. (2010), for example, cite six disparate estimates ranging in numbers from 15,000 to 234,000 with employee numbers of 227,000 to 475,000 and turnover of 8.5 to 97 billion UK pounds.

An in-depth survey of organization characteristics in the UK was conducted by the Social Enterprise Coalition (Leahy and Villeneuve-Smith 2009, pp. 6–7). The report provides quantitative documentation to support their key findings: (1) *Social enterprises operate at a wide variety of scales, but their economic impact is significant and growing*. They are recession busters, profitable, vary widely in scale, are different from the voluntary sector, and scale is important; (2) *Social impact is both the fundamental objective behind social enterprise and a daily fact of life through profit reinvestment*. Social enterprise is a fundamentally different proposition from corporate social responsibility, profit reinvestment for social goals is a reality, and these enterprises are a natural home for women entrepreneurs; (3) *Social enterprise is a very diverse sector*. There are few business sectors that don't include social enterprises; these enterprises choose a wide variety of legal forms; the sector is very diverse; the scope of operations is mainly, but not universally, very local; the public sector is already a key customer; and community interest companies are, on balance, happy with their legal form; and (4) *Finance is vital and possible to raise*. Finance is the oxygen of social enterprise, social enterprise is as capital hungry as small business, finance is mainly for growth, and business support isn't fully meeting social enterprise needs.

## GLOBAL DIVERSITY IN SOCIAL ENTERPRISE

While the United States and the United Kingdom and several countries in Western Europe have been leaders in the development of the theory and practice of social enterprise, there are both similarities and differences in their approach to this organizational phenomenon. Authors such as Kerlin (2009) and Defourny and Kim (2011) have identified three spheres of influence on social enterprise: the market, the state, and civil society.[1] An additional sphere, international aid, is of particular relevance to the developing world and the former states of the Soviet bloc. Not surprising, the strong market ethic combined with a common suspicion of big government in the United States has bred a social enterprise model embedded in both civil society and the market. In contrast, the tradition of government intervention in Europe coupled with a somewhat less enthusiastic embrace of the free market has dictated that social enterprise in the UK and on the continent tends to be a product of civil society and the state. [See also Defourny and Nyssens 2010.]

The more formalized and structured approach to social enterprise in Europe led to the creation of a research network in 1996 called "The Emergence of Social Enterprise in Europe" (EMES), which has conceptualized an "ideal type" social enterprise with several distinctive characteristics (OECD n.d.; Defourny 2001, pp. 26–27; Kerlin 2006). They are directly engaged in the production and/or sale of goods and services; are voluntarily created and managed by groups of citizens; enjoy a high degree of autonomy; dependent on the efforts of their members for their financial viability; face a significant level of economic risk; reliant on a minimum number of paid workers; are the result of an initiative by citizens involving people belonging to a community or to a group that shares a certain need or aim; are characterized by decision-making power not based on capital ownership; are participatory in nature; avoid profit maximizing behaviour, as they involve a limited distribution of profit; and pursue an explicit aim to benefit the community or a specific group of people. Within the last two decades there has been a literal explosion of social enterprise across the globe (Salamon et al. 2004; Noya 2009). In each country, various manifestations of this phenomenon have emerged in response to perceived needs, particularly widespread poverty, often flowing from the absence of a strong market environment, legal system, or effectively functioning government. Extensive research has already documented the array of unique models of social enterprise in such diverse regions as Latin America (*Harvard Review of Latin America* 2006), Africa (Minard 2009), South Asia (Hackett 2010; McKague and Tinsley 2012), and Eastern Asia (Curtis 2012; Defourny and Kim 2011). By way of example, Defourny and Kim have identified five distinct models of social enterprise in China, Hong Kong, Taiwan, and South Korea: trading nonprofit organizations (NPO), work integration social enterprise, nonprofit cooperative, NPO-for-Profit partnership, and community development enterprises. Kerlin (2009) has conducted an extensive comparative overview of social enterprise in seven world regions and countries, summarized in Table 26–3. She differentiates among these regions on the basis of six variables: outcome emphasis, program area focus, common organizational type, legal framework, societal sector, and strategic development base.

The most extensive dataset available on global social enterprise has been developed at Johns Hopkins University with its Global Civil Society Index (http://ccss.jhu.edu/wp-content/uploads/downloads/2011/12/Civil-Society-Index_FINAL_11.15.2011.pdf). The data summarized by Salamon et al. (2004) include 36 countries and cover the size of the civil society workforce; the number of volunteers by field and the value of their work; sources of support; the share of civil society sector revenue from government, philanthropy, and fees by field (culture and recreation; education and research; health; social services; environment; development and housing; civic and advocacy; philanthropic intermediaries; international, religious worship; business, profession, labor; and n.e.c.) As of 2004, the authors estimated the size of the civil society sector as $1.3 trillion representing 5.4% of the combined GDP of the countries surveyed. This represented the world's seventh largest sector with an aggregate workforce in the 36 countries of 45.5 million full-time equivalents, or 4.4% of the economically active population (p. 26). Table 26–4 summarizes some of the national data.

Perhaps the archetypal social enterprise in the developing world was the Grameen Bank, which pioneered the development of microcredit, a phenomenon now ubiquitous in much of the Third World. First developed in Bangladesh by Mohammad Yunus, the Grameen Bank was designed to raise the standard of living of the poorest levels of society, particularly women, by bringing them into the market

**TABLE 26.3**

*Comparative Overview of Social Enterprise in Seven World Regions and Countries*

| | USA | WESTERN EUROPE | JAPAN | EAST-CENTRAL EUROPE | ARGENTINA | ZIMBABWE / ZAMBIA | SOUTHEAST ASIA |
|---|---|---|---|---|---|---|---|
| **Outcome emphasis** | sustainability | social benefit | social / economic benefit | social benefit | social / economic benefits | self-sustainability | sustainable development |
| **Program area focus** | all nonprofit activities | human services / employment | services / employment | human services / employment | human services / employment | employment | employment / services |
| **Common organizational type** | nonprofit company | association / cooperative | nonprofit / company | association / cooperative | cooperative / mutual benefits | Microfinance institutions / small enterprise | small enterprise / association |
| **Legal framework** | under discussion | developing | not yet considered | developing | not yet considered | not yet considered | not yet considered |
| **Societal sector** | market economy | social economy | market economy | social economy | social economy | market economy | market economy |
| **Strategic development base** | foundations | government / EU | government | international donors / EU | civil society | international donors | mixed |

*Source:* Kerlin 2009, Table 9.1

*Status:* Reproduced with permission Kerlin 2009, Table 9.1, reproduced with the permission of the University of New England Press

**TABLE 26.4**

*Summary Dimensions of the Nonprofit Sector*

| | LOW | AVERAGE | HIGH |
|---|---|---|---|
| Civil society sector workforce as % of economically active population - TOTAL | Mexico: 0.4% | 4.4% | Netherlands: 14.4% |
| Civil society sector workforce as % of economically active population - PAID STAFF | Mexico: 0.3% | 2.7% | Netherlands: 9.2% |
| Civil society sector workforce as % of economically active population - VOLUNTEERS | Mexico: 0.1% | 1.6% | Netherlands: 5.1% |
| Value of Volunteer Work (million US$) | Slovakia: $7.3 | $8,789 | USA: $109,013 |
| Number of volunteers ('000) | Mexico: 30 | 3654 | USA: 44,564 |
| Percent of adult population volunteering | Mexico: 0.1% | 10.0% | Norway: 52% |

**Civil society sector FTE by field - % of total civil society workforce**

| | LOW | AVERAGE | HIGH |
|---|---|---|---|
| culture | Peru: 2.5% | 18.8% | Sweden: 45.5% |
| education | Sweden: 6.8% | 22.9% | Pakistan: 56.6% |
| health | Sweden: 0.9% | 13.7% | Japan: 37.3% |
| social services | Philippines: 6.2% | 19.7% | Peru: 38.3% |
| environment | India: 0% | 2.3% | Tanzania: 10.6% |
| development | India: 0% | 7.5% | Philippines: 21.3% |
| civic /adv. | India: 0% | 4.0% | Finland: 16.8% |
| foundations | India: 0% | 1.1% | Tanzania: 7.8% |
| international | India: 0% | 1.0% | Romania: 4.0% |
| professional | India: 0% | 6.9% | Mexico: 33.6% |
| n.e.c. | Belgium: 0% | 2.2% | Kenya: 24.5% |
| Total number ('000) | Slovakia: 23 | 1138 | USA: 13549 |

**Sources of support [including volunteers]**

| | LOW | AVERAGE | HIGH |
|---|---|---|---|
| Government | Philippines: 3.1% | 26.5% | Ireland: 67.6% |
| Philanthropy | Peru: 14.7% | 31.1% | Romania: 66.5% |
| Fees | Romania: 13.0% | 42.4% | Mexico: 74.7% |
| Total support (million US$) | $139 | $48,517 | $675,973 |

**Sources of civil society sector in relation to GDP (%)**

| | LOW | AVERAGE | HIGH |
|---|---|---|---|
| Government | Pakistan: 0.03% | 1.80% | Netherlands: 9.04% |
| Philanthropy | Mexico: 0.04% | 0.37% | Israel: 1.29% |
| Volunteering | Slovakia: 0.04% | 1.07% | Netherlands: 4.13% |
| Fees | Romania:0.10% | 1.94% | Netherlands: 5.90% |

*Source:* derived from Salamon et al. 2004

economy (Yunus 2003, 2007). It is somewhat ironic that Yunus was awarded the Nobel Peace Prize rather than the comparable prize in Economics in light of the fact that his inspirational achievement has radically transformed the economic plight of millions of people across the world.[2]

## A NOTE ON THE EMERGENCE OF BASE-OF-THE-PYRAMID COMMERCE

A significant proportion of social enterprise in the Third World is focused on the alleviation of poverty. Paralleling this phenomenon in the last two decades has been the emergence of a for-profit business model that has developed to capitalize on a heretofore unrecognized market opportunity of large proportions by selling goods and services to the poorest members of the global population who have largely subsisted outside the global capitalist market. Termed Base-of-the-Pyramid [BoP], this population grouping has been estimated to number approximately 4 billion people, that is, a majority of the human population (Prahalad 2009; Prahalad and Hart 2002). According to London and Hart (2011), however, this marketing concept is seriously flawed as it focuses on "finding a fortune at the base of the pyramid" through the mass merchandising of low-cost goods with potentially detrimental environmental impacts. At its worst, this marketing phenomenon can be exploitative and spur rampant consumerism among the poor. An example of this perverse result is the takeover of microcredit by large banks focused principally on the pursuit of profit as opposed to Yunus's original goal of poverty alleviation (*New York Times*, April 14, 2010).

London and Hart make the case for a fundamental transformation in the BoP model, arguing strongly for a transition from "fortune finding" to "fortune creating" through business *with* four billion by co-creating new business models and technological solutions. As the authors state: "the most effective BoP strategies can actually build capacity and generate income among the poor, not simply extract wealth in the form of increased consumer spending" (p. 7). These strategies would not only succeed in raising the standard of living of the bottom four billion, but also attempt to do so in an environmentally sustainable manner. [See also London 2009 and Hart 2010.]

## METRICS FOR MEASURING THE IMPACT OF SOCIAL ENTERPRISE

With the emergence of the social enterprise as a major player in sustainability, there is a pressing need to generate metrics that can be used to evaluate not only the attractiveness of such ventures for potential investors, but also to measure both temporally and across enterprises the impact of the broad range of initiatives undertaken. In many cases the transference of conventional financial measures is inappropriate or insufficient to measure the unique characteristics of these ventures. Table 26–5 presents nine alternative approaches to measuring the performance of social enterprise (Social Capital Partners and Vancity Community Foundation n.d). Of these metrics, the one most conceptually similar to conventional for-profit analysis is the social return on investment (SROI). Several comprehensive guides have already been produced on this

**TABLE 26.5**

*Different Approaches to Social Enterprise Performance Measurement*

| APPROACH | WHAT IT MEASURES | KEY ASPECTS | WHO PROMOTES | FURTHER INFORMATION |
|---|---|---|---|---|
| Outcome measurement | Short, medium & long-term benefits of programs / services | Logic model that can be modified to the enterprise situation | United Way of America | www.national.unitedway.org/outcomes/ |
| Program measurement and management | The difference between planned goals and actual achievements | Logic model and goal-setting process to help identify improvement needs | Seedco | www.seedco.org |
| Benchmarking | Compares processes used by one enterprise with one or more others | Involves building partnerships with other businesses to look at efficiencies | Used in industries, usually with large-scale production processes | www.benchmarkingnetwork.com; see also Chapter 27, this volume |
| Balanced scorecard | Creates an information-based feedback loop to ensure that internal processes align with the mission as seen by external stakeholders | Sets goals according to the enterprise mission, then tracks progress on internal and external indicators | The Balanced Scorecard Institute | www.balancedscorecard.org; see also Chapter 25, this volume |
| Sustainable livelihoods framework | Client assets and constraints and progress related to their ability to realize a sustainable livelihood | Interviews individuals and tracks over time to improve program design and outcomes | Department for International Development (UK) | www.livelihoods.org; www.ekonomos.com |
| Triple bottom-line | Identifies overall impact in three areas: social, environmental, financial | Separates and identifies intentional and unintentional effects of enterprise | Frequently used in private sector | www.bsdglobal.com; see also Chapter 24, this volume |

**TABLE 26.5**
*continued*

| | | | |
|---|---|---|---|
| NESsT | Assesses impact in four areas: financial impact; financial sustainability; social impact; and organizational sustainability | Looks at organizational impact of enterprise in addition to business and social impact | Non-Profit Enterprise and Self sustainability Team | www.nesst.org/ |
| Social return on investment (SROI) | Calculates the net benefit of a financial investment in monetary terms | Translates social benefits into monetary terms to compare investment in the enterprise to resulting social benefit | Roberts Enterprise Development Fund (San Francisco) | www.blendedvalue.org; www.redf.org; see this Chapter |
| Social Capital Partners | Combines sustainable livelihoods and SROI approach | Uses sustainable livelihoods framework to set baseline indicators, then uses SROI analysis to translate the social impact into monetary terms | Social Capital Partners (Toronto) | www.socialcapitalpartners. ca for an example, go to the "Ideas" section of the site and check out the ICR report cards. |

*Source*: Social Capital Partners and Vancity Community Foundation, n.d., reproduced with permission of the authors

subject, most notably "SROI Methodology" by the Roberts Enterprise Development Fund (REDF) in San Francisco (2001), and "A Guide to Social Return on Investment" from the British Government in cooperation with several NGOs (2009).

REDF (2001) has developed six key SRPI stages and accompanying quantitative metrics to help inform investors on the degree of value creation from their philanthropic investments in social enterprises. These metrics are divided into two general categories (measures of value and indices of return) as illustrated in Tables 26–6 and 26–7.

As explained by REDF:

These first three metrics measure what a social purpose enterprise is 'returning' to the community. The next three metrics compare these returns against the philanthropic investments required to generate them. This comparison of returns generated to investments required is articulated in the Index of Return. The Index of Return (Index) is a ratio used to determine impact of an investment. It compares an investment to the value created by the investment. The

| **TABLE 26.6**<br><br>*Measures of Value* | TYPE OF VALUE CREATED | METRIC | DEFINITION |
|---|---|---|---|
| | Economic | Entreprise Value | Present value of excess cash generated by enterprise's business operations (excluding social operating expenses and subsidies) |
| | Socio-economic | Social Purpose Value | Present value of projected social savings and new tax revenue generated by employees of social purpose enterprses less social operating expenses |
| | Socio-economic | Blended Value | Enterprise Value + Social Purpose Value - Long-term debt |
| | Social | | |

*Source:* REDF 2001, Chapter 2, p. 7

| **TABLE 26.7**<br><br>*Indices of Return* | | |
|---|---|---|
| | Enterprise Index of Return | = Enterprise Value / Present Value of Investment to Date |
| | Social Purpose Index of Return | = Social Purpose Value / Present Value of Investment to Date |
| | Blended Index of Return | = Blended Value / Present Value of Investment to Date |

*Source:* REDF 2001, Chapter 2, p. 9

resulting number shows whether the investment lost, maintained, or created value. An Index of one means that all investors will receive their required rate of return. An Index greater than one shows that excess value is generated. If the Index is less than one, value is lost. However, it is important to remember that the SROI metrics only measure monetizable value. Social Purpose Enterprises create value that is not captured by these measures. An Index of Return less than one does not necessarily imply a poor investment.

The British government guide is also designed to give detailed, hands-on instructions to stakeholders in social enterprises on how to construct and interpret measures of social value from social enterprises. The manual outlines six stages in SROI analysis: (1) establishing scope and identifying key stakeholders, (2) mapping anticipated or realized outcomes, (3) finding evidence of outcome occurrence and valuing them, (4) establishing impacts, (5) calculating the SROI, and (6) verifying and reporting the results and embedding processes that produce the desired outcomes. The underlying principles of analysis are similar in kind to standard financial analysis but require their adaptation to situations where outcome measures may be somewhat more difficult to measure and monetize. Key outcomes are identified for all major stakeholders, and then appropriate indicators for each outcome are also identified. The final step is determining possible financial proxies that accurately capture and reflect the underlying processes.

There are several complexities in this analysis, as adjustments must be made to reflect four important factors: (1) deadweight—the amount of outcome that would have occurred without the social enterprise; (2) displacement—any net losses elsewhere that might offset the gains from the activities of the social enterprise; (3) attribution—separating out the effect of other organizations and people on the final outcomes; and (4) predicting or tracking the effect of the program over time that may decline due to reduced effort or external factors.

Finally, the monetized results can be presented in one or more of several formats: net present value, SROI, and payback period. Wherever a stream of future costs and benefits must be included, it is recommended that a social rate of discount be applied somewhere in the range of 3.0–3.5%. A real-life example of the approach to calculating a SROI is presented in the following section.

## CASE STUDY: MILLRACE IT

MillRace IT is a social enterprise with two related goals: to increase the employability of disabled people, and to reduce the flow of electronic equipment to landfills (Nicholls et al. n.d.; UK Cabinet Office 2009). It accomplishes these tasks by employing and training people with mental disabilities to repair and refurbish old computers and peripheral electronic equipment. Some of these employees will eventually move into the normal work stream; other may remain working at MillRace, thereby reducing their risk of falling back into their former state of reliance on state support. Table 26–8 identifies the key variables in the analysis: relevant stakeholders, financial and other inputs, principal outputs, indicators, and impacts. Figure 26–2 maps the process of analysis in the derivation of net impact, and Table 26–9 provides

| TABLE 26.8 | STAKEHOLDER | INPUT | OUTPUTS | OUTCOME INDICATORS | IMPACT |
|---|---|---|---|---|---|
| *MillRace IT Indicator Map* | Participants | Number of participants | (1) Number of tonnes of computers recycled AND (2) Length of time in programme | (1) Length of time in recovery AND (2) change in medical costs AND (3) change in income | Deadweight: Number of computers that would have been recycled anyway<br><br>Displacement: Assumed nil given nature of participant population |
| | Government | Funding | (1) Number of trained participants AND (2) Number of tonnes of computers recycled | (1) Number who obtain jobs AND (2) Number who extend recover AND (3) Number of decrease use of the local health care system | Deadweight: Number of computers that would have been recycled anyway<br><br>Displacement: Assumed nil given nature of participant population |

*Source:* Based on NEF, n.d., p. 32

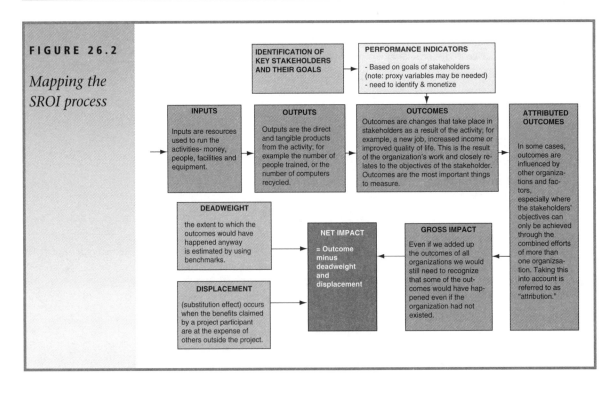

**FIGURE 26.2**

*Mapping the SROI process*

| INDICATOR | VALUE (UK POUNDS) | |
|---|---:|---|
| **Benefits to participants** | | **TABLE 26.9** |
| Employee wages (for some participants) | £13,500 | |
| Less welfare benefits lost (weighted average) | –£6,900 | *MillRace IT* |
| Less increase in tax contribution | –£1,600 | *SROI Model* |
| Less increase in National Insurance | –£500 | |
| Net benefit per participant that moves on to full-time employment | £4,500 | |
| Number of participants that move on to full time employment per annum | 3 | |
| **Total benefits to participants** | **£13,500** | |
| **Benefits to local government** | | |
| Cost to send one tonne of waste to landfill | £39 | |
| Number of tonnes recycled per annum | 50 | |
| **Net savings to local government** | **£1,950** | |
| **Benefits to national government (per employee)** | | |
| Welfare benefits saved (weighted average) | £6,900 | |
| Number of participants that no longer require welfare benefits per annum | 3 | |
| **Net savings in welfare benefit expenditure** | **£20,700** | |
| Savings in the cost of mental health provision | £20,500 | |
| Number of participants who do not require intensive care | 4 | |
| **Total health care savings** | **£82,000** | |
| **Net benefit to national government** | **£102,700** | |
| **Combined net benefit** | | |
| Payback period (in months) | 1 | |
| Aggregate annual benefits | £118,150 | |
| Less deadweight from computer recycling (118,150-1950) | £116,200 | |
| Less attribution | 75% | |
| **MillRace IT share of outcome** | **£87,150** | |

*Source:* NEF, n.d., p. 40

monetized estimates of total social benefits. The final step in this analytical process is calculation of the SROI, as illustrated in Figure 26–3, the results of which are reported in Table 26–10.

Clearly, the application of metrics such as SROI and others will be somewhat more complex in a Third World environment in the absence of clear market signals

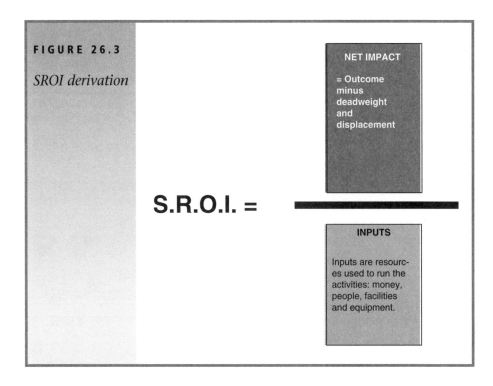

**FIGURE 26.3**

*SROI derivation*

**NET IMPACT**

= Outcome minus deadweight and displacement

**S.R.O.I. =**

**INPUTS**

Inputs are resources used to run the activities: money, people, facilities and equipment.

**TABLE 26.10**

*MillRace IT SROI*

CASE STUDY: MILLRACE IT

SROI

The returns are calculated annually due to the nature of Social Firms, in that their 'output' is the ongoing training and support for disabled people. Therefore, no benefits are projected forward. Therefore, the calculations that we do in this instance for SROI are simply:

$$SROI = \frac{Net\ benefits}{Net\ investment}$$

Therefore, to determine the SROI we complete the following calculation:

$$SROI = \frac{£76,825}{£10,325}$$

**SROI generated by MillRace IT**

|  | Total value created | MillRace IT share | Investment | SROI | MillRace IT share |
|---|---|---|---|---|---|
| Aggregate Benefits | £107,825 | £78,288 | £10,325 | 10.44 | 7.58 |
| Less Deadweight | £105,875 | £76,825 | £10,325 | 10.25 | 7.44 |

*Source:* NEF, n.d., p. 51

to aid in evaluation and the frequent inability to gauge the full extent and reach of any social enterprise program.

In summary, the past several decades have witnessed the formal emergence of a major new form of organization linking philanthropy, venture capital, and entrepreneurial talent to the goals of social and environmental amelioration. With this development has come the need to generate useful measures of social return, and such measures have been forthcoming. Further work is required even in the United States to measure more accurately the total extent and impact of social enterprise as well as to modify the legal framework of organizational law to facilitate the growth of this sustainable industry.

## DISCUSSION QUESTIONS

1. To what extent do any of the forms of social enterprise satisfy the criteria for a sustainable organization enunciated by Anderson, McDonough-Braungart, or Robert? [See Table 24–4.]
2. How scalable is social enterprise? Specifically, how large a contribution toward a sustainable economy can be made by this form of enterprise?

## CITED REFERENCES AND RECOMMENDED READINGS

B Lab (2011) *B Corporation Annual Report*. Berwyn, PA.

Borzaga, C. and J. Defourny (eds.) (2001) *The Emergence of Social Enterprise*. London: Routledge.

Curtis, Timothy (2011) " 'Newness' in Social Entrepreneurship Discourse: The Concept of 'Danwei' in the Chinese Experience." *Journal of Social Entrepreneurship*, 2(2), October, pp. 198–217.

Dacin, Peter A. et al. (2010) "Social Entrepreneurship: Why We Don't Need a New Theory and How We Move Forward From Here." *Academy of Management Perspectives*, August, pp. 37–57.

Defourny, Jacques and Marthe Nyssens (2008) "Social Enterprise in Europe: Recent Trends and Developments." *Social Enterprise Journal*, 4(3), pp. 202–228.

Defourny, Jacques and Marthe Nyssens (2010) "Conceptions of Social Enterprise in Europe and the United States: Convergences and Divergences." *Journal of Social Entrepreneurship*, 1(1), March, pp. 32–53.

Defourny, Jacques and Shin-Yang Kim (2011) "Emerging Models of Social Enterprise in Eastern Asia: A Cross-Country Analysis." *Social Enterprise Journal*, 7(1), pp. 86–111.

*Forbes* Magazine (2011) "Corporate Responsibility Nonprofit, B Lab, Shows Strong Growth," March 16.

Hackett, Michelle Therese (2010) "Challenging Social Enterprise Debates in Bangladesh." *Social Enterprise Journal*, 6(2), pp. 210–224.

Hart, Stuart L. (2010) *Capitalism at the Crossroads: Next Generation Business Strategies for a Post-Crisis World*. Third Edition, Upper Saddle River, NJ: Prentice Hall.

*Harvard Review of Latin America* (2006) "Social Enterprise. Making a Difference." Special Issue. Fall.

Henriques, Adrian (2010) *Corporate Impact. Measuring and Managing Your Social Footprint.*

http://ccss.jhu.edu/wp-content/uploads/downloads/2011/12/Civil-Society-Index_FINAL_11.15.2011.pdf [website of Johns Hopkins Global Civil Society Index].

http://www.bcorporation.net [website of B Corporation, Berwyn, PA].

IFF Research (2005) *A Survey of Social Enterprise across the UK.* Research Report prepared for the Small Business Service (SBS), London.

Kerlin, Janelle A. (ed.) (2009) *Social Enterprise: A Global Comparison.* Medford, MA: Tufts University Press.

Kerlin, Janelle A. (2006) "Social Enterprise in the United States and Europe: Understanding and Learning from Differences." *Voluntas*, 17, pp. 247–263.

Kerlin, Janelle A. and Tom Pollak (2010) "Nonprofit Commercial Revenue: A Replacement for Declining Government Grants and Private Contributions?" *The American Review of Public Administration*, 41(6), pp. 686–704.

Leahy, George and Frank Villeneuve-Smith (2009) *State of Social Enterprise Survey 2009.* London: Social Enterprise Coalition.

London, Ted (2009) "Making Better Investments at the Base of the Pyramid." *Harvard Business Review*, May, pp. 106–113.

London, Ted and Stuart L. Hart (2010) *Next Generation Business Strategies for the Base of the Pyramid: New Approaches for Building Mutual Value.* Upper Saddle River, NJ: F.T. Press.

Lyon, Fergus et al. (2010) "Approaches to Measuring the Scale of the Social Enterprise Sector in the UK." Third Sector Research Centre, Birmingham, working paper 43, September.

Mair, Johanna et al. (eds.) (2006) *Social Entrepreneurship.* Houndmills: Palgrave Macmillan.

McKague. Kevin and Sarah Tinsley (2012) "Bangladesh's Rural Sales Program: Towards a Scalable Rural Sales Agent Model for Distributing Socially Beneficial Goods to the Poor." *Social Enterprise Journal*, 8(1), pp. 16–30.

Minard, C. Sara L. (2009) "Valuing Entrepreneurship in the Informal Economy in Senegal." *Social Enterprise Journal*, 5(3), pp. 186–209.

*New York Times* (2011) "A Quest for Hybrid Companies That Profit but Can Tap Charity." October 12.

Nicholls, Jeremy et al. (n.d.) *Measuring Real Value: A DIY Guide to Social Return on Investment.* London: New Economics Foundation (NEF).

Noya, Anonella (ed.) (2009) *The Changing Boundaries of Social Enterprise.* Paris: Organisation for Economic Co-operation and Development (OECD).

Organisation for Economic Co-operation and Development (OECD) (n.d.) "The Social Enterprise Sector: A Conceptual Framework."

Prahalad, C.K. (2009) *The Fortune at the Bottom of the Pyramid: Eradicating Poverty through Profits.* Revised and updated 5th Anniversary Edition. Upper Saddle River, NJ: Prentice Hall.

Prahalad, C.K. and Stuart L. Hart (2002) "The Fortune at the Bottom of the Pyramid." *Strategy + Business.* January, Issue 26, pp. 54–67.

Roberts Enterprise Development Fund (REDF) (2001) *SROI Methodology. Analyzing the Value of Social Purpose Enterprise within a Social Return on Investment Framework*, San Francisco.

Salamon, Lester M. et al. (2004) *Global Civil Society. Dimensions of the Nonprofit Sector*. Volume Two. Sterling, VA: Kumarian Press.

Salamon, Lester M. et al. (2012) "Holding the Fort: Nonprofit Employment during a Decade of Turmoil." Nonprofit Employment Bulletin No. 39. Baltimore, MD: The Johns Hopkins Nonprofit Economic Data Project.

Social Capital Partners and Vancity Community Foundation (n.d.) "Is It Working? Social Enterprise Performance Measurement." Vancouver, BC: Workshop Handouts.

UK Cabinet Office. Office of the Third Sector. (2009) *A Guide to Social Return on Investment*.

U.S. Internal Revenue Service (IRS) "SOI Tax Stats—Charities & Other Tax-Exempt Organizations Statistics."

Young, Dennis R. (2001) "Social Enterprise in the United States: Alternate Identities and Forms," prepared for the EMES Conference, The Social Enterprise: A Comparative Perspective, Trento, Italy, December 13–15.

Yunus, Mohammad (2003) *Banker to the Poor*. New York: Public Affairs.

Yunus, Mohammad (2008) *Creating a World without Poverty: Social Business and the Future of Capitalism*. New York: Public Affairs.

## NOTES

1. The term *civil society* has been defined as "as a 'third sector,' distinct from government and business. In this view, civil society refers essentially to the so-called 'intermediary institutions' such as professional associations, religious groups, labor unions, citizen advocacy organizations, that give voice to various sectors of society and enrich public participation in democracies" (CSI 2003).

2. Under the terms of Alfred Nobel's will of 1895, the Nobel Prize was established to recognize "those who, during the preceding year, shall have conferred the greatest benefit on mankind." Nobel's intent was to focus on physics, chemistry, physiology-medicine, literature and peace, although an award for Economics, funded by Sweden's central bank, was added in 1968.

# CHAPTER 27

# Sustainability and Corporate Culture

A S OUTLINED IN THIS BOOK, THE SUCCESSFUL TRANSITION from tradi-tional corporate management to sustainability requires a number of critical prerequisites: first, a change of worldview that recognizes the economy as a subset of our ecological system; second, a method for monetizing the non-priced externali-ties of human industrial activity; third, an accounting system that allows the inte-gration of social and environmental accounts with traditional financial statements; and, finally, a cultural shift in attitudes and behavior not only among the general public as citizens and consumers, but also a fundamental change in the culture of the corporate entity.

In a recent working paper from the Harvard Business School, Eccles et al. (2011) examine the impact of corporate culture on corporate behavior and performance by studying 180 companies over an 18-year period. They have found that *high sustain-ability* firms (defined as those who voluntarily adopted environmental and social policies many years ago) significantly outperform their *low sustainability* competi-tors on both stock market and standard accounting measures. The authors posit that "these policies reflect the underlying culture of the organization, a culture of sustainability, where environmental and social performances, in addition to finan-cial performance, are important, but also forge a stronger culture by making explicit the values and beliefs that underlie the mission of the organization" (p. 2).

In contrast to social enterprise where both management and employees have usually self-selected into the organization and fully subscribe to its social and envi-ronmental goals, there is a major challenge to introducing the principles of sustain-ability into a conventional business entity, as management culture is embedded in a system of economic organization—the corporation—which has been one of the most resilient and productive inventions of modern society. While it has been posited that the successful integration of social and environmental values into cor-porate profit and loss statements will go a long way toward shifting corporate cul-ture, the question remains as to whether this is sufficient in and by itself. If recent examples of corporations realizing that "waste is lost profit" have heightened aware-ness of issues of sustainability at the upper levels of corporate management, several questions might be legitimately asked: "Why only now? Why weren't these obvious opportunities to increase profits not realized before?"

As Michael Porter has stressed, the traditional corporate mindset viewed envi-ronmental concerns solely as cost centers. Some of this has changed with increas-ing public and governmental influence on corporate decision making but, clearly, this process of transition is incomplete. It is here that the issue of corporate culture assumes importance. As Hoffman (2001, p. 21) has observed, "The essence of how environmentalism changes the corporate enterprise lies not primarily in its technical adjustments but more important, in its structural, strategic and cultural transformation."

Corporate culture has been characterized as the mind and soul of a company, and many corporations have well-established cultural identities. Exxon, for example, has gained notoriety for funding anti-environmental groups and initiatives (Coll 2012; Hoggan 2009; McKibben 2010; Michaels 2008; Oreskes and Conway 2010; UCS 2007; *The Guardian* 2006), and other companies such as Shell and BP have adopted the language of sustainability in their public persona despite debate over the seriousness of their commitment to the principle in an industry characterized by massive negative externalities from the production and consumption of energy (Greenpeace 1992; Magner 2011).[1] Nevertheless, there are many other companies that have established positive records with respect to environmental issues. Table 27–1 lists companies that have appeared in the top 10 in *Newsweek's*

| TABLE 27.1 | GREENEST U.S. COMPANIES | LEAST GREEN U.S. COMPANIES |
|---|---|---|
| *Greenest and Least Green U.S. Companies* | 1. IBM | 1. T. Rowe Price Group |
| | 2. Hewlett-Packard | 2. BlackRock |
| | 3. Sprint Nextel | 3. Monsanto |
| | 4. Baxter | 4. Invesco |
| | 5. Dell | 5. CONSOL Energy |
| | 6. Johnson & Johnson | 6. Archer-Daniels-Midland |
| | 7. Accenture | 7. Ameren |
| | 8. Office Depot | 8. Bunge |
| | 9. CA Inc. | 9. Peabody Energy |
| | 10. NVIDIA | 10. Ralcorp Holdings |
| | 11. Agilent Technologies | 11. FirstEnergy |
| | 12. Hartford Financials | 12. SCANA |
| | 13. EMC Corp. | 13. Mead Johnson Nutrition |
| | 14. Adobe | 14. PPL |
| | 15. Intel Corp. | 15. Ameriprise Financial |
| | | 16. Tyson Foods |
| | | 17. AES |
| | | 18. Edison International |
| | | 19. Allegheny Technologies |
| | | 20. KeyCorp |

*Source:* Newsweek.com

annual survey of the most green and least green companies in the United States over the past three years. How do companies earn such reputations? There is a consensus among most scholars of organizational behavior that the role of the chief executive officer is critical in forming and maintaining corporate culture. One need only think of such visionary CEOs as Apple's Steven Jobs, Interface's Ray Anderson, IBM's Tom Watson Jr., Polaroid's Edwin Land, Chrysler's Lee Iacocca, Microsoft's Bill Gates, Berkshire Hathaway's Warren Buffett, and GE's Jack Welch and Jeff Immelt to understand the central role of such key individuals in the lifeblood of their corporations. The influence of the CEO is particularly important when that person is the organizational founder. Hillestad et al. (2010, p. 442) characterize the founder's role as a *cultural architect* "crafting and energizing organizational culture in the early years of an organization."

When leadership changes, corporate culture can be significantly impacted and, again, this is especially critical when the leader is the founder who has retired, died, or been replaced. There are several possible outcomes. On the one hand, a new leader may carry on the corporate traditions established by his/her predecessor, supplementing them with a new set of values that are gradually absorbed by the organization (Jackofsky et al. 1988, p. 39) or, on the other hand, may consciously or unconsciously alter the culture and performance of the organization for better or for worse. In a study of public sector organizations, Boyne et al. (2011) found that succession has a positive effect where prior performance is low and the opposite effect when it is high. Succession can lead to dramatic change—as aptly illustrated by the volte-face in British Petroleum (BP) when Tony Hayward replaced Lord John Browne as CEO and moved the corporation away from its emerging interest in renewable energy sources (characterized by the slogan "Beyond Petroleum") back toward a primary focus on petroleum (Magner 2011). Hayward's philosophy of corporate governance and behavior became apparent in the United States in the wake of the massive oil spill from BP's Deepwater Horizon oil rig in the Gulf of Mexico on April 20, 2010.

The central and critical role of the CEO in corporate affairs does not necessarily mean that the CEO has an unfettered ability to change corporate culture. Gagliardi (1986) has identified two polar views on this subject: one that postulates a limited scope for action; the other suggesting that there are numerous direct and indirect levers of influence at the command of an organizational leader. It is possible to posit at least three factors that may constrain the role of a CEO in molding corporate culture: (1) organizational complexity, (2) organizational inertia, and (3) organizational entropy.

## ORGANIZATIONAL COMPLEXITY

One of the seminal works in organizational theory was published in 1971 by Graham Allison. Focusing on the events of the Cuban Missile Crisis of 1962, Allison developed several conceptual models that transcended the traditional view of government policy as being a unified and rationale approach to critical issues of public policy. In essence, Allison opened up the black box of organizational strategy and focused on the existence of both competing suborganizational units or groups and individuals within an organization. An interesting and modern example of this complexity is the recent emergence of a strong environmental ethic at the highest level of the Chinese central government. Realizing that environmental despoliation poses a significant threat to continued economic growth and prosperity, Beijing has put in place a large array of new legislation and regulations intended to reduce air and water pollution, soil contamination, and excessive reliance on fossil fuels. China has encountered serious challenges to the achievement of these ambitious goals for many reasons, some of which are due to the competing goals of regional actors such as provincial and urban governments and local businesses that are focused principally on social stability and direct economic outcomes (Economy 2004, 2005).

Howard-Grenville (2008) has taken a somewhat similar conceptual approach by attempting to deconstruct corporate decision making with respect to environmental issues. To quote:

> If we treat the organization as a "black box" and regard external factors, including regulation, scientific information, public pressure, new technology, and competitive and economic forces, as the primary drivers of environmental practice (Porter and van der Linde, 1995), we cannot necessarily understand why organizations respond to some environmental issues rather than others and why organizations facing similar issues show a range of responses. (p. 46)

Howard-Grenville focuses her attention on the existence of competing subcultures with asymmetrical power and influence.

> Organizational cultures are rarely monolithic, however, and subcultural differentiation may be more the norm than the exception. Indeed, researchers have found that subcultures form around occupational groupings, organizational roles, hierarchical levels, and functional or professional identifications. Subcultures can also emerge around shared understandings of tasks, mission, and authority structures. Some have even shown that subcultures cut across organizations or exist at the level of industries. (p. 50)

In a companion work, Howard-Grenville et al. (2008) identified five specific factors that contribute to problem solving within a corporation and its strategies for action: managerial incentives, organizational culture, organizational identity, organizational self-monitoring, and personal commitment and affiliations. [See Table 27–2.] Synthesizing the work of other scholars in the field, the authors distinguish between *organizational culture*, which is embedded in the everyday actions that people take throughout the company and influences how things are done; and *organizational identity*, which refers to "an overarching sense among members of what the organization stands for and where it intends to go."

| FACTOR | DEFINITION | SOURCES OF EVIDENCE | |
|---|---|---|---|
| Managerial incentives | Opportunities (or lack thereof) for managerial initiatives and actions, stemming from the structure, rules, and routines of the organization and the informal patterns of influence and control | formal reporting structure; patterns of information flow; approval procedures; compensation schemes | **TABLE 27.2** *Organizational Factors Contributing to Problem Setting and Strategies for Action* |
| Organizational culture | System of meanings and norms that shape daily action and interactions within a company; i.e. "the way things are done" | Tacit norms of behavior; observed, repeated patterns of interaction; rules revealed through actions that breach them | |
| Organizational identity | Members' perceptions of what is central, enduring and distinctive about their company; i.e. "what kind of company we are" | Member's statements of what the organization "is about"; reflections of what is threatened when outsiders are critical of the organization | |
| Organizational self-monitoring | Choices about how an organization portrays its actions to outsiders, in response to its impressions of those outsiders and the value it places on adhering to socially appropriate portrayals | Public portrayals through media, web site, and commercial outreach; number, variety, and scope of partnerships or associations with external groups | |
| Personal commitment and affiliations | Individual members' profession experiences, education and training, and personal interests and values that influence their awareness of and perspectives on environmental issues | Professional backgrounds; memberships in other business or environmental organizations; stated values | |

Howard-Grenville et al. 2008, p. 80, reproduced with permission of Law & Policy

## ORGANIZATIONAL INERTIA

Over a period of time, successful corporations develop standard operating procedures and cultural norms. When new leadership attempts to change the philosophical direction of a corporation, a type of organizational inertia can pose a significant barrier to change. As Gagliardi (1986, p. 119) states, "the more deeply rooted and diffuse these values are, the more tenacious and unalterable is the culture." Bartunek and Moch (1987) outline several types of organizational development interventions and their increasing degrees of complexity. The analysis is cast in terms of changes to "schemata," defined as organizing frameworks that guide cognitions, interpretations, or ways of understanding events. The authors distinguish among three orders of schematic change: "*First order change*: the tacit reinforcement of present understandings; *second-order change*: the conscious modification of present schemata in a particular direction; and *third-order change*: the training of organizational members to be aware of their present schemata and thereby more able to change these schemata as they see fit" (p. 486).

The apparent ease with which Tony Hayward was able to redirect the strategic initiatives of Lord John Browne in BP may ironically reinforce the concept of organizational inertia. It could be posited that Browne had not succeeded in dramatically altering the culture of a long-established and successful multinational energy company and that Hayward had only reinforced the pre-existing culture.

## ORGANIZATIONAL ENTROPY

Chapter 1 introduced the theory of *strategic decay* where corporations face the risk of loss of competitive advantage through changes in their external environment and/or a loss of exceptionalism through a type of regression to the mean in internal strategies and processes due to loss of zeal or innovation, internal political and personal distractions, acceptance of the status quo, increase in bureaucratic red tape, and rule-driven decision-making systems. The remedy to this problem is a process of rejuvenation and reinforcement of corporate goals and direct and indirect systems of influence and control within the organization.

Bertels et al. (2011) have produced one of the most comprehensive summaries for chief executives and other senior management on how to embed the principles and practice of sustainability in organizational culture. The authors organize their study into four general categories: fostering commitment, clarifying expectations, building momentum for change, and instilling capacity for change. Under each of these headings, they provide a list of individual practices with examples and an assessment of their effectiveness. [See Figure 27–1.]

This chapter ends with several brief examples that illustrate the interacting roles of complexity, inertia, and entropy in both corporate success and failure.

## CASE STUDIES

In a book entitled *When Good Companies Do Bad Things*, Schwartz and Gibb (1999) studied companies who had run afoul of government regulation and public perception in the environment and other high visibility public policy arenas. Among

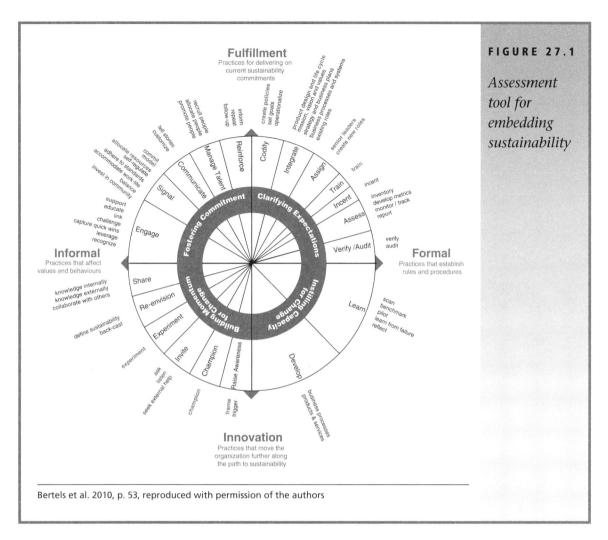

FIGURE 27.1

*Assessment
tool for
embedding
sustainability*

Bertels et al. 2010, p. 53, reproduced with permission of the authors

these were Royal Dutch Shell, Unocal, Texaco, Union Carbide, and Tor Chemicals. The reasons for these problems were, according to the authors: (1) failing to create a culture that tolerates dissent or one in which planning processes are encouraged to take nonfinancial risks seriously; (2) focusing exclusively on financial measures of performance; and (3) discouraging employees from thinking about their work as whole people, from using their moral and social intelligence as well as their business intelligence; (4) talking to the same circle of people and information sources all the time and avoiding people or organizations who disagree with or criticize them; (5) letting their commitment to a particular project or product overwhelm all other considerations—financial, ethical, or social; and (6) senior managers considering ethical or social issues as matters for somebody else to resolve (pp. 177–178). The authors conclude that companies are more vulnerable to these types of problems if they have not examined their operations *from a long-term perspective in a social context*.

In light of these challenges, what levers are available to a company and its CEO, in particular, to rectify these problems? First, the leader must be a visionary, able to communicate and motivate others; second, systems for influencing corporate culture must be designed to induce buy-in at all levels of the corporation, among all subcultural groups and individuals; and third, these messages must be reinforced through a process of continued monitoring, feedback, and renewal. A 10-point list of recommended elements to embed sustainability has been assembled by a team of advisors to HRH The Prince of Wales and published as *The Prince's Accounting for Sustainability Project* (2007). These elements are (1) board and senior management commitment; (2) understanding and analyzing the key sustainability drivers for the organization; (3) integrating the key sustainability drivers into the organization's strategy; (4) ensuring that sustainability is the responsibility of everyone in the organization (and not just of a specific department); (5) breaking down sustainability targets and objectives for the organization as a whole into targets and objectives that are meaningful for individual subsidiaries, divisions, and departments; (6) processes that enable sustainability issues to be taken into account clearly and consistently in day-to-day decision making; (7) extensive and effective sustainability training; (8) including sustainability targets and objectives in performance appraisal; (9) champions to promote sustainability and celebrate success; and (10) monitoring and reporting sustainability performance.

An outstanding example of this integrated approach to inculcating the ideals of sustainability throughout an organization is Ray Anderson's Interface Carpets (Anderson et al. 2010). Anderson's guiding principles are based on the realization that

> Vital to the transition of the economy is the very institution that serves as its primary engine: business and industry. To lead this shift, business must delve much deeper than just the array of eco or clean technologies that are in vogue, to the core beliefs that drive actions. While a few visionary companies have been founded on the principles of sustainability, most businesses will require radical change. (p. 96)

Anderson and his coauthors describe five development phases of change at their company in pursuit of this goal: (i) awakening—defining the vision; (ii) cocooning—creating the road map that included goals, timelines, resource allocation, and metrics; (iii) metamorphosis—aligning the organization; (iv) emergence—ongoing integration; and (v) engagement—a continuing effort to influence others.

Several important initiatives have been undertaken by Interface and other companies in a broad range of endeavors to maintain the momentum of sustainability and reverse any tendency toward corporate entropy. These include regular training and feedback session for employees, flattened hierarchical organizational structures, shortened lines of intrafirm communication, and regular internal peer review of major staffing and strategic decisions. By way of example, Sun Microsystems instituted a system where any employee could e-mail the CEO at any time and expect to receive a timely reply (personal communication). Mayo Clinic has maintained its reputation as a world leader in the delivery of health care through continuous committee peer-based quality control, participative and collaborative management, and publication of performance metrics on both its Intranet and Internet, which have been used as benchmarks for other health-care delivery organizations (Berry and Seltman 2008; Heskett 2011). Central to this effort is the *Mayo Clinic Model of Care*, which codifies its values, culture, and expectations in a document given to all employees and available on the web as a 21-page publication.

Many major corporations now have mission statements that attempt to elucidate and communicate their underlying philosophy of business. Such an exercise is not without risks however, as companies must beware of situations where their behavior is inconsistent with their cultivated public image. One of the most prominent of such statements is Johnson & Johnson's *Credo* directed at both internal and external stakeholders, which outlines their responsibility to doctors, nurses and patients, employees, communities in which they live and work, and shareholders. Over the years, Johnson & Johnson has achieved an unsurpassed level of recognition as one of the country's most respected brands (Reputation Institute 2011). Despite this achievement, Johnson & Johnson has been bedeviled with a series of controversies and lawsuits over the last two decades concerning some of its practices, drugs and medical devices. The problems facing the company were summarized in a *New York Times* article of January 17, 2010, entitled "In Recall, A Role Model Stumbles."

> The Harvard Business School teaches future executives the gold standard in brand crisis management. . . . The template is based on Johnson & Johnson's conduct in 1982, when several people died after taking tainted Tylenol pills. The company's reaction to the crisis is widely regarded as exemplary. But last week, Johnson & Johnson appeared to abandon its own template, stunning a few business school professors. Its conduct also drew harsh criticism from federal officials.

The event that prompted this strongly negative reaction was the recall of several well-known, over-the-counter medicines such as Benadryl, Motrin, Rolaids, Simply Sleep, St. Joseph Aspirin, and Tylenol by McNeil Consumer Healthcare, a division of Johnson & Johnson. This precipitated a warning letter from the FDA after an internal agency study found a 20-month delay in the recall after initial consumer complaints about tainted products. Just two days earlier, the *New York Times* (January 15, 2010) had reported that Johnson & Johnson was the subject of a complaint filed by the Office of the U.S. Attorney in Boston, accusing the company of paying kickbacks to nursing homes for prescribing some of its problem pharmaceuticals. In fairness to Johnson & Johnson, there is no reason to believe that the *Credo* had been rendered totally inoperative by this pattern of recent behavior. What is more likely to have been the cause is the confluence of at least two of the three factors described above: the existence of an entropic process where the company in several notable circumstances allowed the principles to be compromised by the short-term pursuit of profitability by subunits and subcultures with different goals, to the exclusion of its philosophical mandate. Unfortunately, this pathology of corporate behavior had not been remedied as of 2012, as the company was engulfed in another public image fiasco over knowingly distributing defective hip implants (*New York Times*, February 21, 2012).

While the J&J example lies outside the area of sustainability, it exemplifies the challenges that corporations may face in attempting to convey to the general public the relationship between their culture and the achievement of society's goals. In a tongue-in-cheek study by Don Watson (2003) entitled *Death Sentences*, the author describes how corporate mission statements may act to misinform rather than education the public. The epitome of such misinformation is one corporate mission statement that reads, in part: "At CACI we take pride in our commitment to quality service and best value for our clients, individual opportunity and respect for each other, integrity and excellence in our work, and distinction and the competitive edge in our work" (p. 75). The problem with this mission statement is that CACI was one of the private contractors at the infamous Abu Ghraib prison near Baghdad.

The clearest manifestation of this type of organizational pathology in the area of sustainability involves the process of greenwashing. [See, for example, Greenpeace 1992; Greer and Bruno 1997.] One of the most exhaustive studies of this phenomenon was published by TerraChoice in 2010. The company conducted a survey of 1,108 consumer products bought in six national big box retail chains in North America. Their conclusion was that "all but one made claims that are demonstrably false or that risk misleading intended audiences." Their findings, as reported in several reports, were that greenwashing is pervasive and can have significant consequences Terrachoice 2007, p.1):

- Well-intentioned consumers may be misled into purchases that do not deliver on their environmental promise. This means both that the individual consumer has been misled and that the potential environmental benefit of his or her purchase has been squandered.

- Competitive pressure from illegitimate environmental claims takes market share away from products that offer more legitimate benefits, thus slowing the penetration of real environmental innovation in the marketplace.

- Greenwashing may create cynicism and doubt about all environmental claims. . . . This would eliminate a significant market-based, financial incentive for green product innovation and leave committed environmental advocates with government regulations as the most likely alternative.

Among the most controversial recent claims relating to sustainability are associated with "ethical oil from the oil sands" [see chapters 23 and 24], and "clean coal" and other fossil fuels from carbon capture and storage [see chapter 24] (Smil 2010; Thompson 2009; U.S. EPA 2008). One of the most important enunciated changes in corporate culture with respect to sustainability—that of Wal-Mart, the world's largest retailer—is detailed in the next and final chapter of this book.

## CITED REFERENCES AND RECOMMENDED READINGS

Allison, Graham (1971) *Essence of Decision: Explaining the Cuban Missile Crisis*. Boston: Little, Brown & Co.

Anderson, Ray et al. (2010) "Changing Business Cultures from Within," in *State of the World 2010. Transforming Cultures. From Consumerism to Sustainability*. Washington, DC: Worldwatch Institute, pp. 96–102.

Bartunek, Jean M. and Michael K. Moch (1987) "First-Order, Second-Order and Third-Order Change and Organization Development Interventions: A Cognitive Approach." *Journal of Applied Behavioral Science*, 23, pp. 483–500.

Berry, Leonard L. and Kent D. Seltman (2008) *Management Lessons from Mayo Clinic: Inside One of the World's Most Admired Service Organizations.* New York: McGraw-Hill.

Bertels, Stephanie et al. (2011) *Embedding Sustainability in Organizational Culture, a Systematic Review of the Body of Knowledge.* London: Network for Business Sustainability.

Boyne, George A. et al. (2011) "Leadership Succession and Organizational Success: When Do New Chief Executives Make a Difference?" *Public Money & Management*, September, pp. 39–346.

Coll, Steve (2012) *Private Empire. ExxonMobil and American Power.* New York: Penguin Press.

Eccles, Robert G. et al. (2011) "The Impact of a Corporate Culture of Sustainability on Corporate Behavior and Performance," Working Paper 12–035, Harvard Business School, November 4.

Economy, Elizabeth C. (2004) *The River Runs Black. The Environmental Challenge to China's Future.* Ithaca, NY: Cornell University Press.

Economy, Elizabeth C. (2005) "Environmental Enforcement in China," Ch. 4 in Kristen A. Day (ed.) *China's Environment and the Challenge of Sustainable Development.* Armonk, NY: M.E. Sharpe, pp. 102–120.

Gagliardi, Pasqaule (1986) "The Creation and Change of Organizational Cultures: A Conceptual Framework." *Organization Studies*, 7, pp. 117–134.

Greenpeace (1992) *The Greenpeace Book of Greenwash*, Washington, D.C.: Greenpeace International.

Greer, Jed and Kenny Bruno (1997) *Greenwash: The Reality behind Corporate Environmentalism.* Penang, Malaysia: Third World Network.

*The Guardian* (2006) "Royal Society Tells Exxon: Stop Funding Climate Change Denial," September 20.

Heskett, James (2011) *The Culture Cycle: How to Shape the Unseen Force That Transforms Performance.* Upper Saddle River, NJ: F.T. Press.

Hillestad, Tore et al. (2010) "Innovative Corporate Social Responsibility: The Founder's Role in Creating a Trustworthy Brand through 'Green Innovation.'" *Journal of Product & Brand Management*, 19(6), pp. 440–451.

Hoffman, Andre J. (2001) *From Heresy to Dogma. An Institutional History of Corporate Environmentalism.* Stanford, CA: Stanford Business Books.

Hofmeister, John (2010) *Why We Hate the Oil Companies, Straight Talk from an Energy Insider.* New York: Palgrave-Macmillan.

Hoggan, James (2009) *Climate Cover-Up. The Crusade to Deny Global Warming.* Vancouver: Greystone.

Howard-Grenville, Jennifer (2008) "Inside the 'Black Box.'" *Organization & Environment*, 19(1), March, pp. 46–73.

Howard-Grenville, Jennifer et al. (2008) "Constructing the License to Operate: Internal Factors and Their Influence on Corporate Environmental Decisions." *Law & Policy*, 30(1), January, pp. 73–107.

HRH The Prince of Wales (2007) *The Prince's Accounting for Sustainability Project.* London. (www.accountingforsustainability.org./)

Jackofsky, Ellen F. et al. (1988) "Cultural Values and the CEO: Alluring Companions?" *The Academy of Management Executive*, II(1), pp. 39–49.

Johnson & Johnson (http: www.jnj.com).

Magner, Mike (2011) *Poisoned Legacy. The Human Cost of BP's Rise to Power.* New York: St. Martin's Press.

McKibben, Bill (2010) *Earth. Making a Life on a Tough New Planet.* Toronto: Alfred A. Knopf Canada.

Michaels, David (2008) *Doubt Is Their Product. How Industry's Assault on Science Threatens Your Health.* Oxford: Oxford University Press.

*New York Times* (2010a) "In Recall, a Role Model Stumbles," January 17.

*New York Times* (2010b) "Johnson & Johnson Accused of Drug Kickbacks," January 15.

*New York Times* (2012) "Hip Maker Discussed Failures," February 21.

Newsweek.com and TheDailyBeast.com.

Oreskes, Naomi and Erik M. Conway (2010) *Merchants of Doubt.* New York: Bloomsbury Press.

Porter, Michael and Claas van der Linde (1995) "Green and Competitive: Ending the Stalemate." *Harvard Business Review*, September/October, pp. 120–134.

Reputation Institute (2011) *2011 Forbes Reputation Institute U.S. RepTrak Pulse Study. Top-Line Summary.* Washington, DC.

Schwartz, Peter and Blair Gibb (1999) *When Good Companies Do Bad Things: Responsibility and Risk in an Age of Globalization.* New York: John Wiley & Sons.

Smil, Vaclav (2010) *Energy Myths and Realities: Bringing Science into the Policy Debate.* Washington, DC: AEI Press.

TerraChoice (2007) *The Six Sins of Greenwashing.* Ottawa, ON.

TerraChoice (2010) *The Sins of Greenwashing.* Ottawa, ON.

Thomson, Graham (2009) *Burying Carbon Dioxide in Underground Saline Aquifers: Political Folly or Climate Change Fix?* Munk Centre for International Studies, University of Toronto.

Union of Concerned Scientists (UCS) (2007) *Smoke, Mirrors & Hot Air: How ExxonMobil Uses Big Tobacco's Tactics to Manufacture Uncertainty on Climate Science.* Cambridge, MA, January.

U.S. Environmental Protection Agency (EPA) (2008) *Vulnerability Evaluation Framework for Geologic Sequestration of Carbon Dioxide*, July 10.

Watson, Don (2003) *Death Sentences. How Clichés, Weasel Words, and Management-Speak Are Strangling Public Language*, Toronto: Viking Canada.

## NOTE

1. John Hofmeister (2011, p. 82), the former president of Shell Oil Company, recently wrote: "Energy companies' hands are not completely clean, however. The money ExxonMobil has put behind anti-climate change research is frequently cited, and a coal industry coalition was outed in August 2009 for hiring a public relations firm that forged letters to legislators opposing the carbon cap-and-trade bill. Such faux grassroots efforts (often referred to as 'astroturfing') are yet another reason that energy companies have such a black eye."

# CHAPTER 28

*Afterword*

IT HAS BEEN A DOMINANT THEME OF THIS BOOK that sustainability can be achieved only with the whole-scale participation of the business sector—the engine of economic prosperity. To some authors, such as Anderson, McDonough, and Braugart, nothing short of a new industrial revolution will suffice. While sustainability brings with it challenges and threats to the established order, it also brings extraordinary opportunities not only for long-run corporate profitability but also for a more stable social, political, and physical environment. Figure 28–1 summarizes the dual nature of the challenge facing business—as epitomized by the Chinese character for "crisis" described in chapter 1. To date, we have witnessed the adoption of numerous incremental steps toward sustainability by many mainstream businesses as well as the emergence of social enterprise dedicated to the advancement of sustainable goals [see chapter 27]. What is ultimately required is the adoption of fundamental principles of sustainable strategy, process and products across *all* sectors of the global economy, and *all* types and sizes of enterprises. This goal still remains a distant hope.

Chapter 26 introduced the concept of the base of the pyramid [BoP]. This is one component in a model that utilizes the pyramid analogy to characterize the multiple layers of global economic activity (Hart 2010; London and Hart 2011). Sitting astride the pyramid are the approximately 800 million citizens of the developed nations with their extensive purchasing power; at the bottom are the 4 billion or so individuals who subsist on meager daily earnings estimated to range from $2 to $5 a day; and sandwiched in between are the 2 billion or so members of the emerging middle class whose annual income adjusted for purchasing power parity ranges anywhere from $1,500 to $20,000 (Hammond et al. 2007; Hart 2010; Prahalad and Hart 2002). Two entirely different models of sustainability emerge from the two extremes of this pyramid, and each is briefly summarized in turn.

## THE TOP OF THE PYRAMID

This is the market predominantly serviced by the large multinationals and their vast networks of suppliers. Wal-Mart is a preeminent example of this model. With an extraordinary capacity to leverage the nature of global business practices, perhaps no company has had such a polarizing effect on public discourse in the United States. While its social impacts on small business, urban cores, and labor have been a lightning rod for criticism, its massive presence in the American economy entails less visible but extraordinary impacts on material throughput and energy use throughout

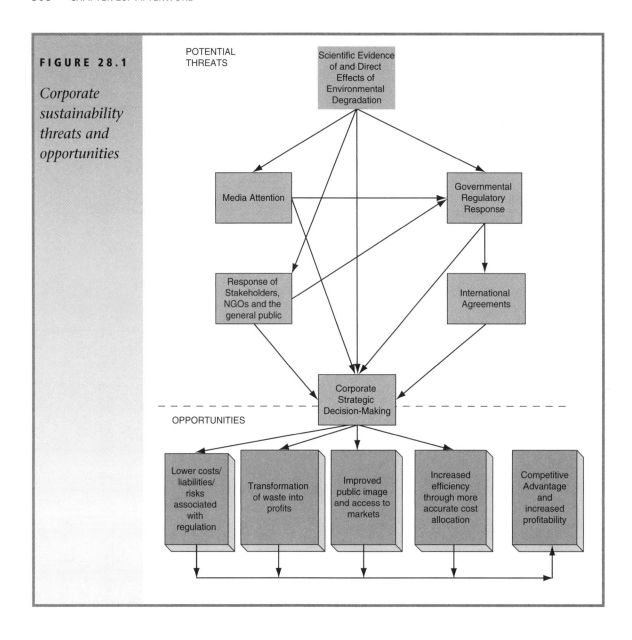

**FIGURE 28.1**

*Corporate sustainability threats and opportunities*

its supply chain. As discussed earlier in this book [see chapter 15], because of its virtually unique role, Wal-Mart has the ability to dramatically change the face of commerce not only in the United States, but also globally. On October 24, 2005, Lee Scott, Wal-Mart's chief executive officer, delivered his "Twenty First Century Leadership Lecture""(Scott 2005), billed as a major reorientation of its strategy toward sustainability. Scott began his speech by molding Hurricane Katrina into a metaphor for the crisis that is facing our physical and business environment. To quote:

We should view the environment as Katrina in slow motion. Environmental loss threatens our health and the health of the natural systems we depend on. The challenges include: increasing greenhouse gases that are contributing to climatic change and weather-related disasters; increasing air pollution which is leading to more asthma and other respiratory diseases in our communities; water pollution which is increasing while safe fresh water supplies are shrinking; water-borne diseases causes millions of death each year, mostly among children; destruction of critical habitat, causing unprecedented threat to the diversity of life, the natural world and us. And that's just to name a few. As one of the largest companies in the world, with an expanding global presence, environmental problems are OUR problems. The supply of natural products (fish, food, water) can only be sustained if the ecosystems that provide them are sustained and protected. There are not two worlds out there, a Wal-Mart world and some other world.

Scott then enunciated Wal-Mart's environmental goals and outlined the intimate relationship between environmental stewardship and good business practice. The principal goals were (1) to be supplied 100% by renewable energy, (2) to create zero waste, and (3) to sell products that sustain resources and the environment. Scott stated that "These goals are both ambitious and aspirational, and I'm not sure how to achieve them. . . . at least not yet. This obviously will take some time. But we do know the way. There is a simple rule about the environment. If there is waste or pollution, someone along the line pays for it."

| AREA | SUGGESTED TOOLS/RESOURCES |
|------|---------------------------|
| Energy & Climate | calculate your carbon footprint |
| | carry out a facility energy audit and review your options for taking action |
| | explore renewable energy options |
| | participate in the Carbon Disclosure Project (CDP) |
| Material Efficiency | conduct a waste audit |
| | establish your water footprint |
| | consider retrofit opportunities in your facilities |
| | drive behavioral change among employees |
| Nature and Resources | develop sustainable purchasing guidelines for your suppliers |
| | explore applicable product certifications and/or standards |
| People & Community | identify the names and locations of your Tier 1 and Tier 2 suppliers |
| | establish a social compliance tam and develop an auditing protocol |
| | understand the life cycle social impacts potentially associated with your product |
| | explore applicable certifications and/or standards |

**TABLE 28.1**

*Wal-Mart's Suggested Tools for Suppliers to Improve Their Sustainability Scores*

*Source*: Wal-Mart no date

Wal-Mart's CEO then presented specific examples in four environmentally related areas to illustrate the nature and magnitude of the potential savings: trucking, store design and operation, waste generation, and product design and sourcing. To assist the multitude of firms in their supply chain coordinate their activities with Wal-Mart's sustainability programs, Wal-Mart (no date) has published an extensive *Suppler Sustainability Assessment* manual. This document first asks each supplier to answer 15 basic questions in the 4 areas of energy and climate, material efficiency, nature and resources, and people and community; scores these responses depending on the level of performance; explains some of the benefits from improving their performance scores in each of the four areas; and finally, lists a group of tools and resources that suppliers can use to improve their performance. [See Table 28–1.]

Several years have passed since the declaration of new goals for Wal-Mart, and the company is now under different leadership. In 2012, the corporation published a scorecard on its progress so far, which is summarized in Table 28–2. Whether its lofty goals will be attainable in the near to midterm future remains an open question, but the contents and import of the talk are remarkable, bearing in mind that if Wal-Mart were a country it "would be the 20th largest in the world."

| **TABLE 28.2** *Wal-Mart's Scorecard on Sustainability* | TARGET | GOAL | MARKET | STATUS | DETAILS |
|---|---|---|---|---|---|
| | **Commitments** | Require all direct-import, nonbranded and private-label suppliers to declare that their factories are compliant with local social and environmental regulations by the end of 2011. | global | Achieved | complete |
| | | Work with The Sustainability Consortium globally to establish the criteria that will be used to gather information from top-tier suppliers and other retailers for products in at least 20 categories. | U.S. | Achieved | 100 product categories |
| | | Accelerate the agricultural focus of the Sustainability Index globally, beginning with a Sustainable Produce Assessment for top producers in its Global Food Sourcing network by the end of 2011. | global | Achieved | complete |
| | | To reduce water use by 20 percent by 2013 (2008 Baseline). | Mexico | Achieved | 21.3% reduction in water use |

| TARGET | GOAL | MARKET | STATUS | DETAILS | |
|--------|------|--------|--------|---------|---|
| | Provide a license for organizations, such as universities, NGOs, government agencies and corporations around the world to the My Sustainability Plan (MSP) employee engagement program by Sept. 1, 2011 | global | Achieved | 35 organizations have signed up for the license | **TABLE 28.2**<br>*continued* |
| | Double the sale of products in the U.S. that help make homes more efficient by 2011 (2008 Baseline). | U.S. | Not met | 35.52% sales increase | |
| | Reduce phosphates in laundry and dish detergents by 70 percent by 2011 (2009 Baseline). | Americas region | Not met | 43% reduction | |
| **Energy** | Be supplied by 100 percent renewable energy. | global | In progress | 22% of total electricity;15% of total energy | |
| | Double fleet efficiency by October 2015 (2005 Baseline). | U.S. | In progress | 69% improvement | |
| | Reduce greenhouse gases (GHG) at our existing store, club and distribution center base by 20 percent (2005 Baseline). | global | In progress | 12.74% reduction | |
| **Waste** | Eliminate landfill waste from stores and Sam's Club locations by 2025. | U.S. | On track | 80.9% landfill waste reduced | |
| | Reduce our global plastic shopping bag waste by an average of 33 percent per store by 2013 (2007 Baseline). | global | On track | 35% reduction | |
| | Reduce food waste in emerging market stores and clubs by 15 percent and in our other markets by 10 percent by the end of 2015 (2009 Baseline). | global | In progress | baselines being established | |
| **Products** | Partner with suppliers to improve energy efficiency by 20 percent per unit of production by the end of 2012 in the top 200 factories in China from which we source directly (2007 Baseline). | global | In progress | 148 factories have reduced energy consumption 20% | |

(Continued)

**TABLE 28.2**

*continued*

| TARGET | GOAL | MARKET | STATUS | DETAILS |
|---|---|---|---|---|
| | Work with suppliers to drive customer returns on defective merchandise virtually out of existence (less than 1 percent) by the end of 2012. | global | In progress | 1.72% returned |
| | Reduce packaging by 5 percent by 2013 (2008 Baseline). | global | In progress | estimates indicate we are on track to reach our goal by 2013 |
| | Be packaging neutral by 2025. | global | In progress | packaging that is recyclable, reusable, made with recycled and/ or sustainably sourced renewable content |
| | Develop a worldwide sustainable product index globally. | global | In progress | beginning business integration |
| | Eliminate 20 million metric tons of greenhouse gas emissions from Walmart's global supply chain by the end of 2015. | global | In progress | more than 120,000 metric tons eliminated, 16 million metric tons identified |
| | Expand the success of Walmart China's Direct Farm program by engaging as many as 1 million farmers by 2011. | China | In progress | supporting 81 farm bases in 23 provinces |
| | Sell $1 billion in food sourced from 1 million small- and medium-sized farmers in emerging markets by the end of 2015. | global | In progress | we expect to report metrics in our next report |
| | By the end of 2012, require that 95 percent of direct-import factories receive one of the two highest ratings in audits for environmental and social practices. | global | On track | 94.8% |

| TARGET | GOAL | MARKET | STATUS | DETAILS | **TABLE 28.2**<br>*continued* |
|---|---|---|---|---|---|
| | Provide training to 1 million farmers and farm workers in our food supply chain, of which we expect half will be women, in emerging markets by the end of 2015. | global | In progress | we expect to report metrics in our next report | |
| | Raise the income of the small- and medium-sized farmers we source from by 10 percent to 15 percent in emerging markets by the end of 2015. | global | In progress | we expect to report metrics in our next report | |
| | Walmart will double sales of locally sourced produce, accounting for 9 percent of all produce sold by the end of 2015 (2009 Baseline). | U.S. | On track | 97% increase | |
| | Require sustainable sourced palm oil in all of our private-brand products globally by the end of 2015. | global | In progress | Walmart baseline calculated | |
| | Expand the existing practice of Walmart Brazil of sourcing only beef that does not contribute to the deforestation of the Amazon rainforest to all of our companies worldwide by the end of 2015. | global | In progress | monitoring system pilot underway | |
| | In the U.S. Walmart will require all fresh and frozen, farmed and wild seafood products sold at Walmart and Sam's Club to become certified as sustainable by a third party using Marine Stewardship Council (MSC), Best Aquaculture Practices (BAP) or equivalent standards. Walmart will require currently uncertified fisheries to develop work plans to achieve certification and report progress biannually. | global | In progress | 76% third-party certified | |
| | Invest more than $1 billion in our perishable supply chain so that we deliver fresher, higher-quality food with a longer shelf life by the end of 2015. | global | In progress | $167 million invested | |

*Source:* Wal-Mart 2012

## THE BOTTOM OF THE PYRAMID

In 2010, Stuart L. Hart published the third edition of a work entitled *Capitalism at the Crossroads*, a distillation of over a decade of analysis and empirical research devoted to the creation of a new model of sustainable business anchored at the bottom of the pyramid. He argues that the centralized solutions used by corporations targeting the market at the top of the pyramid cannot provide global sustainable solutions due to a wide array of factors. These include the environmental impact of most First World products, consumer inertia in the face of familiar and entrenched products (what one might call *the inertia of affluence*), established corporate culture, prices which do not reflect social cost, the vested interests of producers, and the inability of top-of-the-pyramid products to meet the needs of the bottom half of humanity. He cites the strategic reorientation of General Electric (Immelt et al. 2009) in calling for "reverse innovation"—the development of "disruptive technologies" or low-cost innovative products specifically designed for the Third World that can be successfully migrated up to the developed world. Hart maintains that the distributed business model that is inherent in this approach can produce more sustainable or "green" products at reasonable cost while raising the standard of living of the poorest members of the global community. Cited examples of corporations that have successfully implemented at least part of this model include Honda, Toyota, Sony, Galanz, Grameen Bank and Grameen Telecom, and Philips (Hart 2010). Hart speaks of a *Great Convergence* that seeks to "fuel growth through the incubation and rapid commercialization of distributed green technologies from the bottom-up (p. 164)."

The fundamental question is whether either one of these two divergent approaches or the variants of smaller-scale sustainable enterprises described in chapter 26 represent an economic model that can meet the aspirations of all global citizens for a higher quality of life while simultaneously reducing the massive throughput of energy and material that threaten to destroy the ecological and social fabric that sustains global civilization. Or, if none of these paths is the right one, is there some other nascent business model yet to emerge that satisfies the rigorous criteria of sustainability established by Anderson, McDonough-Braungart, and Robert, which can meet this most extraordinary of challenges?

### Discussion Questions

1. Assess Wal-Mart's sustainability strategy in light of the three principal models of the sustainable corporation presented in this book (Anderson, McDonough-Braungart, and Robert). [See Table 24–4.]
2. Is Wal-Mart's mass marketing business model compatible with a sustainable corporation?
3. Is Wal-Mart on the path of eco-efficiency or eco-effectiveness?
4. Compare Wal-Mart's environmental strategy with its social strategy (particularly its wage policies and impact on small business).
5. How important are changes in Wal-Mart's supply chain in such countries as China and Mexico to its goal of sustainability?
6. Which of the two models described above are more likely to lead to a sustainable world?

## CITED REFERENCES AND RECOMMENDED READINGS

Hammond, Allen L. et al. (2007) *The Next 4 Billion. Market Size and Business Strategy at the Base of the Pyramid.* Washington, DC: World Resources Institute.

Hart, Stuart L. (2010) *Capitalism at the Crossroads. Next Generation Business Strategies for a Post-Crisis World.* Third Edition. Upper Saddle River, NJ: Prentice Hall.

Humes, Edward (2011) *Force of Nature. The Unlikely Story of Wal-Mart's Green Revolution. How It Could Transform Business and Save the World.* New York: Harper Business.

Immelt, Jeffrey R. et al. (2009) "How GE is Disrupting Itself." *Harvard Business Review*, October, pp. 56–65.

London, Ted and Stuart L. Hart (2011) *Next Generation Business Strategies for the Base of the Pyramid. New Approaches for Building Mutual Value.* Upper Saddle River, NJ: F.T. Press.

Prahalad, C.K. and Stuart L. Hart (2002) "The Fortune at the Bottom of the Pyramid." *Strategy + Business*, January, Issue 26, pp. 54–67.

Scott, Lee (2005) "Twenty First Century Leadership," Wal-Mart, October 24, available at http://walmartwatch.com/wp-content/blogs.dir/2/files/pdf/21st_Century_Leadership.pdf.

Wal-Mart (2012) *Beyond 50 Years Building as Sustainable Future. 2012 Global Responsibility Report.*

Wal-Mart (no date) *Supplier Sustainability Assessment.*

# Index

LIBRARY, UNIVERSITY OF CHESTER

# Taylor & Francis

# eBooks
## FOR LIBRARIES

ORDER YOUR FREE 30 DAY INSTITUTIONAL TRIAL TODAY!

Over 22,000 eBook titles in the Humanities, Social Sciences, STM and Law from some of the world's leading imprints.

**Choose from a range of subject packages or create your own!**

Benefits for **you**

▶ Free MARC records
▶ COUNTER-compliant usage statistics
▶ Flexible purchase and pricing options

Benefits for your **user**

▶ Off-site, anytime access via Athens or referring URL
▶ Print or copy pages or chapters
▶ Full content search
▶ Bookmark, highlight and annotate text
▶ Access to thousands of pages of quality research at the click of a button

For more information, pricing enquiries or to order a free trial, contact your local online sales team.

UK and Rest of World: **online.sales@tandf.co.uk**

US, Canada and Latin America:
**e-reference@taylorandfrancis.com**

**www.ebooksubscriptions.com**

ALPSP Award for BEST eBOOK PUBLISHER **2009 Finalist**

Taylor & Francis eBooks
Taylor & Francis Group

A flexible and dynamic resource for teaching, learning and research.